WORLD SPORTS RECORDS

ISBN: 978-1-84732-158-9   53500

Editor: Martin Corteel
Designer: Luke Griffin
Project Art Editor: Paul Chattaway
Picture Research: Paul Langan
Production: Lisa Cook

Printed in Dubai

Picture Credits:
The publishers would like to thank the following sources for their kind permission to reproduce the pictures in this book.
PHOTOGRAPHY SUPPLIED BY GETTY IMAGES

Except for the following:
Action Images: /Reuters: 442, 454t, 486b; /Sporting Pictures: 255t. Alamy Images: /Buzz Pictures: 465t; /PBP Galleries: 373t; /Popperfoto: 19t, 68b, 110b, 241. Courtesy of
Dick Bass: 336t. Canadian Football Hall of Fame and Museum: 103b. Corbis: /Bettmann: 122t, 124t, 127t, 142t, 212t, 228t, 236, 293b, 302t; /Ully Bleil: 514t; /Carlos De Saa/
EPA: 539; /Rick Doyle: 318t; /Hulton-Deutsch Collection: 252b; /Robert Garvey: 364t; /Gerard Rancinan/Sygma: 323t. GSP Images: 474t. Hockey Hall of Fame: 35b, 69b.
Inpho: 280. International Tennis Hall of Fame & Museum, Newport, Rhode Island: 28b. Judophotos.com: /David Finch: 371b. LAT Photographic: /Robert Fellowes:
116. Library of Congress: /L. Van Oeyen: 40b. Lord Price Collection: 42b, 54b. Newspix: 86t, 133, 262, 384. Offside Sports Photography: /L'Equipe: 73b, 106t, 148t, 160b,
368b; /Mark Leech Sports Photography: 250b. PA Photos: 23t, 196b, 225t, 298t, 309b, 320b, 420b, 547t; /AP: 26t, 188b, 191b, 221t, 228b, 248t, 265, 278t, 287t, 306b, 310b,
334b, 351t, 389b, 424b, 478, 499b, 580b; /DPA: 292t; /Empics Sport: 17b, 74t, 239, 266b, 282, 307b, 314t, 337b, 346t, 380b; /Frank Gunn/AP: 580t; /Panoramic: 347b; /S&G and
Barratts: 52t, 128t, 148t, 172b, 178t, 217b, 254t, 266t, 269, 271, 314b, 315t, 339t, 350t; /Sutton: 301; /Topham Picturepoint: 300t. Private Collection: 13t, 14t, 16t, 20b, 26b, 31t, 34t,
36b, 41, 106b, 118b, 119, 140b, 184b. Ralph V. Harvey: 328b. Rex Features: /I.B.L.: 330; /Neale Haynes: 447b. Courtesy of Ueli Steck: /Daniel Mader: 574b. Tony Bijkerk: 81b.
Topham Picturepoint: 45, 81t, 82b, 98b, 126t, 168b, 214t; /Alinari: 217t; /Collection Roger-Viollet: 74b. Ullstein Bild: 89t. University Libraries of Notre Dame: /Harry E
Winkler Collection: 60b

Every effort has been made to acknowledge correctly and contact the source and/or copyright holder of each picture and Carlton Books Limited apologises for any
unintentional omissions which will be corrected in future editions of this book.

WORLD SPORTS RECORDS

CHRIS HAWKES

CARLTON

CONTENTS

Opposite: Michael Phelps got off to a blistering start in his much-hyped quest at the 2004
Olympic Games by breaking the 400m medley world record in his first event.

After spending about 15 minutes on the summit of Everest on 29 May 1953, Edmund Hillary and Tenzing Norgay made it back to base camp on 2 June 1953.

INTRODUCTION

The human capacity for progression has found no better vehicle over the years than in the world of sports. The need to run faster, to climb higher, to drive quicker or to sail further has captivated both sportsmen, sportswriters and sports fans throughout the world, and the consequence of such needs have been an array of feats that have provided motivation and inspiration to generations of athletes.

Every entrant in *Greatest Moments In Sports* is proof that the human pioneering spirit – the need to extend boundaries of achievement – lives on; they have all achieved something in their chosen domain that no human (or team) has ever done before and have, for the most part, become a benchmark against which others have been judged, as well as providing new challenges for new sportsmen to conquer. How often is it said of dominant sportsmen that they are no longer competing against their peers but against history? This book could quite easily have been called Greatest Sports Trailblazers.

The starting point is the opening years of the 20th century,, and clearly there will be widespread debate as to who has been included and who has not. There are the obvious records: the first four-minute mile, the first sub-10-second 100m run, the most World Cup goals, the most wins by a jockey in the season, the single-season home run record; the list goes on, but then there are defining moments in human achievement, beyond the boundaries of a sporting field, that fully deserve inclusion.

Do extreme sports have a place in this book? It is a simple question to answer: if you are to include the feat of an athlete throwing a javelin a record distance or a Formula One driver outshining his peers, then man's battles against nature – conquering windswept, mountain-top wildernesses or challenging the hellish and unforgiving seas of the Southern Ocean – stand just as tall in the milestones of human achievement. Edmund Hillary and Tenzing Norgay's ascent of Everest in 1953, for example, remains one of the defining moments of the twentieth century, and is a more than worthy entrant in this book.

Then there are the fame-seekers: Marilyn Bell or Annie Edson Taylor, whose death-defying feats on Lake Ontario and at Niagara Falls brought crowds in their thousands – more one suspects out of the prospect of seeing them fail than out of hopes of success – or the early racing drivers who sought to save their reputations – and their capacity to earn a living – by tackling the land speed record. In short, every entrant in this book has produced a feat that will raise even the most stubborn of eyebrows.

The result is a chronicle of sporting success that spans more than a century. and there will be names in this book that even the most widely read sports fan may never have stumbled across. I hope that it will be as much fun to read as it was to compile.

Chris Hawkes

KRAENZLEIN'S RECORD MEDAL HAUL

ALVIN KRAENZLEIN BREAKS RECORD FOR MOST INDIVIDUAL TRACK-AND-FIELD GOLD MEDALS
May–October 1900, Paris, France

Kraenzlein retired from athletics the following year as the holder of six world records.

The Games of the II Olympiad were staged in Paris, France, to coincide with the city hosting the 1900 World's Fair. Spread, nonsensically, over a period of six months, the Games saw the participation of women for the first time and also prompted a moral debate about competing on Sundays. But one man, Alvin Kraenzlein, a Wisconsin-born dental student, rose above the clamour to stake a place in the history books. He won gold in the 60m, the 110m, the 220m hurdles and the long jump to become the only person in Olympic history to win four individual track-and-field golds – the long jump by the slenderest of margins: 1cm.

➲ Controversy reigned over the long jump. The silver medallist, Meyer Prinstein, had set his mark during qualification and, due to a gentleman's agreement with Kraenzlein not to compete on a Sunday, failed to turn up for the final. Kraenzlein did … and bettered his countryman's mark by 1cm. On hearing the news, Prinstein, less than impressed, sought out Kraenzlein and, according to some sources, landed one or two hefty blows.

GOING, GOING, GONE ... FOR 10,000 GUINEAS

SCEPTRE BOUGHT FOR 10,000 GUINEAS, A RECORD FOR A YEARLING
July 1900, England

Bred by the 1st Duke of Westminster, Sceptre – a horse with an immense pedigree – became one of the greatest fillies in the history of racing. Sadly the duke never saw her race. Still a weanling upon the duke's death, she was put up for auction. Bidding was intense, but Robert Sievier – the owner of the Winning Post and a voracious gambler – snapped Sceptre up for the staggering sum of 10,000 guineas, a record price for a yearling. She turned out to be quite an investment: in 1902, she won 13 of 21 starts, including four of that year's Classics – 1,000 Guineas, 2,000 Guineas, the Oaks and the St Leger.

➲ Sceptre is the last of four fillies to have claimed the 1,000 and 2,000 Guineas double.

Sceptre's race winnings in 1902 alone came to more than 20,000 guineas.

LAJOIE'S IMPREGNABLE SINGLE-SEASON MARK

NAP LAJOIE AVERAGES .426 OVER THE COURSE OF A BASEBALL SEASON

April–September 1901, USA

In 1901, with the birth of the American League, legendary owner and manager Connie Mack persuaded Nap Lajoie to jump ship from the Philadelphia Phillies and join Mack's cross-town arch-rivals the Philadelphia Athletics on a four-year contract worth some $6,000 a year. Lajoie, the Rhode Island-born youngest of eight children of French-Canadian parents, was worth every cent. He had an amazing year, leading the league in batting average (.426), slugging percentage (.643), runs (145), RBI (125), hits (232), total bases (350), doubles (48), home runs (14), singles (156), runs created (158), extra base hits (76) and times on base (269).

No one has come close to matching Lajoie's .426 single-season mark ... and most are in agreement no one ever will.

➲ 1901 was Lajoie's only season with the A's. Before the start of the following campaign, the Phillies took out a court injunction preventing him from playing for another club in the city, so he joined the Cleveland Broncos.

FRY'S SIX OF THE BEST

C.B. FRY SCORES A CENTURY IN SIX CONSECUTIVE INNINGS

8 August–14 September 1901, England

C.B. Fry was an elegant right-handed batsman who played first-class cricket for Sussex over a 30-year period (1892–1922) and who represented England 26 times (captaining them on six occasions). He scored an impressive 94 centuries during his first-class career, 13 of them coming in his stellar 1901 season – including a record run of six consecutive hundreds that has been equalled twice – by Donald Bradman (1938–39) and Mike Proctor (1970–71) – but never beaten. Starting on 8 August, Fry's next six scores ran as follows: 106, 209, 149, 105, 140 and 105. The record-breaking sequence came to an end with the close of the season.

➲ You would be hard pressed to find a more talented individual than Charles Burgess Fry. In addition to his impressive cricket career, Fry, an Oxford University graduate, tied the world long jump record in 1893 (the record lasted for a year), played in the 1902 FA Cup final for Southampton (he also played soccer once for England), served as a deputy for the Indian delegation at the League of Nations and stood (unsuccessfully) for the British parliament.

According to legend, such was his athletic ability that C.B. Fry was able to jump onto a mantelpiece while performing a back flip.

TAKING ON THE HORSESHOE FALLS

ANNIE EDSON TAYLOR BECOMES THE FIRST PERSON TO GO OVER NIAGARA FALLS IN A BARREL

11 24 October 1901, Niagara Falls, USA/Canada

Sadly, fame and fortune did not last long: soon afterwards, her manager disappeared with the barrel, and Taylor spent a considerable sum on private detectives trying to track him down. The barrel was eventually found in Chicago, but disappeared again some time afterwards, this time for good.

Down on her luck – her personal savings had been wiped out twice – Annie Taylor, a 63-year-old former teacher, decided to undertake the stunt of stunts to assure her fame and fortune into old age: she decided to become the first to negotiate the Niagara Falls in a barrel. Choosing an oak barrel, padded on the inside with a mattress, she was launched near the American shore, north of Goat Island, and was soon swept over Horseshoe Falls by the current. Reached by rescuers moments after the plunge, she was found to be alive and well, with only a small cut over her head to show for her death-defying stunt.

➲ Afterwards, Taylor declared: "If it was with my dying breath, I would caution against anyone attempting the feat. I would sooner walk up to the mouth of a cannon, knowing it was going to blow me to pieces, than make another trip over the falls."

GILBERT JESSOP: ENGLAND'S MASTER BLASTER

ENGLAND'S GILBERT JESSOP HITS THE FASTEST CENTURY IN ASHES HISTORY

11–13 August 1902, The Oval, London, England

Gilbert Jessop is best remembered as one of the greatest attacking batsmen Test cricket has ever seen. Short and stocky, he possessed quick feet and a dazzling array of shots and garnered a reputation for being able to master wickets others found treacherous. His most famous innings came for England in the fifth Test against Australia at The Oval in 1902: with England in desperate trouble on 48 for 5 – needing 263 to avoid a 3–0 series defeat – Jessop strode to the crease and smashed an unbeaten 104 out of 139 in 75 pulsating minutes to lead England to an improbable victory.

➲ Jessop faced only 76 balls to reach his Test century, a record in Ashes history until Adam Gilchrist struck 102 of 59 balls at Perth in 2006.

Gilbert Jessop played a total of 18 Test matches, but his unbeaten 104 at The Oval in 1902 was the only Test century of his career.

HILL REACHES 1,000-RUN MILESTONE

CLEM HILL BECOMES FIRST BATSMAN TO SCORE 1,000 TEST RUNS IN CALENDAR YEAR

8–11 November 1902, Cape Town, South Africa

So good was Clem Hill in 1902 that no one came close to matching his 12-month total of Test runs until Dennis Compton's stellar year in 1947. The year started inauspiciously for the left-hander, as he fell short of three figures in three successive Tests against England (99, 98 and 97), but the runs continued to flow. Back in England the following summer, Hill scored the only century of the second Test at Sheffield to guide Australia to victory. The 1,000th run of his remarkable year came against South Africa in Cape Town during an unbeaten innings of 91. Hill ended the year with 1,060 Test runs to his name.

➲ By the time Dennis Compton broke Hill's record in 1947, 70 years of Test cricket had been played and Hill was the only batsman to have scored 1,000 runs in a calendar year.

Clem Hill, the South Australian left-hander, played 49 times for Australia, scoring 3,412 runs at an average of 39.21. A thousand of those runs came in 1902.

TRUMBLE TAKES RECORD WICKET HAUL

HUGH TRUMBLE FIRST BOWLER TO TAKE 50 TEST WICKETS IN CALENDAR YEAR

8–11 November 1902, Cape Town, South Africa

Clem Hill wasn't the only Australian to enjoy a record-breaking year in 1902. Hugh Trumble, a tall off-spinner who bowled at medium pace, started the New Year in spectacular fashion, taking a hat-trick to win the match and level the series against England at the Melbourne Cricket Ground. Later in the summer, back in England at The Oval on a damp wicket, he recorded a Test-best 8 for 65, although a Gilbert Jessop-inspired England edged to a one-wicket victory. By the end of the year, after playing eight Test matches, he had taken five wickets on four occasions and ended up with 53 wickets.

➲ The record stood for a decade, until England's S.F. Barnes took 61 wickets in 1912.

In the final innings of his final Test match, in March 1904, Hugh Trumble became the first player to take two Test hat-tricks. Only two other men have repeated the feat: Australia's T.J. Matthews and Pakistan's Wasim Akram.

TWO-TIME ANDERSON WINS OPEN

WILLIE ANDERSON FIRST TWO-TIME WINNER OF US OPEN

July 1903, Baltusrol Golf Club, Springfield, New Jersey, USA

Willie Anderson, a Scottish emigrant to the United States, first made US Open headlines in 1897, when he finished second. He went one better in 1901, dramatically snatching his first major following a playoff victory over Alex Smith. So when Anderson arrived at the 1903 championships at Baltusrol, he was among the favourites for the crown. He started in splendid fashion, shooting a new US Open record low 71, but a disappointing final-round 82 condemned him to another playoff, against David Brown. He shot 82 once again, but this time there was no disappointment: Brown shot 84 and Willie Anderson had become the US Open's first multiple winner.

➲ Anderson defended the crown in 1904 and 1905 to become not only the first to win three successive US Opens, but one of only four four-time winners. The others: Bobby Jones (1923, 1926, 1929, 1930), Ben Hogan (1948, 1950, 1951, 1953) and Jack Nicklaus (1962, 1967, 1972, 1980).

Willie Anderson (left, with Alex Smith) was one of a number of British golfers who crossed the Atlantic and spread golf's gospel, working as club professionals. Indeed, British-born golfers won the first 16 US Opens played.

THE FIRST TOUR

MAURICE GARIN FIRST WINNER OF TOUR DE FRANCE

19 July 1903, Paris, France

The first Tour de France was inspired by the newspaper L'Auto in an attempt to increase circulation figures. The first of just six stages – a gruelling 467km ride from Paris to Lyon – started on 1 July and was won by Maurice Garin, an Italian-born naturalized Frenchman, in a time of 27h47m. Garin completed his second win on the fifth stage, from Bordeaux to Nantes, by which time only 32 of the 60 starters remained. By the time he crossed the finishing line in Paris to record his third stage success, he had finished the 2,428km course in 84h33m14s, almost three hours ahead of second-placed Louis Pothier.

➲ Most of the stages were in excess of 400km and many lasted more than 24 hours, meaning riders were forced to ride through the night.

Garin was initially declared winner of the second Tour de France in 1904, until news emerged that he had taken a train through part of the route. He was promptly disqualified and never rode in the Tour again.

RELIANCE CAUSES A STIR

RELIANCE, LARGEST YACHT EVER BUILT FOR THE AMERICA'S CUP, ROMPS TO VICTORY

3 September 1903, New York, USA

The 13th running of the America's Cup saw the introduction of one of the most celebrated boats in the competition's history, but the massive scale of the USA's *Reliance* caused quite a stir. At the time, the only restriction on designers was to ensure the load waterline length did not exceed 27.43m. *Reliance*'s designer, Nathanael Greene Herreshoff, overcame this restriction by adding 13.5m of overhang. The result: an increased waterline in heavier seas and an increase in speed. The challenger *Shamrock III* could not live with her: mystically *Reliance* and her 64-man crew emerged from dense fog in the final race to cross the finishing line; *Shamrock*, meanwhile, had lost her route and headed back to her moorings.

➲ *Reliance* had the largest overall sail area of any yacht in America's Cup history, 1,501m². The next largest was America's 1937 entrant, *Ranger*, with 701m².

Reliance's racing career was short. In 1904, following the introduction of the 90ft rule, she was obsolete as a racing yacht and, just a year after her America's Cup success, was broken up.

Pound-for-pound, there were few harder punchers in boxing history than Bob Fitzsimmons.

BOXING'S FIRST TRIPLE CROWN CHAMPION

BOB FITZSIMMONS FIRST TO WIN THREE WORLD TITLES AT DIFFERENT WEIGHTS

25 November 1903, Mechanics Pavilion, San Francisco, California, USA

Bob Fitzsimmons was a middleweight with a heavyweight's punch. Patient, powerful and precise, he was a supreme master of the art of ring craft. In 1890, he knocked out Jack "Nonpareil" Dempsey in the 13th round to claim the middleweight championship. He defended the title just once: his eyes were fixed on the heavyweight crown. He finally got his chance against James J. Corbett in 1897 and, despite weighing 16lb less than his opponent, Fitzsimmons sent the champion crashing to the canvas in the 14th round. He lost his title two years later, but carried on boxing and, in 1903, aged 40, sensationally knocked out George Gardner in 14 rounds to become light-heavyweight champion.

➲ During a 30-year career, Fitzsimmons is believed to have fought over 300 bouts.

WE HAVE LIFT-OFF

THE *WRIGHT FLYER* BECOMES WORLD'S FIRST SUCCESSFUL AIRPLANE
17 December 1903, Kitty Hawk, North Carolina, USA

By 1902, as part of a broad experimental program, the Wright brothers, Orville and Wilbur, had developed a successful glider. Next they needed to understand how propellers worked: the notion of a propeller serving as a movable wing rotating on an axis and moving the plane forward. They developed propeller designs, testing them in their wind tunnel until they were satisfied. Then they needed power: they built a state-of-the-art four-cylinder crankshaft engine and the *Wright Flyer* was ready. On 14 December they made an unsuccessful attempt at flight with Wilbur at the helm; three days later they were back, this time with Orville in command. The plane took off from a launching ramp on the sands of Kitty Hawk beach and flew for 12 seconds over a distance of 37m (120ft). Man had finally achieved sustained controlled flight.

➲ The *Wright Flyer* was flown three more times that day with the brothers alternating as pilot. The longest flight, with Wilbur at the controls, was 260m (852ft), lasted 59 seconds.

The Wright brothers' major breakthrough came with their understanding of three-axis control, which enabled the pilot to steer the plane.

15

BREAKING THROUGH THE BARRIER

LOUIS RIGOLLY FIRST TO BREAK 100MPH BARRIER

24 May 1904, Ostend, Belgium

With the automobile industry very much in its infancy, the career of a racing driver lived and died on reputation, and reputation was secured by winning races. So when French driver Louis Rigolly lost a standing-mile drag race to fellow countryman Paul Baras, he needed to save face. He declared he would make an attempt on the land speed record, set on the same Ostend sands a few months earlier by Frenchman Pierre de Caters (97.258mph). Rigolly powered across the sands in his Gobron-Brillie car, and thrilled the crowds when news emerged of his speed: 103.561mph. He had become the first to break the fabled 100mph barrier and, more importantly, his reputation was secure.

➲ The record lasted until 13 November 1904 when Paul Baras returned to Ostend and clocked 104.53mph.

Louis Rigolly was widely considered to have been the first true star of drag racing and being the first to break the 100mph barrier merely added fuel to his legend.

CORNET BEATS THE CHEATS

HENRI CORNET BECOMES YOUNGEST WINNER OF TOUR DE FRANCE

December 1904, Paris, France

There was a sense of déjà vu about the 1904 edition of the Tour de France as Maurice Garin was the first to cross the finishing line for the second straight year. But there were more headlines to come. Initial whispers of irregularities soon grew into a public clamour and the French cycling union established an investigative committee. Their findings, released in December 1904, were sensational: 11 of the riders, including the top four finishers, had received the aid of either a train or car during the race. They were summarily disqualified and fifth-placed Henri Cornet was awarded the win: at 20 years old, he remains the youngest winner in Tour history.

➲ Public distaste towards the 1904 Tour de France manifested itself during the final stage: because spectators had thrown nails onto the course, Henri Cornet was forced to ride the last 40km with two flat tyres.

Cornet did not enjoy such success in the Tour again. In subsequent races his best finish came in 1908, when he was eighth.

CHESBRO WINS 41 GAMES

JACK CHESBRO SETS SINGLE-SEASON MARK FOR MOST WINS

April–October 1904, USA

By the time Jack Chesbro finished his playing career in 1909, he had started in 332 games and won 198 of them.

The last thing Jack Chesbro would have been thinking about as he watched his spitball crash and burn against his Boston opponent's bat and sail over the catcher's head was his place in the history books. Chesbro had just conceded the winning run and his New York Highlanders team (now the Yankees) had been dumped out of the pennant. But that moment temporarily overshadowed what had otherwise been a phenomenal year for the right-handed pitcher. He had started 51 games, completed 48 of them, pitched 454 innings and had recorded a staggering 41 wins: a figure never likely to be broken in MLB history.

➲ Old Hoss Radbourn had a 60-game winning season in 1884, but because he was playing under different regulations, Chesbro's mark is considered the modern-day record. The closest anyone came to breaking Chesbro's record was Christy Mathewson in 1908 with 37. Under current practices, the chances of anyone breaking it in the future are negligible.

MIDDLESBROUGH SIGN COMMON FOR £1,000

ALF COMMON SUBJECT OF SOCCER'S FIRST FOUR-FIGURE TRANSFER DEAL

February 1905, Middlesbrough, England

Alf Common more than justified his record price tag, scoring 58 times for Middlesbrough in 168 appearances.

Alf Common was no stranger to the big-money deal. Eyebrows were raised when, three years after having left the club for Sheffield United (where he scored 21 goals in 67 appearances), the centre-forward returned to Sunderland for a record fee of £520. But his time at Roker Park was short-lived. In February he was off to Middlesbrough for the staggering fee of £1,000 – a world record that caused a sensation. Common won the hearts of the Ayresome Park faithful on 25 November 1905, his very first game for the club, when he scored a penalty to secure a 1–0 win over Sheffield United, one of his former clubs.

➲ Common remained Britain's most expensive soccer player for 13½ years, until Charlie Roberts moved from Manchester United to Oldham Athletic in October 1913 for £1,500.

TWO-WHEEL WORLD SPEED RECORD

GLENN CURTISS BREAKS MOTORBIKE WORLD SPEED RECORD

23 January 1907, Ormond Beach, Florida, USA

Remembered in history more as one of the aviation industry's early pioneers, Glenn Curtiss developed a keen interest in motorcycles and internal combustion engines in his youth while working as a bicycle messenger for Western Union. Before long he was manufacturing his own single-cylinder motorcycles. He made quite a stir in 1903 when he clocked an average speed of 64mph over a mile-long course ... but he was convinced he could go faster. In 1907, racing his Curtiss V8 motorcycle over the sands of Ormond Beach, Florida, he went faster than any human had ever been before, recording the sensational speed of 136.27mph (219.31km/h) to earn the accolade "The Fastest Man on Earth".

Glenn Curtiss is perhaps best known for his impact on the early aviation industry, but his early love for motorcycles culminated in him breaking the world two-wheel land speed record.

➲ Curtiss's land speed record stood until 6 July 1924, when Rene Thomas clocked 143.21mph (230.47km/h) in Arpajon, France. The motorbike record lasted for some 30 years.

WHO ATE ALL THE PIES?

WILLIAM "FATTY" FOULKE, HEAVIEST MAN TO PLAY SENIOR SOCCER, RETIRES

May 1907, Bradford, England

The general trend for modern goalkeepers is for height and a cat-like agility between the sticks. William Henry Foulke certainly ticked all the boxes when it came to the first of those requirements, measuring a mighty 6ft 7in, but it was his weight that attracted the jibes of visiting supporters: at his heaviest, Foulke tipped the scales at 336lbs (153 kilos). But he made for a considerable presence between the posts and forged a decade-long career with Sheffield United (1895 to 1905), with the highlight coming in the Blades' 2–1 replay victory over Southampton in the 1902 FA Cup final, during which Foulke made a series of crucial saves.

It is an apocryphal story that the taunt "Who ate all the pies?" was first directed at William "Fatty" Foulke. He earned one international cap for England, against Wales in 1897. He is thought to have been England's tallest-ever player until Peter Crouch.

➲ Foulke left Sheffield United to join newly formed Chelsea in 1905. A year later he moved back to his roots in the north to play for Bradford City, his last season in senior soccer. He died aged 42 on 1 May 1916.

12 ALL OUT!

NORTHAMPTONSHIRE DISMISSED FOR LOWEST FIRST-CLASS TOTAL

10 June 1907, Gloucester, England

Northamptonshire may well have been relative newcomers to the County Championship, having played first-class cricket for just two seasons, but when they travelled to the Spa Ground in Gloucester to play four-time champions Gloucestershire, nobody could have foreseen the rout that was to follow. Not that the visitors got off to the worst of starts, dismissing the hosts for a paltry 66, but that was as good as it got. George Dennett, Gloucestershire's number 11, no doubt frustrated by the disappointing efforts of his batsmen, unleashed his fury on the Northants batsmen and flattened them with a devastating spell of 8 for 9. A stunned Northamptonshire capitulated to a miserable 12 all out.

➲ This is not the shortest completed first-class innings in terms of balls received. That accolade falls to Hampshire, all out for 15 in 53 balls against Warwickshire at Edgbaston in 1922.

On what clearly must have been a treacherous wicket, Gloucestershire (above) scraped to 88 all out in their second innings. Northamptonshire didn't get close to their victory target (143), crashing to 40 all out with Dennett again coming to the fore, taking 7 for 12.

Massy's Open Championship success in 1907 did much to accelerate the game's popularity on the continent.

MASSY FIRST OVERSEAS CHAMPION GOLFER

ARNAUD MASSY BECOMES FIRST OVERSEAS PLAYER TO WIN OPEN CHAMPIONSHIP

July 1907, Hoylake, England

The Open Championship title was the preserve of the British. The previous 46 Opens had only ever seen a British winner and when the tournament returned to Hoylake in 1907 there was little reason to believe anything would be different this time round. But on the first day the wind blew. France's Arnaud Massy and Walter Toogood produced the best damage-limitation exercise, shooting 76. Normality resumed after the third round. J.H. Taylor had found his swing and moved into a one-shot lead over Massy, but it was the Frenchman who won the day, shooting a final-round 77 to Taylor's 80 to become the Open Championship's first overseas winner.

➲ There have since been 65 overseas winners, but Massy remains the only Frenchman to have tasted Open Championship success and remained the only continental player to win the tournament until Seve Ballesteros' triumph at Royal Lytham in 1979.

EWRY WINS EIGHTH GOLD

RAY EWRY BECOMES ONLY PERSON IN OLYMPIC HISTORY TO WIN EIGHT TRACK-AND-FIELD GOLDS

27 April–31 October 1908, White City, London, England

The eruption of Mount Vesuvius on 7 April 1906 may have led to the Games' switch from Rome to London, but it was Indiana-born Ray Ewry who sent shockwaves around the sporting world during the 1908 Summer Olympics. By the time he arrived at the newly constructed 68,000-capacity White City, he was already a six-time champion, having won all three standing jump competitions – long jump, high jump and triple jump – at both the 1900 (Paris) and 1904 (St Louis) Olympics. He added two more golds to his haul in London, successfully defending both his high jump and long jump crowns, and became the only man in history to win eight track-and-field gold medals.

➲ Ewry did not have a chance to defend his standing triple jump title: the discipline was dropped for the 1908 Games, thus making him the event's only Olympic champion.

The fact that Ewry overcame polio as a child – at one time it was feared he would spend the rest of his life in a wheelchair – made his Olympic achievements all the more remarkable.

Madge Syers (pictured here with her husband Edgar) eased to singles skating gold at the 1908 Olympics. At 27, she remains the oldest-ever winner of the competition.

SYERS DOMINATES OLYMPIC SKATING

MADGE SYERS ONLY PERSON TO WIN MEDALS IN SINGLES AND PAIRS AT SAME OLYMPICS

27 April–31 October 1908, White City, London, England

In 1902, upon discovering the rulebook did not specify gender, Madge Syers, an accomplished British skater, decided to enter the world championships. Skating in an ankle-length skirt, she finished second, although many present thought she should have won; afterwards the judges defended their decision by saying they could not see her feet because of the skirt. Four years later a world championships for women was created: Syers won. So when skating was included in the program for the 1908 Summer Olympics, Syers was the hot favourite. She did not disappoint, picking up gold in the singles and bronze in the pairs, with her husband Edgar, to become skating's only multi-medallist at a single Olympics.

➲ Ill health forced Madge Syers to retire from skating soon after her 1908 Olympic success, but she will be remembered as the first true pioneer of women's figure skating.

PETIT-BRETON AT THE DOUBLE

LUCIEN PETIT-BRETON FIRST BACK-TO-BACK WINNER OF TOUR DE FRANCE

9 August 1908, Paris, France

In 1907, as the Tour continued to break free from the shackles of its inglorious recent past, you would have been hard pressed to find anyone backing French rider Lucien Petit-Breton, other perhaps than Petit-Breton himself. However, despite not being affiliated to a team – meaning he had no mechanical help during the race – he took two stage victories en route to an improbable win. He more than justified the champion's tag the following year, showing everyone his skill, as he won five stages and cruised into Paris with a comfortable lead to become the Tour de France's first back-to-back winner.

➲ Petit-Breton was never as successful in the Tour de France again. He lost his best racing years to the First World War and died in 1917, when he crashed into the front of a car during a race.

Lucien Petit-Breton, the French-born Argentine, caused quite a stir with his maiden Tour de France success in 1907, but defended his title with majestic ease the following year.

JOHNSON KO'S THE COLOUR BARRIER

JACK JOHNSON BECOMES FIRST AFRICAN-AMERICAN TO WIN WORLD HEAVYWEIGHT CHAMPIONSHIP

26 December 1908, Sydney, Australia

Jack Johnson was the best heavyweight boxer of his generation. Having turned professional in 1897, he captured his first major title when he beat Ed Martin to become the "Coloured Champion", but James J. Craddock, the reigning heavyweight champion, refused to fight him; the heavyweight title was considered too sacrosanct for coloureds to compete for. Johnson's shot at the biggest title in boxing finally came when Canadian Tommy Burns became champion. Johnson goaded him in the press and chased him to Australia, with the two fighting on 26 December in Sydney: the police broke the fight up after 14 rounds, but Johnson was declared the winner.

➲ Johnson held on to the title until 1915, when Jess Willard knocked him out in the 26th of 45 rounds in Havana, Cuba. He never had another shot at the world championship, but continued fighting through to 1938.

Jack Johnson had to wait 11 long years for his shot at the world heavyweight championship, and when he finally got his hands on boxing's biggest prize he held onto it for seven years.

PEARY AND HENSON WIN RACE TO NORTH POLE

ROBERT PEARY AND MATTHEW HENSON FIRST TO REACH NORTH POLE

6 April 1909, North Pole

Polar expeditions fired the public's imagination in the early part of the 20th century and assaults on the North Pole were not uncommon. Just days after Robert Peary left New York harbour with a crew of 23 men on his latest attempt on the North Pole, news emerged of another claimant to the honour, although Dr Frederick Cook's claims were later dismissed. Peary, a keen student of Inuit survival techniques, arrived in Ellesmere Island near Greenland and set off for the pole on foot on 1 March 1909. Aided by a team of Inuit and his personal assistant of many previous expeditions, Matthew Henson, Peary and his group finally reached the North Pole on 6 April 1909.

Veteran polar explorer Robert Peary and his long-time assistant Matthew Henson were celebrated as the first to have reached the North Pole.

➲ Although Peary and Henson were recognized by the National Geographic Society as being the first to have reached the North Pole, it is now thought that, due to navigational errors, they may have been as much as 30–50 miles (50–80km) short of their intended destination.

AGE WILL NOT DIMINISH HIM

ARTHUR GORE BECOMES OLDEST WINNER OF WIMBLEDON MEN'S SINGLES TITLE

July 1909, Wimbledon, London, England

Having played in every All-England tournament for over two decades, Arthur Gore arrived at the 1909 Wimbledon Championships with plenty of experience on his side, and considerable pedigree: he had enjoyed a bumper year in 1908, taking singles and doubles gold at the London Olympics as well as securing a second Wimbledon crown to add to the title he won in 1901. But the defending champion was forced to call on every resource at his disposal during the 1909 final, losing the first two sets before rallying in style to emerge 6–8, 1–6, 6–2, 6–2, 6–2 winner. At 41 years 182 days, he had become the tournament's oldest winner.

Three-time Wimbledon champion Arthur Gore holds the record for the most championship appearances (30) and is also the oldest winner of the men's singles crown.

➲ To cap a remarkable tournament for the Englishman, he partnered Roper Barrett to the men's doubles crown.

GARDNER BREAKS THE MOULD

ROBERT A. GARDNER BECOMES YOUNGEST WINNER OF US AMATEUR

11 September 1909, Chicago Golf Club, Wheaton, Illinois, USA

Tommy Morris'sstellar performances in the 1860s and '70s had opened the British golfing fraternity's eyes to the possibility of a prodigy, but things were slightly different on the other side of the pond; in the United States, golf was still the preserve of the tweed-clad elders. But one-time Yale student Robert A. Gardner was cut from a different cloth. Tall, slender and dressed in white flannels, he arrived at the 1909 US Amateur championships at the Chicago Golf Club as an unknown. Everybody knew his name when he left: he battled his way through the matchplay-format tournament to the final, where he beat Chandler Egan 4&2 to become the championship's youngest winner.

➲ Tiger Woods now holds the record as the US Amateur's youngest winner: he captured the trophy on the first of three occasions in 1994 aged 18 years 7 months and 29 days.

Robert A. Gardner (left) was an accomplished all-round athlete: a pole-vaulter for Yale, a national doubles racquets champion and a two-time winner of the US Amateur championships.

TREBLE TROUBLE FOR THE TIGERS

DETROIT TIGERS FIRST TO LOSE THREE CONSECUTIVE WORLD SERIES

16 October 1909, Forbes Field, Philadelphia, Pennsylvania, USA

The Detroit Tigers were the class act of the American League: they had swept to three consecutive pennants – in 1907, 1908 and 1909 – but always came unstuck when it really mattered, losing the 1907 World Series in five games to the Chicago Cubs and suffering the same fate to the same opponents the following year. After that, the Tigers would have approached their third consecutive Fall Classic – this time against the Philadelphia Phillies – with a degree of trepidation. But a change of opponent did little to prompt a change of fortune: the Tigers slumped to an 8–0 defeat in game seven to become the first team to lose three consecutive World Series.

➲ Another 25 years would pass before the Tigers reached the World Series again. In 1934, they lost in seven games to the St Louis Cardinals, but Tigers fans did not have to wait much longer to taste World Series success: they beat the Chicago Cubs 4–2 the following year to win baseball's biggest prize for the first time.

Detroit may have had the masterful batting of Ty Cobb and a formidable pitching staff at their disposal but, between 1907 and 1909, Sam Crawford (above) and the rest of the Tigers endured nothing but World Series misery.

YOUNG BOWS OUT OF BASEBALL

CY YOUNG RETIRES FROM BASEBALL WITH RECORD NUMBER OF CAREER WINS

15 October 1911, Boston, Massachusetts, USA

Such was the impact made by Denton "Cy" Young during his 22-year professional career – he was nicknamed "Cyclone" because of the speed of his fastball – that Major League Baseball created a trophy bearing his name and presented it each year to the best pitcher in each of the American and National Leagues. Born in Gilmore, an Ohio farming community, in 1867, Young made his MLB debut with the Cleveland Spiders in 1890. A pitcher with phenomenal control – he led the league with fewest walks issued 13 times – he soon acquired a reputation as the hardest fastball pitcher in the game. By the time he appeared on the mound for the final time, for the Boston Braves aged 44 on 11 October 1911, some 815 games later (an all-time MLB best for a starting pitcher), he held the record for the most wins (511 – 94 more than second-placed Walter Johnson), the most innings pitched (7,356), the most completed games (749) and, more dubiously, the most losses.

➲ Cy Young pitched the first-ever game in the inaugural World Series in 1903; he lost that one, but would go on to win two, as the Red Sox upset the National League's Pittsburgh Pirates to become the first winners.

Few believe Cy Young's career record of 511 wins will ever be beaten.

GREEN LIGHT FOR INDY 500

RAY HARROUN FIRST TO TAKE CHEQUERED FLAG IN INDIANAPOLIS 500

30 May 1911, Indianapolis, Indiana, USA

Built in 1909 as a gravel-and-dirt track but only attracting a series of small events, the track's owners decided that the Indianapolis Motor Speedway needed something new. They resurfaced the track with 3.2 million bricks and set about trying to host the biggest race the United States had ever seen, offering a staggering first prize of $25,000: the temptation was too great to resist. On 30 May 1911, in front of 80,000 spectators all paying an entrance fee of $1, the leading drivers of the time lined up on the starting grid for the first running of the Indianapolis 500. Ray Harroun, in his Mormon Wasp, was the first winner.

⊃ A local Indiana boy racing for a local Indiana manufacturer, Harroun had come out of retirement to compete in the first Indy 500; he never competed in the event again.

Ray Harroun's average race speed during the 1911 Indy 500 was 74.602mph (129.060km/h).

McDERMOTT BREAKS BRITISH MONOPOLY

JOHN McDERMOTT BECOMES FIRST AMERICAN AND YOUNGEST TO WIN US OPEN

27 June 1911, Chicago Golf Club, Wheaton, Illinois, USA

The last time one of the USA's national golf events had been played at Chicago Golf Club, Robert A. Gardner had upset the formbook to become the US Amateur's youngest winner. When the US Open tournament arrived at the Illinois course in 1911, no such surprises were anticipated: a British-born player had won all 16 previous Opens. But American golf was on the up, the march led by 19-year-old John J. McDermott, a self-assured graduate of the Philadelphia caddie sheds who knew his own game inside-out. McDermott had finished runner-up in 1910, but went one better the following year to become not only the first American-born winner of the tournament, but also, at 19 years, 10 months and 14 days, the youngest.

⊃ McDermott defended his title the following year, at the Buffalo Country Club, shooting 294 over four rounds and becoming the first player in US Open history to shoot a sub-par 72-hole total.

Although McDermott was the first American-born player to win the US Open, Francis Ouimet, whose victory in 1913 rocked the golfing establishment, is credited with being the man who started the USA's golf boom.

LAMBERT-CHAMBERS RECORDS DOUBLE BAGEL

DOROTHEA LAMBERT-CHAMBERS FIRST TO WIN WIMBLEDON FINAL 6–0, 6–0
July 1911, Wimbledon, London, England

London-born Dorothea Lambert-Chambers may have been the daughter of a clergyman, but she put any ideas of charity to one side the moment she arrived on the tennis court. Possessing a ruthless competitive streak, she had a mentality focused on just one thing: winning. And win she did. By the time she arrived to defend her Wimbledon crown in 1911 – she had beaten Dora Boothby 6–2, 6–2 in the 1910 final – the four-time winner already had her sights firmly set on Lottie Dod's all-time record of five singles titles. She squared off against Boothby for the crown once more and nobody could have predicted the outcome. The match saw some of the most formidable tennis ever seen as Lambert-Chambers dispatched Boothby 6–0, 6–0 in a match lasting a mere 22 minutes.

➲ The match was the shortest in Wimbledon final history. Lambert-Chambers would go on to record two further successes in the tournament, in 1913 and 1914, and also played her part in the longest women's singles final ever played, when she lost 10–8, 4–6, 9–7 to Suzanne Lenglen in 1919.

Dorothea Lambert-Chambers picked up five women's singles titles in the space of nine years (1906–14), but none was won more comfortably than her 1911 triumph.

BIG KAHUNA BREAKS SWIMMING WORLD RECORD

DUKE KAHANAMOKU BREAKS WORLD RECORD FOR 100 YARDS

11 August 1911, Honolulu, Hawaii

Duke Kahanamoku was the ultimate beach boy. Brought up on the sands of Waikiki beach, he developed such an affinity with the sea he became the leading watersportsman of his day and, arguably, of all time. One of the pioneers of modern surfing, he was also the world's fastest swimmer. On 11 August 1911, in a timed swimming feat in the still waters of Honolulu harbour, he swam 100 yards (91m) in 55.4 seconds, breaking the existing record by the massive margin of 4.6 seconds. He also broke the record for the 220 yards (201m) and 50 yards (46m): they were records a disbelieving Amateur Athletic Association refused to accept for some years.

Best known as the father of modern surfing, Duke Kahanamoku – aka "The Big Kahuna" – was also a world-record-breaking swimmer.

➲ Kahanamoku qualified comfortably for the US team for the 1912 Olympics in Stockholm, breaking the 200m world record in the trials, and went on to capture a gold medal in the 100m freestyle.

VETERAN LARNED EASES TO SEVENTH TITLE

WILLIAM LARNED BECOMES OLDEST WINNER OF US OPEN SINGLES CROWN

4 September 1911, Newport, Rhode Island, USA

Born into a family that could trace its roots to shortly after the arrival of the Mayflower, William Larned enjoyed a privileged upbringing. He went to Cornell and made a name for himself when he became the only Cornellian to win the inter-collegiate tennis tournament and soon transferred that promise onto the international stage. Having already won the US Open six times (in 1901, 1902, 1907, 1908, 1909 and 1910), he enjoyed one last hurrah in 1911, beating countryman Maurice McLoughlin 6–4, 6–4, 6–2 in the final to become the first player to win seven titles and, at 38 years 242 days, the tournament's oldest-ever winner.

➲ William Larned invented the steel-framed tennis racket in 1922 and went on to found a company to manufacture them.

Along with Richard Sears and Bill Tilden, William Larned was considered to be one of the US Open's "Big Three".

AMUNDSEN WINS RACE TO SOUTH POLE

ROALD AMUNDSEN FIRST TO LEAD TEAM TO SOUTH POLE
14 December 1911, South Pole

Richard Peary's successful assault on the North Pole in 1909 led to a change of plan. Roald Amundsen, an experienced Norwegian polar explorer – he had been the first to successfully traverse the Northwest Passage in 1903 – decided to turn Robert Falcon Scott's attempt on the South Pole into a race. Utilizing survival skills learned from the Arctic Inuit, Amundsen and his party of four other men, 52 dogs and four sledges left their base camp in the Bay of Whales and made their way along a direct line to the South Pole, stopping at provisions dumps strategically placed en route. Overcoming treacherous conditions, the group (along with 16 of the dogs) finally reached 90°S (the South Pole) on 14 December 1911, beating Scott and his crew by 35 days.

➲ Amundsen returned to base camp on 25 January 1912; in contrast, Scott and his team were never to return.

Lessons learned during previous Arctic expeditions undoubtedly helped Amundsen become the first to reach the South Pole.

THORPE SETS DECATHLON BEST

JIM THORPE BREAKS THE DECATHLON WORLD RECORD
May–July 1912, Stockholm, Sweden

Of Native American ancestry, raised as a Sac and Fox and named "Wa-Tho-Huk" (literally meaning "Bright Path"), Jim Thorpe poured the frustration of a difficult life into sports and excelled ... in track and field, baseball, basketball, lacrosse and even ballroom dancing. But it was his exploits on the American football field that earned him nationwide fame: in 1911, he scored all of Carlisle Indian Institute's goals when they shocked Harvard in the inter-collegiate tournament. He made international headlines the following year, when he won pentathlon and decathlon gold at the Olympic Games in Stockholm, the latter with a world record haul of 8,413 points.

➲ Thorpe's decathlon mark would stand for over two decades, but he was stripped of his Olympic titles when it was discovered he had played minor league baseball prior to the Games, thus breaking the amateur status rules.

A prolific athlete who excelled in track and field and who played American football, baseball and basketball professionally, Jim Thorpe was named "Greatest Athlete of the First Half of the Century" by the Associated Press in 1950.

During his time, Sydney Barnes was universally accepted as being the world's best bowler; you would be hard pressed to find any other bowler in cricket history to receive such a universal accolade.

BARNES'S YEAR OF YEARS
ENGLAND'S S.F. BARNES BREAKS RECORD FOR MOST TEST WICKETS IN CALENDAR YEAR
12–13 August 1912, The Oval, London, England

Sydney Barnes possessed the fast bowler's greatest weapon: the ability to swing the ball both ways, late and at pace. The Staffordshire-born tearaway put his skills to especially good use during 1912. In 12 months that year, Barnes took 61 wickets in nine Tests, including 26 wickets in four matches against Australia to help England overturn a 1–0 deficit and record a memorable 4–1 Ashes victory. But the highlight came against South Africa at The Oval in August, when he ended up with match figures of 13 for 57 as England routed South Africa and won by 10 wickets inside two days.

➲ Barnes's record would last 52 years until 1964, when Australia's Graham McKenzie took 71 wickets in 14 Test matches.

GOUX TASTES INDY SUCCESS

JULES GOUX WINS INDIANAPOLIS 500 BY RECORD MARGIN

30 May 1913, Indianapolis, Indiana, USA

Jules Goux made five appearances at the Indianapolis 500, but none was more impressive than his record-breaking victory in 1913.

It may only have been the third running of the event, but the 1913 Indianapolis 500 marked the first time the race possessed a truly international flavour. Cars from England, Germany, France and Italy crossed the Atlantic to take on the United States' finest and it was a Frenchman who stole the day: Jules Goux, driving the number 16 four-cylinder Peugeot, led 138 of the 200 laps and stole such a march on his rivals that, after he took the chequered flag, 13 minutes and eight seconds passed before second-placed Spencer Wishart crossed the finishing line. It was the largest margin of victory in Indy 500 history.

⮞ So comfortable was the victory, legend has it that Goux was drinking champagne throughout the entire race.

VETERAN TAYLOR WINS OPEN

J.H. TAYLOR COLLECTS FIFTH OPEN CHAMPIONSHIP WITH EIGHT-STROKE WIN

24 June 1913, Hoylake, Liverpool, England

John Henry Taylor stole the headlines after the first round of the 53rd Open Championship: the four-time champion (1893, 1895, 1900 and 1909) had rolled back the years to share the first-round lead. And his championship form continued through the first nine of the second round, before he slipped up in the homeward nine to trail the leader by one. But then the wind blew, and Taylor, a master of the low shot, produced the round of the day to lead by three with 18 holes remaining. He kept his nerve and more, extending his lead to eight shots to secure his fifth Open success, 19 years after his first – a tournament record.

⮞ In securing his fourth title at the 1909 Open Championship in Deal, Taylor had become the first player in the tournament's history to shoot all four rounds under 80 shots.

In 1913, J.H. Taylor joined his fellow members of the Great Triumvirate, Harry Vardon and James Braid, as a five-time winner of the Open Championship.

AMATEUR'S US OPEN WIN STUNS GOLF

FRANCIS OUIMET BECOMES FIRST AMATEUR TO WIN US OPEN

19 September 1913, The Country Club, Brookline, Massachusetts, USA

Former caddie Francis Ouimet's 1913 US Open triumph triggered a rapid growth in the game in the United States. No longer was golf simply a game for the wealthy.

The United States may already have enjoyed its first home-born US Open champion – John McDermott had won the previous two events – but golf still remained beyond the mainstream of American sporting consciousness. That all changed at Brookline in 1913, when 20-year-old Francis Ouimet returned to the club where he used to caddie as a boy and took on the game's greatest players. Eyebrows were raised when his four-round total of 304 left him in a tie for first place with the leading English golfers of the day, Harry Vardon and Ted Ray, but his victory – he shot 72 in the play-off to Vardon's 77 and Ray's 78 – didn't just shock the golfing fraternity, it changed the entire perception of the sport: a former caddie could win the US Open…

➲ Ouimet, with the help of his ten-year-old caddie Eddie Lowery, became the first amateur to win the US Open championship. He used to live in a house that lay across the street from The Country Club's 17th green.

LEONARD SETS NEW ERA LOW

DUTCH LEONARD SETS MODERN-DAY ERA RECORD WITH 0.96

October 1914, USA

Herbert Benjamin "Dutch" Leonard had played two seasons in college, plus one in the minor leagues before getting his shot at the big time with the Boston Red Sox as a 20-year-old at the start of the 1913 season. And he soon showed he was a fearsome pitcher, quickly cementing his place in the Red Sox pitching rotation. It is quite common for players to suffer in their second Major League season, but Leonard excelled in 1914, winning 19 games and setting a modern-day record for ERA with 0.96 to secure long-lasting fame.

➲ Leonard went on to win three World Series with the Red Sox, in 1915, 1916 and 1918.

Dutch Leonard's pitching performances at the Red Sox in 1914 earned him a permanent place in the record books.

BARNES BATTERS SOUTH AFRICA

S.F. BARNES TAKES RECORD 49 WICKETS IN SERIES

18 February 1914, Durban, South Africa

South African batsmen would have been sick of the sight of Sydney Barnes following England's 1913–14 winter tour: as he had done throughout his impressive career, the Staffordshire-born bowler confirmed his status as the most dynamic tearaway bowler of his generation. As England romped to a comfortable 4–0 series victory, Barnes, playing in only four of the five Tests, collected a record series haul of 49 wickets. His dominance started in the first Test in Durban – he collected 10 wickets in the match as England eased to an innings victory – and five further five-wicket hauls followed, including 17 in the second Test.

➲ In what would turn out to be his last appearance for England, in the fourth Test v South Africa in Durban, Barnes took his 49th wicket of the series to end with match figures of 14 for 144.

Sydney Barnes claimed the record for most wickets in a five-Test series, despite playing in only four of England's five matches against South Africa in 1913–14.

REGRET WINS THE DERBY

REGRET BECOMES FIRST FILLY TO WIN THE KENTUCKY DERBY

9 May 1915, Louisville, Kentucky, USA

Bred by Harry Payne Whitney, a leading American owner and breeder, Regret, a big, chestnut filly, went to the post for the first time in the 1914 Saratoga Special: she beat the top colt in the race, Pebbles, by a length to take the win. Over the course of the next 14 days, Regret won two further races and amassed $17,390 in winnings: now recognized as the champion two-year-old filly, she did not race again that year. Her next outing came in the 1915 Kentucky Derby and the red-hot favourite did not disappoint the punters, leading the race wire-to-wire to become the first filly in history to win America's biggest horse race.

➲ Regret would only race 11 times through her career, winning on nine occasions and collecting $34,093 in career earnings.

Regret, the 1915 Kentucky Derby winner, was ranked 71st when the magazine *Blood-Horse* produced its list of the 20th century's top horses.

16 SHUTOUTS FOR ALEXANDER

GROVER CLEVELAND ALEXANDER SETS MLB SINGLE-SEASON SHUTOUT RECORD

October 1916, Philadelphia, Pennsylvania, USA

Suffering from epilepsy, living beneath the shadow of alcoholism and, later in his career, haunted by experiences during the First World War, Grover Cleveland Alexander somehow managed to put his problematic life behind him the moment he stepped on the mound. He came to prominence in 1915, winning the Triple Crown as his Philadelphia Phillies team lost out to the Red Sox in five games in the World Series. In 1916, Alexander picked up where he had left off: winning 33 games, leading the league in ERA (1.55) and strikeouts (167) to win a second Triple Crown and recording 16 shutouts, a record never likely to be broken.

➲ In 1999, the Sporting News ranked Grover Cleveland Alexander 12th out of the 20th century's best baseball players: during his 20-year career he notched up an impressive 373 wins.

Grover Cleveland Alexander's record-breaking exploits in 1916 were not enough to secure the Philadelphia Phillies the National League pennant; they finished second.

ALCOCK AND BROWN CONQUER ATLANTIC

JOHN ALCOCK AND ARTHUR BROWN COMPLETE FIRST SOLO FLIGHT ACROSS ATLANTIC

14–15 June 1919, St John's, Newfoundland–Clifden, near Connemara, Ireland

In 1913, the *Daily Mail* had offered a prize of £10,000 for the first successful non-stop flight across the Atlantic. Such an enormous sum was hard to ignore and John Alcock (as pilot) and Arthur Brown (as navigator) were selected to take on the feat. They took off from Lester's airfield in St John's, Newfoundland, in the late afternoon of 14 June 1919 in their modified Vickers Vimy IV plane. Overcoming engine trouble, snow, fog and ice, they made a "successful" crash-landing in a bog in southern Ireland at 8.50 a.m. on 15 June 1919. The 1,890-mile (3,040km) journey had taken them 15 hours and 57 minutes.

➲ A month earlier, a United States navy plane also crossed the Atlantic, but it had made multiple stops along the way and the journey had taken 19 days.

Alcock and Brown both flew for the Royal Air Force during the First World War and both had been shot down and taken prisoner, Alcock in Turkey and Brown in Germany. They became heroes after their successful crossing and both were later knighted.

SEVENTH HEAVEN FOR JOE MALONE

JOE MALONE SETS NHL RECORD FOR MOST GOALS SCORED IN ONE GAME

31 January 1920, Quebec, Canada

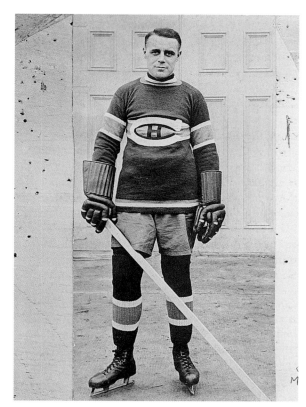

Joe Malone was the greatest goal-scorer of the NHL's formative years. He began his professional career playing for the Quebec Bulldogs, but when his team decided not to enter the newly founded National Hockey League in 1917, he moved to the Montreal Canadiens. He was an instant star, scoring five goals in his first game and ending the season with 44 goals in 20 games – a record single-season mark that would last until 1945. He returned to Quebec in 1919 for the franchise's first NHL season and, on 31 January 1920, shocked the world by scoring a record seven goals (an eighth was disallowed) in a 10–6 victory over Toronto.

➲ Malone broke Newsy Lalonde's record of six goals in a game set just three weeks earlier in December 1919. No one has come close to breaking it since.

NHL history books abound with goal-scoring legends – Howe, Gretzky, Lemieux, Bossy *et al.* – but only Joe Malone can lay claim to averaging two goals per game throughout his career.

FRANCE'S NINE-YEAR LOSING STREAK

FRANCE SUFFER RECORD 18 CONSECUTIVE DEFEATS
28 January 1911–17 February 1920

Those who thought France's 16–15 win over Scotland on 2 January 1911 – their first win in international history – would trigger an upturn in their rugby fortunes were proved sadly wrong. Three weeks later, Les Bleus travelled to London to play England and were trounced 37–0: it triggered the worst sequence of results in international rugby history. For nine years, over 18 matches, France simply could not win. They came close – 8–11 against Wales in 1913, 0–5 to Scotland in 1920, 5–6 to Wales later the same year – but it wasn't until they played Ireland in Dublin on 3 April 1920 and won 15–7 that they could finally exorcize their losing demons.

➲ The taste of victory must have been sweet: France went on to win their next two games 14–5 against the United States and 3–0 against Scotland.

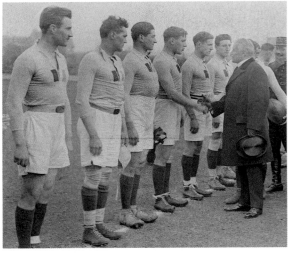

Not all records are cherished ones. French rugby was in the mire between 1911 and 1920: the national team lost every one of the 18 games they played.

LES HABS BLITZ THE BULLDOGS

MONTREAL CANADIENS SCORE AN NHL RECORD 16 GOALS IN ONE GAME
3 March 1920, Quebec City, Canada

The Montreal Canadiens moved to a new home for the start of the 1919–20 season – the NHL's third – and marked their first game there by trouncing Toronto St Patricks 14–7, with Newsy Lalonde scoring a then-record six goals: the 21 goals scored that night were the most in a game in NHL history (eventually equalled when Edmonton Oilers beat Chicago Blackhawks 12–9 on 11 December 1985). They did even better on 3 March, travelling to play the Quebec Bulldogs and beating them 16–3 on their own ice to set an all-time NHL record for the most goals scored by one team in a single game.

➲ The Montreal Canadiens may well have broken some records during the 1919–20 season, but they missed out on the prize they really wanted: they finished runner-up to the Ottawa Senators.

The Montreal Canadiens were prolific scorers in 1919–20, but they were not so good at winning games and finished 13–11 for 26 points, 12 behind the Ottawa Senators, who won the Stanley Cup against the Seattle Metropolitans.

Billy Meredith, the Welsh Wizard, pictured right, enjoyed a phenomenal 30-year career in professional soccer that spanned four decades.

WELSH WIZARD CASTS HIS FINAL SPELL

BILLY MEREDITH BECOMES OLDEST INTERNATIONAL IN SOCCER HISTORY

15 March 1920, Highbury, London, England

Billy Meredith's dazzling displays for soccer's most attacking team in the early part of the 20th century, Manchester United, saw the Welshman become the game's first true superstar. His bursts of speed, runs down the wing and deadly accurate crosses helped bring the Old Trafford club the championship in 1908 and 1911 and the FA Cup in 1909. The First World War may have ended the careers of many players, but not that of the Welsh Wizard, who played the last of his 48 internationals against England at Highbury on 15 March 1920. Aged 45 years 229 days, he bowed out in style as Wales recorded a memorable 2–1 win.

➲ His international retirement marked anything but the end of the road for Billy Meredith. He moved to Manchester City in 1921 and played his last match for the Blues in the FA Cup semi-final against Newcastle, aged 49 years 245 days.

42-YEAR-OLD MACDONALD STRIKES GOLD

PATRICK MACDONALD BECOMES OLDEST OLYMPIC TRACK-AND-FIELD GOLD MEDALLIST

24 August 1920, Antwerp, Belgium

Patrick "Babe" MacDonald was a giant of a man: at 6ft 5in and weighing in at almost 18 stone, the New York City policeman produced the throw of his life in the 1912 Olympics in Stockholm to win shot-putt gold. The cancellation of the 1916 Games due to the First World War meant MacDonald had to wait until shortly after his 42nd birthday before having the chance to defend his crown, at the 1920 Olympic Games in Antwerp. He missed out on shot-putt gold, finishing fourth, but his victory in the 56lb throw saw him become the oldest track-and-field gold medallist in Olympic Games history.

➲ MacDonald served in the New York Police Department for 41 years (1905–46) and was one of the most recognizable officers in the city: his job was to direct the traffic in Times Square.

Patrick MacDonald was 42 years 26 days old when he became an Olympic champion for the second time.

BRITAIN MAKE SPLASH IN WATER POLO

BRITAIN BECOME FIRST TO WIN THREE CONSECUTIVE OLYMPIC WATER POLO GOLD MEDALS

April–September 1920, Antwerp, Belgium

Over a 12-year period, covering three Olympic Games, the British water polo team were the side to beat. After winning gold in both 1908 and 1912 they were forced to wait eight years before having a shot at an Olympic hat-trick. Britain and Belgium were the form teams of the early rounds when Olympic competition resumed in Antwerp in 1920 following the end of the First World War, and it was no surprise when both made it through to the final. With the scores tied at 2–2, Britain scored a late goal to silence the vociferous partisan crowd and claim an unprecedented third successive gold.

➲ Two of Britain's players appeared in all three Olympic triumphs: goalkeeper and captain Charles Sydney Smith and Paul Radmilovic, who scored the winning goal in the 1920 final. In addition to the three water polo gold medals, Radmilovic also won gold as part of the 1908 4 x 200m freestyle relay: his haul of four gold medals was unbeaten by any British Olympian until Steve Redgrave won his fifth gold medal at the 2000 Olympics in Sydney.

Britain completed a hat-trick of water polo gold medals in 1920, but any dreams of a fourth title in Paris in 1924 were soon shattered: Britain were eliminated from the competition in the first round.

With little left to lose after the first 36 holes, George Duncan switched to a new driver he had recently bought at the championship exhibition of golf equipment. The results were immediate, and Duncan had his first taste of major success.

DUNCAN FINDS SOME LATE FORM

GEORGE DUNCAN STAGES GREATEST TURNAROUND IN OPEN HISTORY TO WIN CLARET JUG

July 1920, Deal, Kent, England

The first post-war Open Championship was played at Royal Cinq Ports, Deal, in 1920. After the first 36 holes had been played, Scot George Duncan would not have thought much of his chances. Having opened up with a pair of 80s, Duncan lay 13 strokes behind halfway leader Abe Mitchell. The time was ripe for experiment: in the third round Duncan decided to switch to a new driver. It was an instant love affair: he shot 71 to haul himself back into contention and a final-round 72 was enough to see him to the Claret Jug by one stroke: Duncan had completed the greatest turnaround in Open Championship history.

➲ Born near Aberdeen in 1887, Duncan turned down the chance of a professional contract with Aberdeen's soccer club to pursue a career in golf. The winner of five tournaments, he also appeared in the Ryder Cup three times.

THYS POWERS TO TOUR HAT-TRICK

PHILIPPE THYS BECOMES FIRST TO WIN TOUR DE FRANCE ON THREE OCCASIONS

27 July 1920, Paris, France

There was no one to defend the Tour de France title in 1919. Belgian Philippe Thys, who had won the last two races before the war (in 1912 and 1913), decided not to participate in a Tour that weaved its way through bomb-damaged villages on pot-holed roads, and the unknown Belgian Firmin Lambot had come through the field to take a surprise victory. But Thys returned in some style the following year, winning the second stage (of 15) and collecting three more en route to crossing the finishing line a crushing 57 minutes-plus ahead of second-placed rider Hector Heusghem to pick up a record third Tour title.

➲ Thys stood alone as a three-time Tour de France winner until 1955, when Louison Bobet became the first to complete a hat-trick of wins. Jacques Anquetil became the Tour's first four-time winner in 1963.

Belgian Philippe Thys may have lost the best years of his career to the First World War, but he returned with a bang in 1920 to win the Tour for an unprecedented third time.

FENDER'S 35-MINUTE CENTURY

PERCY FENDER HITS FASTEST FIRST-CLASS HUNDRED

25–27 August 1920, County Ground, Northampton, England

Early in his career, Surrey captain Percy Fender adopted a policy when batting to hit the ball as fiercely as he could, whatever the state of the wicket. A tremendous driver of the ball and strong square of the wicket on both sides, he could gather runs in quick time. One of the most successful examples of his flashing-blade policy came against Northampton in 1920. Fender strode to the wicket with his side five wickets down but already holding a 142-run first-innings lead. Forty minutes later another 171 runs had been added, with Fender (113 not out) reaching his century in just 35 minutes.

➲ Fender's record stood untouched until the introduction of "declaration" bowling in the 1990s – teams in the County Championship would deliberately concede runs to try and force a declaration and thus have a chance of winning the game and securing more points – after which 30-minute centuries became a more regular occurrence.

Surrey and England's Percy Fender was one of early cricket's most colourful characters and was renowned as being one of the shrewdest captains in the game.

SIZZLING SISLER STORMS INTO RECORD BOOKS

GEORGE SISLER BREAKS TY COBB'S RECORD FOR MOST HITS IN A SEASON

September 1920, St Louis, Missouri, USA

One of the most dynamic first basemen baseball has ever seen, George Sisler is one of only three men – along with Ty Cobb and Rogers Hornsby – to have recorded .400 seasons on more than one occasion. One of those seasons came during his stellar year of 1920. It was an early-season shift up the St Louis Browns' batting order that triggered a change in fortune for Sisler: by September his average had rocketed past the .400 mark and he could now set his sights on Ty Cobb's record for the highest number of hits in a season – with eight games remaining, Sisler lay nine short of Cobb's 1911 mark. He collected another 18 hits to take his place in the record books.

➲ Between 1920 and 1977 nobody came within 20 hits of Sisler's record, which ended up lasting for 84 years, until the Seattle Mariners' Ichiro Suzuki broke it in 2004 with 262.

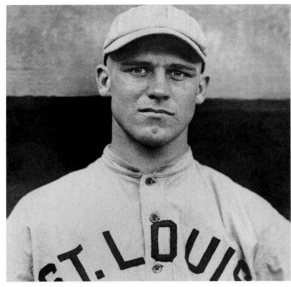

George Sisler's mark for hits would stand as a record for 84 years and it took Ichiro Suzuki an extra eight games to break it.

WAMBSGANSS'S WORLD SERIES MAGIC

BILL WAMBSGANSS BECOMES ONLY PLAYER TO RECORD UNASSISTED TRIPLE PLAY IN WORLD SERIES

10 October 1920, League Park, Cleveland, Ohio, USA

Until 1920 there had only ever been one recorded instance of an unassisted triple play in baseball history, but under modern regulations even that would have been deemed an unassisted double play. That all changed on 10 October 1920 when the Cleveland Indians took on the Brooklyn Dodgers in game five of the World Series. In the fifth inning, with Cleveland holding a 4–0 lead, the Indians' Bill Wambsganss caught a line drive batted by Clarence Mitchell, stepped on second base to retire Pete Kilduff and tagged Otto Miller coming from first base to end the innings and record the first instance of an unassisted triple play on the biggest stage of all.

➲ An unassisted triple play occurs when one fielder makes all three outs in a continuous play. There have only been 13 such occurrences in Major League Baseball history.

Bill Wambsganss – left, with his three victims – turned an unassisted triple play to help the Cleveland Indians to an 8–1 game-five win to take a lead they never surrendered in the World Series, winning the nine-match Fall Classic 5–2.

HANGING UP HIS BOOTS

HARRY "VIC" CUMBERLAND RETIRES AT 43, OLDEST PLAYER IN VFL HISTORY
December 1920, Melbourne, Australia

Harry Cumberland epitomized the spirit of the era: a strong and natural ruckman, with a strong mark and an excellent box kick, he enjoyed a career that spanned four decades. Born in Victoria, he had his first taste of senior football on the other side of the Bass Straits in Tasmania: he soon caught the eye of the big league scouts and joined professional outfit Melbourne in the Victoria Football League in 1898. In 1920, aged 43, after enjoying spells with Sturt and St Kilda, spending time in New Zealand and serving in the First World War – where he was wounded three times – he finally decided to call time on a remarkable playing career.

➲ Journalists twice named Cumberland the best player in the Victoria Football League: in 1904 and 1913.

Tragically, seven years after he retired as a player, Vic Cumberland was killed in a motorcycle accident.

RUTH TOPS THE BILL WITH 177 RUNS

BABE RUTH SETS ALL-TIME MLB SINGLE-SEASON RUN MARK

13 October 1921, Polo Grounds, New York, USA

Having pushed aside any self-doubt following his controversial and much-fabled transfer from the Boston Red Sox to the New York Yankees in 1920 by swatting a record 54 home runs in his first season at the New York franchise, Babe Ruth found his second season with the Yankees turning out to be quite an encore – in fact, arguably the best season of Ruth's stellar career. He set Major League records in home runs (59), total bases (457), RBI (171) and one that has stood the test of time: runs. The closest anyone has come to Ruth's 177 mark was Jeff Bagwell in 2000 with 152.

➲ Ruth's performances helped the New York Yankees to the American League pennant and secured a debut appearance in the World Series, but the Fall Classic proved too much for them and they crashed in eight games to cross-town rivals New York Giants.

Babe Ruth was only 26 years old when he set the all-time single-season record for runs. By this early stage of his career he had already hit more home runs than any other player in baseball history ... and was already the biggest sports star the United States had ever seen.

BIG BUCKS FOR BUCK

HAROLD BUCK BECOMES RUGBY LEAGUE'S FIRST £1,000 PLAYER

5 November 1921, Leeds, England

Leeds created a sensation in 1921 when they offered £1,000 for the services of Hunslet winger Harold Buck – and according to some sources one other player – to smash the previous transfer record by some £400 (Hull had paid £600 for the services of Billy Batten in 1912). Buck turned out to be worth every penny, soon becoming part of Leeds's infamous backline "The Busy Bs" and terrorizing defences throughout the league. The highlight of his 99 appearances for the club came when he scored one try and set up another two as Leeds demolished Hull in the 1923 Challenge Cup final.

➲ The transfer remained a rugby league record until Stanley Smith, an established international, moved from Wakefield to Leeds for the same sum in 1930.

Harold Buck (far right) may have demanded the highest price tag in rugby league, but he never received an international call-up; the closest he came was in 1924, when he made an appearance as a replacement in a Test trial.

FALKIRK GRAB WEST HAM STAR

FALKIRK PAY WEST HAM £5,000 WORLD RECORD FEE FOR SERVICES OF SYD PUDDEFOOT
February 1922, Upton Park, London, England

In 1922, West Ham soccer club was faced with a catastrophic financial crisis. Two years earlier, the club's directors had agreed to undertake a building program to increase the capacity of their Upton Park ground and the club had run out of money to pay the bills. Only one choice remained: West Ham were forced to sell their best players and one name above all was on the top of everybody's shopping list: Syd Puddefoot. The Bow-born striker had found the net 69 times in the previous three seasons and carried a high price tag. Falkirk were not deterred and paid a world record £5,000 for his services.

➲ The transfer record did not last long: just months later Sunderland forked out £5,500 for South Shields's Warney Cresswell.

Syd Puddefoot returned to his home club ten years later and stands 13th on West Ham's all-time scoring list.

THE SQUIRE TAKES THE SPOTLIGHT

GENE SARAZEN BECOMES US PGA'S YOUNGEST WINNER
12–18 August 1922, Oakmont Country Club, Oakmont, Pennsylvania, USA

Defending champion Walter Hagen may have decided to skip the tournament in favour of a heavy program of exhibition matches, but the fifth incarnation of the US PGA Championships, this time staged at the Oakmont Country Club, Philadelphia, still attracted plenty of the game's biggest names, among them the man who, a month earlier, had won the US Open – 20-year-old Gene Sarazen, the man they called "The Squire". And the diminutive New Yorker picked up where he had left off at the Stokie Country Club, beating former champion Jock Hutchinson 3&1 in the quarter-finals, Bobby Cruikshank 3&2 in the semis and Emmett French 4&3 in the final to become, at 20 years, five months and 22 days, the tournament's youngest winner.

➲ Sarazen's Oakmont victory meant he became the first in golf history to win the US Open and the US PGA in the same year.

Two years after turning professional at the age of 18, Gene Sarazen was a two-time major winner.

One of the greatest swimmers the world has ever seen, Weissmuller would become an on-screen star, featuring as Tarzan in 12 movies between 1932 and 1948.

WEISSMULLER BECOMES PRINCE OF WAVES

JOHNNY WEISSMULLER BREAKS 100M FREESTYLE WORLD RECORD

9 July 1922, Alameda, California, USA

As a 17-year-old in 1921, Johnny Weissmuller entered an amateur 100 yards freestyle race and lost. He was never to lose again. The Romanian-born immigrant (his parents had migrated to the States when he was just seven years old) worked hard with his coach William Bachrach to develop his revolutionary front-crawl style: he tended to hold his head high out of the water, perhaps because he had learned to swim in less-than-clean waters. Either way it was quick. Already the holder of the 50-yard world record (he broke his own mark in 1922, with 23 seconds), he set about challenging Duke Kahanamoku's 1920 record of 1m00.4s set at the Olympic Games in Antwerp, Belgium. His chance came in Alameda, California, on 9 July 1922 and he smashed it by nearly two seconds – the new time: 58.6s.

➲ Weissmuller would lower the mark by over a second the following year (57.4s) and the record would stand for a decade. During his career the man who would be Tarzan set 67 world swimming records, won 52 national swimming championships and won five Olympic gold medals.

TWO-TIME LAMBOT DEFIES THE YEARS

FIRMIN LAMBOT BECOMES TOUR DE FRANCE'S OLDEST WINNER

23 July 1922, Paris, France

Firmin Lambot, who had ridden through the bomb-damaged course in 1919 to become the Tour's first post-war winner, was at it again in 1922, but he had a few strokes of luck along the way. First, defending champion Philippe Thys crashed and fell out of contention; then, just as had been the case in both 1913 and 1919, home favourite Eugene Christophe was forced to retire with a broken fork. It left Lambot, who had not registered a single stage win, with a clear run to Paris, and he took the win by 41 minutes from fellow countryman Jean Alavoine.

➲ Lambot's second Tour victory made him, at 36 years and four months, the event's oldest-ever winner.

Firmin Lambot's second Tour de France victory owed something to chance: benefiting from the misfortunes of others, in 1922 he became the first to win the event without having claimed a single stage win.

BLINK AND YOU'VE MISSED IT

BART PRICE SCORES FASTEST TRY IN INTERNATIONAL RUGBY HISTORY

20 January 1923, Twickenham, London, England

If England wanted to put the frustrations of what had been a disappointing 1922 Five Nations campaign behind them, then there was no better time to exorcize any demons than in their opening game of the Five Nations championship against defending champions Wales at Twickenham. And what a start they made. As the cheers echoed around the ground and the referee signalled the start of the game, England's flanker, H.L. "Bart" Price, stole over the line just ten seconds after kick-off to give the home side a lead they would never surrender. England won the game 7–3 and Bart Price had scored the fastest try in international rugby history.

➲ England continued the momentum gained from their victory over Wales and went on to win their fourth grand slam in history.

Oxford University and Leicester Tigers flanker Bart Price (back row, middle) would appear only once more for his country, against Ireland later in the 1923 Five Nations championship; he scored a try in that match, too.

THE WHITE HORSE FINAL

FIRST WEMBLEY FA CUP FINAL ATTRACTS LARGEST CROWD IN SOCCER HISTORY
28 April 1923, Wembley Stadium, London, England

The prospect of taking a look inside England's new national stadium proved too hard to resist. Built with 25,000 tons of concrete, 1,500 tons of steel and over half a million rivets, at a cost of £750,000 in just 300 days, Wembley Stadium was ready to open its doors for its first match: the 1923 FA Cup final between Bolton Wanderers and West Ham United. The massed supporters could not wait that long: amid scenes unparalleled in soccer history the crowds rushed the gates, burst through them and swarmed on to the pitch. Kick-off was delayed and mounted policemen were called in to calm the mob – among them PC George Scorey on his white horse Billy. Were it not for the presence of King George V in the royal box it is unlikely the match would have been played but, 45 minutes later than scheduled, the 1923 FA Cup final got under way in front of an estimated minimum of 240,000 spectators, the largest number ever to watch a soccer match.

➲ Bolton, with goals from David Jack (after two minutes) and J.R. Smith (53 minutes), won the day, beating West Ham 2–0 to win the FA Cup for the second time in their history.

A record crowd packed into the 127,000-capacity Wembley Stadium for the 1923 FA Cup final. Estimates put the number of people present at between 240,000 and 300,000; the exact figure will never be known.

CHANGING OF THE GUARD

HELEN WILLS BECOMES YOUNGEST SINGLES WINNER AT US OPEN

19 August 1923, Forest Hills, New York, USA

There are moments in sports when the accepted order of
things is shattered and a future of new possibilities presents
itself. Norwegian Molla Bjurstedt Mallory was the Queen of
the US Open; the seven-time champion and winner for the
last three years had made it through to the final yet again.
And nobody bet against her securing an eighth title. She was
up against 17-year-old Helen Wills, a Californian who played
the game with detached poise … and immense power. It
was a no-contest: Wills blew the defending champion off
the court – 6–2, 6–1 – to become the tournament's youngest
winner. All of a sudden the future of women's tennis was
different.

➲ Wills defended her title in 1924 and again in 1925. In all she
would win the US Open on seven occasions, to add to her eight
Wimbledon championships and four French Open triumphs – 19
grand slam singles titles.

American sports writer Grantland Rice famously labelled Wills "Little Miss
Poker Face": on the court she was detached and introverted, ignoring
everything but her own game. It may not have won over the crowds or the
sports writers, but it was a mighty effective way to win matches.

After an inauspicious Olympic debut, aged 11, Sonja Henie would dominate
women's figure skating for more than a decade. She is credited with being the
first to incorporate ballet moves into a skating routine.

YOUNG HENIE TAUGHT A LESSON

SONJA HENIE, AGED 11, BECOMES YOUNGEST PARTICIPANT IN THE WINTER OLYMPICS

29 January 1924, Chamonix, France

Wilhelm Henie had grand plans for his daughter Sonja.
The one-time world cycling champion and now successful
Norwegian fur trader introduced his six-year-old daughter
to a pair of ice skates and hired world-famous Russian
ballerina Tamara Karsavina under strict instructions: to
turn his daughter into a sporting celebrity. She appeared in
the first-ever Winter Olympics held in Chamonix, France,
in 1924, aged just 11 and, although she showed glimpses
of potential, her routine – punctuated by frequent visits
to the side of the rink – left her in eighth place out of a total
of eight competitors. Mr Henie would have to wait for his
moment of glory.

➲ But success was imminent: Sonja Henie won the first of ten
consecutive World Championships in 1927 and the first of three
successive Olympic gold medals the following year.

CANADA, FIRST NATION IN ICE HOCKEY

CANADIAN PLAYERS CRUSH THE US TO THE TUNE OF 6–1 TO BRING HOME FIRST WINTER OLYMPIC GOLD IN ICE HOCKEY

25 January–4 February 1924, Chamonix, France

The first Winter Olympics was an event largely dominated by Scandinavians, with 17 of the 49 medals going to Norway and 11 to Finland. Canada's only medal came from ice hockey, but the Canadian team pulled its first-place finish off with aplomb, starting the tournament by flattening Switzerland 33–0, Czechoslovakia 30–0 and Sweden 22–0. Great Britain put up more of a fight but still went down by a score of 19–2. At the same time, the US won a 20–0 shutout over Sweden and advanced to meet Canada in the finals. The Canada–US match was a hard-fought affair, but the Canucks still came through, conceding only one first-period goal. At the end of the game, Canada had won 6–1.

He shoots, he scores! Canada racks up another goal against the USA in the gold medal match at Chamonix. Aside from 1936, Canada won gold every Winter Olympics until 1952. After that, their next Olympic gold finish was at Salt Lake City in 2002.

➲ Canada in fact pulled off the unlikely feat of winning the first Olympic gold in ice hockey *twice*. Though the sport made its Winter Olympics debut at the 1924 Winter Games, ice hockey had first appeared in the 1920 Summer games in Antwerp, Belgium, where Canada had obliterated Sweden 12–1. So Canada was, in fact, defending its gold medal from 1920.

Paavo Nurmi overcame a packed schedule to pick up five gold medals in the space of just five days in the 1924 Olympic Games.

KING OF RUNNERS IS CROWNED

PAAVO NURMI WINS RECORD FIVE TRACK-AND-FIELD GOLD MEDALS AT SUMMER OLYMPICS

15 July 1924, Paris, France

Finland's Paavo Nurmi was the greatest middle- to long-distance runner of his generation, if not of all time. By the time he arrived for the eighth Olympiad in Paris he was already a three-time Olympic gold medallist (he won 10,000m, individual and team cross-country golds in 1920 in Antwerp) and was a serial world-record breaker. But a seven-day period in July 1924 defined his career and confirmed his place among the pantheon of athletics greats. He started his Olympic campaign on 8 July with two days of qualifying; then came a five-day gold rush, with wins in the 1,500m, 5,000m and the 10,000m cross-country, as well as team and individual gold in the 3,000m cross-county event.

➲ In a bid to protect Nurmi from the packed program, Finnish officials did not enter him in the 10,000m, thus denying him the chance to defend his Olympic title. Angry, Nurmi promptly returned to Finland and broke the 10,000m world record, setting a mark (30m06s) which would last for 13 years.

49

WHITE SPRINGS TO OLYMPIC DOUBLE

ALBERT WHITE FIRST TO WIN DOUBLE OLYMPIC DIVING GOLD

4 May–27 July 1924, Paris, France

The United States' Clarence Pinkston had come mighty close to becoming the first to complete a 10m and 3m springboard diving sweep at the 1920 Olympic Games – missing out on 3m gold by a whisker – but no one had successfully completed the diving double. That all changed in Paris in 1924. Pinkston finished third in the 10m springboard, but top of the pile after the eight-dive competition (four compulsory dives and four of the diver's choice), was his compatriot Albert White. The new 10m champion leapt to further glory in the 3m, seeing off team-mate Peter Desjardins in the 12-dive competition to take the unprecedented diving double.

➲ Desjardins – who had lost out to White in Paris in the 3m springboard – went on to repeat the 10m-3m double at the 1928 Olympic Games in Amsterdam, the Netherlands.

Albert White dominated the diving competition at the 1924 Olympic Games in Paris.

NORTON'S CLOSE CALL WITH EVEREST

EDWARD NORTON CLIMBS TO RECORD ALTITUDE OF 28,126FT WITHOUT OXYGEN

June 1924, Mount Everest, Nepal/Tibet

George Mallory and Sandy Irvine were not the only climbers to have made an attempt on the summit during the 1924 Everest expedition. Two days before the pair's ill-fated assault on the world's highest peak, expedition leader Lt Col. Edward Norton and Howard Somervell made an attempt without oxygen, using equipment that, by today's standards, was woefully inadequate. Somervell was forced to abandon at 28,000ft, but Norton continued, painstakingly dragging himself across every inch of ice. Eight hundred feet below the summit, exhausted, he turned back to camp. He had reached a height of 28,126ft and no man would climb higher without the aid of oxygen for 54 years.

➲ At one point during his climb Norton removed his goggles to make sure of his footing. It was a grave error: hours later he was afflicted by double vision – a significant factor behind him turning back to camp – and, by the next day, he was snow-blind.

Edward Norton (front row, second left) may have failed in his attempt on Everest in 1924, but no man would climb higher for 29 years.

HORNSBY HITS A HOT STREAK

ROGERS HORNSBY SETS NATIONAL LEAGUE SINGLE-SEASON BATTING RECORD AT .424

October 1924, St Louis, Missouri, USA

Sometimes extremes work. So dedicated was St Louis Cardinals second baseman Rogers Hornsby to his craft of batting, he refused to read newspapers or watch movies in case they had a detrimental effect on his eyesight. Between 1920 and 1925 he averaged .402, a figure never likely to be broken, but during that stellar stretch, 1924 was his 20/20 year. After going two-for-five against the Chicago Cubs' Vic Aldridge on the opening day, only one pitcher held him hitless three times during the year – Johnny Cooney – and he only went hitless in 24 games. By the end of the season he had accumulated a batting average of .424.

➲ The figure of .424 still stands as the all-time National League record. In addition, Hornsby is the only right-handed hitter in the 20th century to have put together three .400 seasons.

A colourful character with a darker side – he was an inveterate gambler – Rogers Hornsby is considered the greatest right-handed hitter of all time.

GILL'S DOUBLE ALL-IRELAND SUCCESS

MICK GILL BECOMES ONLY PLAYER IN HURLING HISTORY TO WIN TWO ALL-IRELAND TITLES IN SAME YEAR

14 December 1924, Dublin, Ireland

As civil war raged around them, the last thing on anyone's mind in Ireland during 1923 was the fact that the latter stages of the All-Ireland hurling championships would be played the following year, but it led to a unique set of circumstances for one man, Mick Gill. By the time Gill's Galway shocked defending champions Tipperary in the delayed 1923 semi-final against them on 18 May 1924, Gill had already joined the police in Dublin. But although he played that day and again in the final, as Galway beat Limerick, he was only a visiting player: by mid-1924 he was already playing regularly in Dublin and found himself in another All-Ireland final in December 1924: Dublin beat Antrim to hand Gill his second success in the space of six months.

➲ Gill captained Dublin to his third All-Ireland title in 1927, but never tasted final success again.

ALL BLACK BROWNLIE SEES RED

CYRIL BROWNLIE FIRST MAN TO BE SENT OFF IN RUGBY INTERNATIONAL

3 January 1925, Twickenham, London, England

It was always going to be an intense contest. England – coming off back-to-back grand slams (in 1923 and 1924) and unbeaten for three years – against New Zealand, unbeaten since 1921 and reaching the end of a 32-match tour in which they had swept all before them. It was a battle from the first moments. Only eight minutes were on the clock when Welsh referee Albert E. Freeth brought the feuding forwards together for a third time and issued his final warning. It had little effect. Moments later All Black loose-forward Cyril Brownlie stamped on a prostrate English forward and left the Neath official with little choice: he issued a player his marching orders for the first time in international rugby.

➲ Despite being a man down so early in the game, New Zealand dug deep to win 17–11. The All Blacks won their final four games on tour as well: the Invincibles had won all 32 games.

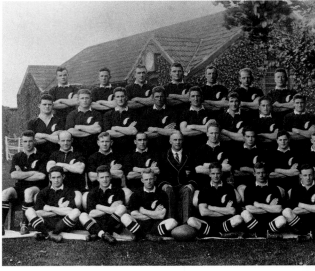

Despite his moment of infamy, Cyril Brownlie – pictured here, one row from back, fourth left, with the 1925 Invincibles – went on to enjoy a lengthy career with the All Blacks, representing them 31 times and scoring 33 points.

Jack Hobbs, known as "The Master", scored 3,024 runs (including his record-breaking 127th century) during the summer of 1925. It would stand as a record season total until Dennis Compton's stellar 1947 season, when he scored 3,816 first-class runs.

THE MASTER OVERTAKES THE DOCTOR

JACK HOBBS BREAKS W.G. GRACE'S RECORD FOR MOST FIRST-CLASS HUNDREDS

18 August 1925, County Ground, Taunton, England

It is early morning in Taunton, Somerset, on 17 August 1925. There is a buzz in the air as the press intermingle with large numbers of spectators in the stands of the County Ground. They are all there for the same reason: the great Jack Hobbs, unbeaten overnight on 92, is within sight of his 126th first-class century, which would equal W.G. Grace's long-standing all-time record. To great cheers, Hobbs flicks Somerset's Jimmy Bridges to leg and raises his bat. He was out shortly afterwards for 101. The next day, with Surrey needing 183 to win the game, Hobbs hit a peerless unbeaten 101, his 127th first-class century, to break the record.

➲ The Surrey and England opening batsman got better with age. Playing well into his 50s, he ended up with 61,237 first-class runs and 199 centuries, both of which are figures never likely to be beaten.

Walter Johnson, aka "The Big Train", stayed with the Washington Nationals/Senators throughout his 20-year career and by the time he retired had set numerous pitching records.

THE BIG TRAIN RUNS OUT OF STEAM

WALTER JOHNSON RETIRES FROM BASEBALL WITH RECORD NUMBER OF SHUTOUTS

October 1926, Washington, DC, USA

Walter Johnson was the leading power pitcher of his generation. With a fastball close on 100mph, the Washington Nationals (then Senators) pitcher terrorized Major League line-ups throughout his 20-year career and by the time the man known as "The Big Train" finally retired from the game he had set new pitching standards. So good were his numbers that only two of his peers were within 1,000 of his career total of 3,509 strikeouts – a figure that would stand as a record for 57 years – but it is another of his milestones that has stood the test of time: his career total of 110 shutouts.

➲ Although the strikeout record has now been passed by eight pitchers (Nolan Ryan is the current record-holder and his 5,714 is more than 1,000 ahead of his nearest rival), Walter Johnson's shutout record has never been touched and, in all likelihood, never will be.

EDERLE THROWS OFF CHANNEL DEMONS TO SET RECORD

GERTRUDE EDERLE BECOMES FIRST WOMAN TO SWIM THE CHANNEL

6 August 1926, Cap Gris-Nez, France–Kingsdown, England

Twelve months earlier, in August 1925, 18-year-old American champion swimmer Gertrude Ederle's attempt to become the first woman to swim the English Channel had ended in disaster; coughing and weeping bitterly, she'd been pulled by her coach from the icy waters just seven miles short of the finishing line. In 1926 she was back: wearing a red cap, a black two-piece bathing suit and smeared in grease to protect her from the cold, she plunged into the waters off Cap Gris-Nez and embarked on her feat. Battling wind, rain and heavy swells, she stepped onto Kingsdown beach 14 hours 31 minutes later to become the first woman to swim the Channel.

➲ The first person to meet the shivering and exhausted swimmer after she set foot on British soil following her epic swim was an immigration officer, who promptly asked her to produce her passport.

Since Matthew Webb first accomplished the feat in 1875, only four other men had managed to swim the English Channel. Gertrude Ederle not only became the first woman to achieve the feat, she also smashed the existing record by nearly two hours.

BYRD AND BENNETT ON TOP OF THE WORLD

RICHARD BYRD AND FLOYD BENNETT FIRST TO FLY OVER NORTH POLE

9 May 1926, Kings Bay, Spitzbergen

The race to the North Pole on foot had already been won, but now a new polar challenge captivated the public's imagination: who would be the first to fly over the "top of the world"? Roald Amundsen and his team had tried and failed in 1925 – mechanical problems left the team stranded in the unforgiving environment for three weeks trying to forge a runway from the ice – but, a year later, US Navy pilots Richard E. Byrd and Floyd Bennett joined the race. They took off in their tri-motored Fokker from Kings Bay, Spitzbergen, on 9 May 1926 and returned some 15-and-a-half hours later claiming to have become the first to fly over the North Pole.

➲ Byrd and Bennett returned to international acclaim – the pair both went on to receive the Congressional Medal of Honor – but doubts later emerged as to whether they had, in fact, reached the Pole. Byrd's log diaries of the flight (found some years later) contain sextant readings which suggest that although they flew from Spitzbergen in a direct line to the Pole they almost certainly turned back before reaching it.

Richard Byrd and Floyd Bennett received a hero's welcome after claiming to have flown over the North Pole in 1926, although doubt was later cast over the validity of their achievement.

VICTORIA PUT NSW BOWLERS TO THE SWORD

VICTORIA COMPILE HIGHEST INNINGS IN FIRST-CLASS HISTORY

24–29 December 1926, Melbourne, Australia

At the top of the Victoria line-up stood the prolific Bill Ponsford: the game of cricket has seen no greater exponent of the art of building an innings and his Victoria team-mates learned well from his fine example … as New South Wales found to their cost in December 1926. Having been dismissed for 221, New South Wales were forced to sit back and watch a fearsome display of batting mastery. The first Victorian wicket fell at 375 (Bill Woodfull for 133); the second at 594 (Stork Hendry). Ponsford finally fell for 352, but Jack Ryder took up the baton, hammering a quick-time 295. By the time John Ellis was run out for 63, Victoria had compiled a record first-class innings of 1,107 all out.

➲ No doubt a shade demoralized after their long stint in the field, New South Wales's batsmen were all out for 230 in their second innings, with Albert Hartkopf the chief destroyer with 6 for 98. Victoria won the game by an innings and 656 runs.

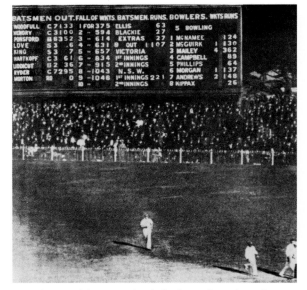

Victoria hammered the New South Wales bowlers to all parts during their 190.7-over first innings in December 1926 and ended up with a record all-out total of 1,107.

SEAGRAVE BREAKS 200MPH BARRIER

HENRY SEAGRAVE AND MYSTERY REGAIN THE LAND SPEED RECORD

29 March 1927, Daytona Beach, Florida, USA

When Henry Seagrave told everyone he was going to become the first man to drive a car at 200mph, people thought he was mad; he had, after all, suffered the trauma of being shot twice during the First World War and had clearly been affected by the experience. But Seagrave loved speed. In 1927, he crossed the Atlantic with his four-litre Sunbeam (called "Mystery") to Daytona Beach to reclaim the record he had lost in 1926 (to John Parry-Jones and, subsequently, to Malcolm Campbell). On 29 March he pushed the Sunbeam to a top speed of 203.79mph (327.97km/h) to reclaim the record and become the first man in history to break the 200mph barrier.

➲ Seagrave's record lasted less than a year. On 19 February 1928 Malcolm Campbell and Bluebird reached 206.95mph (333.05km/h).

Born in Maryland, United States, but raised in Ireland and schooled at Eton College, Henry Seagrave broke the land speed record on three occasions and, on 13 June 1930, the water speed world record. However, he died later the same day in an accident during a renewed assault on a world best.

JONES EXORCIZES OLD COURSE DEMONS

BOBBY JONES DEFENDS OPEN CHAMPIONSHIP CROWN WITH RECORD AGGREGATE SCORE

16 July 1927, St Andrews, Scotland

The last time Bobby Jones played at the Old Course, St Andrews, was as a 19-year-old prodigy in the 1921 Open Championship. He took four shots to extricate himself from the depths of Hill bunker on the 11th during his third round, picked up his ball and retired. Seven years later he was back as the defending Open champion and pushed any lingering demons over the course to one side with a stunning opening round of 68 to take a four-shot lead. By the time the cheering crowds carried him from the 18th green after the final round, he had extended the lead to six: his four-round total of 285 was the lowest in Open Championship history.

➲ Jones's aggregate score (285) stood as an Open Championship record until 1932, when Gene Sarazen shot 283 at the Prince's Club in Sandwich. The current championship best of 267 was set by Greg Norman at Royal St George's in 1993.

After his humbling St Andrews experience as a 19-year-old in 1921, Bobby Jones was reported to say: "Master Bobby is just a boy, and an ordinary boy at that." Seven years later he returned to the Old Course in record-breaking style, his reputation as the game's supreme player complete.

LINDBERGH MASTERS THE ATLANTIC

CHARLES LINDBERGH COMPLETES FIRST NON-STOP FLIGHT ACROSS ATLANTIC
20–21 May 1927, Roosevelt Airfield, New York, USA–Le Bourget Field, Paris, France

The Orteig Prize – a $25,000 award offered by rich French hotelier Raymond Orteig for the first non-stop flight from New York to Paris – was still up for grabs. Many had tried, and a number had lost their lives in the attempt; as a result the prize captured the public's imagination in an unprecedented fashion. Millions tuned in their radios as Charles Lindbergh took off in the Spirit of St Louis from Roosevelt Airfield on 20 May 1927, and listened in for regular updates. Lindbergh was spotted over Nova Scotia and again over Newfoundland, but then came silence. Lindbergh had turned right and headed across the Atlantic for Ireland. The world held its breath. The following morning he was spotted over the Irish coast; 100,000 excited spectators flocked to Le Bourget Field in Paris to await his arrival. Thirty-three-and-a-half hours after take-off, Lindbergh flew into sight and eased to the ground. He had done it and his place in aviation history was secure.

⮑ Lindbergh was convinced that the more engines a plane had, the higher the chance of failure; he opted for the single-engine Spirit of St Louis to guide him over the Atlantic.

After his arrival in Paris, Charles Lindbergh became an instant celebrity. The French president bestowed the Legion of Honour on him and he was escorted back to the United States by warships and aircraft ... followed by a tickertape parade through Manhattan.

THE BAMBINO SWATS 60 LONG BALLS

BABE RUTH BREAKS OWN SINGLE-SEASON HOME RUN RECORD
30 September 1927, New York, USA

By the mid-1920s, Babe Ruth had become the most visible, most popular and, above all, the most dominant sportsman the United States had ever seen. His legendary power hitting had earned him the moniker "The Sultan of Swat". In 1919 the Bambino struck 29 homers; it was deemed "the unbeatable mark" – until the following year, when he smashed an incredible 54 long balls. The home run record was now his personal domain. In 1921 he was at it again, edging his record to 59. Already head and shoulders above his peers, the Bambino had one more power year up his sleeve and, in 1927, no ballpark in the land was big enough to contain him. The Yankees slugger hit more home runs as an individual (60) than any team combined in the American League. Babe Ruth was assured of his place at the head of the table when it came to baseball greats.

⮑ "Sixty, count 'em, 60. Let's see some son of a bitch match that," said Babe Ruth on 30 September 1927 after hitting his 60th home run of the season; the record would last for 34 years.

It took Babe Ruth just 155 games to reach 60 home runs in 1927. His homer total amounted to 14 per cent of the total long balls hit in the American League that year.

WELCOME TO MURDERER'S ROW

NEW YORK YANKEES WIN A SEASON-RECORD 100 GAMES
30 September 1927, New York, USA

The New York Yankees' pitching staff may have led the American League in almost every category following the 1927 baseball season, but their endeavours were totally overshadowed by a batting line-up that simply blitzed the opposition. And it wasn't just Babe Ruth (with 60 home runs) who caused opposing pitchers sleepless nights: Earle Combs (with a season's average of .356), Bob Meusel (.337) and Lou Gehrig (.376 with 47 homers and a league-leading 175 RBI) all played their part as the Yankees combined to score 975 runs in 400-plus games to earn themselves the moniker "Murderer's Row". By the end of the season the Yankees had won the American League pennant by a record 19 games and their total of 110 wins was the highest in Major League history.

➲ The Yankees continued their form into the Fall Classic, sweeping the Pittsburgh Pirates in four games to secure World Series glory – the first team from the American League to secure a World Series sweep. The Yankees' 110 wins would stand as a record until 1998 (broken by a new generation of New York Yankees).

The 1927 New York Yankees led the American League from start to finish and ended the season with a record 110 wins: they became the first team in baseball history to secure a season winning percentage of over .700 (.714).

BABY BRINGS HOME THE BREAD

ALBERTO "BABY" ARIZMENDI BECOMES YOUNGEST PROFESSIONAL BOXER IN HISTORY
11 October 1927, San Antonio, Texas, USA

Adversity often triggers a change in direction. Following a bout of polio, Mexican-born Alberto Arizmendi paid a visit to the doctor and was told he needed to take up a physical pursuit to aid his recovery: at the age of 11, little Alberto chose boxing. Two years later, he was making his professional debut. At 13 years, six months and 24 days, he strode into the ring in San Antonio, Texas, to challenge Kid Laredo – the bout ended in a draw. He was back in the ring just two months later and recorded his first victory, beating Caveman Ferrici on points after ten close-fought rounds.

➲ Nicknamed "Baby" because of his ceaselessly smiling face, Alberto Arizmendi had a charging, bruising style of boxing. His only shot at the world featherweight title came on 28 February 1933: he lost on points to Freddie Miller.

Although his early boxing record is incomplete, Ring magazine – boxing's most trusted source – believes Alberto Arizmendi made his professional boxing debut at the tender age of 13.

FIVE UP FOR THE HAIG

WALTER HAGEN WINS US PGA CHAMPIONSHIP FOR RECORD FIFTH TIME
November 1927, Cedar Crest Country Club, Texas, USA

Walter Hagen had the uncanny ability to produce his best golf when it really mattered. He was a master in matchplay and of one tournament in particular – the US PGA Championship, which until 1958 was played in a matchplay format. Hagen was in his element. He collected his first win in 1921 (beating Jim Barnes 3&2 in the final) and triumphed again in 1924. Then Haig could not stop winning: further triumphs followed in 1925 and 1926, and nobody bet against him picking up a fifth title in 1927. Hagen did not disappoint: surviving the odd scare along the way, he defeated Jim Turnesa 1up in the final to notch up his tournament record fifth win.

➲ The most exciting and assertive player of his era, Walter Hagen still holds the record for the most wins in the US PGA Championship.

Hagen added two US Opens (1914 and 1919) and four Open Championships (1922, 1924, 1928 and 1929) to his five US PGA Championships. Only two players – Jack Nicklaus and Tiger Woods – have won more than Hagen's 11 major championships.

1927

PROLIFIC PONSFORD PASSES 400 AGAIN

BILL PONSFORD BREAKS HIS OWN RECORD HIGHEST FIRST-CLASS SCORE

16–21 December 1927, Melbourne, Australia

You did not have to be a talent-spotting genius to recognize Bill Ponsford's uncanny adhesion to the batting crease. In February 1922, in only his second first-class game for Victoria, the opening batsman scored 162: his reward was to miss out on selection for the state side for the next 12 months. He made quite a statement when he returned to the Victoria line-up the following year, hitting a world-record 429 against Tasmania to break A.C. MacLaren's 27-year-old record for the highest score in first-class cricket. With only his own record to beat, Ponsford was at it again in 1927: hammering 437 off Queensland's hapless bowlers to set a new mark and become the first batsman in history to pass the 400 mark for a second time.

➲ Ponsford and Brian Lara are the only two batsmen in cricket history to have compiled two first-class innings of 400 or more.

Bill Ponsford's run-scoring feats did not end with his record knock of 437. Continuing his rich vein of form his next three scores read 202, 38 and 336. His four-innings total of 1,013 runs remains a record in first-class cricket.

THREE IN A ROW FOR GRAFSTRÖM

GILLIS GRAFSTRÖM WINS THIRD SUCCESSIVE FIGURE-SKATING GOLD

11–19 February 1928, St Moritz, France

An endless innovator who never ceased in his search for figure-skating perfection, Norway's Gillis Grafström left his mark on the sport by inventing three moves: the Grafström pirouette (on the back outside edge of the blade), the flying sit spin and the change sit spin. He also left his mark in the Olympic record books. He gained his first figure-skating gold in Antwerp in 1920, claiming the vote of all six judges, despite having to perform with unfamiliar curved skates (he had broken his own). He defended his crown four years later in Chamonix, France – the first figure skater in Olympic history to do so – and won an unprecedented triple when he narrowly beat Austria's Willy Böckl in St Moritz, France, in the 1928 Olympics.

➲ Grafström's bid for a fourth consecutive gold medal ended in disappointment in Lake Placid in 1932 when he finished in second place behind Austria's Karl Schäfer.

Norwegian Gillis Grafström was a triple Olympic champion who later went on to coach his nation's other figure-skating prodigy, Sonja Henie.

RANK OUTSIDER WINS THE NATIONAL

100–1 TIPPERARY TIM WINS THE GRAND NATIONAL AS 40 OUT OF 42 HORSES FALL
30 March 1928, Aintree, Liverpool, England

Mist enveloped the Aintree racecourse as the 42 horses emerged from the paddock and lined up under starter's orders. They were off. The crowd of 250,000 roared as the horses approached the first of 30 obstacles: one fell. Three fell at the fourth and another three, including one of the favourites, Amber-wave, succumbed at Becher's Brook. On the horses ran, hidden by the mist, until the Canal Turn prompted mayhem. Easter Hill fell, carnage ensued; jockeys were strewn over the course and only seven horses were still in the race. With two fences to go only two remained: American horse Billy Barton and 100–1 rank outsider Tipperary Tim. The American challenger succumbed and Tipperary Tim, ridden by Billy Dutton, staggered to the line to take a most unexpected win.

➲ The 1928 Grand National saw the fewest finishers in the event's long history (two), but it was still a crowd-pleaser. The majority of the 250,000 spectators were glad an English horse had beaten off Billy Barton's American challenge.

The weather may have been appalling – it had rained heavily for most of the day and stopped just moments before the race – but the 1928 Grand National left all those who saw it with a warm glow. It was the most eventful race in Grand National history, with only two horses out of the field of 42 completing the course.

DEAN POWER PROPELS EVERTON TO LEAGUE TITLE

DIXIE DEAN SCORES RECORD 60 GOALS IN A LEAGUE SEASON
6 May 1928, Highbury, London, England

He was quick, sharp and intelligent. Everton knew they had got themselves a bargain when they signed William Ralph Dean – aka "Dixie" – from Tranmere Rovers for the substantial fee of £3,000. The centre-forward made an immediate impact for the Toffees, scoring 32 goals in his first full season, just eight shy of Bert Freeman's record. But then disaster struck: in May 1926 while riding his motorcycle in Holywell, North Wales, Dean suffered a near-fatal accident that had doctors fearing for his life. A fractured skull left him requiring life-saving surgery and the majority doubted whether he would ever play soccer again. Yet he roared back to action in the 1927–28 season and in some style, scoring in each of his first nine matches – including all five in Everton's 5–2 crushing of Manchester United – and ended the campaign with 60 goals in 39 games. Everton romped to the Division One title and Dean had overcome the odds to take a lasting place in the history books.

⮞ Dean was three goals short of the 60 mark with just one game of the season remaining, an away trip to Herbert Chapman's Arsenal. He completed his hat-trick with just five minutes of the match to go, breaking George Camsell's record of 59 goals scored for Middlesbrough in the Second Division the previous season.

Dixie Dean overcame terrible injuries suffered in a motorcycle accident – including a steel plate in his skull – to fire a record 60 league goals in the 1927–28 season.

ENIGMATIC "SASKATOON LILY" LIGHTS UP THE GAMES

ETHEL CATHERWOOD STILL ONLY CANADIAN WOMAN ATHLETE TO WIN INDIVIDUAL GOLD IN OLYMPIC TRACK AND FIELD

17 May–12 August 1928, Amsterdam, The Netherlands

The Games of the IX Olympiad saw the advent of both the Olympic Flame and women's events in athletics and gymnastics. The inclusion of the women's events came about despite resistance to the idea, and Canada's Matchless Six practised tirelessly on the ship to Amsterdam, intent on showing the nay-sayers that women were ready to compete on the world stage. And they sure did: Canada's women came away with two golds, one silver and one bronze – but the brightest spot was Catherwood's amazing high jump coup on the last day of competition. The Saskatoon Lily psyched out her opponents by jumping in her track suit until she missed a jump, then removing it to jump in the usual sports togs. And it worked very well: Catherwood sailed easily to a world record by jumping 1.60 metres, beating the record she had set on Labour Day two years earlier.

The press corps at the 1928 Games emphasized Catherwood's girl-next-door looks, dubbing her the "Saskatoon Lily." Her Olympic gold medal remains the only one Canada has ever won in women's individual track-and-field events.

➲ The 1928 Games were good for Canada: Catherwood's gold in the high jump was joined by a gold for Canada's women's team in the 4x100 metre relay and team-mate Fanny Rosenfeld's silver in the 100 metres – as well as Percy Williams's 100m and 200m gold medals and James Ball's silver in the 400m on the men's side.

GAUDIN GETS HIS JUST DESERTS

LUCIEN GAUDIN FIRST TO TAKE OLYMPIC FENCING DOUBLE GOLD

17 May–12 August, Amsterdam, the Netherlands

Frenchman Lucien Gaudin started his extraordinary fencing career in 1904 and within a year had collected his first individual world title, but he had to wait much longer before tasting sole Olympic success. Gaudin made his first Olympic appearance in 1920, but was wounded in the individual competition, withdrew, and missed out on a medal. Team gold in both epee and foil came in Paris in 1924, but once again he was forced to retire from the individual competition, this time with an acute pain in his left hand. His moment of Olympic glory came when he snatched individual epee and foil gold in Amsterdam in 1928 – the first Olympian to do so.

➲ Gaudin missed out on selection for the French squad for the 1908 Olympics and his country chose not to attend the 1912 Games in Stockholm, and then came the First World War: he finally made his Olympic debut 24 years after his competitive debut.

Just when it seemed as though fate would deny Lucien Gaudin the Olympic glory he so deserved, the Frenchman had his moment of moments in the 1928 Olympic Games in Amsterdam at the tender age of 42.

According to legend, during negotiations over the David Jack transfer, Arsenal manager Herbert Chapman offered the Bolton board members hefty gin and tonics while he sat there drinking just tonic. Whatever his tactics, he got his man, and David Jack became soccer's first five-figure player.

JACK SOCCER'S FIRST FIVE-FIGURE MAN

DAVID JACK MOVES FROM BOLTON TO ARSENAL FOR WORLD RECORD TRANSFER FEE
October 1928, Highbury, London, England

The son of a soccer player, David Jack made his professional debut with Plymouth Argyle in 1919 and did enough in his first year to impress Bolton Wanderers, for whom he signed the following year. Thus started an eight-year association with the Trotters, yielding 144 goals in 295 league matches, including two FA Cup triumphs, in 1923 (when Jack became the first player to score at Wembley) and 1926 (where he scored the only goal in Bolton's 1–0 win over Manchester City). So when Bolton experienced financial problems in 1928, Arsenal manager Herbert Chapman knew the time was ripe to swoop for one of the game's most prolific centre-forwards. His staggering offer of £10,890 (the transfer record stood at £6,500) was too good to ignore and Jack was on his way to Highbury.

➲ Jack made his debut for the Gunners on 28 October 1928 and soon became a regular in the line-up, ending the season as the club's top scorer. When Arsenal won the FA Cup in 1930, Jack became the first player to win the FA Cup with two different clubs.

COBB CALLS IT A DAY

TY COBB RETIRES FROM BASEBALL WITH RECORD .366 CAREER BATTING AVERAGE

11 September 1928, Philadelphia, Pennsylvania, USA

When Ty Cobb stepped to the plate as a pinch hitter in the ninth inning for the Philadelphia Athletics and popped out against Washington Senators' pitcher Hank Johnson to shortstop Mark Koenig, he brought down the curtain on a prolific 23-year career which had brought 12 batting titles, a Triple Crown in 1909 and new standards to the game of baseball. Some of his career numbers stood as records for many years – most career hits (4,189 until 1985), career runs (2,246 until 2001), most stolen bases (892, as a modern record until 1977) – but one of his records has stood the test of time: his career batting average of .366.

➲ Ty Cobb broke some 90 records during his 24-year career (the first 22, 1905–26, with the Detroit Tigers and 1927–28 with Philadelphia As), some of which have stood the test of time.

Such was his influence on the early years of baseball, Ty Cobb received more votes than any other player at the inaugural Hall of Fame ballot in 1936.

ENGLAND CRUSH SORRY AUSSIES

ENGLAND RECORD THE HIGHEST TEST VICTORY BY RUNS

30 November–5 December 1928, Exhibition Ground, Brisbane, Australia

As the first to bat in the first match of a long series on foreign soil, the 1928–29 England tourists knew the importance of putting a satisfactory total on the scoreboard. They did just that: Patsy Hendren top-scored with 169 and Harold Larwood chipped in with a dogged 70 as England posted an imposing 521 all out. Larwood picked up with the ball where he had left off with the bat, ripping through the home side's top order as Australia reached a paltry 122 all out. England did not let up, cruising to 342 for 8 in their second innings to set Australia an unlikely victory target of 742. They slipped to a sorry 66 all out and England had won by a record 675 runs.

➲ England carried their early momentum into the rest of the series, winning the next four matches before losing the final Test in Melbourne to record a memorable 4–1 victory.

The 1928–29 Marylebone Cricket Club tourists got off to a record-breaking start in the first Test against Australia, winning by a staggering 675 runs – the highest margin of victory by runs in Test history.

HOBBS ROLLS BACK THE YEARS

46-YEAR-OLD JACK HOBBS BECOMES OLDEST TEST CENTURION IN CRICKET HISTORY

8–16 March 1929, Melbourne, Australia

The 1928–29 MCC tour to Australia had been one of unending triumph for England. They had won the first four Tests comfortably and headed into the final match of the five-match series in Melbourne looking for the clean sweep. But it hadn't been all smiles in the England camp: by his own high standards, veteran opener Jack Hobbs, looking to enjoy one final hurrah Down Under, was enduring a torrid time, with just 244 runs to show from seven innings. That all changed in Melbourne. England may have gone on to lose the match by five wickets, but Hobbs hit a peerless 142 in the first innings to become, at 46 years, 82 days, Test cricket's oldest centurion.

➲ Hobbs hit 65 in England's second innings to end the series with 451 runs at an average of 50.11 (against a career average of 56.94). His first-innings 142 was the last of his 15 Test centuries.

Twenty-one years after making his Test debut, Jack Hobbs bowed out of his final overseas tour in style, hitting 142 in the final match of the 1928–29 series against Australia to become, at 46, the oldest player in Test history to reach three figures.

HAINSWORTH PROVES HARD TO BEAT

GEORGE HAINSWORTH SETS NHL SINGLE-SEASON RECORD FOR SHUTOUTS

March 1929, Montreal, Canada

George Hainsworth had difficult shoes to step into. He arrived in Montreal for the 1926–27 season as the recommended replacement for Georges Vezina, the Canadiens' long-serving goaltender who was stricken with tuberculosis and who would soon die of the illness. Hainsworth excelled: with his laid-back approach belying his bravery, and possessing an uncanny puck-stopping ability, he was the league's leading goalkeeper in his first two seasons with the Montreal franchise. But the best was still to come. His greatest season came in 1928–29, when he conceded just 43 goals in 42 games, including an NHL record 22 consecutive shutouts.

➲ "Little George" Hainsworth retired in 1937 with a career goals-against average of 1.91 per game, the equal lowest (along with Alex Connell) in NHL history.

George Hainsworth's 1928–29 shutout exploits helped Montreal to the top of the Canadian League table, but they lost in the semi-finals to the Boston Bruins, who would go on to lift the Stanley Cup.

SIXTY-SIX HORSES AND GRAND NATIONAL CHAOS

100–1 SHOT GREGALACH EMERGES FROM LARGEST FIELD IN GRAND NATIONAL HISTORY TO TAKE WIN

23 March 1929, Aintree, Liverpool, England

Following the carnage of the previous year's race, in which only two out of a field of 44 horses had finished the race amid scenes of scattered jockeys and rider-less horses, one or two eyebrows would have been raised when the final entry list for the 1929 Grand National was published. This time round a staggering 66 horses would line up at the starter's post. The doom-mongers forecast disaster … and they were right. For the second year running, horses fell by the wayside in alarming numbers – only nine would go on to finish the race – and for the second year in succession it was a 100–1 outsider, this time Gregalach, ridden by Robert Everett and trained by Tom Leader, who emerged from the carnage to take a surprise win.

Gregalach (partly hidden by the riderless No. 34), a 100–1 outsider, was the surprise winner of the 66-horse 1929 Grand National. The race was chaotic in the extreme and prompted calls to make the race less hazardous by restricting the size of the field. It was limited to 40 in the 1990s, since when the quality of the horses entering the race has improved dramatically.

➲ Neither horse nor rider would appear in the top four again. Gregalach is one of only four horses to have won the Grand National with odds of 100–1, the others being Tipperary Tim (1928), Caughoo (1947) and Foinavon (1967).

AROUND THE WORLD IN 20 DAYS

THE AIRSHIP *GRAF ZEPPELIN* COMPLETES FIRST AERIAL CIRCUMNAVIGATION

29 August 1929, Lakehurst, New Jersey, USA

It was nothing more than a publicity stunt; in the words of company chairman Hugo Eckener – who would also pilot the flight – the attempt to guide the LZ-127 Graf Zeppelin airship around the world would show "the expediency of her mode of travel". Securing sponsorship – including that of US press tycoon William Randolph Hearst, who placed a reporter on board – the airship took off from Lakehurst, New Jersey, on 9 August and crossed the Atlantic for Friedrichshafen, Germany. From there it passed over Siberia before refuelling in Tokyo. Then came the first non-stop flight across the Pacific before the craft refuelled in Los Angeles, and then it was back to Lakehurst. The entire trip took 20 days, four hours.

Hugo Eckener piloted the *Graf Zeppelin* to the greatest moment in airship history. Within nine years – following the *Hindenburg* disaster in 1937, which killed 36 people – airships as a viable mode of mass passenger transport became more or less extinct.

➲ The stunt worked. Within days of completing the flight, Eckener took four more orders for a Zeppelin.

BYRD HEADS SOUTH AND FLIES OVER BOTTOM OF WORLD

RICHARD BYRD AND CREW FIRST TO FLY OVER THE SOUTH POLE
29 November 1929, South Pole

At 3.29 p.m., on 28 November 1929, a Ford Tri-motor plane – containing Richard Byrd (who had claimed the first successful flight over the North Pole in 1926) as navigator, pilot Bernt Balchen, co-pilot and radioman Harold June and photographer Ashley McKinley – took off from base camp on the Ross Ice Shelf, Antarctica, on a mission to become the first to fly over the South Pole. As the plane struggled to gain enough altitude to pass the 11,000ft Polar Plateau, the desperate crew dumped empty gas tanks and emergency supplies; they passed over the plateau's edge with a few hundred feet to spare. They passed over the South Pole shortly after midnight on 29 November, flying a few miles beyond and to the left and right of it to account for any navigational errors.

➲ The Ford Tri-motor plane was called *Floyd Bennett*, after Byrd's 1926 North Pole pilot, who had died in 1928 from injuries suffered during an attempt on the Orteig Prize – the award for a non-stop flight from New York to Paris ultimately won by Charles Lindbergh – in 1927.

Richard Byrd – one from left – and his crew flew over the South Pole on 29 November 1929 as part of an Antarctic expedition between 1928 and 1930.

1930

MICK THE MILLER AT THE DOUBLE

MICK THE MILLER BECOMES FIRST GREYHOUND TO WIN ENGLISH DERBY TWICE

28 June 1930, White City, London, England

Mick the Miller brought greyhound racing to the masses. Bred in the backwoods of Ireland by a gambling-mad priest called Father Martin Brophy, Mick the Miller was lucky to make it through his first year, but somehow survived distemper and took the survival instincts gained from that experience on to the track. During a three-year career he won five Classic races, including the 1929 English Derby, but his finest moment came the following year, when he returned to White City to defend his title and he stormed to victory in front of a 50,000-strong crowd to become the first greyhound to win the English Derby in successive years.

➲ Mick the Miller's feat was repeated by Patricia's Hope in 1973.

On 28 June 1930, Mick the Miller stormed to a second straight English Derby win to thrill the 50,000-strong White City crowd, among them King Alfonso XIII of Spain.

THE DON PUTS ENGLAND'S BOWLERS TO THE SWORD

DONALD BRADMAN SETS NEW TEST RECORD FOR HIGHEST INDIVIDUAL SCORE

12 July 1930, Headingley, Leeds, England

England and Australia went into the third Test of the five-match 1930 series at Headingley with the tie delicately balanced at 1–1. So when England took the early wicket of Archie Jackson to leave the Australians 2 for 1, there would have been a certain level of discomfort in the visitors' dressing-room. There needn't have been. The prodigious Donald Bradman strode to the crease and put the England bowlers to the sword: by the time he was out for 334 (to set a new Test record), Australia had moved on to a dominating 508 for 6 (they would ultimately be all out for 566). Bradman was demonstrating the talent that would make him the greatest batsman Test cricket has ever seen.

Donald Bradman had a memorable series against England in 1930, scoring 974 runs in the five Tests – an all-time record for a five-match series – including 232 in the final Test at The Oval to help Australia to a 2–1 series win.

➲ Bradman's record-breaking innings came just three months after England's Andy Sandham (325) had broken fellow countryman Tip Foster's 27-year Test record (287) score; Bradman's mark would last for two-and-a-half years, until Walter Hammond smashed an unbeaten 336 against New Zealand in Auckland in 1933.

AGE NO BARRIER FOR TRAMUTOLA

JUAN JOSÉ TRAMUTOLA BECOMES YOUNGEST MANAGER IN WORLD CUP HISTORY

15 July 1930, Montevideo, Uruguay

FIFA president Jules Rimet had finally achieved his dream. On 26 May 1928, Uruguay, the reigning Olympic soccer champions, were granted the right to host the first-ever World Cup. The decision did not meet with unanimous acclaim. Europe was ravaged by economic depression and only four of its nations decided to undertake the long sea voyage to participate. It left pundits predicting a South American win and among the favourites were reigning Copa America champions Argentina, coached by Juan José Tramutola who, when he led his side out for his country's first World Cup match, against France on 15 July 1930, became, at 27 years, 267 days, the youngest manager in World Cup history.

Twenty-seven-year-old Juan José Tramutola, the youngest manager in World Cup history (seen leading his team out before the match), guided his side all the way to the final, where they lost 4–2 to hosts Uruguay.

➲ Argentina won the game 1–0 thanks to an 81st-minute goal from Luis Monti, but the match is remembered for the actions of the Brazilian referee Mr Rege, who blew for full time with France's Marcel Langiller dribbling through the Argentine defence ... with six minutes still on the clock. After a pitch invasion and mass protests – some players were already in the shower – it was decided to play out the extra six minutes. It did not affect the result.

PATENAUDE WORLD CUP'S HAT-TRICK HERO

USA'S BERT PATENAUDE SCORES FIRST HAT-TRICK IN WORLD CUP HISTORY

17 July 1930, Montevideo, Uruguay

There may be 48 of them in history, but the debate as to who scored the first World Cup hat-trick raged on for 76 years. According to the US Soccer Federation, the first occurrence came on 17 July 1930, when Bert Patenaude scored in the 10th, 18th and 50th minutes to secure a 3–0 victory over Paraguay. FIFA disagreed, crediting the second goal to Tom Florie, and awarding the accolade of the World Cup's first hat-trick scorer to Argentina's Guillermo Stabile (who had scored three times two days after Patenaude's effort). That all changed on 10 November 2006, when FIFA finally decreed that Bert Patenaude had indeed scored the United States' second goal; officially he had become the first person to score a hat-trick in World Cup history.

➲ Sadly for Bert Patenaude, his place in the World Cup record books was not ratified until 32 years after his death.

The United States' Bert Patenaude (front, squatting over the ball) was one of the World Cup's first hot shots, but his claim to being the first to score a World Cup hat-trick was debated for many years.

RECORD EIGHT STAGE WINS BUT STILL THE BRIDESMAID

CHARLES PELISSIER WINS TOUR RECORD EIGHT STAGES BUT STILL FINISHES IN NINTH PLACE

27 July 1930, Paris, France

The announcement of a new national team structure for the 1930 Tour de France excited an entire nation. The French had not enjoyed home success for seven years and their team for 1930 was packed with stars. One of them, Charles Pelissier, won two of the first three stages, but by the time he picked up his fourth stage win (in stage 11), he was already forced to play second fiddle to team-mate André Leducq, the yellow jersey-holder since the ninth stage. Pelissier won the final four stages to bring his overall haul to a record eight, but still found himself over an hour behind new champion Leducq and ninth in the final standings.

➲ Charles Pelissier must have wondered what more he could have done to win the Tour de France: he finished runner-up seven times. His record number of stage wins has since been equalled – by Eddy Merckx (1970 and 1974) and Freddy Maertens (in 1976) – but never beaten.

Charles Pelissier notched up a Tour de France record eight stage wins in 1930, but still finished only in ninth place.

IT'S A RECORD!

PERCY WILLIAMS, OLYMPIC 100M AND 200M LAUREATE, BREAKS WORLD RECORD
9 August 1930, Toronto, Canada

Percy Williams overcame a bout of rheumatic fever, which had damaged his heart when he was 15, to become an early track and field superstar. He ran his way into history by winning gold in both the 100m and 200m races in the 1928 Olympics in Amsterdam. He then kept on running – and winning – over the next few years, culminating in his record-breaking time of 10.3 seconds in the 100m in 1930. Canadians were elated, but Americans were unimpressed at having their domination of the sport upset by the skinny kid from Canada. They planned a series of 21 track meets throughout the US, on surfaces that were unfamiliar to Williams. He dazzled the Americans on their own turf, winning all but one of the races. Williams remains the only non US-runner to take home double golds in the 100m and 200m Olympic races.

Dubbed the "Human Flash," Williams's spectacular double-gold Olympic performance remains an unequalled feat of individual track-and-field achievement by a Canadian athlete at the international level.

➲ Nothing lasts forever. Williams later pulled a thigh muscle and never fully recovered. After being eliminated in the quarter-finals of the 1932 Olympics in Los Angeles, he gave up running and pursued a career in insurance. Depressed by the death of his mother and suffering chronic arthritis pain, Williams took his own life in 1982.

RBI RECORD CONSOLATION FOR WILSON

HACK WILSON FALLS SHORT OF BABE RUTH'S HOME RUN RECORD BUT SETS ALL-TIME MARK FOR RBI
28 September 1930, Chicago, Illinois, USA

Chicago Cubs centerfielder Hack Wilson may well have been short of stature, but he lacked nothing when it came to the power department. Standing only 5ft 6in, he weighed in at 195lb (88kg), had an 18-inch neck and could hit the ball a mighty distance. He was a three-time league leader in home runs and in 1930 set tongues wagging as he launched an assault on Babe Ruth's home run record (60). He fell short by four – his 56 home runs stood as a National League record until Mark McGwire (70) and Sammy Sosa's (66) personal homer duel in 1998 – but set an RBI mark (191) that has stood the test of time.

For years Hack Wilson was credited with having recorded "only" 190 RBIs. In 1999, additional research found that a run initially attributed to Charlie Grimm was actually batted in by Wilson.

➲ Despite his home run exploits, it was his RBI heroics that earned Wilson a long-standing place in the history books. During his 12-year Major League career he passed the 100 RBI mark on six occasions.

JONES WINS GOLF'S GRAND SLAM

BOBBY JONES WINS ALL FOUR MAJOR TOURNAMENTS IN SAME YEAR
30 September 1930, Merion Country Club, Pennsylvania, USA

Bobby Jones produced the greatest year golf has ever seen in 1930, winning all four of the major championships available to him. He retired from the game soon afterwards having won four US Opens, three Open championships, five US Amateur championships and one British Amateur championship.

If there was ever any doubt about Bobby Jones's place among the greats of golf history, it was eradicated in 1930. Having worked hard on his fitness through the winter, Jones sailed for England in March 1930 as part of the Walker Cup team in the best shape of his life and as a man on a mission. The United States took the Walker Cup 10–2. He then travelled to St Andrews for the British Amateur championship and made it to the final, where he trounced 1923 champion Roger Wethered 7&6. Success in the Open Championship followed two weeks later at Hoylake, before Jones returned to a ticker-tape parade through the streets of Manhattan. He then birdied the final hole to win the US Open at Interlachen Country Club by two shots. Only one leg of the grand slam remained, the US Amateur … and an entire country was caught up in the drama. Jones delighted in the leading role, winning the 36-hole final against Gene Homan on the 29th hole. Bobby Jones had achieved the impossible.

➲ Journalists later asked Bobby Jones whether he himself had ever thought the feat possible. "I felt reluctant to admit that I considered myself capable of such an accomplishment … actually, I did make plans for that golfing year with precisely this view in end," came the reply.

WOOD AND *MISS AMERICA* MAKE A SPLASH

GAR WOOD BECOMES FIRST TO BREAK 100MPH BARRIER ON WATER

20 March 1931, Miami Beach, Florida, USA

An innovator and a man who simply loved speed, Gar Wood experimented with placing aircraft engines in his boats – critics told him he was mad – and crossed the Atlantic in 1920 to compete in the prestigious Harmsworth Trophy, the speedboat equivalent of the America's Cup. He won and went on to defend the trophy eight times. In 1931, with his reputation at an all-time high, he took one of his boats – *Miss America IX* – to Miami Beach and, powered by twin Packard 3A-250s, guided her to a top speed of 102.25mph (164.5km/h), to become the first man in history to break the 100mph barrier on water.

➲Wood's record lasted barely a month. On 15 April 1931, England's Kaye Don guided his confrontationally named craft *Miss England II* to 103.49mph (166.55km/h) on South America's Parana River.

Gar Wood was one of the men vying for the title King of the Waters in the 1920s and '30s: he would break the world water speed record on six separate occasions.

POST SETS THE RECORD STRAIGHT

WILEY POST AND HAROLD GATTY BREAK RECORD FOR FASTEST AERIAL CIRCUMNAVIGATION

1 July 1931, Roosevelt Field, Long Island, New York, USA

Angered by the fact that a fixed-wing craft did not hold the record for the world's fastest aerial circumnavigation, Wiley Post, the personal pilot of two wealthy Oklahoma oilmen and a one-time parachutist with a flying circus, decided to put the Zeppelins in their place. On 23 June 1931, along with navigator Harold Gatty, he took off from Roosevelt Field in Long Island in his single-engine Lockheed Vega – called *Winnie Mae* – and embarked on a 14-stop journey around the world. Eight days, 15 hours and 31 minutes later, on 1 July 1931, they returned as record-breakers, and duly received a reception not seen since the days of Charles Lindbergh.

➲ Post was killed on 15 August 1935 when an engine failure caused his plane to crash on take-off from a lagoon near Point Barrow, Alaska.

Compensation received following an oilfield accident in 1926 – which led to him losing the sight in one eye – allowed Wiley Post to buy his first aircraft. Five years later, he broke the record for the fastest flight around the world.

TILDEN'S BULLET SERVE

BILL TILDEN SETS UNOFFICIAL RECORD FOR WORLD'S FASTEST SERVE

USA

Tall, lean and with shoulders as broad as the Delaware River that flows through the city of his birth, Philadelphia, Bill Tilden allied his great strength to a mastery of imparting spin on the ball to stand at the top of the world rankings for seven long years and to become tennis's first true superstar. His raw physical power manifested itself mostly in his serve, a beautiful fluid motion combined with perfect ball striking. At a tournament in 1931, one of his serves was measured – using a ballistic chronometer – at 163.6mph (263.1km/h). However, the ITF refuse to ratify it as a record because they consider the measuring equipment unreliable.

➲ Tilden's unofficial mark stands some 8mph (12.9km/h) faster than the official record, 155mph (249.44km/h) set by Andy Roddick in a Davis Cup tie against Belarus in 2004, but given the rackets players were using at the time it seems unlikely Tilden reached the mark.

Bill Tilden's all-power game brought him ten grand slam singles titles (seven US Open wins and three at Wimbledon) and, according to the Guinness Book of World Records at least, a claim on the fastest serve ever delivered.

DOMINANT CANADA SWEEP ALL-COMERS OFF THE ICE

CANADA WIN RECORD FOURTH SUCCESSIVE OLYMPIC ICE HOCKEY GOLD

13 February 1932, Lake Placid, New York, USA

It was the Winnipeg Falcons, representing Canada, who got the ball rolling, taking gold the first time ice hockey appeared in the Olympics at the 1920 summer games in Antwerp. Ice hockey found its rightful home four years later with the first staging of the Winter Olympics in Chamonix, France, but the result was still the same: Canada marched through the tournament unbeaten to claim a second successive gold. And after they had made it three in a row in St Moritz in 1928 it was hardly a surprise when only three other teams turned up for the 1932 Olympic ice hockey tournament in Lake Placid. Canada waltzed through the competition, winning five of their six games to claim an unprecedented fourth successive gold.

Canada were untouchable in the first four Olympic ice hockey tournaments, sweeping all before them to claim a record four consecutive gold medals.

➲ Canada entered the 1936 Winter Olympics in Garmisch-Partenkirchen, Bavaria, Germany, as firm favourites, but found themselves on the receiving end of one of the biggest shocks in Olympic history when Great Britain beat them 2–1 in the medal round to bring their record run to an end. Britain went on to snatch a shock gold.

AUSTRALIA STEAMROLLER SORRY SOUTH AFRICA

AUSTRALIA BEAT SOUTH AFRICA IN SHORTEST COMPLETED TEST IN HISTORY

12 February 1932, Melbourne, Australia

By the time South Africa arrived in Melbourne for the final Test in 1932 they were on their knees: trailing 4–0 in the series, they had been on the receiving end of Bradman at his best – the Don had scored four centuries in five innings – and had been thrashed into submission. South Africa collapsed to a sorry 36 all out in their first innings in just 23.2 overs, but fought back, dismissing Australia, without the injured Bradman, for 153. That was as good as it got for the Boks. A mere 31.3 overs later it was all over: South Africa were dismissed for a paltry 45 and Australia had won by an innings and 72 runs in just five hours 53 minutes.

➲ The 1931–32 series between Australia and South Africa saw the great Don Bradman close to, if not at, his peak. He scored 806 runs in his five innings in the series at a mighty average of 201.5.

Donald Bradman was injured during the first innings of the final Test of the 1931–32 series at the MCG. His batting was barely missed as Australia's 153 proved too much for the South Africans, who capitulated for 36 and 45, off 54.5 overs, to lose by an innings and 72 runs. Twenty-one wickets fell on the first day.

THE BRADMAN OF BILLIARDS' RECORD BREAK

WALTER LINDRUM COMPILES WORLD-RECORD BILLIARDS BREAK

19 February 1932, Thurston Hall, London, England

The grandson of Australia's first world billiards champion, Friedrich Wilhelm von Lindrum, and the son of the 1909 Australian champion, Frederick Lindrum, Perth-born Walter Lindrum played his first professional match at the age of 13 and by 16 was regularly hitting breaks of over 1,000. By the 1930s he was the star of the circuit – one journalist dubbed him "the Bradman of Billiards" – and such was his status that even the great Donald Bradman himself came to watch his matches. But the day he outshone his illustrious ancestors came on 19 February 1932 – during a game he ultimately lost to the great Joe Davis – when he compiled a world-record break of 4,137.

➲ Lindrum's world-record break lasted for two hours 55 minutes and comprised some 1,900 consecutive scoring shots.

The star turn in billiards in the 1930s, Walter Lindrum set some 57 world records during the course of his career; none was more impressive than his record break of 4,137.

SOLARIO FETCHES STAGGERING SUM OF 47,000 GUINEAS

CHAMPION HORSE SOLARIO SOLD AT PUBLIC AUCTION FOR RECORD SUM

March 1932, England

Sir John Rutherford paid a record 3,500 guineas for Solario, a well-made, strong, handsome, yearling colt in 1923, and it turned out to be worth every penny. Solario won all three starts as a juvenile and two years later, in 1925, cantered to an easy victory at the St Leger. A year later he caused a sensation, setting a pace in the 1926 Coronation Cup that no one could live with and strolling to a 15-length victory. Offers for Solario came flooding in – including some in excess of £100,000, an astonishing amount for those days – but Rutherford resisted all bids for his star horse until the day of his death in 1932. Solario was put up for public auction shortly afterwards and was sold for the staggering sum of 47,000 guineas – a record that would last for 35 years.

➲ Solario proved as successful on the stud farm as he had been on the racecourse, siring two Derby winners – Mid-day Sun (1937) and Straight Deal (1943) – as well as Exhibitionist, who took the 1,000 Guineas and the Oaks in 1937.

Jockey Joseph Childs guided Solario to a stunning success in the 1926 Coronation Cup, easing to victory by 15 lengths and attracting the eyes of many. Soon afterwards offers for the star horse came flooding in.

FLYING DUTCHWOMAN BREAKS 12-SECOND BARRIER

TOLLIEN SCHUURMAN FIRST WOMAN TO RUN 100M IN UNDER 12 SECONDS

5 June 1932, Haarlem, the Netherlands

Born in the Dutch province of Drenthe in the north-east of the Netherlands in 1913, by the age of 17 Tollien Schuurman had already broken the national 100m record and was beginning to be recognized as one of the fastest women on the planet. Later that year she became one of five athletes to run the 100m in 12 seconds dead. The United States' Betty Cook had been the first to run 12 seconds on 2 June 1928 in Chicago but, four years on, nobody had run faster and the 12-second mark was fast becoming women's athletics' unbreakable barrier. That all changed on 5 June 1932 in Haarlem, the Netherlands, when Schuurman clocked 11.9 seconds.

➲ Schuurman matched the feat a week later in Amsterdam and again on another four occasions to equal her own record, which finally fell on 4 September 1933 when Poland's Stanislawa Walasiewicz ran 11.8s in Warsaw.

Tollien Schuurman travelled to the 1932 Olympic Games as the joint world record-holder and one of the strong favourites for the 100m title. However, any gold medal dreams were dashed when she was eliminated from the competition at the semi-final stage.

VERITY STRIKES PERFECT NOTE WITH 10 FOR 10

YORKSHIRE'S HEDLEY VERITY RECORDS BEST BOWLING FIGURES IN FIRST-CLASS HISTORY

12 July 1932, Trent Bridge, Nottingham, England

Hedley Verity's sense of application to his craft bordered on obsessive scientific research, but the results – a high left-arm action, an unflinching mastery of length and a masterly control of pace – marked him out as one of cricket's greatest-ever bowlers. His finest moment came in just his second year of first-class cricket, playing for Yorkshire against Nottinghamshire at Trent Bridge in July 1932. On a rain-affected wicket and with the match edging to the home side's favour (Nottinghamshire held a 71-run first-innings lead), Verity proved unplayable, taking all 10 wickets – including a hat-trick – for just 10 runs in 19.4 mesmerizing overs. Nottinghamshire were all out for 67 and Yorkshire strolled to a comfortable 10-wicket victory.

➲ Verity died on 31 July 1943, a prisoner of war, from wounds received during the Eighth Army's first assault on German positions in Catania, Sicily. News of his death emerged on 1 September 1943, exactly four years after he had played his final match for Yorkshire.

A veteran of 40 Test matches for England, Hedley Verity took 144 wickets at an average of 24.37 and became the fastest English bowler in history to take 100 wickets, reaching the milestone in his 26th match.

Charles Pahud de Mortanges put the disappointment of losing out on a hat-trick of team three-day eventing Olympic golds behind him to defend his individual eventing crown successfully and become the first rider in history to win four equestrian gold medals.

DUTCH DELIGHT AS DE MORTANGES TAKES FOURTH GOLD

CHARLES PAHUD DE MORTANGES WINS RECORD FOURTH OLYMPIC EQUESTRIAN GOLD

30 July–14 August 1932, Los Angeles, California, USA

With the world gripped in the midst of the Great Depression, Los Angeles was the only city to bid for the 1932 Olympic Games and only half as many competitors as had appeared in Amsterdam in 1928 dug deep enough into their pockets to attend. Among them was Dutch equestrian star Charles Pahud de Mortanges, the defending individual event champion and part of a Dutch team seeking a hat-trick of three-day eventing golds. The United States edged out the Dutch into silver place in the team event, but de Mortanges successfully defended his eventing crown to become the first equestrian athlete to win four Olympic golds.

➲ The Los Angeles Games featured never-before-seen facilities for the athletes, including the first Olympic village in history.

Walter Hammond hit a rich vein of scoring form against New Zealand in 1933, hitting 563 runs in two innings, including a world-record 336 not out in the second Test in Auckland.

HAMMOND'S HEROICS IN VAIN AS KIWIS CLING ON

WALTER HAMMOND BREAKS RECORD FOR THE HIGHEST SCORE IN TEST CRICKET

31 March–2 April 1933, Auckland, New Zealand

Having been on the receiving end of a 4–1 hammering at the hands of Australia in the recent Test series – and seen Don Bradman confirm his status as the best batsman the world had ever seen – England would have been thankful to cross the Tasman Sea and round off their 1932–33 Australasian tour with a two-Test series against a New Zealand side still very much finding its feet in the international cricket arena. The drop in standard was manna from heaven for one England batsman: Wally Hammond. Having scored an unbeaten 227 in the first drawn match in Christchurch, he carried his form into the second and final Test in Auckland and hammered an unbeaten 336 to break Bradman's record for the highest Test score.

➲ Despite taking a massive 390-run first-innings lead, England's bowlers were left with next to no time to secure the win. New Zealand faced just 8.3 overs in their second innings and the series ended in a draw.

HAMMOND HAMMERS RECORD 10 SIXES

HAMMOND BREAKS RECORD FOR THE MOST SIXES IN A TEST INNINGS

31 March–2 April 1933, Auckland, New Zealand

It was the brutal manner of Walter Hammond's innings against New Zealand that sent shockwaves around the cricket world. Famous for the masterly fashion in which he could nurture an innings (with his textbook drives, his fleeting footwork and his dashing strokeplay), it was often said that watching a Hammond innings was worth the entrance fee alone; in 1933 he simply bludgeoned the New Zealand bowling. If his unbeaten 227 in the first Test in Christchurch had been aggressive (he faced just 301 balls), then his second-Test display was murderous: it took him just 318 balls and contained 34 fours and a Test record ten sixes.

➲ Hammond's tally of ten sixes stood as a Test record until October 1996, when Pakistan's Wasim Akram hit 12 sixes during his innings of 257 not out against Zimbabwe.

Walter Hammond made 22 centuries during his illustrious Test career, but none was more murderous than his electrifying triple-century in Auckland in 1933.

SOARING OVER THE ROOF OF THE WORLD

BRITISH EXPEDITION TEAM FIRST TO FLY OVER SUMMIT OF MOUNT EVEREST

3 April 1933, Mount Everest, Nepal/Tibet

By 1932 there weren't many aviation firsts left to achieve, but still nobody had flown over the world's highest peak. In 1933 all that was to change: both France and Germany were planning expeditions to fly over the peak of Everest. But it was the British team, led by Col. Stewart Blacker, who held the ace up their sleeve: a supercharged Bristol IS3 Pegasus engine that could already lay claim to the world altitude record (43,976ft). By March 1933 the British challenge was ready and on 3 April, battling high winds and with the Pegasus engine roaring at full power, the Houston-Westland, piloted by Lord Clydesdale and accompanied by Blacker, passed over the summit of Everest.

➲ The aircraft spent some 15 minutes circling around the summit – so that Blacker could take as many photographs of the peak as possible – before returning to base camp, in Lalbalu Airdrome, Bihar, northern India, and international acclaim.

Col. Stewart Blacker and his Houston-Westland expedition members pulled off a logistical and engineering tour de force when they completed the first flight over the summit of Mount Everest in 1933.

RECORD-BREAKING RICHARDS SURPASSES ARCHER'S MARK

GORDON RICHARDS BREAKS RECORD FOR NUMBER OF WINNERS IN SEASON

April–November 1933, England

At the age of 15, on the recommendation of a friend, Gordon Richards applied to become a stable boy at Fox Hollies and was accepted. He notched up his first winner by the age of 17 and by 1925, at the age of 21, became champion jockey for the first time. His reputation was beginning to grow: by 1932 he was the leading jockey of his day and joined forces with star trainer Fred Darling. It was a marriage made in heaven: the following year Richards notched up 249 winners – including wins in the Challenge Stakes and the King George Stakes – to beat Fred Archer's record of 246 winners set in 1885.

➲ Tony McCoy has since eclipsed Gordon Richards'srecord number of wins, but life for a jockey was somewhat different in Richards'sday than it is today. While modern jockeys can flit between races with helicopters, Richards would often have to ride his horse to the station to catch a train to reach his next race.

Gordon Richards, the only jockey in history to have been knighted, recorded a staggering 4,870 winners during his career: 249 of them came during his stellar 1932–33 season.

ROACH RECORDS KING PAIR AT HOME OF CRICKET

CLIFFORD ROACH ONLY MAN IN TEST HISTORY TO BE DISMISSED FIRST BALL IN BOTH INNINGS

24–27 June 1933, Lord's, London, England

The last time England had played the West Indies, Clifford Roach had become the first Caribbean batsman to score a Test double hundred, so when the West Indian tourists arrived in England in the summer of 1933, Roach would have been keen to lock horns with England's bowlers once again. But the West Indies had not played in a Test match for over two years … and the rust showed. England made 296 all out in their first innings; the West Indies' reply started with Roach being clean bowled first ball by Gubby Allen and they slipped to 97 all out. Things got no better second time round: forced to follow on, Roach fell first ball for a second time as the West Indies slipped to 172 all out and England swept to an innings-and-21-run victory.

➲ It turned out to be a miserable series for both Roach and the West Indies: the attacking opening batsman scored just 141 runs in six innings (at an average of 23.5) as England eased to a 2–0 win in the best-of-three-match series.

Clifford Roach (left) may have become the first West Indian batsman to record a double hundred in Test cricket (against England at Georgetown, Guyana, in February 1930), but three years later he had a more chastening experience when, against the same opponents (at Lord's), he became one of the few batsmen in Test history to suffer a King pair.

Garrison Savannah and L'Escargot both won the Gold Cup and the Grand National, but Golden Miller (shown leading at Cheltenham) is the only horse in history to have won both of Britain's premier steeplechases in the same year.

GOLDEN MILLER'S GOLDEN YEAR

GOLDEN MILLER BECOMES ONLY HORSE TO LAND CHELTENHAM GOLD CUP AND GRAND NATIONAL DOUBLE

24 March 1934, Aintree, Liverpool, England

When Golden Miller arrived at Aintree for the 1934 Grand National, the Irish-bred, seven-year-old bay gelding was one of the favourites and already recognized as one of the greatest horses in jump-racing history: he arrived at the world's most famous steeplechase race following a hat-trick of wins in the Cheltenham Gold Cup. And, after a few wobbles over Becher's Brook, as the race entered its final half-mile, Golden Miller found himself neck and neck for the lead with Dalaneige. The pair eased over the final fence together, before Golden Miller found his characteristic turn of pace to win the National in a new record time – which would stand until Red Rum came along some 40 years later – and claim an unprecedented double.

➲ Golden Miller made four further appearances at Aintree but failed to complete the course on each occasion. In contrast, he enjoyed continued success at the Cheltenham Gold Cup, taking the race in both 1935 and 1936 to record five straight victories.

PRATT'S HEROICS CANNOT SAVE THE SWANS

SOUTH MELBOURNE'S BOB PRATT KICKS VFL SEASON RECORD 150 GOALS

October 1934, Victoria, Australia

Born in Mitcham, Victoria, in 1912, Bob Pratt made his debut for South Melbourne (who, in 1982, would evolve into the Sydney Swans) as a 17-year-old in 1930. He would go on to become one of the finest full forwards ever to have graced an Australian Rules pitch and his achievements in the game resonate through the sport's history. Pratt soon got into his stride, leading the Swans' scoring tables in 1932 (71 goals) and again the following year (with 109). He went even better in 1934, breaking the 100-goal mark for the second year in a row and kicking his 150th during the Swans' Grand Final loss to Richmond.

➲ Pratt continued to lead the way for the Swans, ending as their leading scorer again in 1935 (103), 1936 (64) and 1938 (72). He left the club in 1939 to play for Colden in the Victoria Football Association and was soon up to his goal-scoring antics again, kicking a VFA record 183 goals – a mark since eclipsed by Ron Todd.

In 1934, South Melbourne's Bob Pratt (centre) kicked a VFL record 150 goals, a mark matched – by Peter Hudson in 1971 – but never beaten.

THE SHOT HEARD ROUND THE WORLD

GENE SARAZEN WINS THE MASTERS TO BECOME FIRST GOLFER IN HISTORY TO WIN CAREER GRAND SLAM

9 April 1935, Augusta National, Georgia, USA

The Masters, in just its second year, was the only major tournament the diminutive Gene Sarazen had yet to win and, having skipped the inaugural 1934 edition, the seven-time major winner was in deep trouble in his first visit to the Augusta National: three behind leader Craig Wood with just four holes remaining and his ball 235 yards away from the flag on the par-five 15th green. He went for it, cracking a four-wood over the water hazard and watching his ball land on the green and snake its way into the hole. A double-eagle ... Sarazen was now tied with Wood for the lead and both held on. They played a 36-hole playoff the next day: Sarazen won by four shots to become the first man in history to complete golf's career grand slam.

➲ Apart from Gene Sarazen, only four other golfers in history have completed the career grand slam: Ben Hogan (in 1953), Gary Player (in 1965), Jack Nicklaus (in 1966) and Tiger Woods (in 2000).

By the time Gene Sarazen stood over his ball on the 15th fairway in his final round at the 1935 Masters, the $1,500 winner's cheque had already been made out to Craig Wood, but then Sarazen produced the "shot heard round the world" – and became the first golfer in history to complete the career grand slam.

PERRY BECOMES THE COMPLETE MASTER OF TENNIS

FRED PERRY WINS FRENCH OPEN TO BECOME FIRST TENNIS PLAYER TO WIN CAREER GRAND SLAM

3 June 1935, Roland Garros, Paris, France

Former world table tennis champion Fred Perry's mastery of the continental grip – which allowed him to take a forehand on the run and get close enough to the net to volley – led to his domination of world tennis in the mid-1930s. He'd already won the US Open in 1933 and 1934 (and the Australian Open and Wimbledon titles in the latter year) and the French Open championship was the last grand slam title to elude him. That all changed in 1935: Perry made it all the way through to the final and beat German Gottfried von Cramm (6–3, 3–6, 6–1, 6–3) to become the first tennis player in history to achieve the career grand slam.

➲ Perry is one of only five players to have completed the career grand slam. The others are Don Budge (in 1938), Rod Laver (1962), Roy Emerson (1964) and Andre Agassi (1999).

Since his feats in the mid-1930s, every British tennis player has been judged against Fred Perry. The son of a Labour MP, he was world No. 1 for five years and ended his career with eight grand slam titles to his name: the US Open (in 1933, 1934 and 1936), the Australian Open (in 1934), Wimbledon (in 1934, 1935 and 1936) and the French Open (in 1935).

SULTAN OF SWAT FINALLY CALLS IT A DAY

BABE RUTH RETIRES WITH ALL-TIME CAREER SLUGGING PERCENTAGE RECORD

3 June 1935, Boston, Massachusetts, USA

Having been released by the New York Yankees in 1934 and with his hopes of managing a Major League outfit hanging by a thread, Babe Ruth jumped at the chance to sign for the Boston Braves on the promise of becoming the franchise's manager the following year. But any managerial hopes were soon dashed once more, and the Sultan of Swat knew that one of the most storied careers in the history of baseball was coming to an end. Three days after swatting the final three home runs of his illustrious career he retired, frustrated, but holding the record for the most career home runs (714 – broken by Hank Aaron in 1973) and the highest career slugging percentage (his mark of .690 has never been beaten).

Babe Ruth's Major League career ground to an undignified halt with the Boston Braves in 1935, but the Bambino still left baseball holding many of the sport's records: one of them – his career slugging percentage of .690 – has never been beaten.

➲ Ruth never did get the chance to manage a Major League franchise. He was still hanging out for the chance to manage the Yankees when the New York franchise instead offered him the chance to manage their Minor League outfit, the Newark Bears. Ruth turned the opportunity down, hoping a better offer would come along. It never did.

SALT FLATS' SURFACE SUITS CAMPBELL AND BLUEBIRD

MALCOLM CAMPBELL SHATTERS LAND SPEED RECORD AND BECOMES FIRST TO BREAK 300MPH BARRIER

3 September 1935, Bonneville Salt Flats, Utah, USA

For Malcolm Campbell, the days of land speed record attempts on a beach were over. It was March 1935, and the British multiple record holder had just broken his own land speed world record for the third time (276.71mph) on Daytona Beach, Florida. But Campbell was convinced he could go faster: soft sand equated to a loss of traction and a loss of speed. By 3 September the same year, Campbell and Bluebird had relocated to the Bonneville Salt Flats, Utah: a 159m² densely packed salt pan ideal for racing and perfect for land speed record attempts. Campbell recorded a top speed of 301.12mph that day to become the first to pass the 300mph barrier.

➲ This was the last land speed record Malcolm Campbell would set; it would last for two years, until George Eyston took his Thunderbolt car to 312mph on 27 August 1937, again at Bonneville Salt Flats.

A change of surface, from sand to salt, was enough to propel Malcolm Campbell and Bluebird past the 300mph barrier in September 1935.

GRIMMETT BECOMES FIRST MEMBER OF 200 CLUB

AUSTRALIA'S CLARRIE GRIMMETT FIRST BOWLER IN HISTORY TO TAKE 200 TEST WICKETS

17 February 1936, Johannesburg, South Africa

Born in New Zealand, Clarrie Grimmett moved to Australia at the age of 17 to pursue a career in cricket (the country of his birth was not a Test-playing nation at that stage). By the time he made his debut for Australia, against England at Brisbane in January 1925, some 16 years later, he was the complete bowler. He took 11 wickets in the match and never looked back. Seventeen matches later, in January 1931, he had taken his 100th Test wicket and, five years later, against South Africa in Johannesburg on 17 February 1936, he trapped Chud Langton leg before to become the first man in Test history to take 200 wickets.

➲ Grimmett would play in only one more Test match, the fifth Test v South Africa in Durban: he took 13 wickets in the match to end his Test career with 216 wickets at an average of 24.21.

In an age when spin bowling dominated Test cricket, leg-spinner Clarrie Grimmett presented the complete package that baffled batsmen the world over and saw him become the first bowler in Test history to reach the 200-wicket mark.

BRADL SOARS TO NEW WORLD RECORD MARK

JOSEF "SEPP" BRADL FIRST SKI-JUMPER TO BREAK THE 100M BARRIER

15 March 1936, Planica, Slovenia

In 1879, a Norwegian commentator had been left speechless when his fellow countryman Olaf Haugann propelled himself down a ramp and flew some 23m to set a new ski-jumping world record. As the years passed by, technical advances in both ski ramps and ski equipment had seen a dramatic improvement in distances jumped, and by the mid-1930s, jumpers were regularly hitting the 90m mark. By 1935, the world record stood at 99.5m, set by Austria's Fritz Kainersdörfer. But it was another Austrian who stole the headlines a year later: Sepp Bradl leapt 101m in Planica, Slovenia, to snatch the world record and become the first man in history to leap a three-figure distance.

➲ Just to show how far ski-jumping has progressed in the intervening years, Britain's Eddie "The Eagle" Edwards – one of the "heroes" of the 1988 Winter Olympics in Calgary, Canada – holds the British record with 105m. The current world record, set by Bjorn Elnar Romoren on 20 March 2005 in Planica, stands at a massive 239m.

Sepp Bradl went on to better his mark of 101m in 1938, when he leapt 107m. That mark stood as a record for three years: until Germany's Rudi Gehring jumped to 108m.

MAHMOUD SPRINTS TO DERBY WIN

AGA KHAN-OWNED MAHMOUD WINS EPSOM DERBY IN RECORD TIME

28 May 1936, Epsom Downs, Surrey, England

More money had been bet on the Epsom Derby in 1936 than in any previous year, but only a fraction of it had been placed on Mahmoud, the big grey Aga Khan-owned stallion, who bookmakers considered too much of a sprinter to win Britain's biggest flat race. The crowd waited expectantly: after a nervous start, the horses got away smoothly. First Carioca, then Thankerton took the lead; Mahmoud's jockey Charlie Smirke held him back until the home straight … and then let him go. Mahmoud darted to the front of the field and he galloped to the line three lengths ahead of Taj Akhbar: he had completed the 1 mile, 4 furlongs and 10 yard course in a record 2m54s.

➲ After the onset of the Second World War, plans were made to ship Mahmoud from Britain to the United States. He was taken to the port, but the ship's captain refused to take the stallion aboard because he did not possess the right papers. Mahmoud remained at the port in a shed; the ship set sail without him and was torpedoed en route. Mahmoud crossed safely in another vessel a few days later.

The bookmakers may not have considered Mahmoud one of the favourites for the 1936 Epsom Derby, but the Aga Khan-owned horse silenced any doubters with a record-breaking run.

OWENS SINGLE-HANDEDLY SILENCES THE NAZI REGIME

JESSE OWENS WINS RECORD FOUR OLYMPIC TRACK-AND-FIELD GOLD MEDALS

3–9 August 1936, Berlin, Germany

The Games of the XI Olympiad in Berlin, awarded to Germany before the rise of the Nazi party, were the Olympic Games Adolf Hitler tried to steal. The German leader wanted to use the showpiece event as a shop window to the world on his theories of Aryan supremacy. The only problem was, one United States athlete, Jesse Owens – the grandson of a slave and the son of a sharecropper – failed to read the script. On 3 August, he claimed the Olympic 100m crown with a start-to-finish win. A day later he took the long jump gold; the day after that he won the 200m and, four days later, on 9 August, made it a record quadruple gold as part of the winning 4x100m relay team … in contrast, Herr Hitler had long since made a hasty retreat from the stadium.

➲ Owens's four track-and-field gold-medal haul at the 1936 Olympics would not be repeated until Carl Lewis's haul in the 1984 Olympic Games in Los Angeles, when he won 100m, 200m, long jump and 4x100m gold.

Jesse Owens not only defeated his fellow competitors at the 1936 Olympic Games in Berlin, he also flattened the host nation's theories of Aryan supremacy.

CAPTAIN CHAND DRIVES INDIA TO OLYMPIC HAT-TRICK

INDIA'S DHYAN CHAND SCORES RECORD SIX GOALS IN OLYMPIC HOCKEY FINAL

15 August 1936, Berlin, Germany

Things weren't panning out well for the Germans at their home Olympics in 1936. If Jesse Owens had done his part to make a mockery of Hitler's theory of racial supremacy, then India's hockey team – and their captain and star player Dhyan Chand – drove the final nail into that particular theory's coffin. India, seeking a hat-trick of Olympic titles, swept all before them to face off for gold against a German side who had beaten them just months earlier. India led 1–0 at half-time, but in the second half ran riot, with Chand scoring six of the goals as India flattened the Germans 8–1.

➲ Legend has it that Hitler was so impressed by Chand's performance he offered him the position of Field Marshal in the German army. The Indian captain politely declined the offer.

Widely considered the greatest ever to play the game, Dhyan Chand reached his crowning moment when he scored six of India's eight goals in the 1936 Olympic hockey final.

HELL HATH NO FURY...

**DOROTHY POYNTON-HILL BECOMES FIRST WOMAN TO DEFEND 10M PLATFORM
OLYMPIC CROWN**
14 August 1936, Berlin, Germany

For one sports writer, at least, Dorothy Poynton-Hill was, as her name suggested, "over the hill". A "veteran" of two Olympics – she had taken gold in the springboard dive in 1928 (when she was aged barely 13) and gold again in the high dive in Los Angeles in 1932 – she was now married, 22 years old, and no longer worthy of a place in the United States diving team. Poynton-Hill had other ideas: she qualified for the team and promptly won the 10m platform crown to become the first woman in history to defend her Olympic diving title. The writer who had criticized her just months before, Frederick Graham of the *Glendale News-Press*, swiftly issued an apology.

⮑ Dorothy Poynton-Hill is one of only two women in history – the other being China's Fu Mingxia (1992, 1996 and 2000) – to win diving medals at three different Olympics.

Dorothy Poynton-Hill (right), the high-diving sweetheart of the United States, defied her critics to pick up her record second successive high-diving gold at the 1936 Olympic Games.

KING CARL PROVES UNPLAYABLE IN RECORD-BREAKING STREAK

CARL HUBBELL SETS ALL-TIME MAJOR LEAGUE RECORD WITH 24 CONSECUTIVE WINS

26 May 1937, New York, USA

A devastating left-handed pitcher from the Oklahoma oilfields, Carl Hubbell was the mainstay of the New York Giants' pitching line-up throughout the 1930s. He earned the moniker "The Meal Ticket" from his team-mates, leading them to three National League pennants, a World Series win in 1933 (where he threw two complete game victories) and two National League MVP awards (in 1933 and 1936). Using the screwball pitch that he perfected, he recorded five consecutive 20-win seasons (1933–37) and led the NL in wins three times (1933, 1936 and 1937). During the latter two seasons he set a record that has stood the test of time: 24 consecutive wins (16 at the end of the 1936 season and eight at the start of 1937).

⮕ In addition to his 24 consecutive wins, Hubbell will always be famed for his performance during the 1934 All Star game at the Polo Grounds, New York, on 10 July 1934. He yielded a single and then a walk before striking the next five batters, all future Hall of Famers – Babe Ruth, Lou Gehrig, Jimmie Foxx, Al Simmons and Joe Cronin – as well as pitcher and number nine hitter Lefty Gomez to achieve an All-Star record six strikeouts.

Carl Hubbell – known as "The Meal Ticket" to his team-mates and "King Carl" to Giants fans – produced many miraculous pitching performances during his 15-year career with the New York franchise; one of them – 24 consecutive wins – has stood the test of time.

BATTLESHIP ROMPS TO UNIQUE DOUBLE

BATTLESHIP BECOMES ONLY HORSE TO HAVE WON AMERICAN GRAND NATIONAL AND GRAND NATIONAL

25 March 1938, Aintree, Liverpool, England

Muscular but small at just 15.2 hands, Battleship was bred for flat racing and disappointed, winning only 10 of 22 starts. He was sold in 1931 to Marion duPont Scott, a steeplechase horse-racing specialist who had developed a state-of-the-art equine training centre in Orange, Virginia. By 1933 Battleship was ready, winning three of his four starts, and the next year came to public attention when he won the American Grand National. It was time for England. Battleship reappeared on the other side of the Atlantic in 1936 and disappointed. But the following year he won five of his 13 races and, in 1938, completed a unique double when he won the Grand National.

⮕ Battleship, sired by the great Man O'War (who won 20 of his 21 starts between 1919 and 1921), remains the smallest horse ever to win the Grand National.

Battleship may have endured a difficult flat-racing career, but a switch to the fences paid dividends: he won the American Grand National in 1934 and completed a unique double when he won the Grand National in 1938.

TEENAGER HOBBS STEERS BATTLESHIP TO GRAND NATIONAL SUCCESS

BRUCE HOBBS BECOMES YOUNGEST JOCKEY TO WIN THE GRAND NATIONAL
25 March 1938, Aintree, Liverpool, England

With the spectre of war looming over Europe for the second time in 20 years, perhaps it was appropriate that a horse called Battleship should win the 1938 Grand National. And just as it was a record-breaking run for the horse – who became the first to win both the American Grand National and the Aintree race – so it was a history-making moment for Battleship's jockey, Bruce Roberston Hobbs, an American-born Brit who, just three months beyond his 17th birthday, successfully steered his steed around the most famous steeplechase course in the world to became the youngest Grand National-winning jockey in history.

➲ The following year Hobbs suffered a terrible fall during a race and sustained multiple injuries, including a broken spine. He recovered from his injuries but never rode again and became a trainer in 1946 at the age of just 25.

Neither the bookmakers nor the public thought much of Battleship and Bruce Hobbs's (pictured left) chances in the 1938 Grand National, backing them at 40–1, but the odd couple came good and both horse and rider claimed separate places in the record books.

SWISS TRIUMPH IN SPITE OF LÖRTSCHER'S OWN-GOAL EMBARRASSMENT

SWITZERLAND'S ERNST LÖRTSCHER SCORES FIRST OWN GOAL IN WORLD CUP HISTORY

9 June 1938, Parc des Princes, Paris, France

As had been the case in 1934, the 1938 World Cup was played on a knockout basis. Switzerland and Germany opened proceedings on 4 June in Parc des Princes, Paris, and drew 1–1 after extra-time (these were the days before penalty shootouts). They met again five days later and the Swiss got off to a terrible start – 2–0 down after 22 minutes following an eighth-minute strike from Wilhelm Hahnemann and an own goal by their midfielder Ernst Lörtscher (the first such instance in World Cup history) – but recovered to win the game 4–2 and take their place in the second round.

➲ Switzerland did not progress far in the tournament, losing 2–0 in the second round to the eventual runners-up Hungary.

Andre "Trello" Abegglen (attempting a scissors kick) scored twice in the last 15 minutes of Switzerland's surprise 4–2 defeat of Germany in their World Cup first-round replay. It saved the blushes of Swiss midfielder Ernst Lörtscher, who had earlier become the first man to be credited with an own goal in the World Cup.

ITALY PROVE THEY ARE WORLD CUP KNOCKOUT KINGS

ITALY BECOME FIRST TEAM TO MAKE SUCCESSFUL DEFENCE OF WORLD CUP CROWN

19 June 1938, Stade Olympique de Colombes, Paris, France

Following their 2–1 win over Czechoslovakia in the 1934 World Cup final, Italy travelled to France four years later seeking to become the first team to regain the World Cup and – following Uruguay's withdrawal – the only team to win the Jules Rimet trophy twice. Vittorio Pozzo's men ground their way to a 2–1 win over Norway after extra-time in the first round. They dispatched France more easily in the quarter-finals, winning 3–1, and then ended Brazil's interest in the tournament with a 2–1 victory. The final against Hungary was one-way traffic: Italy won 4–2 and became the first nation to complete a successful defence of the World Cup crown.

➲ Italy would fail in their quest to complete a hat-trick of tournament wins when, following the end of the Second World War, the World Cup returned to the sporting calendar. In Brazil 1950 they failed to get beyond the group stages.

Defending champions Italy may have been advantaged by the absence of both Argentina and Uruguay from the 1938 World Cup, but they beat all who were placed before them to defend their title.

EIGER'S INFAMOUS NORTH FACE YIELDS AT LAST

GERMAN-AUSTRIAN TEAM OF CLIMBERS FIRST TO COMPLETE SUCCESSFUL ASCENT OF NORTH FACE OF EIGER

21–24 July 1938, Eiger, Switzerland

By the mid-1930s the north wall of the Eiger – one of the six great north faces of the Alps – had acquired a fearsome reputation. The first ascent of the 13,025ft (3,970m) peak had been made in 1858 (via the west flank and west ridge), but the north face – a vertical 5,000ft wall – remained unconquered … and many had died trying to conquer it. The key to unlocking what was starting to be called the Murder Wall came with a new 12-point crampon and on 21–24 July 1938, Anderl Heckmair, Ludwig Vörg, Heinrich Harrer and Fritz Kasparec, a German-Austrian team of climbers, put the new equipment to good use to complete the first successful ascent.

➲ Nine years would pass before Frenchmen Louis Lachenal and Lionel Terray completed the second successful ascent of the Eiger's north face.

Although the north face of the Eiger has been climbed on numerous occasions since the Heckmair-Vörg-Harrer-Kasparec expedition – with many of the climbers still opting for the classic 1938 route – in recent years much of the snow and ice has melted back to reveal bare rock, thus making the climb fractionally easier.

THE DON PASSES MILESTONE AT RECORD PACE

DONALD BRADMAN BREAKS RECORD FOR FASTEST 5,000 RUNS IN TEST HISTORY

22–25 July 1938, Headingley, Leeds, England

Donald Bradman did his utmost to put paid to Benjamin Disraeli's oft-quoted theory that there are "lies, damned lies and statistics". During the course of his distinguished career, the Don set landmarks in Test cricket that stand as giant monuments to the fact that he was head and shoulders above anyone else in Test history to have picked up a bat. In June 1938, during the fourth Test match against England at Headingley, Bradman notched up his 5,000th Test run in record time. He had required just 56 innings to achieve the feat: the next best in history is England's Jack Hobbs, who took 91 innings to reach the landmark.

➲ Bradman's first 5,000 runs contained nine centuries, eight double-centuries and two triple-centuries, with a top score of 334 against England at Headingley in July 1930. He ended his career with 6,996 Test runs to his name.

Donald Bradman eased past the 5,000 Test-run mark in 1938: it had taken him 35 innings fewer than the next fastest man in Test history to achieve the milestone.

HUTTON THRILLS OVAL CROWD WITH RECORD 364

LEN HUTTON BREAKS BRADMAN'S RECORD FOR HIGHEST TEST SCORE

20–24 August 1938, The Oval, London, England

Even the great cricket writer Neville Cardus was moved to suggest at the end of the match that the wicket "was unfair to skilled bowlers and not in the interests of the game"... unless you were an England supporter or a fan of the great Len Hutton. One down in the series against Australia with just one match to go, England won the toss at The Oval and elected to bat, knowing they needed to post a big first-innings score to have any chance of winning the game. Len Hutton produced a 797-minute vigil to score 364 – a new Test record – and lead England to 903 for 7 declared. The home side went on to win the game by the massive margin of an innings and 579 runs.

⟳ Hutton's new mark would stand as a Test best for nearly 20 years, until Garfield Sobers hit an unbeaten 365 against Pakistan in Jamaica in March 1958.

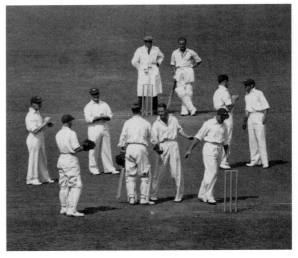

The greatest of Len Hutton's 19 Test centuries came at The Oval against the Australians in August 1938. Legend has it that England captain Walter Hammond wanted to put 1,000 runs on the board to put the Aussies under extreme pressure; led by Hutton's 364, England declared 97 runs short of fulfilling their captain's wishes, but still went on to win the game and square the series.

Don Budge ended his Grand Slam-winning year by helping the United States to retain the Davis Cup. He left the amateur ranks shortly afterwards to join the professional circuit, comprised mostly of lucrative exhibition matches.

BUDGE BLOWS ALL COMERS OFF THE COURT TO WIN GRAND SLAM

DON BUDGE BECOMES FIRST MALE PLAYER IN TENNIS HISTORY TO WIN GRAND SLAM

24 September 1938, Forest Hills, New York, USA

In 1938 Don Budge, tall, red-haired and with a game based on power, was beginning to be mentioned by tennis followers in the same breath as the legendary Bill Tilden. With a thunderous serve and the greatest backhand tennis has ever seen, Budge started the year by winning the Australian Open; he then beat Roderick Menzel in the Roland Garros final before sweeping all before him at Wimbledon to take the All-England crown without losing a set. Only the US Open title remained between Budge and his place among tennis immortals. He was too strong again, beating Gene Mako 6–3, 6–8, 6–2, 6–1 in the final to become the first player in tennis history to win the Grand Slam.

⟳ Don Budge is one of only two men in tennis history to have won the Grand Slam; the other, Rod Laver, achieved the feat twice, in 1962 and 1969.

England captain Walter Hammond scored 140 in the second innings as England amassed 654–5, chasing a target of 696. It remains, by more than 200 runs, the highest ever fourth-innings total in a Test match (the highest winning score in the fourth innings is 418–7, by the West Indies against Australia at Antigua in May 2003).

THE TIMELESS TEST

SOUTH AFRICA AND ENGLAND PLAY LONGEST TEST MATCH BY DAYS IN CRICKET HISTORY

3–14 March 1939, Kingsmead, Durban, South Africa

In the era of timeless Test matches, where both sides would continue to play until there was an eventual winner, one match became known as "The Timeless Test". On 3 March 1939, South Africa captain Alan Melville won the toss in the final match of the five-Test series and elected to bat. Ten days later, with an aggregate 1,981 runs scored, the rain, which had disrupted proceedings throughout the match, fell again with England needing 42 runs for victory but, more importantly, in desperate need of getting to Cape Town to catch their steamship home. The captains agreed upon a draw, England won the series 1–0 and made it to Cape Town in time to catch their boat.

➲ This match was the final nail in the coffin for timeless Tests. Although convenient in theory, the idea of continuing until there was a winner made scheduling matches a nightmare: South Africa v England in Durban in March 1939 was the last timeless Test ever played.

THE IRON HORSE FINALLY DRAWS TO A HALT

LOU GEHRIG'S MLB RECORD CONSECUTIVE-GAME STREAK COMES TO AN END

2 May 1939, Yankee Stadium, New York, USA

It all started on 2 June 1925 and, despite a broken thumb, a broken toe and numerous back strains, Lou Gehrig kept his place in the Yankees' starting line-up for more than a decade. By the end of the 1938 season, though, his performances were starting to wane. Media observers suggested there was something wrong with him and by the time 1939 spring training came around it was obvious Gehrig no longer possessed the power that had made him one of baseball's biggest draws. But still Yankees manager Joe McCarthy could not find it in himself to drop him. Then, on 2 May 1939, Gehrig approached McCarthy and said: "I'm benching myself." The legendary consecutive-game streak had stopped at 2,130.

➲ Long believed to be one of baseball's unbreakable records, Lou Gehrig's consecutive-game record was at last broken by the Baltimore Orioles' Cal Ripken Jr on 6 September 1995.

Shortly after his record-breaking consecutive-game streak had come to an end, doctors diagnosed Gehrig with a very rare and incurable form of degenerative disease – amyotrophic lateral sclerosis (ALS). It would kill him within two years and is now known as Lou Gehrig's disease.

Having learned to defend himself as a youth on the streets of St Louis, Henry Armstrong, the man they called "Homicide Hank" and the 11th of 15 children, picked up three world titles at different weights in the space of three years (1937–39).

HOMICIDE HANK TAKES THIRD WORLD CROWN

HENRY ARMSTRONG BECOMES FIRST BOXER TO HOLD THREE WORLD TITLES IN DIFFERENT WEIGHTS SIMULTANEOUSLY

22 August 1939, Yankee Stadium, New York, USA

Henry Armstrong fought his first professional bout in 1931 at the age of 18 and was knocked out in the third round. His first shot at a world title came on 29 October 1937 (off the back of a 22-bout unbeaten run) and Armstrong knocked out Petey Sarron in the sixth at Madison Square Gardens to take the world featherweight title. The following year he challenged Barney Ross for the welterweight crown and won by a unanimous decision. Then, on 22 August 1939, Armstrong made history when he beat Lou Ambers on points to take the world lightweight crown: he had become the first boxer in history to hold three world titles at three different weights simultaneously.

➲ Although Henry Armstrong is one of a number of boxers to have won world titles at three separate weights, he is the only one to have held them all at the same time.

SHAW AND HIS MASERATI DEFEND INDY CROWN

WILBUR SHAW BECOMES FIRST TO RECORD BACK-TO-BACK WINS AT INDY 500

30 May 1940, Indianapolis Motor Speedway, Indiana, USA

A former worker in a Detroit battery company, Wilbur Shaw, who used to watch events at Indianapolis as a child from the stands, finally went racing in 1921 at the age of 19. He had his first taste of Indy 500 success in 1937 and travelled to race in Europe. It was there he encountered a Maserati for the first time. Shaw returned to the States and persuaded a Chicago businessman to sponsor him to drive a Maserati in the 1939 Indy 500. He won. Reunited with his car the following year, Shaw won again, starting from second on the grid and leading 136 of 200 laps to become the first driver in history to win back-to-back Indy 500s.

➲ Shaw is perhaps best remembered as the man responsible for saving the Indianapolis Motor Speedway from becoming an industrial park. In November 1945, he persuaded Tolman Hulman to buy the dilapidated speedway – it had been severely neglected during the Second World War – for $750,000.

Wilbur Shaw is one of only five men in history to record back-to-back wins in the Indianapolis 500. The others are Mauri Rose (1947–48), Bill Vukovich (1953–54), Al Unser (1970–71) and Helio Castroneves (2001–02).

JOLTIN' JOE'S 56-GAME STREAK

JOE DIMAGGIO SETS THE CONSECUTIVE-GAME HITTING RECORD WITH 56
15 May–17 July 1941, USA

It all started on 15 May 1941. The New York Yankees' Joe DiMaggio, a man who was no stranger to making the headlines, went a seemingly innocuous one-for-four against Eddie Smith and the Chicago White Sox. And on it went: Joltin' Joe simply could not stop, hitting safely for 56 games in a row to record one of the greatest achievements in baseball's much-storied history. The legendary streak finally came to an end on 17 July 1941 against the Cleveland Indians, but only just: it took two magnificent backhanded stops from third baseman Ken Keltner to halt DiMaggio's march.

➲ DiMaggio reignited the Yankees' charge that year and they went on to win the World Series with their star player picking up the Most Valuable Player award.

On the day of the Yankees' match-up with the Indians, DiMaggio and team-mate Lefty Gomez were heading to the ballpark in a taxi when the cabbie piped up: "I've got a feeling that if you don't get a hit your first time up tonight they're going to stop you." Gomez snapped: "What are you trying to do, jinx him?"

Nothing could go wrong for patient hitter Ted Williams during the 1941 baseball season and he became the last in Major League history to average above .400 over the course of a season.

THE SPLENDID SPLINTER FINDS HIS FORM

TED WILLIAMS BECOMES LAST PLAYER TO END MLB SEASON WITH AVERAGE OVER .400

28 September 1941, Fenway Park, Boston, Massachusetts, USA

While Joe DiMaggio was putting together his 56-game hitting streak, a 22-year-old from further up the east coast was starting to make headlines of his own. Nobody liked hitting more than Boston Red Sox leftfielder Ted Williams, and in 1941 he embarked on one of the most storied hitting seasons in Major League Baseball history. It all started on 15 April when he went 1-for-1 against the Washington Senators. By 24 July, his average stood at .397: a day later he went 2-for-3 against Cleveland to take it above .400 … and it never slipped below the mark again. In his last outing of the season, on 28 September against Philadelphia, he went 2-for-3 to become the last player in Major League history to end the season with an average above .400 (.406).

➲ Ted Williams did not just lead the league's averages that year, he also led the way in home runs (37), base on balls (147), runs (135), slugging average (.735) and on base percentage (.551 – a figure that would stand as a record until 2002). As a consequence he beat Joe DiMaggio to that season's batting crown.

COPPI TAKES BREAK FROM WAR EFFORT TO EDGE RECORD

FAUSTO COPPI SETS NEW MARK FOR WORLD HOUR CYCLING RECORD

7 November 1942, Vigorelli Velodrome, Milan, Italy

Enrolled in the Italian army in an infantry regiment based in Tortona, Piemonte, northern Italy, Fausto Coppi, who had won the Giro d'Italia as a 19-year-old in 1940, was granted leave to take his bicycle to the Vigorelli Velodrome in Milan and make an assault on the world hour record held by Frenchman Maurice Archambaud. At 2 p.m. on 7 November 1942, his record bid got underway. But he set off too quickly and by the half-hour mark was trailing the Frenchman's record pace. Coppi dug deep, grinding out lap after lap and edging himself towards record-breaking pace. The hour was up and he had done it: Coppi had beaten Archambaud's mark by a mere 31m (102ft).

➲ Coppi's world hour mark of 45.798km (28.46 miles) stood as a record for 14 years until beaten by Frenchman Jacques Anquetil on 29 June 1956.

A world record-breaker during the Second World War, Coppi went on to enjoy a successful career when peace had finally settled over Europe. In 1949, he became the first cyclist in history to win the Giro d'Italia and the Tour de France in the same year.

ROCKET FIRES 50 FOR THE HABS

MAURICE RICHARD BECOMES FIRST IN NHL HISTORY TO SCORE 50 GOALS IN A SEASON

March 1945, Montreal, Canada

After his debut season with the Montreal Canadiens had been cut short by a broken ankle, Maurice Richard bounced back in style in the 1943–44 season, scoring 32 goals in 46 games to help the Habs to a first Stanley Cup triumph in 13 years. A star was born, but the man they started to call "Rocket" had even more up his sleeve the following season. In 1944–45, Richard went on a scoring spree unprecedented in NHL history: on 28 December 1944, he notched eight points – five goals and three assists – in a game against Detroit, setting a record that would stand until 1976 – and ended the season with a staggering 50 goals in 50 games.

➲ "50 goals in 50 games" has become one of hockey's most celebrated milestones. Only four other players in NHL history have been able to score 50 goals in 50 – or fewer – games: (Mike Bossy (1980–81), Wayne Gretzky (1981–82, 1983–84 and 1984–85), Mario Lemieux (1988–89) and Brett Hull (1990–91 and 1991–92).

Having made his mark in the NHL the previous season, Maurice Richard took his place among ice hockey legends in 1944–45 by scoring 50 goals in 50 games.

In 1945, Byron Nelson produced one of the best years in golf history, winning a record 18 times, including a record considered the most unattainable in golf – 11 consecutive tournament wins.

BRILLIANT BYRON LEAVES OPPONENTS TRAILING IN HIS WAKE

BYRON NELSON WINS PGA TOUR RECORD 18 TOURNAMENTS DURING THE SEASON

17 December 1945, Fort Worth, Texas, USA

Many have laid claim to putting together the greatest season in the history of golf – Bobby Jones in 1930, Ben Hogan in 1953 and Tiger Woods in 2000–01 – but a prime candidate was Byron Nelson's vaunted 1945 season. Tall and with an upright swing that became the model for the modern swing, in 1945 Nelson notched up a record 18 tournament wins – including a run of 11 successive victories and victory in the PGA Championship (his fifth major). He also produced 19 consecutive rounds of under 70 and finished the year with a scoring average of 68.33 – which stood as a PGA Tour record until Tiger Woods's 68.22 during the 2000 season.

➲ Nelson retired at the end of the 1946 season, at the age of 34, and settled into life on the ranch he had bought with his golf winnings. He lived there until his death in 2006 at the age of 94.

"SULLY" FINALLY HANGS UP HIS GOLDEN BOOTS

JIM SULLIVAN RETIRES FROM RUGBY LEAGUE HOLDING RECORD FOR MOST GOALS KICKED

23 February 1946, Wigan, Lancashire, England

Arguably the greatest Welsh player ever to appear in the ranks of rugby league, Jim Sullivan switched codes in 1921 when he joined Wigan from Cardiff RFC (for whom he had been first-choice full-back since the age of 16) for the record-breaking sum of £750. He was worth every penny of the investment: possessing prolific goal-kicking skills – in 1925 he scored a record 22 goals in a Challenge Cup match against Flimby and Fothergill – he went on to enjoy a prolific career, including three tours with Great Britain (in 1924, 1928 and 1932). By the time he hung up his boots in 1946, he had made 774 appearances for Wigan, kicked 2,317 goals and scored 4,833 points, numbers which have not been challenged since.

➲ Upon his retirement, Sullivan became Wigan's manager, leading them to Challenge Cup success in 1948 and 1951 before becoming manager of St Helens in 1952.

Such was Jim Sullivan's kicking prowess that every rugby league kicker since has had to live in his shadow: he kicked 2,317 goals in a phenomenal 25-year career with Wigan.

Having won his 15th straight world title in 1946, Joe Davis, still at the height of his abilities, took a step away from the world championship spotlight.

DAVIS ON CUE FOR 15TH WORLD SNOOKER CROWN

JOE DAVIS WINS WORLD SNOOKER CHAMPIONSHIP FOR RECORD 15TH TIME

20 May 1946, London, England

Born in the Derbyshire coal-mining village of Whitwell in 1901, Joe Davis became a professional billiards player at the age of 18. But despite forging an impressive career, he was convinced the future lay with the game of snooker, and set about organizing the first world snooker championship in 1927. He won, beating Tom Dennis 20–10 in the final, and would go on to win every world championship until 1946 – a total of 15 (the tournament was not played between 1941 and 1945). Believing such dominance to be detrimental to the game's development, he never contested the tournament again, although he continued to play the game professionally.

➲ During his distinguished career, Joe Davis, considered the father of modern snooker, was officially beaten on level terms just four times.

A KICKOFF FOR MULTICULTURALISM

HERB TRAWICK BECOMES FIRST BLACK PRO FOOTBALL PLAYER IN CANADA

1946, Montreal, Canada

CFL football in the mid-'40s was a uniformly white game, a situation that the management of the nascent Montreal Alouettes wanted to change. They'd watched as Jackie Robinson electrified baseball with the Montreal Royals, and they wanted some of that for football. Head coach Lew Hayman searched for a black player who would be as popular with fans as Robinson was, and he found him in a Kentucky State University graduate who had also been a college football star. Herb Trawick arrived in Montreal for the 1946 season and never left, playing 12 seasons with the team before retiring in 1957. As a pro player, he helped sweep the Als into four Grey Cup games and was voted CFL Eastern Division All Star seven times. He has since been voted one of the CFL's all-time top 50 players of the modern era.

Trawick was nothing short of amazing: quick and agile despite is large size, his speed made his a household name – though offensive linemen are not usually considered stars. He was also one of the few linemen to sore a touchdown at the Grey Cup.

➲ Trawick was known for his charity work and community involvement as well as his on-field prowess. After his retirement, the Alouettes retired his jersey number and he was inducted into the Canadian Football Hall of Fame. Trawick lived in Montreal up to his death in 1985. Twelve years later, the City of Montreal named a park in his honour.

ROBINSON CROSSES BASEBALL'S COLOUR LINE

JACKIE ROBINSON BECOMES FIRST AFRICAN-AMERICAN PLAYER TO PLAY IN MAJOR LEAGUE BASEBALL
15 April 1947, Brooklyn, New York, USA

The colour barrier in baseball had not been crossed for some 50 years, but Brooklyn Dodgers president Branch Rickey knew he had found the man to break it. Jackie Robinson, a talented all-round sportsman – and the first in UCLA history to win varsity letters in four sports – had been farmed out to Montreal Royals in 1946 and led the International League in both batting (av. .349) and fielding (.985). Rickey knew Robinson was ready for the big time, even if the rest of the United States didn't. Amid great media attention, Robinson made his Major League debut for the Brooklyn Dodgers on 15 April 1947 against the Boston Braves and went 0-for-3, but went on to excel. A drawing card from the word go – some came out of curiosity, others to see his electrifying play – he ignored the constant catcalls that came his way and went on to enjoy a stellar nine-year career.

➲ Robinson adapted to big-time baseball so quickly that he collected Rookie of the Year honours after the 1947 season. He was a six-time National League All-Star, and an integral part of the Dodgers line-up that won six NL pennants. In 1949 Robinson won both the batting title and the MVP award in 1949. He retired after just nine seasons, but went out with a bang as the Dodgers won their first World Series.

Jackie Robinson's first appearance in the Major League did more than shake baseball to the very core; such was its social impact, it changed the United States for ever and stands as one of the most significant moments in the civil rights movement.

An unusual set of circumstances created Albert Bourlon's day in the sun in the 1947 Tour de France. Whispers of a prize for the first past 5km in the 14th stage led to him securing the largest breakaway victory in the event's history.

BOURLON GOES IT ALONE FOR RECORD WIN

ALBERT BOURLON SECURES LARGEST BREAKAWAY VICTORY IN TOUR DE FRANCE HISTORY
11 July 1947, Luchon, France

It is 11 July 1947 and the 14th stage of the Tour de France – a 253km slog from Carcassonne through the mountains of the Pyrenees to Luchon – is about to start. Frenchman Albert Bourlon, already out of contention for the overall title, wants to take something from his second Tour. Shortly before the start of the stage he hears of a 20,000-franc prize on offer for the first rider to reach 5km: almost as much money as was on offer for the stage winner. Bourlon starts the stage like a bat out of hell … and no one follows him. Talk of the prize had been a ruse. In a unique set of circumstances, Bourlon ploughed a lonely furrow at the front of the field and crossed the winning line in 8h10m11s, some 16m20s ahead of the second-placed man to earn the biggest breakaway victory in Tour history.

➲ Bourlon may have won the 14th stage of the 1947 Tour de France – the first to be staged following the end of the Second World War – but it did little to help his overall classification by the time he had reached Paris: he was 21st overall, some 2h38m18s behind winner Jean Robic.

FANNING BOWS OUT IN RECORD-BREAKING STYLE

FRED FANNING SCORES AFL/VFL RECORD 18 GOALS IN A GAME
27 July 1947, Junction Oval, Melbourne, Australia

Only a paltry crowd of 6,000 turned up at Junction Oval for the final game of the 1947 VFL season: after all, the Melbourne Demons had already missed out on a place in the semi-finals and their opponents for the day, St Kilda, had been the league's whipping boys for much of the season. But for those present, the Demons' full-forward Fred Fanning, a mountain of a man with a huge leap, huge hands and quick feet, made it a day to remember. In 19 shots at goal that day, Fanning scored 18 of them to break the record set by Gordon Coventry when he scored 17 times against Fitzroy in 1930.

➲ Ironically it was the last professional game Fanning would play. He joined Hamilton as coach the following year, aged 25, for £10 a week, three times the salary he was getting with the Demons.

Fred Fanning's feat of scoring 18 goals in a game remains an AFL record unlikely ever to be broken.

His Test career spanned some 20 years, and none was more successful for Dennis Compton than 1947: a year in which he scored 1,159 runs in 15 innings.

COMPTON REMAINS CONSTANT AS ENGLAND RETURN TO FORM

DENNIS COMPTON BREAKS CLEM HILL'S 45-YEAR RECORD FOR MOST TEST RUNS IN CALENDAR YEAR

16–20 August, The Oval, London, England

The summer of 1947 saw a return to winning ways for the English cricket team … and for one man a place in the record books. England bounced back from a 3–0 defeat Down Under and a failure to get their hands on the Ashes, to beat South Africa 3–0 in the five-match home series. But Dennis Compton was one man whose form had remained constant throughout the course of the year. The Middlesex star scored six centuries during the course of the calendar year, including two in the failed Ashes campaign and a knock of 208 in the second Test against the Boks at Lord's, en route to a total of 1,159 runs (at an average of 82.78) to break the record for most Test runs in a calendar year set by Clem Hill (1,060) back in 1902.

➲ Compton's total of runs in a calendar year would stand as a Test record for 11 years, until Garfield Sobers scored 1,299 runs in 1958.

1947

Already the holder of the world land speed record, John Cobb died in a 200mph accident on Loch Ness in Scotland in 1952 during an attempt on the world water speed record.

COBB CONFIRMS STATUS AS THE FASTEST MAN ON EARTH

JOHN COBB BREAKS HIS OWN WORLD LAND SPEED RECORD

2 February 1948, St Moritz, Switzerland

16 September 1947, Bonneville Salt Flats, Utah, USA

A director of fur brokers Anning and a wealthy man in his own right, John Cobb was a British motor-racing enthusiast who, during the 1930s and '40s, was conducting a private battle with fellow countryman George E.T. Eyston for the tag of the fastest man in the world. Cobb had held the record since 1939, when he took his Railton car to 369.74mph (595.02km/h) on Bonneville Salt Flats in Utah to break Eyston's record by 12mph. Eight years later he was back … and this time he had the tools at his disposal to go even faster: a newly made Railton Special powered by two supercharged W12-block Napier Lion VIID aircraft engines, each of which produced 1,250bhp. It worked: Cobb averaged 394.19mph (634.37km/h) over a measured mile to write yet another line in the history books.

➲ Cobb's mark would stand as the world land speed record for 16 years until Craig Breedlove guided his Spirit of America car to 408.312mph (663.54km/h) on 15 September 1963 over the same Bonneville Salt Flats.

INNOVATIVE BUTTON DAZZLES JUDGES

DICK BUTTON BECOMES YOUNGEST-EVER GOLD MEDALLIST AT WINTER OLYMPICS

2 February 1948, St Moritz, Switzerland

Having claimed the United States championships the previous year, 17-year-old Dick Button was prompted to become more artistically daring after a second-place finish in the 1947 world figure-skating championships. When the 1948 Winter Olympics came around, the American sensation was ready to dazzle the world. During his free skate program he attempted two routines never seen on ice before – the double axel (which included two-and-a-half rotations) and the first version of a camel jump (a jump into a spin) – and nailed them both. The judges were impressed: eight out of nine put him in first place, and Button, aged 18, had become the youngest gold medallist in Winter Olympic history.

➲ 1948 turned out to be a golden year for Dick Button as he became the only man in history to complete what could be termed the "figure-skating grand slam". As well as the Olympic title, he also walked away with the United States, North American, European and World crowns.

Widely considered one of the premier skaters of all time, Dick Button was a five-time world champion (1948–52) and went on to defend his Olympic crown in 1952 in Oslo, Norway. He later became an Emmy-winning sports broadcaster.

BOY WONDER MATHIAS STEALS THE SHOW

BOB MATHIAS BECOMES YOUNGEST ATHLETE IN HISTORY TO WIN TRACK-AND-FIELD OLYMPIC GOLD

29 July–14 August 1948, London, England

In the spring of 1948, Tulare High School coach Virgil Jackson suggested that his protégé Bob Mathias, a high-school standout in athletics, should try his hand at the decathlon. Three weeks later Mathias won his first event and travelled in hope more than expectation to the National AAU competition, which would serve as a trial for the XIV Olympiad in London. Against all the odds, Mathias won. And his fairytale rise to world stardom continued. He may have been inexperienced, but he was too strong for his fellow competitors at the 1948 Olympic Games and swept to a comfortable decathlon gold. At 17 years, 263 days he had become the youngest track-and-field gold medallist in Olympic history.

⊃ Four years later, at the 1952 Olympics in Helsinki, Finland, Bob Mathias cemented his legend as one of the world's greatest athletes when he crushed his opponents to retain his Olympic title – the winning margin over second-placed Milt Campbell was a staggering 912 points.

1948 was a fairytale year for 17-year-old Bob Mathias. In the space of a few short months he went from being a high-school star to becoming the youngest track-and-field gold medallist in Olympic history.

Scott pulled off her gold medal win on a rink that was slushy and uneven, thanks to rising temperatures and the previous day's hockey match. Scott went on to turn pro in June of that year. After retiring from skating, Scott became a successful horse trainer.

CANADA'S SWEETHEART IS PURE GOLD IN ST-MORITZ

FIRST FEMALE FIGURE SKATER TO LAND A DOUBLE LUTZ IN COMPETITION WINS CANADA'S FIRST OLYMPIC GOLD IN FIGURE

9 August 1948, St-Moritz, Switzerland

In 1948, Canadians needed a symbol to help them forget the ravages of World War II – and they got it in Barbara Ann Scott. Scott began skating at the age of seven, winning the Canadian Junior Championship at 11 and the Senior title at 15. As a 13-year-old, Scott was the first female to successfully land a double Lutz in competition skating. She was North America's skating champ from 1945–48, and became the first North American to win the European Championship and Worlds in 1947 – then won them again in 1948. Scott capped off an amazing career by becoming the first Canadian to win the gold medal in Olympic figure skating.

⊃ Scott was awarded the Lou Marsh Trophy for Canadian athlete of the year in 1945 1947 and again in 1948. In 1955, she married Chicago publicist Tom King and moved to the US, where she lives to this day.

After her record four-gold-medal-winning performance in the 1948 Olympic Games in London, 30-year-old mother of two Fanny Blankers-Koen was nicknamed "The Flying Housewife".

THE FLYING HOUSEWIFE GRABS QUADRUPLE GOLD

FANNY BLANKERS-KOEN BECOMES ONLY WOMAN TO WIN FOUR TRACK-AND-FIELD GOLD MEDALS IN SINGLE OLYMPICS

29 July–14 August 1948, London, England

Two fifth-placed finishes were all 17-year-old Fanny Koen could manage in the 1936 Olympics. Then came the war, followed by marriage to Jan Blankers, and the birth of her two children. By the time of the first post-war Olympics in 1948 she was 30 years old and considered by many to be over the hill. But on 2 August, with the rain sweeping down and turning the track to mud, she ran 11.9s to take 100m gold. Two days later, she recovered from a poor start to take her second gold in a photo finish. On 6 August, with the rain lashing down once more, she won the 200m by seven-tenths of a second – the largest winning margin in the event's history. Her record fourth gold came when she anchored the Dutch to victory in the 4x100m relay.

➲ Fanny Blankers-Koen is the only woman in history to have won four track-and-field gold medals in a single Olympics. Only three men in history have equalled the feat: Alvin Kraenstein (1900), Jesse Owens (1936) and Carl Lewis (1984).

COACHMAN LEAPS TO A PLACE IN THE RECORD BOOKS

ALICE COACHMAN BECOMES FIRST AFRICAN-AMERICAN WOMAN TO WIN OLYMPIC GOLD

29 July–14 August 1948, London, England

Born in the USA's Deep South, Alice Coachman learned to jump barefoot in a neighbourhood park. The US national high jump champion between 1939 and 1948, she also forged a formidable reputation as a sprinter – setting national records in both the 50m dash and the 100m. By the 1948 Olympics she was in her prime – she had qualified for the US team in high jump by leaping to a new world record mark of 5ft 4in – and, battling back pain, jumped through the pain barrier to record a competition-winning 5ft 6^1/8 in in her first jump. In the process, she became not only the first American female athlete to win an Olympic track-and-field gold, but also the first African-American athlete to do so.

➲ Coachman's main rival, Britain's Dorothy Tyler, matched her leap, but because she did so in her second jump, the gold medal was awarded to the American athlete.

Just a year after Jackie Robinson had broken the colour barrier in baseball, Alice Coachman became the first African-American woman to win an Olympic gold medal. She returned from the 1948 Games in London to a hero's welcome.

Vicki Manalo Draves had to overcome racial discrimination as a child to become the first woman to win both springboard and high-diving competitions at the Olympic Games.

MANALO DRAVES BECOMES FIRST TO CLAIM DOUBLE DIVING GOLD

VICKI MANALO DRAVES FIRST TO COMPLETE SPRINGBOARD AND PLATFORM DIVING DOUBLE

29 July–14 August 1948, London, England

Born to a Filipino father and an English mother in California in 1924, Vicki Manalo began diving when she was 16 and soon ran into problems with her culturally mixed background when the diving club she attended suggested she might consider changing her name. She left the club and worked with a new coach, Lyle Draves – the pair later married. Under his guidance she won the national championships in 1943, before returning to her wartime job as a secretary. She resumed her diving career after the end of the Second World War and etched her place in legend when she became the first woman to sweep both 3m springboard and 10m platform gold medals at the 1948 Olympic Games in London.

➲ Vicki Manalo Draves turned professional directly after the Games had finished and put on her first exhibitions in the Philippines.

THE MOST FAMOUS DUCK IN TEST HISTORY

DONALD BRADMAN RETIRES WITH HIGHEST AVERAGE IN TEST HISTORY (99.94)
14–18 August 1948, The Oval, London, England

The whole cricket world knew that, at 40 years of age, the great career of Donald Bradman was coming to end. And if the Australian tour to England in 1948 was scheduled as the Don's farewell tour, it turned into little more than a royal procession. Australia swept all before them and Bradman arrived for his final Test, at The Oval, having scored 508 runs in the series – including a match-winning unbeaten 173 in the fourth Test at Headingley – and needing just four runs to reach 7,000 career runs and ensure a 100.00 average. As he walked onto the sun-drenched ground, the crowd rose to a man to acknowledge him; the England players formed a guard of honour and gave him three cheers. Bradman took guard and blocked the first ball from Eric Hollies. He played all around the next: D.G. Bradman b Hollies 0. There was stunned silence: Bradman had failed in his quest and ended his career with an average of 99.94.

➲ To put Donald Bradman's achievements on a cricket pitch into some perspective, the next best career batting average in Test history is Graeme Pollock's 60.97.

The great Don Bradman may well have bowed out of Test cricket with a whimper, but his career figures (6,996 runs at an average of 99.94) have never been beaten and, in all probability, never will be.

THE INVINCIBLES TRIUMPH IN ENGLAND

AUSTRALIA BECOME FIRST TEAM TO TOUR ENGLAND WITHOUT LOSING A SINGLE MATCH

14–18 August 1948, The Oval, London, England

The Don might have fluffed his lines in the final scene, but his Australian team-mates played the perfect supporting role in what was billed as Bradman's farewell tour. For the most part, victory followed victory during their three-and-a-half-month, 32-match tour: over half of them by an innings, two of them by 10 wickets and one of them by nine. Eleven of their batsmen combined to score 50 centuries and seven of the touring party of 17 passed 1,000 runs. And the bowlers did just as well, dismissing opponents for under 200 on 37 occasions. They certainly proved too strong for England in the five-match Test series: the home side's hopes of winning the Ashes for the first time since 1934 ended in a 4–0 series drubbing.

➲ The scores from the Test series underline Australia's superiority. They won the first Test at Lord's by eight wickets; the second in Manchester by 409 runs; the third Test in Manchester ended in a rain-affected draw; the Australians won the fourth Test at Headingley by seven wickets and rounded off the tour with an innings-and-149-run win in the final Test at The Oval.

Dubbed the Invincibles and considered the most united team ever to have stepped into the Test arena, the 1948 Australian touring team to England retained the Ashes and ended their 32-match tour unbeaten.

BROWN BOMBER HANGS UP THE GLOVES ... FOR NOW

JOE LOUIS RETIRES AFTER RECORD 25 SUCCESSFUL DEFENCES OF WORLD HEAVYWEIGHT CROWN

1 March 1949, Detroit, Michigan, USA

After a successful and lucrative amateur career, Joe Louis turned professional on 4 July 1934 and in his first pro fight knocked out his opponent Jack Kracken in the first round. His performances quickly caught the eye. His first shot at the world heavyweight title came against "Cinderella Man" James J. Craddock on 22 June 1937: Louis was knocked down in the first, but recovered to KO the champion in the eighth to take the crown. He then made a career out of defending it. Over 11 years and 10 months, the "Brown Bomber" made 25 successful defences, including a record ten defences in 15 months between 1940 and 1942. After two gruelling fights against Jersey Joe Walcott in 1947 and 1948, which went a combined 26 of 30 rounds, he announced his retirement on 1 March 1949.

➲ It didn't last long. Louis was lured back into the ring the following year, but lost to Ezzard Charles on a unanimous decision. A year later he fought Lee Savold, recognized by the British as world heavyweight champion. Louis won by KO in the sixth: it was his record 27th world heavyweight championship contest.

Joe Louis, rated by *Ring* magazine as the No. 1 puncher of all time in 2003, made a record 25 successful defences of his world heavyweight crown.

BIONDETTI CRUISES TO MILLE MIGLIA HAT-TRICK

CLEMENTE BIONDETTI BECOMES ONLY DRIVER TO SECURE HAT-TRICK OF MILLE MIGLIE WINS

24 April 1949, Brescia, Italy

Born in Sardinia in 1898, Clemente Biondetti's racing career did not get underway until his family moved to Florence in the early 1920s. Starting with motorbikes, he switched to cars in 1927 and went on to win the Italian championship. Success in the Mille Miglia, a 1,000-mile-long road race around Italy, would come in 1938, but then came the Second World War and normal life was put on hold. Biondetti was 49 years old by the time the race resumed in 1947, but drove his Alfa Romeo through the bombed-out country to take his second win. He won again the following year in a Ferrari sports car; and car and driver combined to good effect in 1949 – Biondetti took the chequered flag to complete a unique hat-trick.

➲ Biondetti fought a close race with Tazio Nuvolari in both 1947 and 1948. In the latter of the two years, Biondetti trailed Nuvolari for most of the race; but Nuvolari was forced to retire with mechanical problems shortly before the end of the race and Biondetti stole through to win.

Already 49 years old when the Mille Miglia resumed after the end of the Second World War, Clemente Biondetti showed age was no barrier by securing a unique hat-trick of wins.

ARGENTINA STEAL WORLD CHAMPIONSHIP CROWN

ARGENTINA FIRST TO WIN THE WORLD POLO CHAMPIONSHIP

April 1949, Buenos Aires, Argentina

The origins of polo – the oldest of all equestrian sports – are both obscure and undocumented. No one knows precisely where or when stick first met ball – some credit India with being the game's source, others Persia – but, as with many other sports, as British colonial fever spread around the world, so polo's popularity spread with it. And, as with many other sports, the pupils went on to excel the teacher. Polo first came to Argentina in the 1920s and developed into something of a national mania. By 1949 they were world champions – they beat the United States in a best-of-three unofficial world championship – and have remained world champions ever since.

➲ Argentina remains to this day the source of many of the world's best polo players.

Three years after her 1950 heroics, Babe Zaharias was diagnosed with colon cancer: she fought it bravely – winning her tenth and final major, the 1953 US Women's Open, just a month after surgery – but died in 1956 at the age of 45.

BABE'S HEROICS SECURE SPOT AMONG SPORTING GREATS

BABE ZAHARIAS BECOMES FIRST WOMAN IN GOLF HISTORY TO WIN GRAND SLAM

24 June 1950, Cherry Hills Country Club, Co, USA

If any further proof were ever needed that Babe Zaharias (born Mildred Didriksen) was the greatest all-round female athlete of all time, then one need look no further than 1950. A double Olympic gold medallist from the 1932 Olympics in Los Angeles (she won the 80m hurdles and the javelin) and an All-American basketball player, Zaharias took up golf in 1935: by the end of the 1940s she had won five majors and was considered one of the leading players of the day – of either sex. In 1950, she stamped her name on the game's history, winning all three available major tournaments – the US Women's Open, the Titleholders' Championship and the Western Open – to become the first woman to do so.

➲ As an athlete, Zaharias once set five world records in a single afternoon. She set other records in golf: in January 1939 she became the first woman to appear in a men's PGA tour event (she shot 81 and 84 to miss the cut) and ended her career with ten major championship victories to her name.

URUGUAY STUN WORLD RECORD CROWD

RECORD CROWD OF 199,954 FLOCKS TO WORLD CUP MATCH BETWEEN BRAZIL AND URUGUAY

16 July 1950, Maracana Stadium, Rio de Janeiro, Brazil

The 1950 World Cup in Brazil was the last World Cup not to feature an actual "final", but the last match of the final-four round robin group. It pitted hosts Brazil against 1930 champions Uruguay and was the equivalent of a final. To the delight of the home crowd Brazil had been in imperious form, beating Sweden 7–1 and Spain 6–1; all they needed was a draw to win the World Cup. Uruguay, a point behind Brazil, needed the win. A crowd of 199,954 flocked to the Maracana Stadium in Rio de Janeiro to watch Brazil's coronation as world champions, but Uruguay had other ideas, coming from a goal down to win 2–1 and take the World Cup for a second time. The record crowd was left stunned.

➲ Goals in the 66th minute from Juan Alberto Schiaffino and in the 79th minute from Alcides Ghiggia were enough to secure Uruguay their second World Cup triumph.

Anticipating a first World Cup win, a record-breaking crowd of 199,954 turned up to the Maracana Stadium in Rio de Janeiro for the final match of the 1950 World Cup. They were left in stunned silence when Uruguay staged a late comeback to spoil the party and win the trophy for a second time.

FARINA FORMULA ONE'S FIRST WORLD CHAMPION

NINO FARINA WINS ITALIAN GP TO BECOME FIRST-EVER FORMULA ONE WORLD CHAMPION

3 September 1950, Monza, Italy

Given the dominance of the Alfa Romeo Alfetta car, it seemed inevitable that one of the three Fs, Alfa Romeo team drivers Juan Manuel Fangio, Luigi Fagioli or Nino Farina, would win the inaugural Formula One World Championship in 1950. As the championship entered its final race, the Italian Grand Prix at Monza, the title had indeed come down to a straight fight between Fangio and Farina. And when Fangio, the younger of the two drivers at 39, took pole and recorded the fastest lap in the early stages of the race, it looked as though the title was going the Argentine's way. But gearbox problems struck on the 23rd lap, and Farina stole through for the win to become Formula One's first-ever world champion.

➲ Farina and Fangio won six of that year's seven World Championship races; the other – the Indianapolis 500 (won by Johnnie Parsons) – they did not attend.

Forty-three-year-old Giuseppe "Nino" Farina, a veteran racing driver renowned for his straight-arm, ruthless and aggressive driving style, saw off the attentions of 39-year-old "upstart" Juan Manuel Fangio to win the first-ever Formula One World Championship.

Johnny Mantz recorded only one victory during his NASCAR career and when he won the 1950 Southern 500 he did so in style, driving through the field from 43rd on the grid to take the win.

MANTZ COMES THROUGH FIELD FOR HISTORIC WIN

JOHNNY MANTZ WINS SOUTHERN 500 STARTING FROM 43RD ON THE GRID

4 September 1950, Darlington Raceway, South Carolina, USA

Things weren't looking so good for Johnny Mantz before the start of the first Southern 500 at Darlington Raceway in South Carolina, the first 500-mile race in NASCAR history (and the only one until the birth of the Daytona 500 in 1959). Mantz and his Plymouth car would be starting from 43rd place on the grid: on row 15. But Mantz survived the war of attrition, averaging 75.250mph (121.1km/h) and taking some 6h39m to complete the course that had been carved out of cotton and peanut patches to finish some nine laps ahead of second-placed Fireball Roberts. No one else in NASCAR history has won from so far back in the field.

➲ Fonty Flock equalled Mantz's feat in the Raleigh 300 at the Raleigh Speedway in 1953.

MAGICAL COLEMAN MAKES HIS MARK

JOHN COLEMAN BECOMES ONLY MAN IN VFL/AFL HISTORY TO START CAREER WITH TWO 100-GOAL SEASONS

October 1950, Essendon, Melbourne, Australia

A child prodigy who was playing for under-18 teams by the age of 12, John Coleman finally forced his way into the Essendon line-up at the start of the 1949 season. The spectacular high-leaping forward scored 12 goals in his first game and never looked back. His star continued to shine all season and in true storybook fashion he scored his 100th goal of the season in the dying moments of a winning Grand Final against Carlton. He was even more prolific the following year, scoring 120 goals as Essendon edged North Melbourne to the Premiership title. Coleman is the only man in VFL/AFL history to have started his career with two 100-goal seasons.

➲ A controversial four-week suspension dished out to Coleman the following season essentially put paid to any chances Essendon might have had of securing a Premiership hat-trick. In 1954, after dislocating his knee in a nasty fall during a game, his career was over at the age of 25.

John Coleman's record-breaking career was brief, as was his life: he died suddenly from a coronary atheroma at the age of 44.

Luigi Fagioli may have driven only 20 of 77 laps at the 1950 French GP, but he was awarded the race win, shared the winning points with Juan Manuel Fangio, earned an extra point for having clocked the fastest lap and was rewarded with a permanent place in the history books as Formula One's oldest-ever race winner.

FAGIOLI HITCHES RIDE INTO HISTORY BOOKS

LUIGI FAGIOLI BECOMES FORMULA ONE'S OLDEST-EVER GRAND PRIX WINNER

1 July 1951, Reims-Gueux, France

A third-place finish in the inaugural season of the Formula One World Championship in 1950 must have disappointed Luigi Fagioli. Both of his team-mates had finished above him and both had notched up three race wins as opposed to Fagioli's none. The Italian competed in only one grand prix the following year, the French, and shared the drive for the No. 8 Alfa Romeo with Juan Manuel Fangio. The Argentine may have driven 57 of the 77 laps, but because the No. 8 car was the first to the chequered flag, the pair shared the points for the win, and Fagioli received the accolade of being Formula One's oldest race-winning driver – aged 53 years, 22 days.

➲ The following season, Fagioli signed to compete for the Lancia team in sports car racing: he crashed during practice for a race in Monaco in June 1952 and died as a result of his injuries.

AUSSIES MAKE THE PERFECT PAIR

FRANK SEDGMAN AND KEN MCGREGOR BECOME ONLY MEN'S DOUBLES PAIR TO WIN GRAND SLAM

2 September 1951, Forest Hills, New York, USA

In an era when the men's doubles carried perhaps more weight than it does today, for a short while one pairing stood head and shoulders above their peers. Australians Frank Sedgman (fleet of foot and renowned for his grace and skill at the net) and Ken McGregor (a 6ft 3in former Australian Rules player who brought power and athleticism to the game) were formidable. They had their year of years in 1951, opening up with victory in the Australian Open. The French and Wimbledon titles soon followed, and when they beat fellow countrymen Mervyn Rose and Don Candy in the final of the US Open at Forest Hills, they became the only men's doubles pair in history to complete the Grand Slam.

➲ The pair were on course to repeat the feat the following year, but after picking up wins in Australia, France and Wimbledon, they fell at the final hurdle, losing to fellow countryman Mervyn Rose and his American partner Vic Seixas.

Frank Sedgman (right) and Ken McGregor combined to perfect effect, forming a formidable men's doubles pairing and winning seven straight major titles in 1951 and '52.

Geoff Duke swept all before him in 1951, winning both the 350cc and 500cc world championships, and set new standards in motorcycling along the way.

THE DUKE BECOMES THE TWO-WHEEL KING

GEOFF DUKE BECOMES FIRST TO WIN 500CC AND 350CC WORLD MOTORCYCLING CHAMPIONSHIPS IN SAME YEAR

September 1951, Monza, Italy

The post-war motorcycling world found its first true superstar in Geoff Duke and the Lancashire-born rider went on to attract a fanatical following. In 1951, he excelled on Norton's new bike frame, adapting his riding style to perfection to suit the new single-cylinder engine, and the pair swept all before them in both the 350cc and 500cc world championships. In his distinctive one-piece leather suits – he even hired a tailor to make them – Duke won five of the eight grand prix in the 350cc championship and four of the eight races in the 500cc world championship – including the Isle of Man TT – to become the first man in history to win both championships in the same season.

➲ Duke ended his career in 1959 with six world championship triumphs and five Isle of Man TT wins to his name.

VAN BROCKLIN MAKES A RECORD-BREAKING POINT

NORM VAN BROCKLIN PASSES FOR NFL RECORD 554 YARDS IN A SINGLE GAME

28 September 1951, Los Angeles, California, USA

Throughout the 1950 NFL season, Norm van Brocklin split quarterback duties with the LA Rams' other star performer, Bob Waterfield. The pair finished one-two in that season's passing ratings as the Rams ended up losing 30–28 to the Cleveland Browns in the title game. The Rams were happy to run with the same quarterback arrangement for the following year, but when Waterford was injured for the Rams' match-up with the New York Yanks, van Brocklin responded by replacing him in the starting line-up and becoming the first passer in history to throw for more than 500 yards. A point, it seems, had been somewhat forcibly made.

➲ Norm van Brocklin connected with five touchdown passes that day. His total of 554 yards passed beat the existing record of 468 yards, set by Johnny Lujack in 1949.

One of the most colourful and competitive players the NFL has ever seen, Norm van Brocklin stamped his name in the record books on 31 September 1951 when he threw for 554 yards against the New York Yanks.

NIGHT TRAIN LANE'S RECORD-BREAKING NFL INTRODUCTION

DICK LANE SETS NFL RECORD FOR MOST INTERCEPTIONS IN A SEASON

December 1952, Los Angeles, California, USA

Receivers throughout the NFL feared playing one-on-one with cornerback Dick "Night Train" Lane. Tall and athletic at 6ft 2in, his ferocious open-field tackling (his preferred method of tackling an opponent was to rip them down by the head and neck – a practice outlawed from the game today), his cat-like qualities and his ability to gamble on the flight of the ball made him the prototypical defensive back. He burst onto the NFL scene in 1952: having gone to the Los Angeles Rams' offices in search of work and having subsequently impressed in spring training, he forced his way into the Rams' starting line-up and in his debut year set an NFL record for the most interceptions made in a single season (14).

➲ During his 15 seasons in the NFL, Dick Lane recorded 1,207 yards returning 68 interceptions.

Born to a prostitute mother, a pimp father and left for dead in a dumpster aged three months, Dick "Night Train" Lane put his unfortunate start in life behind him to forge a successful career in the NFL.

PRODIGY BAUER FINALLY GETS FIRST TOUR VICTORY

MARLENE BAUER BECOMES YOUNGEST-EVER LPGA TOUR WINNER

2 March 1952, Sarasota, Florida, USA

Marlene Bauer (later Hagge) first played golf at the age of three, and by the age of ten won the Long Beach City boys' title. She went on to win a number of adult amateur events and achieved nationwide fame in 1947 when, aged 13, she became the youngest player in history to make the cut at the US Women's Open – she finished in eighth place. A founder member of the LPGA Tour (aged 16) in 1950, she was forced to wait before she could enjoy her first taste of success. Two years after turning professional she claimed her first title, the 1952 Sarasota Open, and at 18 years, 14 days became the youngest tournament winner in LPGA history.

➲ Marlene Bauer, 5ft 2in, petite, blonde, and often considered golf's first glamour girl, visited the winner's circle 26 times during her 20-year career, but only once in the majors, where her sole success came in the 1956 LPGA Championships.

Having turned professional shortly before her 16th birthday to become one of the founding members of the LPGA Tour, Marlene Bauer (pictured here, right, with her sister Alice, who also was a pro golfer) gained her first victory at the 1952 Sarasota Open to become the youngest winner in LPGA Tour history.

ZAHARIAS LEADS THE WAY

BABE ZAHARIAS FASTEST IN HISTORY TO RECORD 20 LPGA TOUR WINS

March 1952, Bakersfield, California, USA

After formally turning professional in 1947 – with a stellar amateur career already behind her – and being one of the 13 founding members of the LPGA Tour in 1950, Babe Zaharias set about ensuring the fledgling tour got the star it so desperately needed to flourish, and in the process ensured her name stood in shining lights in women's golf history. In the first year of the tour she notched up eight tournament wins (including what was then considered the grand slam of women's golf – the US Women's Open, the Titleholders' Championship and the Western Open; the following year she won nine times, and when she won the Bakersfield Open in 1952, her 20th tour win, she achieved the milestone more quickly than any other woman in history.

➲ During the course of her grand slam-winning year in 1950, Babe Zaharias also became the fastest in history to record ten LPGA victories.

Record-breaking sports star Babe Zaharias made golfing history when she recorded her 20th LPGA Tour win in record time in 1952.

Bill Mosienko may have played 19 seasons of professional hockey, but he will always be remembered for the 21 seconds of magic he produced against the New York Rangers on 23 March 1952.

MOSIENKO PRODUCES 21 SECONDS OF MAGIC TO STUN RANGERS

BILL MOSIENKO SCORES THE FASTEST HAT-TRICK IN NHL HISTORY

23 March 1952, Chicago, Illinois, USA

Having grown up in Winnipeg, Manitoba, Canada, Bill Mosienko turned pro with the Chicago Black Hawks aged 18 in 1940. After spending a few years in the minor leagues, he forced his way into the starting line-up by the 1943–44 season and went on to form a part of the Black Hawks' famous "Pony Line", along with the Bentley brothers, Max and Bob. It was said that, with his amazing speed across the ice and his exceptional stick-handling ability, Mosienko was a magician on the ice ... and he put his wizardry to good use against the New York Rangers on 23 March 1952. With both teams at full strength, Mosienko scored three goals in the space of just 21 seconds – an NHL record that has never been beaten.

➲ For the New York Rangers goaltender Lorne Anderson, 23 March 1952 was quite a swansong: in his final game in the NHL he conceded a hat-trick in just 21 seconds. Mosienko's new mark broke the previous record of 1m04s set by the Detroit Red Wings' Carl Liscombe in 1938.

HILL GAIL LANDS ARCARO RECORD FIFTH DERBY WIN

JOCKEY EDDIE ARCARO BECOMES FIRST FIVE-TIME WINNER OF KENTUCKY DERBY

3 May 1952, Churchill Downs, Louisville, Kentucky, USA

By the time Eddie Arcaro won the Kentucky Derby for the first time on Lawrin in 1938 he was one of the sport's most established jockeys. Smart, aggressive and strong, he possessed a fine sense of pace ... and the respect of many of the day's leading trainers. Through a combination of great skill and choice rides, he won all of the important races of the day ... and enjoyed particular success in the Kentucky Derby. His second Churchill Downs victory came in 1941 when he rode Whirlaway to victory in record-breaking time; further wins followed in 1945 (on Hoop Jr) and Citation (1948), and when he rode Hill Gail to victory in 1952, Arcaro became the first jockey in history to win the Kentucky Derby five times.

➲ Bill Hartack equalled Eddie Arcaro's feat of five Kentucky Derby wins when he rode Majestic Prince to victory over the Churchill Downs course in 1969.

Eddie Arcaro finished as leading jockey six times during his 18-year career. His Derby victory on Citation in 1948 made him the only US rider in history to win the Triple Crown (winning the Preakness Stakes, the Belmont Stakes and the Kentucky Derby in the same year) twice.

RECORD SIXTH DERBY SUCCESS FOR TRAINER JONES

TRAINER BEN JONES BECOMES FIRST SIX-TIME WINNER OF KENTUCKY DERBY
3 May 1952, Churchill Downs, Louisville, Kentucky, USA

By the 1920s Ben A. Jones was recognized as one of the best trainers the United States had to offer. In 1931 he took up a position with Woolford Farm in Kansas and trained one Kentucky Derby winner (Lawrin in 1938) during his eight-year stay. In 1939 he moved to Calumet Farm in Kentucky, and proceeded to transform it into one of the greatest stables in US racing history, producing a number of winners, including five more Derby winners – Whirlaway (1941), Pensive (1944), Citation (1948), Ponder (1949) and Hill Gail (1952) – making Jones the only trainer in history to have won the Kentucky Derby on six occasions.

➲ Ben Jones'srecord-breaking sixth Kentucky Derby victory in 1952 was the first to be broadcast live on television.

Ben Jones (second left, white hat, being congratulated by some of his happy owners) rubber-stamped his reputation as the leading trainer of his day when he saddled Hill Gail to success in the 1952 Kentucky Derby: his sixth victory in the race.

KID RUTTMAN SECURES FAMOUS BRICKYARD WIN

TROY RUTTMAN BECOMES YOUNGEST-EVER WINNER OF THE INDIANAPOLIS 500

30 May 1952, Indianapolis Motor Speedway, Indianapolis, USA

Troy Ruttman was a natural-born racer. In 1945, at the age of 15, he entered the family car in a roadster race in California and won. Four years later, having won the California roadster championships in both 1947 and 1948, he left to try his luck on the AAA Sprint and Champion Car circuits in the midwest. By 1952 he had competed in the Indianapolis 500 on three occasions, with a best finish of 12th in 1949. But things were looking better this time round. Ruttman qualified seventh on the grid and trailed Bill Vukovich for most of the race, but when Vukovich was forced to retire with steering problems, Ruttman stole into the lead and stayed there for the final 44 laps to become the Indy 500's youngest-ever winner.

⮞ At just 22 years, 80 days, Ruttman also held the distinction of becoming the youngest driver to win a Formula One race (the Indy 500 was part of the F1 schedule at the time), a record that stood until Bruce McLaren won the United States GP in Sebring in 1959.

Troy Ruttman's 1952 success marked the only time he finished on the podium in 12 Indianapolis 500 outings.

COPPI DOMINATES MOUNTAIN STAGES EN ROUTE TO RECORD VICTORY

FAUSTO COPPI TAKES TOUR DE FRANCE WIN BY A RECORD-BREAKING MARGIN

19 July 1952, Paris, France

Talk before the 39th running of the Tour de France suggested it would be one of the most open races for years. And, initially at least, so it turned out to be – until the tour reached the mountain stages and one man, Italian Fausto Coppi, took centre stage. No stranger to success – he had won the Tour in 1949 and was a four-time winner of the Giro d'Italia – Coppi won every single one of the Alpine stages to leave his opponents reeling in his wake. By the time the Tour arrived in Paris, Coppi was on cruise control and finished a record 28m27s ahead of second-placed Stan Ockers.

⮞ Having become the first rider in history to win the Tour de France and the Giro d'Italia in 1949, Fausto Coppi cemented his place in cycling legend when he repeated the feat three years later.

Fausto Coppi dominated the mountain stages during the 1952 Tour de France and built up a record-breaking lead he would never relinquish.

TEENAGER JONES GRABS GOLD

BARBARA JONES, AGED 15, BECOMES YOUNGEST-EVER OLYMPIC TRACK-AND-FIELD GOLD MEDALLIST
19 July–3 August 1952, Helsinki, Finland

The 1952 Olympic Games in Helsinki saw a record number of participants, with many countries, including the Soviet Union, competing for the first time. The Cold War had just started and was getting colder by the day. The Soviets built an entire Olympic village for the sole use of Eastern Bloc athletes in an attempt to show their supremacy over the United States. They lost: the Americans claimed 40 gold medals to the USSR's 22, among them a gold for US 4x100m women's relay member Barbara Jones who, at 15 years, 123 days, became the youngest-ever winner of an Olympic track-and-field gold medal.

➲ The Games went without a hitch and were considered to have been a model of efficiency and organization. So much so, in fact, that an idea was mooted to host every future Olympic Games in Scandinavia. The idea was, of course, rejected.

The United States' team of, left to right, Catherine Hardy, Barbara Jones, Mae Faggs and Janet Moreau, won the women's 4x100m relay in the 1952 Olympic Games in Helsinki and it gave Jones the honour of being the youngest-ever winner of an Olympic gold medal in a track-and-field event.

ZATOPEK BECOMES OLYMPIC LONG-DISTANCE KING

EMIL ZATOPEK WINS UNIQUE OLYMPIC HAT-TRICK: 5,000M, 10,000M AND MARATHON
19 July–3 August 1952, Helsinki, Finland

After the Olympic flame had been lit at the opening ceremony by two Finnish long-distance running heroes, Paavo Nurmi and Hannes Kolehmainen, it seemed only appropriate that the star of the 1952 Olympic Games should be another long-distance runner. Czech Emil Zatopek started by winning the 10,000m with a margin of 100m. Next up came the 5,000m and, with 400m to go, Zatopek was in fourth place and struggling; he dug deep, put in a ferocious lap and claimed his second gold. Then, at the last minute, he decided to do something he had never done before: tackle his first-ever marathon – in the Olympics, no less. He won sensationally, completing a unique treble.

➲ Nicknamed the "Czech Locomotive" for the puffing and panting manner in which he ran his races, Zatopek once famously said: "I was not talented enough to run and smile at the same time."

Emil Zatopek (leading), who had been suffering from a gland infection only months before the 1952 Olympics began, ignored his doctor's advice and won a unique hat-trick of gold medals, all of them in Olympic record-breaking times.

JEPPSON BECOMES WORLD'S MOST EXPENSIVE PLAYER

NAPOLI PAY WORLD-RECORD TRANSFER FEE FOR SWEDISH STRIKER HASSE JEPPSON

Summer 1952, Naples, Italy

While still playing amateur soccer in Sweden, striker Hasse Jeppson captained his country at the 1950 World Cup to a shock opening-game victory over Italy, scoring two of the goals in his side's 3–2 win. A year later, he became the first Swede in history to be transferred to an English club when he joined Charlton. But the love affair did not last long and, after appearing just 12 times for the Addicks, Jeppson was off to Italy and Serie A with Atlanta. Just a year later Jeppson made headlines in the sports sections of newspapers around the world when Napoli lodged a world-record bid of £52,000 for his services.

➲ Because of the hefty price tag, Napoli fans nicknamed Jeppson the "Bank of Naples", but he did not disappoint them, scoring 52 goals in his four seasons with the club.

Having shocked the Italians with two goals for his country during the 1950 World Cup, Hasse Jeppson became the world's most expensive player when he signed for Napoli in the summer of 1952.

ASCARI PUTS DOMINANT FERRARI TO GOOD USE

ALBERTO ASCARI WINS F1 WORLD CHAMPIONSHIP BY WINNING RECORD SIX OF SEASON'S SEVEN RACES

7 September 1952, Monza, Italy

By the end of the 1951 Formula One World Championship season, it was becoming clear that the immediate future of the sport lay in normally aspirated engines (as opposed to the fuel-heavy, supercharged engines that were then in use). But such advances would mark the end of the line for the government-funded and previously dominant Alfa Romeo team, who withdrew from the competition. It meant the Ferrari was the car to have for the 1952 season and Alberto Ascari put it to very good use, winning six of the seven races he entered to win the World Championship for the first time.

➲ The only World Championship race he entered but did not win came in the Indianapolis 500 – which was considered part of the Formula One calendar, despite the absence of many F1 drivers – a race in which he finished in 31st place.

In 1952, Alberto Ascari won 86 per cent of the races he entered to become Formula One world champion for the first time.

HOWE ACHIEVES ART ROSS HAT-TRICK

GORDIE HOWE FIRST TO WIN ART ROSS MEMORIAL TROPHY THREE YEARS IN A ROW
April 1953, Detroit, Michigan, USA

Gordie Howe may have finished top of the points-scoring charts for the first time in his NHL career, but the taste in his mouth come the end of the 1950–51 season would have been one of lingering disappointment: his beloved Detroit Red Wings had been defeated by the Montreal Canadiens in the playoff semi-finals. Forming part of the now-infamous "Production Line" – along with Sid Abel and Ted Lindsay – Howe bounced back in style in 1951–52, leading the league in points once again as the Red Wings notched up their fifth Stanley Cup success, but disappointment shrouded Detroit once again the following year: the Red Wings fell in the playoff semi-finals once again. Every cloud has a silver lining, though: Howe led the points-scoring charts to become the first man in history to win the Art Ross Memorial Trophy three years in succession.

⮎Howe won the Art Ross Memorial Trophy the following year as well, and again on a further two occasions. Between 1980 and 1987, Wayne Gretzky won the trophy for a record seven consecutive years.

Gordie Howe set his stamp on the NHL in the early 1950s, winning the Art Ross Memorial Trophy for the league's leading points-scorer four times in a row.

MAN CONQUERS THE ROOF OF THE WORLD

EDMUND HILLARY AND TENZING NORGAY BECOME FIRST TO CLIMB EVEREST

29 May 1953, Mount Everest, Nepal/Tibet

After spending the night at camp at 27,900ft (8,500m), Edmund Hillary and Tenzing Norgay set off early the following morning and had reached the south summit of Everest by 9 a.m. Beyond them lay the route to Everest's summit: a 400ft (120m) long level ridge of rock, flanked by ice cornices and sheer drops on both the east and west sides. They passed over successfully. Then came the final obstacle: a 55ft (17m) spur of rock and ice, set at an extreme pitch (it is now known as the "Hillary Step"). First Hillary and then Tenzing hauled himself up the spur, with backs to the wall, placing their feet in cracks and hauling themselves up inch by desperate inch. The final major obstacle to Everest's summit had been cleared and by 11.30 a.m. on 29 May 1953, Edmund Hillary and Tenzing Norgay were looking down on the rest of mankind from the roof of the world.

➲Part of a British expedition sponsored by the Royal Geographical Society and the Alpine Club, Hillary and Tenzing were not the first to have made an assault on the summit of the world's highest peak. Two days earlier, Tom Bourdillon and Charles Evans had reached the south summit, but they had arrived there late in the day and had been forced to return to camp.

After spending about 15 minutes on the summit of Everest on 29 May 1953, Edmund Hillary and Tenzing Norgay made it back to base camp on 2 June 1953. News of their achievement flashed around the world and the first ascent of Everest turned out to be one of the defining moments of the 20th century.

In his one and only appearance in the Open Championship, at Carnoustie in 1953, Ben Hogan pulled clear of the field in the final round to collect his third major of the year.

HOGAN'S VINTAGE YEAR

BEN HOGAN BECOMES FIRST GOLFER IN HISTORY TO WIN THREE OF YEAR'S FOUR PROFESSIONAL MAJORS

11 July 1953, Carnoustie, Scotland

What made Ben Hogan's achievements in 1953 all the more impressive was that, just four years earlier, he had survived a head-on crash with a Greyhound bus that left doctors fearing he would never walk again. But walk he did and, with his legs heavily bandaged, he used his finely honed swing to great effect … and thrived. He won the first two majors of 1953, the Masters and the US Open, and was left with a choice to make: play in the Open Championship or compete in the US PGA (the two tournaments overlapped). The choice was easy: the latter required players to play 36 holes a day; Hogan crossed the Atlantic and won the Open Championship at Carnoustie by four shots to complete a unique treble.

➲ Ben Hogan stood alone as the only golfer to have won three major tournaments in a year until Tiger Woods won the US Open, the Open Championship and the US PGA in 2000.

VETERAN HOGAN OLDEST TO COMPLETE CAREER GRAND SLAM

BEN HOGAN BECOMES OLDEST OF FIVE PLAYERS TO WIN GOLF'S CAREER GRAND SLAM

11 July 1953, Carnoustie, Scotland

The Open Championship was the only major tournament trophy missing from Ben Hogan's mantelpiece and, in 1953, he crossed the Atlantic two weeks before the tournament at Carnoustie got underway and set about mastering links-style golf. Player and course were a perfect fit. By the end of the third round of the 1953 Open, Hogan had a share of the lead. Then, displaying the stuff of true champions, he shot a course-record 68 to get his hands on the Claret Jug for the first time. In the process he became only the second person in golf history to have won all four majors and, at 41 years, 10 months, the oldest to do so.

➲ The 1953 Open Championship at Carnoustie was the last time Ben Hogan tasted major success – it was his ninth victory in a major tournament and only three men (Jack Nicklaus, Tiger Woods and Walter Hagen) have won more.

Ben Hogan endeared himself to the locals during his assault on the 1953 Open Championship at Carnoustie. Impressed with his meticulous approach and iron-willed demeanour, they nicknamed him the "Wee Ice Man".

THE MAGPIES STUN THE CATS AS RECORD RUN ENDS

GEELONG'S RECORD-BREAKING UNBEATEN RUN IN THE VFL COMES TO AN END

1 August 1953, Geelong, Melbourne, Australia

On 12 July 1952, Geelong Cats coach Reg Hickey's vision seemed to click into place. His team had strolled to a comfortable 29-point win over Collingwood, and the majority of the 36,145 crowd were treated to a masterclass of speed and sensational ball handling. The Cats had clicked into gear and no one could stop them: they marched through the rest of the season unbeaten and crushed the Magpies by 46 points in the Grand Final. The run continued into the following season and had stretched to 26 games when Collingwood came to town on 1 August 1953 and, on a pitch more akin to a mudbath than a football field, won by 22 points.

➲ Geelong would go on to lose their next match as well, an 11-point loss to Essendon, and they would not repeat their Grand Final heroics of 1952, losing to arch-rivals Collingwood by 22 points.

The record-breaking Geelong side of 1952–53 contained three future members of the Team of the Century – Fred Flanagan (above), Bernie Smith and Bob Davis, all playing at the peak of their powers – as well as a supporting cast including the likes of Leo Turner, Neil Tresize, George Goninon and Peter Pianto.

LITTLE MO GUNS HER WAY TO GRAND SLAM GLORY

MAUREEN CONNOLLY BECOMES FIRST WOMAN TO WIN TENNIS GRAND SLAM
7 September 1953, Forest Hills, New York, USA

In 1954, just a year after her grand slam heroics, Maureen Connolly was hit by a truck while riding her horse and suffered career-ending injuries to her leg, aged just 20. She had nine grand slam singles titles to her name.

Blessed with tremendous power and big-gunning accuracy from the baseline, Maureen Connolly, known as "Little Mo", won the US national championships for girls when she was 15. In 1951, aged 16 years, 11 months, she became the youngest-ever winner of the US Open. But she was only just getting started. The following year she defended her US Open crown and added the Wimbledon title to her collection. In 1953, she entered all four grand slam tournaments for the first time and excelled, winning the Australian Open (defeating Julie Sampson Heywood in the final), the French Open, Wimbledon and the US Open (beating Doris Hart in all three finals), to become the first woman, and only the second tennis player in history, to win the grand slam.

➲ Only two other women in history have gone on to repeat the feat: Margaret Smith Court (1970) and Steffi Graf (1988).

BRONX BOMBERS' FIVE-IN-A-ROW GLORY

NEW YORK YANKEES WIN THE WORLD SERIES FOR FIFTH CONSECUTIVE YEAR

5 October 1953, Yankee Stadium, New York, USA

The 1953 World Series was a re-run of the 1952 Fall Classic, in which the New York Yankees had edged the Brooklyn Dodgers in seven games to win their fourth consecutive World Series and equal the feats of the Yankee class of 1936–39. And the smart money was on the Dodgers – backed by their impressive line-up – bringing the Bronx Bombers' reign to an end. But the Yankees had other ideas. They won game one, 9–5, to knock the wind out of the Dodgers' sails, and continued their momentum with a 4–2 win in game two. The Dodgers regrouped, winning the next two games to tie the series at 2–2. But the Yankees bounced back, winning game five, 11–7, and sealing a record fifth consecutive World Series with a 4–3 win in game six.

❍ The Yankees' reign came to an end the following season when the Cleveland Indians eased to the American League pennant by eight games. Since the Yankees' five consecutive World Series wins, no team has won more than three in a row.

Clockwise, from bottom left, Gil McDougald, Billy Martin, Mickey Mantle, Gene Woodling and Jim McDonald wrote their names into New York Yankees history when they won the 1953 Fall Classic to record a fifth consecutive World Series victory.

The New York press may not have thought much of him when he first arrived at the Yankees, but Casey Stengel became the talk of the town when he masterminded the franchise to five straight World Series crowns.

STENGEL MASTERMINDS FIVE IN A ROW FOR THE YANKEES

CASEY STENGEL ONLY MANAGER IN HISTORY TO LEAD SIDE TO FIVE CONSECUTIVE WORLD SERIES WINS

5 October 1953, Yankee Stadium, New York, USA

Nicknamed K.C. during his playing days (he was born in Kansas City), Casey Stengel enjoyed a 13-year playing career in which he played in three World Series. But it is for his success as a manager that he is most remembered today – not that the New York press thought that would be the case when the Yankees hired him as manager in 1949. However, despite his limited previous managerial success, Stengel turned out to be one of the most innovative tacticians the game of baseball has ever seen. He turned the Yankees into a juggernaut and masterminded their march to five consecutive World Series wins.

➲ Stengel would go on to enjoy further World Series success with the Yankees in 1956 and 1958. He retired after the 1960 season, but joined the newly formed New York Mets as manager in 1961 and led them for four years. He died in 1975 at the age of 85.

VETERAN FARINA PRODUCES ONE LAST MAGICAL LAP

NINO FARINA BECOMES FORMULA ONE'S OLDEST-EVER POLE WINNER

17 January 1954, Buenos Aires, Argentina

Giuseppe "Nino" Farina, nicknamed the "Gentleman of Turin" because of his privileged upbringing, had used his aggressive, high-stakes driving style to optimum effect in 1950 to become Formula One's first-ever world champion, but by 1954 he was drawing to the end of his illustrious career. He still had one final trick up his sleeve, though. In the first qualifying session of the season, at the Autodromo Oscar Alfredo Galvez, in the southern part of Buenos Aires, he produced a lap of 1m44.8s to put his Ferrari 625 on pole position, ahead of the much stronger Maseratis. At 47 years, 97 days, he was the oldest pole winner in Formula One history.

➲ The Maseratis and Juan Manuel Fangio had the last laugh, though, as the Argentine champion won his home grand prix for the first time. Farina finished in second place, to notch up a then-record 22nd points-scoring race.

Nino Farina may have been coming towards the end of his career, but he produced one final flourish when he put his labouring Ferrari on pole position at the Argentine GP in 1954 at the age of 47 years, 97 days.

MAGICAL SELVY SHOOTS 100 POINTS

FRANK SELVY BECOMES ONLY PLAYER IN NCAA BASKETBALL HISTORY TO SHOOT 100 POINTS IN A GAME

13 February 1954, Greenville, South Carolina, USA

In many ways the events of 13 February 1954 were preordained. Furman coach Lyles Alley had already designated the match the "Frank Selvy Night" in an attempt to get his star player All-American first-team recognition for the second successive year. Selvy's family and friends had made the six-hour trek from Corbin, Kentucky, to Greenville, South Carolina, and television cameras would broadcast the match live for the first time. Alley's instructions to the Furman team were simple: get the ball to Selvy as often as possible so he could score as many points as possible. Neither the players nor Selvy let their coach down: the Furman guard shocked opponents Newberry College by shooting 41 of 66 field goals and 18 of 22 free-throws to become the first and only player in NCAA basketball history to shoot 100 points (Selvy's 100th point of the evening came just moments before the final buzzer).

⮑ The game was played well before the introduction of the three-point line (it wasn't introduced into the NBA until 1979). Selvy later estimated that, on today's courts, a dozen of his shots on the evening of 13 February 1954 would have been three-pointers.

Nicknamed "The Corbin Comet", Kentucky-born Frank Selvy found a permanent place on the college basketball map when he scored 100 points in Furman's 149–95 victory over Newberry College in February 1954.

THE MIRACLE MILE

ROGER BANNISTER BECOMES THE FIRST MAN TO RUN A SUB-FOUR-MINUTE MILE
6 May 1954, Iffley Road track, Oxford, England

It was hardly the ideal day for record-breaking, with crosswinds of up to 25mph gusting across the Iffley Road track. But still a 3,000-strong crowd came out in force to witness a moment of history: the first sub-four-minute mile. The starting gun fired ... but it was a false start. It fired a second time and they were off. "Faster", Roger Bannister screamed to his leading pacemaker Chris Brasher, but the steady pace was maintained. They completed the first lap in 57.5 seconds. The half-mile mark was reached in 1m58s; the second pacemaker Chris Chataway burst into the lead. They crossed the three-quarter-mile mark in 3m07s and the expectant crowd started to roar. With 300 yards to go Bannister surged into the lead, his tired legs forcing him to the finishing line as he surged through the tape. Then came the timekeeper's announcement: "Here is the result of ... the one mile ... The time was three..." The crowd roared again: they knew history had been made.

➲ Six weeks later, Australian John Landy bettered Bannister's mark with a time of 3m57.9s. The world mile record (3m43.13s) is currently held by Morocco's Hicham El Guerrouj.

Some years later Bannister reflected: "When the time was announced – 3m59s – I grabbed Chris Brasher and Chris Chataway. I was incredibly proud that we'd managed to do it on the first opportunity of the year. We realized, too, that we had done something of more significance than we might have imagined. By the time we saw the newspapers at two o'clock the next morning, we were in no doubt at all."

TEENAGER PIGGOTT STROLLS TO DERBY SUCCESS

LESTER PIGGOTT BECOMES THE YOUNGEST JOCKEY TO WIN EPSOM DERBY

2 June 1954, Epsom Downs, Surrey

The most gifted apprentice of his generation, who went on to become one of the greatest jockeys of all time, Lester Piggott rode his first race winner at the age of 12. Four years later he competed in the Epsom Derby for the first time and finished ninth. In 1954, aged 18, he was given the ride on American-bred horse Never Say Die – named to celebrate the Blitz mentality during the Second World War. The bookmakers may not have thought much of the pair, pricing them at 33–1, but Piggott defied the odds, and eased to a two-length victory to become, at just 18 years of age, the youngest-ever jockey to taste Derby success.

➲ The last of Lester Piggott's record nine Derby wins came some 29 years later, on Teenoso in 1983.

Champion jockey 11 times, Lester Piggott first captured the hearts and minds of an entire nation when he rode Never Say Die to Derby success in 1954 while still a teenager.

After spending some months studying the world's second highest peak, lead climber Achille Campagnoni (right) and his assistant Lino Lacedelli – part of an Italian expedition group led by Ardito Desio – became the first men in history to conquer K2.

ITALIANS CONQUER WORLD'S SECOND HIGHEST PEAK

ITALY'S ACHILLE CAMPAGNONI AND LINO LACEDELLI FIRST TO CLIMB K2

31 July 1954, K2, Pakistan/China border

By 1954, with Everest having been conquered the year before, K2 – the world's second highest peak at 28,500ft (8,616m) – was the greatest mountaineering prize of the day, and also the hardest to attain. The enormity of the challenge lay in the supreme steepness of K2's ridges and faces; attempts on the summit had been made since 1902 and all had failed, with too many climbers for comfort having paid the ultimate price: the mountain had acquired a reputation as the deadliest in the world. But on 31 July 1954, at 6 p.m., two Italians, 40-year-old Achille Campagnoni and 29-year-old Lino Lacedelli, did what others before them had failed to do when they became the first to reach the summit.

➲ Even this climb almost ended in disaster. Two hundred metres below the summit the pair's oxygen ran out and they were left with a difficult choice, to turn back to safety or to continue into the unknown: they chose the latter and became the first to climb K2.

ONE LAST HURRAH FOR BABE

BABE ZAHARIAS BECOMES FIRST THREE-TIME WINNER OF THE US WOMEN'S OPEN

3 July 1954, Salem Country Club, Peabody, Massachusetts, USA

It was the context of Babe Zaharias's third US Women's Open victory at the Salem Country Club, Massachusetts, in 1954 that made it all the more remarkable. Just a year earlier, after a period of prolonged illness, she had been diagnosed with colon cancer and had undergone major surgery to remove a malignant tumour. A year later she was back. She started the 1954 season with three victories and arrived for the ninth US Women's Open full of confidence. In what has since been described as the greatest comeback in the history of sports, she blew her opponents off the course to complete a record third tournament victory by a stunning 12 shots.

⊃ The following year, complaining of hip pain, Zaharias visited the specialists once more and discovered the cancer had returned. Playing a limited schedule of just eight events in 1955, she won the last event she ever played, the Peach Blossom Classic, and died the following year, battling her illness to the end.

Babe Zaharias picked up the last of her ten major tournament victories – a record third US Women's Open title – just a year after undergoing major surgery for cancer.

Sandor Kocsis (arms raised) celebrates one of his two extra-time goals that saw off Uruguay 4–2 in the semi-final at Lausanne. Kocsis scored 11 of Hungary's 27 goals in their five-match 1954 World Cup campaign, which ended in a 3–2 final defeat by West Germany.

MIGHTY MAGYARS' GOAL BLITZ NOT ENOUGH

HUNGARY SET RECORD FOR MOST GOALS SCORED IN A SINGLE WORLD CUP TOURNAMENT

4 July 1954, Wankdorf Stadium, Berne, Switzerland

Hungary were the heavy favourites to win the 1954 World Cup, staged in Switzerland to celebrate FIFA's 50th anniversary, and with television cameras beaming live pictures of the tournament around the world for the first time, the Magyars duly responded to the tag. They won their opening game against Korea 9–0 and followed it up with an 8–3 victory over West Germany to qualify for the quarter-finals: they beat Brazil 4–2, then ended Uruguay's reign by the same score in the semi-final and looked forward to their crowning moment – a final against a West German team they had already comfortably beaten. But the Germans stole the day, coming back from two goals down to win the World Cup for the first time. Hungary's record tally of goals (27) came as only a minor consolation.

⊃ Seven of the Hungarian side got their names on the scoresheet during the course of the competition: Sandor Kocsis (11 goals – a tournament record, breaking Brazilian Ademir's mark of nine set in 1950), Nandor Hidegkuti (4), Ferenc Puskas (4), Zoltan Czibor (3), Mihaky Lantos (2), Peter Palotas (2) and Jozsef Toth (1).

Inspired by national pride, Bell decided to attempt the Lake Ontario crossing only after the Toronto-based event organizers failed to encourage Canadian swimmers to take part. Her triumphant achievement catapulted her to international celebrity.

A FIRST FOR LAKE ONTARIO

MARILYN BELL BRAVES COLD AND EELS TO BECOME THE FIRST PERSON TO SWIM LAKE ONTARIO

9 September 1954, Toronto, Canada

When an exhausted Marilyn Bell emerged from the frigid water of Lake Ontario before 300,000 cheering fans, she had not only beaten out the two swimmers who had begun with her at Youngstown, New York, but also the many swimmers who had tried before her. The distance between Youngstown and Toronto is 32 km, but strong winds and currents turned Bell's crossing into a 52-km, 21-hour ordeal, rife with five-metre waves, icy temperatures and attacking lamprey eels. But the 16-year-old swimmer refused to give up, even as her main challenger (renowned US long-distance swimmer Florence Chadwick) failed. When Marilyn Bell stumbled from the water, she had become the first person ever to successfully swim across Lake Ontario.

➲ The next year, Bell became the youngest person to swim the English Channel (a record broken in 1972 by US swimmer Lynne Cox), then swam the Juan de Fuca strait on the Pacific northwest coast. Soon afterwards, she gave up marathon swimming, got married and moved to New Jersey.

DAVIS DELIVERS SNOOKER'S FIRST MAXIMUM

JOE DAVIS COMPILES FIRST 147 BREAK UNDER TOURNAMENT CONDITIONS IN SNOOKER HISTORY

22 January 1955, Leicester Square Hall, London

He may have retired from the world championship scene to aid the development of the game, but Joe Davis still had one more burning ambition in snooker: to hit a maximum 147 break under tournament conditions. His chance came in an exhibition match against his former mentor Willy Smith at Leicester Square Hall in January 1955. Davis potted 13 reds followed by 13 blacks but lost position. He produced a magical pot on the 14th red, shouting "It's in" as he potted it, and scrambled the rest of the balls into the pockets. As the final black crept towards the pocket, Smith threw his arms around Davis: he had become the first player in snooker history to achieve the magical 147.

➲ It was one of the last exhibition matches ever played at the Leicester Square Hall; it was closed shortly after Davis's feat.

Multiple world champion Joe Davis was the father of modern snooker ... and the first to record a maximum break under tournament conditions.

Bert Sutcliffe made 11 and was New Zealand's top scorer when they were bowled out for a record low 26 by England in the second innings of the second Test at Eden Park, Auckland.

KIWIS COLLAPSE TO ALL-TIME TEST LOW

ENGLAND DISMISS NEW ZEALAND FOR 26 – THE LOWEST TEAM SCORE IN TEST HISTORY

25–28 March 1955, Eden Park, Auckland, New Zealand

1955

The New Zealand batsmen's difficulties against England's bowling attack had been apparent during the first Test of the 1954–55 series: they had mustered just 257 runs in the match and suffered an eight-wicket defeat. So hopes would have been somewhat higher in the second Test after they had made 200 in their first innings and then dismissed England for 246, restricting the visitors to a first-innings lead of just 46 runs. The talk in the dressing room would have been to build a steady lead and set England a challenging target. But then the wheels fell off: only Bert Sutcliffe made it into double figures, as the home side slipped to a humble 26 all out, the lowest score in Test history and defeat by an innings and 20 runs.

➲ New Zealand's mark of 26 beat the previous lowest score of 30, set by South Africa on two occasions (in 1895–96 and 1924).

VETERAN CHIRON BIDS FAREWELL IN FRONT OF HOME CROWD

LOUIS CHIRON BECOMES OLDEST FORMULA ONE DRIVER IN HISTORY

22 May 1955, Monte Carlo, Monaco

Monaco-born Louis Chiron joined the grand prix racing circuit after the end of the First World War and won his first local race in 1928, at the age of 29. His racing career was winding down by 1938 and was brought to a halt by the Second World War. But by the end of hostilities, like many of the drivers of the day beyond his racing peak, Chiron was back racing again and duly entered the first Formula One World Championship in 1950. In 15 starts he recorded just one podium finish, but he made history when he competed in the 1955 Monaco GP at 55 years, 292 days to become the oldest driver in history to take part in a Formula One race. He finished in sixth place, five laps behind the winner Maurice Trintignant.

➲ Chiron endeavoured to make another appearance in Formula One three years later, but failed to qualify for the 1958 Monaco GP.

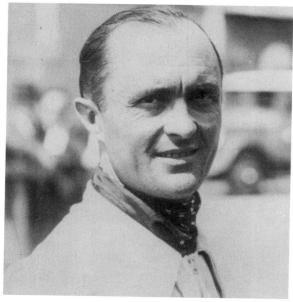

In an otherwise undistinguished Formula One World Championship career that yielded just one podium finish in 15 starts, Louis Chiron took his place in the sport's history books when he competed in the 1955 Monaco GP just a few months short of his 56th birthday.

Louison Bobet may not have been loved by everyone – his penchant for the Hollywood matinee look upset many of his contemporaries – but no one could question his on-road approach: it was good enough to secure three consecutive Tour de France victories in 1953–55.

BOBET COMPLETES TOUR DE FRANCE HAT-TRICK

LOUISON BOBET BECOMES FIRST TO WIN THREE SUCCESSIVE TOUR DE FRANCE TITLES

30 July 1955, Paris, France

Born in Brittany, north-west France, in 1925, Louison Bobet was blessed with natural ability, a pure pedal stroke and the stuff all great champions are made of ... dedication. He used all three to great effect to become the first great French post-war rider. He truly made a name for himself in 1953 when, during the course of his first overall victory, he blitzed the peleton in the Vars Mountains to win the stage by five minutes, and entered Paris with a 14-minute lead. He had increased the winning margin to 15 minutes the following year and, in 1955, a lead of nearly five minutes was enough to ensure Bobet became the first rider in history to secure three consecutive overall Tour de France wins.

➲ Bobet would make only one further appearance in the world's greatest cycling race, finishing seventh overall in 1958. He is one of only eight riders to have won the Tour on three or more occasions.

Donald Campbell followed in his father's illustrious footsteps when he broke the world water speed record on Ullswater in the Lake District in July 1955.

CAMPBELL KEEPS FAMILY NAME ALIVE WITH WATER SPEED RECORD

DONALD CAMPBELL FIRST TO BREAK THE 200MPH (321.86KM/H) BARRIER ON WATER

23 July 1955, Ullswater, Lake District, England

Following the death of his father, Sir Malcolm Campbell – the holder of 13 world land and water speed records in the 1920s and '30s – in 1949, Donald Campbell purchased Bluebird K4 and set about reviving his family's pastime of breaking speed records. He first took the Bluebird K4 to Coniston Water in the Lake District in 1951, but when the boat suffered structural failure at 170mph (270km/h) it was back to the drawing board. Campbell and his team developed the Bluebird K7, a metal three-point hydroplane powered by an engine capable of 3,500lb of thrust. On 23 July 1955, Campbell powered his newly developed craft to 202.15mph (324km/h) over the waters of Ullswater to become the first man in history to break the 200mph (321.86km/h) barrier on water.

➲ Campbell went on to break his own record on 16 November that year, when he pushed Bluebird K7 to 216.20mph (347.94km/h) across Lake Mead in the United States. He would break the record again on a further five occasions.

FANGIO POWERS HIS WAY TO WORLD TITLE No. 3

JUAN MANUEL FANGIO WINS RECORD THIRD FORMULA ONE WORLD CHAMPIONSHIP

11 September 1955, Monza, Italy

Considered a youthful upstart and too inexperienced for the first staging of the Formula One World Championship in 1950 at the tender age of 39, Juan Manuel Fangio answered his critics by winning three races to finish second in the overall standings and carried his form into the following season, winning three races en route to a first world title. Sidelined for a year with a neck injury in 1952, he claimed the runner-up spot in 1953 before a mid-season switch to Mercedes in 1954 paid dividends as Fangio picked up six race wins and a second world title. The Argentine revelled in the W196 Monoposto once again in 1955, picking up four race wins and a record third world title.

➲ Further championships would follow in 1956 and '57. Fangio's haul of five Formula One titles stood as a record for 45 years until Michael Schumacher won his sixth F1 crown in 2003.

The dominant driver of the early years of the Formula One World Championship, Argentina's Juan Manuel Fangio was the first driver to collect three world titles.

MARCIANO MAINTAINS 100 PER CENT FIGHT RECORD

ROCKY MARCIANO ONLY HEAVYWEIGHT IN HISTORY TO WIN ALL PROFESSIONAL BOUTS
21 September 1955, Yankee Stadium, New York, USA

An Italian-American born in Brockton, Massachusetts, Rocky Marciano first started to box seriously during time spent in the US Army. He officially turned professional on 12 July 1948 and opened his career with a first-round knockout win over Harry Bilzerian. He went on to win his next 15 fights as well – all of them by knockouts and all of them by the fifth round, with nine coming in the first round. Before long, and helped by an eighth-round knockout win against Joe Louis, he became a leading contender for the heavyweight championship of the world. His title chance came against Jersey Joe Walcott on 23 September 1952: he survived a first-round knockdown to KO the champion in the 13th round. Marciano won the rematch against Walcott – repeating the first win with a first-round knockout – and went on to defend the title five more times. His last fight came on 21 September 1955, when he KO'd Archie Moore in the ninth round.

⮑ Marciano announced his retirement from the ring on 27 April 1956. His professional fight record stood at 49 fights, 49 wins (43 by KO). He remains the only heavyweight champion in history to retire without a defeat or a draw to his name.

Rocky Marciano may have enjoyed a less-than-scintillating amateur career (11 wins and three losses in 14 fights), but he was unbeatable as a pro, winning all 49 of his fights, including this eighth-round knockout of Ezzard Charles at Yankee Stadium, New York, in 1954.

John Reid, seen here on the Nursery at Lord's, struck 84 as New Zealand built what proved to be a match-winning lead in the fourth and final Test against the West Indies at Eden Park, Auckland, ending their 26-year wait for a Test victory.

KIWIS FINALLY STRIKE A WINNING NOTE

NEW ZEALAND RECORD FIRST-EVER TEST WIN: IT HAD TAKEN THEM A RECORD 26 YEARS TO DO SO
9–13 March 1956, Eden Park, Auckland, New Zealand

The patient New Zealand cricket public deserved a medal. Since their national team entered the Test arena in January 1930 some 26 years had elapsed and still the Kiwis had failed to record a win – and there had been plenty of lows along the way. And as the four-Test home series against the West Indies entered its final match, it appeared as though the champagne would have to stay on ice a little longer. The West Indies had won the first three matches of the series and travelled to Auckland for the final Test full of confidence and ready to complete a series sweep. New Zealand had other ideas, though, gaining a 110-run first-innings lead and dismissing the West Indies for 77 in their second innings to record their first-ever Test victory.

➲ Not that New Zealand's cricket-lovers could afford to get too carried away: they would have to wait a further 13 years before they could celebrate a series win – it came when the Kiwis beat Pakistan 1–0 in a three-match away series in October/November 1969.

REAL RALLY TO SECURE FIRST FINAL WIN

REAL MADRID BECOME FIRST-EVER WINNERS OF THE EUROPEAN CUP
13 June 1956, Parc des Princes, Paris, France

The brainchild of Gabriel Henot, the editor of L'Equipe magazine, who suggested an annual European inter-club cup competition, the European Cup was first staged in the 1955–56 season. Sixteen teams contested the knockout tournament played on a home-and-away basis, but none of them was English (champions Wolverhampton Wanderers declined to take part). No matter; there were still plenty of star attractions among the entrants, including Real Madrid, who brushed off the attentions of Servette FC (7–0 on aggregate), FK Partizan (4–3) and AC Milan (5–4) to reach the final against Reims. The French side were 2–0 up after ten minutes, but the Spaniards rallied to take the trophy 4–3 to become the European Cup's first-ever winners.

➲ Goals from Alfredo di Stefano, Hector Rial (two) and Marcos Alonso Marquitos were enough to take Real Madrid to the first European Cup. They would defend their title for the next four years.

Captains Robert Jonquet (Stade de Reims, left) and Miguel Muñoz (Real Madrid) pose together with English referee Arthur Ellis, before the first European Cup final, won 4–3 by Real Madrid.

ANQUETIL BREAKS COPPI'S 14-YEAR RECORD

JACQUES ANQUETIL BREAKS WORLD HOUR RECORD FOR BICYCLES
29 June 1956, Vigorelli Velodrome, Milan, Italy

By the 1950s, Fausto Coppi's 1942 world hour record for bicycles was starting to be mentioned in the same breath as the word "unbeatable", not particularly because of the record itself, but because of the legend, in every sense of the word, Coppi had since gone on to become. And it took another rider on the verge of greatness to break it. Frenchman Jacques Anquetil had won the French amateur championships in 1952 and had taken the Grand Prix des Nations time trial the following year, but he truly stamped his name on the world cycling map when he went to Milan and bettered Coppi's world hour mark by 361m to set a new record at 46.159km (28.68 miles).

➲ After it had remained unconquered for 14 years, Anquetil suddenly made the world hour record vulnerable again: it would be broken a further three times over the course of the next 18 months.

Jacques Anquetil first came to the attention of the global cycling fraternity when he broke Fausto Coppi's long-standing world hour record. He would go on to far greater things, winning the Tour de France five times between 1957 and 1964.

149

SPIN WIZARD LAKER CASTS A SPELL OVER AUSTRALIA

JIM LAKER RECORDS BEST BOWLING FIGURES IN HISTORY OF TEST AND FIRST-CLASS CRICKET

26–31 July 1956, Old Trafford, Manchester, England

The good times were back for English cricket. With Don Bradman now out of the equation, England had finally regained the Ashes in 1953 (after a wait of some 19 years), defended the urn in Australia in 1954–55, and headed to the fourth Test of the 1956 series off the back of a memorable win at Headingley and with the series delicately poised. England compiled an impressive 459 all out in their first innings before Jim Laker (who had taken 11 for 113 in Leeds) produced the performance of his lifetime, taking 9 for 37 as Australia fell for a paltry 84 in their first innings and then a staggering 10 for 53 off 51.2 overs as Australia slipped to 205 all out second time round. England won by an innings and 170 runs to hold onto the Ashes for a third time and Laker, with match figures of 19 for 90, had produced the best match bowling performance in the history of Test cricket.

➲ Only one other bowler in Test history has taken all ten wickets in an innings: Anil Kumble for India v Pakistan at Delhi in February 1999.

Surrey and England off-spinner Jim Laker came up with the goods in Ashes-winning style against Australia at Old Trafford in 1956, recording the best-ever match figures (and single-innings figures) in Test history – 19 for 90 (9 for 37 and 10 for 53). The only other England wicket-taker at Old Trafford in 1956 was Tony Lock, who took the third Australian wicket to fall in the first innings.

DON LARSEN'S PERFECT GAME

DON LARSEN PITCHES THE ONLY PERFECT GAME IN WORLD SERIES HISTORY
8 October 1956, Yankee Stadium, New York, USA

Pitching perfection, otherwise known as the "perfect game" (27 up, 27 down), is not unheard of in the history of Major League Baseball. There have been 17 official perfect games, but only one on the biggest stage of them all – the World Series. It happened in game five of the 1956 Fall Classic between the New York Yankees and the Brooklyn Dodgers, with the series tied at 2–2. The Yankees named Don Larsen as their starting pitcher, a surprise given his performance in game two, when he had lasted barely two innings as the Dodgers mounted a come-from-behind victory. But this time his control did not desert him and Larsen needed just 97 pitches to complete the game, with only one opposing batsman able to get to the three-ball count. Larsen, considered in some quarters as being little more than a journeyman pitcher, had become the first, and to date only, pitcher to deliver a perfect game in the World Series.

⊃ Don Larsen's perfect game in the 1956 World Series remains the only no-hitter of any type ever pitched in post-season play.

With the 1956 Fall Classic evenly poised – the Yankees had come back from two games down to the Dodgers – Don Larsen found the perfect time to produce the World Series' first perfect game. The Yankees eventually won the classic Subway Series 4–3 and Larsen's name has stayed up in lights ever since.

THE GALLOPING MAJOR'S FINAL SALUTE

FERENC PUSKAS SCORES HIS RECORD 84TH AND FINAL INTERNATIONAL GOAL

14 October 1956, Vienna, Austria

Stocky and barrel-chested, Ferenc Puskas stamped his name on soccer folklore during his time with Real Madrid in the late 1950s and early '60s, but it was his performances for club side Honved and the Hungarian national team that initially grabbed the public's attention. He scored on his international debut against Austria in 1945 and went on to form part of the legendary Mighty Magyars team that shocked England 6–3 at Wembley (with Puskas scoring twice). And although he ended up on the losing side in the 1954 World Cup (he had a goal disallowed for offside in the dying moments of the game), still the goals flowed. He netted for the final time in an international (his 84th in 85 appearances) during a 2–0 win over Austria in October 1956. Shortly afterwards, with Puskas away in Spain with Honved, the Russian tanks rolled into Hungary: Puskas and several of his team-mates defected to the West.

➲ Puskas's goal haul stood as a record for 47 years until Iran's Ali Daei scored his 85th international goal against Lebanon on 28 November 2003 in Tehran.

Blessed with arguably the greatest left foot the game of soccer has ever seen, Ferenc Puskas, known as "The Galloping Major", scored 84 times for Hungary in just 85 international appearances. He also made four appearances for Spain in 1960 and 1961, but did not add to his international goal tally.

Patricia McCormick's margin of victory in the 1956 Olympic springboard competition – more than 16 points – was the largest winning margin in Olympic diving history, but that was the least remembered of the milestones she reached at the XVI Olympiad.

McCORMICK DIVES HER WAY INTO OLYMPIC HISTORY

PATRICIA McCORMICK BECOMES FIRST IN HISTORY TO WIN OLYMPIC DIVING'S DOUBLE-DOUBLE

22 November–8 December 1956, Melbourne, Australia

Patricia McCormick used to perform flips into the sea off a bridge on Muscle Beach, Santa Monica, as a child and entered as many diving competitions as she could. A coach soon spotted her raw potential and introduced her to legendary divers Vicky Draves and Sammy Lee. A dream was ignited. She learned to perform difficult and dangerous dives – usually ones only attempted by men and banned in international competition for women until 1952. When the ban was lifted, McCormick was in her element, winning springboard and platform gold in Helsinki in 1952 and becoming the only woman in history to complete the double-double in Melbourne in 1956.

➲ McCormick accomplished her feat just eight months after giving birth to her first son. Only one other diver in Olympic history has achieved the double-double: Greg Louganis in 1984 and 1988.

MATTHEWS IS EUROPE'S FIRST SOCCER PLAYER OF THE YEAR

STANLEY MATTHEWS BECOMES INAUGURAL WINNER OF THE BALLON D'OR

December 1956, Paris, France

Created by the French soccer magazine *France Football* in 1956, the Ballon d'Or (otherwise known as the European Soccer Player of the Year award), voted for by soccer journalists across the continent, has gone on to become one of the most prestigious awards in soccer. Players from Barcelona, Real Madrid, Manchester United and Bayern Munich have all gone on to win it, but the accolade of being the first winner fell to a 41-year-old right-winger from Blackpool who was coming towards the end of an illustrious career: Stanley Matthews. It was a just reward for a player who played 701 league games (scoring 71 goals) and 54 internationals for England (scoring 11 times).

⮑ In January 1965, Stanley Matthews became the first soccer player in history to receive a knighthood.

Stanley Matthews, one of the greatest players English soccer has ever produced, was voted Europe's No. 1 player in 1956 at the tender age of 41. It was the first time the Ballon d'Or had been awarded.

FROM SEGREGATION TO TICKER-TAPE PARADES

ALTHEA GIBSON BECOMES FIRST AFRICAN-AMERICAN WOMAN TO WIN WIMBLEDON

6 July 1957, Wimbledon, London, England

Tennis in post-war America was a segregated game and although Althea Gibson won the first of her ten consecutive national coloured titles in 1947, aged 20, she would have to wait until 1950 before making her first appearance in the US Open – she lost in the second round. She joined the main Tour later that year – becoming the first African-American woman to do so – and slowly found her feet, winning the Italian Championships in 1955 and her first grand slam tournament, the French Open, the following year. Grand slam glory continued in 1957 when she beat Doris Hart 6–3, 6–2 in the Wimbledon final to become the first African-American player to win the All-England crown. She returned to the United States a hero.

➲ Gibson would go on to defend her Wimbledon crown in 1958 when she beat Angela Mortimer 8–6, 6–2 in the final.

Sometimes described as the "Jackie Robinson of tennis", Althea Gibson had to overcome more hurdles than most to get her hands on the Wimbledon crown in 1957.

MOSCONI PRODUCES MAGIC ONE LAST TIME

WILLIE MOSCONI WINS HIS RECORD 15TH AND LAST WORLD POOL CHAMPIONSHIP

November 1957, New York, USA

Born in 1913, the son of a pool hall owner, Willie Mosconi became a pool child prodigy. His father, seeing his son as a potential source of extra income, set up challenge matches: as a six-year-old Mosconi pushed the reigning world pool champion all the way before losing a closely fought match. He entered his first major tournament in 1939 and, after several near misses, won the Billiards Congress of America world pool championship for the first time in 1941 (in league play) and again the following year (this time in tournament play). He would go on to win the title a further 13 times, with his last victory coming in 1957.

➲ A few months after his victory in the BCA world championship, Mosconi suffered a stroke and retired from tournament play.

Fifteen-time world pool champion Willie Mosconi set numerous records, among them the record run of 526 (the number of consecutive balls potted without a miss), set in Springfield, Ohio, in 1954.

FORTY-SIX-YEAR-OLD FANGIO STILL FIRING

JUAN MANUEL FANGIO WINS RECORD FIFTH F1 TITLE AND BECOMES OLDEST-EVER WORLD CHAMPION

4 August 1957, Nürburgring, Germany

1957

Juan Manuel Fangio simply got better with age. In 1954 – having already won the championship in 1951 – the Argentine, now 43 years old, benefited from a mid-season switch from Maserati to Mercedes. He won four times in it to win a second title. It was more of the same in 1955 as Fangio claimed a third world crown. And a switch from Mercedes to Ferrari in 1956 did little to trigger a switch in fortune: Fangio took a fourth title by three points. It was an altogether more comfortable ride back in a Maserati in 1957: Fangio's fourth race win of the season, at the Nürburgring, secured a record fifth title and a place in the history books: at 46 years, 41 days, he had become Formula One's oldest-ever world champion.

➲ The next-oldest world champion in Formula One history was Nino Farina, who won the inaugural championship in 1950 aged 43 years, 308 days.

In the last full season of his stellar career, Argentine Juan Manuel Fangio eased to a fifth World Championship in 1957 to become the sport's oldest-ever world champion.

THE END OF HOCKEY'S COLOUR BARRIER

WILLIE O'REE SKATES QUIETLY INTO HISTORY

18 January 1958, Montreal, Canada

New Brunswick native Willie O'Ree was picked out of the minor-league Quebec Aces to replace an injured member of the Boston Bruins halfway through the 1957–58 season. He played in two games before returning to the minors for the next season. O'Ree was again tapped by the Bruins for the 60–61 season, then spent the rest of his career in the minors, retiring from hockey in 1979. During his second stint with the Bruins, O'Ree received a pass from team-mate Leo Boivin and snapped the puck past the Canadiens' goalie to score the first goal by a black player in the NHL. But perhaps the most amazing thing about O'Ree breaking the colour barrier was the news it *didn't* make: the media didn't play up the milestone event, and it would be another dozen years before another black player would appear in the league.

Willie O'Ree's NHL career lasted only 45 games, four goals and ten assists – but his claim to fame is as the first black player in the history of the NHL.

➲ Willie O'Ree would probably have been in the majors for much longer if he'd played right-wing: He was 95-per cent blind in his right eye, and should never have been allowed to play in the NHL at all with this condition – but he kept quiet about it.

SWASHBUCKLING SOBERS HITS NEW TEST HIGH

GARFIELD SOBERS BREAKS THE RECORD FOR TEST CRICKET'S HIGHEST SCORE

1 March 1958, Sabina Park, Kingston, Jamaica

Born in Bridgetown, Barbados, in 1936, Garfield Sobers made his first-class debut at the age of 16 and his first Test appearance for the West Indies a year later. Initially, at least, he was primarily picked as a bowler – capable of bowling left-arm spin (orthodox or wrist spin) or medium-fast deliveries, he went on to collect 235 Test wickets – and although he was a world-class performer with the ball, it was his feats with the bat that made him one of the standout performers in Test history. The left-hander scored 26 Test centuries: his first, and also his highest, came in the third Test against Pakistan in March 1958. Sobers came to the crease with the West Indies on a comfortable 87 for 1; by the time he left the field his team had a stranglehold on the game – he had scored an unbeaten 365 (including 38 fours) in 614 minutes. It was the highest-ever Test score (beating the 364 set by Len Hutton in 1958) and Sobers had become the biggest star cricket had seen since the glory days of Don Bradman.

➲ Sobers's record stood for 36 years, until Brian Lara scored 375 against England in Antigua in 1994. However, it still remains the highest maiden Test century in cricket history.

Seven months before Garfield Sobers set a new record Test score of 365 at Kingston, Jamaica, he was in England and, at The Oval in the final Test, he top-scored in both innings, but the West Indies were still defeated by an innings and 237 runs.

SUGAR RAY ROBINSON: THE FIVE-TIME CHAMPION

SUGAR RAY ROBINSON WINS WORLD MIDDLEWEIGHT CHAMPIONSHIP FOR RECORD FIFTH TIME
25 March 1958, Chicago Stadium, Chicago, Illinois, USA

It must have felt as though Father Time was finally catching up with Sugar Ray Robinson. The 38-year-old former world welterweight champion (1946–51) and four-time middleweight title-holder had gone without food for 20 hours in an attempt to make the weight for his rematch with Carmen Basilio for the world middleweight crown. Six months earlier, Basilio had won the favour of the judges during a brutal 15-round bout, and Robinson was going to need all of his experience if he was to achieve a record fifth divisional world championship title. The fight went the distance once again: this time, with Basilio nursing a badly injured eye, Robinson took the judges' vote by two to one: he had cemented his reputation as one of the greatest fighters of all time.

⮰ Robinson lost the title two years later – on a split decision to Paul Pender – and failed in his bid to win the middleweight world championship for a sixth time in the rematch, again on a split decision. He carried on fighting until 1965, but never fought for a world title again.

Widely considered one of the best pound-for-pound fighters of all time, Sugar Ray Robinson, pictured right, won or regained the world middleweight title a record five times.

When Suzy Kormoczy won the French Open singles title in 1958, she not only became the tournament's oldest-ever champion but also the first and only Jewish player to win a grand slam tournament.

HUNGARIAN HOUSEWIFE TRIUMPHS IN PARIS

SUZY KORMOCZY BECOMES OLDEST WINNER OF FRENCH OPEN WOMEN'S TITLE
2 June 1958, Roland Garros, Paris, France

Thirty-three-year-old, Budapest-born Suzy Kormoczy arrived at Roland Garros for the 1958 French Open in the shape of her life. Ranked No. 2 in the world, she had embarked on a program of running and gymnastics before the start of the tournament and had breezed through to the final without losing a set and having barely drawn breath. But with the scores tied at one set all (6–4, 1–6) in the final, against defending champion Shirley Bloomer, she found the perfect time to put her newfound stamina to good use and took the final set 6–2 to become, at 33 years, 284 days, the oldest winner of the French Open women's title.

⮰ Kormoczy narrowly failed to defend her title the following year, losing 6–4, 7–5 in the final to Christine Truman who, in a sharp twist of irony, became the tournament's youngest-ever winner.

The world got its first glimpse of Pele – the man who would go on to become the greatest player soccer has ever seen – at the 1958 World Cup finals, when, at just 17 years of age, he played a starring role in Brazil's first tournament success.

HOT SHOT PELE OPENS WORLD CUP ACCOUNT

PELE BECOMES YOUNGEST PLAYER TO SCORE IN THE WORLD CUP FINALS

19 June 1958, Gothenburg, Sweden

Pele made his debut for Santos FC in Brazil at the age of 15 in a pre-season friendly against Corinthians, and scored one goal in a 7–1 win. He ended his first season as the league's leading goalscorer and recognition from the national team came a year later, just ten months after his professional debut. The following year, in 1958 in Sweden, he became the youngest player to appear in the World Cup finals when he lined up for Brazil in their final group game against the USSR. He kept his place for the quarter-final clash against Wales, and when he scored the only goal of the game in the 66th minute became, aged 17 years, 239 days, the tournament's youngest-ever goalscorer.

➲ Pele was just finding his World Cup feet: he went on to score a hat-trick in Brazil's 5–2 semi-final destruction of France and twice in the final as Brazil beat Sweden by the same scoreline to win the World Cup for the first time.

FOUR-GOAL FONTAINE BOWS OUT WITH RECORD

JUST FONTAINE SETS RECORD FOR MOST GOALS SCORED IN THE WORLD CUP FINALS

28 June 1958, Gothenburg, Sweden

Eventual winners Brazil may have beaten France in the semi-finals, but the tournament had been a personal triumph for Morocco-born French striker Just Fontaine. He scored six goals in the group stages (including a hat-trick in France's 7–3 win over Paraguay), twice in the quarter-finals (in a 4–0 win over Northern Ireland) and once in the semi-final loss to Brazil (2–5). And both he and the French bowed out of the tournament in style as they hammered West Germany 6–3 in the third-place playoff game in Gothenburg, with Fontaine finding the back of the net four times to end the tournament with a record 13 goals.

➲ Fontaine's record is considered the most unbreakable in soccer. The next best tournament tally is 11, by Hungary's Sandor Kocsis in 1954; since 1958, the most goals anyone has managed to score in a single World Cup finals is eight (Eusebio in 1966 and Ronaldo in 2002).

Stade de Reims striker Just Fontaine scored 30 goals for France in 21 matches before a recurring injury brought a premature end to his career: 13 of those goals came in six games during the 1958 World Cup finals.

BRAZIL MARK CORONATION WITH RECORD GOAL HAUL

BRAZIL RECORD HIGHEST-EVER SCORE IN THE WORLD CUP FINAL

29 June 1958, Rasunda Stadium, Stockholm, Sweden

If the 1958 World Cup in Sweden showcased the emergence of Brazil as one of the world powers of soccer, then the final, against the hosts, served as a triumphant procession towards their coronation as world champions. The home crowd were cheering when their side took the lead after four minutes, but were subdued by half-time: Vava had scored twice to hand the Brazilians a 2–1 lead. Their third was one of the great World Cup goals: a piece of audacious skill from 17-year-old Pele. Zagallo scored another, and although the plucky Swedes pulled one back, Pele added a fifth before full-time. Brazil, a country where soccer is religion, had won the game's greatest prize ... and in sumptuous style.

➲ Brazil's 5–2 win remains the highest winning score in a World Cup final. There have been three instances of a 4–2 scoreline, in 1930, 1938 and 1966.

Brazil captured their first World Cup in style in 1958, scoring a record five goals in the final against Sweden.

CONSISTENCY THE KEY TO HAWTHORN'S SUCCESS

MIKE HAWTHORN BECOMES FORMULA ONE'S YOUNGEST WORLD CHAMPION

19 October 1958, Ain-Diab, Morocco

The 1958 French Grand Prix was significant for two reasons. First, it saw the last-ever involvement of five-time world champion Juan Manuel Fangio in the Formula One World Championship – his retirement meant no active driver had won the championship – and, secondly, Ferrari's Mike Hawthorn would go on to win the race. It was the only race he would win that season – compared to Stirling Moss, who would take four race wins that year – but Hawthorn added five second places and one third to that solitary success to take the championship from Moss by one point. At 29 years, 192 days, he had become Formula One's youngest world champion.

➲ Mike Hawthorn's record would last until 1963, when Jim Clark became world champion for the first time at 27 years, 188 days. Sadly Hawthorn did not live to see the feat: he was killed in a car accident in Guildford, England, four months after becoming world champion.

Mike Hawthorn's first and only Formula One World Championship success came in 1958: he became the sport's youngest-ever champion but was tragically killed just four months later.

CANADA FIRST IN CURLING

UPSTART PRAIRIE TEAM OBLITERATES SCOTTISH HOPEFULS IN FIRST WORLD CURLING CHAMPIONSHIP

1959, Falkirk, Scotland

1959's inaugural Scotch Cup was a meeting of Scottish experience and youthful New World exuberance. The Canadian team, fresh from their victory at the 1959 Brier in Quebec City, arrived in Scotland for a five-game series against the older Scottish champions – then gave them a right thumping, winning all five games by margins ranging from one point (8–7) to seven (9–2). Though the world championships have changed names several times since then, one thing has remained the same: Canada dominates the sport, winning more championships than any other country (30 out of 43 in men's; 14 out of 25 in women's). .

➲ The curse of LaBonte occurred at the 1972 championship, when an inadvertent slip by US skip Bob LaBonte knocked a Canadian rock into the winning position. Canada went on to win the championship, much to LaBonte's chagrin. They say that the US skip cursed the Canadian team because they would fail to win the championship again until 1980.

MOHAMMAD BREAKS BRADMAN'S 30-YEAR RECORD

HANIF MOHAMMAD BREAKS RECORD FOR HIGHEST FIRST-CLASS SCORE

11 January 1959, Karachi, Pakistan

Garfield Sobers wasn't the only batsman capturing the sports headlines in 1958–59. In the first Test match between the West Indies and Pakistan at Bridgetown, Barbados, Pakistan batsman Hanif Mohammad had set the record for the longest-ever Test innings (970 minutes) and became the first player from his country to score a triple-century. Less than a year later, the "Little Master" – he was the first batsman from the subcontinent to assume the moniker – showed his powers of concentration and his faultless technique once again: playing for Karachi against Bahawalpur, he hit 499 to break Don Bradman's 1929–30 record for the highest first-class score (452 not out). He was run out attempting his 500th run in the last over of the day.

➲ Hanif Mohammad's 499 would stand as a first-class record for 35 years, until Brian Lara hit 501 not out for Warwickshire against Durham at Edgbaston in 1994.

Hanif Mohammad, the first star of Pakistan cricket, thrust himself into the world cricket spotlight when he hit 499 runs in a day for Karachi against Bahawalpur on 11 January 1959.

THE IRONBRIDGE ROCKET FIRST TO 100-CAP LANDMARK

BILLY WRIGHT WINS A RECORD 100TH CAP FOR ENGLAND

11 April 1959, Wembley Stadium, London, England

Born in Ironbridge, Shropshire, Billy Wright was the first real showbiz star of soccer – he was married to one of the Beverley Sisters, the leading female pop group of the day – and arguably the greatest club-and-country servant ever to play the game. He made his debut for Wolves as a 15-year-old in 1939, and his international debut, as a wing-half, in 1946. He captained his country to the World Cup in 1950 (where England suffered a humiliating 1–0 loss to the United States), 1954 and 1958. A switch to central defence was a revelation and extended his career. Wright won his 100th cap against Scotland in April 1959: England won the day 1–0 and Wright was carried off the pitch on the shoulders of his team-mates to a standing ovation.

➲ Wright's international haul of caps (104) stood as a record until fellow countryman Bobby Charlton won his 105th cap against East Germany on 14 June 1970. Wright also captained England a record 90 times (equalled by Bobby Moore) and made a record of 70 consecutive appearances, which has never been equalled.

Billy Wright of Wolverhampton Wanderers and England became the first man in soccer history to reach the landmark of 100 international caps when he led his country to a 1–0 win against Scotland in April 1959.

YOUTH HAS ITS DAY AS TRUMAN WINS TITLE

CHRISTINE TRUMAN BECOMES YOUNGEST WINNER OF THE FRENCH OPEN

31 May 1959, Roland Garros, Paris, France

Either way a record was going to be broken in the 1959 French Open ladies' singles final. Suzy Kormoczy, who had shocked the tennis world the previous year when she had become the tournament's oldest winner aged 33, had made it through to the final once again. She would be up against Britain's Christine Truman, the hard-hitting new kid on the block who, aged 17, had made it through to the quarter-finals the previous year and who was bidding to become the tournament's youngest-ever winner. Youth would win the day: Truman took the title 6–4, 7–5 to earn her place in the record books.

➲ The 1959 French Open title was the only grand slam tournament Truman would win: she finished as runner-up at the US Open later in the year and again at Wimbledon in 1961.

Just a year after leading Britain to success in the Wightman Cup for the first time in 28 years, Christine Truman won the 1959 French Open to become the tournament's youngest-ever champion.

AT FACE VALUE

CANADIENS' GOALIE JACQUES PLANTE FIRST TO DON MASK ON-ICE

1 November 1959, New York City, USA

These days, the ice hockey goalie's mask is a familiar piece of the uniform, but this was not always so. The mask first appeared on-ice when Jacques Plante, the Montreal Canadiens' goalie from 1953–63, suffered one bad gash too many during a game against the New York Rangers at Madison Square Garden. A puck to the face sent Plante to the changing room for stitches, and when he emerged again, he was wearing the homemade mask he wore for practise. Plante refused to go back on the ice without it, and coach Toe Blake furiously relented and let him go on. The Canadiens won the game, then embarked on a winning streak that took them straight to that season's Stanley Cup.

⮑ Plante finally took the mask off again for a 1960 game against Detroit. The Habs' 3–0 loss that night ended an 18-game winning streak for the Canadiens. The mask went back on for the next game and all those that followed.

Plante went on to design masks for other goalies as well, bringing many innovations to the design and helping bring about today's joined mask and helmet concept. After Plante retired, he moved to Switzerland, where he died of stomach cancer in 1986.

A former chicken farmer from Utah, Lamar Clark's mauling-and-brawling style brought him a record 44 consecutive wins by knockout between January 1958 and January 1960.

CLARK COMPLETES RECORD 44TH KNOCKOUT

LAMAR CLARK SETS RECORD FOR MOST CONSECUTIVE KNOCKOUT WINS

11 January 1960, Las Vegas, Nevada, USA

Lamar Clark started his pro career in winning style, beating John Hicks on points on 4 January 1958, and then embarked on a whirlwind campaign of fights that would cement his place in the record books. Starting on 11 January 1958, Clark knocked out 44 consecutive opponents, many of them unknowns, sometimes more than one of them in a night – he knocked out six opponents in one evening in December 1958 – and 29 of them in the first round. He achieved his record 44th KO win when he knocked out Kenneth Hayden in the first round in Las Vegas in January 1960.

⮑ The record-breaking streak came to an end on 8 April 1960, when Clark lost to Dominican heavyweight champion Bartoli Soni in the ninth round. He had a chance to get his career back on track the following year when he fought Cassius Clay (later Muhammad Ali), but was knocked out in the second round, suffered a broken nose and never fought again.

FIVE IN A ROW FOR LOS MERENGUES

REAL MADRID WIN THE EUROPEAN CUP FOR THE FIFTH SUCCESSIVE YEAR

15 May 1960, Hampden Park, Glasgow, Scotland

If anyone were ever in any doubt as to how Real Madrid became one of the most feted clubs in world soccer, they need look no further than the club's exploits in the early years of the European Cup. But, having won the tournament four years in a row between 1956 and 1959, their position as European kings was coming under threat from the ambitions of rivals Barcelona. The pair met in the semi-finals of the 1960 European Cup; just a week earlier the Catalan giants had wrested the Spanish league on goals scored from Real. But this was Europe: Real won the two-match tie 6–2 on aggregate and, in front of a record crowd of 127,621 at Hampden Park, beat Eintracht Frankfurt 7–3 in the final to win the European Cup for a record fifth consecutive year.

In front of the biggest crowd a European final has ever seen, and before an estimated 70 million television viewers worldwide, Real Madrid steamrollered Eintracht Frankfurt 7–3 in the 1960 European Cup final to take the trophy for a record fifth consecutive year.

➲ Barcelona gained their revenge the following year, ending Real Madrid's five-year reign as European champions with a 4–3 aggregate victory in the first round. Barca went all the way to the final, where they lost 3–2 to Benfica.

DI STEFANO HAT-TRICK MAKES IT FIVE OUT OF FIVE

ALFREDO DI STEFANO SCORES IN HIS FIFTH SUCCESSIVE EUROPEAN CUP FINAL

15 May 1960, Hampden Park, Glasgow, Scotland

Alfredo Di Stefano was living proof that the greatest players are able to perform at the top of their game on the biggest stage of all. The Argentine-born striker, perhaps the original "total soccer player", possessed extraordinary versatility, incredible stamina (he would be defending one moment then popping up in the opponents' penalty area the next), remarkable selflessness and an eye for goal that has rarely been matched in soccer history. The man they called the "Blond Arrow" scored in every one of Real Madrid's European final successes, capping Los Merengues' fifth victory with a hat-trick during their 7–3 demolition of Eintracht Frankfurt. It is a record never likely to be beaten.

Cometh the hour ... Alfredo Di Stefano played a pivotal role in Real Madrid's early domination of the European Cup, scoring in all five of their final wins from 1956 to 1960, including a hat-trick in the 1960 final.

➲ By the end of his career, Alfredo Di Stefano had scored 49 goals in 58 European matches. It stood as a record tally until 2005 when another great servant of Real Madrid, Raul, broke it.

PATTERSON STUNS JOHANNSON TO REGAIN HEAVYWEIGHT CROWN

FLOYD PATTERSON BECOMES FIRST PERSON TO REGAIN WORLD HEAVYWEIGHT CROWN

20 June 1960, Polo Grounds, New York, USA

Trained by the legendary Cus D'Amato, 21-year-old Floyd Patterson – the 1952 Olympic heavyweight champion – became the youngest, and the first Olympic gold medallist, to win the heavyweight championship of the world when he knocked out Archie Moore for the vacant title on 30 November 1956. Four routine title defences followed, before Patterson faced Ingemar Johannson on 26 June 1959: the Swede floored the champion seven times before the fight was stopped in the third round. The smart money was on the Swede to repeat his performance in the rematch a year later, but Patterson had other ideas, producing a devastating left hook in the fifth round to KO Johannson and become the first boxer in history to regain the world heavyweight title.

➲ To complete what many consider to be one of the greatest trilogies in boxing history, the pair fought for a third time in 1961. Patterson won by KO in the sixth round. However, he would lose his title the following year when Sonny Liston flattened him in the first round.

Having been humiliated by the same opponent just a year earlier, Floyd Patterson defied his doubters when he knocked out Sweden's Ingemar Johannson in the fifth round at the Polo Grounds, New York, to become the first man in history to regain the world heavyweight crown.

167

ARMIN HARY: THE FASTEST MAN ON EARTH

ARMIN HARY BREAKS WORLD 100M RECORD AND BECOMES FIRST TO CLOCK TEN SECONDS FLAT

21 June 1960, Zurich, Switzerland

A former youth soccer player, Armin Hary switched to sprinting at the age of 16 and thrived. Within five years the West German sprinter had won his first major international title – the 100m European Championship crown – and then set his sights on breaking Willie Williams's 1956 world record of 10.1 seconds. Later that year he thought he had done it: clocking ten seconds dead, only to be informed that the 11cm slope on the track had been deemed illegal. Then, in Zurich in 1960, he thought he had done it again, clocking the same time, only to be informed by the judges that he had made a false start. He clocked the same time (ten seconds flat) later the same day: this time the judges were happy. Armin Hary had become the fastest man on earth.

➲ No one would better Hary's mark for six years: it was equalled on nine occasions, until Jim Hines from the United States ran 9.9 seconds in Sacramento, California, on 20 June 1968.

After breaking the 100m world record earlier in the year, Armin Hary completed a memorable season by winning 100m gold at the 1962 Olympics in Rome, becoming the first non-American to win the event since Canada's Percy Williams in 1928.

UNWITTINGLY SWEPT TO A PLACE IN THE RECORD BOOKS

ROGER WOODWARD BECOMES FIRST TO SURVIVE PLUNGE OVER FALLS WITHOUT A BARREL

9 July 1960, Niagara Falls, USA/Canada

If ever proof were required that not all records are intended, here it is. During the afternoon of Saturday, 9 July 1960, Jim Honeycutt took his co-workers' children – 17-year-old Deanne Woodward and her seven-year-old brother Roger – on a boat trip on the upper Niagara River. They soon got into difficulties: the engine failed, the boat capsized and the three were pitched into the raging rapids. Deanne Woodward was rescued feet from the edge of the Horseshoe Falls; the other two were not so lucky. Honeycutt disappeared over the edge and was never seen alive again; Roger, wearing nothing but a swimsuit and life jacket, survived and was picked up by a passing tourist boat. Somewhat unwittingly, he had become the first person to survive a plunge over Niagara Falls without a barrel.

➲ Roger Woodward was taken to hospital and stayed there for three days suffering from concussion. A day after his release, the river yielded Honeycutt's body from its depths.

In 1960, Roger Woodward became the first to survive an unaided plunge over the Niagara River's Horseshoe Falls. The feat has been repeated once, during a failed suicide attempt in 2003.

RAWLS RIDES LUCK TO CLAIM RECORD FOURTH OPEN TITLE

BETSY RAWLS BECOMES FIRST FOUR-TIME WINNER OF THE US WOMEN'S OPEN

23 July 1960, Worcester Country Club, Worcester, Massachusetts, USA

Betsy Rawls may not have picked up a golf club until the age of 17, but she was a quick learner. Within four years she was the Texas amateur champion, won the title for the second successive year in 1950 and turned professional a year later, winning the US Women's Open in her rookie year. A second Open triumph came in 1953 when she beat Jacqueline Pung in a playoff, and Pung's misfortune in 1957 – she was disqualified after signing for the wrong card – turned into Rawls's joy as she completed a hat-trick of wins. Her record fourth title came in 1960, when Joyce Ziske missed a five-foot putt on the last to hand her a one-shot victory.

Betsy Rawls enjoyed eight triumphs in major tournaments: four of them came in the US Women's Open.

➲ Rawls's feat has been equalled – by Mickey Wright, who won the event in 1958, 1959, 1961 and 1964 – but never beaten.

BOSTON LEAPS INTO THE RECORD BOOKS

RALPH BOSTON BREAKS JESSE OWENS'S 25-YEAR WORLD LONG JUMP RECORD

12 August 1960, Mount San Antonio College, Walnut, California, USA

Ralph Boston leapt to a place in both the history books and American consciousness when he broke Jesse Owens's 25-year-old world long jump record in 1960: he went on to break the record on numerous occasions, before Bob Beamon shattered it in 1968.

A talented all-round athlete who excelled in sprinting, high hurdles and high jump (he was ranked fourth in the country in the event), Tennessee University student Ralph Boston decided to concentrate solely on the long jump in his senior season in an attempt to make the US team for the 1960 Olympic Games in Rome. It was a worthwhile decision: Boston went on to become the 1960 NCAA champion, qualified for the Olympics and, two weeks before setting off for Rome, broke Jesse Owens's 25-year record for long jump by 8cm, setting a new mark of 8.21m in Walnut, California. To round off a spectacular year, he took Olympic gold as well (by 1cm from team-mate Bo Roberson), breaking Owens's 24-year-old Olympic record in the process.

➲ The long jump world record became the hot potato of the athletics world over the next few years. Boston would go on to break his own record twice, before Russia's Igor Ter-Ovanesjan jumped 8.31m in Moscow in June 1962. At the height of the Cold War, the pressure on Boston to break the record was intense: he responded with 8.34m in Los Angeles in 1964 and 8.35m a year later. Ter-Ovanesjan equalled the mark in 1967 ... and then Bob Beamon arrived on the scene.

KITTINGER MAKES HISTORIC LEAP FROM THE HEAVENS

US AIR FORCE PILOT JOSEPH KITTINGER MAKES WORLD'S HIGHEST PARACHUTE JUMP

16 August 1960, Holloman Air Force Base, Alamogordo, New Mexico, USA

As jet engines allowed planes to go higher, the US Air Force became concerned about what would happen to pilots should they be forced to eject at extreme high altitude. Tests on dummies had shown that a body in freefall could rotate as many as 200 times per minute – a potentially fatal figure. Project Excelsior was established to create a multi-stage parachute system (including timers and altitude sensors) capable of producing a controlled descent, pilot Joseph Kittinger was chosen to test it and a helium balloon was developed to lift him into the stratosphere. In the last of the three tests, the balloon rose to 102,800ft (31,300m) above the New Mexico desert and, 13m45s after jumping, Kittinger landed safely.

➲ The ascent to 102,800ft (almost 20 miles above the earth's surface) took 1h31m. Kittinger waited in the gondola for 12 minutes before the balloon drifted over the landing site and then jumped. A small stabilizer parachute opened immediately, and Kittinger was in controlled freefall for 4m36s before opening his main chute at 17,500ft (5,300m) and landing safely in the New Mexico desert.

During a US Air Force test in 1960, pilot and career military officer Joseph Kittinger broke the world records for the highest parachute jump and the longest parachute freefall in history: neither record has been broken, although some question the validity of the records because of Kittinger's use of a stabilizer chute.

RECORD-BREAKING ELLIOTT EASES TO 1,500M GOLD

HERB ELLIOTT BREAKS WORLD 1,500M RECORD TO WIN FIRST OLYMPIC GOLD

6 September 1960, Rome, Italy

Herb Elliott trained harder than any of his contemporaries, sprinting up and down sand dunes until he dropped – but that's what happens when all you have to race against is the history books. During his distinguished career, the Western Australian never lost a race over 1,500m or a mile. His battle was with the stopwatch. On 6 August 1958, then 20, he broke Derek Ibbotson's 1957 world mile record mark by 2.7 seconds in Dublin; later that month he broke Olavi Salonen's 1,500m world record by almost two seconds (3m36s). But his crowning moment came in the 1,500m final at the 1960 Olympic Games in Rome. In one of the most commanding performances in history, Elliott struck gold and broke his own world record in the process. The new record: 3m35.6s.

The greatest middle-distance runner of his generation, Herb Elliott produced a stellar performance in the 1960 Olympic 1,500m final, breaking his own world record to win the only Olympic gold of his short career. He retired from athletics in 1961 at the age of 23.

➲ Elliott's time would stand as a record for seven years, until America's Jim Ryun set a new mark on 8 January 1967 in Los Angeles, California, when he clocked 3m33.13s.

PAKISTAN SHOCK INDIA TO WIN HOCKEY GOLD

INDIA'S OLYMPIC HOCKEY RECORD 28-GAME WINNING STREAK COMES TO AN END
9 September 1960, Rome, Italy

Hockey, along with cricket, would have been one of the few welcome British leftovers from the days of the Raj, and whereas India may have initially struggled to establish themselves in cricket, they steamrollered allcomers in hockey to become the most dominant force in the game. They took the first-ever Olympic hockey gold medal in Amsterdam in 1928 and defended their title in the next five Olympics. And when they got to the final in Rome in 1960, few would have bet against them winning the title for a seventh consecutive time. Their opponents, Pakistan, had other ideas, however, and won the game 1–0 to end India's 32-year winning streak in the Olympic Games.

➲ India rebounded to win hockey gold in Tokyo four years later, but Pakistan's 1960 victory removed the gloss of invincibility from their play. Since 1964, India have picked up only one more hockey gold, in Moscow in 1980.

Pakistan defeated Australia in a group match on their way to winning the gold medal at the 1960 Olympic hockey tournament, so ending more than three decades of domination for India, who lost 1–0 in the final.

171

BRILLIANT BIKILA TAKES MARATHON GOLD

ABEBE BIKILA BECOMES FIRST AFRICAN TO WIN AN OLYMPIC GOLD MEDAL

11 September 1960, Rome, Italy

When Abebe Bikila arrived in Rome for the 1960 Olympic Games he was relatively unknown and unfancied, but just two weeks earlier the Ethiopian had completed a marathon at altitude in 2h21m23s and was in the shape of his life. Before the Olympic marathon, Bikila decided he should stay with the pack until the obelisk of Axum – a monument that had been plundered from Ethiopia by Italian troops in 1937 – 1km from the finishing line. The plan worked like clockwork: Bikila pulled away from the pack and went on to win the race by 200m in a world record time of 2h15m16.2s: he had become the first African in history to win an Olympic gold medal and, what's more, now everybody knew his name.

➲ In 1964 in Tokyo, just 40 days after undergoing an appendectomy, Bikila went on to become the first person in history to defend an Olympic marathon title – and did so in a world record-breaking time of 2h12m11.2s.

The image of Abebe Bikila running and winning the 1960 Olympic marathon in his bare feet is one of the most striking in sporting history. Bikila claimed he had run the race without shoes because he "wanted the world to know that my country, Ethiopia, has always won with determination and heroism". It was a point perfectly made.

FREDRIKSSON BECOMES MOST SUCCESSFUL CANOEIST IN OLYMPIC HISTORY

GERT FREDRIKSSON WINS RECORD SIXTH OLYMPIC CANOEING GOLD MEDAL

25 August–11 September 1960, Rome, Italy

Working on the principle that if he trained harder than everyone else he would be the best, Swede Gert Fredriksson won his first Olympic gold medal in the 10,000m kayak in London in 1948, his winning margin of 30.5s being the largest in the sport's history. The next day he took 1,000m gold, this time by 6.7s (the second-largest margin of victory in an Olympic canoeing event). He defended his 1,000m K1 title in 1952 (also winning gold in the 10,000m K1) and again in 1956. Although he failed to make it four in a row in Rome in 1960, Fredriksson closed out his Olympic career in style, teaming up with Sven-Olov Sjodelius to win the 1,000m K2 race and claim a record sixth canoeing gold medal.

➲ The greatest canoeist the world has ever seen, Gert Fredriksson won seven world canoeing championship gold medals between 1948 and 1954.

Six-time gold-medal winner Gert Fredriksson is the most decorated Swedish athlete and the most successful canoeist in Olympic history.

ELVSTROM CONFIRMS STATUS AS KING OF THE WAVES

DENMARK'S PAUL ELVSTROM WINS RECORD FOURTH SUCCESSIVE SAILING GOLD MEDAL

25 August–11 September 1960, Rome, Italy

Paul Elvstrom started sailing at the age of five and went on to become the greatest sailor in Olympic history. Terrifically fit and keen to pioneer new methods – he was the first to use "hiking", the practice of leaning over the side of the boat in order to keep it level in stronger winds and get more speed – he won his first Olympic gold medal at the age of 20 in the Firefly sailing class in the 1948 Games in London. The class was modified to Finn for the 1952 Olympics and Elvstrom won again. He defended his title once more in Melbourne in 1956 and again in Rome to become one of only three men to win the same individual Olympic event four times in a row.

➲ No one has come close to matching Elvstrom's sailing record. The only other two men in history to have won the same Olympic event four times in a row are Al Oerter (discus) and Carl Lewis (long jump).

A gold medal winner in 1948, 1952, 1956 and 1960, Denmark's Paul Elvstrom went on to compete in the Olympic Games in 1968, 1972, 1984 and 1988 to become one of only four athletes to participate in eight Olympic Games. In Los Angeles 1984 he teamed up with his daughter Trine in a Tornado catamaran: they finished outside the medals, but remain the only father–daughter combination ever to compete at an Olympic Games.

BUENO REACHES DOUBLES PERFECTION

MARIA BUENO BECOMES FIRST WOMAN IN HISTORY TO WIN DOUBLES GRAND SLAM

September 1960, Forest Hills, New York, USA

Born in Brazil in 1939, Maria Bueno was the country's women's champion at age 14 and went on to win her first grand slam tournament (the women's doubles title at Wimbledon) as a 19-year-old in 1958. The following year she won her first grand slam singles title (the US Open) and ended the year as the world No. 1. And although she may have picked up the Wimbledon singles title the following year, it was her performances as a doubles player in 1960 that set tongues wagging. She won the Australian Open (with Christine Truman) and went on to collect the French, Wimbledon and US doubles titles as well (with Darlene Hard), to become the first woman in history to complete the doubles grand slam.

➲ Only three other women have repeated the feat. Martina Navratilova and Pam Shriver in 1984 and Martina Hingis – with Leslie Turner Bowrey (at the Australian Open) and Jana Novotna (French Open, Wimbledon and US Open) – did the same in 1998.

A graceful and proficient athlete, and the best female tennis player ever to have emerged from Latin America, Maria Bueno (pictured, right, with her regular doubles partner Darlene Hard) ended her career with 19 grand slam titles to her name: seven singles titles, 11 doubles – including all four in 1960 – and one mixed doubles title.

MAZEROSKI SWATS HIS WAY INTO THE HISTORY BOOKS

BILL MAZEROSKI BECOMES FIRST PLAYER TO SECURE WORLD SERIES WITH GAME-ENDING HOME RUN

13 October 1960, Forbes Field, Pittsburgh, Pennsylvania, USA

Nicknamed "The Glove", Bill Mazeroski went on to become the greatest second baseman of his day and, perhaps, of all time – he recorded a lifetime .983 fielding percentage – but it is for one particular exploit with the bat that he will always be remembered. The Pittsburgh Pirates had made it through to their first World Series for 35 years; their opponents, the New York Yankees, were appearing in their eighth Fall Classic in ten years. The series was matched at 3–3. After the Yankees had tied the game at 9–9 in the top of the ninth inning, Ralph Terry came into the game to pitch to Mazeroski in the bottom of the ninth. On a one ball and no strikes count, Maseroski slammed a long drive over the left-field wall: it was game over. Pittsburgh were the world champions and Mazeroski had become the first person in history to win the World Series with a game-ending home run.

➲ The ball was caught in the stands by 13-year-old Ted Szafranski, who swapped it back to Mazeroski for two crates of beer. It is now displayed in the Baseball Hall of Fame.

A game-winning home run in the ninth inning of Game 7 of the 1960 World Series made Bill Mazeroski, middle, a household name across the United States. Toronto's Joe Carter matched his feat in 1993, albeit in Game 6.

THE TIED TEST

AUSTRALIA AND WEST INDIES PLAY OUT FIRST INSTANCE OF TIED TEST IN CRICKET HISTORY

14 December 1960, Gabba, Brisbane, Australia

The first Test between Australia and the West Indies for the Frank Worrell trophy in 1960 came down to the wire. Australia, needing 233 for victory, found themselves on 227 for 7 with just one over (they were playing eight-ball overs) to go. Wes Hall rolled up his sleeves and summoned the energy for one final effort. First ball: Australia scramble a single. Second ball: Richie Benaud is caught behind (Australia 222 for 8). Third ball: no run. Fourth ball: single. Fifth ball: single. Sixth ball: Ian Meckiff hits the ball towards the midwicket boundary; Grout is run out attempting the third and winning run (Australia 232 for 9, the scores are tied). Seventh ball: Lindsay Kline pushes the ball to square leg. The Australians attempt the run. Joe Solomon scoops up the ball and throws down the stumps. Ian Meckiff is run out. The greatest Test match ever played has ended in the first tie in 84 years of Test cricket.

➲ There has only ever been one other instance of a tied Test in cricket history. It occurred between India and Australia in Chennai in 1986.

1960

It had taken 498 matches and 84 years of Test cricket before Australia and the West Indies completed the first-ever tied Test match, at Brisbane in 1960.

UNITAS'S STREAK FINALLY RUNS OUT OF STEAM AT 47

JOHNNY UNITAS'S RECORD-BREAKING STREAK OF THROWING AT LEAST ONE TOUCHDOWN PER GAME COMES TO AN END
11 December 1960, Los Angeles, California, USA

Born in Pittsburgh, Pennsylvania, Johnny Unitas must have thought his professional American football career was almost finished before he had even thrown a pass in anger. After an impressive four-year college career at the University of Louisville, he was a ninth-round draft choice for the Pittsburgh Steelers in 1955, but was cut from their squad before he had even played a game. He went back to playing in the semi-professional leagues – for $6 a game – and was finally spotted by the Baltimore Colts in 1956. He signed a professional contract with the Colts for $17,000 but got off to an inauspicious start: his first-ever pass in pro football was intercepted for a touchdown. However, from that moment on, he never looked back. Starting on 9 December 1956, he proceeded to throw at least one touchdown per game over the next four years: a 47-game streak that finally came to an end on 11 December 1960 against the Los Angeles Rams.

➲ Unitas's record was considered at the time to be the American Football equivalent of Joe DiMaggio's 56-game hitting streak and is the Everest of NFL records. The closest anyone has come to challenging it was the Green Bay Packers' Brett Favre, who threw touchdown passes in 37 consecutive games between 2002 and 2004.

His professional career almost failed to get off the ground, but when it did Johnny Unitas (19) soon hit his stride: starting in his rookie year, he put together a 47-game streak of throwing at least one touchdown per game.

TEENAGER MOHAMMAD KEEPS INDIA AT BAY

MUSHTAQ MOHAMMAD BECOMES YOUNGEST CENTURION IN TEST CRICKET

8–13 February 1961, Feroz Shah Kotla Stadium, Delhi, India

One of five Mohammad brothers, Mushtaq was not the most talented of the four who went on to play Test cricket but certainly became the most prolific. He made his first-class debut aged 13, scoring 87 and taking 5 for 28. Within two years he had followed older brothers Wazir and Hanif into the Pakistan Test side (at 15 years, 124 days he became the youngest to play Test cricket) and scored 18 on his debut against the West Indies. His record-breaking moment came in his sixth Test, against India in Delhi in 1961, when, during Pakistan's first innings, he scored 101 to become, at 17 years, 78 days, the youngest player in Test cricket to score a century.

➲ Mohammad broke Giff Vivian's record that had stood for 29 years (he had scored 100 for New Zealand against the West Indies aged 19 years, 121 days). The record stood until 2001, when Bangladesh's Mohammad Ashraful (17 years, 61 days) scored 114 against Sri Lanka in Colombo.

Although his exact age is not certain – birth certificates are not commonplace in Pakistan – Mushtaq Mohammad (pictured, middle, with brothers Hanif and Sadiq, left and right, respectively), who went on to play 57 Test matches for Pakistan (19 of them as captain), is credited with scoring a Test century at 17 years, 78 days (the second youngest Test centurion in cricket history).

PLAYER BREAKS US STRANGLEHOLD ON THE MASTERS

GARY PLAYER BECOMES FIRST NON-AMERICAN TO WIN THE US MASTERS

10 April 1961, Augusta National, Augusta, Georgia, USA

By 1961, the US Masters had been played on 27 previous occasions and had yielded a total of 27 American winners, but if any foreign player had the game to succeed over the Augusta National set-up it was South Africa's Gary Player. An uncompromising perfectionist, Player had collected his first major championship at the 1959 Open Championship and was fast becoming one of the biggest names in the game. He started his 1961 Masters campaign with three successive rounds in the 60s (69, 68, 69) to hold a four-shot lead going into the last 18 holes. And, despite a final-round wobble, he found himself in a greenside bunker on the 18th needing to get down in two to win the green jacket for the first time. He did just that to become the US Masters' first non-American winner.

➲ Player would have to wait another 13 years before enjoying similar success at the US Masters and a third title came in 1979. To date only nine non-Americans have won the green jacket.

It was only right that Gary Player, the man they nicknamed the "Black Knight" and the most successful international golfer of all time, should be the first non-American to don the green jacket when he won the US Masters in 1961.

INTER PAY WORLD RECORD FEE FOR SUAREZ

BARCELONA'S LUIS SUAREZ BECOMES SOCCER'S FIRST £100,000 PLAYER

June 1961, Milan, Italy

Having impressed Barcelona while playing in a game against them for Deportivo la Coruna, Luis Suarez signed for the Catalan giants in 1953 and played an integral part in their rise to becoming one of the most formidable clubs in Europe. During his nine seasons with the club he won three league titles, in 1953, 1959 and 1960, and the Fairs Cup twice in 1958 and 1960, and all but the first league title under Argentine coach Helenio Herrera. But Herrero left the club in 1960 and went to build a team at Inter Milan: he knew exactly where to find his star player and, a year after he left, persuaded Inter to offer a world record fee of £152,000 for the services of Suarez. The offer was too good to refuse for the Catalan club and Suarez had become the world's most expensive player.

➲ Suarez was an instant hit in Milan. With his perceptive passing and powerful shot, the Spanish midfielder went on to become the driving force behind the team that came to be known as "Great Inter", winning two league titles, two European Cups and two Intercontinental Cups.

Shortly after becoming the only Spanish-born player to be voted European Soccer Player of the Year, in 1960, Luis Suarez became the subject of the biggest transfer ever seen when he joined Inter Milan from Barcelona for £152,000 in June 1961.

RODRIGUEZ SENDS SHOCKWAVES THROUGH FORMULA ONE

RICARDO RODRIGUEZ BECOMES YOUNGEST-EVER F1 DRIVER TO QUALIFY ON THE FRONT ROW OF THE GRID

10 September 1960, Monza, Italy

The younger brother of Pedro, Ricardo Rodriguez used his wild, ragged, fearless driving style to wring as much speed out the car as possible. In 1960, he became the youngest driver in history to record a podium finish (second) in the Le Mans 24 Hour race in his North American Racing Team Testa Rossa car – NART were arguably Ferrari's best privateer sports outfit. His performance caught the eye of Enzo Ferrari, who invited the Mexican to appear as a guest driver for his team at the 1961 Italian GP. In qualifying Rodriguez caused a storm, putting his Ferrari second on the grid just one tenth of a second behind pole-sitter Wolfgang von Trips. At 19 years, 208 days, he remains the youngest driver in history to qualify on the front row of the grid.

➲ The race itself turned out to be one of the darkest in Formula One history. On the second lap, Wolgang von Trips and Jim Clark touched; von Trips span into the crowd, killing himself and 14 spectators. Rodriguez was forced to retire from the race on the 13th lap with fuel pump problems.

Ricardo Rodriguez looked a world champion in the making when, aged 19, he qualified his Ferrari on the front row of the grid at the 1960 Italian GP. A year later he was dead, killed in the dying moments of qualifying for the inaugural Mexican GP.

1961

MARIS DARES TO BREAK RUTH'S HOME RUN RECORD

ROGER MARIS BREAKS BABE RUTH'S 34-YEAR SINGLE-SEASON HOME RUN RECORD

1 October 1961, Yankee Stadium, New York, USA

Babe Ruth's legend had grown since his death in 1948 and his home run record was deemed unbeatable. When Mickey Mantle briefly threatened it in 1956 (with 52) even the New York press had been pro-Ruth. But in 1961, when the American League expanded from eight teams to ten, the pitching diluted and the home runs started to flow. Ruth's record was under threat. Leading the race were Mantle and his Yankee team-mate Roger Maris. The press had a field day. Mantle was the favourite, Maris the outsider. But then Mantle was felled by a leg injury which left Maris as the sole runner in the race. Then came another hurdle. Baseball commissioner Ford Frick, a close friend of Ruth's, announced that, because the season was eight games longer, the record had to be broken in 154 games (as Ruth had done). Maris failed in that quest, but hit his 61st home run of the season in the Yankees' final game. Despite Frick's wishes, Maris's mark stood as a record. Babe's home run mark had finally been toppled and, for the most part, a country mourned.

➲ Maris was deeply affected by the experience. Legend has it that such was the stress, Maris's hair often fell out in large chunks during the course of his record-breaking season. The record stood until 1998, when Mark McGwire hit 70 home runs.

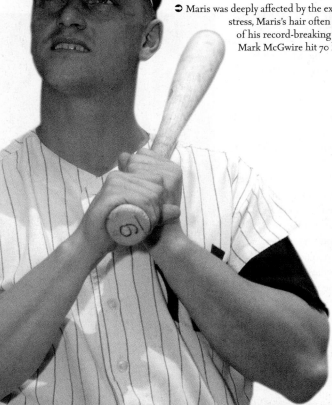

Dubbed the outsider by the pro-Ruth New York press, Roger Maris hit his 61st home run in the final game of the 1961 season to take his place in the record books, but lived the rest of his life (he died in 1985) as one of the most unwanted record-breakers in history.

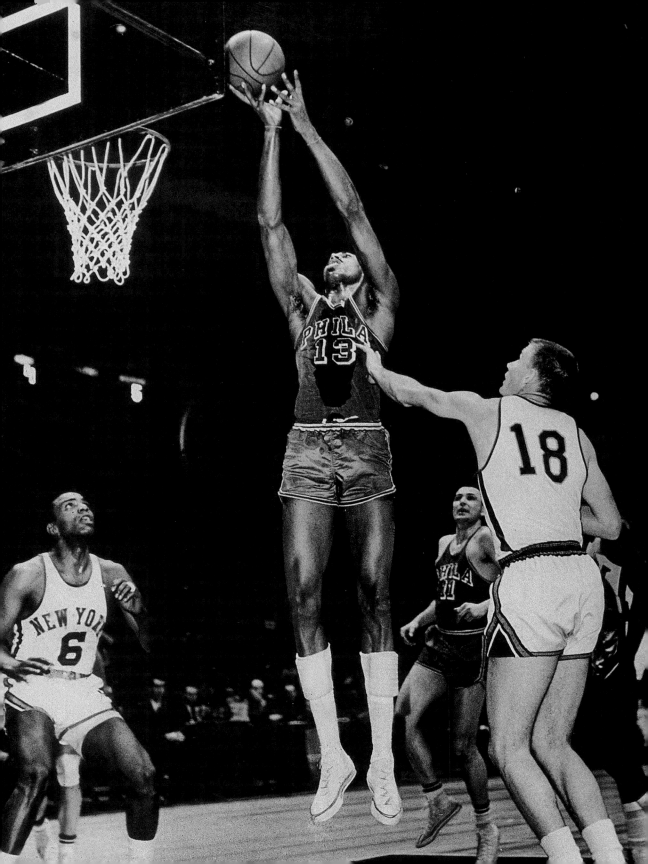

THE BIG DIPPER HITS THE PEAK OF HIS POWERS

WILT CHAMBERLAIN BECOMES ONLY PERSON IN NBA HISTORY TO SCORE 100 POINTS IN A GAME

2 March 1962, Hershey, Pennsylvania, USA

Wilt Chamberlain was used to fighting. His enormous height attracted plenty of attention, mostly of the unwanted kind, but, despite catcalls from the crowd and suffering foul after foul from his opponents, the 7ft 1in centre backed up his stellar amateur career with the most impressive rookie season in NBA history. Playing for the Philadelphia Warriors in 1959–60 he averaged 37.6 points per game and 27 rebounds (both all-time NBA records) and became one of only two players in history to collect both the MVP and Rookie of the Season awards in the same year. He beat his own record a year later, but the best was still to come. In the 1961–62 season he became the first player in NBA history to score more than 4,000 points, producing unbelievable performances, including one that still stands as the greatest in basketball history. On 2 March 1962, playing for the Warriors against the New York Knicks, he became the first and only player in NBA history to score 100 points in a game. Chamberlain connected on 36 of 63 field goal attempts – the 3-point shot was introduced many years later – but the big surprise was Wilt's accuracy from the free-throw line on this night. Normally a liability from the charity stripe – his career average was a paltry .511 – he sank 28 of 32 attempts (.875) to bring up the 100 points.

➲ The 316 points – Philadelphia won 169–147 – scored on 2 March 1962 in the game between the Warriors and the New York Knicks, played in Hershey, Pennsylvania, broke the record for the highest aggregate score in NBA history. Nobody has come close to Chamberlain's mark of 4,029 regular season points in 1961–62 (only one other player in history has passed the 3,000 mark, Michael Jordan in 1986–87).

Nicknamed the "Big Dipper", because he always had to dip his head when he entered the room, Wilt Chamberlain used his 7ft 1in frame to great effect on 2 March 1962. With the 4,124-strong crowd screaming "Give the ball to Wilt", he sank shot after shot to become the first player in NBA history to score 100 points in a game.

ROBERTSON MAKES HIS MARK IN THE NBA

OSCAR ROBERTSON FIRST IN NBA HISTORY TO AVERAGE A TRIPLE-DOUBLE OVER THE COURSE OF A SEASON

20 March 1962, Cincinnati, Ohio, USA

A star high-school player, Oscar Robertson went to the University of Cincinnati and put together one of the most impressive college careers in history (only Pete Maravich scored more points during his college career than the "Big O"). After leading the US team to gold in the 1960 Olympic Games, he signed professional terms with the Cincinnati Royals in 1960 and went on to win Rookie of the Year honours at the end of his first season. The following season, 1961–62, he became the only player in history to average a triple-double – ten or more in any three of the following categories: points, rebounds, assists, steals or blocked shots – over the course of an entire season (30.8 points, 12.5 rebounds, 11.4 points).

➲ Oscar Roberston also leads the way in the career triple-double category. During the course of his 14-year career he achieved the feat 181 times. The next best in history is Magic Johnson's 138.

With an arsenal of shots and an array of moves the likes of Magic Johnson and Michael Jordan would go on to emulate, Oscar Roberston defined the role of the modern guard: he is the only player in history to average the triple-double over the course of an entire NBA season.

DUBY AND *MISS US I* BREAK WORLD WATER SPEED RECORD

ROY DUBY BECOMES FIRST TO BREAK 200MPH BARRIER IN PROPELLER-DRIVEN CRAFT

17 April 1962, Guntersville Lake, Alabama, USA

Donald Campbell may have passed the 200mph mark in his jet-propelled hydroplane on Ullswater in 1955, but the same barrier was proving somewhat harder to attain for propeller-driven craft: in simple terms, they simply could not stand up to the strain of such speed. That all changed on 17 April 1962. *Miss US I* – powered by a Rolls-Royce-Packard Merlin engine and guided by Roy Duby – powered its way to 204mph on its first run of three across the waters of Lake Guntersville, Alabama. Duby believed he had reached 215mph on the second run, but the electric timing scanner broke and the speed was not recorded. On the third run he got to 196.33mph: the average speed of 200.419mph set a new mark for the world water speed record for propeller-driven craft.

Roy Duby's 1962 world water speed record remained unbroken for 38 years: it became the longest-standing major speed record in motorsports history.

➲ Duby's mark would stand as a record for 38 years, until Russ Wicks (205.494mph) broke it on Lake Washington on 16 June 2000.

VAVA ON THE MARK YET AGAIN AS BRAZIL RETAIN CROWN

VAVA BECOMES FIRST PLAYER TO SCORE IN TWO CONSECUTIVE WORLD CUP FINALS

17 June 1962, Estadio Nacional, Santiago, Chile

Two goals each for teenage sensation Pele and his strike partner Vava (and another goal from Zagallo) had helped Brazil win the World Cup for the first time in 1958, and the kings of soccer travelled to Chile in 1962 full of confidence about retaining their crown. They won their group, but at a price: Pele suffered a tournament-ending injury in the second game. But still the goals kept coming: Brazil beat England (3–1) and Chile (4–2) to take their place in the final, against Czechoslovakia, where goals from Amarildo (Pele's replacement), Zito and Vava helped them to a 3–1 win. In the process, Vava became the first player in history to score in two consecutive World Cup finals.

➲ Only three other players in history have scored in two separate World Cup finals: Pele (1958 and 1970), Paul Breitner (1974 and 1982) and Zinedine Zidane (1998 and 2006).

One of the greatest strikers Brazil has ever produced, Vava helped his side overcome the early loss of Pele to injury to win the World Cup for a second consecutive time, in Chile in 1962.

185

As famous today for his malapropisms, Yogi Berra had a stellar baseball career that should not be underestimated. He holds or held many World Series records: most games (75), at-bats (259), hits (71), doubles (10), singles (49), games caught (63) and catcher putouts (457).

EVER-PRESENT BERRA ENJOYS TENTH FALL CLASSIC SUCCESS

YOGI BERRA BECOMES ONLY PLAYER IN HISTORY TO COLLECT TEN WORLD SERIES WINNERS' RINGS

16 October 1962, Candlestick Park, San Francisco, California, USA

Yogi Berra was an efficient batter who could hit for power and for average and who became one of the most feared clutch hitters of his day. He was also a truly outstanding catcher, who went on to forge a 19-year career with a New York Yankees franchise which, once again, dominated the baseball world. World Series success followed World Series success, five between 1947 and 1953, and a sixth followed after Berra's Game 7-winning performance in 1956, when he hit two home runs and drove in four runs. The Yankees steamroller rumbled on: they enjoyed further Fall Classic wins in 1958 and 1961 and, the following year, Berra, aged 37, picked up his record tenth winners' ring.

➲ In 1963, Berra's last season with the New York franchise, the Los Angeles Dodgers swept the Yankees in four games in the World Series. Berra would never taste the atmosphere of the Fall Classic again.

THE OLD MONGOOSE GOES OUT WITH A BANG

ARCHIE MOORE COMPLETES LAST OF RECORD 145 CAREER KNOCKOUTS

15 March 1963, Phoenix, Arizona, USA

Clever and crafty in the ring, Archie Moore started his professional boxing career at the age of 25 in 1938 as a middleweight, slowly working his way up the world rankings before announcing his retirement in 1941. He was back the following year, moved up to light-middleweight and carried on fighting. His first shot at the world title came in 1952: he beat Joey Maxim on points and made nine title defences before being stripped of the belt. It mattered not; Moore simply stepped up a weight and carried on fighting, until March 1963 when, aged 50, he flattened Mike Dibiase in the third round. The following year he announced his retirement. His fight record: 221 fights, 194 wins (a record 145 of them by knockout).

➲ Archie Moore is the only fighter to have fought both Rocky Marciano and Muhammad Ali. The Marciano fight came in 1955, with Moore losing in the ninth. His fight against Ali, seven years later, also ended in a knockout defeat, this time in the fourth round.

Archie Moore enjoyed an incredible 27-year career, fighting a mammoth 221 bouts and winning a record 145 of them by knockout. Above, left, he takes on Yolande Pompey for the world light-heavyweight title at the Harringay Arena, London. Moore won on a technical knockout in the tenth of 15 rounds.

KIWI CHARLES WINS OPEN TO MAKE HISTORY

BOB CHARLES BECOMES FIRST LEFT-HANDED GOLFER TO WIN A MAJOR TOURNAMENT

13 July 1963, Royal Lytham & St Anne's, Lancashire, England

In the 224 major tournaments played since 1860 there had never been a left-handed winner, but after 72 holes of the 92nd Open Championship at Royal Lytham & St Anne's in 1963, there remained a distinct possibility that that golfing anomaly might be addressed. Bob Charles, the tall, softly spoken, smooth-swinging left-hander from New Zealand with a deadeye putter, had tied with ex-marine Phil Rodgers on 277 strokes and faced a 36-hole playoff the following day for the chance to become a history-maker. The force was with the Kiwi, as rounds of 69 and 71 were enough to secure an eight-shot win and a place in the history books.

⮑ It took 40 years before another left-hander collected a major tournament victory: Mike Weir won the US Masters in 2003. The following year Phil Mickelson made it a club of three when he became the second left-hander to win the Masters in two years (Mickelson won the Masters again in 2006 and the US PGA Championship in 2005).

Bob Charles collected a career total of six PGA Tour victories: none was more memorable than his 1963 Open Championship win, when he became the first left-hander in 103 years of major tournament golf to record a victory.

A speedster since his early teens – he won his first drag car race at the age of 16 – Craig Breedlove powered *Spirit of America* into the history books on 5 September 1963 when he became the first man to break the 400mph barrier, over the Bonneville Salt Flats in Utah.

BREEDLOVE BRINGS WORLD LAND SPEED RECORD BACK TO STATES

CRAIG BREEDLOVE AND *SPIRIT OF AMERICA* BECOME FIRST TO BREAK 400MPH (643.72KM/H) BARRIER

5 September 1963, Bonneville Salt Flats, Utah, USA

Twenty-eight years had passed since Donald Campbell became the first to guide an internal-combustion-engine car past the 300mph (482.79km/h) barrier and although the location may have been the same – the Bonneville Salt Flats in Utah was the place to attempt world land speed records – the rules for the latest attempt on the world land speed record were different. On 5 September 1963, 26-year-old Craig Breedlove unveiled Spirit of America, his challenger for the record. It was space-aged and beautiful: three-wheeled, streamlined and powered by a surplus J-47 jet engine out of a US Navy F-4 Phantom. Breedlove hit a top speed of 408.312mph (657.114km/h) that day – the first to pass the 400mph (643.72km/h) barrier – to bring the world land speed record back to the United States for the first time since 1929.

⮑ Breedlove's record was broken the following year by compatriot Tom Green. Green's record fell two days later to Art Arfons, who held the title of "fastest man on earth" for a total of one week, before Breedlove returned on 15 October 1964 to become the first person to break the 500mph barrier. A year later, on 15 November 1965, he became the first to pass the 600mph barrier as well.

PALMER FIRST TO POCKET IN EXCESS OF $100,000

ARNOLD PALMER BECOMES FIRST GOLFER TO WIN MORE THAN $100,000 IN A SINGLE SEASON

7 October 1963, Philadelphia, Pennsylvania, USA

As the cameras started to broadcast the game around the United States, golf could not have chosen its first television star more wisely. From a humble background (his father was a club professional), Arnold Palmer's affable, down-to-earth personality, coupled with his grip-it-and-rip-it, daredevil approach to the game, brought him a legion of fans – they became known as "Arnie's Army" – and brought golf out of the exclusive country clubs and into the mainstream of American consciousness. And the money finally started to flow into the game. So it was entirely appropriate when, in 1963, seven tournament wins were enough to see Arnold Palmer become the first player in PGA Tour history to earn more than $100,000 in a single season's winnings ($128,230).

➲ In 1967, Palmer became the first golfer to pass $1 million in career earnings. The current record for most money earned in a single season is $10,905,166, by Vijay Singh in 2004.

Between 1960 and 1963 Arnold Palmer won 29 PGA Tour events; in the latter of those years he became the first golfer in history to pass the $100,000 mark in single-season earnings.

WRIGHT SWINGS HER WAY INTO THE RECORD BOOKS

MICKEY WRIGHT WINS RECORD 13 LPGA TOURNAMENTS DURING COURSE OF THE SEASON

13 October 1963, Stardust Country Club, Las Vegas, Nevada, USA

No less an authority than Ben Hogan thought Mickey Wright's swing the finest he had ever seen in the game of golf, and the San Diego-born Wright used it to great effect. She won her first tournament in 1956 and could not stop winning. Victory in the 1962 Western Open saw her become the only woman in history to hold all four major titles simultaneously (following victories at the US Women's Open, the Titleholders' Championship and the LPGA Championships in 1962). She took the Western Open in 1963 as well and, when she won the LPGA Championships for the second time in three years, became the only woman in history to win 13 LPGA events in a season.

➲ Only four other golfers in history have recorded ten or more LPGA tournament victories in a single season: Carol Mann (ten in 1958), Betsy Rawls (ten in 1959), Kathy Whitworth (ten in 1968) and Annika Sorentsam (11 in 2002).

Arguably the greatest golfer ever to grace the women's game, Mickey Wright notched up 82 career titles – only Kathy Whitworth (88) has more – with 13 of her wins, including two of her total of 13 major championship wins, coming during her stellar 1963 season.

BENAUD FIRST TO REACH ALL-ROUNDER MILESTONE

RICHIE BENAUD BECOMES FIRST IN TEST HISTORY TO SCORE 2,000 RUNS AND TAKE 200 WICKETS

6 December 1963, Woolloongabba, Brisbane, Queensland, Australia

Richie Benaud's masterful insights into the game of cricket from behind the microphone come from his not inconsiderable exploits on the field of play. He made a slow start to his Test career (his debut came in 1952), but within a few years had become an integral part of the side. A bowling all-rounder – he was one of the greatest leg-spinners to have played the game and a hard-hitting lower-order batsman – he took his 200th Test wicket against South Africa in 1958 and made history when, against the same opponents at Brisbane in December 1963, he scored his 2,000th Test run during his first-innings knock of 43. He became the first in history to complete the 2,000-run/200-wicket double.

➲ Benaud took 60 Test matches to achieve the feat and only six players have reached the milestone in fewer games: Ian Botham (42), Kapil Dev (50), Imran Khan (50), Richard Hadlee (54), Shaun Pollock (56) and Chris Cairns (58).

A master leg-spinner and a hard-hitting lower-order batsman, Richie Benaud played a huge part in Australia's rise back to the top of the world game in the 1960s following their slump in the middle of the 1950s. He was the first player in Test history to score 2,000 runs and take 200 wickets.

CLASSY CLARK EASES TO FIRST WORLD TITLE

JIM CLARK BECOMES YOUNGEST DRIVER TO WIN FORMULA ONE WORLD CHAMPIONSHIP

28 December 1963, East London, South Africa

Jim Clark may only have finished second in his Lotus Elite on Boxing Day 1958, but he had impressed race-winner Colin Chapman (Lotus's owner) so much that, within two years, the young Scot was making his debut for the Lotus F1 team, at the 1960 Dutch GP. He retired that day and went on to finish tenth in the end-of-season standings. He improved to eighth the following season and, but for mechanical failure in the final race of the season, would have won the World Championship. He suffered no such ill-luck the following year, winning seven of the season's ten races to become, at 27 years 188 days, the youngest driver to win the Formula One World Championship.

➲ Clark would remain Formula One's youngest world champion until Emerson Fittipaldi won the title in 1972, aged 25 years, 273 days.

Jim Clark won the first of his two World Championships in 1963, winning seven of the season's ten races to become the sport's youngest world champion. His second title came in 1965.

SENSATIONAL BROWN'S SIGNATURE YEAR

JIM BROWN BECOMES FIRST RUNNING BACK IN NFL HISTORY TO LEAD LEAGUE IN ALL SEVEN RUSHING CATEGORIES

15 December 1963, DC Stadium, Washington, USA

Jim Brown's job was to run and no running back in NFL history has done it better. His supreme physicality – he was 6ft 2in and weighed 230lb – saw him take to NFL action with the Cleveland Browns like a duck to water, and when he came to the end of his sensational but all-too-short nine-year career he held every rushing record known to man. In a career littered with body-scattering runs, his signature year came in 1963, when he led the league in all seven rushing categories, including his astonishing average of 6.4 yards per rush (2.3 yards better than the NFL average – both of which are all-time records) and the record for single-season rushing yards (1,863, broken by O.J. Simpson in 1973 with 2,003).

➲ Having dominated the position like no other running back in NFL history, Jim Brown shocked the world when he announced his retirement on 4 June 1966, aged 29, at the peak of his powers. Nearly all of his records have since gone on to be broken, but had he enjoyed a lengthier career...

Playing the game without emotion, just raw power and talent, Jim Brown heads the list of most when asked to name the greatest running back in NFL history: in 1963 he led every rushing category in the league and set two records that last to this day.

BLACK PANTHER GRABS THE GOLDEN BALL

LEV YASHIN BECOMES ONLY GOALKEEPER IN HISTORY TO WIN EUROPEAN SOCCER PLAYER OF THE YEAR AWARD

December 1963, Paris, France

Lev Yashin joined Dynamo Moscow in 1949 and stayed there for 22 years. Tall, athletic and unflinchingly courageous, he made his debut for the USSR in 1954 and helped them to Olympic success in Melbourne in 1956 and to European Championship glory four years later. His reputation as the best keeper in world soccer was confirmed when he played for the Rest of the World against England in the 1963 FA Centenary game: the Wembley crowd were left stunned as the Russian pulled off stunning save after stunning save. *France Football* magazine had seen enough: at the end of the year they named him European Soccer Player of the Year, the only goalkeeper in history to receive the honour.

➲ The International Federation of Football History and Statistics voted Lev Yashin the best goalkeeper of the 20th century.

His all-black attire earned Lev Yashin the nickname "Black Panther"; a string of fine performances during 1963 earned him the European Soccer Player of the Year award, the only goalkeeper in history to receive the honour.

SKOBLIKOVA RACES TO SPEED SKATING GLORY

LIDIA SKOBLIKOVA BECOMES FIRST WINTER OLYMPIAN TO WIN FOUR GOLD MEDALS AT SINGLE GAMES

29 January–9 February 1964, Innsbruck, Austria

In her first Olympics, in 1960, Russian speed skater Lidia Skoblikova had taken gold in the 1,500m and the 3,000m. Within three years she was the dominant force in the sport, winning all four distances she contested in the 1963 world championships, and travelled to the 1964 Winter Olympics looking to repeat the feat. She silenced critics who thought she might be vulnerable in the opening 500m event by leading a Russian sweep of the medals; the next day she took the 1,500m by 2.5s – the largest winning margin in the event's history – and when she followed that up with successes in the 1,000m and 3,000m, she became the first Winter Olympian in history to win four gold medals at a single Games.

➲ Eric Heiden broke Skoblikova's record in the 1980 Winter Olympic Games at Lake Placid, when the American collected five speed skating gold medals.

The most successful female speed skater of all time, Russia's Lidia Skoblikova won two gold medals at the 1960 Winter Olympics in Squaw Valley, USA, and an astonishing four in Innsbruck, Austria, in 1964. Her attempts at adding to her medal haul in 1968, however, came to nought.

GOOD HORSE SENSE

NORTHERN DANCER WINS KENTUCKY DERBY IN A RECORD-SETTING TWO MINUTES FLAT

2 May 1964, Kentucky, USA

As a colt, Northern Dancer wasn't expected to be much: when his breeder, millionaire EP Taylor, put him up for sale along with several other yearlings, he was considered too small and stocky to make a good racer, especially for the $25,000 price. Unsold, Northern Dancer returned to the farm's racing stable, where he won seven and came in second in two of nine races. The rest of Northern Dancer's career would look much the same: he ultimately won 14 of the 18 races he started, including an amazing record-breaker at the 1964 Kentucky Derby, where he clocked in at 2:00:00, beating the second-place Hill Rise by a neck. That was Northern Dancer's best and final year. He won the Flamingo Stakes, Preakness Stakes, Florida Derby, Blue Grass Stakes and Queen's Plate before a bowed tendon retired him from racing. Northern Dancer's Kentucky Derby record was broken in 1973 by Secretariat, who crossed the finish at 1:59:40.

Northern Dancer, described by American horse-racing journalist Joe Hirsch as "a pugnacious little horse," single-handedly established Canada as a force to be reckoned with on the international thoroughbred racing and breeding scene.

➲ Northern Dancer went on to become the 20th century's sire of sires. He has sired over 140 stakes winners, including British triple-crown winner Nijinsky. There are currently more winners of the Breeder's Cup in Northern Dancer's line than that of any other sire.

ANQUETIL AT IT AGAIN TO RECORD HISTORIC FIFTH TOUR WIN

JACQUES ANQUETIL BECOMES FIRST PERSON IN HISTORY TO WIN THE TOUR DE FRANCE FIVE TIMES

14 July 1964, Paris, France

A year after breaking Fausto Coppi's legendary mark for cycling's world hour record, Jacques Anquetil became a national hero when, at his first attempt, he won the 1957 Tour de France. But the Rouen-born son of a peasant farmer failed to live up to his sensational start in the professional ranks. Three moderate performances on the Tour followed before a return to form in 1961 saw the Frenchman claim his second overall title. Anquetil had remembered how to win cycling's toughest race and for the next three years refused to forget. He defended his crown in 1962 – picking up two stage wins – and became the first in history to win the Tour four times with a third successive victory in 1963. The following year he held off the attentions of up-and-coming compatriot Raymond Poulidor to collect an historic fifth win.

➲ Three riders have equalled Anquetil's feat of winning the Tour de France five times – Eddy Merckx, Bernard Hinault and Miguel Indurain – but the Frenchman's haul would stand as a record until 2004, when Lance Armstrong notched up his sixth successive victory in the world's greatest cycling race (the Texan would go on to add a seventh win in 2005).

Famous for the manner in which he prepared for races – he would stay up all night drinking – Jacques Anquetil put any physical excesses to one side once he was in the saddle. One of the most successful cyclists in history, he was the first to win the Tour de France five times and the first to win all three of the Grand Tours: the Tour de France (1957, 1961–64), the Giro d'Italia (1960 and 1964) and the Vuelta a Espana (1963).

FIERY FRED BECOMES FIRST MEMBER OF 300 CLUB

FRED TRUEMAN BECOMES FIRST BOWLER IN HISTORY TO TAKE 300 TEST WICKETS

15 August 1964, The Oval, London, England

Five years after making one of the most impressive debuts in the history of Test cricket in 1952, Fred Trueman had earned only six more caps. The greatest fast bowler England had ever produced did not fit in: enormously talented and, with his classical action, genuinely quick, he was also sharp-tongued and insubordinate – and as a result, of the 118 Tests he could have played for England, he made only 67 appearances. But when he was selected, he excelled to such an extent that in his 65th Test, against Australia at The Oval in 1964, he dismissed Neil Hawke to become the first bowler in history to take 300 Test wickets.

➲ After the close of play, Trueman was asked whether he thought the record would ever be broken. Ever the showman, he replied: "I don't know, but whoever does it will be bloody tired."

An intimidating presence on the field (the legendary cricket writer and broadcaster John Arlott once described his bowling as "like a storm wave breaking on the beach"), Fiery Fred Trueman overcame problems with the England selection committee to take a record 307 Test wickets. The record would stand for 12 years.

MAN OF IRON STRIKES GOLD FOR RECORD SIXTH TIME

GYMNAST BORIS SHAKHLIN WINS RECORD SIXTH INDIVIDUAL OLYMPIC GOLD MEDAL
10–24 October 1964, Tokyo, Japan

Born in Siberia in 1932, Boris Shakhlin's steely determination and calm consistency earned him the nickname "Man of Iron" and led to him becoming one of the most decorated athletes in gymnastics history. Unusually tall for a gymnast – which helped him on the horizontal bars but hindered him in floor exercises – he won his first gold on the pommel horse at the 1956 Olympics. Four years later he enjoyed quadruple gold success – in all-round, vault, pommel horse and parallel bars. Victory in the horizontal bars in Tokyo in 1964 meant the Russian, with six gold medals to his name, had become the most decorated male gymnast in Olympic history.

➲ No man has ever bettered Shakhlin's haul of individual Olympic gold gymnastics medals, but his feat has been beaten by a woman: Vera Caslavska won her seventh individual medal at the 1968 Olympic Games in Mexico City.

A winner of 13 Olympic medals (seven gold, four silver and two bronze), Russia's Boris Shakhlin is tied for third in the all-time list of Olympic medal-winners. He still holds the record for the most individual gold medals ever won by a male gymnast.

FRASER COMPLETES HAT-TRICK TO MAKE SWIMMING HISTORY

DAWN FRASER BECOMES FIRST WOMAN TO WIN THREE GOLDS IN SAME EVENT IN THREE CONSECUTIVE OLYMPICS

10–24 October 1964, Tokyo, Japan

An asthmatic who started swimming to aid her breathing, Dawn Fraser began swimming seriously at the age of 16 and went on to become one of the most iconic figures in Australian sports history, as much for her larrikin behaviour out of the pool as for her prodigious talent in it. She won her first Olympic gold at the 1956 Olympic Games in Melbourne, breaking both the world and Olympic records to win the 100m freestyle. She repeated her success in Rome four years later and when she completed a hat-trick of 100m freestyle wins in Tokyo in 1964, she became the first woman swimmer in history to win gold in the same event at three consecutive Olympic Games.

⊃ Hungary's Kristina Egerszegi equalled Dawn Fraser's feat of winning the same swimming event at three consecutive Olympic Games when she won the 200m backstroke in 1992, 1996 and 2000.

Dawn Fraser's antics at the start of the 1964 Olympic Games caused a sensation. Her relationship with the Australian Swimming Union hit the point of no return when she turned up uninvited at the opening ceremony wearing an old swim suit – thus upsetting the sponsors. She was later accused (falsely) of having climbed a flagpole at Emperor Hirohito's palace and stealing the Olympic flag. In 1965, a year after winning 100m freestyle gold for the third successive Olympics, the ASU banned her for ten years. The ban was lifted four years later but, by then, Fraser's career was already over.

LATYNINA SECURES LEGEND WITH 18TH OLYMPIC MEDAL

LARISSA LATYNINA WINS 18TH MEDAL TO BECOME MOST DECORATED ATHLETE IN OLYMPIC HISTORY

10–24 October 1964, Tokyo, Japan

Russia's Larissa Latynina debuted aged 21 in the 1956 Olympics in Melbourne: her duel with Hungary's Agnes Keleti was one of the highlights of the Games and both emerged with four gold medals. Latynina defended her all-round and floor exercise titles four years later and added a second successive team gold to her growing tally of medals. The Russian bowed out of Olympic competition in style in Tokyo in 1964, winning a third successive floor title and being part of the Russian line-up that completed a hat-trick of team titles. Latynina's Olympic career was over, but she had a record 18 medals to her name (nine gold, five silver and four bronze).

⊃ Larissa Latynina shares or holds numerous other records. She is one of only four athletes to have won nine gold medals (the others being Paavo Nurmi, Mark Spitz and Carl Lewis). She is the only athlete to have won 14 medals in individual Olympic events and one of only three women to have won the same individual event at three consecutive Games (the others being swimmers Dawn Fraser and Kristina Egerszegi).

Russian gymnast Larissa Latynina's Olympic record is better than that of any other athlete in history. She attended three Olympic Games and collected a record haul of 18 medals.

TWO-WHEEL CHAMPION SURTEES BECOMES F1 KING

JOHN SURTEES FIRST MAN TO BECOME WORLD CHAMPION ON TWO WHEELS AND FOUR

25 October 1964, Autodromo Hermanos Rodriguez, Mexico City, Mexico

A multiple world champion on two wheels and in need of a new challenge, John Surtees switched to Formula One in 1960 and, four years later, won the drivers' championship.

In 1960, at the age of 26, John Surtees, having won all there was to win on two wheels – the 500cc world championship in 1956, 1958, 1959 and 1960, the 350cc title between 1958 and 1960 and the first three-time winner of the Senior Isle of Man TT (1958–60) – decided to switch to Formula One. He had to wait until 1963 – and a move to Ferrari – before he could celebrate his first win (at the German GP). Two more wins in 1964 – at the German and Italian Grands Prix – coupled with four other podium finishes (including the season-ending Mexican GP) were enough to see him become the first and only man in history to be crowned world champion on both two wheels and four.

➲ 1964 proved John Surtees's best season in Formula One: he made only one more serious assault on the title, in 1966, where he won two races to finish second in the championship standings.

D'ORIOLA MAKES HISTORY WITH SECOND GOLD

PIERRE JONQUERES D'ORIOLA BECOMES ONLY RIDER IN HISTORY TO WIN TWO SHOWJUMPING GOLD MEDALS

24 August 1964, Tokyo, Japan

Born in the western Pyrenees in the south of France in 1920, Pierre Jonqueres d'Oriola started riding at the age of 12. A plain-speaking man who had numerous run-ins with the authorities, he won his first major event in 1946, the Zurich Grand Prix. He earned selection for the French team for the 1952 Olympic Games in Helsinki and rode Ali Baba to first place in the individual showjumping event. Twelve years later, now 44 years of age, he appeared in the 1964 Olympics in Tokyo, the first Olympiad to be held in a non-Western nation, and became the only man in history to win two individual showjumping gold medals when he rode Lutteur B to victory on the final day of the games.

➲ D'Oriola added to his medal haul in the 1964 Olympics with a silver medal in the team showjumping competition; something both he and the French team would repeat at the 1968 Olympic Games in Mexico City.

Outspoken, but a master in the art of horsemanship, Pierre Jonqueres d'Oriola (middle) is the only man in history to have won two gold medals in the Olympic individual showjumping competition.

SIMPSON LEADS FROM THE FRONT IN RECORD-BREAKING STYLE

BOBBY SIMPSON BREAKS GARFIELD SOBERS'S RECORD FOR MOST TEST RUNS IN A CALENDAR YEAR

8 December 1964, MCG, Melbourne, Victoria, Australia

Having played in 30 Test matches for Australia (seven of them as captain), opening batsman Bobby Simpson still had not reached three figures for his country. When he finally reached the milestone, he did so in style, hitting a patient 311 against England at Old Trafford in 1964 to record the fifth-highest score seen in Test cricket. Technically correct and immensely dedicated, Simpson continued to accrue runs throughout the year, including two centuries against Pakistan in Karachi (150 and 115), and by the time he had scored 48 runs in the match against the same opponents in the final Test of the year, he had scored a record 1,381 runs, to beat Garfield Sobers's 1958 mark by 82 runs.

➲ Bobby Simpson's record for most Test runs in a calendar year stood for 12 years until 1976, when a young Viv Richards swashbuckled his way onto the international cricket scene with a staggering 1,710 runs.

Bobby Simpson made his debut for Australia in 1957 as a leg-spinner and a useful lower-order batsman. After a spell out of the side he transformed himself into an opening batsman, forming one of the greatest opening partnerships in Test history with Bill Lawrie and excelling in his own right: in 1964, he set a record for the most Test runs scored in a calendar year (1,381).

SPEEDSTER McKENZIE MARCHES TO NEW RECORD

GRAHAM McKENZIE BREAKS MAURICE TATE'S RECORD FOR MOST TEST WICKETS IN A CALENDAR YEAR

8 December 1964, MCG, Melbourne, Victoria, Australia

Graham McKenzie made his debut for Australia as a 19-year-old, against England at Lord's, appearing as a stand-in for the injured Richie Benaud. And the Western Australian tearaway bowler made quite an impression, taking the last three England wickets to fall in 12 balls as Australia won by five wickets. Soon McKenzie became an integral part of the Australian side, and the nemesis of batsmen around the globe. His best spell came between 11 December 1963 and 8 December 1964: in the 15 Tests he played in that period he took 73 wickets (including four five-wicket hauls) – a record number of Test wickets in a calendar year.

➲ McKenzie's total of 73 wickets in a calendar year stood as a Test record until 1979, when India's Kapil Dev took 74 wickets in 17 Tests matches. His haul is still the 13th best in the history of Test cricket.

During Graham McKenzie's record-breaking season in 1964, he became the youngest player in history, aged 23, to reach the 100-Test-wicket landmark.

Jim Clark powered his way to victory in the 1965 season-opening South African GP and claimed a record sixth career Grand Chelem in the process: numbers seven and eight would follow at that year's French and German Grands Prix.

CLARK LAYS DOWN MARKER TO RIVALS IN SEASON-OPENER

JIM CLARK BREAKS ALBERTO ASCARI'S RECORD FOR MOST GRAND CHELEMS IN FORMULA ONE

1 January 1965, Prince George Circuit, East London, South Africa

Having been denied a second successive Formula One driver title by an oil leak in the closing stages of the 1964 Mexican Grand Prix, Jim Clark and Lotus arrived at the Prince George Circuit in East London on New Year's Day 1965 for the season-opening South African GP with a point to prove. And how the Scot made it, taking the chequered flag some 26s ahead of defending world champion John Surtees. In doing so he had produced Formula One perfection, the "Grand Chelem" – leading the entire race from pole position and setting the fastest lap – for the sixth time in his career (breaking Alberto Ascari's all-time record). The Scot would claim a further five race victories that season – including the final two Grand Chelems of his career – en route to a second world title.

➲ The Grand Chelem is a rare feat in Formula One. The list of drivers who have achieved two or more in their career proves this is a true mark of Formula One greatness. Behind Jim Clark's eight Grand Chelems are: Alberto Ascari and Michael Schumacher with five; Jackie Stewart, Ayrton Senna and Nigel Mansell (four); Nelson Piquet (three); Juan Manuel Fangio, Jack Brabham and Mika Hakkinen (two).

SLAMMIN' SAM COLLECTS RECORD

SAM SNEAD BECOMES OLDEST-EVER WINNER OF A US PGA TOUR EVENT

4 April 1965, Greensboro, North Carolina, USA

Sam Snead burst onto the PGA Tour in 1937, driving enormous distances down fairways – earning him the nickname "Slammin' Sam" – with one of the most graceful and smooth swings ever seen in golf and picking up five wins in his rookie year. Winning was something that seemed to come easy to the Virginia native: he collected an all-time record 82 wins on the PGA Tour during his career, including seven major tournaments – although to both his and an entire nation's despair he never hoisted the US Open trophy, finishing runner-up on four occasions. The last of his record haul of wins came when he won the Greater Greensboro Open in 1965: at 52 years, ten months and eight days he became the oldest-ever winner in the history of the US PGA Tour.

➲ Snead's success in the 1965 Greater Greensboro Open completed his eighth victory in the competition: no other golfer in history has won a single tournament on more occasions.

Snead set numerous PGA Tour records. He won the most events, was the oldest-ever winner of a tournament and, in the 1979 Quad City Open, at the age of 67, became the first person in PGA Tour history to shoot a number lower than his age: he went round in 66.

KING CLARK AT THE PEAK OF HIS POWERS

JIM CLARK BECOMES FIRST DRIVER IN HISTORY TO WIN INDY 500 AND F1 WORLD CHAMPIONSHIP IN SAME YEAR

1 August 1965, Nurburgring, Germany

Fresh off his record-breaking success at the 1965 South African Grand Prix, Jim Clark took a break from the Formula One schedule to make a third attempt on the Indianapolis 500. Qualifying in second, he traded the lead with A.J. Foyt, before the defending champion ran out of fuel and the Scot cantered to victory by almost two minutes. He continued his dominance back in the Formula One arena, winning his next five races – the Belgian, British, Dutch, French and German Grands Prix: victory at the Nurburgring saw him become the first and only driver in history to win the Indianapolis 500 and the Formula One World Championship in the same year.

➲ Clark would win neither the Indy 500 nor the Formula One World Championship again: he finished runner-up at the Brickyard in 1966 and his best effort in F1 came in 1967 when he finished third.

During his most dominant year behind the wheel, in 1965, Jim Clark became the first and only man in history win the Indy 500–F1 World Championship double in the same year.

THE PITCHIN' MAN ROLLS BACK THE YEARS

SATCHEL PAIGE, AGED 59, BECOMES THE OLDEST PITCHER IN MAJOR LEAGUE HISTORY
25 September 1965, Kansas City, Missouri, USA

Satchel Paige was sent to a correctional institution at the age of 12 and it was there he learned the art of pitching. He would go on to make a career out of putting that art to good use. He played wherever he was paid: in the Negro League, in Cuba, Mexico, the Dominican Republic and finally, in 1948, in the Major Leagues, where he was part of the Cleveland Indians team which won the World Series. On he went until the early 1960s, before he settled down to retirement. It did not last long: he was lured back onto the mound (for cash) in 1965 for the Kansas City Athletics and pitched four innings to become, aged 59, the oldest-ever pitcher in baseball history.

➲ There would have been no Jackie Robinson had it not been for the exploits of Satchel Paige: he was the first African-American baseball star and he was the man who opened up Major League baseball parks to multi-racial crowds. His inclusion as pitcher in the 1953 All-Star Game (at the age of 47) was recognition of both his talent and his impact on the game of baseball.

Seventeen years after enjoying the taste of victory in the World Series, Leroy "Satchel" Paige, aged 59, was lured out of retirement by Kansas City Athletics owner Charles O. Finley to appear in one game for his club. He pitched four innings against the Boston Red Sox to become the oldest pitcher in Major League history.

1965

KOUFAX DEFIES PAIN TO BREAK STRIKEOUT RECORD

SANDY KOUFAX BREAKS MAJOR LEAGUE RECORD FOR SINGLE-SEASON STRIKEOUTS

14 October 1965, Metropolitan Stadium, Bloomington, Minnesota, USA

After suffering pain in his left elbow towards the end of the 1964 season, Sandy Koufax was diagnosed with arthritis. By 1965 the situation had deteriorated: Koufax would wake up in the morning, his arm black and blue from overnight haemorrhaging, and it would take a cocktail of painkillers to get him on the mound and buckets of ice to ease the pain afterwards. Still, Koufax ground out 335²/₃ innings for the Los Angeles Dodgers that season, hurling his thunderbolt fastballs through the pain barrier to deliver one of the most successful pitching seasons in Major League history. By the end of 1965, Koufax had won his second pitching Triple Crown, leading the league in wins (26), ERA (2.04) and strikeouts (382, to break his own record of 269 set in 1961), and rounded off a memorable year by dragging himself onto the mound to record a three-hit shutout in game seven as the Dodgers overcame the Minnesota Twins 2–0 to win the World Series.

➲ Although doctors warned him his arm could not withstand another full season's pitching, Sandy Koufax played on for one final year. He announced his retirement after the Baltimore Orioles had swept the Dodgers 4–0 in the 1966 World Series.

Delivering blazing fastballs through the pain barrier in 1965, Sandy Koufax set a new single-season strikeout record of 382. It would stand until 1973, when Nolan Ryan threw 383.

MIKE THE BIKE FREEWHEELS TO TITLE NO. 4

MIKE HAILWOOD BECOMES FIRST TO WIN FOUR SUCCESSIVE 500CC WORLD CHAMPIONSHIPS
4 November 1965, Monza, Italy

Born in 1940, Mike Hailwood, whose father owned a large motorcycle distributorship, began riding at an early age. He entered his first professional race shortly after his 17th birthday, finished 11th, and decided to spend the winter in South Africa honing his driving skills: he returned as the country's national champion. By 1961 he was racing for Honda and brought home the 250cc world championship: he switched to MV Agusta in 1962 for a shot at the big time. It was a marriage made in heaven: over the next four years Hailwood won a staggering 28 of the 37 races he entered to become the first person in history to win four successive 500cc world championships.

Versatile, brave and outstandingly talented, Mike Hailwood left behind his wealthy upbringing to become a true man of the people. He dominated the motorcycle scene between 1962 and '65, winning 76 per cent of the races he entered en route to four successive 500cc world titles.

➲ One of the finest riders of all time, Hailwood ended his career with nine world championships, 75 grands prix wins and 14 Isle of Man TT titles to his name. He was killed in a car accident, along with his nine-year-old daughter Michelle, in March 1981.

RUSSELL TAKES CHARGE OF THE CELTICS

BILL RUSSELL BECOMES FIRST AFRICAN-AMERICAN TO BE A HEAD COACH IN NORTH AMERICAN SPORTING HISTORY
18 April 1966, Boston, Massachusetts, USA

Bill Russell made a name for himself defying racism off the court to produce stellar performance after stellar performance once he found himself on the hardwood. When he joined the Boston Celtics in 1956, the 6ft 9in star became the centrepiece of a franchise that would go on to become one of the greatest dynasties in American sporting history. The first African-American to achieve superstar status in basketball found another place for himself in the history books when, a week into the 1966 NBA playoff finals against the LA Lakers, Red Auerbach announced that he would be retiring at the end of the season and that Russell would become the franchise's new player-coach: he would become the first African-American in history to assume a managerial position in North American sports.

Bill Russell, one of the best defensive players in NBA history who went on to enjoy a record 11 NBA Championship victories, was another to break the colour barrier in sports when he became the Boston Celtics' player-coach before the 1966–67 season.

➲ Russell's stint as player-coach lasted for three years. During that time he suffered frequent battles with racism – many fans shunned the Celtics and Russell received little support from the press – but he led Boston to the NBA Championships in both 1967–68 and 1968–69.

EIGHT IN A ROW FOR ALL-CONQUERING CELTICS

BOSTON CELTICS WIN THE NBA CHAMPIONSHIPS FOR A RECORD EIGHTH CONSECUTIVE YEAR

28 April 1966, Boston, Massachusetts, USA

Legendary coach Red Auerbach is the man credited with creating perhaps the most outstanding dynasty in sporting history, but his impact on the ailing Boston Celtics was far from immediate, more the patient creation of a masterpiece. First Bob Cousy was added to the Celtics canvas; then Bill Russell and Tommy Heinsohn joined the mix in 1956–57. The Celtics beat the St Louis Hawks in the playoffs to win the NBA Championships for the first time in their history that year – but it was the capture of K.C. Jones following the Celtics' 1958 finals loss to the Hawks that, for Auerbach, made it picture perfect. The Celtics were unstoppable, winning the championship for the next eight seasons to record the longest championship-winning streak in the history of North American sports.

➲ The Celtics' record run came to an end in the 1966–67 season when the Philadelphia 76ers beat them in the Eastern Championship finals.

The Boston Celtics were unstoppable between 1959 and 1966, winning an NBA record eight consecutive championships.

CLASSY CLARKE CRUISES TO 5,000M TITLE ONCE AGAIN

RON CLARKE BREAKS THE WORLD 5,000M RECORD FOR THE FOURTH TIME IN 18 MONTHS

5 July 1966, Stockholm, Sweden

Ron Clarke, a former world junior mile record-holder, first came to the public's attention when he lit the Olympic flame at the 1956 Games in Melbourne. After a time in the wilderness, the middle-distance runner resurfaced in spectacular fashion nine years later: during a 44-day period in 1965, he competed on 18 occasions and broke a staggering 12 world records – including Vladimir Kuts's 5,000m world record (13m35.0s, which had stood since 1957), which he improved on two further occasions (to 13m25.8s). The following year – after having seen Kenya's Kipchoge Keino run 13m24.2s in November 1965 – he ran 13m16.60s in Stockholm. The record was his once again: during the course of 18 months he had lowered it by some 18 seconds.

➲ Ron Clarke's 13m16.60s for the 5,000m would stand as a world record for six years: Finland's Lasse Viren set a new mark in 1972 when he ran 13m13.4s in Helsinki.

Ron Clarke went on a record-breaking spree between January 1965 and July 1966: at one stage he held every world record between two miles and 20km.

Antonio Carbajal retired at the end of the tournament (Mexico drew two and lost one of their group matches to suffer an early tournament exit), as the holder of several unwanted records: no other player had lost more World Cup matches (10) and no goalkeeper had conceded more World Cup goals.

CARBAJAL MAKES IT WORLD CUP NO. 5

ANTONIO CARBAJAL BECOMES FIRST PLAYER TO APPEAR IN FIVE WORLD CUPS

13 July 1966, Wembley Stadium, London, England

Antonio Carbajal's World Cup debut was a true baptism of fire: playing in front of 80,000 screaming supporters against Brazil at the Maracana Stadium in Rio de Janeiro, the 21-year-old Mexican goalkeeper picked the ball out of the back of the net four times as the hosts ran riot. Things may not have got any better for Mexico either in that World Cup or the next three – they won only once (3–1 against Czechoslovakia in 1962), but Carbajal was an ever-present between the posts. When he appeared in the Mexican goal for his country's opening match in the 1966 World Cup against France, he became the first man in history to appear in the tournament on five occasions.

➲ It would be 32 years before anyone repeated the feat: Lothar Matthäus appeared in his fifth World Cup finals tournament in 1998.

HURST HAT-TRICK SEALS WORLD CUP GLORY FOR ENGLAND

GEOFF HURST BECOMES THE FIRST PLAYER TO SCORE A HAT-TRICK IN A WORLD CUP FINAL

30 July 1966, Wembley Stadium, London, England

A crowd of 98,000 hopeful fans flocked to Wembley to see England play West Germany in the 1966 World Cup final. West Germany started the stronger and took the lead in the 12th minute. But, seven minutes later, England fans were cheering once more, with Geoff Hurst getting on the end of a Bobby Moore free-kick. It looked as though Martin Peters had handed England the Jules Rimet trophy with a 77th-minute lead, but a last-gasp German goal took the game into extra-time. England took a controversial lead 11 minutes into extra-time when a Hurst shot was adjudged to have crossed the line. West Germany pressed for an equalizer; the clock ticked down. Moore found Hurst with a long ball. The England striker raced into the opposition penalty area – people were running onto the pitch – before unleashing a thunderbolt into the top left-hand corner of the net. England had won the World Cup and Geoff Hurst had become the first, and to date only, man in history to score a hat-trick in a World Cup final.

➲ Geoff Hurst also holds the joint record for the most goals scored in World Cup finals (three). The others: Vava (Brazil, scored in 1958 (2) and 1962 (1)), Pele (Brazil, 1958 (2) and 1970 (1)) and Zinedine Zidane (France, 1998 (2) and 2006 (1)).

Geoff Hurst scored 24 times in his 49 career appearances for England: three of them came during England's finest hour, the 1966 World Cup final.

BRAND BRABHAM STRIKES PERFECT TUNE

JACK BRABHAM BECOMES ONLY MAN IN HISTORY TO WIN F1 CHAMPIONSHIP IN A CAR OF HIS OWN MAKING

23 October 1966, Autodromo Hermanos Rodriguez, Mexico City, Mexico

Already a two-time world champion (in 1959 and 1960), Jack Brabham made history when he claimed his third and final title in 1966 as the team owner of his own car.

It was a switch to the Cooper team in 1959 that truly sparked Jack Brabham's career. Throughout the course of an impressive two seasons, the Australian showed everyone that Cooper's new rear-engined cars were the racing cars of the future as he swept to two consecutive drivers' championships. Needing a fresh challenge, Brabham set up his own team in 1961 (the Brabham Racing Organization) and although the team struggled for consistency in its early years, excitement abounded ahead of 1966 with the new Brabham-Repco car. Brabham guided it to four wins that year to become the first man in history to win the Formula One World Championship in a car of his own making.

➲ Brabham's four victories during the 1966 season came in four consecutive races: the French GP, the British GP, the Dutch GP and the German GP. He eventually finished 14 points clear of Ferrari's John Surtees to collect his third drivers' championship.

FOINAVON SURVIVES CARNAGE TO TAKE SHOCK NATIONAL WIN

FOINAVON AT 100–1 BECOMES HIGHEST-PRICED WINNER OF THE GRAND NATIONAL

9 April 1967, Aintree, Liverpool, England

Rank outsider Foinavon, whose 100–1 odds were considered by many to be over-generous, was so far behind the carnage that ensued at the 23rd fence in the 1967 Grand National that he was able to weave his way through the mayhem to cause the biggest upset in the race's illustrious history.

With one-and-a-half circuits completed, the favourites all still in the hunt and the treacherous Becher's Brook safely negotiated, there seemed nothing unusual about the 1967 Grand National. But then mayhem ensued: riderless Popham Down refused the 23rd fence – at 4ft 6in one of the smallest on the course – causing the rest of the field to either fall, stop or refuse. It looked as though the race was over for everybody, until back-marker Foinavon and jockey Johnny Buckingham arrived on the scene and weaved their way through the carnage. The 100–1 outsider was the only horse running and cantered to a 15-length victory ahead of 17 remounted horses, setting the record for the highest-priced horse ever to win the Grand National.

➲ The fence after Becher's Brook (the seventh obstacle on the first circuit and 23rd on the second in the Grand National) is now called the Foinavon Fence in memory of the bizarre events of 1967.

Defying age and an ill-equipped boat, Francis Chichester set numerous records in his epic 1966–67 voyage: he completed the fastest voyage around the world by a small vessel; covered the greatest distance without entering a port of call (15,500 miles/24,945km); twice exceeded the single-handed speed record; and achieved the first true circumnavigation via the three capes (Good Hope, Leeuwin and Horn).

CHICHESTER COMPLETES EPIC VOYAGE

FRANCIS CHICHESTER COMPLETES FIRST ONE-STOP SINGLE-HANDED CIRCUMNAVIGATION

28 May 1967, Plymouth, England

In 1958, at the age of 57, Francis Chichester was diagnosed with lung cancer and given six months to live. Nursed back to health by his wife, the former aviation pioneer commissioned a yacht – Gypsy Moth IV – in an attempt to see whether he could race single-handed around the world against the average time of Australian wool clippers (230 days) from the Victorian era. It was an unrealistic attempt: Gypsy Moth IV, at 53ft, was some 180ft shorter than the clippers, slower, unwieldy and unbalanced: Chichester arrived in Sydney 107 days after his departure from Plymouth, a week behind schedule. On his return leg he became the first to complete a true circumnavigation (where the journey passes over the same point twice) and, 119 days after leaving Sydney, returned to Plymouth to a hero's welcome. At 65 years of age, Francis Chichester had single-handedly sailed into the record books.

➲ Chichester's journey inspired a nation. On his arrival in Sydney, he heard he had been awarded a knighthood. He received his honour shortly after his return, with Queen Elizabeth II using the sword that had originally been used by Elizabeth I to knight Francis Drake on 4 April 1581.

TEN-YEAR-OLD KLASS SHOCKS GOLFING WORLD

BEVERLY KLASS BECOMES YOUNGEST PLAYER IN HISTORY TO COMPETE IN AN LPGA TOUR EVENT

15 May 1967, Dallas, Texas, USA

Californian Beverly Klass started playing golf under the instruction of her father Jack at the age of three. It was an uneasy relationship between the two: Jack Klass had high hopes for his daughter and adopted a ruthless approach to make sure she lived up to them. In 1967, at her father's insistence, Beverly Klass shocked the golfing world when she turned professional at the age of ten. She made her first appearance on the LPGA Tour at the 1967 Dallas Open: it turned out to be a tournament to forget, with Klass shooting rounds of 88-88-90-99 for a total of 365 and last place.

➲ Klass would appear in three further events in 1967 – including the US Women's Open – she holds the record as the tournament's youngest participant – and won the grand total of $31. She was reinstated as an amateur the following year.

EMERSON EASES TO RECORD 12TH GRAND SLAM SUCCESS

ROY EMERSON WINS FRENCH OPEN TO COLLECT RECORD 12TH GRAND SLAM SINGLES TITLE

3 June 1967, Roland Garros, Paris, France

Athleticism was the key to Roy Emerson's success. The Australian allied great strength and sharp reflexes to a prodigious work ethic: the result was a seven-year period of dominance (1961–67) during which he collected 12 grand slam singles titles. His first came in the 1961 Australian Open, when he beat Rod Laver in the final. Laver got his revenge the following year, but between 1963 and 1967 Emerson could call the tournament his own, picking up five successive wins. Primarily a serve-and-volleyer, Emerson could adapt his game to all surfaces: he won the US Open twice (1961 and 1964), Wimbledon twice (1964 and 1965) and the French Open twice (first in 1963 and again in 1967, when he beat Tony Roche 6–1, 6–4, 2–6, 6–2 to notch up the last of his 12 titles).

➲ Emerson's haul of grand slam titles would stand as a record for 33 years, until Pete Sampras collected his 13th grand slam crown when he won Wimbledon in 2000.

In addition to his 12 grand slam singles wins, Roy Emerson also collected 16 doubles titles. His total haul of 28 is a record for a male tennis player. He is also the only man in history to have won singles and doubles titles at all four grand slam tournaments.

FIVE IN A ROW FOR
TT KING HAILWOOD

**MIKE HAILWOOD WINS THE ISLE OF MAN SENIOR TT
RACE FOR FIFTH CONSECUTIVE YEAR**
16 June 1967, Isle of Man

Off the back of four consecutive wins in the Senior TT race, an event
on the grand prix motorcycling calendar between 1949 and 1976,
Mike Hailwood's duel with Giacomo Agostini for a fifth successive
crown is remembered as one of the greatest races in history.
Agostini, on his MV Agusta, broke the lap record on lap one
of the six-lap race; Hailwood, on his fast but unwieldy
Honda, responded with a lap record of his own on lap
two, but he was seven seconds adrift of the Italian.
He closed the gap to a couple of seconds by the mid-
race pitstop, but dropped 10 seconds behind once
more. He drove to the limit – at times beyond it – and
reeled the Italian in by the fifth lap. Then disaster struck:
Agostini's chain snapped, leaving Hailwood to cruise to a
record-breaking fifth consecutive win.

➲ Hailwood's average speed of 108.77mph stood as a lap record
until 1975, when Mick Grant achieved 109.82mph.

Following his 1967 Senior TT victory,
Mike Hailwood did not return to the
Isle of Man for 11 years: when he did,
in 1978, he did so in winning style,
sensationally claiming victory in the
Formula One TT.

THE CORONATION OF KING RICHARD

RICHARD PETTY WINS AN ASTONISHING 27 RACES EN ROUTE TO SECOND NASCAR CHAMPIONSHIP

2 October 1967, North Wilkesboro, North Carolina, USA

The son of Lee Petty, a three-time NASCAR champion and the inaugural winner of the Daytona 500 in 1959, Richard Petty was born to race, but not before his father said so. Lee Petty insisted his son wait until he had reached the legal age (21) before he could compete: Richard Petty's NASCAR career started just 16 days after his 21st birthday. Six years later, he won the Daytona 500 for the first time en route to his first championship crown. He then took time out of the sport to compete in drag car racing, but returned in 1966 and became the first person to win the Daytona 500 twice. But 1967 was his signature year. Driving a potent Plymouth he was unbeatable: in 48 races that season Petty never finished outside the top ten, had 11 top-five finishes and marched to victory lane an astonishing 27 times. The championship was his by some distance, and the title "King Richard" would stick with Petty from that moment on.

➲ An example of Petty's dominance that year came during a race at Nashville. Petty crashed into the wall during the race and limped into the pits with a badly damaged car. He rejoined the track seven laps down on the leader, but went on to win with an astonishing five-lap lead.

The greatest NASCAR racer of all time, Richard Petty competed until 1992. By the time he retired he held numerous records, including: most career wins (200), most championships (seven, tied with Dale Earnhardt), most Daytona 500 wins (seven) and most career poles (127).

Charlie Sifford had to defy more than most – phone calls in the middle of the night and constant death threats – but through iron-willed determination became the first African-American in history to play and win on the PGA Tour.

SIFFORD DEFIES THE ODDS TO PICK UP FIRST TOUR CROWN

CHARLIE SIFFORD BECOMES FIRST AFRICAN-AMERICAN TO WIN A PGA TOUR EVENT

20 August 1967, Hartford, Connecticut, USA

By the mid-1960s golf was an exclusive all-white, country-club sport and white America was steadfast in its determination to keep it so; but six-time Negro champion Charlie Sifford wanted the chance to compete at the highest level. In 1961 he challenged the PGA's white-only clause and won: at the Greensboro Open that year he became, aged 39 and past his prime, the first African-American to play in a PGA Tour event. Subjected to death threats and racial abuse from the galleries, Sifford had to wait six years before enjoying the taste of victory, but when the moment finally came it did so in some style: Sifford shot a final-round 64 to win the 1967 Greater Hartford Open.

❐ Sifford picked up his second tournament victory in 1969 when he won the Los Angeles Open. He then went on to enjoy a successful senior career, the highlight of which came when he won the Senior PGA Championship in 1975.

FLYING FOX MAKES IT WORLD CHAMPIONSHIP NO. 5

OVE FUNDIN BECOMES FIRST FIVE-TIME SPEEDWAY WORLD CHAMPION IN HISTORY

16 September 1967, Wembley Stadium, London, England

Born in Sweden in 1933, Ove Fundin, nicknamed "The Fox" on account of his flaming red hair, started his speedway career with the Monakerna club at the age of 19. After stints in both Britain and Australia honing his technique, he joined the Norwich Stars in 1955 and finished fifth in the world championship. He rebounded the following year to become the first continental European to become world champion and added the European and Swedish titles for good measure. Four years would pass before he got his hands on the world title again, but victories in 1960, 1961 and 1963 confirmed Fundin's status as the hottest speedway star of his day. He rode to a record fifth title in 1967.

❐ Ove Fundin's haul of five world speedway championships stood as a record until 1979, when New Zealand's Ivan Mauger claimed his sixth title.

His ruthless pursuit of success may have alienated him from the crowds, but it took Ove Fundin to five world speedway titles in 11 years and made him the hottest property in the sport for many years.

GRENOBLE GOLD FOR GREENE

"TIGER" GETS GOLD FROM GRENOBLE OLYMPICS
15 February 1968, Grenoble, France

By the time Nancy Greene showed up at the 1968 Winter Games, her aggressive style and attitude had already won her championships at home and abroad, including the first Alpine skiing World Cup. At the Olympics, Greene started off in a less-than-stellar fashion, pulling down a middling 10th-place finish in the downhill contest. But she wasn't done yet: disturbed by her performance in the downhill, Greene threw herself to a silver finish in slalom, then pushed her way to the giant slalom gold medal, a cool 2.64 seconds faster than second-place finisher Annie Famose of France – at that point the widest winning margin in the event's history. Greene then went on to win the World Cup again for 1968. After retirement, she served as coach of the Canadian ski team until 1973, and was inducted as an Officer of the Order of Canada on 26 April 1968.

⟳Greene and her husband, Al Raine, played an integral role in the development of British Columbia's Whistler-Backcomb Resort, and are still heavily involved in skiing: Greene is the director of skiing at the Sun Peaks Resort, where the couple built, and still live in, Nancy Greene's Cahilty Lodge.

Greene is active the promotion of skiing. The Nancy Greene Ski League is a program that helps Canadian kids get started in competitive skiing. In 1999, Greene was voted Canada's female athlete of the century and given a star on Canada's Walk of Fame.

Fortune may well have been on his side, but Jean-Claude Killy became France's favourite son when he achieved triple gold success in the 1968 Winter Olympics in his home country.

KILLY WINS THE HEART OF A NATION

JEAN-CLAUDE KILLY COMPLETES ALPINE SKIING'S TRIPLE CROWN
6–18 February 1968, Grenoble, France

Jean-Claude Killy was his country's big gold-medal hope at the 1968 Winter Olympics, but it almost went wrong for the Frenchman before it had started. As he arrived at the starting gate for the downhill, he realized he had picked up the wrong pair of skis – the ones he was wearing were un-waxed. No matter: showing the daredevil, speed-at-all-costs style that had propelled him to two world championships, he took gold by eight hundredths of a second. It was merely the prelude: a few days later he picked up gold again in the giant slalom and, when he took gold in the slalom to complete the clean sweep, his place in the pantheon of skiing greats was assured.

⟳No skier has won more than two Alpine golds at the Winter Olympics since.

Judy Wills Cline (left) was the first dominant force in women's trampolining, winning five world championships in a row after the competition's inception in 1964.

WILLS CLINE SPRINGS TO TRAMPOLINE GLORY

JUDY WILLS CLINE BECOMES TRAMPOLINING'S FIRST AND ONLY FIVE-TIME WORLD CHAMPION
April 1968, Amersfoot, the Netherlands

When George Nissen and Larry Griswold stood in a garage in 1935 and stretched a piece of canvas over an iron frame, they had little idea that they had created one of the most popular pieces of gymnastic equipment in history. Named after the Spanish world el *trampolino*, meaning "diving board", the first world trampoline championships were held in Frankfurt in 1964. Mississippi-born Judy Wills Cline took the women's title, which she would defend the following year in London. She became the dominant force in the sport, completing a hat-trick of wins in 1966, making it four in a row the following year and becoming the only person in history to win the title five consecutive times when she won in the Netherlands in 1968.

↪In recognition of her contribution to the sport of trampolining, Judy Wills Cline was elected to the United States Gymnastics Hall of Fame in 1993.

START OF THE OPEN ERA IN TENNIS

PROFESSIONALS AND AMATEUR TENNIS PLAYERS COMPETE AGAINST EACH OTHER FOR FIRST TIME
27 May 1968, Roland Garros, Paris, France

Time had finally caught up with tennis. Since the first Wimbledon Championships in 1877, the sport had stuck firmly to its amateur principles, but at a price: in order to make a living, the game's best players tended towards the exhibition circuit and, branded professionals, were barred from the grand slam tournaments. By 1968, however, commercial interests led to a change of strategy: money coming into the game from external sources was too hard to resist and the "open era" of tennis began. The first open tournament in history was the 1968 French Open and, from that moment on, tennis was never the same again.

↪The final at Roland Garros in 1968 turned out to be an all-Australian affair with Ken Rosewall beating Rod Laver 6–3, 6–3, 6–1 in the final to win his second French Open crown, some 15 years after he had collected his first.

Promises of television money and the establishment of an international tennis circuit including each and every one of the world's best players forced the world tennis authorities to abandon their amateur principles in 1968 and declare the game open. It was the birth of professional tennis as we know it today.

DEADLY DRYSDALE PROVES UNHITTABLE

DON DRYSDALE THROWS MLB RECORD 58²/₃ CONSECUTIVE SCORELESS INNINGS

8 June 1968, Los Angeles, California, USA

In the late 1950s and early '60s, Don Drysdale and Sandy Koufax formed one of the most deadly pitching duos in the history of baseball. The pair swept the LA Dodgers to three World Series titles (1959, 1963 and 1965) with Drysdale, pitching ferocious brushbacks and sidearm fastballs – all delivered with supreme control – intimidating batsmen throughout the National League. Winner of the Cy Young Award in 1962 for his 25 wins, his most storied year came in 1968, the "Year of the Pitcher", when he threw 58²/₃ consecutive scoreless innings, including a Major League record six consecutive shutouts, to break Walter Johnson's mark of 56 set in 1913.

⮯ Drysdale's record would stand for some 20 years, until Orel Hershiser pitched 59 consecutive scoreless innings in 1988.

The 1968 season proved the final hurrah for Don Drysdale. After pitching a record 58²/₃ consecutive scoreless innings, he was forced to retire the following season after failing to shrug off a persistent arm injury.

BIRDIE SPREE TAKES POST TO LPGA TITLE

SANDRA POST BECOMES YOUNGEST WOMAN IN HISTORY TO WIN A MAJOR

23 June 1968, Pleasant Valley Country Club, Sutton, Massachusetts, USA

A three-time winner of the Ontario youth and Canadian youth titles, Sandra Post, arguably the greatest golfer to have emerged from Canada, turned professional in 1968 and became the first woman from her country to appear on the LPGA Tour. And what an impression she made. After tying with defending champion Kathy Whitworth over 72 holes at the LPGA Championship in her rookie year, she went on a birdie spree in the 18-hole playoff – shooting 68 to Whitworth's 75 – to become the first non-US-born golfer to win the tournament and, at 20 years, 11 days, the youngest major winner in the history of women's golf.

⮯ Sandra Post held the distinction until 2007, when Morgan Pressel won the Kraft Nabisco tournament at the age of 18 years, 313 days.

During a 16-year career on the LPGA Tour, Canada's Sandra Post collected nine tournament victories, including three majors (the LPGA Championship in 1968) – to become the youngest female winner of a major – and back-to-back wins in the Dinah Shore in 1978 and '79.

COWDREY CELEBRATES 100-CAP MILESTONE IN STYLE

COLIN COWDREY BECOMES FIRST CRICKETER IN HISTORY TO WIN 100 TEST CAPS

11 July 1968, Edgbaston, Birmingham, England

Having made his first-class debut for Kent in 1949 at the age of 17, four years later Colin Cowdrey was a surprise inclusion for the 1954–55 Ashes tour to Australia, but two hundreds in the match against a strong New South Wales team cemented his place in the batting line-up for the upcoming Test series. A maiden century came in the third Test, England won the Ashes 1–0 and a star was born. Cowdrey remained on the England scene for the next two decades, captaining them on 26 occasions, and during the third Test against Australia in 1968 became the first man in history to win 100 Test caps. He marked the occasion in fine style, hitting 104 in the first innings as the match petered out into a draw.

⮑Cowdrey made his final appearance for England against Australia in 1974–75. Flown out as a replacement following a series of injuries, he appeared in the second Test at Perth, aged 41 and some three-and-a-half years after his previous appearance.

The first player in Test history to reach the 100-cap milestone, Colin Cowdrey played for England 114 times, scoring 7,624 runs at an average of 44.06 (with 22 centuries).

BOROS DEFIES THE YEARS TO WIN US PGA CHAMPIONSHIP

JULIUS BOROS BECOMES OLDEST-EVER WINNER OF ONE OF GOLF'S MAJOR TOURNAMENTS

22 July 1968, Pecan Valley Golf Club, San Antonio, Texas, USA

The son of Hungarian immigrants, Julius Boros was a practising accountant when he discovered golf in his 20s. Working on the maxim "swing easy, hit hard", he turned professional in 1949 at the age of 29, and successfully made his way from tee to green on the PGA Tour for the next 16 years. His effortless iron play and touch around the greens brought him two US Open championships (in 1952 and 1963), five Ryder Cup appearances and a third major championship in 1968: the US PGA Championship when, at the age of 48 years, 8 months and 18 days, he beat Arnold Palmer down the stretch to win by one stroke and become the oldest major winner in golf history.

⮑Boros broke the record set by Tom Morris Sr, who won the 1867 Open Championship at Prestwick aged 46 years, 99 days.

Julius Boros defied the notion that golf was a young man's game when he won the US PGA Championship in 1968 at 48 years of age.

In the space of three short years, Pietro Anastasi went from being a Serie D soccer player with his hometown club in Catania, Sicily, to become the most expensive soccer player on the planet.

JUVENTUS PAY RECORD FEE FOR HOTSHOT ANASTASI

PIETRO ANASTASI BECOMES WORLD'S MOST EXPENSIVE SOCCER PLAYER

July 1968, Turin, Italy

Eighteen goals for Massiminiana in Italy's Serie D in his debut season (1965–66) were enough to secure Pietro Anastasi a move to Serie B side Varese. The northern Italian side won promotion during Anastasi's first season and the young striker took to Serie A soccer in 1967–68 like a duck to water, scoring 11 goals. A national call-up came later in the summer, in the 1968 European Championship final against Yugoslavia. After the game ended 1–1, Anastasi scored the second goal in the replay as Italy won 2–0. The 20-year-old was now one of the hottest properties in soccer. So hot, in fact, that Juventus paid a world-record £500,000 for his services shortly after the end of the tournament.

➲Anastasi went on to enjoy a successful career with the Old Lady of Italian soccer, scoring 78 goals in 205 appearances and collecting championship-winners' medals in 1972, '73 and '75 before moving on to Inter Milan in 1976.

Already the holder of the highest score in Test cricket, Garfield Sobers's place among the pantheon of cricket greats was secured when he became the first player in the history of first-class cricket to score six sixes off an over. The unfortunate bowler was Glamorgan's Malcolm Nash.

SIX SIXES IN AN OVER FOR SOBERS

GARFIELD SOBERS FIRST BATSMAN TO HIT SIX SIXES OFF AN OVER IN FIRST-CLASS CRICKET

31 August 1968, Swansea, Wales

With his side in a strong first-innings position against Glamorgan in their final match of the 1968 County Championship, Nottinghamshire captain Garfield Sobers faced up to Malcolm Nash with one thing on his mind: to up the run-rate. And how. The first two balls disappeared beyond the boundary rope; Nash's next two balls suffered a similar fate – one a lavish drive over long-off, the other an agricultural slog over midwicket. Sobers lofted the fifth ball towards the long-off boundary and was caught, only for the fielder to fall backwards over the boundary rope. Six. Then came the final ball: Nash, seeking to avoid an unwanted place in the history books, bowled it fuller and flatter. Sobers pivoted and hoisted the ball beyond the midwicket boundary. Another six: Sobers had become the first batsman in cricket history to swipe six sixes in an over.

➲Sobers's feat has been equalled once in first-class cricket – by Ravi Shastri for Bombay in 1985 – and once in a one-day international, by Herschelle Gibbs for South Africa in 2007.

Having won the 100m Olympic final in record-breaking style, Hines also won gold with the US 4x100m team. Running the anchor leg, he picked up the baton in third place, rocketed past his opponents and crossed the line in 38.2s for a new world record with Hines being timed at an astonishing 8.2s for the final leg.

JIM HINES BREAKS OWN 100M WORLD RECORD TO CLAIM GOLD

SPRINTER HINES SETS NEW 100M WORLD RECORD AS HE WINS OLYMPIC GOLD

14 October 1968, Mexico City, Mexico

Raised in Oakland, California, Jim Hines was a promising baseball player in his youth before a track-and-field coach spotted his potential and persuaded him to try his hand at athletics. It was an epochal moment: by 1967, at the age of 21, the supremely quick Hines had equalled the world record for the 100-yard dash (clocking 9.1 seconds). The following year, at the US national championships, he became the first man in history to clock under 10 seconds for the 100m: hand-timing registered him at 9.9s, although the real mark was 10.03s. No matter: Hines qualified for the US team for the 1968 Olympics, made it through to the 100m final and recorded a new world's best mark – timed electronically on this occasion – of 9.95s. Jim Hines was officially the fastest man on the planet.

⮑ Jim Hines's record would stand for some 20 years, an astonishing duration for a sprint record, until fellow American Calvin Smith ran 9.93s in 1983.

AMAZING OERTER MAKES IT DISCUS GOLD NO. 4

AL OERTER BECOMES FIRST IN HISTORY TO WIN SAME OLYMPIC EVENT FOUR TIMES IN A ROW

15 October 1968, Mexico City, Mexico

When Al Oerter was 15, a discus landed at his feet. He picked it up and threw it back: the discus sailed over the heads of the crowd from whence it had come and a supreme talent had been discovered. Five years later, in 1956, Oerter claimed his first Olympic gold. He defended his crown in 1960, throwing 59.18m to break the Olympic record. Title number three came in Tokyo in 1964. He entered his fourth Olympic discus competition in Mexico in 1968 as the underdog, but broke his own Olympic record in the first round with a throw of 64.78m: it was enough to see him become the first man in history to win the same Olympic event on four consecutive occasions.

⮑ Only one other man has equalled Al Oerter's feat: Carl Lewis, who won the long jump title at the 1984, 1988, 1992 and 1996 Olympic Games.

Al Oerter threw an Olympic best (64.78m) in the discus in Mexico in 1968 to claim his fourth consecutive gold medal in the event. The record would stand for eight years, until fellow countryman Mac Wilkins threw 68.28m in the 1976 Olympics in Montreal.

TERRIFIC TYUS DEFENDS OLYMPIC CROWN IN SENSATIONAL STYLE

WYOMIA TYUS BECOMES FIRST IN HISTORY TO RETAIN OLYMPIC 100M CROWN
15 October 1968, Mexico City, Mexico

As a student at Tennessee State University, Wyomia Tyus fell under the influence of legendary track-and-field coach Ed Temple, who spotted her early potential and groomed her for stardom. After narrowly earning selection for the US team for the 1964 Olympics in Tokyo, only 19 years old, she equalled Wilma Rudolph's 100m record during the qualifying rounds (11.2s) and went on to claim gold in the final. She returned to the Olympic arena in Mexico four years later, attempting to become the first athlete in history to defend a 100m title – and did so in world-record-breaking style, clocking 11s dead to create her own slice of history.

After collecting her second successive gold in the 100m final, Wyomia Tyus (middle) would also take the top step of the podium after anchoring the US 4x100m team to gold medal glory. She retired soon afterwards.

➲ Only one other person in Olympic history has equalled her feat: Carl Lewis who claimed 100m gold in 1984 in Los Angeles and 1988 in Seoul.

SMITH SPRINTS TO OLYMPIC GOLD IN WORLD-RECORD-BREAKING FASHION

TOMMY SMITH BECOMES FIRST PERSON TO RECORD OFFICIAL SUB-20S TIME FOR 200M
17 October 1968, Mexico City, Mexico

Tommy Smith's display of Black Power during the playing of the national anthems at the medal ceremony in Mexico 1968 is one of the most powerful and controversial images in Olympic history. It overshadowed his performance of just a few hours earlier when he won 200m gold in a world-record-breaking time of 19.83s.

A former professional American footballer with the Cincinnati Bengals, Tommy Smith switched to athletics when he started teaching sociology at Obin College in Ohio, and with some effect. He may have finished second to John Carlos in the US Olympic trials for the 200m in 1968 – Carlos ran a world-record time of 19.92s, but it was never ratified because the spike formation on his running shoes was deemed illegal – but entered the 200m final in Mexico City as one of the favourites. He produced a staggering performance, clocking 19.83s to become the first person in history to run the 200m officially in under 20s. Carlos finished in third place.

➲ Smith and Carlos took to the podium after the race in bare feet and wearing black gloves. During the national anthem, both raised clenched fists to protest at the level of poverty in black America. It caused a sensation.

EVANS RUNS RACE OF HIS LIFE TO SECURE OLYMPIC GOLD

LEE EVANS WINS 400M GOLD AT THE 1968 OLYMPICS IN RECORD-BREAKING STYLE

18 October 1968, Mexico City, Mexico

Following a successful high-school career in California, during which he went undefeated in the 400m, Lee Evans became the United States national champion for 440 yards for the first time as a 19-year-old in 1966. Later that year he achieved his first taste of world-record-breaking success, when he formed part of the US 4x100m relay team that clocked sub-three minutes for the first time in history. He qualified for the US 1968 Olympic team in style, breaking the 400m world record en route to booking his ticket to Mexico. And he chose the biggest stage of all, the 400m Olympic final, to run the race of his life. He ran 43.86s to collect the only individual gold medal of his career and became the first man in history to run the 400m in under 44s.

⟳ Evans's time would stand as a record for almost 20 years, until compatriot Butch Reynolds ran 43.29s in Zurich on 17 August 1988.

Lee Evans underlined his dominance in the 400m by becoming the first man in history to break the 44s barrier and did so on the biggest stage of all, in the Olympic final in Mexico in 1968.

Such was the impact of Beamon's jump that 1962 Olympic champion Lynn Davies, who had just lost his title, went up to the American and said: "You have just destroyed this event."

THE JUMP THAT SHOOK THE WORLD

AMERICA'S BOB BEAMON SHATTERS THE WORLD LONG-JUMP RECORD

18 October 1968, Mexico City, Mexico

The fact of the matter is that Bob Beamon barely made it into the Olympic long-jump final. Two no-jumps in his first two attempts left him in a precarious position, until a steady third jump took him through. He would not make the same mistake in the final. Instead he would produce one of the most thrilling moments in Olympic history. It took just 19 strides, a jump and a total of six seconds for Bob Beamon to send shockwaves around the sporting world and, when he landed, the 22-year-old American had obliterated the world long-jump record. During the previous 33 years the world-record mark had literally crept forwards: by just 21.6cm to 8.35m (achieved by the USA's Ralph Boston). Beamon jumped a staggering 8.90m, 55cm further than any man had jumped before him.

⟳ Beamon's world record stood for almost 23 years until it was broken by another American, Mike Powell, who jumped 8.95m at the 1991 World Championships in Tokyo.

MANOLIU PRODUCES THROW OF HER LIFE TO WIN DISCUS CROWN

LIA MANOLIU BECOMES OLDEST PERSON IN HISTORY TO WIN TRACK-AND-FIELD OLYMPIC GOLD

19 October 1968, Mexico City, Mexico

Already a veteran of four Olympic Games, which included bronze medals in 1960 and 1964, Lia Manoliu must have thought her discus career was over when the Romanian Athletics Federation informed her that, at the age of 35, she was too old to compete and should not attend the national training camps. Manoliu dug deeper than ever before, underwent an intense training period and duly qualified for the Romanian Olympic team. But then disaster struck: she injured herself before the start of the discus tournament and was told by a doctor that her arm was good for only one throw. That was all she needed: her 58.28m was enough to win gold. At 36 years, 176 days, Lia Manoliu had become track-and-field's oldest-ever Olympic champion.

➲ Manoliu's Olympic career was far from over. She went on to appear in a record sixth Olympic Games in Munich in 1972, finishing ninth in the discus final.

Lia Manoliu (pictured left, after her bronze-medal-winning performance at Tokyo in 1964) produced perhaps the greatest against-the-odds victory in Olympic history in Mexico City in 1968. The oldest competitor in the field, and restricted to just one throw by injury, she became the oldest track-and-field athlete in history to win an Olympic gold medal.

DICK FOSBURY FLOPS TO HIGH-JUMP GLORY

DICK FOSBURY BREAKS OLYMPIC HIGH-JUMP RECORD WITH STYLE THAT WOULD REVOLUTIONIZE THE SPORT

20 October 1968, Mexico City, Mexico

By the 1960s there were several accepted high-jump techniques: scissors, western roll or straddle, all of which required the competitor to attack the bar from front-on and to take off using the inside leg. At the age of 16, Dick Fosbury started experimenting with a different approach: to attack the bar with a curved run-up (which would allow him to attack it with more speed), take off with his outside leg and to twist his body over the bar back first. The results were sensational: he won the US national championships in 1968 and headed to the Olympic Games in Mexico as one of the favourites. He did not disappoint, jumping 2.24m in his last attempt to break the Olympic record and claim gold.

➲ Fosbury's jump would stand as an Olympic best until 1976, when Poland's Jacek Wszola jumped 2.25m in Montreal.

Dick Fosbury's performance in the 1968 Olympic Games revolutionized high jump: now every jumper in the world uses the technique that has since come to be known as the "Fosbury Flop".

USA CRUISE TO 4X400M GOLD

UNITED STATES SHATTER 4X400M RELAY WORLD RECORD

22 October 1968, Mexico City, Mexico

To say that the American line-up for the men's 4x400m relay was strong at the 1968 Olympics would be a gross understatement. Up for the first leg was Vincent Matthews, who would go on to become 400m Olympic champion in 1972. Next came Ron Freeman. Then came the real firepower: legs three and four would be run by two men who, just four days earlier, had both run inside world-record time – Larry James (who took silver) and Lee Evans (gold and the world record). In truth they were racing against the clock, the baton … and history. They steamrollered the existing world record (2m59.6s) by some three-and-a-half seconds. The new mark: 2m56.16s.

↪ The record time was equalled by another US team in Seoul in 1988, but would not be bettered for 24 years. In 1992 in Barcelona, a new generation of American athletes, including a certain Michael Johnson, clocked 2m55.74s.

Such was the strength of the United States' 4x400m relay team that, even though Kenya finished inside the old world record time, they found themselves some three-and-a-half seconds behind the gold-medal winners.

MEXICO FALL FLAT IN FRONT OF RECORD CROWD

MEXICO AND JAPAN PLAY IN FRONT OF LARGEST CROWD EVER SEEN FOR AN OLYMPIC SOCCER MATCH

24 October 1968, Azteca Stadium, Mexico City, Mexico

Hosts Mexico had flattered to deceive in the 1968 Olympic soccer tournament: impressive wins over Colombia and Guinea sandwiched a sorry 4–1 defeat by France; and a 2–0 victory over Spain in the quarter-finals was followed by a devastating 3–2 reverse to Bulgaria. But still the Mexicans turned out in force to see their heroes take on Japan in the third-place playoff game. However, in front of a colossal 105,000 people in the Azteca Stadium – the largest crowd ever assembled for an Olympic soccer match – Mexico disappointed once again, losing the game 2–0 and finishing outside of the medals.

↪ The 1968 Olympic soccer tournament was won by Hungary, who beat Bulgaria 4–1 in the final to record the last of their three successes in the competition.

It may only have been a playoff for the bronze medal, but 105,000 partisan fans turned out to see Mexico play Japan in the 1968 Olympics: the largest crowd ever seen in the competition's history.

A record four gold medals in the 1968 Olympics added to the three she collected in Toyko in 1964 made Vera Caslavska the most decorated female gymnast in Olympic history.

GUTSY CASLAVSKA DOMINATES WOMEN'S GYMNASTICS

VERA CASLAVSKA BECOMES ONLY FEMALE GYMNAST IN HISTORY TO WIN FOUR GOLDS AT SINGLE OLYMPICS
12–27 October 1968, Mexico City, Mexico

Just weeks before the start of the 1968 Olympic Games, three-time gold-medal-winning Czech gymnast Vera Caslavska had been in hiding, fearing for her safety after a series of outspoken comments against the Soviet regime in her native Czechoslovakia, but, against the backdrop of unrest in her homeland, she was finally granted permission to travel to Mexico. Once she was there, Caslavska put in one of the most dominant performances in gymnastic history, retaining her all-round title (becoming only the second woman in history to do so) and capturing gold in the vault, uneven bars and floor (tied) to become the only female gymnast in history to collect four gold medals in a single Olympics.

⊃ As the Soviet national anthem was played at the medal ceremony for the floor competition, Caslavska controversially lowered her head and turned away from the Soviet flag in protest against events occurring in her homeland. Shortly after the Games, the government deprived her of her right of travel, effectively ending her career.

THE RAIDERS TURN TO YOUNG GUN MADDEN

JOHN MADDEN BECOMES THE YOUNGEST HEAD COACH IN NFL HISTORY
4 February 1969, Oakland, California, USA

After being drafted in the 21st round by the Philadelphia Eagles in 1958, John Madden suffered a career-ending knee injury during training camp and never appeared in a professional game. His coaching career started while studying for a master's degree at California Polytechnic State University and he continued to advance through the coaching ranks; the Oakland Raiders hired him as their linebackers' coach in 1967 – the year they reached the Super Bowl. Two years later, Raiders head coach John Rauch resigned to take the helm at the Buffalo Bills. The Raiders turned to Madden to fill the void: at 32 years of age he had become the youngest head coach in NFL history.

⊃Madden went on to enjoy a successful nine-year stint with the Raiders – the highlight coming with a Super Bowl win in 1976 – before switching to the commentary booth in 1979.

Taking the reins of the Oakland Raiders as a 32-year-old in 1969, John Madden became the youngest coach in NFL history. During a successful career, he would also become the youngest head coach in history to record 100 career regular-season victories.

The National League team immediately captured the hearts of Montreal fans, who would pack north-end Jarry Park to cheer on such perennial local favourites as Rusty Staub ("Le Grand Orange" – seen swinging in 1969), Mack Jones, Jose "Coco" Laboy, and Bill Stoneman.

MAJOR LEAGUE BASEBALL GETS A TASTE OF CANADA

FIRST APPEARANCE BY A NON-US MLB TEAM LEAVES NEW YORK SMARTING

8 April 1969, New York, USA

In 1960 Montreal had lost its International League baseball team, the Royals, but by the late '60s, the city had its wind back. Expo 67 had left behind a town that simply scintillated, and everybody knew that the Olympics were on their way for 1976. It was time to get back in the game – the baseball game. Snowdon councilman Gerry Snider submitted a bid to MLB management on 2 December 1967. On 8 April 1969, after overcoming numerous obstacles, the new Montreal team took to the field with a roar, beating the New York Mets at Shea Stadium 11–10. Six days later, the Expos' first home game resulted in a win against the St Louis Cardinals. But Montreal's subsequent ride would be rocky: the team suffered ten losing seasons before perking up in 1979 for five winning seasons. The team became the Washington Nationals in 2004.

➲The Expos also made history by being first non-US franchise awarded by a major sports organization originating in the US. Impressed by Montreal's early performance, the MLB would launch the Toronto Blue Jays in 1977. Felipe Alou became the Major League's first Dominican-born field manager when the Expos promoted him from bench coach in 1992.

ELEVEN NBA CHAMPIONSHIPS AND OUT FOR RUSSELL

BOSTON CELTIC'S BILL RUSSELL WINS HIS RECORD 11TH AND LAST NBA CHAMPIONSHIP

5 May 1969, Los Angeles, California, USA

Boston Celtics coach Red Auerbach had seen enough of Bill Russell to know he was the missing piece in his jigsaw. Russell had made a name for himself at college as a supreme defensive player, showing awesome abilities in shot-blocking, rebounding and man-to-man marking: in other words, he was the ideal addition to a high-scoring Celtics team with a propensity to leak points – too many points if they were going to win their first-ever NBA Championship. It was a marriage made in heaven: the Celtics and Russell went on to enjoy a spell of near-complete dominance as title followed title. When the Celtics beat the LA Lakers in game seven of the playoff finals in 1969, Bill Russell picked up his record 11th and final NBA Championship.

➲Bill Russell still holds the record for the most rebounds made in NBA finals history, with 1,718.

Bill Russell's 13-year career with the Boston Celtics, including a three-year spell as player-manager, brought massive success: Russell and the Celtics collected the first 11 NBA Championships in the franchise's history.

Inspired by a book recounting Harbo and Samuelsen's 1896 feat of rowing across the Atlantic ocean, in 1969 John Fairfax became the first rower in history to make a solo Atlantic crossing.

COURAGEOUS FAIRFAX COMPLETES ATLANTIC CROSSING

JOHN FAIRFAX BECOMES FIRST ROWER IN HISTORY TO COMPLETE SUCCESSFUL SOLO ATLANTIC CROSSING

19 July 1969, Miami, Florida, USA

John Fairfax's first 31 years on the planet had been colourful: born in Italy and raised in Argentina, he had left home aged 13 to live in the jungle before later going to the United States, working on a Colombian ship and then spending three years with pirates. But throughout these varied experiences there had been one constant in his life: a desire to become the first rower in history to complete a solo crossing of the Atlantic. He got his chance in 1969, setting out from the Canary Islands in a 24ft rowing boat called *Britannia* in an attempt to make history: 180 days later, the 31-year-old Briton touched ashore on a beach in Florida. His lifelong desire had been fulfilled.

➲ Eight days after Fairfax had completed his feat, another British rower, Tom McLean, completed his journey from Newfoundland to Ireland to complete the first successful west-to-east Atlantic crossing.

DEBUTANT MERCKX DELIVERS TOUR CLEAN SWEEP

EDDY MERCKX BECOMES ONLY MAN TO WIN YELLOW, GREEN AND POLKA-DOT JERSEYS AT TOUR DE FRANCE

20 July 1969, Paris, France

Having won the amateur world cycling championship the previous year, Eddy Merckx turned professional in 1965 and was the world professional champion within two years. In 1968 he continued his climb up the cycling ranks when he became the first Belgian in history to win the Giro d'Italia, but this performance was merely an aperitif compared to what was to come the following year. In 1969, Merckx made his first appearance in the Tour de France and simply blew his opponents away, winning six stages, including the last in Paris, en route to becoming the only man in Tour history to win the yellow jersey (overall race leader), the green jersey (best sprinter) and polka-dot jersey (King of the Mountains) in the same race.

➲Although never equalled in the Tour de France, Merckx's feat of winning all three jerseys has been achieved twice on another Grand Tour race – the Vuelta a Espana – by Tony Rominger (1993) and Laurent Jalabert (1995).

Eddy Merckx's dominance in his debut Tour in 1969 handed the event a glimpse into its immediate future. The Belgian would claim the yellow jersey four further times over the next five years.

ROCKHAMPTON ROCKET COMPLETES SECOND GRAND SLAM

ROD LAVER BECOMES THE ONLY TENNIS PLAYER IN HISTORY TO WIN THE GRAND SLAM TWICE
9 September 1969, Forest Hills, New York, USA

After completing the grand slam for the first time in 1962, Rod Laver signed a professional contract for $50,000 and disappeared from tennis's amateur ranks. He soon established himself as one of the best professionals on the world stage and was approaching his 30th birthday by the time the sport's governing body announced the start of the "open era" from 1968. By then, Laver still had the game to compete at the very top: incisive from the baseline and clinical at the net, he became Wimbledon's first open-era champion in 1968. He opened his 1969 grand slam campaign with a win at the Australian Open; the switch to clay did little to dampen his form and he beat Ken Rosewall in the French Open final. A Wimbledon win soon followed and when he beat Tony Roche 7–9, 6–1, 6–2, 6–2 in the US Open final, he had become the only man in history to win the grand slam twice.

⮑Only one other man in the history of the game has completed a grand slam: America's Don Budge in 1938. Three women have achieved the feat: Maureen Connolly (1953), Margaret Smith Court (1970) and Steffi Graf (1988).

1969

Two grand slams (in 1962 and 1969) and a total of 11 grand slam tournament victories marked Australian Rod Laver out as one of the greatest tennis players in history. Who knows how high that tally of wins would be had he not lost five years of grand slam tournament play to professionalism?

BALCZO DELIGHTS HOME FANS WITH RECORD FIFTH PENTATHLON CROWN

ANDRAS BALCZO WINS WORLD PENTATHLON CHAMPIONSHIP FOR RECORD FIFTH CONSECUTIVE TIME

26 September 1969, Budapest, Hungary

Five individual world championships and an Olympic gold medal mark Hungary's Andras Balczo as the greatest modern pentathlete of recent times.

A fourth-place finish in the individual event, coupled with gold for Hungary in the pentathlon team event, at the 1960 Olympic Games in Rome highlighted 22-year-old Andras Balczo as a potential star of the future. A typewriter mechanic outside of competition, he combined his strength in swimming and cross-country with an all-round competence in shooting, fencing and horse riding to win the world championship for the first time in 1963: he would hold on to his title until 1969 – for four further championships (the tournament is not held during Olympic years). His fifth and final triumph came in front of his adoring home fans in 1969.

➲Although the reigning world champion, Balczo chose not to compete in the 1964 Olympics. He took individual silver in 1968 (along with a second team gold), but the greatest moment of his career came in 1972 when, aged 34, he took individual pentathlon gold in Munich.

QUALIFYING KING ISAAC FLATTERS TO DECEIVE

BOBBY ISAAC SETS NASCAR WINSTON CUP SINGLE-SEASON RECORD FOR THE MOST POLES

8 December 1969, Texas World Speedway, Texas, USA

Bobby Isaac secured a record 19 pole positions during the 1969 Winston Cup campaign – including a streak of ten consecutive – but still finished only in sixth place in the end-of-season overall drivers' standings.

A North Carolina native who left school before sixth grade to go and work in a sawmill, Bobby Isaac started to race full-time at the age of 24 in 1956. His first appearance in the Winston Cup came in 1961: his race lasted just two laps. His first win came three years later and by 1968 Isaac and his Dodge were ever-present on the starting grid, with three wins enough to secure the championship runner-up spot. The following year promised much, but delivered little: a king in qualifying, Isaac placed his car on pole a record 19 times during the course of the season (including ten consecutive) and although he visited victory lane 17 times, he couldn't translate his qualifying supremacy into championship dominance, ending the year in sixth place in the drivers' standings.

➲Isaac would not have to wait long for that elusive Winston Cup championship: he won 11 times in 1970 – with 13 pole positions – to become champion for the only time in his career.

SAWCHUK ADDS FINAL SHUTOUT TO CAREER RECORD

TERRY SAWCHUK COMPLETES NHL RECORD 103RD AND LAST SHUTOUT
2 February 1970, New York, USA

Born in Winnipeg, Manitoba, Canada, in 1929, goaltender Terry Sawchuk was signed to the Detroit Red Wings organization when he was 16 years old. Agile and, above all, fearless, Sawchuk played his first full season in the NHL in 1951–52: a 1.99 goals against average was enough to earn him the Calder Trophy as the league's top rookie, as well as his first Stanley Cup-winners' medal. Within five seasons he had recorded 199 wins and 57 shutouts, but was then traded to the Boston Bruins in 1954–55. He endured two miserable seasons before a move back to Detroit in 1957–58 revitalized his career. He went on to break George Hainsworth's career shutout record of 95 and continued playing until 1970, by which time he had recorded 103 shutouts, a record that remains unbroken to this day.

➲Less than three months after achieving his record 103rd shutout, Sawchuk died as a result of injuries sustained in a household accident. He was just 40 years old and was inducted into the NHL Hall of Fame the following year.

In a 19-year NHL career, during which he required some 600 stitches, Terry Sawchuk recorded 447 wins – a total that would stand as a record for 30 years – and an all-time record 103 career regular-season shutouts.

With his dazzling ball-handling, incredible shooting ability and creative passing, Pete Maravich broke every record standing during his three-year college career (1968–70) and ended his collegiate career in style, breaking the NCAA single-season points record with 1,381.

PISTOL PETE BOWS OUT IN STYLE

PETE MARAVICH BREAKS THE NCAA SINGLE-SEASON POINTS RECORD

March 1970, Baton Rouge, Louisiana, USA

Born in 1947, Pete Maravich showed remarkable basketball abilities from a young age and wowed university scouts with his dazzling on-court skills. But his father gave him a choice of one university: Louisiana State University, where the elder Maravich served as basketball coach. Young Pete made a spectacular start to his college career, averaging a staggering 43.8 points per game in an era before the three-point line. Yet it would turn out to be the worst season of his college career. The 6ft 5in guard, continuing to astound the crowds with his sleight-of-hand artistry, upped the average to 44.2 the following year. He did even better in his final year, 1970, averaging 44.5 points per game en route to scoring an NCAA record 1,381 points.

➲Maravich graduated from Louisiana State University in 1970 and made history when he signed a record $1.6 million deal with the Atlanta Hawks. He went on to enjoy a ten-year career in the NBA and was voted to the All-Star team five times.

Brazil's magnificent displays in the 1970 World Cup in Mexico helped Pele to a slice of history: he became the only man ever to have won the World Cup three times.

➲Pele's goal in the final meant he became only the second player in World Cup history (along with Vava) to score in two separate World Cup finals. Paul Breitner (1974 and 1982) and Zinedine Zidane (1996 and 2004) are the only two other players to achieve the feat.

PELE SHINES IN WORLD CUP SWANSONG

PELE BECOMES FIRST SOCCER PLAYER IN HISTORY TO WIN THREE WORLD CUP-WINNERS' MEDALS

21 June 1970, Azteca Stadium, Mexico City, Mexico

Pele had burst on to the international soccer stage with some stunning performances during the 1958 World Cup as Brazil won the tournament for the first time. But an injury picked up in the first game of the 1962 World Cup meant he played little part in Brazil's World Cup defence (although he still picked up a winners' medal) and when he announced his international retirement following England's win in 1966, it seemed Pele's World Cup odyssey had come to a disappointing end. But the lure of one last World Cup proved too hard to resist, and Pele stamped his name in the annals of World Cup legend, contributing four goals – including the first in the 4–1 final win over Italy – as Brazil romped to their third World Cup crown. Pele had become the first soccer player in history to win the competition three times.

ZAGALLO'S BRAZILIAN BLEND A WORLD CUP WINNER

MARIO ZAGALLO BECOMES FIRST MAN IN HISTORY TO WIN WORLD CUP AS BOTH PLAYER AND MANAGER

21 June 1970, Azteca Stadium, Mexico City, Mexico

A World Cup winner with Brazil in both 1958 and 1962, playing in the left-forward position, Mario Zagallo took charge of his national team shortly before the start of the 1970 World Cup in Mexico. His brief was short and to the point: to create a system to accommodate the stellar talents of Pele, Jairzinho, Rivelino, Gerson et al. and to retain the world crown they had ceded to England four years earlier. Zagallo came up with the never-before-seen, interchangeable, 3-5-2/5-3-2 formation and it suited Brazil to a tee: they scored 19 times en route to a third title and Zagallo became the first man in World Cup history to have won the tournament both as a player and manager.

➲ Zagallo also played a part in Brazil's fourth World Cup win in the United States in 1994, serving as an assistant coach to Carlos Alberto Parreira.

Mario Zagallo guided Brazil to World Cup success in Mexico in 1970 to become one of only two men to have won the tournament both as a player and manager (the other being West Germany's Franz Beckenbauer, as a player in 1974 and as manager in 1990).

COURT PRODUCES GREATEST SEASON IN TENNIS HISTORY

MARGARET COURT WINS WTA RECORD 21 TOURNAMENTS DURING SEASON

13 September 1970, Forest Hills, New York, USA

By numbers alone, Margaret Court compiled the most successful career in tennis history: in 1970 she put together the greatest season the sport has ever seen, winning a staggering 21 of the 27 tournaments she entered.

When she announced her retirement in 1967 at the age of 25, 12-time grand slam winner Margaret Court was already assured a place in the history books. But the lure of competition was too strong for the tall, athletic Australian and by 1968 she was back on the trail of more championships. She added three more grand slam titles to her collection in 1969 (missing out only on Wimbledon), but that merely served as a prelude to the greatest year of her career, and perhaps in tennis. In 1970, Court won 21 of the 27 tournaments she entered, a WTA record, and compiled a match record of 104–6. In the process, she also became the second woman in history to win the grand slam.

➲By the time she retired in 1977, Margaret Court had compiled a record total of 62 grand slam titles: 24 singles, 19 doubles and 19 mixed doubles. She is one of only three players in tennis history to have completed the boxed set of winning every grand slam title available to them (singles, doubles, mixed doubles).

Gary Gabelich's need for speed took him to the world land speed record in Blue Flame in 1970; 14 years later it would take his life when he was killed in a motorcycle accident in Long Beach, California.

GABELICH JETS TO WORLD LAND SPEED RECORD

GARY GABELICH AND *BLUE FLAME* BECOME FIRST TO BREAK THE 1,000KM/H BARRIER
23 October 1970, Bonneville Salt Flats, Utah, USA

➲Gabelich's record would last for 13 years, until Britain's Richard Noble and *Thrust I* powered to 633.468mph (1,019.47km/h) on 4 October 1983.

Born in San Pedro, California, in 1940, Gary Gabelich almost certainly claimed a slice of history for himself (records are inconclusive) when, as a 19-year-old, he propelled a car to 356mph (587.39km/h) over the Bonneville Salt Flats. Eight years later, he made a name for himself when he became the first man in drag racing history to break into the seven-second bracket. The Californian simply liked speed and so was the perfect man to steer the high-performing, ultra-high-speed, rocket-powered *Blue Flame* car in its attempt on the world land speed record at the same Utah salt flat in 1970. They reached an average speed of 622.407mph (1,001.67km/h) to become the first in history to pass through the 1,000km/h barrier.

RINDT'S MEMORY SECURED WITH WORLD CHAMPIONSHIP SUCCESS

JOCHEN RINDT BECOMES FORMULA ONE'S ONLY POSTHUMOUS WORLD CHAMPION

25 October 1970, Autodromo Hermanos Rodriguez, Mexico City, Mexico

It wasn't until 1969 that Austrian Jochen Rindt finally found a drive worthy of his enormous talent. Five years into his Formula One career Rindt moved to Lotus and tasted his first race victory, in the 1969 US Grand Prix at Watkins Glen, en route to a fourth-place finish in the drivers' championship. He took his Lotus 72 to victory in the 1970 season-opening Monaco GP and four further wins put him in command of the drivers' championship. Then disaster struck: Rindt was killed during practice for the Italian GP. However, no driver could overtake his points haul and, come the end of the season, the Austrian became the first man in history to win the Formula One World Championship posthumously.

Jochen Rindt did not live to see his greatest day. In complete control of the 1970 Formula One World Championship, he was killed during practice for the Italian GP at Monza, but nobody could overtake him at the top of the drivers' rankings come the end of the season.

➲The trophy was awarded to Rindt's widow, Nina, the daughter of famous Finnish racer Curt Lincoln. She revealed that, ironically, her husband had promised to retire if he won the drivers' title.

THE START OF CRICKET'S REVOLUTION

AUSTRALIA AND ENGLAND CONTEST CRICKET'S FIRST-EVER ONE-DAY INTERNATIONAL

5 January 1971, Melbourne Cricket Ground, Melbourne, Australia

Three days of prolonged rain had left the third Test match of the 1970–71 Ashes series between Australia and England in tatters and a disquieted Melbourne public restless. So, on the scheduled final day of the abandoned Test match, officials decided to host the first-ever one-day international, on the same ground where Test cricket had begun 94 years earlier. A crowd of 46,000 flocked to the Melbourne Cricket Ground as England, batting first, reached a disappointing 190 all out in their 40 overs. To the joy of the crowd, Australia cantered to a five-wicket victory with five overs to spare. The officials were happy too: they received a record $33,894.60 (Australian dollars) in gate receipts. Cricket's revolution had begun.

Prolonged rain and a restless holiday public prompted the staging of the first one-day international in history, between Australia and England at Melbourne in January 1971. Australia won the day.

➲England would enjoy more success in the seven-match Test series. Under the leadership of Ray Illingworth they won 2–0 to regain the Ashes.

Renowned for their showmanship, all-round basketball ability and their seeming inability to lose a game, the Harlem Globetrotters were forced to regroup after suffering a shock loss to the New Jersey Reds in 1971. They recovered well: no one would beat them again for 24 years.

REDS SHOCK THE GLOBETROTTERS TO END RECORD-BREAKING RUN

HARLEM GLOBETROTTERS' 2,495-GAME WINNING STREAK COMES TO AN END

5 January 1971, Martin, Tennessee, USA

They were founded in 1926 in Chicago as the Savoy Big Five, but when sports promoter Abe Saperstein acquired the rights to the club's players the following year he decided to give them a new name: the Harlem Globetrotters. Saperstein chose the name because of its resonance with the African-American community (all of his players were black). Originally a competitive team, the Globetrotters evolved into one of the greatest entertainment franchises in history, touring the world and playing exhibition matches against hand-picked, and usually weaker, opposition. But on 5 January 1971, the New Jersey Reds were having none of their under-card status and shocked the Globetrotters 100–99 to end their 2,495-game winning streak.

➲The Globetrotters recovered by embarking on an unbeaten run that would stretch some 24 years and 8,829 games, before falling to Kareem Abdul-Jabbar's All-Star team in Vienna, Austria, on 12 September 1995.

Knighted in 1968 after masterminding Manchester United's successful assault on the European Cup, Matt Busby spent 21 years turning the Reds into one of the giants of the modern game.

SIR MATT FINALLY CALLS IT A DAY

MATT BUSBY RETIRES AS LONGEST-SERVING MANAGER IN ENGLISH SOCCER

2 June 1971, Manchester, England

Matt Busby took over the reins at Manchester United in October 1946 aged 36 promising a more "hands-on" approach. Considered the first tracksuit manager, he led an ageing United team to their first championship in 40 years in 1952 before constructing a team that came to be known as the "Busby Babes"; they won championships in 1956 and 1957 before a plane crash in Munich in 1958 left the Babes decimated and Busby fighting for his life. He recovered and went on to build a new dynasty, the highlight of which came with victory in the 1968 European Cup final. Busby retired the following year, but returned for one more season in 1970–71 before bringing the curtain down on his record-breaking 21-year stint at the managerial helm.

➲Busby retired as one of the most successful managers in the history of English soccer: he collected five championships (1952, 1956, 1957, 1965 and 1967), won the FA Cup twice (in 1948 and 1963) and the European Cup once (in 1968).

SVEDLUND CONQUERS THE INDIAN OCEAN

ANDERS SVEDLUND BECOMES FIRST ROWER TO COMPLETE SOLO CROSSING OF THE INDIAN OCEAN

23 June 1971, Ankirikiriyr, Madagascar

After two previous aborted efforts which had seen him desperately paddling back to the Australian shore, 43-year-old Swede Anders Svedlund, a naturalized New Zealander, finally set off from Kalbarri, Western Australia, in his quest to row across the Indian Ocean on 29 April 1971. All he had with him for company in his 21ft glass-fibre boat, *Roslagena*, was four pairs of spare oars, 50 gallons of drinking water, a desalination plant, some food and some fishing tackle. Sixty-four days later he came ashore on the island of Madagascar, completing a 4,400-mile (7,081km) journey, to become the first rower in history to complete a solo crossing of the Indian Ocean.

⮑ The feat has been equalled only twice: by Britain's Simon Chalk in 2003 and by Ukrainian Pavel Rezvoy in 2005. In 1974, Svedlund completed a 6,462-mile (10,399km) crossing from Chile to Western Samoa to become the first rower to complete a mid-Pacific Ocean crossing.

FALCK SMASHES THROUGH TWO-MINUTE BARRIER

HILDEGARD FALCK BECOMES FIRST WOMAN TO RUN THE 800M IN UNDER TWO MINUTES

11 July 1971, Stuttgart, Germany

Born in Nettelrede, near Hannover, West Germany, in 1949, Hildegard Falck (née Janze), at 1.73m tall and weighing 58kg, had the ideal build for middle-distance running. She first came to the world's attention when she won the German indoor championships in 1970 at the age of 20 and, when she won the European indoor championships a year later, was being talked of as a contender to become the first woman to break the mythical two-minute barrier for 800m; the best anyone had previously done was Yugoslavia's Vera Nikolic, with 2m00.5s in 1968. The whisperers were right: in front of her home fans in Stuttgart, West Germany, in July 1971, Falck shattered the existing world record by two seconds. Her record-breaking time: 1m58.45s.

⮑ Falck's record would stand for little more than two years. On 24 August 1973 in Athens, Bulgaria's Svetla Zlateva clocked 1m57.5s.

Falck was at her best in front of a home crowd: the following year, in Munich, she won gold in the 800m final with an Olympic record-breaking time (one-tenth of a second outside of her world record time).

BEAMES BREAKS THREE-HOUR BARRIER FOR MARATHON

ADRIENNE BEAMES FIRST WOMAN TO RUN A MARATHON IN UNDER THREE HOURS

31 August 1971, Werribee, Victoria, Australia

For too many years, the 26-mile-365-yard (42.195km) marathon course was considered too demanding, too brutal for women to tackle. Indeed, in the early Olympics women were barred from competing in any distance longer than 200m. But by the early 1970s, competition rules had been relaxed – even though the longest event for women at the 1972 Olympic Games was the 1,500m – and women no longer had to hide in bushes or disguise themselves as men to compete in marathons. On 31 August 1971, on the same day American Dave Scott became the first man to drive a car on the moon, Australia's Adrienne Beames became the first woman to run a marathon in under three hours: her record-breaking time in Werribee, Australia, was 2h46.30m.

➲The marathon formed part of the women's Olympic schedule for the first time in Los Angeles in 1984. USA's Joan Benoit won in a time of 2h24m52s.

MUSCLES ROLLS BACK THE YEARS TO CLAIM TENTH GRAND SLAM TITLE

KEN ROSEWALL BECOMES OLDEST-EVER MALE WINNER OF THE AUSTRALIAN OPEN

2 January 1972, Melbourne, Australia

Ken Rosewall had put paid to any whispers that his first Australian Open win in 1953 was a flash in the pan when he claimed the French Open title a few months later: the 18-year-old Sydney-born left-hander was one of the hottest properties in tennis. With a game built around athleticism and precision rather than power – his fellow competitors nicknamed him "Muscles" on account of his slight stature – Rosewall's tennis shelf life was always going to be longer than most and, by 1972, with nine grand slam tournament victories to his name and with his renowned backhand still functioning smoothly, he found time for one last hurrah in the Australian Open, beating Mal Anderson 7–6, 6–3, 7–5 in the final to become, at 37 years, 2 months, the tournament's oldest-ever winner.

➲To round off a memorable tournament for Rosewall, he also partnered Owen Davidson to the doubles crown when they beat Ross Case and Geoff Masters 3–6, 7–6, 6–2 in the final.

Aged 37, Ken Rosewall won the Australian Open for the fourth time to collect the last of his ten grand slam tournament victories.

LAKERS WIN 33 TIMES ON THE BOUNCE

LOS ANGELES LAKERS RECORD 33-GAME WINNING STREAK IN THE NBA

9 January 1972, Los Angeles, California, USA

When the Boston Celtics' period of dominance finally came to an end in the early 1970s, the Los Angeles Lakers were only too happy to become basketball's top dog. Under new coach Bill Sharman for the 1971–72 NBA season, the Lakers went 6–3 through the first month of the season. On 5 November 1971 they beat Baltimore 110–106 to mark the first of 14 straight victories; a 16–0 record in December saw them breeze past the Milwaukee Bucks' record of 20 straight wins set the previous year. Three further wins at the start of the New Year saw the Lakers extend their streak to 33, before the Bucks brought it to an end on 9 January 1972 when they ran out 120–104 winners.

➲ The Lakers ended the year with 69 wins (a record that would last until the Chicago Bulls went 72–10 in 1995–96) and went on to beat the New York Knicks 4–1 in the playoff finals to win their first NBA Championship for 18 years.

Coach Bill Sharman led the Los Angeles Lakers to a then-record 69 wins and the NBA Championship in his first season in charge in 1971–72; 33 of those wins came consecutively.

THE HURRICANE BLOWS INTO TOWN

ALEX HIGGINS BECOMES YOUNGEST-EVER WINNER OF WORLD SNOOKER CHAMPIONSHIP

28 February 1972, Selly Park, Birmingham, England

Alex Higgins learned his trade at the Jampot snooker club in Belfast in his youth. By the age of 19 he had won the All-Ireland and Northern Ireland amateur championships and turned professional in 1972. Snooker had never seen anything like him: unorthodox and brash (both on and off the table), Higgins twitched his way round the table and advanced through to the final of the world championship – that year the tournament was played on a knockout basis throughout the year – to face defending world champion John Spencer. The fans that flocked to the Selly Park British Legion in Birmingham saw a slice of history: Higgins won 37–32 to become, aged 23, the youngest world snooker champion in history.

➲ Higgins remained the world snooker championship's youngest winner until Stephen Hendry won the title in 1990 aged 21.

Nicknamed the "Hurricane" because of his speed around the table, Alex Higgins lived up to his name when he won the world snooker championships at his first attempt in 1972.

FAIRFAX AND COOK CONQUER THE PACIFIC

JOHN FAIRFAX AND SYLVIA COOK BECOME THE FIRST ROWERS TO COMPLETE CROSSING OF PACIFIC OCEAN

22 April 1972, Hayman Island, Queensland, Australia

A successful solo crossing of the Atlantic in *Britannia* in 1969 did little to quell the spirit of adventure coursing through John Fairfax's veins. Two years later he set off on a death-defying attempt, along with Sylvia Cook, to become the first to complete a successful crossing of the Pacific Ocean. The pair started out, without GPS, from San Francisco in *Britannia* II on 26 April 1971. They defied hurricanes – they were caught up in Cyclone Emily and feared lost – and a lack of water, which forced them to make three stops to replenish fresh water supplies. They even had battles with sharks – Fairfax was severely bitten by one before Cook dragged him into the boat, sewed him up and rowed on. The pair reached Hayman Island, off the coast of Queensland, Australia, 361 days after their departure to international acclaim.

⮣ Britain's Peter Bird completed the first solo crossing of the Pacific on 14 June 1982; it took him 294 days. Sylvia Cook remains one of only two women, the other being America's Kathleen Saville in 1984, to have achieved the feat.

John Fairfax and Sylvia Cook defied all nature could throw at them to haul themselves across the Pacific Ocean inch by agonizing inch in 1971–72.

GROSSE SOARS TO NEW WORLD BEST

HANS WERNER GROSSE BREAKS DISTANCE GLIDING WORLD RECORD

25 April 1972, Biarritz, France

A Luftwaffe pilot during the Second World War and a glider enthusiast since his teens, Germany's Hans Werner Grosse, winner of the 1970 glider world championships, had dominated the gliding world record scene for many years, breaking some 47 world records. A 48th came when he attempted to break the straight line distance soaring record in his ASW12 in 1972. Setting off from Lübeck on the coast of the Baltic Sea, he soared his way across Europe before touching down in Biarritz, France, just short of the Spanish border. Grosse had covered a colossal 907.7 miles (1,460.8km) to break the existing world record by 170 miles (274km).

⮣ Grosse's record would stand for over 30 years. On 4 December 2004, New Zealand's Terry Delore set a new mark at 1,362.6 miles (2,192.9km) in Argentina.

DER BOMBER CONTINUES TO HIT THE BACK OF THE NET

GERD MULLER BECOMES THE FIRST TWO-TIME WINNER OF SOCCER'S GOLDEN BOOT

May 1972, Munich, Germany

Short and stocky, but notoriously fast and strong, Gerd Muller joined Bayern Munich as an 18-year-old when the side were still in the West German second division: the pint-sized striker found the net 33 times in 26 games as Bayern achieved promotion to the Bundesliga. And still the goals continued to flow: 62 of them in three seasons before Muller's 30 goals in 30 appearances helped Bayern to the first championship success in their history in 1969. He did even better the following year, scoring 38 goals in 33 matches to win the Golden Boot, as Europe's top scorer, for the first time. He became the first person to win it twice two years later, scoring 40 goals in 34 games as Bayern took the Bundesliga title for a second time.

⊃Only one other player in history has won the Golden Boot twice: Rangers' Ally McCoist in 1992 and 1993 (with 34 goals in both seasons). Muller did not restrict his goal-scoring prowess to the Bundesliga; he was prolific on the international scene as well, scoring 68 goals in 62 appearances for West Germany.

A true "fox in the box", Gerd Muller scored goals with every team he played for: his 365 goals in 427 career appearances for Bayern Munich helped establish the Bavarian club as one of the giants of European soccer and took the diminutive striker to two Golden Boot awards (in 1970 and 1972).

A losing finalist in the 1969 Australian Open, Andres Gimeno had his day of days in the 1972 French Open, winning the last title of his career and his first grand slam at 34 years of age.

GIMENO ENJOYS GRAND SLAM SUCCESS IN TWILIGHT OF CAREER

ANDRES GIMENO BECOMES OLDEST-EVER MEN'S CHAMPION AT THE FRENCH OPEN

5 June 1972, Roland Garros, Paris, France

Tall, at 6ft 2in, supremely fit and the possessor of rapier-like ground-strokes and a booming serve, Barcelona-born Andres Gimeno had the game to achieve far more in the tennis world than his career numbers suggest. A winner of the Wimbledon men's doubles crown, along with Pancho Gonzalez, in 1967, he enjoyed four tournament wins. By the time of the 1972 French Open, it seemed Gimeno's career was coming to an undistinguished end, but the veteran found his form, battling through to the final against home favourite Patrick Proisy. Experience won the day and, at 34 years, 301 days, Gimeno became the oldest-ever winner of the men's French Open singles title.

⊃Gimeno retired the following year and set up a state-of-the-art tennis-training complex in Barcelona. He went on to coach a number of world stars, including Arantxa Sanchez Vicario, Mary Jo Fernandez and Alex Corretja.

IL SIGNOR DAVIS CUP

NICOLA PIETRANGELI WINS THE LAST OF HIS RECORD 120 DAVIS CUP RUBBERS

16–18 June 1972, Bucharest, Romania

Solidly built but deceptively fleet of foot, Nicola Pietrangeli was at his most comfortable on clay, winning the Roland Garros title in both 1959 and 1960. But he also flourished in the Davis Cup arena, almost single-handedly pulling Italy through the competition between 1954 and 1972. In all he played in a record 66 Davis Cup ties, appearing in a record 164 rubbers in singles and doubles and winning 120 of them. He led his country to the Davis Cup final in 1960 and 1961, but on both occasions they lost to Australia. Pietrangeli's final Davis Cup appearance came when he partnered Adriano Panatta to a doubles loss against Romania's Ilie Nastase and Ion Tiriac in Budapest in 1972. Italy lost the tie 4–1.

⊃After his retirement, Pietrangeli became Italy's captain and guided them to their first-ever Davis Cup win in 1976 (they beat Chile 4–1).

Nobody has played or won more Davis Cup matches than Italy's Nicola Pietrangeli: over 18 years he played in 164 rubbers with a record of 78–32 in singles and 42–12 in doubles.

DOMINANT AGOSTINI ROMPS TO SEVENTH 500CC SUCCESS

GIACOMO AGOSTINI WINS 11 RACES EN ROUTE TO CLAIMING RECORD SEVENTH CONSECUTIVE 500CC WORLD TITLE

30 July 1972, Imatra, Finland

Giacomo Agostini got his break when he was chosen as factory driver for the Morini team in 1964. He won that year's 350cc Italian championship and finished fourth in the Italian GP. His performances earned him a ride with the MV Agusta team for 1965. He recovered from a last-gasp runner-up finish in his first season to win the 500cc championship in 1966. The following year, he fought a season-long battle with Mike Hailwood (both had five race wins) before winning the title on account of his three second-place finishes to Hailwood's two. It was the last close call Agostini would experience for the next five years. During his period of dominance he won an astonishing 49 races of the 56 he entered, including a record 11 out of 13 in 1972 en route to a unique seventh consecutive 500cc world championship.

➲ Agostini's dominance during that period was not restricted just to the 500cc arena. Between 1968 and 1974 the Italian also won seven consecutive 350cc world championships.

Giacomo Agostini was the true king of the road between 1966 and 1972, collecting seven consecutive 500cc world championships and winning an astonishing 76 per cent of the races he entered during that time.

SPITZ'S MAGNIFICENT SEVEN

SWIMMER MARK SPITZ WINS A RECORD SEVEN GOLD MEDALS AT MUNICH OLYMPICS
26 August–11 September 1972, Munich, Germany

Disappointed by his performances during the 1968 Olympic Games in Mexico (two relay gold medals did little to hide his sense of failure following silver in the 100m butterfly and bronze in the 100m freestyle), Mark Spitz moved to Indiana University to spend time with legendary swimming coach Doc Counsilman. The results were immediate: the following year, Spitz, of Jewish origins, competed in the Maccabiah Games – the Jewish Olympics held every four years in Israel – and walked away with six gold medals. He travelled to the 1972 Olympic Games in Munich vowing to repeat the feat. In fact he did even better. Putting together one of the most prolonged periods of swimming excellence the world has seen, Spitz won every event he entered – 100m freestyle, 200m freestyle, 100m butterfly, 200m butterfly, 4x100m freestyle, 4x200m freestyle and 4x100m medley – all of them in world-record times, to become the first swimmer in history to win seven gold medals at a single Olympic Games.

➲Sadly Spitz's achievements were overshadowed by events beyond the fields of competition. During the Games, a Palestinian terrorist group called "Black September" took a number of Israeli athletes hostage. By the time it was all over, 11 athletes, one police officer and five of the eight terrorists were dead. The ramifications of the incident sent shockwaves around the world.

Champion swimmer Mark Spitz arrived in Munich for the 1972 Olympic Games vowing to win six gold medals. He exceeded his boast, winning all seven events he entered in world-record times.

Olga Korbut changed the face of gymnastics for ever at the 1972 Olympic Games in Munich, thrilling the crowds with her compelling displays of grace and power, including a never-before-seen backward somersault on the balance beam.

KORBUT CHARMS WORLD WITH SKILL AND COURAGE

OLGA KORBUT PERFORMS BACKWARD SOMERSAULT ON BALANCE BEAM FOR THE FIRST TIME

26 August–11 September 1972, Munich, Germany

In 1966, at the age of 11, Belarus-born Soviet gymnast Olga Korbut joined up with coach Renald Kynsh and the pair set about devising routines that would shift the emphasis in the sport from grace to power. Indeed, so dangerous were these routines considered at the time that the sport's governing body thought of banning them. The entire world was glad they didn't. In the 1972 Munich Olympics, Korbut was the star of the show, thrilling the packed stadium with her radiant smile, her bubbling personality and, above all, her gymnastic brilliance. The 17-year-old took gold in the team event, the floor exercise and on the balance beam. In the latter she was astonishing, thrilling the crowd when she became the first gymnast in history to complete a backward somersault on the beam as part of her gold-medal winning routine.

⟳Korbut was strongly fancied to win the individual title as well, but missed her mount on the bars three times and her disastrous score of 7.5 allowed team-mate Ludmilla Tourischeva to take the title.

WINKLER DELIGHTS HOME CROWD WITH FIFTH GOLD

HANS-GUNTHER WINKLER COLLECTS RECORD FIFTH OLYMPIC SHOW-JUMPING GOLD MEDAL

26 August–10 September 1972, Munich, Germany

The son of a horse and jockey trainer born in Wuppertal, West Germany, in 1924, Hans-Gunther Winkler seemed destined to spend his life associated with horses. And, indeed, he displayed such horsemanship over numerous years that he is widely considered one of the greatest horsemen of all time. World champion in 1954 and 1955, the following year he took Olympic gold in both the team and show-jumping competitions (staged in Stockholm, Sweden, because of quarantine restrictions in Melbourne). The West German team repeated the feat in both 1960 (Rome) and 1964 (Japan) and, although they missed out on a hat-trick in Mexico in 1968 (they won bronze), their 1972 success in front of their home fans in Munich meant Winkler had become the only show-jumper in history to collect five Olympic gold medals.

➲With a silver medal in Montreal four years later Winkler became one of only four people in history to collect medals at six separate Olympic Games.

Hans-Gunther Winkler, the most decorated equestrian rider in Olympic history, won seven medals – five of them gold – in a 24-year Olympic career.

Mary Peters, a 33-year-old secretary from Belfast, needed to produce a world-record-breaking performance to win Britain's sole gold medal at the 1972 Olympics in Munich, and even that was only enough to secure pentathlon gold by the slender margin of ten points.

NEW WORLD BEST JUST ENOUGH FOR PETERS

MARY PETERS TAKES OLYMPIC PENTATHLON GOLD WITH WORLD RECORD POINTS HAUL

3 September 1972, Munich, Germany

A prodigious work ethic helped Mary Peters turn her raw talent into a successful two-decade-long career. The Commonwealth pentathlon champion in 1970 and 1974, her crowning moment came with a spectacular performance in the 1972 Olympic Games. On day one, she set personal bests in all three events – hurdles, shot and high jump – to lead local favourite Heide Rosendahl by 301 points. The following day Peters suffered disappointment in the long jump – Rosendahl's strongest discipline. It meant the competition was wide open going into the final event, the 200m. The German won again; but Peters – running a personal best – finished fourth, enough to claim gold by a meagre ten points. In addition, her total of 4,801 points stood as a new world and Olympic record.

➲The pentathlon became the heptathlon from the 1984 Olympics, when the javelin and 800m were added to the other five events.

FLYING FITTIPALDI BECOMES F1'S YOUNGEST CHAMPION

BRAZILIAN BLASTS OPPOSITION ASIDE TO BECOME FORMULA ONE'S BEST

10 September 1972, Monza, Italy

A national champion in Formula Vee by the age of 21, Emerson Fittipaldi left Brazil in 1969 seeking fame and fortune in Europe. Some dazzling performances in Formula Ford caught the attention of Lotus boss Colin Chapman, who signed Fittipaldi to his team to partner Jochen Rindt for the 1970 Formula One season. By the end of the season, following Rindt's death at Monza, the Brazilian had become team leader. If 1971 was all about car development, then 1972 was a demonstration of what hard work can achieve. Fittipaldi and his Lotus 72D proved unstoppable, and their fifth victory of the season, at Monza, was enough to see him secure his first drivers' world championship. At 25 years, 273 days, Fittipaldi had become the sport's youngest world champion.

⟳ Fittipaldi would go on to repeat his World Championship success in 1974, this time with McLaren. He was also successful on the other side of the Atlantic, winning the CART championship in 1989 and claiming wins in the Indianapolis 500 in 1989 and 1993.

The Lotus 72D was certainly the car to be driving during the 1972 Formula One World Championship, powering 25-year-old Emerson Fittipaldi to five race wins and the world title. His status as Formula One's youngest-ever world champion lasted until 2005, when Fernando Alonso claimed his first drivers' World Championship aged 24 years, 59 days.

Already a four-time winner of the Tour de France, Eddy Merckx made sure his cycling legend was complete when he broke the world hour record in Mexico City in 1972.

MERCKX SHATTERS ANOTHER CYCLING MILESTONE

EDDY MERCKX BREAKS CYCLING'S WORLD HOUR RECORD

25 October 1972, Mexico City, Mexico

Cycling's world hour record had been a feather in the cap of all the sport's greats. It had been Fausto Coppi's first statement of intent in the cycling world in 1942, before going on to win the Tour de France in 1949 and 1952, and for Jacques Anquetil in 1956 it served as a prelude to five Tour wins in eight years. For Belgium's Eddy Merckx – nicknamed "The Cannibal" following his four successive Tour victories (1969–72) – it was the only thing missing from an already immaculate resumé. On 25 October 1972, in Mexico City, Merckx challenged Ole Ritter's world hour record distance of 48.653km set in Mexico City in 1968. He shattered it by 0.778km and afterwards described it as the hardest thing he had ever done.

⟳ Merckx's record would stand for 28 years and became one of the most legendary milestones in cycling. Britain's Chris Boardman finally broke it in 2000 when he covered 49.441km in Manchester.

PERFECT DOLPHINS WIN SUPER BOWL VII

MIAMI DOLPHINS FIRST TO RECORD A PERFECT REGULAR SEASON AND A PERFECT POSTSEASON

14 January 1973, LA Coliseum, Los Angeles, California, USA

If Miami Dolphins coach Don Shula had been looking for a response from his players following the team's 24–3 Super Bowl VI loss to the Dallas Cowboys, then he could have asked for no more. The Dolphins swept through the regular season, astounding onlookers with their attacking zest and winning 14 games out of 14. They breezed through the playoffs to take their place in Super Bowl VII against the Washington Redskins and it was the Dolphins' defence that won the day – nicknamed the "No Name Defence" because all the plaudits went to the attackers – as a 14–7 victory ended the first and only perfect season in NFL history.

A season of perfection in 1972 – played 17 won 17 – culminated in the Miami Dolphins winning the Super Bowl for the first time in the franchise's history.

➲ The Dolphins reached Super Bowl VIII the following year – becoming the first team in NFL history to reach three consecutive Super Bowls – and beat the Minnesota Vikings 24–7.

DOMINANT THÖNI COMPLETES SKIING HAT-TRICK

GUSTAV THÖNI FIRST TO WIN THE SKIING WORLD CUP THREE YEARS IN A ROW

24 March 1973, Heavenly Valley, California/Nevada, USA

The skiing World Cup – a series of downhill, slalom and giant slalom races around the world (the combined was added in 1974–75 and the Super G in 1982–83), with points allocated to each race – suited Italy's Gustav Thöni to a tee. A master in slalom and giant slalom, he dominated both events during the 1970–71 season to win the competition for the first time. After winning giant slalom gold in the 1972 Winter Olympics, he took his second successive World Cup in 1972–73, by 14 points. A hat-trick of titles came the following year, as Thöni became the first skier in history to win the competition three years in a row.

➲ Thöni won the World Cup for a fourth time in 1974–75. Only Marc Girardelli, with five, has won more.

A specialist in slalom and giant slalom, Italy's Gustav Thöni dominated the skiing World Cup in the early 1970s, winning it four times in five years.

Secretariat, a large chestnut thoroughbred, stole a nation's heart when he collected the Triple Crown, winning two of the three races in record-breaking time.

SUPERHORSE SECRETARIAT SPRINTS TO DERBY GLORY

SECRETARIAT WINS THE KENTUCKY DERBY IN RECORD-BREAKING TIME

5 May 1973, Churchill Downs, Louisville, Kentucky, USA

Sired by Bold Ruler, a fine mix of speed and stamina, Secretariat was jostled out of the gates in his first-ever race, as a two-year-old, and ended up in fourth place – the only time he would finish out of the money in 21 races. He won seven out of his next eight races to enter the 1973 Kentucky Derby as one of the favourites. Secretariat went on to produce one of the most measured displays of controlled perfection ever seen. Midway in the field entering the backstretch, he moved effortlessly past his rivals, before edging past his main rival Sham and sprinting past the winning post. His time of 1m59.4s was a new course record.

➲ Secretariat's victory in the Preakness Stakes – the second leg of the Triple Crown – a few weeks later sparked mass interest in the horse. When he won the Belmont Stakes in record-breaking time, to become the first horse to win the Triple Crown for a quarter of a century, he was declared a "Superhorse".

WILT THE STILT BOWS OUT AT THE TOP OF HIS GAME

WILT CHAMBERLAIN REGISTERS THE LAST OF CAREER RECORD 23,924 REBOUNDS

10 May 1973, Los Angeles, California, USA

If Wilt Chamberlain's stellar 14-year career in the NBA was supposed to be coming to an end, then someone forgot to tell him. Playing for the LA Lakers, the 36-year-old centre played like a man 15 years his junior, averaging 13.2 points and 18.6 rebounds per game (enough to lead the league for rebounds for the 11th time in his career) and recording an all-time NBA shooting accuracy from the field record with .727. The Lakers made it through to the NBA finals, losing in five games to the New York Knicks. It was the last the NBA saw of Chamberlain and he left with many records to his name: the most impressive being his career rebound total of 23,924 – a figure that will take some beating.

Wilt Chamberlain, the most dominant player the NBA has ever seen, played for the last time in the 1973 NBA finals and left the game with numerous records to his name.

➲ The following season Chamberlain took up a player-coach position with the San Diego Conquistadores, but the Lakers filed a lawsuit to prevent him from playing and won. Chamberlain remained with the Conquistadores in a coaching capacity, suffered a disappointing season and retired from both playing and coaching at the end of the season.

After years of failing to become the first woman in history to break the 11-second barrier for 100m – she clocked 11 seconds dead on three occasions – Renate Stecher clocked 10.9s in June 1973.

STECHER FINALLY GETS HER HANDS ON 100M RECORD

RENATE STECHER FIRST WOMAN TO BREAK THE 11-SECOND BARRIER IN 100 METRES

7 June 1973, Ostrava, Czechoslovakia

Since America's Wyomia Tyus had clocked 11 seconds dead to break the world record in the 100m final of the 1968 Olympic Games in Mexico City, four women had matched her feat, but none had bettered it. Among the new joint record-holders was East Germany's Renate Stecher and the smart money suggested that if anyone could break the now-infamous 11-second barrier it would be her: she had, after all, equalled the record on three occasions between 1970 and 1972, and by 1973 was the reigning 100m and 200m Olympic champion. Stecher finally lived up to her record-breaking billing on 7 June 1973 in Ostrava, Czechoslovakia, when she ran the 100m in 10.9s.

➲ The record would stand for over four years. On 1 July 1977, Marlies Oelsner-Göhr clocked 10.88s in Dresden in her native East Germany.

BEDFORD FINALLY MAKES MARK ON WORLD STAGE

DAVE BEDFORD BREAKS 10,000M WORLD RECORD IN FRONT OF HOME CROWD

13 July 1973, Crystal Palace, London, England

For the average athletics fan, following Dave Bedford's career provided nothing but disappointment. Brash and outspoken off the track, on it he was an enormously talented middle-distance runner – and a former world cross-country champion – who singularly failed to come up with the goods in the major championships; a sixth-place finish in the 10,000m final at the 1972 Olympic Games in Munich being his best showing in a major. Still his fans believed the British national record-holder could deliver more, and he did: in the 1973 AAA national championships in London, Bedford produced one of the most sensational runs in history to break Finn Lasse Viren's 10,000m world record by almost eight seconds. The new mark: 27m30.8s.

➲ Bedford's record would last until 30 June 1977, when Kenya's Samson Kimobwa clocked 27m30.47s.

Considered by many a serial underperformer, Dave Bedford finally gave his British fans something to cheer about when he set a world's best time for the 10,000m in 1973 in London.

No one ever doubted the speed of Nolan Ryan's fastballs, merely their accuracy, but a switch to the California sun did the trick. In his first season with the California Angels, Ryan struck out 329 batters; the following season, 1973, he set an all-time MLB single-season strikeout record with 383.

RYAN'S BLAZING FASTBALLS FINALLY FIND THEIR RANGE

NOLAN RYAN BREAKS SANDY KOUFAX'S SINGLE-SEASON STRIKEOUT RECORD

27 September 1973, Anaheim Stadium, Anaheim, California, USA

Nolan Ryan signed professional terms with the New York Mets as an 18-year-old and became the youngest player in the league when he was called up to the Major League in 1966, but his time with the New York club was a far from happy one. The right-handed pitcher may have possessed a blazing fastball, but his inability to find the strike zone meant he struggled to establish a regular place in the talented Mets pitching rotation. Ryan handed in a trade request in 1971, moved to the California Angels the following year and almost immediately found his range. In his first season he had a league-leading 329 strikeouts; in his second, 1973, he struck out 383 batters to beat Sandy Koufax's single-season record (382) by one.

➲Ryan went on to enjoy a record-tying 28-year career in the Major Leagues – he went on to play for the Houston Astros (1980–88) and the Texas Rangers (1989–93) – and holds several all-time records, including: most career strikeouts (5,714) and most bases on balls (2,795).

LOS PUMAS HAVE NO PEERS IN SOUTH AMERICAN RUGBY

ARGENTINA WIN THEIR 20TH CONSECUTIVE MATCH, A RECORD IN INTERNATIONAL RUGBY

21 October 1973, Buenos Aires, Argentina

Few could doubt Argentina's claim to being the greatest rugby nation in South America. They have dominated the rugby scene on the continent ever since they organized, and won, the first-ever South American rugby championship staged in Buenos Aires in 1951 and, following a 29–6 defeat by France on 17 August 1960, put together a 14-year, 20-game winning streak that has never been matched in international rugby. True, their opponents were all, bar two Tests against Romania, South American, but their record of 883 points for and 77 against during that period makes for impressive reading. Their 20th consecutive win came against Chile on 21 October 1973; then the French came to town in June 1974 and won 20–15.

➲Argentina's dominance over South American opposition continues to this day, and, finally, they are starting to enjoy success on the wider international stage. In 2007 they reached the Rugby World Cup semi-finals, losing only to champions elect South Africa.

Limited to playing against South American opponents for a 14-year stretch between 1960 and 1974, Argentina put together a winning streak of games never matched in international rugby.

THE JUICE FINALLY LIVES UP TO HIS REPUTATION

O.J. SIMPSON BECOMES FIRST IN NFL HISTORY TO RUSH FOR MORE THAN 2,000 YARDS IN A SINGLE SEASON

16 December 1973, Shea Stadium, New York, USA

After a stellar collegiate career that had seen him become a two-time All-American and the winner of the Heisman Trophy in 1968, O.J. Simpson was one of the most celebrated rookies in NFL history when the Buffalo Bills drafted him in 1969. His first three years were a struggle: used only sparingly as a running back, he averaged 622 yards over the first three seasons. Things improved when Lou Saban took charge of the Bills in 1972 and created a team whose primary concern was to unleash Simpson's attacking potential. The 6ft 1in, 210lb speedster responded in style, rushing for 1,251 yards. He did even better the following year, easing past Jim Brown's all-time single-season rushing record of 1,863 in the final game to end with 2,003.

⮑ Simpson's career came to an end in 1979; his career total of 11,236 rushing yards stands 14th on the all-time NFL list. He later became more famous for his alleged involvement in the killing of his estranged wife Nicole Brown and her friend Ronald Goldman. The "Trial of the Century" culminated on 3 October 1995 with the jury returning a not guilty verdict, but the rumours rumble on.

O.J. Simpson finally matched up to the reputation he had garnered as a college player in 1973, when he rushed for a then NFL record 2,003 yards.

BRILLIANT BAYI STUNS CROWD WITH 1,500M WORLD BEST

FILBERT BAYI BREAKS THE WORLD 1,500M RECORD BY NINE-TENTHS OF A SECOND

2 February 1974, Christchurch, New Zealand

Tanzania's Filbert Bayi silenced the home fans when his world-record-breaking performance in the 1,500m final pushed Kiwi John Walker into second place at the 1974 Commonwealth Games in Christchurch, New Zealand.

The highlight of the tenth staging of the Commonwealth Games, held in Christchurch, New Zealand, came in the final of the 1,500m. Anticipation swept through the crowd as home favourite John Walker took to the starting blocks; his major challenge for the Commonwealth crown would come from All-Africa champion Filbert Bayi from Tanzania and Kenya's Ben Jipcho. Sensationally, Walker ran inside Jim Ryun's 1967 world-record time of 3m33.1s, but the crowd were silent. Walker had finished second to Bayi, and the Tanzanian's time of 3m32.2s – almost nine-tenths of a second better than the previous world best – sent shockwaves around the athletics world.

⮑Bayi's record stood until Sebastian Coe ran 3m32.03s in Zurich on 15 August 1979. Race fans looking to enjoy further clashes between Bayi and Walker were disappointed when Tanzania withdrew from the 1976 Olympic Games, although Bayi did appear in Moscow in 1980, winning silver in the 3,000m steeplechase.

Austria's Annemarie Proll was untouchable in the women's skiing World Cup in the early 1970s, winning five consecutive titles between 1971 and 1975.

THE QUEEN OF THE SLOPES

ANNEMARIE PROLL BECOMES ONLY FEMALE SKIER TO WIN FOUR CONSECUTIVE WORLD CUPS

7 March 1974, Vysoke Tatry, Czechoslovakia

Born in Kleinarl, Austria, in 1953, Annemarie Proll learned her trade on the alpine slopes next to her village and went on to become the most dominant female skier ever seen. A specialist in downhill, giant slalom and combined, Proll won the World Cup for the first time in 1971 and defended her crown the following year. Her team-mate Monika Kaserer managed to reduce the deficit between first and second to 74 points in 1973, but could not prevent Proll from claiming a third successive victory, and a 115-point lead over Kaserer in 1974 was enough to secure Proll a place in skiing legend: she had become the only female skier in history to win the World Cup four times in a row.

⮑Proll would record a fifth successive World Cup win in 1975 and a sixth and final title in 1979. She rounded out her career in magnificent style with downhill gold at the 1980 Winter Olympics in Lake Placid, USA.

RECORD CROWD CHEERS AARON TO RECORD

HANK AARON BREAKS BABE RUTH'S RECORD FOR MOST CAREER HOME RUNS
8 April 1974, Atlanta, Georgia, USA

Far from being restricted by an unconventional cross-handed batting grip, Hank Aaron made his Major League debut for the Milwaukee Braves in 1954 and went on to become one of the most feared power hitters in baseball. He hit home runs for fun – 30 or more homers in a season 15 times – and by 1973 was closing in fast on Babe Ruth's all-time career home run record (714). The press stirred into action: Aaron finished the season on 713. The off-season was a difficult time: Aaron received death threats and feared for his life but, on 8 April 1974, in front of a record 53,775 crowd in Atlanta (the Braves had relocated there in 1966), he hit the 715th home run of his career. Ruth's sacrosanct record was no more.

❑Aaron ended his career in 1976 with 755 home runs to his name. The record stood until San Francisco Giants' Barry Bonds hit the 756th homer of his career on 7 August 2007.

Hank Aaron's chase for Babe Ruth's all-time career home run record became a national obsession, but the Braves slugger defied intrusive press coverage and death threats to take his place in the history books.

CHILE'S CASZELY FIRST TO SEE WORLD CUP RED

CHILE'S CARLOS CASZELY FIRST TO BE RED-CARDED IN A WORLD CUP FINALS MATCH

14 June 1974, Olympiastadion, Berlin, Germany

A crowd of 83,168 flocked to the Olympiastadion in Berlin to see the opening match between the hosts, West Germany, hot favourites for the tournament following their European Championship win in 1972, and Chile, who had qualified for their fifth World Cup after a controversial playoff victory over the Soviet Union. The match was uneventful: Paul Breitner scored from long range in the 18th minute to hand the hosts an expected advantage and they held on for a 1–0 win. But the 67th minute saw a slice of World Cup history when Chile striker Carlos Caszely became the first player to be red-carded in the tournament's history. (Others had been sent-off before).

Chile's Carlos Caszely claimed an unwanted piece of history when he became the first player in World Cup history to be red-carded, against West Germany in the opening game of the 1974 tournament.

➲The red-and-yellow card system had been introduced at the 1970 World Cup, but only yellow cards had been awarded. The World Cup's second red card came the following day when Uruguay's Julio Montero was sent off during his country's 2–0 defeat by the Netherlands.

NEESKENS GETS DUTCH OFF TO FLYING START

JOHANN NEESKENS FIRST PLAYER TO SCORE FROM PENALTY SPOT IN A WORLD CUP FINAL

7 July 1974, Olympiastadion, Munich, Germany

After a protracted second group phase the tournament's two best teams made it through to the 1974 World Cup final: hosts West Germany and the Netherlands, who had dazzled the world with their unique brand of "Total Soccer". With a buzz of anticipation sweeping around Munich's Olympiastadion, the Netherlands kicked off, stroked the ball around, then probed the right side of West Germany's defence. Now Johan Cruyff, the tournament's star player, darted on an incisive run and was brought down in the box by Uli Hoeness. Referee Jack Taylor pointed to the spot: penalty – the first in World Cup final history. Johann Neeskens slammed the spot-kick into the back of the net and West Germany, yet to touch the ball, found themselves 1–0 down.

The 1974 World Cup final got off to a sensational start when the Netherlands scored the first penalty in World Cup final history inside two minutes before finally falling 2–1 to hosts West Germany.

➲The second penalty in World Cup final history came 23 minutes later, this time awarded to West Germany, and Paul Breitner converted it. The Germans took the lead in the 43rd minute through Gerd Muller and held on to win 2–1 and claim the World Cup for the second time.

GIACOMO AGOSTINI: THE TWO-WHEEL KING

AGOSTINI WINS 350CC WORLD CHAMPIONSHIP FOR RECORD SEVENTH CONSECUTIVE YEAR

September 1974, Montjuich Park, Barcelona, Spain

Giacomo Agostini and his MV Agusta motorbike had been unstoppable in the 500cc division between 1966 and 1972, winning seven consecutive world championships in dominant fashion, and the combination of man and bike was no less impressive when they stepped down a formula and competed at 350cc level. He may have been forced to play second fiddle to Honda's Mike Hailwood in 1966 and 1967, but seven wins in seven races in 1968 were enough to secure the Italian his first-ever 350cc world championship. He would keep a firm grip on it for the next six years, winning 38 of the 64 races he entered (an astonishing 59.4 per cent rate over seven years of racing).

Only one rider managed two consecutive 350cc world championships (South Africa's Kork Ballington in 1978 and '79), before the formula was scrapped at the end of the 1982 season.

Italian Giacomo Agostini was the true master of two wheels and the man with whom all modern racing champions are compared. He won 15 world championships, eight of them in the 500cc division (seven consecutively) and seven in the 350cc (all of them consecutively).

Accompanied by a pack mule called Willie Makeit, brothers Dave and John Kunst set off on their journey around the world on foot on 20 June 1970. Over three years later only Dave Kunst returned.

THE EARTHWALKER RETURNS

DAVE KUNST FIRST VERIFIED PERSON TO WALK EARTH'S ENTIRE LAND MASS ON FOOT

5 October 1974, Waseca, Minnesota, USA

On 20 June 1970, Dave Kunst and his brother John set off from Waseca, Minnesota, and walked to New York, where they touched the Atlantic Ocean. They then flew to Lisbon, Portugal, touched the Atlantic and set off through Europe, Iran, Afghanistan – and disaster: they were attacked by bandits and shot, John fatally. Four months later, Dave and another brother, Pete, continued the journey from the spot of the attack and walked to Calcutta, touched the Indian Ocean, flew to Perth, Australia, touched the Indian Ocean and walked to Sydney, where they touched the Pacific Ocean. They then flew to the USA and touched the Pacific Ocean at Newport Beach, California. Dave arrived back in Waseca on 5 October 1974.

The entire 14,450-mile journey took 3 years, 3 months and 15 days.

CRUYFF VOTED EUROPE'S BEST FOR RECORD THIRD TIME

JOHAN CRUYFF BECOMES FIRST THREE-TIME WINNER OF EUROPEAN SOCCER PLAYER OF THE YEAR AWARD

December 1974, Paris, France

Johan Cruyff emerged from the shadows of Pele to become the finest soccer player in the world. Perhaps the greatest exponent of Total Soccer, he thrilled soccer fans the world over with his technical ability, speed and acceleration. He starred for Ajax when they won the European Cup for the first time in 1971 and ended the season as European Soccer Player of the Year. Cruyff scored both goals as Ajax defeated Inter Milan 2–0 in the 1972 European Cup final and, following a hat-trick of wins in 1973, collected his second European Soccer Player of the Year award. A switch to Barcelona in 1974 did little to affect his form: the Catalan giants won the league for the first time in 14 years, Cruyff helped the Netherlands to the World Cup final and ended the season as the first three-time winner of the European Soccer Player of the Year award in history.

Johan Cruyff's status as the finest player in the world in the early 1970s was confirmed with three European Soccer Player of the Year awards in four years between 1971 and '74.

➲Two other players have won the European Soccer Player of the Year award on three occasions: Michel Platini (1983, '84 and '85) and Marco van Basten (1988, '89 and '92).

They may have had a state-of-the-art stadium to play in – the boast was that no seat was more than 200ft away from the ice – but Yvon Labre and the Washington Capitals enjoyed little success in their debut season in the NHL in 1974–75, winning just eight games en route to compiling the worst season in NHL history.

CAPITALS CAPITULATE DURING DEBUT SEASON

WASHINGTON CAPITALS PRODUCE THE WORST SEASON IN NHL HISTORY

8 April 1975, Capital Center, Washington DC, USA

Abe Pollin had just built a state-of-the-art stadium, the Capital Center, to house his NBA team Washington Wizards and then turned his attentions to the NHL, forming the Washington Capitals as part of the NHL expansion for the 1974–75 season. He may have regretted his decision: the expansion and the increasing popularity of the World Hockey League provided a drain on experienced players and it showed. The Capitals went on to record the worst season in NHL history, losing 39 times out of 40 on the road, recording a paltry .131 winning average, collecting a miserable 21 points and ending the season with an 8–67–5 record. Their final-match 8–4 victory over Pittsburgh would have come as little consolation.

➲The following season saw little improvement for the Capitals. They opened the 1975–76 season by going 25 games without a win and finished with 32 points and an 11–59–10 record.

LOMBARDI LASTS DISTANCE TO EARN HISTORIC F1 HALF-POINT

LELLA LOMBARDI BECOMES ONLY WOMAN IN HISTORY TO SECURE A POINTS FINISH IN A FORMULA ONE RACE

27 April 1975, Montjuic Park, Barcelona, Spain

Hooked on the thrill of speed since a young age, Lella Lombardi caught the attention of those who mattered driving in the lower formulae and entered her first-ever Formula One World Championship event at the 1974 British GP in a privately entered Brabham. She failed to qualify. She switched to March and prepared for her first full season in 1975. Her first race saw a disappointing retirement and then came the Spanish GP and one of Formula One's darkest days, when Rolf Stommelen's car flipped into the Montjuic Park crowd and killed four. The race was stopped at three-quarter distance and there, two laps down on the leaders, was Lombardi in sixth place: she had become the only woman in history to achieve a points finish in a Formula One race.

➲ Lombardi's single point was reduced to half a point shortly afterwards when stewards decided to award half points for the race because it had not run the full distance.

A 21st-place finish in the end-of-season standings for the 1975 Formula One World Championship may not be much to shout about, but in the season's second race, the Spanish GP, Lella Lombardi had become the only woman in history to collect points in a Formula One race.

TINY TABEI CONQUERS THE ROOF OF THE WORLD

JUNKO TABEI BECOMES THE FIRST WOMAN TO CLIMB MOUNT EVEREST

16 May 1975, Mount Everest, Nepal/Tibet

Considered weak and fragile as a child – even as an adult she measured only 4ft 9in – by 1974 Junko Tabei had become the foremost female climber in her native Japan and was selected by the *Yomiuri* newspaper and Nihon television company to lead an all-woman expedition to conquer Everest. The trip was not without problems: the group fell prey to an avalanche which covered Tabei for six minutes before her Sherpa guide dug her out. Twelve days later, on 16 May 1975, battered and bruised, she undertook the route taken by Edmund Hillary and Tenzing Norgay in 1953 and crawled her way to the summit to become the first woman in history to conquer the world's highest peak.

➲ In 1976, a year after her conquest of Everest, Junko Tabei became the first woman in history to climb the Seven Summits, the highest mountains of the Earth's seven continents.

Diminutive in stature and suffering from the effects of an avalanche, Junko Tabei pushed herself to the very limit in May 1975 to stand on the roof of the world – the first woman in history to do so.

ASHE PRODUCES MAGICAL DISPLAY TO SHOCK CONNORS

ARTHUR ASHE BECOMES THE FIRST AFRICAN-AMERICAN TO WIN THE ALL-ENGLAND TITLE

6 July 1975, Wimbledon, London, England

In 1968 Arthur Ashe became a worldwide sensation, winning the US Amateur championships and the US Open within a few weeks of each other (the only person in history to do so and the first American winner of the US Open since 1955) and helping the US to a first Davis Cup win in five years. He turned professional soon afterwards and collected a second grand slam title in 1970, the Australian Open. By 1975 it seemed as though Ashe's best days were behind him, but he produced the form of his life at the Wimbledon Championships that year, shocking Jimmy Connors 6–1, 6–1, 5–7, 6–4 in the final to become the first African-American winner of the All-England title.

➲Ashe had beaten a young Bjorn Borg 2–6, 6–4, 8–6, 6–1 in the quarter-finals en route to his championship success. He would be the last person to beat the Swede on the hallowed grass of the All-England club for five years.

Arthur Ashe (1968 US Open, 1970 Australian Open and 1975 Wimbledon) is one of only two men of black African origin to have won a grand slam title, the other being France's Yannick Noah (1983 French Open).

MERCKX SETS ALL-TIME TOUR RECORD IN LOSING BID

EDDY MERCKX WINS THE LAST OF HIS RECORD 34 TOUR DE FRANCE STAGE WINS

7 July 1975, Auch, France

Five-time champion (1969–72 and 1974) Eddy Merckx returned to the Tour de France in 1975 intent on becoming the event's first six-time winner and wins on stages six and nine (the 33rd and record 34th stage wins of his career) saw him surge into the yellow jersey in the early stages of the race. Then he hit trouble. There had been an outpouring of horror around France at the thought of a Belgian breaking Jacques Anquetil's record: and that horror manifested itself in a sickening way on stage 14 when a spectator leapt from the crowd and punched Merckx in the liver. Valuable time was lost and even more when he suffered a broken jaw in a later stage. The Belgian finished in second, 2m47s behind winner Bernard Thevenet.

➲Merckx's eight-day stint in the yellow jersey during the 1975 Tour de France meant he had spent a record career total of 96 days as the Tour de France leader, a figure never beaten. His last Tour came in 1976: he finished sixth.

Eddy Merckx may well have preferred to forget the 1975 Tour de France, but although he failed in his quest to become the event's first six-time winner, he went down fighting, winning two stages (including the 34th and final stage win of his career). It is a record that stands to this day.

WALKER PUTS HIS NAME UP IN LIGHTS WITH WORLD MILE BEST

JOHN WALKER FIRST TO RUN THE MILE IN UNDER 3M50S

12 August 1975, Gothenburg, Sweden

At the 1974 Commonwealth Games in Christchurch, New Zealand, the world got to see just how good John Walker was. In the final of the 1,500m, considered one of the greatest middle-distance racers of all time, he ran the second-quickest time in history, but still had to settle for the silver medal behind Tanzania's Filbert Bayi. And Walker had to sit back and watch the following year as the Tanzanian broke the world mile record too. But in 1975, the New Zealander would have his revenge: in Gothenburg, Sweden, he broke Bayi's record and became the first man in history to run the mile in under 3m50s – his time: 3m49.4s.

➲Walker's record would stand for nearly four years until Sebastian Coe ran 3m48.95s in Oslo, Norway, on 17 July 1979.

After breaking the world mile record in 1975, the highlight of John Walker's career came the following year when he won the 1,500m final at the Olympic Games in Montreal.

COURT BOWS OUT IN WINNING STYLE

MARGARET COURT COLLECTS RECORD 62ND AND FINAL GRAND SLAM VICTORY

25 August 1975, Forest Hills, New York, USA

With 24 singles, 18 women's doubles and 19 mixed doubles grand slam titles already to her name, Margaret Court could have been forgiven for taking her final grand slam tournament, the 1975 US Open, a little easier. But the Australian was not built that way. Any hopes of adding to her record grand slam tally seemed to come to an end when she lost 6–2, 6–4 in the quarter-finals to up-and-coming Czech star Martina Navratilova. All was not lost: Court and her partner Virginia Wade made it through to the women's doubles final and their victory over Billie Jean King and Rosemary Casals saw Court collect the 62nd and final grand slam winner's trophy of her career.

The only tennis player to have completed a calendar grand slam in both singles and doubles, Margaret Court rounded out her career in memorable style by partnering Britain's Virginia Wade to doubles success in the 1975 US Open. It was the 62nd grand slam title of her illustrious career.

➲Second in the list of all-time grand slam tournament wins is Martina Navratilova with 59 – 18 in singles, 31 in doubles and 10 in mixed doubles.

THE GOLDEN BEAR PASSES BOBBY JONES'S HISTORIC MARK

JACK NICKLAUS WINS HIS RECORD 14TH MAJOR CHAMPIONSHIP
11 August 1975, Firestone Country Club, Akron, Ohio, USA

Jack Nicklaus burst on to the professional scene in spectacular style when he won the US Open in his rookie year. He carried that form into 1963, winning not only the Masters but also the US PGA. Further triumphs followed at Augusta in 1965 and again in 1966; later the same year he won the Open Championship to become the youngest golfer (aged 26) to complete the career grand slam. His second US Open title came in 1967, but three years would pass before Nicklaus added to his major tally. He won the Open Championship at St Andrews in 1970, and proved he was back to winning ways when he won the US PGA in 1971. A possible grand slam following wins at the Masters and US Open in 1972 did not materialize, but still Nicklaus's major tally continued to grow: the US PGA in 1973; the Masters in 1975; and when he won the US PGA for a third time, in 1975, for his 14th major tournament victory, he had overtaken Bobby Jones's record haul of 13 major championships.

➲Nicklaus added four more majors to his tally, the last of them coming at the Masters in 1986, to end his career with 18 major tournament victories. Some claim he has won 20 (because of his two US Amateur wins in 1959 and 1961), but the official take on the matter is that he won 18.

Aged 35 and still firing, Jack Nicklaus won his fourth US PGA title at the Firestone Country Club in 1975 to overtake Bobby Jones as the player to have won the most major tournaments.

BEPPEGOAL BECOMES SOCCER'S FIRST MILLION MAN

GIUSEPPE SAVOLDI SIGNS FOR NAPOLI FROM ATALANTA FOR WORLD RECORD FEE OF £1.2 MILLION

September 1975, Naples, Italy

A formidable header of the ball with an eye for goal and impeccable technique, Giuseppe "Beppe" Savoldi made his debut for Atalanta in 1965, but made a name for himself with his performances for Bologna between 1968 and 1975: in 201 appearances for the *Rossoblù* he found the back of the net on 85 occasions. It was enough to attract the attention of FC Napoli, the southern Italian club who were desperate to make an impact on their domestic league. Their staggering offer of two billion Lire (around £1.2 million) was too good to refuse and Savoldi promptly became the first million-pound player in soccer history.

⮑ The £1.2 million paid by Napoli to Bologna for the services of Beppe Savoldi eclipsed the £922,000 paid by Barcelona to Ajax in 1973 for Johan Cruyff.

KART KING GOLDSTEIN TAKES FIFTH WORLD TITLE

FRANÇOIS GOLDSTEIN BECOMES FIRST FIVE-TIME WINNER OF THE WORLD KARTING CHAMPIONSHIP

5 October 1975, Le Castellet, France

Giving that the karting circuit is considered a breeding ground for supreme driving talent, it may come as some surprise to learn that the most dominant figure in the sport's history never went on to enjoy a career in cars. Belgium's François Goldstein first came to the karting public's attention when he finished runner-up in the 1967 world championship. Renowned for his toughness on the track – he was not beyond shunting opponents from behind – he won his first title two years later and won the next three world championships in succession (1970–72). Following a two-year lull, he was back to his best in 1975, beating Elio de Angelis to the chequered flag to win a record fifth world karting championship.

⮑ Only one karting world champion has ever gone on to win a Formula One race. Italy's Riccardo Patrese won the 1974 world karting championship and went on to race in 257 grands prix – more than any other racer in history – winning on six occasions.

KANGAROOS UNDERLINE STATUS AS WORLD NO. 1

AUSTRALIA BECOME THE FIRST FOUR-TIME CHAMPIONS OF THE RUGBY LEAGUE WORLD CUP

12 November 1975, Headingley, Leeds

The first six rugby league World Cups were played on a single-tournament, league basis between Australia, Great Britain, France and New Zealand, with Britain and Australia winning three times each. For 1975, the tournament received a radical overhaul. Great Britain was divided into England and Wales and the tournament would be played on a home-and-away basis throughout the year. Australia led the standings after all the matches had been played. A hoo-ha erupted: they had played England twice during the tournament and had failed to win on both occasions. How could they be crowned world champions? A challenge match was hastily arranged between the two teams: Australia won 25–0 to become the first four-time winners in the tournament's history.

⮑ Australia have not lost the title since, winning in 1977, 1988, 1992, 1995 and 2000 to confirm their status as the premier rugby league nation on the planet.

Australia's 1975 rugby league victory was not without controversy: having won the tournament once (they finished top of the league standings), the Kangaroos were forced to play England in a one-off challenge match for the title because in the two matches between the teams the Australians had won neither (10–10 in Sydney and 13–16 in Wigan). No matter: the Australians won the day 25–0 in front of a paltry 7,727 crowd at Headingley and were confirmed as champions.

GIBBS PASSES MILESTONE IN FINAL TEST APPEARANCE

LANCE GIBBS TAKES THE 309TH WICKET TO BECOME THE LEADING WICKET-TAKER IN TEST HISTORY

31 January–5 February 1976, Melbourne Cricket Ground, Melbourne, Australia

Tall and lithe, Lance Gibbs used his high, chest-on action – and his extraordinarily long fingers – to deliver high-bouncing, big-spinning off-breaks with deadly accuracy (throughout his Test career he conceded a miserly 1.99 runs per over). After making his Test debut against Pakistan in 1957–58, it was three years before he established himself in the West Indies side. He took 18 wickets in three Tests against Australia in 1960–61; the following year he recorded his Test-best figures of 8 for 38 against India. The wickets kept coming: he passed the 300 milestone dismissing Gary Gilmour in Perth in his final tour and, in his last-ever Test appearance, at Melbourne, dismissed the same player again to take his record 309th and last wicket.

➲ Gibbs's record would last for almost six years before Dennis Lillee dismissed West Indies keeper Jeff Dujon in December 1981 in Melbourne to claim his 310th Test victim.

Lance Gibbs's record haul of 309 wickets came in 79 Test matches for the West Indies. He took five wickets or more in an innings on 18 occasions. In his Test-best haul of 8 for 38 against India, all eight wickets came in a 15-over spell costing six runs.

Darryl Sittler produced the greatest offensive display in NHL history on 7 February 1976 when he registered four assists and scored six goals for a single-game record of ten points.

SIZZLING SITTLER TAKES THE BOSTON BRUINS APART

DARRYL SITTLER SETS ALL-TIME NHL RECORD FOR THE MOST POINTS IN SINGLE GAME

7 February 1976, Toronto, Canada

The Boston Bruins arrived in Toronto in February 1976 off the back of a seven-game winning run and full of confidence; so much so that their coach, Don Cherry, decided the time was right to rest star goaltender Gerry Cheevers and play rookie Dave Reece in his place. The plan backfired spectacularly and the Bruins crashed to an 11–4 defeat, but it was the performance of Maple Leafs' captain Darryl Sittler that captured the following day's headlines. In the first period he registered two assists; in the second he scored three goals and two more assists; and in the final period he scored another hat-trick to become the first person in NHL history to score ten points in a game (six goals, four assists).

➲ The Montreal Canadiens' Maurice Richard held the previous record: eight points against the Detroit Red Wings on 28 December 1944.

MITTERMAIER'S NEAR-MISS ON ALPINE SKIING MEDAL SWEEP

ROSI MITTERMAIER COMPLETES BEST MEDAL HAUL BY FEMALE SKIER IN SINGLE WINTER OLYMPICS

4–15 February 1976, Innsbruck, Austria

During her ten-year career on the skiing World Cup circuit, West Germany's Rosi Mittermaier had cemented her reputation as a fine slalom skier, but she produced the greatest downhill performance of her career to win the Olympic gold medal at Innsbruck by over half a second – it would be the only downhill win of her career. Three days later, she recorded the quickest time in the second slalom run to take her second gold. Excitement levels rose: could Mittermaier emulate Jean-Claude Killy's 1968 feat and complete a clean sweep of the alpine skiing medals? No, she lost out in the giant slalom by one-tenth of a second to Canada's Kathy Kreiner, but there was one consolation: her haul of three medals (two gold, one silver) was the finest by any female skier in history.

➲ Before she arrived at the XII Winter Olympic Games in Innsbruck, Mittermaier had won only seven times on the World Cup circuit and every win had been in the slalom.

Rosi Mittermaier found the form of her life at the 1976 Winter Olympics, winning the downhill and the slalom and picking up silver in the giant slalom. Her haul of three medals was a record for a female skier.

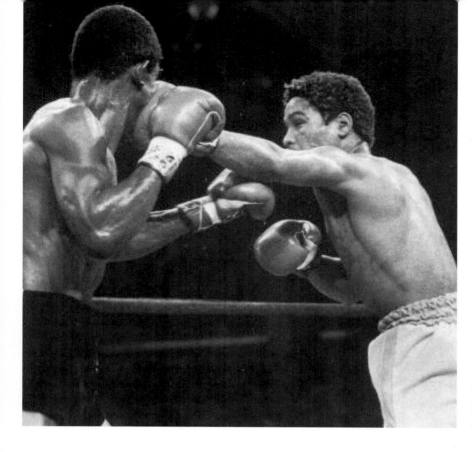

Seventeen-year-old Wilfred Benitez became the youngest world champion in boxing history when he beat two-time champion Antonio Cervantes on points in March 1976.

THE KID WHO PACKED A POWERFUL PUNCH

WILFRED BENITEZ BECOMES YOUNGEST WORLD CHAMPION IN BOXING HISTORY
6 March 1976, Hiram Bithorn Stadium, Puerto Rico

Born in the Bronx, New York, in 1958 into a boxing family – his father and two brothers were boxers – Wilfred Benitez learned the art of boxing during his childhood and turned professional at the age of 15. His fast hands, exemplary defence and sensational punching power shocked many of his early opponents: he won his first fight by a first-round knockout, went undefeated through his first 28 bouts and soon became a championship contender. In 1976, he managed to lure champion Antonio Cervantes from Colombia to Puerto Rico to defend his WBA light-welterweight crown. Benitez won the fight by decision to become, aged 17, the youngest world champion in boxing history.

➲ Benitez retained his title three times before succumbing to the lure of fighting 1976 Olympic champion Sugar Ray Leonard in 1979. Moving up a division to welterweight, he lost by technical knockout in the 15th round. He reverted to light-middleweight, won the title in March 1981 and held on to it for eight months.

RAG TRADE NETS RIMELL RECORD FOURTH GRAND NATIONAL WIN

TRAINER FRED RIMELL WINS THE GRAND NATIONAL FOR A RECORD FOURTH TIME

4 April 1976, Aintree, Liverpool, England

An outstanding jockey in his day who won the champion jockey title four times between 1939 and 1946, Fred Rimell had his career cut short when he broke his neck not once but twice during the 1947 season. It was time to find another career: Rimell turned his hand to training and became one of the most successful trainers in the sport's history. He recorded his first win in the Grand National in 1956 with E.S.B.; a second came five years later with Nicolaus Silver. Gay Trip provided him with win No. 3 in 1970 and, with Rag Trade's Aintree success in 1976, Rimell became the first trainer in history to win the world's greatest steeplechase race four times.

➲The only other trainer in history to have won the Grand National on four occasions is Ginger McCain, with Red Rum in 1973, '74 and '77 and with Amberleigh House in 2004.

Four-time champion jockey Fred Rimell achieved such success when he turned his hand to training – he won the Grand National on four occasions (the last with Rag Trade) – that his outstanding record as a jockey remains largely forgotten.

Having made a serious statement of intent shortly before the 1976 Olympic Games, the new world-record-holder added to her legend when she completed the 800-1,500m double in Montreal.

KAZANKINA SHATTERS 1,500M RECORD BY OVER FIVE SECONDS

TATYANA KAZANKINA FIRST TO BREAK FOUR-MINUTE BARRIER FOR 1,500M

28 June 1976, Podolsk, Moscow, Russia

By 1976, 24-year-old Soviet athlete Tatyana Kazankina was being talked of as a contender for the 1,500m final in the upcoming Olympic Games in Montreal, Canada. Two years earlier she had clocked a personal best in the event of 4m05.94s – the ninth-best time on the all-time list – just four-and-a-half seconds off the world record of 4m01.4s set by Ludmila Bragina in the 1972 Munich Olympics. And, in June, the fragile-looking athlete with the killer kick only added to her growing reputation when she shattered the 1,500m world record, clocking an astonishing time of 3m56s in Podolsk to break the old record by over five seconds and become the first woman in history to run the 1,500m in under four minutes.

➲Kazankina broke her own world record in the 1980 Olympic Games in Moscow with 3m55s and broke it again on 13 August 1980 with 3m52.47s. That mark would stand as the record for 13 years until China's Qu Yungxi clocked 3m50.46s in Beijing on 11 September 1993.

POULIDOR THE BRIDESMAID ONCE AGAIN

RAYMOND POULIDOR NOTCHES UP RECORD EIGHTH PODIUM FINISH IN THE TOUR DE FRANCE

18 July 1976, Paris, France

During 14 years of Tour de France racing Raymond Poulidor recorded seven stage wins, but never once wore the yellow jersey and never once won the most challenging cycle race on the planet. Yet take a poll around France for the most popular rider of the twentieth century and the man they affectionately nicknamed "Pou Pou" comes out on top every time. Why? He was the "eternal second", always the bridesmaid. Between 1962 and 1976, as the Tour's dominance shifted from Jacques Anquetil to Eddy Merckx, Poulidor's supremacy in the mountains translated itself into a record number of podium finishes – eight of them (second in 1964, '65 and '74 and third in 1962, '66, '69, '72 and '76 – as the time-trial specialists took the spoils.

➲ Poulidor narrowly missed out on success in the world road race championships as well, placing second in 1974 and third in 1961, '64 and '66.

The chances are Raymond Poulidor would have exchanged a small part of the love the French nation had for him for just one Tour de France victory. Over a period of 14 years, Poulidor finished on the podium a record eight times without ever winning the race.

DIBIASI COMPLETES OLYMPIC DIVING HAT-TRICK

KLAUS DIBIASI FIRST TO WIN SPRINGBOARD DIVING GOLD AT THREE CONSECUTIVE OLYMPICS

17 July–1 August 1976, Montreal, Canada

Klaus Dibiasi's father, Carlo, a former Italian diving champion (1933–36) and a 1936 Olympian, taught his son all the tricks of the trade as he was growing up and, as is so often the case, the pupil went on to outpace the master. Klaus picked up his first national diving title in 1963 and finished second in the platform in the 1964 Olympics. He would not taste Olympic defeat in the event again. He took platform gold in Mexico in 1968, retained his title in Munich four years later and recorded a staggering 600.51 points in Montreal in 1976 – breaking both the world and Olympic record – to become the first diver in Olympic history to win the same event at three consecutive Olympic Games.

Between 1968 and '76, Italy's Klaus Dibiasi was the king of the boards, winning three consecutive gold medals in platform diving. His dominance in the event has never been matched.

↪Three men have managed back-to-back Olympic wins in platform diving: Sammy Lee (1948–52), Robert Webster (1960–64) and Greg Louganis (1984–88).

ENDER MAKES A SPLASH AND CAUSES A STIR

KORNELIA ENDER FIRST WOMAN TO WIN FOUR SWIMMING GOLD MEDALS AT SINGLE OLYMPICS

17 July–1 August 1976, Montreal, Canada

A three-time silver medallist at the 1972 Olympic Games in Munich as a 13-year-old, Kornelia Ender became the first wonder girl of an East German regime which was later found to have fuelled its country's athletes with a state-run drugs program, often without the knowledge of the athletes themselves – Ender later admitted to being given injections after training to help her recuperate. In the months leading up to the 1976 Olympic Games in Montreal, Ender gained 18lb (8.1kg) in muscle and was raring to go. She tore up the pool, winning a record four gold medals – the 110m freestyle, 200m freestyle, 100m butterfly and 4x100m medley – all in world-record-breaking times.

↪The East Germans remained the dominant force in women's swimming until the fall of the Iron Curtain in the late 1980s.

With many convinced she was using performance-enhancing drugs, East German swimmer Kornelia Ender muscled her way to four swimming gold medals at the Montreal Olympics, winning all of the events in world-record-breaking times.

MASTERFUL MOSES
EASES TO GOLD

ED MOSES WINS THE 1976 OLYMPIC 400M HURDLES FINAL IN WORLD-RECORD-BREAKING TIME

25 July 1976, Montreal, Canada

Born in Dayton, Ohio, in 1955, Ed Moses accepted a scholarship to Morehouse College in Atlanta, a school renowned for its academic success as opposed to its ability to produce world-class athletes. Initially a 180-yard and 440-yard dash specialist, he switched to the 400m hurdles event in March 1976 and the results were dramatic. He made immediate progress, bringing a languid, never-before-seen style to the event with his trademark 13 steps (sometimes 12) between hurdles, as opposed to the usual 14: the result was to see him pull away from his opponents as they switched stride patterns in the latter part of the race. Moses qualified for the US team for the 1976 Olympic Games. In his first international meet he made it to the Olympic final, and won it in spectacular fashion, clocking 47.64s to win gold and break John Akii-Bua's 1972 world record.

⟳Moses broke his own record in June the following year (47.45s) before he lost to West Germany's Harald Schmidt on 26 August 1977. It was the last race Moses would lose for nine years, nine months and nine days (a stretch of 122 consecutive race wins in which he improved his world-record time twice – reducing it to 47.02s).

1976

Ed Moses brought an analytical approach to the 400m hurdles and the world got a first glimpse of how effective he was in the 1976 Olympic Games, when he won the event in world-record-breaking fashion.

Nadia Comaneci picked up in 1976 where Olga Korbut had left off in Munich in 1972: she captivated both the crowds and the judges, recording the first of six perfect scores in Olympic history, and did much to popularize gymnastics'new status as a mainstream sport.

PERFECTION FOR COMANECI

NADIA COMANECI THE FIRST GYMNAST TO RECORD PERFECT SCORE IN OLYMPIC COMPETITION
17 July–1 August 1976, Montreal, Canada

Born in Romania in 1961, Nadia Comaneci started gymnastics at the age of six and and was her country's champion by the age of nine. She made her first splash on the international circuit at the 1975 European Championships in Norway, winning every event she entered bar one, the floor exercise in which she finished second. In March 1976 she competed in the American Cup and registered a perfect score of 10.0 in the vault. The 14-year-old travelled to Montreal full of confidence and did not disappoint: she scored 10.0 on the uneven bars during the team competition (the first instance of a perfect score in Olympic gymnastics history) and went on to record another six en route to winning the all-round title (the youngest gymnast ever to achieve the feat) as well as gold medals in the vault and beam events.

➲Comaneci competed in the 1980 Olympic Games in Moscow, finishing second in the all-round competition but defending her balance beam title and winning the floor exercise for the first time. The following year she defected to the United States

THE MASTER BLASTER SMASHES HIS WAY TO NEW RECORD

VIV RICHARDS BREAKS THE RECORD FOR THE MOST TEST RUNS IN A CALENDAR YEAR
12–17 August 1976, The Oval, London, England

Viv Richards swaggered his way onto the international cricket scene in 1974 when, in only his second Test match, he smashed an unbeaten century against India. The following year, the gum-chewing swashbuckler helped his country to win the inaugural Cricket World Cup. But it was his performances in 1975–76 that sent shockwaves around the world and fuelled Richards'simage as the most destructive and powerful hitter ever to have played the game. Awesomely strong on both sides of the wicket, in a 12-month span he played in 11 Tests, batted on 19 occasions, scored seven centuries and five half-centuries to tally an incredible 1,710 runs, including 291 against England in the final match of the 1976 series between the two teams at The Oval.

➲Richards'smark stood as a record until 2006, when Pakistan's Mohammed Yousuf scored 1,788 runs (also in 11 matches and also in 19 innings).

In a 17-year Test career for the West Indies, Viv Richards scored 8,540 runs at an average of 50.23: 1,710 of those runs came in a 12-month spell in 1975–76.

AGOSTINI FINDS WINNING NOTE IN FINAL GRAND PRIX

GIACOMO AGOSTINI WINS THE LAST OF HIS CAREER RECORD 68 RACES

September 1976, Nurburgring, Germany

In 1974, having already set the standards in motorcycle racing by which every future racer would be judged, Giacomo Agostini shocked the sport to its very core when he announced he was leaving the MV Agusta team, with which he had won 13 world championships, to join Yamaha. The switch did little to stop his winning ways: he collected the 350cc title in 1974 and the 500cc title in 1975, the last of his record 15 world championships, but not the last of his record 68 race wins in the 500cc arena. That came in 1976 at the Nurburgring at the West German GP, back on his beloved MV Agusta, in the last world championship race he ever contested.

➲ Agostini also collected 54 race wins in the 350cc formula: his combined career total of 122 wins is also a record.

Fifteen-time world champion Giacomo Agostini ended his stellar career in fine style, winning for the 62nd time in his final grand prix at the Nurburgring in 1976.

13-YEAR-OLD PRODIGY WINS WINDSURFING WORLD CHAMPIONSHIP

ROBBY NAISH BECOMES WINDSURFING'S YOUNGEST-EVER WORLD CHAMPION

10–15 November 1976, Cable Beach, Nassau, Bahamas

Robby Naish grew up around the waters of the Hawaiian island of Oahu and started to windsurf as soon as he was tall enough to reach the boom. He entered the world championships for the first time when he was just 13 years old, and brushed aside the challenge of opponents at least twice his age to become the sport's youngest-ever world champion. Over the next 12 years, as both techniques and equipment in the sport changed beyond recognition, Naish continued to stand at the top of the tree, winning 12 world championships and, with his trademark pink sail bearing the number US1111, becoming the most recognizable face the sport has ever seen.

⮌ Naish also went on to become a noted competitor in the fledgling sport of kiteboarding, winning the world slalom title in 1998 and 1999 and the world jumping title in 1999.

SOUTH AMERICAN HAT-TRICK FOR CHILE'S FIGUEROA

ELIAS FIGUEROA IS SOUTH AMERICA'S SOCCER PLAYER OF THE YEAR AWARD FOR THIRD CONSECUTIVE YEAR

December 1976, Beira-Rio, Porto Alegra, Brazil

Elias Figueroa played the game with great poise and is considered one of the best defenders in soccer history. FIFA certainly thought so following his performances for Chile during the 1974 World Cup when they voted him the tournament's best defender; the same year he won the South American Player of the Year title for the first time. In 1975, he scored the winning goal to secure his club, Internacional, a historic first success in the Brazilian championship and was once again voted South America's best player. He played a major part in Internacional's title defence the following year and was voted the continent's best player once again to become the only man in history to claim the award in three consecutive years.

⮌ Brazil's Zico (or Arthur Antunes Coimbra to give him his full name) was also voted South American Player of the Year on three occasions (1977, '81 and '82), but not in consecutive years.

Voted as one of FIFA's 100 greatest players, defender Elias Figueroa (right, No. 5) was the only man in history to be voted South America's best player three years in a row.

McKAY MAINTAINS PERFECT BRITISH OPEN RECORD

HEATHER McKAY WINS BRITISH OPEN SQUASH TOURNAMENT FOR 16TH CONSECUTIVE YEAR

March 1977, Wembley Conference Centre, London, England

In the absence of a *bona fide* world championship, the British Open tournament, the oldest in the sport, was considered the most prestigious title on the squash calendar and, over a period of 16 years, one woman made it her own: Heather McKay. During a stellar career – she has a rightful claim on being the most successful athlete in history – McKay lost only twice: once in 1960 (to Yvonne West in the quarter-finals of the New South Wales Championship) and again in 1962 (to Fran Marshall in the final of the Scottish Open). It was the last time she tasted defeat until her retirement in 1981. In between times she recorded an astonishing 16 consecutive wins in the British Open from 1962 to '77.

➲Remarkably, McKay did not lose a single game during those 16 consecutive title wins. The highlight came in the 1967 final, when she defeated Bev Johnson 9–0, 9–0, 9–0.

No other sportsman or woman has produced a career to compare with that of Heather McKay and none has dominated their respective sport to such an extent. In her 19-year career she lost only two competitive matches.

KING RICHARD MAKES IT 18 YEARS IN A ROW

RICHARD PETTY RECORDS RACE WIN IN 18TH CONSECUTIVE SEASON

13 March 1977, Rockingham, North Carolina, USA

Richard Petty won his first NASCAR race as a 22-year-old in 1960 and once he had sampled the taste of victory he wanted more of it, winning a race every year – including a single-season record 27 victories in 1967 – through to 1976 and in the process capturing the drivers' championship on six occasions. By 1977, King Richard was still the most feared competitor on the track, and he won the season's fourth race, the Carolina 500, to ensure the winning streak stretched into an 18th year. Four more wins followed that year en route to second place in the season's standings. In 1978, Petty went winless for the first time since 1959, finishing sixth in the championship.

➲Petty bounced back in style the following year, winning five times and capturing his record seventh drivers' title (equalled only by Dale Earnhardt).

The holder of many records in NASCAR, including the most wins in a season (27), most career wins (200) and most career poles (123), Richard Petty also holds the record for the most consecutive years with at least one win (18).

RED RUM COMPLETES GRAND NATIONAL HAT-TRICK

RED RUM BECOMES ONLY HORSE TO WIN THE GRAND NATIONAL THREE TIMES
2 April 1977, Aintree, Liverpool, England

There was a time when Red Rum was considered no more than an average flat racer, but his future was secured in 1968 when trainer Ginger McCain bought him and took him to the sands of Southport Beach in Lancashire. The soft sands, salt water and sea air were clearly to Red Rum's liking. Ridden by Brian Fletcher, Red Rum made his first Aintree appearance in 1973 and won by three lengths. In 1974 he defended his title by holding off the challenge of L'Escargot, but when the roles were reversed the following year, Fletcher, accused of holding Red Rum back, lost the ride. Tommy Stack replaced him for 1976 as Red Rum lost out to Rag Trade by three lengths. But Red Rum was back to his best in 1977, defying the soft ground and jumping to perfection to produce one of the most dominant displays in Grand National history, winning by an astonishing 25 lengths to become the only three-time winner of the most famous steeplechase in the world.

⮑ In a career consisting of more than 100 races, Red Rum won three flat races, three hurdle races and 21 steeplechase races, in addition to finishing second or third on 37 occasions, thus placing him in the money in 64 per cent of the races he entered throughout his career.

A three-time winner of the Grand National, Red Rum's remains are now buried by the winning post on the Aintree racecourse.

CLINICAL CANADIENS BREAK THEIR OWN REGULAR SEASON RECORD

MONTREAL CANADIENS BREAK SINGLE-SEASON NHL RECORD FOR MOST POINTS AND MOST WINS

March 1977, Montreal, Canada

During the 1975–76 NHL season, under the stewardship of head coach Scotty Bowman, the Montreal Canadiens set an all-time regular season record for most wins (58) and most points (127) en route to thwarting the Philadelphia Flyers' assault on a third successive Stanley Cup. And they went even better the following season, the 60th of the National Hockey League: with Guy Lafleur leading the points-scoring charts for the second straight year with 56 goals, 80 assists and Steve Shutt heading the goal charts with 60, the Habs ended the year with an incredible 60 wins and 132 points to break their own all-time record.

The Montreal Canadiens picked up in 1976–77 where they had left off the previous season, compiling the greatest regular season in NHL history: played 80, won 60, lost 8, tied 12 with 132 points.

➲The Canadiens' form continued into the playoffs, where they beat St Louis Blues (4–0) and the New York Islanders (4–2) before sweeping the Boston Bruins 4–0 in the Stanley Cup final.

BREW MAKES GRAND NATIONAL HISTORY

CHARLOTTE BREW BECOMES FIRST WOMAN JOCKEY TO RIDE IN THE GRAND NATIONAL

3 April 1977, Aintree, Liverpool, England

In 1976, following recent equality legislation, the door was opened for women to compete in the Grand National and 20-year-old Charlotte Brew was the first to grab the opportunity, finishing in fourth place at the Foxhunters' Chase over the Aintree course on Barony Fort to qualify for the following year's Grand National. The build-up to the race was extraordinary: amid a whirlwind of media excitement, Brew's face was splashed across the tabloids and expectations rose to almost fanatic levels. The reality was that Brew was riding, at best, a long shot and that a clear round over the demanding Aintree course would have been an achievement. As it was, Brew and Barony Fort fell at the fourth fence from home.

➲Only 13 women have ever ridden in the Grand National and only three of them have completed the race: Geraldine Rees (1982), Rosemary Henderson (1994) and Carrie Ford (2005).

Twenty-one-year-old Charlotte Brew made history in 1977 when she became the first woman in history to ride in the Grand National. She fell four fences from home. It would be another five years before a female jockey finished the race.

The first four-time winner at the Brickyard, A.J. Foyt is the only driver in history to have won the Indianapolis 500, the Daytona 500 (in 1972), the Daytona 24 Hours (1983 and '85) and the Le Mans 24 Hours (1967).

FOURTH INDY 500 VICTORY LANE VISIT FOR FOYT

A.J. FOYT BECOMES THE FIRST FOUR-TIME WINNER OF THE INDIANAPOLIS 500

29 May 1977, Indianapolis Motor Speedway, Indiana, USA

In 1961, Houston-born A.J. Foyt made history when he became the first man in history to defend his championship points-total and win the Indianapolis 500 in the same year. In 1964, in a race remembered best for the deaths of Eddie Sachs and Dave MacDonald, he lapped the field to collect his second Indy win. He benefited from the failure of Parnelli Jones's turbo-engined car in 1967 to win for a third time, and his fourth and final win, 1975, came in dramatic circumstances: after running out of fuel, Foyt found himself 36s down on leader Gordon Johncock; turning up the turbo on his car he reduced the deficit to 8s before Johncock's engine blew. Foyt cantered to a record-breaking fourth win.

⟳Two other drivers have won the Indy 500 four times: Al Unser (1970, '71, '78 and '87) and Rick Mears (1979, '84, '88 and '91).

GUTHRIE TAKES A STAND FOR WOMEN DRIVERS

JANET GUTHRIE FIRST WOMAN TO COMPETE IN THE INDIANAPOLIS 500

29 May 1977, Indianapolis Motor Speedway, Indiana, USA

Janet Guthrie's first employment was with the Republic Aviation company as a flight instructor and aerospace engineer, but she dabbled in car racing on the side, first competing in 1963. By 1972 it had become her passion and she became a full-time racer. Her big break came in 1976 when team owner Rolla Vollstedt invited her to try and qualify for that year's Indianapolis 500; she failed, but took some consolation when, later in the year, she became the first woman in history to qualify for a NASCAR Winston Cup race. However, it was second time lucky in 1977: Guthrie qualified for the Indy 500 – the first woman to do so – and recorded a 29th-place finish.

⟳Guthrie created a further slice of history later in 1977 when she became the first woman to qualify for and race in the Daytona 500. She returned to Indianapolis in 1978 and recorded a ninth-place finish: the best result by a woman until 2005, when Danica Patrick finished fourth.

Janet Guthrie made history in 1977 when she became the first woman in history to qualify for the Indianapolis 500, and made a stir on the first practice day when she set the quickest time. Engine problems curtailed her hopes in the race, however, and she finished in 29th place.

THE MAKING OF MR 59

AL GEIBERGER THE FIRST IN PGA TOUR HISTORY TO SHOOT A ROUND OF 59

10 June 1977, Colonial Country Club, Memphis, Tennessee, USA

As Al Geiberger stood on the tee to start his second round at the Memphis Classic in June 1977, low numbers would have been the furthest thing from his mind. It was a hot, muggy, 102-degree day; a day about survival, not low numbers. He got off to a steady start with two birdies and three pars over the first five holes. Then came the fireworks: he played the next seven holes in eight under par. He was ten under for his round with six holes to play. When he birdied the 15th hole, the gallery shouted "59, 59" – they knew history was on the cards. Geiberger stood on the 18th needing a birdie to break the magical 60 mark: he sank his birdie putt from 9ft to take his place in golfing folklore.

➲The feat has been repeated twice – by Chip Beck in the third round of the 1991 Las Vegas Invitational and by David Duval in the final round of the 1999 Bob Hope Classic – but never beaten.

1966 US PGA champion Al Geiberger produced a near-perfect round in the 1977 Memphis Classic, hitting a bogey-free round of six pars, 11 birdies and an eagle, to become the first man to shoot 59 in PGA Tour history.

Tom Watson edged Jack Nicklaus at Turnberry in the 1977 Open Championship in an epic encounter that became known as the "Duel in the Sun". He needed the lowest score in the tournament's history to do so.

WATSON BEATS NICKLAUS IN THE DUEL IN THE SUN

TOM WATSON WINS OPEN CHAMPIONSHIP WITH RECORD LOWEST AGGREGATE SCORE

10 July 1977, Turnberry, Scotland

Two titans at the top of their game, with one needing to beat history if he were going to break the other: that is exactly what happened at the 1977 Open Championship at Turnberry. Through the first 54 holes, 14-time major-winner Jack Nicklaus and Tom Watson, defending Masters champion and 1975 Open winner, stood locked on seven-under par. In the final round they traded blow for blow; putts roared into the back of the hole as neither could shake off the other's attentions. They reached the par-five 17th all square: Nicklaus got a par; Watson a birdie. It was enough: the pair parred the final hole and Watson was champion. His aggregate score of 268 was the lowest in the tournament's storied history.

➲Watson's total of 268 stood as a tournament best for 16 years, until Greg Norman shot a 72-hole score of 267 at Royal St George's en route to becoming the 1993 Open champion.

END OF THE ROAD FOR RECORD-BREAKER GRIFFITH

EMILE GRIFFITH FIGHTS LAST OF RECORD 339 TITLE-FIGHT ROUNDS

30 July 1977, Stade Louis II, Monte Carlo, Monaco

Emile Griffith turned professional in 1958 and quickly climbed up the welterweight ranks. His most infamous bout came in 1962 during his clash with Benny Paret: the fight went into the 12th round until Griffith cornered Paret and landed a series of unanswered punches. Paret slipped to the floor and into unconsciousness and died ten days later. The ramifications for boxing were dramatic; the trauma suffered by Griffith intense. But he recovered, defeating Dick Tiger for the middleweight title and completing a classic trilogy of fights with Nino Benvenuti. Never quite the same boxer after the Paret fight – some said he punched softer – he fought the last of his record 339 title-fight rounds in Monaco in 1977.

Emile Griffith overcame severe trauma to forge a successful 19-year career in which he won or regained a world championship belt five times and boxed a record-breaking 339 title-fight rounds.

➲ Griffith won or regained a world title on five occasions, a figure surpassed only by Sugar Ray Robinson (six).

ACKERMANN LEAPS INTO UNKNOWN TERRITORY

ROSEMARIE ACKERMANN FIRST FEMALE HIGH-JUMPER TO BREAK THE 2M BARRIER

26 August 1977, Berlin, Germany

Born in Lohsa, Saxony, in 1952, Rosemarie Ackermann (née Witschas) competed for East Germany in the 1972 Olympic Games high jump competition and finished in seventh place. Over the next few years she honed her raw potential, collecting her first international title at the 1974 European Championships in Rome, jumping 1.95m to break the world record she had previously shared with Bulgaria's Jordanka Blagojeva. She improved the mark to 1.96m shortly before the 1976 Olympic Games and travelled to Montreal as the world's premier high-jumper: she lived up to her legend and won gold. The following year, on 26 August 1977 in Berlin, she became the first woman in history to jump 2.00m.

Rosemarie Ackermann emerged as the leading female high-jumper in the 1970s, winning Olympic gold at Montreal in 1976 and becoming the first in history to clear 2.00m the following year.

➲ It was as high as she would ever jump. Not only that, her world record lasted less than 12 months because, on 4 August 1978, Italy's Sara Simenoni cleared 2.01m in Brescia.

1977

After a short-lived retirement in 1973, Jimmy Keaveney returned to the Dubs' line-up and enjoyed considerable success, picking up three All-Ireland Championships and breaking the sport's single-game scoring record in his side's 1979 All-Ireland win.

MR DUBLIN LEADS HIS SIDE TO VICTORY WITH RECORD POINTS HAUL

JIMMY KEAVENEY BREAKS GAELIC FOOTBALL'S SINGLE-GAME SCORING RECORD

25 September 1977, Croke Park, Dublin, Ireland

Born and educated in Dublin, Jimmy Keaveney went on to become one of the most popular and effective Gaelic Football players in history. A stalwart St Vincent's club man, his legendary accuracy with the boot – and his incredible free-taking abilities – meant he played a significant role in the infamous Heffo's Army Dublin team of the 1970s that swept to National Football League wins in 1974 and '76 and All-Ireland Senior Football Championship success in 1974, '76 and '77. His most celebrated feat came in the last of those All-Ireland finals in 1977, when he scored a record two goals and six points (12 points) during the Dubs' victory over Armagh.

➲ Keaveney's feat was equalled in 1979 when Kerry's Mike Sheehy went 2–6 during his side's All-Ireland final win over Dublin.

FOMITCHEVA FREEFALLS INTO THE RECORD BOOKS

ELVIRA FOMITCHEVA COMPLETES LARGEST FREEFALL PARACHUTE JUMP WITHOUT OXYGEN BY A WOMAN
26 October 1977, Odensk, Soviet Union

Parachuting had come a long way since Frenchman Jacques Garnerin first leapt out of a hot-air balloon in 1797. Advances in technology had prompted the US military to test leaps from hitherto-unknown heights in the hope of trying to ascertain what would happen to pilots should they be forced to eject from planes at high altitudes. At the height of the Cold War, the Soviet military were no different. On 26 October 1977, Elvira Fomitcheva, as part of a military test, completed the highest freefall parachute jump without the use of oxygen by a woman in history: leaping from a staggering 48,446ft (14,800m) in Odensk, hitting a maximum speed in freefall of around 280mph (450km/h).

⮑The chances of such a feat happening again are slim. Huge resources are required to transport humans to altitudes in excess of 50,000ft; resources usually available only to governments or multi-millionaires.

SWEET 16 FOR VILAS

GUILLERMO VILAS BREAKS RECORD FOR MOST ATP TOUR TITLES IN A SINGLE SEASON
12 November 1977, Forest Hills, New York, USA

An incisive baseline player, Argentina's Guillermo Vilas was a member of tennis's elite in the 1970s and put together his most impressive season in 1977. His fourth title of the campaign came when he dismissed Brian Gottfried 6–0, 6–3, 6–0 in the final of the French Open to become the first South American player in history to win a grand slam tournament. Following a disappointing grass-court season, a return to hard and clay courts brought a return to form as he collected six further titles, culminating in a US Open win on clay at Forest Hills. The titles continued to come, six of them: his 16th and final tournament victory of the year came in Johannesburg, South Africa, in November.

⮑During the course of his record-breaking 1977 campaign, Guillermo Vilas put together a winning streak of 46 consecutive victories.

At his best on hard courts and clay, Argentina's Guillermo Vilas put together the most successful season in ATP Tour history in 1977, winning 16 titles, including the first two grand slam titles of his career.

THE FIRST LADY OF THE OCEANS

KRYSTYNA CHOJNOWSKA-LISKIEWICZ BECOMES FIRST WOMAN TO COMPLETE A SOLO CIRCUMNAVIGATION

21 April 1978, Las Palmas de Gran Canaria, Gran Canaria, Canary Islands

A shipbuilding engineer and sea captain, Krystyna Chojnowska-Liskiewicz left the Canary Islands on 28 February 1976 to take on the world's oceans in her 31ft (9.5m) sloop *Mazurek*, constructed by a team of Polish engineers headed by her husband. She sailed westwards across the Atlantic to Barbados before heading through the Caribbean Sea and into the Pacific Ocean via the Panama Canal. She then sailed via Tahiti to Australia, across the Indian Ocean to Mauritius and rounded the Cape of Good Hope. She completed the big loop on 20 March 1978 before entering port at Las Palmas de Gran Canaria on 21 April 1978 to become the first woman in history to complete a solo circumnavigation.

➲Chojnowska-Liskiewicz only narrowly defeated New Zealander Naomi James, who completed her own solo circumnavigation on 8 June 1978. Interestingly, James'sjourney had taken just 272 days, beating Sir Francis Chichester's record time by two days.

A POINTS-FEST AT THE MCG

ST KILDA BEAT MELBOURNE IN VFL'S ALL-TIME HIGHEST-SCORING MATCH

6 May 1978, Melbourne Cricket Ground, Melbourne, Australia

Melbourne Football Club, an offshoot of the Melbourne Cricket Club, may have played their home games in one of the finest stadiums in the world, the Melbourne Cricket Ground, but their performances during the 1970s did little to warrant such magnificent surroundings. They were the VFL's whipping boys and continually found themselves at the wrong end of the championship ladder. In 1978, en route to another wooden spoon finish, they managed to secure a place for themselves in the record books. St Kilda came to town and won in the sixth round – there was nothing new about that – but the aggregate score for the game of 345 points – St Kilda 31.18 (204) Melbourne 21.15 (141) – was the highest in AFL/VFL history.

➲At No. 2 on the list comes the match between Richmond – 29.14 (188) – and Hawthorn – 21.23 (189) – on 27 April 1985, with 337 points.

BRANDTS MAKES AMENDS FOR EARLY BLUNDER

ERNIE BRANDTS BECOMES FIRST PLAYER TO SCORE AT BOTH ENDS IN ONE WORLD CUP MATCH

21 June 1978, Estadio Monumental, Buenos Aires, Argentina

As the Netherlands and Italy prepared for their final game of the second group phase at the 1978 World Cup in Argentina, the situation was crystal-clear. With the two sides tied at the top of the table with three points after two games, and with only the group winner progressing to the World Cup final, it was a winner-takes-all showdown. So Dutch defender Ernie Brandts must have been far from thrilled when he put the ball in the back of his own net in the 18th minute to hand the Italians an early lead. He made amends in the 50th minute when he netted the equalizer, and must have left the pitch a relieved man when Arie Hann's 75th-minute goal was enough to hand the Netherlands a 2–1 win.

➲The Netherlands went on to lose the 1978 World Cup final to hosts Argentina, 3–1 after extra-time.

In arguably the biggest game of his career to that point, PSV Eindhoven and Netherlands defender Ernie Brandts became the first player in World Cup history to score both a goal and an own goal in the same game, but his country still won the day.

RONO'S WORLD-RECORD-BREAKING SPREE

HENRY RONO BREAKS FOUR DISTANCE-RUNNING WORLD RECORDS IN 81 DAYS

27 June 1978, Oslo, Norway

Born into the Nandi tribe in the Nandi Hills on the edge of the Great Rift Valley in Kenya, Henry Rono had an aptitude for running that gained him a place at Washington State University. There, under the auspices of legendary coach John Chaplin, he developed into a world-class runner, winning the national collegiate cross-country title three times (in 1976, '77 and '79) and, in 1978, producing one of the most blistering displays of sustained performance ever seen on an athletics track. In the space of 81 days he broke the 5,000m world record (by four-and-a-half seconds), the 3,000m steeplechase record (by 2.6 seconds), the 10,000m record (by a staggering eight seconds) and the 3,000m world record (by three seconds).

➲Rono improved his own 5,000m record in 1981, running 13m06.2s in Knarvik, Norway. His 3,000m steeplechase record lasted until 1989; his 10,000m record lasted until 1984; and his 3,000m record lasted until 1989.

Henry Rono put together one of the most remarkable feats of running ever seen between April and June 1978. In the space of 81 days he broke four world records in four different events.

283

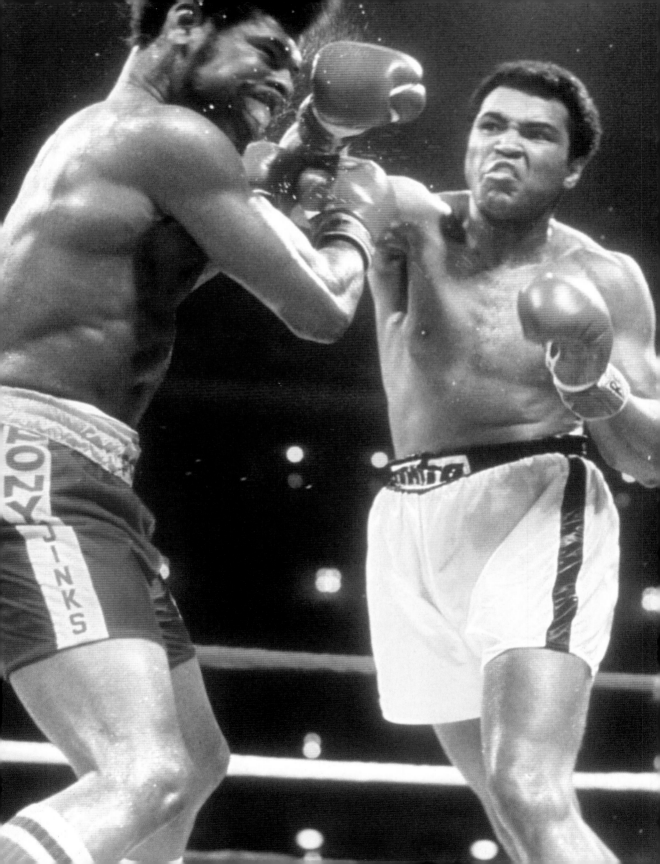

ALI WORLD HEAVYWEIGHT CHAMP FOR A THIRD TIME

MUHAMMAD ALI BECOMES FIRST AND ONLY THREE-TIME WORLD HEAVYWEIGHT CHAMPION

15 September 1978, New Orleans, Louisiana, USA

After being stripped of the WBA and WBC heavyweight title belts in 1967 for refusing induction into the US Army, Muhammad Ali regained the world heavyweight title for the first time when he outlasted George Foreman in the "Rumble in the Jungle" in 1974, taking a terrible beating before dropping the champion in the ninth round. Ali defended his WBA/WBC titles ten times – including a gruelling victory over Joe Frazier in the "Thriller in Manila" in 1975 – before succumbing to a surprise loss, by a split decision, to 1978 Olympic light-heavyweight champion Leon Spinks, who was having only his seventh professional fight. Maligned for not having taken the fight seriously enough, Ali vowed not to make the same mistake second time round in the rematch. Spinks may have gone the distance, but it was Ali who caught the eye of the judges, winning a unanimous decision to become the only fighter in history to win the world heavyweight title on three occasions.

⮑ On 6 September 1978, Muhammad Ali vacated the title and, the following year, announced what would be a short-lived retirement. He returned to the ring in 1980, losing to Larry Holmes, and then again in 1981, losing to Trevor Berbick in what would be his last fight.

At 36 years of age, Muhammad Ali outgunned Leon Spinks in New Orleans to regain the world heavyweight title for a record third time. No other boxer in history has equalled the feat.

MAGICAL MARIO COMPLETES THE SWEEP

MARIO ANDRETTI BECOMES ONLY MAN TO WIN DAYTONA 500, INDY 500 AND F1 WORLD CHAMPIONSHIP

10 September 1978, Monza, Italy

Midget cars, sprint cars, drag cars, sports cars: Mario Andretti won in them all, but his real love was for open-wheeled racing, although he dabbled in NASCAR, competing in 14 races throughout his career, including a sensational win at the Daytona 500 in 1967. He added more silverware to his trophy cabinet in 1969, winning both the Champ Car season championship and the Indianapolis 500; then it was time for Formula One. Andretti drove his first full season in 1975, won his first grand prix the following year and, by 1977, was a title contender. The following season he drove the Lotus 79 to six wins, clinching the championship with two races still to run. He had completed the sweep.

⮌Andretti's feat is unique. Only one other driver in history has managed to win the Indianapolis 500 and a race in both Formula One and NASCAR: Juan Pablo Montoya, who won the 2000 Indy 500, seven Formula One races, 2001–06, and in NASCAR in 2007.

There has been perhaps no more complete driver than Mario Andretti. He won in all forms of race car and during his illustrious career picked up motor-racing's three most prestigious prizes: the Daytona 500 (1967), the Indianapolis 500 (1969) and the Formula One World Championship (1978).

THE FASTEST MAN ON WATER

KEN WARBY BREAKS WORLD WATER SPEED RECORD IN *SPIRIT OF AUSTRALIA*

8 October 1978, Blowering Dam, New South Wales, Australia

Ken Warby designed and built *Spirit of Australia* out of balsa wood and fibreglass, added a 6,000-horsepower Westinghouse jet engine and had one intention in mind: to break the world water speed record and become the first man to break the 300mph barrier on water. It was dangerous: Donald Campbell had attempted the feat in 1967 and had lost his life in the process. After taking *Spirit of Australia* through several test sessions, in which he broke the Australian water speed record on seven occasions, Warby and his boat were ready. On 8 October 1978, he propelled the boat to a combined speed over two runs of 317.59mph (511.1km/h) over the waters of the Blowering Dam in New South Wales to shatter the existing record of 285.21mph (458.99km/h).

⮌The record has stood ever since and at least 50 per cent of the attempts to break it have ended in a fatality. It's the most dangerous of world speed records, and some claim Warby's record will never be broken.

On 8 October 1978, Australian Ken Warby became the first person to travel in excess of both 300mph and 500km/h on water. He shattered the existing world record by 32.39mph.

Grete Waitz started her love affair with the New York marathon in 1978, winning the inaugural race in world-record-breaking time and enjoying a further eight wins up until 1988.

WAITZ BECOMES THE TOAST OF THE BIG APPLE

GRETE WAITZ BREAKS WORLD MARATHON RECORD AT THE INAUGURAL NEW YORK MARATHON
3 December 1978, New York, USA

A talented junior runner who carried her form into adulthood, Norway's Grete Waitz became one of the most impressive long-distance runners of her generation. She broke the 3,000m world record in 1975 with a time of 8m46.6s and within two years had lowered the mark by almost 15 seconds to 8m31.75s. Such performances clearly caught the eye of Fred Lebow, race organizer and director of the New York marathon, who invited the Norwegian to participate in the first-ever edition of the race. Waitz not only won, but did so in the fastest time ever recorded by a woman, clocking 2h32m29.8s to break the existing record – 2h34m29.8s set by Christa Vahlensieck in 1977 – by a full two minutes.

➲ Having improved her world marathon record mark on two occasions, Waitz broke it again at the London marathon in 1983, clocking 2h25m28.7s. The record stood for barely 24 hours: the following day, USA's Joan Benoit won the Boston marathon in 2h22m43s.

LOPEZ HITS THE GROUND RUNNING

NANCY LOPEZ FIRST IN LPGA TOUR HISTORY TO END SEASON AS PLAYER AND YOUNG PLAYER OF THE YEAR
3 December 1978, Daytona Beach, Florida, USA

Nancy Lopez started playing golf at the age of eight and took to it immediately: by the age of 12 she had won the New Mexico women's amateur title before adding the US Girls' Junior title to her growing collection of trophies in 1972 and 1974. Aged 18, she qualified for the 1975 US Open and finished second. Inevitably, she turned professional in 1977 and played six events on the tour, finishing second twice. But in her first full season she was unstoppable, winning nine times, including her first major, the LPGA Championships. At the end of the year she was voted the Player of the Year and the Young Player of the Year, the only player in history to achieve the feat.

➲ Five of Nancy Lopez's nine victories in 1978 came in consecutive tournaments, a record since equalled by Annika Sorentsam (in 2005).

Nancy Lopez's first full season will go down as one of the greatest years for a rookie in history: she won nine times and ended the season as both the Player and Young Player of the Year.

CLOUGH ORCHESTRATES RECORD UNBEATEN STREAK

NOTTINGHAM FOREST'S RECORD 42-GAME WINNING STREAK COMES TO AN END

9 December 1978, Anfield, Liverpool, England

Until Brian Clough arrived on the scene on 6 January 1975, Nottingham Forest were little more than a small club in the East Midlands. In his first full season at the club, 1976–77, Clough dragged his charges into third place in the Second Division and secured promotion to English soccer's top flight. Forest excelled, ending their first season in Division One in style by putting together a 26-match end-of-season unbeaten run – including a 4–0 away win at Manchester United – to secure the first league title in the club's 114-year history. Forest continued their title defence in 1978–79 where they had left off in their championship-winning season, putting together 16 unbeaten games – taking their unbeaten streak to 42 games – before losing 2–0 to Liverpool at Anfield.

➲ Nottingham Forest's record would last for 26 years until Arsenal – dubbed "The Invincibles" – put together a 49-match unbeaten streak from 2003 to '04.

Nottingham Forest made an immediate impact on English soccer following their promotion to the First Division in 1977, winning the title at their first attempt and embarking on a 42-game unbeaten run that would stretch into the following season. Clough's Forest team also won the League Cup in 1977–78, beating Liverpool in a replay after a draw at Wembley.

The best female skier in race history, Annemarie Moser-Pröll recorded 62 World Cup race wins and six overall titles in a 12-year period.

MOSER-PRÖLL EDGES TO SIXTH WORLD CUP WIN

ANNEMARIE MOSER-PRÖLL WINS OVERALL ALPINE WORLD CUP TITLE FOR RECORD SIXTH TIME

19 March 1979, Furano, Japan

Annemarie Moser-Pröll took her Alpine World Cup bow in 1967 at the tender age of 14 over the treacherous downhill course at Badgastein in her native Austria. It was a debut to forget: she crashed three times and finished bottom of the pile. But if any lessons needed to be learned from that day, she learned them well. Over the course of the next 12 years she would become the most dominant force women's skiing has ever seen, winning the overall World Cup title on a record six occasions. The first five titles came in consecutive years from 1971 to 1975. The last came in 1979, three years after she had temporarily retired to tend to her ill father.

➲ Moser-Pröll rounded off her career in spectacular style, capturing Olympic gold for the first time in her career when she won the women's downhill at Lake Placid in 1980.

KOCH SMASHES HER OWN 200M WORLD RECORD

MARITA KOCH RUNS THE FIRST SUB-22-SECOND 200M RACE IN HISTORY

10 June 1979, Karl-Marx-Stadt, Germany

Evidence received of the state-sponsored systematic doping of East German athletes may well have tarnished both Marita Koch's reputation and her place in the history books, but there is no doubting the impact she made on the athletics world when she was at her peak. Her first outdoor record came in 1978 when she broke Irena Szewinska's 1974 200m world-record time (22.21s) clocking 22.06s; she broke Szewinska's 400m world record by a tenth of a second (to 49.19s) and improved it to 48.94s by the end of the year. Back on the record trail in 1979, on 10 June 1979 she broke her own 200m world record, clocking 21.71s in Karl-Marx-Stadt, East Germany.

↪The 200m world record would stand until 1988, when Florence Griffith-Joyner ran 21.56s in the Seoul Olympics. She would hold the 400m world record until 1983, when Jarmila Kratochilova ran 47.99s, but regained it in 1985, running 47.6s in Canberra, a time that has not been beaten to this day.

Her reputation since tarnished by doping allegations, Marita Koch produced some of the most exhilarating moments in athletics history, breaking world records on 16 occasions. She was also the first woman in history to run the 200m in under 22 seconds.

MAROONS MURDER MELBOURNE IN RECORD-BREAKING WIN

FITZROY BEAT MELBOURNE BY A VFL/AFL RECORD 190 POINTS

28 July 1979, Waverly Park, Melbourne, Australia

Tired of years of mediocrity that had seen his team finish in the bottom three no fewer than 11 times between 1962 and 1978 (with a best finish of sixth place in 1971) and in the face of growing unrest among the club's supporters, Fitzroy president Henry Bibby went on a recruitment drive. In came Robert Walls and Brendan Quinlan among others and the results started to improve. In 1978 the Maroons won the VFL night premiership, upsetting North Melbourne 13–18–96 to 2–8–20 in the final. They carried the form into the following season, equalling the club record with nine straight wins, including posting the greatest margin of victory in VFL/AFL history when they thumped Melbourne by a staggering 190 points: 36–22–238 to 6–12–48.

➲ The recruitment drive came at a price for Fitzroy: by the end of the season they were in financial straits, a situation that worsened over the years until they were forced to merge with the Brisbane Bears in 1996. They still play in Queensland.

SCHOOLBOY HOOPER SWIMS THE CHANNEL

MARCUS HOOPER BECOMES YOUNGEST PERSON TO SWIM THE ENGLISH CHANNEL

5 August 1979, English Channel, England/France

First achieved by Captain Matthew Webb in 1875, the Channel swim is still considered one of the ultimate feats of endurance swimming. The rules are simple: a swimmer has to cross the 21-mile stretch of choppy, 50-degree water between the coasts of England and France (in either direction), without assistance or aid of any type, although the swimmer is allowed to grease his body, use goggles and wear one cap and one costume, the costume is not allowed to aid either body temperature or buoyancy. A tough task? Not for 12-year-old South London schoolboy Marcus Hooper who, on 5 August 1978, completed the crossing from Dover to Cap Gris-Nez in 14h37m to become the youngest swimmer to achieve the feat.

➲ Hooper's record lasted until 6 September 1988 when another English schoolboy, Thomas Gregory, completed the swim from France to England in 11h54m, aged 11 years 11 months.

Her all-American looks, pigtails and pinafore belied Tracy Austin's iron-willed determination and she showed the tennis world she was a fearsome competitor when she collected the first of her two US Open titles at the age of 16.

AWESOME AUSTIN BRUSHES OFF EVERT'S TITLE CHALLENGE

TRACY AUSTIN BECOMES YOUNGEST-EVER WINNER OF THE US OPEN
10 September 1979, Flushing Meadows, New York, USA

Tracy Austin was a tennis prodigy. The winner of the United States Under-12 title by the age of ten, she added a further 21 age-group titles to her name before shocking the tennis establishment by winning a professional title in Portland, Oregon, in 1977, aged 14 years 28 days to become the youngest tournament winner in LTA history. She made her bow in the grand slam arena later that year, reaching the third round at Wimbledon and, sensationally, the quarter-finals of the US Open. In 1979, after falling to Martina Navratilova in the semi-finals at Wimbledon, she beat Chris Evert 6–4, 6–3 in the final of the US Open to become, aged 16 years 271 days, the tournament's youngest-ever winner.

➲Austin started the 1980 season as the world's No. 1-ranked women's player, ending the Navratilova-Evert domination. She went on to collect the mixed doubles title at Wimbledon in 1980 and a second US Open singles title in 1981, before a series of injuries cut short her career.

After breaking the 200m world record in 1979, Pietro Mennea finally got his hands on an Olympic gold medal when he won the 200m in the 1980 Games in Moscow.

MENNEA ENJOYS THE THIN AIR OF MEXICO CITY

PIETRO MENNEA BREAKS THE 200M WORLD RECORD
12 September 1979, Mexico City, Mexico

Having finished fourth in the 200m in the 1971 European Championships in Helsinki, Italy's Pietro Mennea made his Olympic bow the following year and this time picked up a bronze medal. The Puglia-born athlete finally made it onto the top step of the podium at the 1974 European Championships in front of his home crowd in Rome (also finishing second in the 100m), but finished a disappointing fourth in the 1976 Olympic Games in Montreal. Three years later, he was invited to attend the World University Games in Mexico City – Mennea was a student in political studies at the time – and won the 200m in a world-record-breaking time, clocking 19.72s to beat Tommy Smith's 1968 record (19.83s, also set in Mexico City) by 0.11 of a second.

➲ Mennea's achievement was often derided because of the fact it had been set at altitude – breaking Tommy Smith's record that had also been set in Mexico City – but the Italian also held the low-altitude record (19.96s) between 1980 and 1983.

MERCURIAL MAUGER MAKES IT TITLE NO. 6

IVAN MAUGER WINS INDIVIDUAL WORLD SPEEDWAY CHAMPIONSHIP FOR RECORD SIXTH TIME
September 1979, Chorzow, Poland

Inspired by the achievements of fellow countryman Ronnie Moore, who in the 1950s had become the first New Zealander to achieve success on the British speedway circuit, Ivan Mauger followed in his hero's path and joined Wimbledon in 1956 at the age of 16. He was back in New Zealand, tail between his legs, by 1958, but continued racing and earned his big break when he joined Newcastle in 1963: within five years he was world champion. He retained his title in 1969 and 1970 to become the sport's first-ever Triple Crown winner and won a fourth title in 1972. In 1977, he equalled Ove Fundin's record haul of five titles, before winning his sixth and final championship in 1979.

➲ Sweden's Tony Rickarsson equalled Ivan Mauger's feat when he won his sixth world championship in 2005 (the other titles coming in 1994, '98, '99, 2001 and '02).

New Zealand's Ivan Mauger overcame disappointment in the early part of his career to become one of the most successful speedway racers in history, winning the world championship six times between 1968 and '79.

A YOUTHFUL HALL-OF-FAMER

BOBBY ORR BECOMES YOUNGEST INDUCTEE INTO HOCKEY HALL OF FAME AT 31

12 September 1979, Montreal, Canada

Chronic knee problems forced Bobby Orr from the ice for the last time a month into the 1978 season. This closed the book on a remarkable career, and one that had taken off at the unlikely age of 14, when he signed with the Boston Bruins. Since he was under 18, the Bruins assigned him to the minor-league Oshawa Generals. Bobby's style and drive made him a player to be reckoned with, and he began his NHL career with a bang, winning the Calder Trophy for rookie of the year in 1967. The 1969–70 season saw Orr emerge as the first defenceman to lead the League in goals scored and helped to sweep the Bruins to their first Stanley Cup victory in 29 years. The circumstances of Orr's retirement, plus his enormous popularity, prompted the NHL to waive the usual three-year waiting period before enshrining him alongside Henri Richard and Harry Howell.

↻That wasn't it for Orr: he was made an Officer of the Order of Canada in 1979. In 1997, Bobby Orr was voted the second-greatest hockey player of all time by an expert committee for the publication *The Hockey News*.

Orr's unique playing style influenced many younger defencemen, who began to adopt his speedy, rushing style to score goals as well as defend the net. After retirement, Orr became a bank manager and player agent in Boston.

A trailblazer in the world of women's basketball, Anne Meyers'scareer reads like a list of firsts: she ended her college career on a high in 1979 when she was voted into the All-America team for a fourth straight year before becoming the first star of the Women's Basketball League.

MEYERS BOWS OUT OF UCLA ON A FOUR-TIME HIGH

ANNE MEYERS FIRST TO BECOME FOUR-TIME ALL-AMERICAN WOMEN'S BASKETBALL PLAYER

5 December 1979, Los Angeles, California, USA

Anne Meyers was an on-court pioneer of women's basketball who pushed the sport to new levels. Her dazzling skills on the hardwood were apparent from an early age and she made history in 1974 when, as a 17-year-old, she became the first player in history to play for a US national team while still at high school. Her standout performances led to her becoming the first woman in history to accept a four-year sports scholarship – she went to the University of California, Los Angeles. And the successes did not stop there: during her stint at UCLA between 1976 and 1979, she became the only basketball player in history – male or female – to be voted onto the All-America team in four consecutive seasons.

↻After her All-America career, Meyers went on to become the first player to be drafted by the Women's Basketball League and also became the first woman in history to try out for an NBA team, the Indiana Pacers.

THE IRON MAN OF THE NFL

JIM MARSHALL PLAYS IN RECORD 282ND AND FINAL CONSECUTIVE NFL GAME

16 December 1979, Schaefer Stadium, Foxborough, Massachusetts, USA

Drafted in the fourth round of the 1960 NFL draft by the Cleveland Browns, defensive end Jim Marshall played one season with the Browns, including the final 12 games, before moving to the Minnesota Vikings in 1961. He would never move teams again, forming an integral and ever-present part of the infamous "Purple People Eaters" – the name given to the Vikings' defensive line in the 1960s and '70s. Over 19 years Marshall did not miss a single game – a testament to his remarkable athleticism – and when he played in his last game for the Vikings, against the New England Patriots in 1979 at the age of 41, he had notched up an NFL all-time record of 282 consecutive games.

↻ Marshall's tally stood as a record until 27 November 2005, when New York Giants' punter Jeff Feagles played in his 283rd consecutive game, but Marshall's haul is still a record for a non-kicker.

The average career span of a defensive end is four-and-a-half years, but Jim Marshall defied the odds, putting together a 19-year career that included a record run of 282 consecutive games.

The Philadelphia Flyers (pictured from left to right: Andre Dupont, Booby Clarke and Reggie Leach) started the 1979–80 NHL season in fine style, putting together an undefeated streak of 35 games – the longest streak in the history of North American sportss.

FLYERS' RECORD WINNING STREAK ENDS AT 35

PHILADELPHIA FLYERS RECORD LONGEST UNBEATEN STREAK IN NHL HISTORY

6 January 1980, Philadelphia, Pennsylvania, USA

Bob McCammon's appointment as coach for the 1978–79 NHL season revitalized the form of the Philadelphia Flyers: they rallied to second place in the regular season standings before losing in the second round of the playoffs. The following season they started with a win and a loss: and nobody could have foreseen what was to follow. From 14 October 1979 through to 6 January 1980, the Flyers were unbeatable, notching up 25 wins and ten ties, passing the Montreal Canadiens' record of 28 consecutive unbeaten games, before losing 7–1 to the Minnesota North Stars on 7th January 1980.

↻ The Flyers eased into the playoffs, before losing the Stanley Cup final in six games to the New York Islanders, who won the championship for the first time in their history.

BOTHAM MAGIC HUMBLES INDIA

IAN BOTHAM FIRST TO SCORE A CENTURY AND TAKE TEN WICKETS IN ONE TEST MATCH
15–19 February 1980, Wankhede Stadium, Mumbai, India

A hard-hitting batsman and an incisive medium-fast bowler, Ian Botham became the talisman of English cricket in the 1970s and '80s, making a generation of young cricketers believe all was possible with his rock 'n' roll lifestyle beyond the boundary rope and his match-winning performances on the field of play. In 1980, in the one-off Test against India, in Mumbai, he confirmed his status as one of the world's leading all-rounders when he took 6 for 58 as India slipped to 242 all out in their first innings. He then hammered 114 out of an England total of 296, before taking seven Indian wickets in the second innings (7 for 48). England won the game by ten wickets and Botham had become the first player in Test history to score a century and take ten wickets in the same Test match.

Botham's achievement has been matched only once, by Pakistan's Imran Khan, who scored 117 and took 6 for 98 and 5 for 82 against India in Faisalabad in January 1983.

Ian Botham made everyone believe Test matches could be won by inspiration alone: in 1980 he became the first of only two men to score a century and take ten wickets in a Test match.

CICHY AND WIELICKI CLIMB TO IMPOSSIBLE HEIGHTS

LESZEK CICHY AND KRZYSTOF WIELICKI COMPLETE FIRST WINTER ASCENT OF MOUNT EVEREST

17 February 1980, Mount Everest, Nepal/Tibet

In 1974, Poland's Andrzej Zawada became the first climber to reach an altitude in excess of 8,000m during the winter climbing season. A seed was sown: could he lead an expedition to achieve the impossible? To become the first to summit the world's highest mountain Mount Everest – a climb dangerous enough in perfect conditions – during the winter season. Some thought it climbing suicide but, in the winter of 1979–80, Zawada persuaded the Nepalese government to grant him the first winter climbing permit in history. On 17 February 1980, two members of the Polish expedition, Leszek Cichy and Krzystof Wielicki, reached the summit. They had completed the first winter ascent of Everest in history.

↻Later that year, on 20 August, Italy's Reinhold Messner became the first person in history to achieve a solo summit of the world's highest mountain.

RODNINA SKATES HER WAY INTO THE HISTORY BOOKS

IRINA RODNINA BECOMES ONLY PAIRS SKATER TO WIN THREE CONSECUTIVE OLYMPIC GOLD MEDALS

14–23 February 1980, Lake Placid, New York, USA

Irina Rodnina was the darling of the Soviet Union. She won the pairs skating world championship for the first time in 1969, with her partner Aleksey Ulanov: she would win three more titles with Ulanov in consecutive years as well as the gold medal at the 1972 Winter Olympics, before the partnership ended. She joined with Aleksandr Zaytsev (the couple would later marry) and the success rolled on: six more world championship titles between 1973 and 1978, seven European titles and a second gold medal in the 1976 Winter Olympics in Innsbruck, Austria. To complete her legend, the pair successfully defended their Olympic title in 1980, making Rodnina the only pairs skater in history to complete a hat-trick of Olympic titles.

↻Her win in Lake Placid also made her the oldest woman ever to win pairs skating Olympic gold (she was 31 years old).

Irina Rodnina was a Soviet national treasure: a ten-time world pairs champion and an 11-time European champion, she became the first in history to win three consecutive Winter Olympic gold medals in pairs skating.

ERIC HEIDEN: THE MAN OF GOLD

SPEED SKATER IS FIRST PERSON IN OLYMPIC HISTORY TO WIN FIVE GOLD MEDALS AT SINGLE WINTER GAMES
14–23 February 1980, Lake Placid, New York, USA

Speed skater Eric Heiden appeared in the 1976 Winter Olympics as a 17-year-old, but made little impact. However, the hours spent on a plastic sheet in his basement paid off the following year when he won the overall world championship for the first time and again in both 1978 and '79. By 1980, those in the know were predicting a possible sweep of the speed skating medals at the upcoming Winter Olympics in Lake Placid. They were spot on: over the course of a spectacular nine days, the doctor's son from the Midwest won the 500m, 1,000m, 1,500m, 5,000m and 10,000m gold medals, all of them in Olympic-record-breaking time and the 10,000m in world-record-breaking time (by an astonishing 6.2 seconds).

⮑ Heiden retired from speed skating after finishing second in the 1980 World Championships and sought other pursuits. In 1985, he became the United States professional cycling champion and competed in the 1986 Tour de France, crashing out of the race in spectacular fashion.

Eric Heiden brought the 1980 Winter Olympics in Lake Placid to life when he became the only Olympian in history to win five gold medals at a single Winter Games.

Multiple world and European luge doubles champions Norbert Hahn and Hans Rinn made history in 1980 when they became the first in history to defend their Olympic title.

HAHN AND RINN COMPLETE LUGE DOUBLES DOUBLE

NORBERT HAHN AND HANS RINN BECOME ONLY PAIR IN OLYMPIC HISTORY TO DEFEND LUGE DOUBLES TITLE
14–23 February 1980, Lake Placid, New York, USA

Twenty-two-year-old East Germans Norbert Hahn and Hans Rinn became the heroes of a nation at the 1976 Winter Olympics in Innsbruck, Austria, when they finished on top of the East Germany–West Germany clash in the doubles luge competition, beating Hans Brandner and Balthasar Shwarm to the gold medal by 0.285s. And they travelled to Lake Placid four years later – the second time the Games had visited the Adirondack Mountains of New York state – as world champions and looking to become the first in history to defend their Olympic crown. They did just that, beating the Italian pairing of Peter Geschnitzer and Karl Brunner by almost three-tenths of a second.

⮑ It was the second time the Winter Olympics had visited Lake Placid (the first was in 1932) and the third time the Winter Games had visited the United States (Squaw Valley in California had played host in 1960).

OXFORD MAKE IT FIVE IN A ROW BY A CANVAS

OXFORD BEAT CAMBRIDGE BY SMALLEST MARGIN OF VICTORY IN UNIVERSITY BOAT RACE HISTORY

5 April 1980, River Thames, London, England

First staged in 1827, the University Boat Race between Oxford University and Cambridge University has been contested on an annual basis (with the exception of the two World Wars) since 1856 on a course measuring 4 miles 374 yards (6,779m) rowing upstream along London's River Thames from Putney to Mortlake. By the end of the 1970s, Oxford were on a roll, winning four races in a row – and the 56th victory in their history – to cut their overall race-win deficit to Cambridge to 12. It was down to 11 in 1980, as Oxford held off a strong charge by Cambridge to win by a canvas or, officially, by four feet (1.22m): the smallest margin of victory in the race's history.

↪In the losing Cambridge eight that day was Hugh Laurie, who would go on to achieve television fame in comedy series with Stephen Fry and in the Emmy-winning hit US TV series *House*.

Oxford edged to their fifth straight victory in the 1980 University Boat Race by the slenderest of margins – four feet. The record stood until 2003, when Oxford won by the margin of one foot (30cm).

After 26 seasons and 1,756 games in the NHL, Gordie Howe – otherwise known as "Mr Hockey" – decided to call time on his illustrious, record-breaking career at the end of the 1979–80 season.

MR HOCKEY CALLS IT A DAY

GORDIE HOWE CALLS TIME ON RECORD-BREAKING 26-YEAR NHL CAREER

5 June 1980, Hartford, Connecticut, USA

Gordie Howe made his debut on the right wing for the Detroit Red Wings at the age of 18 in 1946. A clinical goal-scorer (he finished in the top five goal-scorers for an NHL-record 20 straight years) and an imaginative playmaker, he was also robust – powerful enough to shrug off the attentions of most opponents. He formed part of the infamous "Production Line" that swept the Red Wings to four Stanley Cups between 1950 and '55 and played on until injury caused him to retire in 1971. But life on the sidelines did not suit him: he underwent surgery to mend his injured wrist, appeared in the World Hockey League between 1973 and '79, and played one last year in the NHL – a record 26th – with the Hartford Whalers in 1979–80, aged 52.

↪No player has played more NHL games than Gordie Howe (1,767). Second on the list is Mark Messier, who played 1,756 games for the Edmonton Oilers, New York Rangers and Vancouver Canucks over a 25-year period, 1979–2004.

A NEW BREED OF GERMANS BUT THE SAME WINNING FORMULA

WEST GERMANY BECOME THE FIRST TWO-TIME WINNERS OF THE EUROPEAN CHAMPIONSHIP

22 June 1980, Olympic Stadium, Rome, Italy

The first eight-team, single-tournament European Championship was far from a success. Attendances were poor and the soccer defensive, but one of the few positives from Italy '80 came with the emergence of a new generation of West German players – not one of the 1972 European Championship or 1974 World Cup-winning team remained. Karl-Heinz Rummenigge, Hans-Peter Briegel, Horst Hrubesch, Klaus Allofs and others were the new names on the block, and they won their group with ease to take their place in the final (the two group winners progressed to the final). Their shock opponents were Belgium. But there would be no more Belgian surprises: West Germany won 2–1 to become the first team to win the European Championship for a second time.

⮌This generation of West Germans made it to the World Cup final two years later in Spain, but lost 3–1 to Italy. Playing as a combined German team in 1996, they became the first country to win the European Championship three times.

A second success in the European Championships in 1980 (following their first tournament victory in 1972) confirmed the rebuilding of the West German soccer team was complete. The Germans beat Belgium 2–1 in the final with Horst Hrubesch netting both goals.

BORG REINS SUPREME AND COLLECTS GRAND SLAM NO. 10

BJORN BORG BECOMES YOUNGEST TENNIS PLAYER TO WIN TEN GRAND SLAM SINGLES TITLES

8 July 1980, Wimbledon, London, England

Athletic and deceptively strong, Bjorn Borg shocked the tennis world when he made his debut for Sweden in the Davis Cup at the age of 16. Two years later, in 1974, he recovered from two sets down in the final to win the French Open and retained his title the following year. In 1976 he won the Wimbledon title for the first time and when he defended his title the following year became the No. 1-ranked player in the world. The position suited him: the ice-cool Swede recorded a back-to-back hat-trick of wins on the clay of Paris and the grass of Wimbledon (1978–80) to become, aged 24 years, 29 days, the youngest player in history to win ten grand slam tournaments.

⮌After collecting a record sixth French Open title in 1981, Borg shocked the tennis world once more when he announced his retirement in 1982 at the age of 26.

With his baseline power and ferocious top-spinning forehand and backhand, Bjorn Borg was the master of Wimbledon and Roland Garros, collecting 11 titles in nine years. His 41-game winning streak at the All-England club is still a record.

299

[Image: Nikolay Andrianov performing on the rings]

A problem child in his youth, Nikolay Andrianov found direction through gymnastics and went on to become the most successful male Olympian in the sport's history.

ANDRIANOV TAKES OLYMPIC MEDAL HAUL UP TO 15

NIKOLAY ANDRIANOV WINS LAST OF RECORD HAUL OF MEDALS FOR A MALE GYMNAST

19 July–3 August 1980, Moscow, Soviet Union

Nikolay Andrianov made his competitive debut in 1969 before enjoying his first international success in the 1971 European Championships, when he took gold in both the uneven bars and vault. He made his Olympic bow the following year – picking up three medals (one gold, one silver and one bronze) – and by the time Olympic competition returned four years later was at the peak of his career. He won the all-round title by the largest margin of victory in 42 years and picked up six other medals – three gold, two silver and one bronze. He continued on the medal trail four years later in Moscow, collecting two golds, two silvers and a bronze. No other male gymnast in history has bettered his haul of 15 Olympic medals.

➲ Only compatriot Larissa Latynina has collected more Olympic medals: between 1956 and 1964 she picked up 18 (nine gold, five silver and four bronze).

MESSNER TAKES ON WORLD'S HIGHEST PEAK UNAIDED

REINHOLD MESSNER FIRST TO COMPLETE SOLO ASCENT OF MOUNT EVEREST (AND WITHOUT SUPPLEMENTAL OXYGEN)

20 August 1980, Mount Everest, Nepal/Tibet

Reinhold Messner spent his formative years climbing the peaks of his native Dolomites and by his early 20s was considered one of the leading climbers in the world. Committed to Alpine-style climbing – fast and unaided, no fixed ropes, no oxygen, no base camps; just you and the mountain – by the 1970s, Messner had turned his attentions to Everest. Fellow mountaineers and doctors warned that an unassisted attempt on the world's highest peak was tantamount to suicide, but Messner defied the critics, making the round trip to the summit and back – via the north-east ridge to the north face – in just four days. Messner had succeeded and mountaineering would never be the same again.

➲ In 1986, Reinhold Messner became the first man to summit all of the world's 14 8,000m-plus summits – and all without supplemental oxygen.

In 1980 Reinhold Messner not only became the first man in history to complete a solo ascent of Everest, he also did so without the use of oxygen or fixed ropes.

YOUNG GUN THACKWELL MAKES FORMULA ONE HISTORY

MIKE THACKWELL BECOMES YOUNGEST DRIVER IN FORMULA ONE RACE TO APPEAR ON STARTING GRID

28 September 1980, Montreal, Canada

Kiwi Mike Thackwell enjoyed huge success in racing's junior formulae – winning five times in the British Formula Three championship in 1979, before being signed to the Tyrrell team for the 1980 season as a test driver. Midway through the season, Thackwell was loaned to the Arrows team for one race, the Dutch GP, following an injury to Arrows driver Jochen Mass. He failed to qualify. All was not lost: a few weeks later he was offered a ride in a third Tyrrell car for the Canadian Grand Prix and duly qualified. At 19 years, 182 days he had become the youngest driver in Formula One World Championship history to appear on the starting grid.

➲ Sadly his race did not last long. He was involved in a massive pile-up on the first lap, the race was stopped and Tyrrell team-leader Jean-Pierre Jarier requisitioned his car for the restart. Thackwell only appeared in one more race: the 1984 Canadian GP.

A fleeting appearance it may have been, but when Mike Thackwell qualified for the 1980 Canadian GP he became the youngest in the sport's history to do so.

Henri Toivonen (left, with co-driver Paul White) announced himself onto the world rally scene in 1980, winning the Lombard RAC Rally and becoming the youngest race winner in WRC history.

YOUNGSTER TOIVONEN TAKES THE SPOILS

HENRI TOIVONEN BECOMES YOUNGEST WINNER OF A WORLD RALLY CHAMPIONSHIP EVENT

16–19 November 1980, England/Wales

Henri Toivonen started racing in karts, switched to saloon cars – winning the Finnish Cup championship – and then to Formula Vee, where he won one round of the Scandinavian championship and ended 1977 as Finnish champion. It was a mere prelude to his entrance into rallying. Toivonen switched to rally driving in 1977 to appease family concerns over the safety of circuit racing, and when he could keep the car on the road was quick. After a series of one-off drives, he showed just how quick he could be when he drove his unfancied Sunbeam Talbot to victory in the 1980 Lombard RAC Rally. At just 24 years, 86 days, he remains the youngest driver in history to win a WRC event.

➲ Toivonen drove his first full WRC season in 1985, winning the RAC Rally and a legion of fans with his exuberant driving style. He was killed the following year in a mysterious accident in the Corsica Rally.

In a 1981 interview with the *Sunday Times* newspaper, the Toronto-born Podborski summed up his approach to downhill skiing: "The only thing I want to do when I go fast is to go faster ... I'm never afraid."

IT'S ALL DOWNHILL FROM HERE

CANADIAN SKIER STEVE PODBORSKI BECOMES THE FIRST NORTH AMERICAN TO WIN ALPINE SKIING MEN'S WORLD CUP DOWNHILL CHAMPIONSHIP

7 December 1980, Val d'Isère, France to 28 March 1981, Laax, Switzerland

Steve Podborski was the youngest member of the infamous "Crazy Canucks" downhill ski team, which was known for fast, almost reckless skiing and winning races – lots of races. He was made a member of the team in 1973 and began the world cup tour in 1974. In 1980, he came home from the Winter Olympics with bronze, which made him the first North American to win an Olympic downhill skiing medal. He then became the first North American to take home the World Cup downhill championship in the 1981–82 season. During Podborski's career, he podiumed in 20 of his 89 races, as well as achieving more than 40 top-ten places. He retired in 1984.

➲ Podborski is still involved in sports, acting as a TV commentator, and speaking at many events. He also serves as athlete ambassador for Right to Play, a Canadian charity that brings sports-based fitness programs to developing-world countries.

RAIDERS DOWN THE EAGLES FOR WILDCARD SUCCESS

OAKLAND RAIDERS BECOME FIRST WILDCARD TEAM TO WIN THE SUPER BOWL

25 January 1981, Louisiana Superdrome, New Orleans, Louisiana, USA

When John Madden decided to relinquish his coaching role with the Oakland Raiders in 1979 to take up a position in the commentary booth, the club turned to former quarterback Tom Flores to control their fortunes. He faced his first crisis after five games when quarterback Dan Pastorini broke his leg: Flores turned to Jim Plunkett, who had spent the previous season languishing on the bench. Plunkett found his form, posting an 11–5 record, enough to earn the Raiders a wildcard berth. The Raiders swept into Super Bowl XV against the Philadelphia Eagles and Plunkett shone once again, completing 13 of 21 passes for three touchdowns as the Raiders won 27–10 to become the first wildcard team in history to win the Super Bowl.

➲ Jim Plunkett completed a Lazarus-like return to form in the 1980–81 NFL season that culminated in him winning the Super Bowl MVP award after throwing 261 yards for three touchdowns.

Having scraped into postseason play in the 1980–81 NFL season, the Oakland Raiders swept past the Houston Oilers, Cleveland Browns and the San Diego Chargers to reach Super Bowl XV. And the shocks were not over: the Raiders pummelled the Philadelphia Eagles 27–10 to record an NFL first.

HISTORY-MAKING BROWN STEERS OXFORD TO SIXTH CONSECUTIVE WIN

SUE BROWN BECOMES FIRST WOMAN TO COMPETE IN THE UNIVERSITY BOAT RACE

4 April 1981, River Thames, London, England

After five successive victories, Oxford made history in 1981 when they announced their selection for the forthcoming University Boat Race: their cox would be Sue Brown, the first woman ever to compete in the event. Oxford were the strong favourites – talk among bookmakers was not about who would win but how much Oxford would win by. Cambridge won the toss and surprised everybody by opting for the Surrey station and, despite getting off to the better start, found themselves on the wrong end of the predicted procession. The dark blues of Oxford won by eight lengths to record their sixth consecutive win.

➲ Sue Brown steered Oxford to a seventh consecutive win the following year, this time by three-and-a-quarter lengths.

Oxford's Sue Brown made history in 1981 when she became the first woman to compete in the University Boat Race. Her first taste of the event was a winning one.

Shergar lit up Epsom Downs with a scintillating performance in the 1981 Derby, pulverizing the field and winning by a record ten lengths.

SHERGAR TAKES DERBY SPOILS IN RECORD-BREAKING FASHION

SHERGAR WINS THE EPSOM DERBY BY A RECORD TEN LENGTHS

3 June 1981, Epsom Downs, Surrey, England

Bred by Prince Karim Aga Khan IV in County Kildare, Ireland, Shergar, a bay colt with a distinctive white blaze who was foaled in 1978, began training with Michael Stoute in Newmarket. His debut race came in the Guardian Classic Trial at Sandown Park in 1981: he shocked onlookers by decimating the field and crossing the winning post ten lengths clear. He confirmed his potential with a 12-length victory in the Chester Vase and by the time he arrived at the Epsom Derby in June was considered a strong favourite. With 19-year-old jockey Walter Swinburn in the saddle, Shergar did not disappoint, pulling ahead of the field early and continuing his blistering, punishing pace before cantering to a ten-length victory: the largest winning margin in the race's history.

➲ Shergar retired from racing in September 1981, but his story did not end there. Eighteen months later, masked gunmen kidnapped him from his stud in County Kildare and he was never seen again.

1981

COE EXCELS UNDER THE TUSCAN SUN

SEBASTIAN COE BREAKS 800M WORLD RECORD WITH MARK THAT WILL STAND FOR 17 YEARS

10 June 1981, Florence, Italy

Along with Steve Ovett and Steve Cram, Sebastian Coe was part of a British triumvirate of middle-distance runners who, for a short time in the late 1970s and early '80s, dominated the world. He first came to the public's attention when he won the European indoor championship in 1977. In 1979 he broke Alberto Juantorena's 800m world record of 1m43.44s (set in 1977) by more than a second in Oslo, Norway (the new record: 1m42.33s) and entered the Olympic Games as one of the favourites for the 800m title. He finished second to Ovett. However, he gained some consolation when he took the 1,500m title – it was Ovett's first loss in the event for three years – and underlined his 800m supremacy in 1981, when he improved his own world record mark to 1m41.73s in Florence, Italy.

➲ Coe's mark would stand as a sole record until Kenya's William Kipketer equalled the time on 7 July 1997 before improving it to 1m41.11s 17 days later in Cologne, Germany. To this day, Kipketer is the only man in history to have run the 800m in a quicker time than Coe.

Although he would never win 800m Olympic gold (he took silver in both 1980 and 1984), Sebastian Coe broke the 800m world record twice and held it for 17 years.

VETERAN WHITWORTH THE FIRST TO A MILLION

KATHY WHITWORTH BECOMES FIRST WOMAN IN GOLF HISTORY TO PASS $1 MILLION IN CAREER EARNINGS
26 July 1981, La Grange Country Club, La Grange, Illinois, USA

Kathy Whitworth first picked up a golf club at the age of 15 and within four years was a two-time New Mexico state amateur champion. She turned professional in 1958 and endured a miserable rookie season, earning a paltry $1,300 in 26 events, but any thoughts of giving up were ended in 1962 when she won her first tournament. She won the first of her six majors in 1965, and by 1981, with 80 titles to her name, was on the verge of making history. She was about to become the first woman in golf history to pass the $1 million mark in career earnings: a third-place finish at the 1981 US Women's Open – ironically the one major tournament that eluded her – took her past the milestone.

➲ It took Kathy Whitworth 23 years to earn $1 million. Fifteen years later, Australia's Karrie Webb became the first woman golfer in history to pass $1 million in a single season.

Whitworth finished her career with a staggering 88 tournament wins to her name, passing the mark of both Mickey Wright (82) and Sam Snead (82): she has a strong claim to being the most successful golfer of all time.

Considered the finest butterfly swimmer of all time, Mary T. Meagher took the 1981 US National Swimming Championships by storm, breaking two world records in the space of three days.

MADAME BUTTERFLY HITS WORLD RECORD-BREAKING NOTE

MARY T. MEAGHER BREAKS WORLD RECORD FOR 100M AND 200M BUTTERFLY IN SAME CHAMPIONSHIPS
13–16 August 1981, Brown Deer, Wisconsin, USA

Louisville-born Mary T. Meagher set her first world record in butterfly as a 14-year-old eighth grader in the 1979 Pan American Games held in San Juan, Puerto Rico. Expected to claim Olympic gold at the Moscow Games in 1980, the withdrawal of the United States team must have come as a bitter disappointment, but the butterfly queen bounced back in sensational style the following year at the 1981 US National Championships and in the process produced what some consider the finest performance ever seen in a swimming pool. In the space of three days she broke the world records in both the 100m (57.93s) and 200m (2m05.96s) butterfly events: both records would stand for almost two decades.

➲ Meagher's 100m record would stand until 1999, when compatriot Jenny Thompson swam 57.88s. Her 200m world record stood until 2001, broken by Australia's Susie O'Neill.

BOTHAM'S HEROICS SECURE ASHES FOR ENGLAND

IAN BOTHAM BREAKS RECORD FOR MOST SIXES IN AN ASHES INNINGS

13–17 August 1981, Old Trafford, Manchester, England

Ian Botham's rollercoaster ride in the summer of 1981 captivated a nation. Talk about extremes: a pair in the losing Lord's Test and losing the captaincy; a match-winning 149 off 148 balls to drag England from the Headingley mire to square the series; and then his Ashes-lead-securing spell of 5 for 11 at Edgbaston. Botham, fuelled by the passion of a nation, was on fire. In the fourth Test at Old Trafford he smashed the bewildered Australians around the park, hitting 118 off 102 balls (including an Ashes record six sixes). Australia fell short second time round, England took an unassailable 3–1 series lead and Ian Botham was the toast of a nation.

➲ Ian Botham's record for sixes in an innings stood until 2005, when Kevin Pietersen hit seven during his Ashes-winning innings of 158 during the fifth Test at The Oval.

Ian Botham's feats during the 1981 Ashes campaign were the centrepiece of the most astonishing few weeks in English cricket. His innings at Headingley may well be a long-established part of cricket lore, but it was his innings in the fifth Test at Old Trafford that found him a place in the record books: he hit six sixes during his second-innings knock of 118 as England won both the Test and the series.

"Skeets" Nehemiah bounced back from the disappointment of a US no-show at the 1980 Moscow Olympics by breaking his own world record the following year: it would stand for almost eight years until Roger Kingdom clocked 12.92s in Zurich on 16 August 1989.

SKEETS MAKES STATEMENT WITH WORLD RECORD NO. 3

"SKEETS" NEHEMIAH FIRST MAN TO RUN 110M HIGH HURDLES IN UNDER 13 SECONDS

19 August 1981, Zurich, Switzerland

A national junior champion in 110m high hurdles in 1977, Renaldo "Skeets" Nehemiah next won three NCAA titles and four national titles before going on to excel on the international stage. In 1979 he showed he was the outstanding athlete in his event when he broke the world record twice, lowering Alejandro Casanas's mark by 0.21s to 13s flat. Untouchable in his event, he must have been devastated by the United States' withdrawal from the 1980 Olympic Games in Moscow, but put any disappointment behind him the following year when he ran 12.93s in Zurich to become the first man in history to run the 110m hurdles in under 13s.

➲ In 1982 Nehemiah signed for the San Francisco 49ers in the NFL. He stayed with them for four years – and was part of the team that won the Super Bowl in 1984 – before returning to athletics in 1986, but by then his best years were behind him.

COE SHOWS CHAMPION STATUS WITH ANOTHER WORLD MILE RECORD

SEBASTIAN COE COMES OUT ON TOP OF THE BATTLE OF THE BRITS TO BREAK WORLD MILE RECORD

28 August 1981, Brussels, Belgium

During the strike-ridden days of the late 1970s and early '80s one sporting rivalry captured the imagination of the British public, and Sebastian Coe finally seemed to have won it when he came out on top of the private Ovett–Coe squabble for the world mile record.

Sebastian Coe and Steve Ovett were polar opposites: Coe, a university graduate with his finely honed, refined running style and Ovett, the long-haired son of a grocer who oozed raw talent. They didn't particularly like each other and the tension translated itself into one of the most prolonged duels in athletics history. In 1979, Coe broke the mile world record in Oslo (3m48.95s); shortly before the Olympics the following year, Ovett improved it to 3m48.8s. On 19 August 1981, Coe bettered Ovett's mile record with 3m48.53s; seven days later, Ovett ran 3m48.40s. For Coe the matter was far from closed: two days later he ran 3m47.33s. He had the record again and, what's more, Ovett failed to beat it.

➲ Coe's record would last for four years until another Brit, Steve Cram, clocked 3m46.32s in Oslo, Norway, on 27 July 1985.

HUNT MAKES IT SIX IN A ROW TO BREAK RECORD

GEOFF HUNT WINS THE BRITISH OPEN SQUASH CHAMPIONSHIP FOR A RECORD EIGHTH TIME

September 1981, Wembley Conference Centre, London, England

Geoff Hunt started playing squash at the age of 12 and within three years had become the Victoria state junior champion; the following year he was Australia's national junior champion. The success continued: by 18 he was the Australian senior champion and, by the end of his career, was considered one of the greatest ever to have played the game. A four-time World Open winner and world No. 1 between 1975 and 1980, he is best remembered for his performances in the British Open. He first took the title in 1969; another win followed four years later, and between 1976 and 1981 Hunt could call the championship his own, winning six consecutive titles to become the tournament's first eight-time winner.

➲ Hunt's record has since been beaten by Pakistan squash star Jahangir Khan, who won the British Open ten consecutive times from 1982 to 1991.

Geoff Hunt put together a stellar squash career and particularly enjoyed the British Open, winning the sport's premier tournament eight times in 13 years between 1969 and 1981.

BLINK AND YOU'VE MISSED IT: SMAIL FINDS THE TARGET IN FIVE SECONDS

DOUG SMAIL SCORES THE FASTEST GOAL IN NHL HISTORY

20 December 1981, Winnipeg Arena, Winnipeg, Manitoba, Canada

Doug Smail was a star of the North Dakota University team for three seasons from 1978 to 1980, producing some stunning performances, culminating in his final year when he scored 87 points in 40 games in the NCAA Championships, was selected to the All-America team and was voted the league's MVP. He had caught the eye of NHL scouts and signed for the Winnipeg Jets as a free agent after college. By 1981 he was a full-time player with the Jets and made history on 20 December 1981 when he scored just five seconds after the opening faceoff, in the Jets' game against the St Louis Blues, to score the fastest goal in NHL history.

➲ Smail's feat has been equalled on two occasions – by Bryan Trottier (22 March 1984) and Alexander Mogilny (21 December 1991) – but never beaten.

The highlight of Doug Smail's 13-year NHL career came in December 1981 when he scored the fastest goal in NHL history, after just five seconds.

DENNIS THE MENACE BACK TO BRILLIANT BEST

DENNIS LILLEE BREAKS THE RECORD FOR THE MOST TEST WICKETS IN A CALENDAR YEAR

26–30 December 1981, Melbourne Cricket Ground, Melbourne, Australia

Dennis Lillee arrived on the international cricket scene in spectacular fashion in 1971, delivering the ball at express pace and frightening the life out of batsmen around the world. But it seemed almost over before it had begun: the following year he broke down with a back injury and his career seemed under threat. Through hard work and grim determination he bounced back: he may have lost some of his pace – he was still rapid – but added extra nous and continued to outfox batsmen through the years. His best season came in 1981, when he took a staggering 85 Test wickets in a mere 13 Test matches to break Kapil Dev's record (75) for the most wickets in a calendar year.

➲ Lillee's record would stand for 24 years until fellow Australian Shane Warne took an all-time record 96 wickets in 15 matches in 2005.

A supreme action and a snarling attitude made Dennis Lillee one of the most feared bowlers on the planet, and he simply got better with age. Ten years after his debut, and having defied serious injury, he took a record 85 wickets in a calendar year.

TELEVISION'S FIRST MAXIMUM BREAK

STEVE DAVIS MAKES FIRST-EVER TELEVISED MAXIMUM BREAK IN SNOOKER

11 January 1982, Queen Elizabeth Hall, Oldham, England

Steve Davis was the new kid on the snooker block. After winning the world championship for the first time in 1981, he started 1982 with a bang in the Lada Cars Snooker Classic. With his best-of-nine match against John Spencer evenly poised at 2–2, Davis reeled off 15 reds and 15 blacks: he was on course for a maximum break. Tension in the crowd mounted. Davis sank the yellow, the green, the brown and the blue, but was horribly out of position for the pink. He pulled off a staggering deep-screw shot with the rest and calmly potted the black. A maximum and, what's more, for the first time television cameras were there to capture it.

Reigning snooker world champion Steve Davis made history in 1982 when he completed the first-ever televised maximum break. His reward: a Lada car.

➲ Davis went on to dominate the snooker scene in the 1980s, winning the world championship on six occasions (1981, 1983, 1984, 1987, 1988 and 1989) and winning 28 ranking titles.

GRITTAR LEADS SAUNDERS TO HISTORIC NATIONAL SUCCESS

DICK SAUNDERS BECOMES OLDEST-EVER JOCKEY TO WIN THE GRAND NATIONAL

3 April 1982, Aintree, Liverpool, England

Dick Saunders was originally posted to ride Steel Bridge in the 1969 Grand National but lost out to professional jockey Richard Pitman and had to watch on the sidelines as the pair finished second. He turned his back on professional racing and forged a successful farming career, appearing as a jockey in the odd point-to-point race or the occasional steeplechase race, and 13 long years would pass before another chance to ride in the world's most famous steeplechase came his way. In 1982, aged 48, he was offered a ride on Grittar, the pre-race favourite, following the pair's victory over the Aintree fences the previous year in the Foxhunter's Classic. The duo lived up to the billing: Grittar won the race by 15 lengths and Saunders became the oldest winning jockey in Grand National history.

One of nine riders in the race gaining their first experience of the Grand National in 1982, 48-year-old Dick Saunders did not put a foot wrong and became the oldest jockey in history to win the illustrious race.

➲ 1982 may have been the one and only occasion Saunders appeared in the National, but Grittar was back to defend his crown the following year, with Paul Barton in the saddle, and finished fifth. He made one more appearance in 1984, ridden by John Francome, but finished in a disappointing 12th place.

THE GREAT ONE SHOWS HIS CLASS

WAYNE GRETZKY SETS NHL SINGLE-SEASON RECORD FOR MOST GOALS

5 April 1982, Northlands Coliseum, Edmonton, Alberta, Canada

In 1979, on his 18th birthday, Wayne Gretzky signed a staggering 20-year contract with the Edmonton Oilers in the World Hockey Association and he finished his debut season as the league's top scorer as well as being voted Rookie of the Year. The WHA folded at the end of the year and the Oilers joined the NHL; critics suggested Gretzky would flounder in the bigger, tougher league. They were wrong: he scored 137 points (the most by a rookie in NHL history) and was voted the league's MVP. In 1980–81 he scored a then-record 164 points. It got better. In 1981–82 he broke Maurice Richard's record of 50 goals in 50 games set in 1944–45 (and equalled by Mike Bossy in 1980–81), passing the mark in 39 games before going on to score a record 92 goals, breaking Phil Esposito's 1970–71 single-season goals record by a staggering 16.

➲ The record has never been broken and only Gretzky himself has come close to breaking it: in 1983–84 he scored 87 goals. The next best mark is 85 by Brett Hull in 1990–91.

Wayne Gretzky's performances in the 1981–82 NHL season earned him the moniker "The Great One": he scored 92 goals and 120 assists for 212 points – the first time in NHL history a player had passed the 200-point mark in a single season.

PEARSON'S POLE STREAK HITS 20TH CONSECUTIVE YEAR

DAVID PEARSON SETS NASCAR RECORD FOR MOST CONSECUTIVE SEASONS WITH A POLE POSITION

28 May 1982, Charlotte Motor Speedway, Concord, North Carolina, USA

During a 26-year NASCAR career that saw him win the Winston Cup title on three occasions (1966, 1968 and 1969), David Pearson, known as the "Silver Fox", was perhaps most famous for his duels with Richard Petty. Between August 1963 and June 1977, the pair finished one-two on 63 occasions, with Pearson coming out on top 33 times – including his legendary win in the 1976 Daytona 500. But the truth is that Pearson had to play second fiddle to Petty for the majority of his career – with one exception. On 28 May 1982, Pearson notched up an all-time Winston Cup record when he secured pole for the World 600 at Charlotte: it was the 20th consecutive year he had managed to achieve at least one pole position.

➲ Pearson lies second in the all-time list of NASCAR race winners with 105: in first place is Richard Petty with 200.

Three-time champion David Pearson remained competitive throughout his 26-year NASCAR career: between 1963 and 1982 (a stretch of 20 years) he recorded at least one pole position per season.

McENROE OUTLASTS WILANDER IN DAVIS CUP EPIC

JOHN McENROE BEATS MATS WILANDER IN LONGEST MATCH IN DAVIS CUP HISTORY
11 June 1982, Checkerdrome, St Louis, Missouri, USA

The Davis Cup world group quarter-final between defending champions USA and Sweden stood delicately poised at 2–2: it all came down to the final match between John McEnroe, the three-time US Open champion and 1981 Wimbledon champion, and Mats Wilander, the reigning French Open champion. Both men had won their opening singles rubbers, with McEnroe also partnering Peter Fleming to doubles success, and this final match threatened to be a classic. It was. McEnroe took the first two sets, 9–7, 6–2 (these were the days before tie-breaks were used in the Davis Cup), before Wilander roared back, taking the next two sets 17–15, 6–3. Amid unbelievable tension, McEnroe took the deciding set 8–6. The USA were through and the delirious crowd had just witnessed the longest match in Davis Cup history.

➲ The United States went on to beat France 4–1 in the final, with McEnroe winning all three of the rubbers he contested, two in singles and one in doubles.

After six hours and 20 minutes, John McEnroe finally got the better of Swede Mats Wilander in the longest match ever played in Davis Cup history, in the quarter-finals of the 1982 competition.

MARADONA BECOMES THE WORLD'S MOST EXPENSIVE SOCCER PLAYER

BARCELONA SIGN DIEGO MARADONA FROM BOCA JUNIORS FOR WORLD-RECORD £3 MILLION

June 1982, Barcelona, Spain

Growing up in Villa Fiorito, a shanty-town in the southern suburbs of Buenos Aires, Argentina, all Diego Maradona had in life was soccer. He was spotted by a talent scout while playing for his neighbourhood club and signed for Argentinos Juniors at the age of 12. His professional debut came ten days before his 16th birthday, in 1976, and within a year he had made his debut for the national team (but missed out on selection for the 1978 World Cup because Argentina coach Cesar Menotti considered him too young). In 1981, after 168 appearances for Argentinos Juniors (scoring 116 goals), he secured a dream move to Boca Juniors, the club he had supported as a youth. He played in all five of Argentina's 1982 World Cup games, including being sent off against Brazil for violent play, and his performances caught the eye of Barcelona: he joined the Catalan giants shortly after the end of the tournament for a world-record fee of £3 million.

➲ Maradona remained at the Catalan club for two seasons, scoring 38 goals in 58 appearances, before signing for Napoli in 1984 for another world-record fee of £6.9 million.

In a true rags-to-riches tale, Diego Maradona overcame a poverty-stricken childhood in which he shared a single room with his seven siblings to becoming the most expensive player on the planet. Some claim he is the greatest player ever to have played the game.

HUNGARY HAMMER SORRY EL SALVADOR

HUNGARY BEAT EL SALVADOR 10–1: THE LARGEST WINNING SCORE IN WORLD CUP FINALS HISTORY

15 June 1982, Nuevo Estadio, Elche, Spain

El Salvador travelled to Spain to make their second appearance in the World Cup finals in 1982. They were desperate to eradicate the disappointment they had experienced during Mexico 1970, when their record read played three lost three, with nine goals against and none for. They opened their 1982 campaign against Hungary and found themselves 3–0 down at half-time. In the second half the floodgates opened and El Salvador were 5–0 down by the time Luis Baltazar Ramirez Zapata scored the first World Cup goal in his country's history. But it was a false dawn: Hungary scored five more times in the final 26 minutes: their 10–1 victory is the largest in World Cup finals history.

➲ Things got no better for El Salvador during Spain '82. They lost their next game, against Belgium, 1–0, and bowed out of the tournament following a 2–0 defeat by Argentina. They have not appeared in the World Cup finals since.

Hungary opened their 1982 World Cup campaign in record-breaking style, beating El Salvador 10–1 (the largest win in the tournament's history), but a 4–1 defeat by Argentina and a 1–1 draw against Belgium meant that they, like El Salvador, were eliminated after the first group phase.

Not many can lay claim to breaking one of Pele's records, but Norman Whiteside did just that in the 1982 World Cup in Spain, when he broke the Brazilian's record to become the youngest player ever to appear in the tournament.

HOTSHOT WHITESIDE IS WORLD CUP'S YOUNGEST PLAYER

NORMAN WHITESIDE BECOMES YOUNGEST PLAYER TO APPEAR IN WORLD CUP FINALS

17 June 1982, La Romareda, Zaragoza, Spain

Brought up in North Belfast, Norman Whiteside was discovered by the same Manchester United scout, Bob Bishop, who had unearthed George Best. Powerful and strong, he made his United debut in the 1981–82 season – becoming the youngest to play for the Reds since Duncan Edwards – and scored in both the League Cup and FA Cup finals. His performances earned him a call-up to the Northern Ireland squad for the 1982 World Cup in Spain and he made his debut in the 0–0 draw against Yugoslavia in his country's opening group game. At 17 years and 42 days he had become the youngest player in history to play in the World Cup finals.

➲ Norman Whiteside played 38 times for Northern Ireland, scoring eight goals before his career was cut short by injury at the age of 26.

FAST FREDDIE SHOWS HE BELONGS WITH THE BEST

FREDDIE SPENCER BECOMES YOUNGEST-EVER RIDER TO WIN A 500CC WORLD CHAMPIONSHIP GRAND PRIX

4 July 1982, Spa-Francorchamps, Belgium

Louisiana-born Freddie Spencer started racing motorcycles at the age of four and by the time he was 12 had numerous dirt-track titles to his name. He continued to rise through the ranks, and his 250cc national championship-winning performances in 1979 caught the eye of the American Honda outfit, who signed him to their Superbike team for the following season. Quick wherever he raced, Spencer divided his time in 1981 between the American Superbike and European Grand Prix scenes, before switching to Europe full-time in 1982. He was a sensation, winning the seventh race of the season, the Belgian Grand Prix at Spa-Francorchamps, to become, aged 20 years, 196 days, the youngest rider in history to win a MotoGP.

➲ Spencer won again that year at the San Marino GP and finished third in the end-of-season standings. In 1983 he fought off the attentions of compatriot Kenny Roberts to become the youngest world champion in the sport's history and collected a second title in 1985.

A breath of fresh air on the 500cc world championship scene, Freddie Spencer won a race in his first full season to become the youngest race winner in the sport's history.

The world got its first taste of the drama of a World Cup penalty shootout in Spain '82. The climax of one of the greatest games in the tournament's history saw West Germany beat France 5–4 on penalties (the semi-final clash had ended 3–3 after extra-time) to take their place in the World Cup final.

WORLD CUP CLASSIC DECIDED BY PENALTY SHOOTOUT FIRST

WEST GERMANY AND FRANCE CONTEST FIRST PENALTY SHOOTOUT IN WORLD CUP HISTORY

8 July 1982, Estadio Ramon Sanchez Pizjuan, Seville, Spain

The 1982 World Cup semi-final between France and West Germany was always going to be a clash of styles: the classy, sleek French against the rugged, iron-willed West Germans. The mix produced a classic, with neither side able to shake off the attentions of the other: 1–1 after 90 minutes, 3–3 after extra-time. It would take the first penalty shootout in history to separate them. The Germans missed first, the French followed suit. With the scores locked at 4–4, German keeper Toni Schumacher parried Alain Bossis's weak penalty attempt away. Up stepped Horst Hrubesch: he slotted the ball past a despairing Jean Ettori and West Germany were in the World Cup final.

➲ The match was not without controversy. Midway through the second half, Michel Platini passed to substitute Patrick Battiston. As Battiston leapt to head the ball, onrushing German keeper Toni Schumacher flattened him. The ball went wide: Battiston lay unconscious on the ground with two teeth missing and a bone in his neck broken. To the astonishment of everybody, the referee gave West Germany a goal-kick.

DECKER CONFIRMS WORLD NO. 1 STATUS WITH RECORD-BREAKING SPREE

MARY DECKER BREAKS SIX WORLD RECORDS IN THE SPACE OF SIX WEEKS

16 July 1982, Eugene, Oregon, USA

Mary Decker first caused a stir when she pulled off a shock victory in the 800m in an international meet between the United States and the Soviet Union in Minsk in 1973, aged just 14. Within two years she was a three-time world record holder (in 1,000m, 880 yards and 800m) but, renowned for pushing her body to its absolute limit, she missed out on the 1976 Olympics through injury. A US boycott in 1980 meant she missed the 1980 Games as well, but in 1982 Decker confirmed her reputation as the world's premier middle-distance runner when she broke six records in the space of six weeks: the mile record (twice), 2,000m, 3,000m (indoor), 5,000m and the 10,000m (breaking Jelena Sipatova's record in her first attempt at the distance by almost 40 seconds).

During a sensational six-week period in 1982, Mary Decker broke six world records. By the end of her career she held every US national record between 800m and 10,000m (and still holds the record for 800m, 1,500m, mile, 2,000m and 3,000m).

➲ Mary Decker went on to become a double world champion in Helsinki in 1983, winning 1,500m and 3,000m gold in what became known as the "Decker Double", but her Olympic woes continued in Los Angeles in 1984: she tripped and fell in the 3,000m final.

THOMPSON UNDERLINES DECATHLON DOMINANCE

DALEY THOMPSON BREAKS THE WORLD DECATHLON RECORD

8 September 1982, Athens, Greece

The greatest all-round athlete Britain has ever produced, Daley Thompson's first taste of the Olympic arena in 1976 was a bitter one: the youngest athlete in the competition, he finished a lowly 18th in the decathlon event. And when he came second in the European Championships two years later, he vowed he would never come second again. He was true to his word: having won Olympic gold for the first time in Moscow 1980 – with a number of his main challengers missing from the event – he broke the decathlon world record on 23 May 1982 (8,704pts) to underline his supremacy; West German Jurgen Hingsen (8,723pts) broke it on 15 August. Three weeks later, the pair squared off in the 1982 European Championships in Athens. Thompson won the day and broke the world record in the process with a haul of 8,743pts.

➲ Thompson would go on to defend his Olympic crown in Los Angeles in 1984, but needed to set a new world record points-haul (8,847 points) to do so.

Daley Thompson was single-handedly responsible for dragging decathlon from being little more than a sideshow into one of the main events of an athletics meeting. He is the only man in decathlon history to hold the world, Olympic, Commonwealth and European titles as well as the world record simultaneously.

HENDERSON AT HIS PICKPOCKETING BEST

RICKY HENDERSON SETS SINGLE-SEASON RECORD FOR MOST STOLEN BASES

3 October 1982, Royals Stadium, Kansas City, Missouri, USA

Signed by the Oakland Athletics in the fourth round of the 1976 MLB draft, Ricky Henderson spent the first four years of his professional career in the minor leagues, batting .309 or better each season and giving everybody a glimpse of what was to come in a 1977 match when he stole a minor league record seven bases in one game. In 1980 (he had made his major league debut the previous year), he became only the third man in history to steal 100 or more bases in a season – Maury Wills (104) and Lou Brock (118) being the others. Henderson's total of 100 set a new American League record. He surpassed it two years later, smashing Brock's 1974 MLB record with a staggering 130 stolen bases.

Dubbed the "Man of Steal" by sportswriters, Ricky Henderson lived up to his name in 1982 when he stole 130 bases to set a new single-season record.

➲ Only one other player has stolen more than 100 bases in a season since: Vince Coleman (1985–87). Henderson also holds the all-time record for stolen bases (1,406) and for most career runs (2,295).

HOOKES HAMMERS 34-BALL CENTURY

DAVID HOOKES SCORES THE FASTEST CENTURY IN THE HISTORY OF FIRST-CLASS CRICKET

25 October 1982, Adelaide Oval, Adelaide, Australia

Blond, broad-shouldered and free-hitting, David Hookes made a name for himself in 1977 when he smashed five centuries in six innings for South Australia. Straight away he was thrust into Australia's middle-order for the 1977 Centenary Test and made an immediate impression, hitting Tony Grieg for five consecutive fours during his second-innings knock of 56. But it was a false dawn. Hookes never grew into the Test arena, playing for Australia just 23 times. He continued to score heavily in the domestic arena, however, and on 25 October 1982 set a record that stands to this day when he scored a century off just 34 balls (with 17 fours and three sixes): the fastest in the history of first-class cricket.

A star of both the domestic and World Series cricket scenes, David Hookes failed to translate his talent onto the international stage. But in domestic cricket he was prolific and hit the fastest-ever century in first-class cricket history in 1982, off just 34 balls in 43 minutes.

➲ Hookes died in mysterious circumstances in January 2004 following an altercation with a bouncer during a post-match evening out with the South Australia and Victoria players. Hookes was punched, fell to the floor, hit his head, suffered a cardiac arrest and never regained consciousness.

THE WOUNDED SEAGULL REACHES NEW SURFING HEIGHTS

MARK RICHARDS WINS RECORD FOURTH SUCCESSIVE WORLD SURFING CHAMPIONSHIP

December 1982, Sunset Beach, Oahu, Hawaii

Australia's Mark Richards started surfing at the age of six and by the age of 16 had left school to pursue careers in both professional surfing and surfboard design. He spent his winters in Hawaii and it was there that he met the legendary surfboard pioneer Dick Brewer, who taught him the art of shaping. Together they developed a highly manoeuvrable twin-fin board: in 1979 it took Richards, who was splitting his time between his business and the professional circuit, to a first world title. The following year he became the first surfer in history to defend his crown. Following titles Nos. 3 and 4 in 1981 and 1982 he became the most famous surfer on the planet.

A pioneer in surfboard design, Australia's Mark Richards – nicknamed "The Wounded Seagull" because of his unconventional surfing technique – used his Twin Fin II board design to great effect, winning the world championship four consecutive times between 1979 and 1982.

➲ Mark Richards's record of four world surfing championships stood until 1997 when the USA's Kelly Slater took the crown for a fifth time – further wins in 1998, 2005 and 2006 took the American's haul to eight world crowns.

DORSETT SETS UNBREAKABLE RECORD

DALLAS COWBOYS RUNNING BACK TONY DORSETT SCORES A 99-YARD TOUCHDOWN

3 January 1983, Metrodome, Minneapolis, Minnesota, USA

After putting together one of the most storied careers in college football history – he was a four-time All-American at the University of Pittsburgh – Tony Dorsett was a celebrity before he had even entered the pro football ranks. He joined the Dallas Cowboys in 1977 and picked up where he had left off, collecting Rookie of the Year honours and winning the Super Bowl in his first season. Success continued to come his way: he rushed for more than 1,000 yards in eight of his first nine seasons and, in 1983, created an unusual slice of history: in the Cowboys' match against the Minnesota Vikings he ran a 99-yard touchdown – a record that can be equalled but never beaten.

One of the greatest running backs in NFL history, Tony Dorsett achieved perfection in 1983 when he scored a 99-yard touchdown.

➲ By the time Dorsett's 12-year career had ground to a halt, he had rushed for 12,739 yards – fifth on the all-time NFL list.

THE ONLY GOLDEN SET IN TENNIS

BILL SCANLON PRODUCES THE ONLY PERFECT SET IN THE HISTORY OF PROFESSIONAL TENNIS
22 February 1983, Delray Beach, Florida, USA

On paper at least, the first-round match between the USA's Bill Scanlon and Brazil's Marcos Hocevar at the WCT Gold Coast Classic in Delray Beach, Florida, looked as though it was going to be a one-sided affair, with everyone expecting a comfortable victory for the American, a former NCAA champion in 1977 and a four-time tournament winner on the professional tour. The first set followed the script, with Scanlon taking it comfortably, 6–2. Then something happened that had never been seen before on the professional tennis circuit … and hasn't been seen since. Scanlon produced a "golden set" by winning the set without conceding a single point.

➲ Scanlon's interest in the tournament came to an abrupt end in the second round when he lost in straight sets, 6–4, 7–6, to Cassio Motta.

KLAMMER COMPLETES COMEBACK WITH RECORD FIFTH DOWNHILL TITLE

FRANZ KLAMMER WINS MEN'S DOWNHILL WORLD CUP FOR A RECORD FIFTH TIME
12 March 1983, Lake Louise, Alberta, Canada

Downhill specialist Franz Klammer made his first splash on the international scene with a second-place finish at St Anton in the 1973 World Cup. The following year he finished second in the overall standings, but he truly came of age in 1975 when he won eight of the season's nine races to claim his first overall world downhill title. He defended his crown in 1976 and entered the Winter Olympics in Innsbrück as favourite for downhill gold: the Austrian did not disappoint and the home crowd celebrated. Further downhill titles followed in 1977 and 1978 before a slump in form saw him omitted from the Austrian team for the 1980 Winter Olympics. Some might have retired; Klammer simply worked harder. He won at Val d'Isère in 1981, before completing his climb back to the top of the skiing ladder with a record fifth downhill World Cup title in 1983.

➲ Klammer finally retired in 1985, with 26 race victories to his name – 25 of them in downhill and one in combined.

Watching Franz Klammer ski was a far from relaxing experience, but the Austrian squeezed everything out of his skiing-on-the-edge-of-disaster style to win a record five World Cup downhill titles.

IT ALL COMES GOOD FOR WATSON ON RACE DAY

JOHN WATSON RECORDS GREATEST THROUGH-THE-FIELD VICTORY IN FORMULA ONE HISTORY

27 March 1983, Long Beach, California, USA

Qualifying for the 1983 United States Grand Prix over the temporary road course in Long Beach, California, had been a disaster for the McLaren team. Problems with both tyres and set-up had seen the cars of John Watson and Niki Lauda line up for the race in 22nd and 23rd place on the 26-car starting grid. On race day, though, it was a completely different story. By lap 28 of the 75-lap race, the McLaren team-mates were lying in third and fourth place respectively. By lap 45 they occupied first and second: it was a position they kept, with Watson heading home an unlikely one-two some 30 seconds ahead of his team-mate. It created a slice of history: Watson's win was the largest through-the-field victory in Formula One history.

➲ The United States Grand Prix was as good as it got for McLaren in the 1983 season: Watson finished seventh in the drivers' championship and Lauda tenth, as Brazil's Nelson Piquet took the World Championship spoils.

What a difference a day makes: 24 hours after qualifying in 22nd place for the 1983 United States GP, John Watson obliterated the opposition, climbing through the field from his lowly grid position to take an historic and unlikely victory.

In 1983, Jenny Pitman achieved what many thought impossible when one of her horses, Corbiere (ridden by Ben De Haan), won the Grand National. She is the only woman in history to have trained a Grand National winner. Her ex-husband, Richard, and son, Mark, both finished second in the race as jockeys.

THE FIRST LADY OF AINTREE

JENNY PITMAN BECOMES THE ONLY FEMALE TRAINER IN HISTORY TO WIN THE GRAND NATIONAL

9 April 1983, Aintree, Liverpool, England

Jenny Pitman left school at the age of 15 to become a stable girl. She married at the age of 19 and turned her attentions to training, becoming one of the first women in history to be granted a trainer's licence by the Jockey Club in 1975; she had her first winner later that year. Her plain-speaking toughness allowed her to prosper in the male-dominated racing world and by 1981 she had become the first woman trainer in history to train more than 21 winners in a season. But still no one believed she could win the big one: the Grand National. In 1983 she proved them wrong: her horse Corbiere took the Grand National spoils and Pitman had made history.

➲ Pitman won the National once again with Royal Athlete in 1995. In 1984, she also became the first woman in history to train a Cheltenham Gold Cup winner (Burrough Hill Lad). In 1991, Mrs Pitman repeated her Gold Cup victory with Garrison Savannah – ridden by her son Mark. They nearly emulated Golden Miller in winning the Grand National in the same year, but finished second.

BRILLIANT BENOIT SETS WORLD MARATHON BEST

JOAN BENOIT BREAKS THE MARATHON WORLD RECORD
19 April 1993, Boston, Massachusetts, USA

After collecting the marathon world record in 1983, Joan Benoit went on to win the first-ever Olympic women's marathon, in Los Angeles in 1984, just 17 days after undergoing arthroscopic surgery on her knee.

Joan Benoit took up long-distance running to aid her recovery from a broken leg suffered while skiing and found it very much to her liking. A time of 2h51m for a second-place finish in her first-ever marathon in Bermuda in January 1979 may not have been the most blistering of starts, but she clearly learned from the experience. A few months later she broke the US national record with a time of 2h35m15s in the Boston marathon. She was barely getting started: three years later, in the same event, she became the first woman in history to run the marathon in under 2h25m, breaking Grete Waitz's world record of 2h25m28.7s set just a day earlier in London with a new time of 2h22m43s.

⮞ Benoit's record would last for more than two years until Norway's Ingrid Kristiansen ran 2h21m06s in London on 21 October 1985.

THE GRINDER MAKES WORLD SNOOKER MAXIMUM

CLIFF THORBURN MAKES FIRST-EVER MAXIMUM BREAK AT THE WORLD SNOOKER CHAMPIONSHIPS
23 April 1983, Crucible Theatre, Sheffield, England

A talented all-round sportsman in his youth, Canada's Cliff Thorburn decided team games weren't for him and turned to the cue and the baize. He possessed true talent and headed to England to try his luck on the professional snooker scene. He made his first appearance in the world championship in 1973, reaching the second round, and within seven years had become the only "overseas" player in history to be crowned world champion. But it is for his feat in 1983 that he will always be remembered. In the fifth frame of his second-round match against Terry Griffiths, the Canadian became the first man in history to record a maximum 147 break in the world snooker championships.

Nicknamed "The Grinder" for his slow, meticulous play, Cliff Thorburn broke the mould in 1983 when he became the first person in history to produce a perfect frame in the world snooker championships.

⮞ Only four other players in history have achieved the feat: Jimmy White (1992), Stephen Hendry (1995), Ronnie O'Sullivan (1997 and 2003) and Mark Williams (2005).

SUPREME PIGGOTT RECORDS NINTH DERBY WIN

LESTER PIGGOTT WINS THE DERBY FOR A RECORD NINTH TIME

1 June 1983, Epsom Downs, Surrey, England

During a stellar 47-year career, Lester Piggott rode to victory some 5,400 times in over 30 countries around the world, but his legend will for ever be associated with one particular race: the Epsom Derby – the one-and-a-half-mile flat race run over the Epsom Downs Racecourse in Surrey. Piggott caused a sensation in 1954 when he became the race's youngest-ever winner on Never Say Die. He repeated the success three years later on Crepello. He added two more Derby triumphs to his growing collection in 1960 (St Paddy) and 1968 (St Ivor), and the 1970s bought even more success, with wins in 1970 (Nijinsky II), 1972 (Roberto), 1976 (Empery) and 1977 (The Minstrel). And Piggott was not finished there: he found time for one last hurrah in 1983, riding Teenoso to a three-length victory over a rain-drenched Epsom Course and a record ninth Derby win.

➲ Only one other man in history has ridden more than three horses to Derby victory: Willie Carson in 1979, 1980, 1989 and 1994.

Lester Piggott's record of nine Derby victories is considered one of the most glorious and unassailable in horse racing.

In her final year of singles play, 39-year-old Billie Jean King successfully defended her DFS Classic crown to become the oldest player in history to win an LTA Tour title.

BILLIE JEAN KING DEFIES THE YEARS

BILLIE JEAN KING BECOMES OLDEST-EVER WINNER OF AN LTA TOUR EVENT

13 June 1983, Birmingham, England

Billie Jean King never strayed far from the spotlight, putting together a formidable career that included 12 singles grand slam victories – Australian Open (1968), French Open (1972), Wimbledon (1966, 1967, 1968, 1972, 1973 and 1975) and the US Open (1967, 1971, 1972 and 1974) – 16 grand slam doubles titles and 11 mixed doubles titles. Competitive through to the end of her career, she retired from singles play in 1983, but she showed a new generation she still knew a thing or two when she won the 1983 DFS Classic in Birmingham – a traditional Wimbledon warm-up tournament – at the age of 39 years, 7 months. She remains the oldest-ever woman to win an LTA Tour title.

➲ Seeded tenth for the 1983 Wimbledon Championships a few weeks later, Billie Jean King defied her years once again, making it through to the semi-finals before losing 6–1, 6–1 to Andrea Jaeger.

In July 1983, Calvin Smith used the thin air of Colorado Springs to launch an assault on Jim Hines's 15-year-old 100m world record: it worked, and Smith ran 0.02s faster to set a mark that would last until 1988.

ALTITUDE THE KEY TO BREAKING UNBEATABLE RECORD

CALVIN SMITH BREAKS THE 100M WORLD RECORD
3 July 1983, Colorado Springs, Colorado, USA

Jim Hines's world record mark for the 100m of 9.95s set in 1969 in the rarefied air of Mexico City – which lies some 7,349ft (2,240m) above sea level – was looking like the most unbeatable mark in athletics, with many claiming that it might never be broken, and certainly not at sea level. The nay-sayers were right on one count: it took another high-altitude run to beat it. On 3 July 1983 in Colorado Springs – some 6,000ft (1,839.5m) above sea level – American athlete Calvin Smith clocked an unbelievable 9.93s. The record was broken, but the doubters continued to have their say.

➲ By 1988, the world of the 100m was in turmoil: Canada's Ben Johnson had broken Smith's record on two occasions but then failed a drugs test following his gold-medal-winning performance in the 1988 Olympics in Seoul, South Korea: he, along with his records, was thrown out of athletics. However, Carl Lewis, who had finished second to Johnson in the 100m final, had clocked 9.92s – this time was recognized as the new world record.

TRAINING RUN TURNS INTO GREATEST-EVER 800M PERFORMANCE

JARMILA KRATOCHVILOVA BREAKS THE WOMEN'S 800M WORLD RECORD
26 July 1983, Munich, West Germany

As Eastern European athletes dominated the women's track-and-field scene in the early 1980s, Czechoslovakia's Jarmila Kratochvilova found herself playing second fiddle to East Germany's Marita Koch, but the 400m specialist enjoyed her year of years in 1983, at the tender age of 32. With one eye on the forthcoming inaugural World Championships in Helsinki, Finland, ten days down the line, Kratochvilova travelled to a minor track-and-field meet in Munich, West Germany, with the sole intention of having a minor 400m workout. A slight thigh injury caused a change of plan … and with some result. Electing to run the 800m instead – she considered the race less demanding – the Czech powerhouse obliterated the field, finishing some 30m clear of her rivals and crossing the finishing line in an astonishing 1m53.28s – breaking Nadesha Olizarenko's record, set in the 1980 Moscow Olympics, by some 0.15s.

What was intended as no more than a training run turned into one of the most dynamic displays in athletics history, but although it made Jarmila Kratochvilova one of the biggest names in the sport, it also raised suspicions of drug use, accusations the Czech star has denied to this day.

➲ Ten days later, at the 1983 World Championships, Kratochvilova took gold in both the 400m and 800m – breaking Marita Koch's world record in the former – and silver in the 4x400m.

REVOLUTIONARY DESIGN ENDS USA'S 132-YEAR WINNING STREAK

AUSTRALIA II BECOMES FIRST CHALLENGER TO BEAT THE UNITED STATES IN THE AMERICA'S CUP

26 September 1983, Newport, Rhode Island, USA

The Australian team for the 1983 America's Cup had a trick up their sleeve. They had developed a revolutionary upside-down keel which gave their boat, *Australia II*, exceptional manoeuvrability and a "light" water displacement – the boat's waterline was the shortest ever seen on a 12m boat. The United States objected; the law courts upheld the legality of the design and the result was that the 32nd running of the America's Cup turned into a classic. The United States' *Liberty* raced into a 3–1 lead following a series of mechanical failures on *Australia II*, but then the Aussie boat roared into life, winning the final three races to become the first team in 132 years to beat the United States in the America's Cup.

◑ *Australia II*'s victory prompted mass celebrations Down Under. Even Prime Minister Bob Hawke was caught up in it all, uttering the famous line: "Any boss who sacks anyone for not turning up today is a bum."

It took a revolutionary keel design and the favour of the law courts to end the United States' 132-year domination of the America's Cup: *Australia II*, skippered by John Bertrand, recovered from a 3–1 deficit to win the seven-race series and earn an historic victory.

THE GREAT ONE GETS THE OILERS OFF TO A FLYER

WAYNE GRETZKY SETS ALL-TIME NHL RECORD FOR LONGEST CONSECUTIVE POINT-SCORING STREAK
28 January 1984, Northlands Coliseum, Edmonton, Alberta, Canada

In 1982–83, his first season as captain of the Edmonton Oilers, Wayne Gretzky had continued to write his name large in hockey's history books but had been forced to suffer the acute disappointment of watching his team being swept 4–0 by the New York Islanders in their first-ever appearance in the Stanley Cup finals. At such times a captain needs to lead from the front and Gretzky was more than happy to oblige. The man the world was starting to call the "Great One" started the 1983–84 season by scoring at least one point in the first 51 games of the campaign – 61 goals and 92 assists for 153 points at an average of over three points per game. It is a record no one has come close to breaking.

Wayne Gretzky got off to a flier in the 1983–84 NHL season, picking up points in each of the first 51 games of the season. The next best streak in NHL history is 46 games, by Mario Lemieux in the 1989–90 season.

➲ Gretzky ended the season by winning his fifth straight Hart Trophy (for the league's most valuable player) and his fourth straight Art Ross Trophy (for the league's leading points-scorer), but the biggest prize of them all that year came when the Oilers beat the Islanders 4–1 to win the Stanley Cup for the first time in their history.

TWO GOLDS ARE BETTER THAN ONE

GAETAN BOUCHER WINS CANADA'S FIRST-EVER OLYMPIC GOLD MEDALS IN SPEED SKATING
7–19 February 1984, Olympic speed-skating oval, Sarajevo, Yugoslavia

Months before the 1984 Winter Olympics were due to begin, Gaetan Boucher looked like a shoo-in for gold. The Quebec-born speed skater had already earned a slew of accolades, including repeat world championships, a world speed record in the 1,000m, and a silver medal at the 1980 Winter Games in Lake Placid. Then the unthinkable happened: he broke an ankle. Time heals all wounds, as the saying goes, but Boucher had just ten months to recover before the Games opened. Still nursing his way back to complete recovery at Sarajevo, Boucher managed to win a bronze medal in the 500m, before racing past Sergei Khlebnikov to take Canada's first-ever Olympic speed-skating gold in the 1,000m. But he wasn't finished. Two days later, the 25-year-old made his third appearance on the podium after edging past Khlebnikov one more time to win the gold medal in the 1,500m.

Boucher credits a training visit with skater Eric Heiden for bumping him from a steady second-place finisher to a gold-medal winner. Heiden's gruelling routine inspired Boucher to challenge his pain threshold and take his game to the next level.

➲ Boucher is one of Canada's most successful Olympic speed skaters. He won four medals in two Winter Olympiads (one in 1980 and three in '84) and competed in a third before the ankle he shattered in 1983 finally caught up with him. In 1984, he was made an Officer of the Order of Canada.

TORVILL AND DEAN DANCE TO OLYMPIC PERFECTION

TORVILL AND DEAN BECOME FIRST ICE-DANCING PAIR IN OLYMPIC HISTORY TO RECEIVE PERFECT MARKS

14 February 1984, Sarajevo, Yugoslavia

Britain's Jayne Torvill and Christopher Dean first skated together in 1975 and three years later finished fourth in the European Championships, but it was the disappointment suffered following a fifth-place finish in the 1980 Winter Olympics that forced them into a re-think. Their solution revolutionized the sport of ice dancing: they ditched performances danced to patched-up fragments of music, now basing their routines around powerful, theme-driven, single pieces of orchestration, and didn't look back. They won the World Championships three times between 1981 and 1983 and arrived at the 1984 Winter Olympics in Sarajevo as firm favourites for gold. Their four-and-a-half-minute routine to Ravel's "Bolero" brought the house down. As the music stopped and the pair fell to the ice, flowers rained down on them from the crowd above. The judges were equally impressed, giving the pair 12 perfect scores out of 18, including nine perfect scores out of nine for artistic impression. They were the first-ever perfect scores in Olympic ice-skating history.

Jayne Torvill and Christopher Dean produced the perfect Valentine's Day performance at the 1984 Winter Olympics: a slow, sensuous routine to Ravel's "Bolero" captivated both the crowd and the judges, who awarded the pair the first perfect scores in Olympic history (12 of them out of a possible 18).

➲ The pair followed up their gold-medal-winning performance in the Olympics by claiming a fourth consecutive world championship. They turned professional a year later, but reclaimed amateur status for the 1994 Winter Olympics in Lillehammer, Norway, and went on to finish third.

327

Hallo Dandy may have taken the spoils in the 1984 Grand National, but the race will be best remembered for the record number of finishers: 23.

HALLO DANDY LEADS RECORD 23 HORSES HOME IN NATIONAL

RECORD NUMBER OF HORSES COMPLETE THE GRAND NATIONAL

31 March 1984, Aintree, Liverpool, England

It was the perfect day for racing and the perfect day for watching. Under clear spring skies, people flocked in their thousands for the 138th running of the Grand National and those who went were afforded a slice of history. Forty horses lined up for the start of the four-mile-four-furlong race over 30 fences. By the last, a 13/1 long shot, ten-year-old Hallo Dandy, ridden by Neale Doughty and trained by Gordon W. Richards, had stolen a march on 9/1 Greasepaint. He held on to win by four lengths in a time of 9m21.4s, but it was what followed that made history: a further 22 horses made it past the finishing line, the largest number of finishers in the race's long history.

➲ The fewest number of finishers to complete the race was two in 1928: the same year 100/1 Tipperary Tim won the race.

CREAMER FOLLOWS THE SUN AND THE STARS AROUND THE WORLD

MARVIN CREAMER BECOMES FIRST TO COMPLETE CIRCUMNAVIGATION WITHOUT NAVIGATIONAL AIDS

17 May 1984, Cape May, New Jersey, USA

Sixty-six-year-old former geography professor Marvin Creamer and his crew set off from Cape May harbour, New Jersey, in a 36ft steel-hulled cutter called *Globe Star*, with a boat packed full of provisions, in an attempt to circumnavigate the globe without the use of any navigational aid: no compass, no sextant, not even a wristwatch – just a transmitter to allow coast guards to track the boat's progress. Using only the sun, the moon and the stars to guide them – and when they were not visible, the wind and the ocean's currents – the crew sailed to South Africa, Australia and New Zealand, before rounding Cape Horn and making their way up the Atlantic. Some 514 days after their departure they returned to Cape May … and history had been made.

➲ Creamer was no novice sailor: he had already made eight transatlantic crossings prior to his circumnavigation, three of them without the use of navigational aids.

Marvin Creamer and his crew made history in 1984 when they became the first in modern times to guide a boat around the world's oceans without any form of navigational aid.

Bruce Grobbelaar's (1) antics between the posts worked to Liverpool's advantage – whereas Roma's players succumbed to the pressure. The Reds held their nerve to become the first team in history to win the European Cup after a penalty shootout.

REDS HOLD THEIR NERVE IN PENALTY SHOOTOUT DRAMA

LIVERPOOL BECOME THE FIRST TEAM TO WIN THE EUROPEAN CUP ON PENALTIES

30 May 1984, Stadio Olimpico, Rome, Italy

If Liverpool wanted to win the European Cup for the fourth time in the club's history they would have to do it the hard way: they would have to beat AS Roma in their own backyard – the Stadio Olimpico, the scene of the Reds' first European Cup win in 1977. One hundred and twenty minutes of soccer failed to separate the two sides: they remained deadlocked at 1–1 and, for the first time in history, the European Cup would be decided by a penalty shootout. Inspired by the leg-wobbling antics of their Zimbabwean keeper Bruce Grobbelaar, Liverpool edged the Italian side 4–2, with Alan Kennedy slotting home the decisive penalty for Joe Fagan's side.

⊃ In the years since, seven European Cup (or Champions League) finals have been decided on penalties with Steaua Bucharest (1986), PSV Eindhoven (1988), Red Star Belgrade (1991), Juventus (1996), Bayern Munich (2001), AC Milan (2003) and Liverpool (2005) all winning the trophy the hard way.

PLATINI LEADS LES BLEUS TO EURO CHAMPIONSHIP GLORY

MICHEL PLATINI SCORES A EUROPEAN CHAMPIONSHIP SINGLE-TOURNAMENT RECORD OF NINE GOALS

27 June 1984, Parc des Princes, Paris, France

As the 1984 European Championships in France loomed, the host nation's coach, Michel Hidalgo, was forced to take a gamble: in the absence of a world-class striker he opted for a flexible 4-4-2 formation designed to bring the best out of the attacking brilliance of his captain Michel Platini. It worked: France romped through the group phase with Platini scoring seven goals, including two hat-tricks. He was on target in the semi-final as well, netting a final-minute extra-time winner as the hosts beat Portugal 3–2. The party did not stop there: Platini scored the opening goal in France's 2–0 final victory over Spain – his record ninth goal of the tournament – and a nation danced in the streets.

⊃ Platini stands at the top of the all-time goal-scoring charts in the European Championships with nine goals. In second place, with seven, is England's Alan Shearer.

Michel Platini was on top of his game in the 1984 European Championships in France, scoring nine times in the tournament as his country won the competition for the first time in their history.

KRISTIANSEN THRILLS HOME CROWD WITH WORLD RECORD RUN

INGRID KRISTIANSEN BECOMES FIRST WOMAN TO RUN 5,000M IN UNDER 15 MINUTES

28 June 1984, Oslo, Norway

Born in Trondheim, Norway, in 1956, Ingrid Kristiansen took some time to emerge from the shadow cast by the achievements of her compatriot Grete Waitz, but she first came to the public's attention when she won the inaugural 3,000m world championships in Sittard, the Netherlands, in 1980. She struggled in the 1982 European Championships in Athens, finishing eighth in the 3,000m, but showed her versatility, and her penchant for longer distances, with a third-place finish in the marathon. The following year she became one of the most talked-about middle-distance runners on the planet when she beat Mary Decker's 5,000m record, clocking 14m58.89s at the Bislett Games in Oslo to become the first woman in history to run the distance in under 15 minutes.

➲ Her record stood for barely two months before Zola Budd, a South African athlete representing Britain, clocked 14m48.07s in London. However, Kristiansen reclaimed the record a year later with a time of 14m37.33s in Stockholm – a mark that would stand for some nine years.

A multiple winner of the London marathon, Norway's Ingrid Kristiansen showed her talent over the shorter distances when she became the first woman in history to run 5,000m in under 15 minutes.

BOENISH LEAPS FROM THE SUMMIT OF THE TROLL WALL

CARL BOENISH COMPLETES THE FIRST LISTED BASE JUMP IN HISTORY

5 July 1984, Trollveggen, Norway

Although the history of jumping from fixed objects dates back some 900 years, BASE jumping (leaping from **B**uilding, **A**ntenna, **S**pan or **E**arth) is an altogether more recent phenomenon. The first unofficial jump may have taken place in 1966, but the first BASE jumping record to make it into the *Guinness Book of World Records* belongs to Carl Boenish, the man considered to be the father of the sport. On 5 July 1984, Boenish made the highest jump ever attempted when he leapt from the Trollveggen (the "Troll Wall") in Norway – the tallest vertical rock face in Europe measuring some 3,690ft (1,100m) from base to summit. He was killed trying to repeat the feat two days later.

➲ The current world record for the highest BASE jump lies with two Australians, Glenn Singleman and Heather Swann, who leapt from Meru Peak in northern India from a height of 21,666ft (6,604m) on 26 May 2006.

HOHN'S RECORD LEADS TO A RULE CHANGE

UWE HOHN BECOMES FIRST MAN IN HISTORY TO THROW THE JAVELIN IN EXCESS OF 100M

20 July 1984, Friedrich Ludwig Jahn Sportpark, Berlin, East Germany

Not many sportsmen have produced a performance so spectacular that it has led to changing the rules of the sport they compete in, but that is exactly what happened to Uwe Hohn following his stunning javelin throw in East Berlin in 1984. On 20 July 1984 in the Friedrich Ludwig Jahn Sportpark, Hohn, the reigning European champion, became the first person in history to throw a javelin in excess of 100m – he threw 104.80m, almost the length of the stadium. For safety reasons the International Amateur Athletics Federation were forced to act: they shifted the centre of mass on the javelin forwards by 4cm, making it under-perform and fall more sharply to the ground. This resulted in shorter, and safer, throws, but also meant that Hohn's record could never be beaten. It had become the "eternal record".

⮞ The current javelin world record stands at 98.48m, set by Jan Zelezny of the Czech Republic in Jena, Germany, on 25 May 1996.

LEWIS THE KING OF THE 1984 OLYMPIC GAMES

US TEAM BREAK 4X100M WORLD RECORD AS CARL LEWIS EQUALS JESSE OWENS'S FEAT OF FOUR GOLDS

28 July–12 August 1984, Los Angeles, California, USA

Carl Lewis travelled to the 1984 Olympic Games in Los Angeles with the stated intention of matching Jesse Owens's feat of winning four gold medals at a single Olympics. The holder of the low-altitude world record for long jump, he won the competition with ease: he knew that his first jump of 8.54m would be enough to win and made only one further attempt, but still took gold by 30cm. His next gold came in the 100m, with his time of 9.99s proving far too strong for his opponents. He was made to work harder in the 200m, needing to produce an Olympic record-breaking time of 19.80s to complete the hat-trick. His fourth and final gold was as much of a procession as it was a coronation, anchoring the US 4x100m team to gold in a world-record-breaking time of 37.83s.

⮞ Carl Lewis would go on to make history by defending his Olympic long jump title at the next three Olympic Games: in Seoul in 1988, Barcelona in 1992 and Atlanta in 1996, although he would fail in his quest to break Bob Beamon's long-standing long jump world record.

The finest all-round athlete in the world by the time the Olympic Games rolled into the United States for the first time in over 50 years in 1984, Carl Lewis achieved his aim of winning four gold medals: one of them (200m) came in an Olympic record-breaking time and he completed the feat by anchoring the US team to the fastest 4x100m time in history.

At the 1984 Olympic Games, Daley Thomson became only the second man in history to defend his Olympic decathlon crown (Bob Mathias had won decathlon gold in 1948 and 1952) and did so in world-record-breaking style.

DALEY COMPLETES OLYMPIC DECATHLON DOUBLE

DALEY THOMPSON DEFENDS OLYMPIC DECATHLON CROWN IN WORLD-RECORD-BREAKING STYLE

28 July–12 August 1984, Los Angeles, California, USA

Defending Olympic and world decathlon champion Daley Thompson travelled to the 1984 Olympic Games having seen his great rival Jurgen Hingsen break his world decathlon record a year earlier and was determined to set the record straight. The two matched each other blow for blow during the first seven rounds of competition before Thompson found his form in both the pole vault and the javelin. The gold was his and all he needed to do was to run the 1,500m in 4m34.98s to reclaim the record. He clocked 4m35s dead, but the drama wasn't over. Officials later decided to take another look at his 110m hurdles time: they improved it by 0.01s to hand Thompson extra points … and the world record.

➲ Thompson's haul of 8,847 points stood as the decathlon world record for over eight years. On 5 September 1992, USA's Dan O'Brien collected 8,891 points in Talence, France, to set a new mark.

EL MOUTAWAKEL RECORDS AN AFRICAN FIRST

NAWAL EL MOUTAWAKEL BECOMES FIRST AFRICAN WOMAN TO WIN OLYMPIC GOLD

28 July–12 August 1984, Los Angeles, California, USA

Born in Casablanca, Morocco, in 1962, Nawal El Moutawakel started running at the age of 15 and showed enough promise as a long-distance runner to win a sports scholarship at Iowa State University in January 1983. Later in the year she switched to the 400m hurdles and went on to reach the semi-finals in the event at the inaugural World Championships in Helsinki. The following year she became the NCAA champion and was selected for the Moroccan team for the 1984 Olympic Games in Los Angeles. Considered an outsider for the race, she pulled off a shock win, leading from start to finish to become the first African woman – and the first woman from an Islamic country – to become an Olympic champion.

➲ As Morocco's first-ever Olympic champion, her performance earned her wide recognition in the country of her birth. Morocco's King, Hassan II, decreed that all girls born on the day of her achievement should be named Nawal.

Considered an outsider for the 400m hurdles title, Morocco's Nawal El Moutawakel pulled off a surprise when she led the race from start to finish to become the first African (and Islamic) female to win an Olympic gold medal. She now serves on the International Olympic Committee.

BUBKA SETS NEW STANDARDS IN POLE VAULT

SERGEI BUBKA BREAKS POLE VAULT WORLD RECORD FOR THE FOURTH TIME IN A YEAR
31 August 1984, Rome, Italy

Between 1983 and 1984 an interesting duel was developing for pole vault supremacy between the USSR's Sergei Bubka and France's Thierry Vigneron. As 1984 dawned the world record lay with the Frenchman at 5.83m. Then Bubka seized the initiative, jumping 5.85 in Bratislava on 26 May; a week later, in Paris, he cleared 5.88m; on 13 July he went higher again, leaping 5.90m. But the drama was far from over: in an international meet in Rome on 31 August, Bubka and Vigneron came face to face. The Frenchman jumped 5.91m, but it was only good enough for second place. Bubka cleared 5.94m and never looked back: his decade-long domination of the pole vault scene had just begun.

➲ The pair's performances during the course of the summer of 1984 fuelled speculation that the 6m barrier would soon be broken. Bubka duly obliged on 13 July 1985 at an international meet in Paris.

A surprise world champion at the inaugural World Championships in Helsinki, Finland, in 1983, the following year Sergei Bubka confirmed his status as one of the greatest pole-vaulters of all time when he broke the world record four times during the course of the season.

Sparky Anderson showed his coaching mettle when he took the AL's Detroit Tigers to the first World Series win for 16 years in 1984. It was a history-making moment, as Anderson had also tasted Fall Classic success with the NL's Cincinnati Reds in 1975 and 1976.

ANDERSON WORKS HIS MAGIC WITH THE TIGERS

SPARKY ANDERSON FIRST MANAGER TO WIN WORLD SERIES WITH TWO DIFFERENT TEAMS FROM DIFFERENT LEAGUES
14 October 1984, Tiger Stadium, Detroit, Michigan, USA

Sparky Anderson joined the National League's Cincinnati Reds as manager in 1970 and immediately made an impact, leading them to World Series glory in 1975. They defended the crown the following year with a four-game sweep over the Yankees, but two years later Anderson was fired. He moved to the American League and the Detroit Tigers in 1979 and immediately turned them into a winning club: they opened the 1984 season 33–5 en route to winning their eighth American League pennant – their first in 16 years – and then beat the San Diego Padres in five games to win the World Series. Anderson had become the first manager in baseball history to win the Fall Classic with two different teams from two different leagues.

➲ Tony La Russa equalled Anderson's feat in 2006 when he led the NL's St Louis Cardinals to World Series glory; he had previously taken the Oakland Athletics (of the AL) to the title in 1989.

MARINO MAKES HIS MARK ON THE NFL

DAN MARINO BREAKS NFL SINGLE-SEASON RECORDS FOR COMPLETION, YARDS AND TOUCHDOWNS

20 January 1985, Stanford Stadium, California, USA

Born and brought up in a blue-collar neighbourhood of Pittsburgh, Pennsylvania, Dan Marino was a star high-school athlete and was courted by numerous universities. He chose to stay close to home, enrolled at the University of Pittsburgh and set about dismantling NCAA season and career records in attempts, completions, passing and touchdowns. He was the Miami Dolphins' No. 1 pick in the 1983 NFL Draft and ended his first season with 20 touchdown passes and Rookie of the Year honours to his name. In 1984 he completed 362 of 564 passes for 5,084 yards and 48 touchdowns – all three were NFL single-season records. The only disappointment came when the Dolphins crashed 38–16 to the San Francisco 49ers in Super Bowl XIX.

⮑ Marino's single-season record for the most touchdown passes stood until 2004 when Indianapolis Colts' Peyton Manning threw 49 passes. Similarly Marino's completion record has also been broken: by Houston Oilers' Warren Moon with 404 in 1991.

In only his second year in the NFL, Dan Marino produced one of the most statistically sensational seasons in the sport's history, breaking the single-season records in completions, yards and touchdowns.

RIDDLES MAKES IDITAROD HISTORY

LIBBY RIDDLES BECOMES THE FIRST WOMAN TO WIN THE IDITAROD TRAIL SLED DOG RACE

20 March 1985, Nome, Alaska, USA

First run in 1973, the Iditarod trail sled dog race is the most popular sporting event in Alaska. Held annually, it challenges mushers and their teams of dogs to cover a trail stretching some 1,151 miles (1,853km) through the Arctic tundra, passing in and out of villages and through pine forests, all under the canopy of the Northern Lights. Conditions for the 8–15-day trip can be insufferable, with competitors having to endure blizzards, whiteouts and gale-force winds that drop the temperature to close on −100°C. However, on 20 March 1985, the race captured more attention than ever before when Libby Riddles, a Wisconsin-born dog breeder, became the first woman in the event's history to win, completing the course in 18 days.

⮑ The Iditarod did not have to wait long for its second female winner. The following year Susan Butcher won the event for the first time and would go on to dominate it, collecting three further titles over the next four years.

After making history in 1985 by becoming the first woman to win the legendary Iditarod dog sled race, Libby Riddles went and lived with Inuits for the next six years.

THE MOST SUCCESSFUL JUDO COMPETITOR OF ALL TIME

YASUHIRO YAMASHITA COMPILES LONGEST UNBEATEN STREAK IN COMPETITIVE JUDO HISTORY
April 1985, Tokyo, Japan

Born in 1959 in Yabecho, 500 miles south of Tokyo, Yasuhiro Yamashita was inspired in his youth by a book about the life of judo founder Jigoro Kano and begged his grandfather to allow him to take up the sport. A black belt by the time he reached junior high school, he went on to study at the renowned Tokaidai Sagami High School and Tokai University before winning the All-Japan championships for the first time in 1977 at the age of 19. It was the start of an unprecedented period of domination in the sport. Between 1977 and his retirement in 1985 – by which time he was the youngest holder of the rank of eighth-grade black belt – Yamashita won a record 203 consecutive bouts.

➲ During his winning streak, Yamashita collected nine consecutive All-Japan championships, four consecutive world championships in the 95kg and over category (the championships are held every other year) and Olympic gold in the same category at the 1984 Games in Los Angeles.

The greatest competitor in the history of judo, Yasuhiro Yamashita enjoyed a nine-year unbeaten record in the sport covering some 203 bouts.

INVINCIBLE McENROE SETS SINGLE-SURFACE RECORD

JOHN McENROE SETS RECORD FOR MOST CONSECUTIVE WINS ON A SINGLE SURFACE
April 1985, Atlanta, Georgia, USA

By 1985 the world had seen the best of John McEnroe. His deft volleying and shot-making skills had brought him seven grand slam singles titles – three Wimbledon triumphs (1981, 1983 and 1984) and four US Open crowns (1979, 1980, 1981 and 1984), seven doubles titles with Peter Fleming – four at Wimbledon (1979, 1981, 1983 and 1984) and three at the US Open (1979, 1981 and 1983) – and over 60 ATP tour titles. But the man the British media labelled "Super Brat" still had one final record up his sleeve: between September 1983 and April 1985 he put together a winning streak in indoor carpets that would last for some 75 matches: the largest winning streak on a single surface in tennis history.

➲ McEnroe's record would stand for 21 years. Rafael Nadal beat it in May 2006 when he won his 76th consecutive match on clay. The Spaniard stretched the streak to 81 games before Roger Federer beat him in the final of the Hamburg Masters.

Between September 1983 and May 1985 John McEnroe was unbeatable on indoor carpets, notching up an incredible 75 consecutive wins on the surface.

BASS COMPLETES SEVEN-SUMMIT CHALLENGE

DICK BASS BECOMES FIRST MAN TO CLIMB HIGHEST PEAK ON EACH CONTINENT

30 April 1985, Mount Everest, Nepal/Tibet

Two American businessmen in their early 50s, Dick Bass and Frank Wells (at the time the head of Warner Bros), had the dream of climbing the highest mountains on each of the world's seven continents. They hired one of America's foremost mountaineers, Rick Ridgeway, as their guide and off they went. Starting on 21 January 1983, in order they climbed Aconcagua (22,841ft/6,962m – South America), Mount McKinley (20,320ft/6,193.6m – North America), Kilimanjaro (19,341ft/5,895m – Africa), Elbrus (18,510ft/5,642m – Europe), Vinson Massif (16,050ft/4,892m – Antarctica) and Mount Kosciuszko (7,310ft/2,228m – Australia). Then came the troublesome final hurdle: after three failed attempts on Everest (29,029ft/8,848m) Wells returned home. Bass continued and on 30 April 1985 reached the roof of the world to become the first man in history to complete the Seven Summit Challenge.

It took him over two years and three months, but Dick Bass achieved the dream of a lifetime – and the admiration of the worldwide mountaineering community – when he became the first person to summit the highest peaks on each of the world's seven continents.

➲ Bass's list is one of two versions of the Seven Summit list. The other, compiled by Italian mountaineering legend Reinhold Messner, names Pancak Jaya peak in Papua New Guinea as Oceania's highest peak.

Tall, powerful and possessing athleticism that belied his tender years, Boris Becker stunned the tennis world when he took the Wimbledon men's crown in 1985 at the age of 17.

BOOM BOOM BECKER TAKES WIMBLEDON CROWN

BORIS BECKER BECOMES YOUNGEST-EVER WINNER OF WIMBLEDON MEN'S SINGLES TITLE

7 July 1985, Wimbledon, London, England

Boris Becker turned professional in 1984 and won his first doubles title later that year in Munich. The following season, 1985, turned out to be a magical year for the 6ft 3in teenager. He raised a few eyebrows when his big-serving, hard-hitting game brought him victory at the traditional pre-Wimbledon warm-up tournament at Queen's Club, London, but he sent shockwaves around the world when, a few weeks later, he went on to win the main event, beating Kevin Curren (who had beaten John McEnroe and Jimmy Connors in the previous rounds) 6–3, 6–7, 7–6, 6–4 in the final to become the first unseeded player and the youngest (aged 17 years, 7 months) to win the All-England crown.

➲ At the time, Becker was also the youngest player in tennis history to win a grand slam singles tournament. That record has since been surpassed by Michael Chang, who won the French Open in 1989 aged 17 years 3 months.

THE JARROW ARROW CLOCKS WORLD MILE BEST

STEVE CRAM SHATTERS THE MILE WORLD RECORD BY A FULL SECOND

27 July 1985, Oslo, Norway

Already the reigning 1,500m world champion, in 1985 Steve Cram finally emerged from the shadows of his countrymen Sebastian Coe and Steve Ovett. On 16 July, he broke Ovett's 1,500m world record, set barely a month before, by nine-tenths of a second. Nine days later, he arrived in Oslo with his eyes firmly focused on Coe's mile world record of 3m47.33s – with Coe among the field of 13 athletes. The pair trailed the pacemaker through the first two laps of the race; by the last lap they were in front, with Coe trailing Cram; then Cram kicked, storming down the home straight towards the finishing line, yards clear of the field. He crossed the line in 3m46.32s to smash Coe's mark by a full second.

➲ Cram's mile mark would stand as a record for over eight years until Morocco's Noureddine Morceli clocked 3m44.39s on 6 September 1992.

During the summer of 1985, Steve Cram (No. 90) showed he was the best middle-distance runner in the world, breaking the 1,500m, mile and 2,000m world records in the space of three weeks.

Nicknamed "Mr Magic" by Bradford Northern fans for his stellar performances in an otherwise average side, Ellery Hanley moved to Wigan after a world-record bid in the summer of 1985.

WIGAN BREAK THE BANK FOR HOTSHOT HANLEY

WIGAN SIGN ELLERY HANLEY FROM BRADFORD NORTHERN FOR RUGBY LEAGUE WORLD RECORD TRANSFER FEE

August 1985, Wigan, Lancashire, England

Ellery Hanley signed for Bradford Northern as a 17-year-old in 1978 and made a try-scoring debut. Success may not have been immediate, but by the early 1980s he was fast acquiring a reputation as the most devastating try-scorer in the game. In the 1984–85 season, he scored an astonishing 55 tries in 37 appearances for the club. His performances single-handedly kept Bradford in the top flight, earned Hanley the Man of Steel award (for the league's most influential player) and made him the hottest property in the game. At season's end Wigan offered Bradford a world-record £150,000 plus two players for his services. The deal made Hanley the most expensive player in rugby league.

➲ Hanley went on to become a sensation at Wigan, scoring 776 points in 202 appearances for the Lancashire club.

AOUITA'S ARRIVAL SIGNALS THE END OF AN ERA

SAID AOUITA BREAKS STEVE CRAM'S 1,500M WORLD RECORD

23 August 1985, Berlin, West Germany

Morocco's Said Aouita first came to prominence when he finished third in the 1,500m final at the inaugural World Championships in Helsinki in 1983. Tactically, though, it had been a poor race for the Moroccan – he had been out-kicked down the home straight – and he decided to concentrate on the 5,000m for the upcoming Olympic Games in Los Angeles. He won gold. But he was not through with the 1,500m: having broken the 5,000m world record in Oslo on 27 July 1985, Aouita turned his attentions to Steve Cram's 1,500m world record time of 3m29.67s and on 23 August in Berlin clocked 3m29.46s. It was the start of a new world order for middle-distance running.

Said Aouita's arrival on the international middle-distance scene marked a shift away from the previous British dominance to a period of unrivalled success for African runners.

➲ Aouita's world-record-breaking spree started a period of total middle-distance domination by the Moroccan. Between 1983 and 1990 he would lose only four of the 119 races he contested over a variety of distances ranging from 800m to 5,000m.

ROSE ROMPS PAST COBB'S UNBEATABLE RECORD

PETE ROSE BREAKS TY COBB'S 57-YEAR RECORD FOR MOST CAREER HITS

11 September 1985, Olympic Stadium, Montreal, Canada

Pete Rose registered the first hit of his career on 13 April 1963 and ended his first full season for the Cincinnati Reds with 170 hits to his name. He passed the 200-hit mark in a season for the first of ten times in 1965; in 1973 he posted a career-high 230 hits and, five years later, became the youngest player in baseball history to pass the 3,000-hit milestone. He joined Philadelphia in 1979 and still the hits kept coming – 209 of them in his first year. On 13 April 1983 – 20 years to the day after his first hit – and now playing for the Montreal Expos – he passed the 4,000-hit mark. The following season, on 11 September 1985, he passed Ty Cobb's all-time record for hits, hitting his 4,192nd.

➲ Rose ended his career with 4,256 hits to his name. He also holds the record for most career games (3,562) and most career at-bats (14,053).

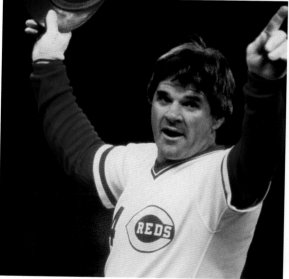

A World Series winner with the Cincinnati Reds in both 1975 and 1976 and with the Philadelphia Phillies in 1980, Pete Rose is best remembered for his assault on the legendary Ty Cobb's career total of 4,191 hits – he would improve the mark by 65.

KOCH CRUSHES FIELD TO SECURE WORLD 400M BEST

MARITA KOCH SHATTERS 400M WORLD RECORD BY A STAGGERING 0.33S

6 October 1985, Canberra, ACT, Australia

Already the holder of the 200m world record, East Germany's Marita Koch travelled to Canberra, Australia, for the IAAF World Cup in 1985 intent on putting one over on her great rival, Czechoslovakia's Jarmila Kratochvilova, who had held the 400m world record since the 1983 World Championships in Helsinki. Koch got off to her customary flier and with the race only half run was competing not against the other athletes in the field but against the clock. In what is considered one of the finest performances in athletics history – despite later revelations of performance-enhancing drug abuse – she decimated the field and crossed the line in 47.6s, shattering the old world record by some 0.33s.

➲ In the 20-years-plus that have passed since Koch set the record, no one has come close to matching it, and given the subsequent admission by East German authorities that they systematically doped their athletes, it seems highly unlikely that any "clean" athlete ever will.

The crowning moment of Marita Koch's controversial athletics career came when she shattered the 400m world record in Canberra in 1985. It is considered athletics' most untouchable record.

Following a highly successful collegiate career, Lynette Woodard made history when she became the first woman to sign for the Harlem Globetrotters in October 1985.

WOODARD MAKES BASKETBALL HISTORY

LYNETTE WOODARD BECOMES THE FIRST FEMALE MEMBER OF HARLEM GLOBETROTTERS

7 October 1985, Phoenix, Arizona, USA

A star of the high-school basketball scene, Lynette Woodard accepted a sports scholarship to the University of Kansas in 1978 and during her time with the Jayhawks saw her fame continue to grow. By the time she graduated in 1981 she was a four-time All-American, averaged 26 points per game and set numerous NCAA records that still stand to this day: most career points (3,649), field goals (1,572), rebounds (1,714), free throws made (505) and steals (522). Success continued to come her way: in 1984 she captained the United States to gold at the Olympic Games in Los Angeles. The following year she made the headlines once more when she became the first woman in history to sign for the legendary Harlem Globetrotters.

➲ Woodard's time with the Globetrotters did much to enhance women's basketball. She stayed with them for two years before travelling to Japan to play in a women's professional league.

THE SUDANESE SULTAN OF SWAT

MANUTE BOL BECOMES TALLEST PLAYER TO APPEAR IN THE NBA

25 October 1985, Capital Center, Landover, Maryland, USA

Born to the chief of the Dinka tribe in southern Sudan, Manute Bol started playing basketball at the age of 15 on the suggestion of his cousin and the first time he tried to slam-dunk the ball he chipped his tooth on the ring. At 7ft 7in (2.31m) his presence was hard to ignore and Farleigh Dickinson University coach Don Feeley spotted him in 1982 while doing a month-long coaching stint with the Sudanese national team. Bol travelled to the States and played one season of college basketball before being drafted in the second round of the 1985 NBA Draft by the Washington Bullets. When he made his debut on 25 October, he became the tallest player in NBA history.

⮑ In 1993 a Romanian, Gheorghe Muresan, also standing at 7ft 7in (2.31m) – but reportedly a few millimetres taller than Bol – made his debut for the Washington Bullets.

In his first season with the Bullets, Manute Bol, the tallest player the NBA had ever seen, blocked a rookie record 397 shots. When his ten-year career came to a close, he held the all-time career record for most shots blocked per minute (.176) to earn the moniker "The Sudanese Sultan of Swat".

A true showman, five-time world champion Eric Bristow took the popularity of darts in the United Kingdom to a level of popularity in the 1980s that has never been matched since.

THE CRAFTY COCKNEY COLLECTS WORLD TITLE NO. 5

ERIC BRISTOW WINS RECORD FIFTH WORLD DARTS CHAMPIONSHIP

12 January 1986, Lakeside Country Club, Frimley Green, Surrey, England

Darts was big business in the 1980s and one man stood at the centre of the stage. Eric Bristow, nicknamed the "Crafty Cockney", was pure box office, a mix of arrogance and wit who would wind up both opponents and crowds in equal measure before revelling in the charged atmosphere he had created. He could play a bit, too: with his unique right-handed delivery – with his trademark little finger pointing in the air – he dominated the sport, winning the world championship for the first time as a 23-year-old in 1980 and reaching the final on a further nine occasions, winning a further four titles (in 1981, 1984, 1985 and 1986).

⮑ Bristow also collected five World Masters crowns (1977, 1979, 1981, 1983 and 1984) and was the winner of the World Cup singles on four occasions (1983, 1985, 1987 and 1989). In the late 1980s he started to suffer from a psychological condition called "dartitis" – the equivalent to a golfer's yips – and was never the same player again.

HARRIS SOARS TO NEW WORLD RECORD

ROBERT HARRIS BREAKS THE WORLD ALTITUDE RECORD IN A GLIDER

17 February 1986, Sierra Nevada Mountains, California, USA

Robert Harris first rode in a Standard Astir III sailplane in 1978 and was so thrilled by the experience that he set about trying to break Paul Bickle's glider altitude world record of 47,267ft (14,065m) that had stood since 1961. It was a slow process. Over the course of five years Harris took his glider higher and higher. On 17 February 1986, he was towed to an altitude of 35,000ft (10,640m) above the Sierra Nevada Mountains. He unhooked the towline, found a strong lift and rose up to 800ft (240m) per minute. Outside temperatures reached -70°C, the canopy froze over, the oxygen system started to fail, but flying solely by the use of his instruments, Harris reached 49,000ft (14,938m) to break the world record.

➲ Harris landed to public acclaim, but not by everybody: the authorities criticized him for flying in controlled airspace without permission.

THE MASTER BLASTER PUTS ENGLAND TO THE SWORD

VIV RICHARDS SCORES THE FASTEST CENTURY IN THE HISTORY OF TEST CRICKET

11–16 April 1986, Recreation Ground, St John's, Antigua

It was the final insult to an England side already heading for a series whitewash. With England 4–0 down in the series and already facing a first-innings deficit of 164 runs in the fifth and final Test, the West Indies captain Viv Richards strode to the crease with his side's score on a comfortable 100 for 1 and decided to entertain his home island fans. He dismantled the England bowling attack and by the time he declared his side's second innings on 246 for 2, Richards had plundered an unbeaten 110 off a mere 58 balls, with his 87-minute vigil at the crease yielding seven fours and a mighty seven sixes. He had reached three figures off just 56 balls, an all-time record for Test cricket.

➲ Predictably England collapsed to 170 all out in their second innings to hand the West Indies a 240-run victory and a second successive "blackwash" over their English opponents.

Viv Richards confirmed his status as the world's best batsman when he swashbuckled his way to the fastest century ever seen in Test cricket, against England in Antigua in 1986: it took him just 56 balls to reach three figures.

THE GOLDEN BEAR ROARS ONE LAST TIME

JACK NICKLAUS BECOMES OLDEST WINNER OF THE MASTERS AND CLAIMS RECORD 18TH MAJOR

14 April 1986, Augusta National, Augusta, Georgia, USA

Prior to the 1986 Masters, 46-year-old Jack Nicklaus had not won a major for six years. In the build-up to the tournament, the *Atlanta Journal-Constitution* labelled the 17-time major winner as "done, washed-up, through". Everyone knew it, perhaps even Nicklaus himself: he was devoting more time to his business interests and spending less time on the fairways. Nicklaus's first two rounds over the Augusta course hardly signalled a return to form: he shot 74 and 71 and found himself six shots off the lead at the halfway stage. A third-round 69 reduced the deficit to four, but still no one gave the Golden Bear a chance, even more so when he covered the first nine holes of his final round in a level-par 35 strokes. But then something remarkable happened: the Golden Bear finally found his bite, shooting 30 on the back nine to win by one and become the tournament's only six-time winner … and its oldest.

➲ Twelve years later, at the age of 58, Nicklaus made another run at the Masters title but faltered over the stretch and finished in sixth place.

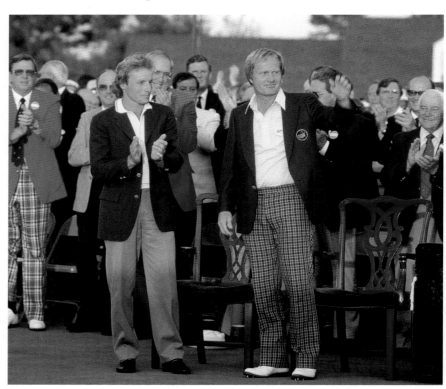

Forty-six years old and without a tournament win of any kind in over two years, Jack Nicklaus found his form when it mattered to claim a record sixth Masters title – and stretch his overall record of major tournament wins to 18.

JORDAN ANNOUNCES HIMSELF TO THE WORLD

MICHAEL JORDAN BREAKS NBA POSTSEASON RECORD FOR MOST POINTS IN A SINGLE GAME

20 April 1986, Boston Garden, Boston, Massachusetts, USA

Michael Jordan tried out for the basketball varsity team in his sophomore year at high school but was considered too small. That summer he went away and worked harder than ever before ... and also grew four inches. Now a shoo-in for the varsity team, he averaged 25 points per game over the next two seasons, became an All-American and earned a basketball scholarship to the University of North Carolina. Following a successful collegiate career with the Tar Heels, the Chicago Bulls selected him as third overall pick in the 1984 NBA Draft and Jordan went on to average 28.2 points per game in his first full season. A broken foot kept him out for most of 1985–86, but he returned in time for the Bulls' assault on the playoffs and created a sensation when he scored an NBA postseason-record 63 points against the Boston Celtics. The Celtics ultimately swept the series 3–0, but no one was left in any doubt that a major NBA star had been born.

➲ Between 1986 and 1993 Michael Jordan would lead the NBA scoring charts for seven consecutive years, establishing his legend as one of the finest players ever to have played the game.

Michael Jordan bounced back from injury in 1985–86 to score a record 63 points in Chicago Bulls' 135–131 defeat by the Boston Celtics in the second game of the team's best-of-five playoff encounter.

343

THE GREAT ONE ADDS TO HIS GROWING LEGEND

WAYNE GRETZKY BREAKS HIS OWN NHL RECORD FOR MOST POINTS SCORED IN A SINGLE SEASON

30 April 1986, Northlands Coliseum, Edmonton, Alberta, Canada

Wayne Gretzky seemed to be getting better with age: in the 1985–86 season he broke his own NHL all-time single-season records for most assists and for most points.

As every year passed Wayne Gretzky simply added to his legend, breaking record after record and becoming fully deserving of the moniker "The Great One". In the 1985–86 season, following the Edmonton Oilers' back-to-back successes in the Stanley Cup (the first two of the franchise's short history), Gretzky returned to the ice and broke his all-time single-season assist record for the third time in four years (notching up 163 assists) and passed the 700 career assists milestone in the process. He also broke his record mark for most points that year, setting a tally of 215 that has never been broken.

⮑ Gretzky's performances were not enough to earn the Oilers a third successive Stanley Cup: they lost in seven games to the Calgary Flames in the second round of the playoffs.

SHOEMAKER ROLLS BACK THE YEARS

BILL SHOEMAKER BECOMES OLDEST JOCKEY IN HISTORY TO WIN THE KENTUCKY DERBY

4 May 1986, Churchill Downs, Louisville, Kentucky, USA

Standing at a mere 4ft 11in (1.50m) and weighing in at just 95lb (43kg), Bill Shoemaker was born to be a jockey. He first rode professionally aged 17 in 1949 and recorded his first win within a month. It was the start of what would become one of the most storied careers in horse-racing history. He picked up his first Triple Crown win on board Swaps in the 1955 Kentucky Derby; a further nine would follow – the Kentucky Derby in 1959 and 1965, the Preakness Stakes in 1963 and 1967, and the Belmont Stakes in 1957, 1959, 1962, 1967 and 1975. His 11th and final win came when, aged 54, he guided 18/1 Ferdinand to an unlikely win at the 1986 Kentucky Derby – he remains the oldest jockey to win the race.

⮑ Bill Shoemaker ended his career in 1990 with 8,833 career wins to his name – an all-time record that would last until 1999.

Bill Shoemaker found time for one last hurrah when he guided 18/1 outsider Ferdinand to victory in the 1986 Kentucky Derby. At 54 years of age, he remains the oldest jockey to win the race.

SCHMIDT SETS ATHLETICS' MOST DURABLE RECORD

JÜRGEN SCHMIDT BREAKS THE WORLD DISCUS RECORD
6 June 1986, Neubrandenburg, East Germany

Born in 1960 in Amt Neuhaus in Lower Saxony, East Germany, Jürgen Schmidt was nearing the peak of his discus-throwing powers when he suffered the acute disappointment of having to watch the 1984 Olympics in Los Angeles from the sidelines following his country's boycott of the Games along with the rest of the Eastern bloc nations. But he stuck to his task with distinction and, two years later, produced one of the most astonishing performances in athletics history when he shattered Soviet athlete Yuri Dumchev's world record of 71.86m set in Moscow in May 1983 with a throw of 74.08m. The mark has stood as a world record ever since and remains the most durable record in track and field.

⮕ Schmidt got his first taste of the Olympic Games in 1988 in Seoul and walked away with the gold medal following a throw of 68.82m. Four years later, in Barcelona, he had to settle for silver.

In the 20-plus years since Jürgen Schmidt broke the discus world record, no one has come close to breaking it.

Chris Evert compiled one of tennis's most impressive records when she bagged at least one grand slam title a year over a period of 13 years between 1974 and 1986.

EVERT'S GRAND SLAM TITLE-WINNING STREAK

CHRIS EVERT WINS A GRAND SLAM SINGLES TITLE FOR A RECORD 13TH STRAIGHT YEAR
8 June 1986, Roland Garros, Paris, France

A 7–6, 7–6 win as a 15-year-old in 1970 over world No. 1 Margaret Court, who had just completed the singles grand slam, marked Chris Evert out for greatness and that was confirmed when, just a year later, she reached the semi-finals of the US Open. She had to settle for second best in 1973 as well, finishing runner-up at both the French Open and Wimbledon, but put any disappointment she may have suffered from those setbacks behind her when she won both titles the following year. It started one of most astonishing streaks in tennis history: over the next 13 years, Evert would claim at least one grand slam win per year, culminating in her 2–6, 6–3, 6–3 triumph over Martina Navratilova in the 1986 French Open final.

⮕ Evert finished her career with 18 grand slam titles to her name: two Australian Opens (1982, 1984), seven French Opens (1974–75, 1979–80, 1983 and 1985–86), three Wimbledons (1974, 1976 and 1981) and six US Opens (1975–78, 1980 and 1982). She is one of only nine women to have won grand slam titles on all four surfaces.

FIRST-MINUTE MARCHING ORDERS FOR BATISTA

JOSE BATISTA RECEIVES A RED CARD AFTER JUST 56 SECONDS, A WORLD CUP RECORD

13 June 1986, Estadia Neza 86, Nezahualcoyotl, Mexico

The message for Uruguay was a simple one: they had to get a result against Scotland in their final game to stand any chance of qualifying for the last 16 of the 1986 World Cup. A win might be enough, should Denmark beat West Germany, and a draw would see them enter the lottery of being the best third-placed team (the top four of the six third-placed teams would progress to the next stage). For Scotland, after two straight defeats, only a win would do. The match ended in a 0–0 stalemate, enough for Uruguay to qualify for the second round, but it was remarkable in another way. Uruguay's Jose Batista, clearly fired up for the match, was sent off after just 56 seconds, an all-time World Cup record.

➲ Uruguay's interest in the tournament ended just three days later when they lost their second-round match to Argentina 1–0.

Uruguay's Jose Batista created a slice of World Cup history when he was sent off after just 56 seconds of his country's final Group E encounter against Scotland in the 1986 World Cup in Mexico.

FLOYD TAKES US OPEN CROWN AT 43

RAY FLOYD BECOMES THE OLDEST WINNER OF THE US OPEN

16 June 1986, Shinnecock Hills, Southampton, New York, USA

Ray Floyd turned professional in 1963 and got off to the worst possible start, missing the cut in the first nine tournaments he entered, but he gained his first PGA Tour title later that year and, when he won the US PGA Championships in 1969, seemed destined for greater things. But the wins dried up and Floyd's reputation as party animal grew. Marriage in 1973 seemed to calm him down and the wins started to flow: he won the Masters in 1976 and a second US PGA crown in 1982, but his greatest moment came in 1986 when he won the US Open for the first time aged 43 years, 284 days to become the oldest winner in the tournament's history.

➲ Floyd's feat was surpassed in 1990 when Hale Irwin won the US Open at the Medinah Country Club, Illinois, aged 45 years, 15 days.

Ray Floyd could count four major successes among his 22 PGA Tour title wins: the last of them came at the US Open in 1986, when he became the oldest winner in the tournament's history.

Certainly the greatest heptathlete in history, Jackie Joyner-Kersee ended her career with the top 11 heptathlon scores in history to her name and 17 out of the top 20. She was also an Olympic gold medallist and two-time world champion in long jump.

JOYNER-KERSEE BEGINS HEPTATHLON WORLD DOMINATION

JACKIE JOYNER-KERSEE BECOMES FIRST WOMAN IN HEPTATHLON HISTORY TO SCORE MORE THAN 7,000 POINTS

7 July 1986, Moscow, Soviet Union

Jackie Joyner-Kersee joined an athletics program at the age of ten and excelled, winning four straight national junior pentathlon titles. She was also a star in basketball and attended UCLA on a basketball scholarship, but following a second-place finish in the heptathlon in the 1984 Olympic Games, basketball was pushed to one side. It was a wise decision. A talented long jumper (she was a two-time world champion in the event), on 7 July 1986 in Moscow she became the first woman in history to score more than 7,000 points in the event: her total of 7,148 points was a staggering 202 points better than the previous mark set by East Germany's Sabine John in 1984.

➲ Joyner-Kersee's domination of the heptathlon had just begun. Less than a month later she bettered her own points haul in Houston, Texas, with 7,158. In 1988 she broke her own world record twice: scoring 7,215 points in Indianapolis on 2 August; and then a staggering 7,291 points in the Olympic Games in Seoul – a record that stands to this day.

CONSISTENCY THE KEY FOR ZOETEMELK

JOOP ZOETEMELK COMPLETES RECORD 16TH AND FINAL TOUR DE FRANCE

27 July 1986, Paris, France

Joop Zoetemelk turned professional shortly after winning a gold medal in the team time trial with the Netherlands at the 1968 Olympic Games in Mexico. He made his first appearance in the Tour de France in 1970 and recorded the first of a record six second-place finishes in the event. His finest moment came in 1980 when, benefiting from Bernard Hinault's withdrawal through a knee injury, he took the title for the first and only time in his career. His final Tour came in 1986 and although he could manage only 24th place, he still found a place for himself in the history books. It was his 16th appearance in the Tour and he had managed to finish every one of them – a record that stands to this day.

➲ Also a winner of the Vuelta a Espana in 1979, Zoetemelk made history in 1985 when he won the cycling world championship at the age of 38 years, 9 months – he remains the sport's oldest-ever world champion.

Longevity was the key to Joop Zoetemelk's place among the pantheon of cycling greats. He appeared in the Tour de France on 16 occasions and finished every single race, including a win in 1980 and six second-place finishes, two of them behind Eddy Merckx and three of them behind Bernard Hinault.

IRON MIKE BECOMES YOUNGEST HEAVYWEIGHT CHAMPION IN HISTORY

20-YEAR-OLD MIKE TYSON KO'S TREVOR BERBICK TO WIN THE WBC HEAVYWEIGHT BELT
22 November 1986, Hilton Hotel, Las Vegas, Nevada, USA

Brought up in the notorious Brownsville section of Brooklyn, Mike Tyson had a problematic childhood, constantly in trouble with the authorities – he was arrested 38 times by the age of 13 – and expelled from school for fighting. Then juvenile detention centre counsellor and former boxer Bobby Stewart discovered his raw talent for boxing. After training him for a few months, he passed Tyson over to legendary trainer Cus D'Amato and together they harnessed Tyson's raw power and turned him into a fearsome fighting machine. Having posted an encouraging 15–2 amateur record, Tyson fought his first professional fight in March 1985 and won by first-round knockout. D'Amato died later that year, but Tyson's routine demolition of opponents – he won 19 of his first 22 fights by knockout – started to attract the media's attention. His first shot at the world title came in November 1986 against WBC champion Trevor Berbick: Tyson floored the champion in the second round to become, aged 20 years, 4 months, the youngest heavyweight champion in boxing history.

➲ By 1 August 1987, Tyson was the owner of all three heavyweight belts (WBA, WBC and IBF), but his problems were just about to start. In February 1990 he suffered a surprise defeat to James "Buster" Douglas; a year later he was in prison, convicted of rape. He returned to the ring in 1995, but was never the same fighter again.

The hottest property in boxing since Muhammad Ali, "Iron Mike" Tyson exploded onto the boxing scene in the mid-1980s and became the youngest world champion in history when he floored WBC champion Trevor Berbick in the second round in November 1986.

KING KHAN RULES THE WORLD OF SQUASH

JAHANGIR KHAN RECORDS LONGEST WINNING STREAK IN HISTORY OF COMPETITIVE SQUASH

November 1986, Toulouse, France

Coached by his father, the 1957 British Open squash champion Roshan Khan, and then by his cousin Rehmat Khan, Jahangir Khan became the world amateur squash champion at the age of 15. Two years later, in 1981, he became the youngest-ever winner of the World Open, aged 17. It signalled the start of an incredible run: in short, over the next five years he was invincible. With a game based on supreme fitness, he set an astonishing pace his opponents simply could not live with and his remarkable winning streak stretched over five years and five months – a total of 555 games – before he was stunned by New Zealand's Ross Norman in the final of the 1986 World Open.

⊃ Khan went on to become a six-time winner of the World Open (1981–85 and 1988) and a ten-time winner of the British Open (he took the title ten years in succession between 1982 and 1991).

A punishing fitness regime, allied to an outrageous talent, paid dividends for Pakistan's Jahangir Khan (right): between 1981 and 1986 he put together a winning streak that stretched some 555 games.

Short in stature at barely 5ft 3in (1.61m), Sunil Gavaskar used his impeccable technique to great effect, becoming the first batsman in the history of Test cricket to score 10,000 runs.

THE LITTLE MASTER PASSES 10,000-RUN MILESTONE

SUNIL GAVASKAR BECOMES FIRST BATSMAN IN HISTORY TO SCORE 10,000 TEST RUNS

4 March 1987, Gujarat Stadium, Ahmedabad, India

Sunil Gavaskar finally burst onto the first-class cricket scene in the 1968–69 season when he scored three centuries in four innings. He made his Test debut for India against the West Indies in the Caribbean and caused a sensation, hitting 774 runs in the series – the most-ever by a Test debutant – at an average of 154.8. He was ever-present in the Indian team from that moment on, never a destructive batsman, but capable of working the ball around the park; the runs flowed. In March 1987, in his penultimate Test match, he became the first player in Test history to pass 10,000 career runs during his innings of 63 against Pakistan in Ahmedabad.

⊃ Gavaskar finished his Test career with 10,122 runs to his name at an average of 51.02. It stood as a record until 26 February 1993, when Australia's Allan Border scored his 10,123rd Test run. Gavaskar also held the record for most Test centuries (34), a mark since beaten by another Mumbai man, Sachin Tendulkar.

Originally omitted from the Penske Racing team's driver line-up for the 1987 Indy 500, 48-year-old Al Unser showed his team what they would have been missing when he won the race for the fourth time in his career.

UNSER EMERGES FROM SHADOWS TO COLLECT FOURTH INDY 500 WIN

AL UNSER BECOMES OLDEST WINNER OF THE INDIANAPOLIS 500

24 May 1987, Indianapolis Motor Speedway, Indiana, USA

A few eyebrows were raised when the Penske Racing team named their line-up for the 1987 Indianapolis 500: there was no place in the team for three-time race winner Al Unser. But that all changed when Danny Ongais crashed into the wall during practice and ruled himself out of the race. Unser was called to fill the breach. Starting from 20th position on the grid, he worked his way slowly through the field and eventually took the lead on the 183rd lap of 200. He held on to win by 4.5s to become, just five days short of his 48th birthday, the oldest driver ever to win the race.

➲ Unser is one of only three four-time winners of the Indy 500 (the others being A.J. Foyt and Rick Mears). He also holds the all-time record for leading more laps of the race than any other driver (644) and is the only man in history to have a sibling (Bobby) and a child (Al Jr) win the race.

SIXTH CONSECUTIVE WIN SECURES BRAGGING RIGHTS FOR PORSCHE

PORSCHE BREAK FERRARI'S RECORD FOR MOST CONSECUTIVE 24 HOURS OF LE MANS WINS

14 June 1987, Le Mans, France

Driven over an 8.3-mile (13.5km) track consisting of a fixed circuit and public roads, the 24 Hours of Le Mans road race is considered the pinnacle of sports car racing and a race that places peculiar demands on manufacturers: they have to build cars that are not only fast but also durable, fuel-efficient and aerodynamic. In short, to win the race is a notable feather in a manufacturer's cap. In the 1960s, Ferrari earned the bragging rights when they won the race five years in a row between 1960 and 1965: it became the mark to beat and it took another massive car brand to do so – Porsche, who took six consecutive race wins between 1982 and 1987.

➲ Porsche also hold the record for most race wins with 16. Ferrari lie in a distant second place with nine victories in the race.

Porsche broke Ferrari's record for most consecutive race wins in the legendary 24 Hours of Le Mans road race with six between 1982 and 1987.

FOX FIRES KIWIS TO INAUGURAL WORLD CUP WIN

GRANT FOX SETS ALL-TIME SINGLE-TOURNAMENT SCORING RECORD FOR RUGBY WORLD CUP

20 June 1987, Eden Park, Auckland, New Zealand

Considered a long shot for the inaugural Rugby World Cup in 1987 – Australia and France were the bookmakers' favourites – New Zealand rugby was trying to bounce back from what had been a difficult year. In 1986, a rebel All Black tour had taken place in South Africa: those who went were banned and the New Zealand rugby public were disgruntled. But by the time the tournament started many of those who had been banned were back in black, including their prolific goal-kicker Grant Fox. To the surprise of many, the All Blacks romped through the tournament, beating France 29–9 in the final, with Fox averaging 21 points per game for an all-time tournament record haul of 126 points.

Considered a pioneer in the art of goal-kicking, New Zealand's Grant Fox was at his prolific best at the inaugural Rugby World Cup in 1987, scoring a tournament-record 126 points as the All Blacks became the first team to lift the William Webb Ellis trophy.

➲ Grant Fox's single-tournament points haul has never been beaten: in second place on the list lies Jonny Wilkinson, who scored 113 points during England's march to the World Cup crown in 2003.

NAVRATILOVA FINDS HER FEET ON THE GRASS COURTS OF WIMBLEDON

MARTINA NAVRATILOVA BECOMES FIRST WOMAN TO WIN SIX SUCCESSIVE WIMBLEDON SINGLES TITLES

5 July 1987, Wimbledon, London, England

Martina Navratilova took women's tennis to a different level. A left-handed serve-and-volley player who based her game around power, aggression and extreme levels of fitness, she had the skills to win on every surface, but found her talents particularly suited to the grass courts of Wimbledon. She won her first grand slam title there in 1978 and defended her crown the following year, before suffering the disappointment of two successive semi-final defeats in 1980 and 1981. But between 1982 and 1987 she could call the All-England title her own: when she beat Steffi Graf 7–5, 6–3 in the 1987 final she became the first woman in history to win the tournament on six consecutive occasions.

➲ Graf would gain her revenge, beating Navratilova in both the 1988 and 1989 Wimbledon finals, before the Czech-born star won a record ninth title in 1990 – it was her tenth consecutive appearance in the final, also a record.

A grand slam winner on all four surfaces, Martina Navratilova loved the grass courts of Wimbledon and, between 1982 and 1987, became the first woman in history to claim six consecutive All-England crowns.

AWESOME AOUITA SETS NEW STANDARDS

SAID AOUITA BREAKS OWN 5,000M WORLD RECORD AND BECOMES FIRST TO BREAK 13 MINUTES IN THE EVENT
22 July 1987, Rome, Italy

The class middle-distance runner of his generation, and often with little to race against but the clock, Said Aouita became the first man in history to break the 13-minute barrier in the 5,000m.

Between 1983 and 1990 Morocco's Said Aouita was the king of middle-distance running and nigh on unbeatable, winning 115 of the 119 races he contested. And although he may have been the reigning world record holder for the 1,500m (he broke Steve Cram's record in Berlin in August 1985), there was little doubt the 5,000m was his strongest event. He had won Olympic gold in the event in 1984 and claimed the world record the following year, running 13m00.40s in Oslo. Two years later, a month prior to the second staging of the World Championships, he broke the record again, clocking 12m58.39s in Rome to become the first man in history to cover the distance in under 13 minutes.

⊃ Aouita went on to claim the one and only World Championship gold medal of his career the following month. His 5,000m world record mark stood until 4 June 1994 when Ethiopia's Haile Gebrselassie clocked 12m56.96s in Hengelo in the Netherlands.

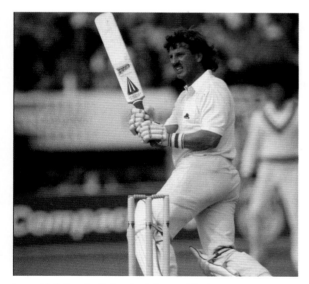

In a match that saw Ian Botham break the record for the most runs ever conceded by an English bowler in a single Test innings (217 v Pakistan in the fifth Test at The Oval in 1987), he also became the first man in Test history to pass the 5,000-run/300-wicket milestone.

BOTHAM CONFIRMS STATUS AS ONE OF THE ALL-ROUND GREATS

IAN BOTHAM BECOMES FIRST IN TEST HISTORY TO SCORE 5,000 RUNS AND TAKE 300 WICKETS
6–11 August 1987, The Oval, London, England

The highs and lows of Ian Botham's spectacular cricket career rumbled on through the 1980s. Having become the fastest in Test history to reach the 1,000-run/100-wicket milestone in 1979 (in just 21 Tests), he lost the England captaincy before winning the hearts of a nation with his epic 1981 Ashes-winning performances. A year later he reached the 2,000-run/200-wicket barrier in record time (42 Tests) and in 1984 passed the 3,000-run/300-wicket mark in his 72nd Test – also a record. Then, in 1986, after admitting to smoking cannabis, he was banned for 63 days – he returned to break Dennis Lillee's then world record wicket haul (with his 356th). The following year he became the first man in Test cricket to pass the 5,000-run/300-wicket milestone.

⊃ Ian Botham ended his 102-Test career in 1992 with 5,200 runs and 383 wickets to his name. He remains one of only two men in Test history to have scored 5,000 runs and taken 300 wickets, the other being India's Kapil Dev (5,248 runs and 434 wickets in 131 Tests).

Johnson's record-breaking run in the 1987 World Championships made him one of the most recognized faces in sports. A year later he was labelled one of the biggest villains in sporting history when he failed a drugs test following his win in the 1988 Olympic Games – he broke his own record in that race, but was later stripped of both that record and the one he set in the World Championships.

BEN JOHNSON: THE FASTEST MAN ON EARTH

BEN JOHNSON BREAKS 100M WORLD RECORD AT WORLD CHAMPIONSHIPS IN ROME

9 January 1988, Candlestick Park, San Francisco, California, USA

30 August 1987, Stadio Olimpico, Rome, Italy

Ben Johnson's first taste of international medal success came when he took silver in the 1982 Commonwealth Games 100m final. The following year, in the inaugural World Championships, he was eliminated from the 100m competition at the semi-final stage (he finished sixth with a time of 10.44s). He fared better in the 1984 Olympic Games, picking up a bronze medal with 10.22s. Then came the transformation. In 1985 he recorded his first victory over Carl Lewis; in 1986 he broke the 10s barrier for the first time. By 1987 he had become the world No. 1 and confirmed his status by running 9.83s in the 100m final at the World Championships in Rome to break Calvin Smith's 1983 record by a full tenth of a second.

➲ Johnson's gold-medal-winning performance prompted Carl Lewis to say: "There are a lot of people coming out of nowhere. I don't think they are doing it without drugs." No one knew it at the time, but those were prophetic words indeed.

JERRY RICE: THE TOUCHDOWN KING

JERRY RICE SETS NFL SINGLE-SEASON RECORD FOR MOST TOUCHDOWNS

9 January 1988, Candlestick Park, San Francisco, California, USA

When he graduated from high school, Jerry Rice attracted the interest of more than 40 NCAA Division 1-A colleges, but none offered him a scholarship to attend. Instead, in 1981, he enrolled Division 1-AA Mississippi Valley State University: after four years there, he had broken many NCAA records (including most career touchdowns – 50). In the 1985 NFL Draft, every team passed on him, except the defending Super Bowl champions, the San Francisco 49ers. Rice took the NFL by storm – in his first year he was named NFC Offensive Rookie of the Year. In 1986 he led the league in both receiving (1,570 yards) and touchdown receptions (15). But the best was yet to come: in the strike-shortened 1987 season he set the single-season record for touchdown receptions with 22, a mark that survived until 2007.

➲ His 22 touchdown receptions in 1987 set another record: he became the only player in history to win a major offensive title with a figure double that of the second-placed man (the Philadelphia Eagles' Mike Quick scored 11 touchdowns).

A players' strike that cut the 1987 season short by 24 days did little to dampen Jerry Rice's scoring ardour: he set the single-season record by catching 22 touchdown passes.

RUNNING BACK PAYTON SETS THE STANDARD

WALTER PAYTON RETIRES WITH MANY NFL RECORDS TO HIS NAME
10 January 1988, Soldier Field, Chicago, Illinois, USA

Walter Payton joined a struggling Chicago Bears in 1975 and suffered a disappointing opening season, but within two years was the league's leading scorer in touchdowns (16) and rushed for over 1,800 yards for the first time – including 275 yards in one game. New coach Mike Ditka started to change the Bears' fortunes; Payton continued to shine and by 1984 he had broken Jim Brown's career rushing record and won his first Super Bowl the following year. After rushing for 1,333 yards in 1986 he announced that the 1987 season would be his last and retired with many records to his name – most rushes (3,838), most 1,000-yard seasons (10), most 100-yard rushing games (77) and most career yards (16,726).

➲ In February 1999, Payton announced he was suffering from a rare liver condition called primary sclerosing cholangitis. He spent the last few months of his life campaigning for organ donors and transplants before his death in November 1999.

With his unique, high-stepping running style and a game based on size, speed and strength, Walter Payton – nicknamed "Sweetness" – lit up the NFL during his 13-year career and left the game at the end of the 1987 season with many all-time records to his name.

Having just seen her great rival break the world record, Bonnie Blair knew she would have to produce the performance of a lifetime if she wanted to win speed-skating gold at the 1988 Winter Olympics. She did just that, breaking the world record for the second time in as many minutes to record a memorable triumph.

BLAIR PRODUCES HER BEST WHEN IT MATTERS

BONNIE BLAIR BREAKS 500M SPEED-SKATING WORLD RECORD TO TAKE OLYMPIC GOLD
13–28 February 1988, Calgary, Canada

Raised in Illinois among a family hooked on speed skating, Bonnie Blair, the youngest of seven children, moved to Milwaukee after graduating from high school to train with the US national speed-skating team. She made her first appearance in the Winter Olympics as a 19-year-old in 1984 in Sarajevo, but finished a disappointing eighth in the 500m. Four years later in Calgary she took to the ice under extreme pressure: minutes earlier East Germany's Christa Rothenburger had broken the 500m world record with a time of 39.12s; if Blair wanted gold she would have to skate faster than any woman in history to get it. She rose to the occasion, clocking 39.10s to take gold in sensational style.

➲ The best was yet to come from Bonnie Blair: she took gold again in the 500m in 1992 in Albertville (as well as the 1,000m title) and defended it for the second time in Lillehammer in 1994. In doing so, Blair became the first American in history to win three gold medals at three different Winter Olympics.

SPINNING INTO HISTORY

KURT BROWNING COMPLETES FIRST QUADRUPLE JUMP IN COMPETITION

25 March 1988, Budapest, Hungary

The 1988 World Skating Championships saw Kurt Browning once again skating against his number-one rival, America's Brian Boitano. Boitano was just coming off a gold-medal win at the Winter Olympics in Calgary and was definitely in his stride. Browning had finished eighth in Calgary and second in that year's Canadian Championships, and was starting to come into his own on the world stage. During the free skating program, Browning executed a perfect quadruple jump and landed on one foot to cheers and accolades from the crowd and International Skating Union VP, Josef Dedic. Boitano then tried a quadruple jump of his own, but landed badly. Boitano still went on to win gold overall, but Browning had skated his way into history.

➲ Kurt Browning's rivalry with Boitano came to a head at the 2006 Ice Wars event, where Browning edged Boitano, leading the World team to victory over the US team. Browning is married to National Ballet of Canada principal dancer Sonia Rodriguez, with whom he has two sons.

Browning is still skating professionally, touring with Stars on Ice and Art on Ice, as well as many other shows. He is also a pet adoption advocate, and commentates on skating events for the CBC.

Galina Chistyakova's finest career moment came during a competition in Leningrad when she equalled the world record in her first jump before breaking it with her second. To this day, no woman has ever jumped further.

CHISTYAKOVA ENJOYS HER DAY OF DAYS

GALINA CHISTYAKOVA BREAKS THE WOMEN'S LONG JUMP WORLD RECORD

11 June 1988, Leningrad, Soviet Union

Considered among the favourites for the long jump title for the 1984 Olympic Games before her country boycotted the event, Galina Chistyakova made amends the following year by claiming her first international title at the European Indoor Championships in Athens. In 1986 she finished second in the outdoor version of the event behind reigning world champion Heike Drechsler, but three months before the start of the 1988 Olympic Games, at a meet in Leningrad, she hit the form of her life: in the first round of the competition she jumped 7.45m to equal the world record held jointly by Drechsler and Jackie Joyner-Kersee, before leaping 7.52m in the next to make the record her own.

➲ It would prove the highlight of her career. She picked up the bronze medal at the Seoul Olympics behind Joyner-Kersee (gold) and Drechsler (silver).

Reynolds shattered Lee Evans's supposedly "unbeatable" 400m record by 0.57s: the mark (43.29s) would stand as a world best until 26 August 1999 when Michael Johnson clocked 43.18s in Seville, Spain.

➲ Sadly, Reynolds's world record-breaking form did not carry him to an Olympic gold medal. He was edged into second place in the 400m final by fellow countryman Steve Lewis, although he did collect a gold medal as part of the US 4x400m relay team.

REYNOLDS RACES TO 400M WORLD RECORD

BUTCH REYNOLDS BREAKS LEE EVANS'S 20-YEAR-OLD 400M WORLD RECORD

17 August 1988, Zurich, Switzerland

Butch Reynolds initially shot onto the world stage as a 23-year-old Ohio State junior in 1987, when he was a 400m individual bronze medallist at the World Championships in Rome before anchoring the US 4x400m relay team to gold. Later in the year he sprang a major surprise by breaking the low-altitude world record for 400m, clocking 44.10s in Ohio at the Jesse Owens Classic. It was now time to set his sights on Lee Evans's world record of 43.86s, set at altitude in Mexico City in 1968 and then considered one of the most unbeatable records in athletics. Reynolds did not share the sentiment and on 17 August 1988, just a few weeks before the start of the Olympic Games in Seoul, he clocked a staggering 43.29s to break the record by a sensational 0.57s.

THE JAVELIN THROW FROM THE HEAVENS

PETRA FELKE BECOMES THE FIRST AND ONLY WOMAN TO THROW A JAVELIN 80M

9 September 1988, Potsdam, East Germany

It always seemed as though Petra Felke, the world's premier javelin thrower in the 1980s, was destined to miss out on a major title. She finished ninth in the 1983 World Championships; suffered from her country's boycott of the 1984 Olympic Games; finished second in the 1986 European Championships; and second once again in the Worlds the following year. But despite her apparent stage fright come the main event, she was a serial world-record-breaker. On 4 June 1985 she broke the record twice in one day (75.26m and 75.40m). In July 1987, she threw 78.90m to reclaim the record from Britain's Fatima Whitbread and on 9 September 1988 she became the first woman in history to hit 80.00m.

➲ A few weeks later, Felke went on to win the major title her talent wholly deserved, throwing 74.68m in Seoul to claim Olympic gold. It was the only gold medal of her career.

In 1988 Petra Felke became the first and only woman to throw a javelin 80m: the specification of the javelin has since been changed – the centre of gravity has been brought forward, reducing the distance a javelin can fly – and the furthest anyone has thrown since is 71.70m (by Cuba's Osleidys Menendez in Helsinki on 14 August 2005).

THE RECORD THAT SHOCKED THE WORLD

BEN JOHNSON STRIPPED OF HIS GOLD MEDAL AT THE 1988 OLYMPICS

24–27 September 1988, Seoul, South Korea

Canada's Ben Johnson eased towards the line with his arm raised in triumph and his opponents left reeling in his wake. He had led the 100m final from start to finish; 48 strides had catapulted him to the line in 9.79 seconds – a new world and Olympic record. Three days later news started to emerge that one of the Canadian's urine samples contained traces of the anabolic steroid Stanozolol. Stripped of the world record – including the one he had set at the World Championships a year earlier – the gold medal and the respect of the world, he was sent packing from Seoul a pariah.

➲ Since 1988, four of that race's top-five finishers have tested positive for drugs at some point in their career. It was almost 11 years before anyone ran as fast again: on 16 June 1999, the USA's Maurice Green clocked 9.79 seconds in Athens.

It rated as perhaps the most sensational three days in athletics history: first Ben Johnson grabbed the headlines when he ran the fastest 100m ever seen; then he became the pariah of the sporting world when news emerged that he had failed a drugs test.

LEWIS BENEFITS FROM JOHNSON'S DISGRACE

CARL LEWIS BECOMES THE FIRST MAN IN OLYMPIC HISTORY TO DEFEND THE 100M CROWN

24–27 September 1988, Seoul, South Korea

Minutes after crossing the finishing line, Ben Johnson gloated to the assembled media: "They can break my record, but they can't take my gold medal away." For Carl Lewis there was nothing but dejection. He had run faster than he had ever run before (9.92s) and had finished second behind his arch-rival. But three days later news emerged that Johnson had failed a drugs test and been stripped of his gold medal (and his world records). While the cameras flashed in front of the disgraced Canadian, Lewis would have afforded himself a slight smile: he was the new 100m world record holder and had become the first man in history to defend the 100m crown.

➲ Lewis's "new" world's best of 9.92s stood as a record until 14 June 1991 when Leroy Burrell raced to 9.90s in New York.

From despair to triumph in the space of 72 hours, Carl Lewis had been slaughtered in the Olympic 100m final by Ben Johnson but, following the Canadian's expulsion from the Games, Lewis was awarded both the gold medal and the world record.

FLO-JO: THE FASTEST WOMAN ON EARTH

FLORENCE GRIFFITH JOYNER SMASHES HER OWN 200M WORLD RECORD

29 September 1988, Seoul, South Korea

Florence Griffith Joyner had always wanted to be the fastest woman on earth. She got her wish at the 1988 US Olympic trials when she set a new 100m mark of 10.49 seconds. At the Olympics itself she strode to 100m gold in 10.54 seconds. Four days later she had a shot at the 100m/200m double. She ran the perfect race, cruising to the line almost half a second ahead of her nearest rival. It got better: she had won in 21.34 seconds, smashing her own world record by 0.22 of a second. Nobody has come close to matching the time since.

➲ It was a magical Olympics for the Los Angeles woman: she went on to add a further gold in the 4x100 relay and a silver in the 4x400. Almost a decade later to the day, though, she was dead, her life cut short by a heart attack at the age of just 38.

There was no doubt Florence Griffith Joyner was the darling of the Seoul Olympics in 1988: she became the first woman since 1948 to leave the Games with three gold medals to her name.

POCKET HERCULES POWERS TO OLYMPIC GLORY

NAIM SULEYMANOGLU BREAKS WEIGHTLIFTING WORLD RECORDS IN BOTH SNATCH AND JERK

17 September–2 October 1988, Seoul, South Korea

Born to Turkish parents living in Bulgaria, Naim Suleymanoglu broke his first weightlifting world record in 1984 when, aged 16, he became only the second person in history to clean and jerk more than three times his body weight. He suffered from Bulgaria's boycott of the 1984 Olympic Games and defected two years later to Turkey: it sparked a controversy. Prior to the 1988 Olympics, Bulgarian authorities demanded and received $1 million from the Turkish government for permission for Suleymanoglu to compete under the Turkish flag. The man dubbed "Pocket Hercules" was worth every penny, winning flyweight gold by a staggering 30kg and breaking the world record in both the snatch and jerk.

➲ He may only have stood at 4ft 11in (1.47m) but Naim Suleymanoglu was weightlifting dynamite: he retained his Olympic titles in both 1992 and 1996.

In 1999, after a sensational career that saw him collect three Olympic gold medals and break the world record on 47 occasions, Naim Suleymanoglu was voted one of the greatest athletes of the 20th century by the international sports journalists' association.

LOUGANIS COMPLETES DIVING'S ONLY DOUBLE DOUBLE

GREG LOUGANIS FIRST IN HISTORY TO WIN SPRINGBOARD-PLATFORM DIVING DOUBLE IN SUCCESSIVE OLYMPICS

17 September–2 October 1988, Seoul, South Korea

Greg Louganis started diving at the age of ten and within six years had already claimed his first Olympic medal, winning silver in the platform competition at the 1976 Olympics. He missed out on the 1980 Games through the United States' boycott, but returned to Olympic competition in style in Los Angeles in 1984 to become the first man in 56 years to win the springboard-platform double. In 1988 he made history again: he recovered from striking the back of his head on the springboard – attempting a reverse two-and-a-half somersault pike – during the preliminaries to become the first man in history to claim the springboard-platform diving double at two consecutive Olympics.

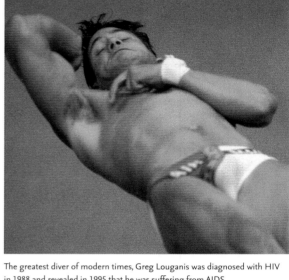

The greatest diver of modern times, Greg Louganis was diagnosed with HIV in 1988 and revealed in 1995 that he was suffering from AIDS.

➲ Louganis did not reserve success solely for the Olympic Games: he was also a six-time world champion and the holder of 47 national titles.

At her peak the covergirl of East Germany's swimming team, Kristen Otto retired in 1989 and her career has since been marred by revelations of a systematic doping regime carried out by the East German authorities.

SIX OF THE BEST FOR OTTO

KRISTEN OTTO BECOMES ONLY WOMAN IN HISTORY TO WIN SIX GOLD MEDALS AT A SINGLE OLYMPIC GAMES

17 September–2 October 1988, Seoul, South Korea

A product of the East German sports academy, Kristen Otto won her first international title at the 1982 World Championships in Ecuador, when she picked up gold in the 100m backstroke. The following year she changed coach and decided to try other strokes. It was a wise decision: in 1984 she broke the 200m freestyle world record. But then came the heartache of the 1984 Olympic Games boycott by Eastern Bloc countries and a back injury that kept her out of the sport for a year. She returned in style, winning four gold medals at the 1986 World Championships, followed by five golds at the following year's European Championships. She did even better in the 1988 Olympic Games, winning a record six.

➲ Otto picked up a gold medal in every event she competed in: 50m freestyle, 100m freestyle, 100m butterfly, 100m backstroke, 4x100m freestyle and 4x100m medley. No female swimmer has ever matched her feat and among men only Mark Spitz has done better, winning seven golds at the 1972 Olympic Games.

EVANS MAKES A SPLASH IN THE POOL

JANET EVANS BREAKS THE 400M FREESTYLE WORLD RECORD
17 September–2 October 1988, Seoul, South Korea

A winner of three gold medals at the 1988 Olympics in Seoul, Evans defended her 800m title in Barcelona in 1992.

The 1988 Olympic swimming gala may have been dominated by the six gold-medal-winning performances of Kristen Otto, but the East German was not the only swimmer making waves in Seoul. Otto was queen of the pool when it came to the short distances, but when it came to the swimming long haul, the USA's Janet Evans was the star of the show. She won the 400m and 800m freestyle gold medals (breaking her own world record by an impressive 1.6s in the former with a time of 4m03.85s) and capped a memorable display by taking gold in the 400m medley.

➲ Evans's 400m freestyle world record would stand for 18 years until France's Laure Manadou swam 4m03.03s in May 2006.

SHARP-SHOOTER COOPER FIRST TO RETAIN OLYMPIC CROWN

MALCOLM COOPER FIRST MAN IN HISTORY TO DEFEND 50M THREE-POSITIONS OLYMPIC SHOOTING CROWN
17 September–2 October 1988, Seoul, South Korea

Malcolm Cooper learned shooting small bore as a child in New Zealand, where his father was based with the Royal Navy. After moving back to England, he started shooting competitively from 1970 and, eight years later, set up his own rifle-making business. A lack of sponsorship meant his appearances in international competitions depended on the state of his business, but things must have been good in the mid-1980s. Cooper travelled to Los Angeles in 1984 and returned as 50m three-positions champion – prone, standing and kneeling; the first British shooting gold medallist since 1908. He won the 300m standing rifle world championships in 1986 and two years later, in Seoul, became the first, and only, man in history to defend his 50m Olympic crown.

➲ Cooper died on 9 June 2001 aged 54 after an eight-month battle with cancer at his home in West Sussex.

Already a European, world and Olympic champion, Britain's Malcolm Cooper became the first man in history to defend his 50m small bore three-position Olympic crown in Seoul in 1988.

GRAF'S GOLDEN SLAM

STEFFI GRAF WINS ALL FOUR GRAND SLAM TOURNAMENTS AND AN OLYMPIC GOLD MEDAL IN THE SAME YEAR

17 September–2 October 1988, Seoul, South Korea

Steffi Graf played her first full season on the professional tour in 1983, aged 13, and within two years had reached No. 6 in the world rankings. She claimed her first Tour title in April 1986 and seven more followed that year. She beat Martina Navratilova in the 1987 French Open to win her first grand slam tournament, but finished runner-up to Navratilova at both Wimbledon and the US Open. In that context, no one was prepared for what was to come. Graf started 1988 in style, winning the Australian Open; she then humiliated Natalia Zvereva 6–0, 6–0 in a 34-minute French Open final. Next she ended Navratilova's six-year reign at Wimbledon, before defeating Gabriela Sabatini in the US Open final to become only the third woman in history to complete the grand slam. The success did not stop there: Graf travelled to Seoul to compete in the Olympic tennis competition – re-introduced to the Games for the first time since 1924 – and beat Sabatini in the final once again to win gold and complete a unique "Golden Slam".

➲ It was just the start of what would be a sensational career. Graf retired in 1999 (at No. 3 in the world rankings – the highest-ever ranking position on retirement in the game's history) with 22 grand slam singles titles to her name (only Margaret Court with 24 has more). Graf is also the only tennis player in history to have won all four grand slam titles at least four times each.

Steffi Graf combined her strong serve, powerful forehand and all-round athleticism to magnificent effect in 1988, winning the Australian Open, the French Open, Wimbledon, the US Open and an Olympic gold medal in the same year.

Jon Sanders waited a long time to fulfil his dream of spending his life at sea, but when it came he grabbed it with both hands. In 1988 he became the first man in history to complete three continuous single-handed non-stop circumnavigations.

SANDERS SAILS INTO THE HISTORY BOOKS

JON SANDERS FIRST TO COMPLETE A TRIPLE NON-STOP SINGLE-HANDED CIRCUMNAVIGATION

September 1988, Fremantle, Western Australia, Australia

Jon Sanders got his first taste of life at sea as a teenager in his native Western Australia, first with the Sea Scouts and then with the Naval Reserve Cadets, but then chose a different career path: he became a sheep shearer for 17 years. He finally gave up a well-paid job to fulfil his lifelong dream of spending his life at sea. In 1970 he completed his first solo navigation; in 1981–82 he became the first to complete a double non-stop circumnavigation. But he wasn't through yet: in 1986 he left Fremantle in his 40ft sloop *Parry Endeavour* in an attempt to become the first to complete a triple single-handed non-stop circumnavigation: he completed his 71,023-mile journey in 657 days.

⮑ Sanders's journey broke many records: he became the first person in history to complete five single-handed non-stop circumnavigations (three of them in one go), had covered the longest distance ever covered by a vessel unassisted and solo (71,023 miles/114,300km) and had spent the longest period alone at sea (657 days).

SOTOMAYOR STARTS HIGH JUMP DOMINATION

JAVIER SOTOMAYOR BREAKS HIGH JUMP WORLD RECORD

8 September 1988, Salamanca, Spain

Cuba's Javier Sotomayor burst into the athletics spotlight as a 16-year-old when he cleared 2.33m in a high jump competition in Havana in 1984; it was an age-group world record and just 6cm less than the then world record. Denied a chance to appear in the 1984 Olympic Games by the Cuban boycott, he won his first international medal (silver) at the 1985 Indoor World Championships. In 1987 he became the Pan-American champion, but disappointed in the World Championships held later that year, finishing ninth. But 1988 saw an upturn in fortunes: Sotomayor set a series of personal bests which culminated in him breaking the world record – set by Sweden's Patrik Sjoberg (2.42m) on 30 June 1987 – with a leap of 2.43m in Salamanca, Spain.

⮑ Sotomayor broke his own world record on 29 July 1989 with 2.44m – becoming the first man in history to clear 8ft – and again on 27 July 1993 with 2.45m. No man since has jumped higher.

Javier Sotomayor started his domination of the men's high jump in 1988 and went on to record 17 of the top 24 jumps in history.

THE BULLDOG REACHES THE PEAK OF HIS POWERS

OREL HERSHISER THROWS MLB ALL-TIME RECORD 59 CONSECUTIVE SCORELESS INNINGS
1 October 1988, Fulton County Stadium, Atlanta, Georgia, USA

1988 proved the perfect year for Orel Hershiser: the National League Cy Young Award, the NL Most Valuable Player, the World Series MVP and an all-time MLB record of 59 consecutive scoreless innings.

After spending four years in the minor leagues, Orel Hershiser made his debut for the Los Angeles Dodgers on 1 September 1983 at the age of 24. Within a year he had become a fully-fledged starting pitcher and in 1985 confirmed his potential by leading the National League in winning percentage (he posted a 19–3 record). By 1987, the man his coach called "Bulldog" had appeared in his first All-Star game; in 1988 he put together one of the greatest seasons in the history of the game, leading the league in wins (23), innings (267) and complete games. What's more, at the end of the season he put together a streak of 59 consecutive scoreless innings to break Don Drysdale's all-time MLB record of 58 set in 1968.

⮞ Hershiser's year only got better: he went on to star in the World Series as well, pitching a complete game shutout in game two as the Dodgers beat the Oakland A's in five games. And, after the season, he was the unanimous choice for the National League Cy Young Award.

In 1988 Curtis Strange became the first golfer in history to earn more than $1 million in a single season. The record for season's earnings is $10,905,166, earned by Fiji's Vijay Singh in 2004.

STRANGE BECOMES GOLF'S FIRST SINGLE-SEASON MILLIONAIRE

CURTIS STRANGE BECOMES FIRST GOLFER IN HISTORY TO WIN MORE THAN £1 MILLION IN A SINGLE SEASON
14 November 1988, Pebble Beach Golf Club, California, USA

When the PGA Tour started in 1934, Paul Runyan won seven titles during the course of the season and finished on top of the end-of-year money list with $6,767 in earnings. It would take a further 30 years before any golfer reached the six-figure mark and that that golfer was Arnold Palmer – $128,320 in 1963 – spoke volumes. Palmer was the man who almost single-handedly made golf cool: television cameras started to appear and money started to pour into the game. Twenty-five years after Palmer's six-figure bounty came the first instance in the game when a player earned more than $1 million in a season: it came in 1988 when Curtis Strange won four times en route to single-season earnings of $1,147,644.

⮞ Two of Strange's four titles that year were prestigious ones: he won the US Open at Brookline Country Club, beating Nick Faldo in an 18-hole playoff, and also took the Tour Championship at Pebble Beach, beating Tom Kite at the second extra hole after the pair had tied over 72 holes.

THE GREATEST ALPINE SKIER OF THEM ALL

INGEMAR STENMARK WINS LAST OF RECORD 86 WORLD CUP SKIING RACES
19 February 1989, Aspen, Colorado, USA

Born in the Swedish province of Lapland in 1956, Ingemar Stenmark moved with his family to the village of Tärbaby, some 60 miles south of the Arctic Circle, at the age of four. He started skiing a year later, practising on a 2,000ft slope ideal for slalom, and won his first race at the age of seven; his first national title followed a year later. He transformed his early success into an incredible career. A specialist in slalom and giant slalom, he dominated the scene, winning seven consecutive giant slalom titles between 1974 and 1981 and eight slalom titles between 1975 and 1983, as well as adding three consecutive overall World Cup titles (1978–80) and double Olympic gold at the 1980 Winter Games in Lake Placid. The last of his giant slalom World Cup titles may have been won in 1984, but still the race wins continued to come his way: he notched up his record 86th and final win in Aspen, Colorado, in 1989.

Ingemar Stenmark's risk-free approach to skiing – he dabbled in downhill, but dismissed it following a heavy accident in 1979 – brought him utter dominance in both slalom and giant slalom. By the end of his career he had notched up more race wins (86) than any other skier in history.

➲ Of Stenmark's 86 career race wins, 46 came in the giant slalom and 40 in the slalom. Only two other skiers in history have recorded more than 50 career race wins: Austria's Hermann Maier (53 – 15 downhill, 23 Super G, 14 giant slalom and one combined) and Italy's Alberto Tomba (50 – 15 slalom and 35 giant slalom). Stenmark also holds the record (shared with Maier) for most race wins in a season, with 13 in 1978–79.

AGE NO BARRIER FOR THE BALD EAGLE

CHARLES WHITTINGHAM BECOMES OLDEST TRAINER TO WIN THE KENTUCKY DERBY

21 May 1989, Churchill Downs, Louisville, Kentucky, USA

An eighth-grade dropout, Charles Whittingham (right) – nicknamed the "Bald Eagle" because of his lack of hair – found his calling with horses and went on to become one of the most successful trainers in the history of American horse racing.

Charles Whittingham took out his trainer's licence in 1934. Three years later the legendary trainer Horatio Luro hired him as his assistant and the pair worked together until the onset of the Second World War, during which Whittingham served with the US Marine Corps. He became a trainer in his own right in 1950 and got his big break when Liz Whitney Tippett hired him to condition her stable. It spawned incredible success: he led the US in purses on seven occasions and trained over 600 stakes winners, including Ferdinand, who gave him his first Kentucky Derby win in 1986 and Sunday Silence, whose Derby victory in 1989 made Whittingham, then aged 76, the oldest winning trainer in the race's history.

◗ Whittingham continued to train horses up until his death on 20 April 1999 at the age of 86.

YOUNG GUN CHANG TAKES FRENCH OPEN CROWN

MICHAEL CHANG BECOMES YOUNGEST-EVER FRENCH OPEN CHAMPION

12 June 1989, Roland Garros, Paris, France

Michael Chang enjoyed an incredible junior career, winning his first national title (the junior hardcourt championship) aged 12 and, in 1987, aged 15, became Under-18 national champion. Later that year, he confirmed his enormous potential by becoming the youngest player in history to win a game in the main draw of the US Open. His first ATP Tour title came in 1988 (aged just 16 years, 7 months), but the most significant event in his "first to achieve" list came the following year at the French Open. Chang rallied from two sets to one down to beat Stefan Edberg in the final to become, at 17 years, 3 months, the youngest French Open champion in history.

◗ Chang retired from tennis in 2003 with 34 career singles titles to his name. His French Open win in 1989 was the only grand slam victory of his career, although he did make three further appearances in grand slam finals, losing the 1995 French Open, 1996 Australian Open and 1996 US Open finals.

Chang's route to the 1989 French Open crown was one of survival. In the fourth round he overcame a severe case of cramp to beat world No. 1 Ivan Lendl in five sets, and was forced to come from behind in the final before rallying to a famous victory by seeing off Stefan Edberg's challenge 6–1, 3–6, 4–6, 6–4, 6–2.

ABDUL-JABBAR CALLS TIME ON 19-YEAR NBA CAREER

KAREEM ABDUL-JABBAR BOWS OUT OF THE NBA WITH NUMEROUS ALL-TIME RECORDS TO HIS NAME
13 June 1989, The Forum, Los Angeles, California, USA

After leading UCLA to three consecutive NCAA Championships between 1967 and 1969, Kareem Abdul-Jabbar burst onto the NBA scene, enjoyed a stellar 19-year career and bowed out of the sport with numerous all-time records to his name.

A star of the UCLA team in the late 1960s, Lew Alcindor became the Milwaukee Bucks' first pick in the 1969 NBA Draft. He was an instant hit, picking up the league's MVP award and his first NBA title in just his second season. Shortly afterwards he announced his conversion to Islam and declared he would be known as Kareem Abdul-Jabbar. He moved to the LA Lakers in 1975 and went on to become an integral part of one of the greatest dynasties in NBA history, picking up championship titles in 1980, 1982, 1985, 1987 and 1988. By the time he retired in 1989 he held the all-time NBA record for most points (38,387), minutes (57,446), field goals (15,837), field goals attempted (28,307), All-Star selections (19), All-Star games (18) and playoff games played (237).

➲ Famous for his "skyhook" shot and distinctive protective goggles – he had twice suffered from a scratched cornea – 7ft 2in (2.18m) Kareem Abdul-Jabbar filled the gap in the NBA left by the retirements of Bill Russell and Wilt Chamberlain.

Two years after being shot accidentally in the back – over 40 shotgun pellets ripped through his body – Greg Lemond edged to his second Tour de France victory by the slenderest of margins: a mere eight seconds.

LEMOND TAKES SECOND TOUR BY A WHISKER

GREG LEMOND WINS HIS SECOND TOUR DE FRANCE BY CLOSEST MARGIN IN THE RACE'S HISTORY
23 July 1989, Paris, France

Greg Lemond made his first appearance in the Tour de France in 1984 and finished third; a year later he complied with team orders and finished second behind Bernard Hinault. The Frenchman returned the favour the following year as Lemond became the Tour's first American winner, but then disaster struck. Lemond was shot in the back while out on a turkey shoot and left fighting for his life. He returned to the Tour in 1989, hoping for little more than a top-20 finish, but as the race entered Paris for the final stage, Lemond found himself second overall, just 50 seconds behind leader Laurent Fignon. The American dug deep, recorded the fastest time-trial in the race's history and won by eight seconds: it is the closest margin of victory in Tour de France history.

➲ Lemond won the Tour again in 1990 – this time by the more comfortable margin of 2m16s – to become one of only eight men to have won the Tour de France on three or more occasions.

KINGDOM FINALLY COMPLETES WORLD RECORD PURSUIT

ROGER KINGDOM BREAKS 110M HURDLES WORLD RECORD

16 August 1989, Zurich, Switzerland

Roger Kingdom may have accepted a football scholarship to attend the University of Pittsburgh, but it was for their track-and-field team that he excelled, particularly in the high hurdles. With his great strength and speed belying a shaky technique – he would often leave flattened hurdles trailing in his wake – he took gold in the 1984 Olympic Games 110m hurdle final aged just 21 years. He defended his Olympic crown four years later in Seoul, running 12.98s in the final to become the first in Olympic history to run the event in under 13 seconds, but still found himself some 0.05s adrift of Skeets Nehemiah's world-record mark of 12.93s. Not for long: the following year he clocked 12.92s in Zurich.

‚ Kingdom's time would stand as a record until Colin Jackson ran 12.91s in the 1993 World Championships in Stuttgart, Germany.

A double Olympic champion (in 1984 and 1988), Roger Kingdom finally added the one missing piece to his already impressive CV when he claimed the 110m hurdles world record in 1989.

DAREDEVILS TAKE ON THE NIAGARA FALLS

PETER DEBERNARDI AND JEFF PETKOVICH COMPLETE FIRST DUO DESCENT OF NIAGARA FALLS

28 September 1989, Niagara Falls, Canada/USA

It had cost Peter Debernardi $1,500 to modify a ten-foot barrel capable of holding two people and surviving a plunge over the Niagara Falls, but his plan hit a last-minute snag: the man he intended to share the trip with pulled out minutes before the "off". Another friend, Jeff Petkovich, stepped into the breach. The pair stood head-to-foot, face-to-face, inside the barrel and were released into the Niagara River 150m (492ft) short of the Horseshoe Falls. The yellow barrel plummeted over the 175ft drop, hit the churning water below and bobbed to the surface near the base of the falls. It slowly drifted to the Canadian side before team members pulled it ashore. Debernardi and Petkovich had suffered only minor injuries.

‚ The pair were arrested shortly afterwards – they were planning on going over the falls once more in a rubber ball – and were charged with infractions under the Niagara Parks Act.

GRETZKY RETURNS TO EDMONTON TO BREAK HOWE'S 29-YEAR RECORD

WAYNE GRETZKY BECOMES MOST PROLIFIC POINTS-SCORER IN NHL HISTORY
15 October 1989, Northlands Coliseum, Edmonton, Alberta, Canada

Wayne Gretzky's trade to the Los Angeles Kings in August 1988 caused uproar in Canada – he was branded a traitor in some quarters – but changed the face of the NHL for ever: ticket sales doubled, merchandise flew off the shelves and the Golden State fell in love with hockey. In his first full season, 1988–89, Gretzky revived the Kings's fortunes, leading them into the playoffs and inspiring them to a 4–3, come-from-behind win against his old club the Edmonton Oilers before the Kings crashed in four games to Calgary. By the start of the 1989–90 season, Gretzky was fast closing in on Gordie Howe's all-time points record. A scriptwriter could not have done better: the Kings travelled to Edmonton with Gretzky one point behind Howe's mark. Gretzky lived up to the occasion, registering his first point, an assist, after just four-and-a-half minutes to equal Howe's mark. It developed into a tight game: with one-and-a-half minutes left on the clock, the Kings trailed 3–4 with their star man beat up and exhausted. He dug deep and, with 60 seconds remaining, scored. The record was his.

⮑ The Northlands Coliseum crowd gave Gretzky a three-minute standing ovation before presenting him with an award. It seemed the Canadians had forgiven him: after all, Gretzky had collected 1,669 of his 1,851 points during his time in Edmonton.

Wayne Gretzky's achievements on the ice were incredible: it had taken Gordie Howe (a player Gretzky idolized as a child), 26 years to amass 1,850 points; the Canadian did it in just ten.

CONNORS STILL FIRING AT 37 YEARS OF AGE

JIMMY CONNORS WINS THE LAST OF HIS ATP RECORD 109 TOURNAMENTS

22 October 1989, Tel Aviv, Israel

Jimmy Connors won his first professional tournament in 1971 while still an amateur studying at UCLA. He turned professional the following year and in 1974 produced one of the greatest years in tennis: he won the Australian Open, Wimbledon and the US Open … and might have won the French Open as well had he not been barred from the tournament because of connections with World Team Tennis. His never-say-die attitude, supreme fitness and hard-hitting game – particularly a devastating double-handed backhand – brought him four more US Open titles (in 1976, 1978, 1982 and 1983), another Wimbledon crown (in 1982) and a record 109 ATP Tour victories, the last of which came in Israel in 1989 when he was 37 years old.

Given the scheduling of tournaments in the modern game, it is unlikely any player will ever beat Jimmy Connors's record of 109 tournament wins.

⊃ Jimmy Connors has played more tournaments and won more matches than any other player in the history of professional tennis. His career record reads 1,337–285 (a winning percentage of 82.4%).

A nine-time European champion and a six-time world champion, Ingrid Berghmans is the most decorated female in judo history.

THE QUEEN OF JUDO

INGRID BERGHMANS WINS RECORD SIXTH JUDO WORLD CHAMPIONSHIP

October 1989, Belgrade, Yugoslavia

Ingrid Berghmans travelled to the inaugural women's world judo championships, held in Madison Square Garden, New York, as a 19-year-old in 1980 and captured the open-class world title. She defended her open-class title two years later and again in 1984, where she also won the under-72kg tournament for the first time. By now the biggest sports star in her native Belgium, she took her fourth successive open-class title in 1986. She may have missed out when the women's world championships was combined with the men's tournament for the first time in 1987, but two years later, in Belgrade, she won her second under-72kg world title. It was the sixth world title of her career and no woman in history has ever won more.

⊃ Ingrid Berghmans also won the under-72kg gold medal in the 1988 Olympic Games in Seoul while judo was still a demonstration sport.

371

DIMINUTIVE SHOEMAKER STANDS TALL WITH JOCKEY RECORD

BILL SHOEMAKER RECORDS THE LAST OF HIS RECORD 8,833 WINNERS

20 January 1990, Goldstream Park, Florida, USA

Bill Shoemaker's first winner came on 20 April 1949 and by the time his first season ended he had added a further 218 race wins to his name. He rode Swaps to victory at the 1955 Kentucky Derby to record the first of 11 Triple Crown wins – four more in the Derby, two in the Preakness Stakes and five in the Belmont Stakes – and the winners continued to flow. By 1970, having overcome two serious injuries – a broken leg in 1968 and a broken pelvis in 1969 – he had overtaken Johnny Longden's all-time jockey record for the most winners (6,032 set in 1966). He raced on until 1990, collecting the last of his 8,833 race wins on board Beau Genius on 20 January. He retired four weeks later.

➲ Shoemaker's tally of winners stood as a record until December 1999 when Laffit Pincay Jr rode his 8,834th winner.

In a career spanning from 1949 to 1990, the diminutive Bill Shoemaker (he stood at just 4ft 11in), won 11 Triple Crown races and 1,009 stake races and took close on 22 per cent of his mounts to the winning post. His career total of 40,350 races is also a record.

HADLEE PASSES THE 400-WICKET MILESTONE

RICHARD HADLEE BECOMES FIRST BOWLER IN HISTORY TO TAKE 400 TEST WICKETS

2–5 February 1990, Lancaster Park, Christchurch, New Zealand

Few players in sports history have carried the fortunes of their team to such an extent. As Richard Hadlee developed from a young, dishevelled, tearaway fast bowler into a refined wicket-taking machine, so the New Zealand cricket team started to enjoy a succession of firsts: a first win over England in 1979; a first win on English soil in 1983, and on Australian soil in 1985 – with Hadlee always to the fore and making his own mark on the record books. In November 1988 he took his 374th wicket, against India in Bangalore, to pass Ian Botham's record for the most Test wickets. Fifteen months later, against the same opposition in Christchurch, he bowled Sanjay Manjrekar to become the first person in history to take 400 Test wickets.

➲ Hadlee finished with 431 Test wickets to his name. It stood as a world record until January 1994 when India's Kapil Dev took his 432nd Test wicket, against Sri Lanka in Bangalore.

Considered one of the finest all-rounders in the history of the game, Richard Hadlee excelled with the ball to such an extent that he became the first bowler in Test history – and one of only ten players – to pass the 400-wicket milestone.

WALDEGARD ROLLS BACK THE YEARS FOR FOURTH SAFARI WIN

BJORN WALDEGARD BECOMES OLDEST RACE WINNER IN THE HISTORY OF THE WORLD RALLY CHAMPIONSHIP
11–16 April 1990, Safari Rally, East Africa

Born on 12 November 1943, Bjorn Waldegard made his first appearance in a rally competition in 1962 and by 1967 had become the Swedish national champion (a title he retained the following year). His first international success came in the 1969 Monte Carlo Rally and in 1979 he became the first winner of the World Rally Championships. His final race win in 1990 is the stuff of rally legend. At the 1990 Safari Rally – the world's toughest rally – Waldegard overcame horrendous conditions, including six days of torrential rain, to cross the finishing line a staggering 38 minutes ahead of second-placed Juha Kankkunen to become, at the age of 46 years, 155 days, the oldest driver in history to win a race in the World Rally Championships.

➲ Waldegard claimed four of his 20 international victories at the Safari Rally, one behind Shekhar Mehta, who holds the record with five (1973, 1979–82).

The inaugural World Rally champion in 1979, Bjorn Waldegard survived a race of attrition in the 1990 Safari Rally – only ten of 52 cars finished the 2,598-mile race – to become the oldest winner in World Rally Championship history.

The consummate break-builder, Stephen Hendry confirmed his early promise in 1990 when he became the youngest snooker world champion in history.

HENDRY ON CUE TO BECOME YOUNGEST SNOOKER CHAMPION

STEPHEN HENDRY BECOMES YOUNGEST-EVER WORLD SNOOKER CHAMPION
29 April 1990, Crucible Theatre, Sheffield, England

Stephen Hendry started playing snooker at the age of 12 and within two years had become the Scottish Under-16 champion. The following year, in 1984, he became Scottish amateur champion. He retained the title in 1985 and in 1986 became the youngest-ever entrant in the world championships, losing 10–8 in the first round to Willie Thorne. He turned professional shortly afterwards and by the end of his first season had made it to No. 23 in the world rankings; by 1988, a year that included his first ranking tournament victory, he was up to fourth in the world. Two years later he made history, beating Jimmy White 18–12 in the final to become, aged 21 years, 106 days, the youngest world champion in snooker history.

➲ It signalled the start of a new era for snooker. Hendry held the No. 1 ranking position for eight years and picked up a further six world championships: 1992–96 and 1999.

GRAF'S GRAND SLAM FINAL STREAK ENDS AT 13

STEFFI GRAF APPEARS IN A RECORD 13TH CONSECUTIVE GRAND SLAM FINAL

10 June 1990, Roland Garros, Paris, France

It may have taken Steffi Graf four years to reach her first grand slam final – at the 1987 French Open (where she beat Martina Navratilova 6–4, 4–6, 8–6) – but once she had found a way to reach the latter stages of the game's biggest tournaments, she could not stop. She reached her next two grand slam finals (losing at both Wimbledon and the US Open); in 1988 she completed her historic "golden slam" and almost repeated the slam the following year, losing only in the French Open final. She started 1990 with victory in the Australian Open, made the final of the French Open for the fourth year in succession (where she lost to Monica Seles) before the run of consecutive grand slam finals came to an end at 13, when Zina Garrison beat her in the 1990 Wimbledon semi-finals.

➲ The record for the most consecutive grand slam finals in men's tennis is ten, held by Roger Federer (from Wimbledon 2005 to the US Open in 2007).

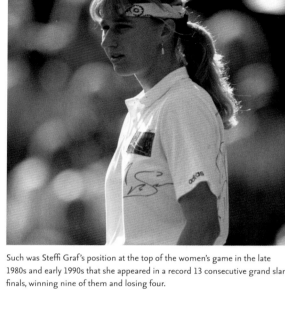

Such was Steffi Graf's position at the top of the women's game in the late 1980s and early 1990s that she appeared in a record 13 consecutive grand slam finals, winning nine of them and losing four.

Hale Irwin's steely game was perfectly suited to the US Open and he won arguably the hardest major of them all on three occasions: in 1974, 1979 and again in 1990 (at the age of 45).

IRWIN DEFIES THE ODDS FOR US OPEN NO. 3

HALE IRWIN BECOMES OLDEST-EVER WINNER OF THE US OPEN

19 June 1990, Medinah Country Club, Illinois, USA

The tougher the conditions, the tougher the course, the more Hale Irwin excelled. In the 1974 US Open he survived the "Massacre of Winged Foot" to claim his first major title. A second US Open followed in 1979, but by the time Irwin arrived at the Medinah Country Club in 1990, there appeared little chance he would add to the tally. However, despite being winless on the Tour for five years, Irwin found time for some more US Open heroics, sinking a 50ft-plus birdie putt on the last to force his way into a playoff with fellow American Mike Donald. The pair could still not be separated after 18 holes, but Irwin won at the first extra hole to become, aged 45 years, 15 days, the US Open's oldest winner.

➲ Hale Irwin is one of only five players to have won the US Open on more than three occasions. The others: Willie Anderson (1901, 1903, 1904 and 1905), Bobby Jones (1923, 1926, 1929 and 1930), Ben Hogan (1948, 1950, 1951 and 1953) and Jack Nicklaus (1962, 1967, 1972 and 1980).

Italy's early form in the 1990 World Cup was menacing. They may not have been dazzling up front, but they were miserly in defence: Claudio Caniggia's equalizing goal in the 67th minute of the semi-final was the first goal the *Azzurri* had conceded in 517 minutes of play and it remains a tournament record.

THE *AZZURRI*'S DEFENSIVE MACHINE GRINDS TO A HALT

ITALY BREAK WORLD CUP RECORD FOR MOST MINUTES PLAYED WITHOUT CONCEDING A GOAL

3 July 1990, Stadio Olimpico, Rome, Italy

Host nation Italy got off to a ruthlessly efficient start at the 1990 World Cup finals: employing their famous *catenaccio* style, they edged to three victories over their Group A rivals without conceding a goal to take their place in the second round. And when they beat former champions Uruguay 2–0 and followed it up with a 1–0 win against the Republic of Ireland in the quarter-finals, a nation started to dream of a fourth World Cup triumph. The *Azzurri* took a 17th-minute lead against Argentina in the semi-final, but then the bandwagon ground to a shuddering halt. Argentina equalized in the 67th minute – thus ending the host nation's tournament record of 517 minutes without conceding a goal – and went on to win the match 4–3 on penalties.

➲ Italy went on to beat England 2–1 in the third-place playoff match.

MONZON FIRST TO SEE WORLD CUP FINAL RED

ARGENTINA'S PEDRO MONZON FIRST PLAYER TO BE SENT OFF IN A WORLD CUP FINAL

8 July 1990, Stadio Olimpico, Rome, Italy

The 1990 World Cup final between two-time winners West Germany and 1978 champions Argentina was always going to be a cagey affair. Neither of the teams was playing at the top of its game and both had ridden their luck to get to the final by surviving a semi-final penalty shootout. But a game that has been described in many quarters as the worst in World Cup final history finally burst into life in the 65th minute, when Argentina's Pedro Monzon cynically scythed down a darting Jürgen Klinsmann. Mexican referee Edgardo Codesal Mendez had no hesitation in flashing a red card in the Argentine's direction and Monzon had become the first player in history to be sent off in a World Cup final.

➲ The second red card in World Cup final history came when, 22 minutes later, Argentina's Gustavo Dezotti was sent off in the 87th minute: West Germany won the game 1–0, thanks to an 85th-minute penalty by Andreas Brehme, to win the World Cup for a third time.

It was more a war of attrition than a flowing soccer match, but the 1990 final in Rome saw a World Cup first when, despite remonstrations from Argentina's players, their team-mate Pedro Monzon was sent off in the 65th minute.

1990

The ultimate professional who simply got better with age, Graham Gooch broke the all-time record for most aggregate runs scored in a Test match with 456 against India at Lord's in 1990. Second on the list is Australia's Mark Taylor with 426 – 334 not out and 92 against Pakistan in Peshawar in October 1998.

GOOCH'S INDIAN SUMMER

GRAHAM GOOCH BREAKS RECORD FOR MOST AGGREGATE RUNS IN A TEST MATCH

26–31 July 1990, Lord's, London, England

Graham Gooch made an inauspicious start to his England career in 1975 when he recorded a pair on debut. Six years later, he led a rebel tour to South Africa, was banned for three years and it seemed Gooch would never fulfil the potential on the international stage his talent deserved. But when England awarded him the captaincy in 1988, the added responsibility saw the Essex stalwart develop into one of the leading opening batsmen of his generation. Against India at Lord's in July 1990, he was in his prime, swatting an unbeaten 333 in the first innings and a belligerent 123 runs in the second to break Greg Chappell's record for the most aggregate runs in a Test match – 380 runs against New Zealand in Wellington in March 1974 – with a staggering 456 runs. England won the match by 247 runs.

➲ Gooch's run heroics did not stop there. He added 116 and 7 in the second Test and 85 and 88 in the third to end the series with 752 runs at an average of 125.33. His haul remains an all-time record for a three-Test series.

1990

HILL CLIMBS HER WAY INTO THE RECORD BOOKS

LYNN HILL BECOMES FIRST WOMAN CLIMBER IN HISTORY TO REDFLAG A 5.14 GRADE CLIMB

July 1990, Cimai Cliffs, Provence, France

A self-professed tomboy, Lynn Hill started climbing at the age of 14 and was instantly hooked. In 1979, she became the first woman in history to complete a 5.12+/5.13 grade climb, when she scaled Ophir Broke in Colorado. By the mid-1980s was an established member of the Camp 4 climbing community in Yosemite National Park. In 1988 she started climbing professionally, winning the prestigious Arco climbing competition for the first time. In 1989 she suffered a potentially fatal fall in Boux, France, but was back competing within four months. In 1990, again in France, she became the first woman in history to climb a 5.14-grade climb – the hardest in the sport – at the Mass Critique, Cimai, in Provence.

➲ French climber J-B Tribout established the Mass Critique route in 1986. Afterwards he famously announced that he thought no woman was capable of climbing it.

Considered one of the finest climbers of all time, of either gender, Lynn Hill became the first woman in history to complete a 5.14-grade climb in 1990, less than a year after surviving a potentially fatal fall.

PISTOL PETE GETS OFF THE MARK

PETE SAMPRAS BECOMES YOUNGEST US OPEN CHAMPION IN HISTORY

10 September 1990, Flushing Meadows, New York, USA

Pete Sampras first stumbled across a tennis racquet in his parents' home as a child and by the age of 11 was showing serious ability. He turned professional in 1988 aged 16 and in 1989 made it to the fourth round of the US Open. His first title came in February 1990 at Philadelphia, a second four months later, but it was his third title that put him on the world tennis map. At the 1990 US Open he beat Ivan Lendl and John McEnroe en route to a final showdown against 20-year-old Andre Agassi. Sampras won the day, beating Agassi 6–4, 6–3, 6–2 to become, aged 19 years, 21 days, the youngest US Open champion in history.

➲ It was the start of major things to come. Sampras would go on to win the US Open on four more occasions (in 1993, 1995–96 and 2002) as well as seven Wimbledon titles (1993–95, 1997–2000) and two Australian Opens (1994 and 1997). His haul of 14 grand slam titles is the largest in men's tennis history.

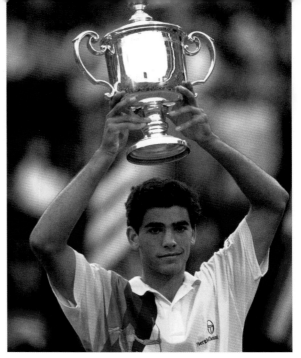

Pete Sampras first announced himself on the world tennis stage when he beat Andre Agassi in straight sets in the final of the 1990 US Open. At just 19 years of age he became the tournament's youngest-ever winner.

ROBINSON'S BATTING FORM HITS AN ALL-TIME LOW

MARK ROBINSON BREAKS WORLD RECORD FOR MOST CONSECUTIVE DUCKS IN FIRST-CLASS CRICKET

15 September 1990, Grace Road, Leicester, England

Mark Robinson made his first-class debut for Northamptonshire in 1987 and in 1988 took an encouraging 46 wickets at an average of 22.93. His performances with the bat were less impressive, however: he scored a mere 37 runs in 17 innings. His consistency with the ball may have ensured he became a regular in the Northants line-up, but it was his batting that started to set tongues wagging. In 1989 he scored 17 runs from 23 innings (including seven straight ducks) and in 1990 his crisis at the batting crease hit a new low: he notched up a world-record 12 consecutive scores of 0 (seven of them not out) before ending the unwanted streak with an imperious 1 not out against Leicestershire at Grace Road on 15 September 1990.

➲ Robinson ended his first-class career in 2002 with 590 runs to his name from 259 innings at an average of 4.01. In contrast, his performances with the ball make for happier reading: he took 584 first-class wickets at an average of 30.49 runs per wicket.

Mark Robinson made the cricket headlines for all the wrong reasons in 1990 when he broke the world record for the most consecutive scoreless innings in the history of first-class cricket (12).

TAR HEELS' UNDEFEATED MARCH STOPS AT 103

UNIVERSITY OF NORTH CAROLINA WOMEN'S SOCCER TEAM'S RECORD-BREAKING 103-GAME UNDEFEATED STREAK COMES TO AN END
22 September 1990, Storrs, Connecticut, USA

Coached by Anson Dorrance (the man who would lead the US to a first World Cup win in 1991) and featuring the likes of Mia Hamm (watching with her chin on her wrist) and Kristine Lilly, between 1986 and 1990 the Tar Heels put together a record 103-game unbeaten streak in the NCAA women's soccer championship.

The University of North Carolina has been the dominant force of the NCAA women's soccer championship since the tournament's inception in 1982 and has played a significant role in shaping the fortunes of the US national team. The Tar Heels were at their strongest in the late 1980s and – able to call on the likes of Mia Hamm, Kristine Lilly, Shannon Higgins and Carla Overbeck, all legendary members of the US national team – they put together an unbeaten stretch of 103 games (winning 97 and drawing six of their matches stretching back to September 1986). The run, which included four straight championships, came to an end when they lost 3–2 to Connecticut on 22 September 1990 after extra-time.

➲ North Carolina recovered from the loss and went on to record a fifth straight NCAA championship success, gaining their revenge over Connecticut by thumping them 6–0 in the final.

Mark McGwire gave a sign of what was to come when, in his first four seasons in the major leagues, he hit 30 or more home runs every year.

BIG MAC SHOWS HIS TASTE FOR THE POWER GAME

MARK McGWIRE FIRST IN MLB HISTORY TO HIT 30 OR MORE HOME RUNS IN FOUR CONSECUTIVE SEASONS
3 October 1990, Oakland-Alameda County Coliseum, Oakland, California, USA

Mark McGwire played his first full season in the major leagues in 1987 and made an awesome impact: his power hitting brought him 49 home runs – smashing the single-season record for a rookie shared by Frank Robinson and Wally Berger (38). The following year his 32 home runs helped the A's to their first World Series appearance since 1974: they lost in five games to the Los Angeles Dodgers. Big Mac hit 33 homers in 1989 and rounded the season off in style as the A's swept the San Francisco Giants in the World Series in four games. In 1990 he hit 39 big ones to become the first player in Major League history to hit 30 or more home runs in four consecutive seasons.

➲ McGwire was traded to the St Louis Cardinals during the 1997 season and continued his power-hitting heroics. In 1998 he became the biggest drawcard in the game following his successful assault on Roger Maris's single-season home run record.

THOMAS HUNTS DOWN KRIEG FOR NFL RECORD

DERRICK THOMAS SETS AN NFL SINGLE-GAME RECORD FOR THE MOST SACKS

11 November 1990, Arrowhead Stadium, Kansas City, Missouri, USA

A standout performer at the University of Alabama, Derrick Thomas was selected by the Kansas City Chiefs in the first round of the 1989 NFL Draft and was an instant success, winning Defensive Rookie of the Year honours in his first season and being elected to the Pro Bowl. Supreme in defence, he was renowned for his "sack and strip" move, where he would close fast on a quarterback's blind side and strip him of the ball. The best example of this came on Veterans' Day 1990, when he sacked Seattle quarterback Dave Krieg an NFL single-game record seven times. Thomas dedicated the performance to his father, who had been killed in the Vietnam War.

An All-Pro in each of his first nine seasons, Derrick Thomas holds the record for the most sacks in a single game. Although Thomas sacked Dave Krieg seven times, the Seattle Seahawks defeated the Kansas City Chiefs 17–16.

➲ On 18 January 2000, Thomas was involved in a car accident and was left paralysed from the waist down. Three weeks later, on 8 February, he died of a heart attack.

GEORGE CHUVALO ENTERS HALL OF FAME

CANADIAN HEAVYWEIGHT CHAMP UNBEATEN IN LIFE

11 October 1990, Fairmont Royal York, Toronto, Canada

George Chuvalo, the Toronto-born heavyweight who was once described by Muhammad Ali as "the toughest man I ever fought," was never knocked out or knocked down. Here he receives his star on Canada's Walk of Fame in 2005.

George Chuvalo's life was rife with punishment – and not all of it was in the ring. He fought some of the greatest boxers of his day, including Muhammad Ali, George Foreman and Joe Frazier – none of whom could knock him down. When Chuvalo retired in 1979, he had been Canadian heavyweight champion for 11 years, and 64 of his 73 victories were by knockout. However, the trials that Chuvalo faced within the ring were soon dwarfed by those without: Heroin claimed the lives of two of his sons; another son and Chuvalo's first wife committed suicide. But Chuvalo wouldn't stay down; he found strength in his grief and now criss-crosses the country, speaking to youth, First Nations communities and inmates about the ravages of drugs. George Chuvalo was inducted into the Canadian Sports Hall of Fame in 1990, an act of recognition for a great athlete – and an even greater man.

➲ In 1997, Chuvalo was inducted into the World Boxing Hall of Fame, and became a Member of the Order of Canada. In a 2005 induction ceremony, Chuvalo was given a star on Canada's Walk of Fame.

WIGAN SNAP UP OFFIAH FOR WORLD-RECORD FEE

MARTIN OFFIAH BECOMES RUGBY LEAGUE'S MOST EXPENSIVE PLAYER

January 1991, Central Park, Wigan, Lancashire, England

Martin Offiah first played club rugby union for Rosslyn Park before signing for Widnes, and rugby league, in 1987. He made up for any deficiencies he may have had in defence with his sensational attacking play and soon developed a reputation as being the most dazzling runner and lethal finisher in the game. He scored a club-record 42 tries in his first season to lead Widnes to the championship and picked up the league's Man of Steel award – the only player to achieve the feat in his first season. His try-scoring feats took Widnes to a second successive championship in 1989, but after he'd scored 181 tries in 145 games for the Lancashire club, Wigan came calling in January 1991 and secured his services for a world-record fee of £440,000.

⊃ Offiah continued his try-scoring ways with Wigan, scoring 186 tries in 158 games for the club – including a rugby league record ten in a game against Leeds in 1992. His fee remained the world's best until 2006, when Wigan paid Bradford Bulls £450,000 for the services of Stuart Fielden.

Dubbed "Chariots Offiah" by the press, Martin Offiah's blistering pace made him a valuable asset for any rugby league team, but it took a world-record transfer fee for Wigan to be able to secure his services. He turned out to be worth every penny.

DEFENCE IS THE BEST FORM OF ATTACK FOR ATLETICO

ATLETICO MADRID SET WORLD RECORD FOR MOST MINUTES WITHOUT CONCEDING A GOAL

19 March 1991, Vicente Calderon Stadium, Madrid, Spain

Atletico Madrid club president Jesus Gil was desperate to bring the good times back to his club in the late 1980s and early 1990s and ploughed a fortune into the club, bringing in prestigious names and hiring and firing managers at will. And for a short time during the 1990–91 season it seemed as though he had finally hit upon the winning formula. Under the stewardship of much-travelled Croat manager Tomislav Ivic – the club's fifth manager in as many years – Atletico embarked on a world-record run of 1,275 minutes (over 14 matches) without conceding a goal. The streak came to an end on 19 March 1991, when Luis Enrique found the back of the net for Sporting Gijon in a game Atletico still managed to win 2–1.

⊃ Sadly for Gil, Atletico's quest for a first La Liga title since 1975–76 ended in disappointment: they finished the season in second place, ten points behind champions Barcelona.

Croat Tomislav Ivic, the fifth coach in the first three years of the Jesus Gil presidency at Atletico Madrid – following Argentina's World Cup-winner Cesar Luis Menotti, Englishmen Ron Atkinson and Colin Addison and future Spanish coach Javier Clemente – couldn't bring a title to the Vicente Calderon Stadium, but his team didn't concede a goal for 1,275 minutes.

THE RYAN EXPRESS IS THE KING OF NO-HITTERS

NOLAN RYAN PITCHES MLB ALL-TIME RECORD SEVENTH NO-HITTER OF HIS CAREER

1 May 1991, Arlington Stadium, Texas, USA

A true legend of baseball, Nolan Ryan holds many all-time pitching records, the most unassailable of which is his record number of no-hitters (7).

The rules of Major League Baseball state that a no-hitter occurs when "a pitcher allows no hits during the entire course of a game, which consists of at least nine innings. In a no-hit game, a batter may reach base via a walk, an error, a hit by pitch, a passed ball or wild pitch on strike three, or catcher's interference." It is a rare occurrence – on average there are roughly two per season – but, when it came to no-hitters, one man stands tall in the record books. Between 1973 and 1991, Nolan Ryan, the man dubbed the "Ryan Express" who went on to set all-time career marks in strikeouts (5,714) and bases on balls (2,795), became the king of the no-hitters, recording an MLB record seven of them. The next best is Sandy Koufax with four.

➲ Ryan is one of only four men in the history of Major League Baseball to have pitched more than two no-hitters in their career. The others are: Koufax (4), Cy Young (3) and Bob Feller (3).

In a speech to the crowd after breaking Brock's all-time record, in which he thanked God and his family, the press latched onto one phrase in which Henderson said, "But today, I am the greatest of all time," and branded him arrogant and selfish. Henderson fights to clear his name to this day.

THE MAN OF STEAL BREAKS BROCK'S RECORD

RICKY HENDERSON BREAKS ALL-TIME MAJOR LEAGUE RECORD FOR STOLEN BASES

1 May 1991, Arlington Stadium, Texas, USA

Ricky Henderson debuted in the Major League in 1979 with the Oakland Athletics and in his third full season shattered Lou Brock's single-season record for stolen bases (118, set in 1974) with a staggering 130. Although one of the premier lead-off hitters of his day, Henderson became renowned for his ability to steal bases, so much so that the press dubbed him the "Man of Steal": between 1982 and 1991 he led the American League every year in the category bar one (1987) and by 1991 he was fast approaching Brock's all-time record of 938 stolen bases, at the time considered one of the most treasured in baseball. The 939th stolen base of Henderson's career came for the Toronto Blue Jays against the Texas Rangers on 1 May 1991 – the achievement was somewhat overshadowed by the fact that Nolan Ryan pitched the seventh no-hitter of his career in the same game.

➲ In 1993, Henderson stole his 1,066th base to break the world record set by Yukata Fukumoto of the Hankyu Braves in the Japanese Baseball League. He ended his nine-club, 25-year career in 2003 with 1,406 stolen bases to his name.

Jenkins was the most prominent pitcher to have started his career in Central America: before his 1963 draft into the Philadelphia Phillies, Jenkins pitched for a pro team in León, Nicaragua.

FERGIE JENKINS HONOURED IN COOPERSTOWN

POPULAR PITCHER FIRST CANADIAN INDUCTED INTO BASEBALL HALL OF FAME

21 July 1991, Cooperstown, NY, USA

Ferguson Jenkins was one of Major League Baseball's best pitchers, using finesse and control to win 20 games in a season seven times. His best season was in 1971, his fifth consecutive 20-win, 200-strikeout campaign. Jenkins also hit six home runs that season and became the first Canadian to win the Cy Young Award as the League's best pitcher. Instead of the triumphant event that it should have been, Jenkins' Hall of Fame investiture was a bittersweet one: just days after being told of his nod, his wife died of injuries sustained in a car accident, leaving him with two children.

➲ Fergie Jenkins was made a Member of the Order of Canada for being Canada's best-known MLB player in 1979, but was finally invested almost 30 years later on 4 May 2007. He now raises horses on his Oklahoma ranch.

A GOLFING STAR IS BORN

TIGER WOODS BECOMES YOUNGEST-EVER WINNER OF US JUNIOR AMATEUR CHAMPIONSHIP

7 August 1991, Bay Hill Club, Orlando, Florida, USA

Tiger Woods first picked up a club aged two and months later was displaying his talents to a national television audience on *The Mike Douglas Show*, by the age of five he was being featured in *Golf Digest* magazine. In 1984, at the age of eight, he won his first international junior title, winning the Junior Under-10 World Championships – the first of what would be six age-group world championship wins. In 1990 he suffered the first disappointment of his career when, as a 14-year-old, he was knocked out of the semi-finals of the US Junior Amateur, but he bounced back the following year, beating Brad Zwetschke at the first extra hole of the 18-hole playoff final, to become the tournament's youngest-ever winner.

➲ Woods retained the title in 1992 to become the tournament's first multiple winner and completed a hat-trick of wins in 1993. The following year, aged 18, he became the youngest-ever winner of the US Amateur championships.

The whole world knew Tiger Woods was coming and in 1991 he confirmed his prodigious talent by becoming the youngest-ever winner of the US Junior Amateur Championships.

MIGHTY MOUSE MAKES A SPLASH IN THE POOL

KRISZTINA EGERSZEGI SHATTERS WOMEN'S 200M BACKSTROKE WORLD RECORD
22 August 1991, Athens, Greece

Born in Budapest, Hungary, on 16 August 1974, Krisztina Egerszegi made her first international appearance as a 14-year-old at the 1988 Olympic Games in Seoul. Emboldened by her silver-medal-winning performance in the 100m backstroke, she sprinted to victory in the 200m backstroke final, breaking the Olympic record and becoming the youngest Olympic swimming champion of all time. In 1991 she became the first to master the newly introduced "no hand touch" turn rule, and put her newfound skill to good use in that year's European long-course championships in Athens, taking 200m backstroke gold and smashing the existing world record – 2m08.60s set by USA's Betsy Mitchell in 1986 – by a staggering 2.38s. Her time of 2m06.22s stands as a record to this day.

She may have been small in stature – she weighed a mere 45kg in her prime – but Krisztina Egerszegi was mighty in the pool, setting a 200m backstroke world record mark in 1991 that has never been broken.

➲ In the 1992 Olympic Games in Barcelona, Egerszegi won gold in the 100m and 200m backstroke as well as the 400m individual medley. In 1996 in Atlanta she completed a hat-trick of wins in the 200m backstroke to become the second swimmer ever to win the same Olympic event three times (Dawn Fraser is the other) and the first woman swimmer in history to win five Olympic gold medals in individual events.

LEWIS WINS THE FASTEST 100M RACE IN HISTORY

CARL LEWIS FIRST TO RUN 100M LEGALLY IN UNDER 9.9 SECONDS
25 August 1991, Tokyo, Japan

The stage was set for the 100m final at the 1991 World Championships. Reigning Olympic champion and former world record holder Carl Lewis (he had inherited both titles following Ben Johnson's expulsion from the sport) faced off against the young pretender, Leroy Burrell, who had broken Lewis's record shortly before the championships (with a run of 9.9s in New York) and was the No. 1 ranked 100m runner in the world, to decide who was the fastest man on earth. It was the fastest 100m race ever held, with six men finishing in under 10 seconds, but there was only one winner: Lewis streaked through the field in the final stages to take gold in a world-record-breaking time of 9.86s.

➲ Lewis's new mark would stand as a record for almost three years until Leroy Burrell reclaimed it with a run of 9.85s on 6 July 1994 in Lausanne, Switzerland.

Carl Lewis made a statement of intent when he completed a hat-trick of 100m World Championship wins in 1991 and broke the world record in the process.

THE LEAP THAT SENT SHOCKWAVES AROUND THE WORLD

MIKE POWELL BREAKS BOB BEAMON'S 23-YEAR LONG JUMP WORLD RECORD

30 August 1991, Tokyo, Japan

It was one of the greatest showdowns athletics has ever seen and as the 1991 World Championship long-jump final in Tokyo progressed not only was the gold medal at stake but also Bob Beamon's 23-year-old world record mark of 8.90m. In conditions ideal for jumping – there was a following wind – Carl Lewis, undefeated in long jump competition for a decade, lay down the marker with a jump of 8.83m. Compatriot Mike Powell responded with a huge leap, but was red-flagged. Lewis responded with another enormous leap: 8.91m, the furthest any man had leapt in history but not considered a world record because the following wind was in excess of 2m per second. Powell's response was massive: the following wind speed was legal (+0.3m per second); the crowd held its breath as Powell launched himself down the runway and produced an enormous leap – 8.95m. Lewis's reign as world champion was over and the most indestructible record in world athletics had finally been broken.

In one of the most breathtaking jump-offs in athletics history, Mike Powell ended Carl Lewis's reign as world champion, but had to produce the greatest leap in history to do so.

➲ Lewis would gain his revenge in the 1992 Olympic Games in Barcelona, beating Powell into second place with a jump of 8.72m to complete a gold medal hat-trick, but Powell's record has never been broken.

Michael Tuck bowed out of Australian Rules at the very top, collecting the seventh Premiership title of his career in his VFL/AFL record 426th and final appearance for Hawthorn in 1991.

RECORD-BREAKING TUCK HANGS UP HIS BOOTS

MICHAEL TUCK RETIRES FROM VFL/AFL HAVING PLAYED IN RECORD NUMBER OF GAMES

28 September 1991, Waverley Park, Melbourne, Victoria, Australia

Stamina and perseverance were the hallmarks of Michael Tuck's game. He made his debut for Hawthorn in the 1972 VFL season, but it would take a further two years – and more than 50 reserve-team games – before he finally established himself in the Hawks' line-up. Once he was there, no one could shift him. He went on to enjoy a stellar 19-year career, picking up seven Premiership titles during his stint with the Hawks (four of those wins coming as captain). Fittingly, the last of his all-time record 426 appearances came in Hawthorn's 53-point Grand Final crushing of the West Coast Eagles in September 1991 in front of 75,230 spectators at Waverley Park.

➲ Tuck also holds the all-time VFL/AFL records for the most finals games played (39), most Grand Final appearances (11) and player with the most Premiership wins (7).

CANADIAN BIATHLETE BLAZES OLYMPIC TRAIL

INTENSE CANADIAN ATHLETE BECOMES THE FIRST NORTH AMERICAN TO WIN A MEDAL FOR BIATHLON AT A WINTER OLYMPIC GAMES

8–23 February 1992, Les Saisies, Savoie, France

Two years before establishing herself as the best female biathlete in the world, Myriam Bedard made her mark at the 16th Winter Games in Albertville, France, as the first North American man or woman to win an Olympic biathlon medal. Heavy snow and the high altitude of Albertville forced the self-described "loner" from Quebec to settle for a disappointing finish in the 7.5km event. However, Bedard came back eight days later to edge out French athlete Veronique Claudel by less than six seconds to win the bronze medal in the 15 km individual event. At the 1994 Winter Games in Lillehammer, Norway, Bedard completely dominated her event, clinching gold in both the 7.5- and 15-km events, thus becoming both the first biathlete and the first Canadian to win two gold medals at a single Winter Olympic Games.

Bedard's first athletic ambition was to become a world-class figure skater, but at age 12, she decided the sport wasn't for her. Three years later, she was invited to join a biathlon team and fell head-over-heels for the sport.

⮑ The three-time Olympian has often courted controversy. In 2004, she went public with allegations that she had been forced out of her job at VIA Rail for blowing the whistle on the transportation company's billing procedures. Three years later, she was charged with child abduction after violating terms of a custody agreement with her ex-husband. She was convicted and received a conditional discharge.

Dramatic performances on the slopes coupled with a playboy lifestyle made Alberto Tomba one of the most popular skiers of all time, but he was also one of the best and in 1992 became the first skier in history to defend an Olympic title.

TOMBA LA BOMBA BACK TO BRILLIANT BEST

ALBERTO TOMBA BECOMES FIRST SKIER IN HISTORY TO DEFEND AN OLYMPIC CROWN

8–23 February 1992, Albertville, France

Alberto Tomba made his World Cup debut in 1985 and announced his enormous potential to the world when he won a bronze medal in the giant slalom in the 1987 World Championships. He was now a force to be reckoned with, and he made sure everyone knew it. He added to his growing reputation at the 1988 Winter Olympics in Calgary when he took gold in both the slalom and giant slalom, but then his form started to fall away, the nadir coming with a seventh-place finish in the giant slalom at the 1989 World Championships. Tomba was stirred into action and by the start of the 1992 Winter Olympics in Albertville, France, was close to his bombastic best. He took silver in the slalom, but cantered to a 0.72s victory in the giant slalom to become the first skier in history to defend an Olympic crown.

⮑ Tomba appeared in the 1994 Winter Olympics in Lillehammer, Norway, and added to his haul of medals by taking silver in the slalom.

After topping the French league's scoring charts in four consecutive years, Jean-Pierre Papin (red and black stripes, playing against Marseille in the 1993 European Cup final) became soccer's first £10 million player when he moved from Marseille to AC Milan, but could not reproduce his scoring form in Serie A.

SOCCER'S FIRST £10 MILLION PLAYER

JEAN-PIERRE PAPIN BECOMES THE WORLD'S MOST EXPENSIVE SOCCER PLAYER

7 March 1992, San Siro Stadium, Milan, Italy

Twenty goals in 30 matches playing for Belgian club side FC Bruges in 1985–86 were enough to guarantee Jean-Pierre Papin a place in France's 1986 World Cup squad – where they finished third – and a lucrative move to Marseille and it was with the *Marseillais* that the fleet-of-foot striker made his name. A typical fox in the box, Papin led the scoring charts for four seasons in a row between 1989 and 1992 (scoring 102 goals) as Marseille dominated La Ligue with four successive championships. Such scoring feats were always going to attract the attention of Europe's big clubs and, on 7 March 1992, Italian giants AC Milan confirmed that they had secured the striker's services for the 1992–93 season for a world-record fee of £10 million.

➲ Papin enjoyed mixed fortunes with Milan, scoring 18 times for them in 40 games before moving on to Bayern Munich for the 1994–95 season. His stint as soccer's most expensive player did not last long: later in the summer of 1992, Juventus paid Sampdoria £12 million for the services of Gianluca Vialli.

THE CATS CRUSH THE BEARS IN RECORD-BREAKING FASHION

GEELONG SCORE AN AFL/VFL RECORD 239 POINTS AGAINST THE BRISBANE BEARS

3 May 1992, Carrara Stadium, Gold Coast, Queensland, Australia

If Geelong wanted to kickstart their 1992 season in the quest for a first Premiership since 1963 – they had started the season with three wins and three losses – then there was no better place for them to go in round seven than to the hapless Brisbane Bears, a club still struggling following its inception in the AFL in 1986. The Cats had a field day: they scored seven goals and four behinds in the first quarter, nine goals and five behinds in the second and seven goals and five behinds in the third quarter (amassing 152 points) before the floodgates well and truly opened in the fourth quarter. Geelong added a further 14 goals (and three behinds) to crush the Bears 239–75 and the record the highest score in AFL history.

➲ Geelong's 239 points beat Fitzroy's record set in 1979 by a single point and the chances are it will never be broken: in recent times the AFL have reduced the length of each quarter by five minutes to 20 minutes.

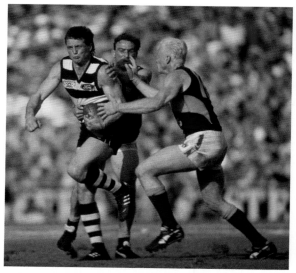

Geelong's (in dark blue and white hoops) record-breaking 239 points against the Brisbane Bears ignited their season: they ended the campaign on top of the Premiership ladder, but suffered heartache in the Grand Final when they lost 113–85 to the West Coast Eagles.

LITTLE AL EDGES TO FIRST INDY WIN

AL UNSER JR WINS THE INDY 500 BY SMALLEST MARGIN OF VICTORY IN THE RACE'S HISTORY

24 May 1992, Indianapolis Motor Speedway, Indiana, USA

A cold breezy day greeted the drivers at the start of the 77th running of the Indianapolis 500 and when pole-sitter Roberto Guerrero crashed out of contention on the parade lap, you could just sense something extraordinary was going to happen. It was a race of attrition: 11 cars dropped out of the stop-start race, including long-time leader Michael Andretti, with just 12 laps to go; it left Al Unser Jr (a savvy, canny driver who had been in exactly the same position three years earlier and lost) and Scott Goodyear (a young Canadian trying to kickstart his career) in a straight dogfight for the crown. Unser Jr held his nerve to win by the slenderest of margins: 0.043s, the smallest in Indy 500 history.

⊃ The 0.043s margin of victory beat Gordon Johncock's existing record of 0.16s set when he beat Rick Mears to the chequered flag in 1979.

Al Unser Jr had been in a winning position in 1989 when he vied for the lead with Emerson Fittipaldi before crashing out in the dying moments of the race. He made no mistake second time round, holding off the charge of Canada's Scott Goodyear in 1992 to take his first Indy 500 by the smallest margin in the race's history.

In 1992, Lyn St James became the second woman, after Janet Guthrie, to qualify for the Indianapolis 500 and the first to win Rookie of the Year honours.

St JAMES LAYS DOWN MARKER FOR WOMEN DRIVERS

LYN St JAMES BECOMES FIRST WOMAN IN HISTORY TO WIN INDY 500 ROOKIE OF THE YEAR HONOURS

24 May 1992, Indianapolis Motor Speedway, Indiana, USA

Lyn St James first went to a drag race at the age of 17 with some friends who had entered a car. One of her friends lost; St James told him she thought she could do better ... and won. Within a decade she had become the leading female driver in motor racing. But she'd had a far from easy ride, facing battles to gain both acceptance among her male peers and sponsorship. In 1988 she switched from road cars to Indy cars and shocked the establishment by winning a race at Watkins Glen; four years later she became only the second woman in history to qualify for the Indianapolis 500. She finished in 11th place and made more history when she became the first woman in Indy 500 history to be voted Rookie of the Year.

⊃ It was the first of seven appearances at the Indy 500 for St James, but she would never enjoy such success again: the best she could do was a 13th-place finish in 1997.

THE DREAM TEAM PUTS ON A SHOW

UNITED STATES BASKETBALL TEAM AVERAGES AN OLYMPIC RECORD 117.3 POINTS PER GAME TO TAKE GOLD

25 July–9 August 1992, Barcelona, Spain

In 1989, the FIBA, basketball's international governing body, allowed players from the NBA to compete in the Olympic Games for the first time, and although the European and South American governing bodies followed suit, all eyes were on the US squad of 12. And what a squad: ten of the members would go on to be named among the NBA's greatest players of all time – in short, the 1992 Olympic basketball competition saw the greatest line-up of talent ever seen on the hardwood and turned out to be little more than an exhibition. No one got close to the Americans, dubbed the "Dream Team". Michael Jordan, Magic Johnson, Patrick Ewing, Larry Bird and co. steamrollered the competition, averaging an Olympic-record 117.3 points per game en route to the gold medal: the closest anyone got to them was 32 points.

➲ The Dream Team's average margin of victory through the tournament was 43.8 points. One other point of interest is that their coach, Chuck Daly, did not use a single timeout throughout the course of the competition.

The greatest array of basketball talent ever assembled, the Dream Team steamrollered the opposition at the 1992 Olympic Games, breaking numerous records en route to a predictable gold medal.

It may have been far from perfect, but Kevin Young produced the performance of his career in the 1992 400m hurdles Olympic final to break Ed Moses's nine-year hold on the world record.

YOUNG CRUSHES REVERED 400M HURDLE WORLD RECORD

KEVIN YOUNG BREAKS ED MOSES'S 400M WORLD RECORD

25 July–9 August 1992, Barcelona, Spain

Ed Moses's monopoly of the 400m hurdles had started in the mid-1970s and took him to two Olympic gold medals and three world records, but although he had bowed out of competition following the 1988 Olympic Games, his world-record time of 47.02s – set in Koblenz, Germany, in 1983 – still stood as a testament to his prodigious talent. If it ever fell, one thought, it would have to fall in some style. It did. In the 1992 Olympic 400m hurdles final in Barcelona, 26-year-old American Kevin Young used his trademark, and unique, 12-stride pattern between the hurdles to obliterate the rest of the world-class field. So crushing was his lead, he found time to stumble over the last hurdle, raise his arms in jubilant celebration and still cross the line 0.24s inside Moses's world-record time.

➲ Young would go on to become world champion the following year. His 400m hurdles world record has never been beaten.

USA'S SPRINTERS SAVE FACE WITH WORLD BEST

USA BREAK MEN'S 4X100M WORLD RECORD
25 July–9 August 1992, Barcelona, Spain

Having suffered the ignominy of not seeing one of their athletes appear on the top two steps of the podium at the Olympic 100m medal ceremony for first time since 1976, America's men's 4x100m relay team had a point to prove. And how they made it. Led off by newly crowned 200m Olympic champion Mike Marsh, who handed over the baton to former world No. 1 Leroy Burrell and then to 100m bronze medallist Dennis Mitchell, the Americans established a healthy lead before Carl Lewis powered to the line half a second ahead of second-placed Nigeria. The time: a new world record of 37.40s, one-tenth of a second faster than the previous world best set by a virtually identical American quartet (Marsh had replaced Andre Cason for the 1992 Olympics) in the 1991 World Championships.

⮱ The time has since been equalled – by an American quartet consisting of Jon Drummond, Cason, Mitchell and Burrell on 21 October 1993 in Stuttgart, Germany – but never beaten.

The US men's 4x100m team finally found their sprinting form when it mattered, taking Olympic gold and breaking their own world record in the process in Barcelona in 1992.

Standing at just 4ft 9in (1.52m), Junko Tabei defied her small stature to become one of the greatest climbers in history. Seventeen years after becoming the first woman to climb Everest, she became the first woman to complete the Seven Summit challenge.

TABEI CLIMBS TO EVEN GREATER HEIGHTS

JUNKO TABEI BECOMES THE FIRST WOMAN TO COMPLETE THE SEVEN SUMMIT CHALLENGE
28 July 1992, Mount Elbrus, Caucasus, Russia

Ten years after becoming the first woman in history to stand on the summit of Mount Everest, Japan's Junko Tabei launched an assault on another first: to become first woman to complete the Seven Summit challenge. She conquered Kilimanjaro in 1981; six years later she took on the 6,960m Aconcagua in Argentina. Mount McKinley (also known as Denali) was next on the list in 1988, followed by a trip to Antarctica in 1992 to tackle the 4,897m Vinson Massif. To make sure she qualified for both the Bass and Messner lists, she climbed both Australia's highest peak (Kosciuszko) and Oceania's highest peak (Carstensz Pyramid) between November 1991 and June 1992, and completed the challenge upon reaching the summit of the West Peak of Mount Elbrus on 28 July 1992, aged 52 years, 310 days.

⮱ Tabei is one of only 11 women to have achieved the feat and it took her 17 years, 74 days to do so. The shortest time taken by a woman to complete the Seven Summit challenge is 2 years, 68 days by Britain's Jo Gambi.

ONE LAST HURRAH FOR HARRY GANT

HARRY GANT BECOMES THE OLDEST RACE-WINNER IN NASCAR WINSTON CUP HISTORY

16 August 1992, Michigan International Speedway, Brooklyn, Michigan, USA

After a successful career in the Busch Series, Harry Gant's first full Winston Cup season came in 1979. Progress was steady if not spectacular: he recorded ten second-place finishes before finally notching up a win – at the Virginia National Bank 500 in April 1982 – in his 107th start. He enjoyed his best season two years later, picking up three race wins en route to a second-place finish in the end-of-season standings, but the most memorable moments of his career came in September 1991 when he won all four of that month's races to earn the moniker "Mr September". The final victory of his career came at the Champion Spark Plug 400 on 16 August 1992. It was a history-making moment – at 52 years, 219 days he became the oldest race-winner in Winston Cup history.

One of the most colourful characters on the Winston Cup racing scene, Harry Gant made history in August 1992 when victory at the Michigan International Speedway made him the oldest race-winner in NASCAR history.

➲ Earlier in the 1992 season, Gant had become the oldest driver in history to win a 500-mile race (52 years, 142 days), taking the chequered flag at the Budweiser 500 on 31 May. He retired at the end of the 1994 season having contested 444 Winston Cup races with 18 career wins.

CAMPO PASSES HALF-CENTURY MARK

DAVID CAMPESE BECOMES FIRST RUGBY UNION PLAYER TO SCORE 50 INTERNATIONAL TRIES

22 August 1992, Newlands, Cape Town, South Africa

David Campese made his full international debut for Australia against the All Blacks at Lancaster Park, Christchurch, on 14 August 1982 and scored a try in a 23–16 defeat. His speed, style and flair soon saw him become the centrepiece of a dazzling Australian backline and the tries continued to flow. He produced his brilliant best in some of the most decisive moments in Australian rugby history: the grand-slam-winning tour of the British Isles in 1984; a first series win on New Zealand soil for 37 years in 1986 and picking up the player of the tournament prize as the Wallabies claimed the Rugby World Cup for the first time in 1991. On 22 August 1992, he became the first player in the history of the game to score 50 international tries during Australia's 26–3 win over South Africa in Cape Town.

As controversial off the pitch as he was brilliant on it, David Campese was once described as the "Bradman of rugby" by Australian coach Alan Jones and lived up to the hype, becoming the first player in history to score 50 international tries.

➲ Campese retired in 1996 having scored 64 tries in 101 appearances for the Wallabies. It stood as a record haul until 14 May 2006, when Japan's Daisuke Ohata scored his 65th international try.

O'BRIEN TAKES OVER THOMPSON'S DECATHLON MANTLE

DAN O'BRIEN BREAKS DALEY THOMPSON'S DECATHLON WORLD RECORD

5 September 1992, Talence, France

Dan O'Brien became American national champion for the first time in 1991 and when he went on to take decathlon gold at that year's world championships, it seemed as though the discipline had finally found the star it so desperately needed to fill the gap left by the retirement of Daley Thompson. But then disaster struck: during the US Olympic trials in 1992, O'Brien fouled out of the pole-vault competition at his first height and no points in the pole vault saw him miss out on Olympic selection. O'Brien bounced back in style: a few weeks after the curtain had come down on the Barcelona Games, O'Brien reminded the world what they had missed in Spain by breaking Thompson's decathlon world record of 8,847 points – recording 8,891 points in Talence, France.

➲ O'Brien's haul of points stood as a record until 4 July 1999, when the Czech Republic's Thomas Dvorak accumulated 8,994 points in a competition in Prague.

Dan O'Brien bounced back from the disappointment of missing out on selection for the 1992 Olympic Games by breaking Daley Thompson's eight-year-old decathlon world record shortly after the Games had finished. He would go on to win the World Championships in 1993 and 1995 and finally got his hands on Olympic gold in Atlanta in 1996.

TANNI GREY'S PARALYMPIC GOLD MEDAL SWEEP

TANNI GREY WINS A RECORD FOUR INDIVIDUAL GOLD MEDALS AT THE 1992 PARALYMPIC GAMES

3–14 September 1992, Barcelona, Spain

Born with spina bifida, but encouraged by her parents from a young age to maintain her independent streak, Tanni Grey first competed for Wales at the Junior National Games and shocked everyone when, aged 15, she won the 100m. By the age of 18 she was a member of the British wheelchair racing team and earned selection for the first World Wheelchair Games in 1987. A year later, she competed in her first Paralympics in Seoul and won bronze in the 100m, before undergoing spinal surgery that kept her out of competition for over a year. She bounced back better than ever before and confirmed her form at the 1992 Paralympics in Barcelona, by completing an unprecedented sweep of the 100m, 200m, 400m and 800m gold medals.

➲ Tanni Grey was back in action at the 1996 Paralympics in Atlanta, but disappointed, picking up a single gold in the 800m. In 2000, at Sydney, she was the star of the show once more, completing the 100m, 200m, 400m, 800m sweep for the second time. She bowed out of Olympic competition in Athens in 2004 with 100m and 400m gold.

Perhaps the greatest wheelchair athlete of all time, Tanni Grey announced her talents in a sensational manner in Barcelona in 1992, winning gold in the 100m, 200m, 400m and 800m as well as picking up a silver medal in the 4x100m relay.

GOALIE STORMS NHL GENDER GAP

MANON RHEAUME MAKES ICE-HOCKEY HISTORY AS THE FIRST WOMAN TO PLAY IN AN NHL GAME

12 September 1992, Florida State Fairgrounds Expo Hall, Lakeland, Florida, USA

After her NHL debut, Manon Rheaume confirmed that she had been asked by *Playboy* magazine to pose nude. Although she was assured that she could make a lot of money modelling, Rheaume rejected the offer.

All she wanted to do was to play hockey with the best of them, but when Manon Rheaume took to the ice in a 1992 exhibition game, she also made sporting history as the first – and last – woman to play in an NHL game. Bearing the uniform of the fledgling Tampa Bay Lightning, the 20-year-old goaltender from Lac Beauport, Quebec, put in a respectable performance, stopping seven of nine shots from the St Louis Blues. Her appearance sparked intense media attention as well as charges that the Lightning hired her as a publicity stunt. Breaking barriers was nothing new to Rheaume: she was the first female to compete at a Quebec International Pee Wee Hockey tournament in 1984 and the first to play at the major-junior level, with the Trois-Rivieres Draveurs. After her two-game NHL stint, Rheaume continued to mind nets with a handful of men's professional teams.

➲ Rheaume, who wrote an autobiography titled *Manon: Alone in Front of the Net*, went on to spend eight years as a goaltender with Canada's National Women's hockey team. She appeared in the first-ever women's hockey tournament at the Olympic level, bringing home a silver medal from the 1998 Winter Olympics in Nagano, Japan.

THE WORLD SERIES EMIGRATES

TORONTO BLUE JAYS BECOME THE FIRST NON-US TEAM TO HOST – AND WIN – MLB'S TOP CONTEST

17–24 October 1992 , Fulton County Stadium, Atlanta, USA, and SkyDome, Toronto, Canada

The Jays became repeat World Series champs when they beat the Philadelphia Phillies the following year. Since the Montreal Expos moved south in 2004, the Jays remain the only non-US team in Major League Baseball.

The 1992 World Series holds a solid place in Major League history as the first time the Series left the USA. The Jays had clinched their second American League East Division crown in a row, and hadn't been swept once that season. The Braves had likewise beaten the Pittsburgh Pirates in the National League Championship to gain a second consecutive World Series berth. The series opened with a home-field 3–1 win for Atlanta, which many thought would set the stage for the rest of the series. But the Jays had other plans: Game 2 resulted in a hard-fought 5–4 victory for Toronto. The action then moved north, where the Jays won two more games before a heartbreaking 7–2 defeat, ending the chances of the Series being decided on Canadian soil. Undaunted, the Jays rebounded in Atlanta, once again slugging it out to an 11th-inning win and the top spot in the League.

➲ There was some pre-game controversy in Game 2, when the US Marines Color Guard paraded an upside-down Maple Leaf onto the field during the singing of the national anthems. Chastised, the Marine Corps offered to make amends before Game 3 in Toronto, where the troops took pains to make sure the flag was right side up.

MANSELL DOMINANT EN ROUTE TO WORLD TITLE

NIGEL MANSELL WINS FORMULA ONE RECORD 14 POLES DURING SEASON

8 November 1992, Adelaide, South Australia, Australia

It seemed the Formula One world championship would always elude Nigel Mansell's grasp. He had suffered a late-race blowout in the final round of the 1986 championship to lose the title by a whisker, and by the end of the 1991 season that was still as close as the popular Briton had come to lifting the title he so craved. But in 1992 it all came together for the Williams man. Driving the FW14B – one of the most sophisticated cars in Formula One history – he opened the season by powering to five straight victories, all of them from pole position. He wrapped up the world title with three months of the season still to run and ended the year with nine wins and a single-season record 14 pole positions to his name.

⮞ In 1993 Mansell crossed the Atlantic and became the first driver in history to win the CART championship in his debut season.

The 1992 Formula One season was a dream for Nigel Mansell: he secured nine race wins – a single-season record that stood until 2002, when Michael Schumacher notched up 11 race wins – and 14 pole positions, a single-season record that has never been broken.

IT'S A NEW DAWN FOR SUMO WRESTLING

AKEBONO TARO BECOMES FIRST NON-JAPANESE WRESTLER TO REACH RANK OF *YOKOZUNA*

27 January 1993, Ryogoku, Tokyo, Japan

Good enough – and tall enough, at 6ft 8in (2.01m) – at basketball to be offered a university scholarship, Hawaiian-born Chad Haaheo Rowan only wanted to be a sumo wrestler. He joined the stable of fellow Hawaiian Azumazeki Oyakata in 1988, adopted the fighting name Akebono Taro (meaning "new dawn") and used his massive frame (his fighting weight was 235kg (517lb)) to make a rapid progression through the sumo ranks. By March 1990 he had been promoted to *juryo* (the second division of six); by September he was in the top division (*makuuchi*). In March 1992 he won a top-division event for the first time and achieved the rank of *ozeki* – lying only behind *yokozuna* in the sumo hierarchy. Not for long: on 27 January 1993, after winning two tournaments in a row, he became the first top-ranked non-Japanese wrestler in history.

Akebono Taro used his massive frame to his advantage and took the world of sumo wrestling by storm. In January 1993, less than five years after making his professional debut, he became the first foreign-born fighter in history to achieve the rank of *yokozuna*.

⮞ Later in 1993, Akebono went on to achieve the rare feat of winning three consecutive tournaments (held in July, September and November – there are six a year, held every other month). He went on to hold the rank of *yokozuna* for an astonishing eight years.

Ranulph Fiennes and Mike Stroud may have failed in their attempt to cross the continent of Antarctica – they were rescued on the Ross Ice Shelf, frostbitten and starving – but they did break the world record for the longest uninterrupted venture trek.

FIENNES AND STROUD TAKE ON ANTARCTICA

RANULPH FIENNES AND MIKE STROUD BREAK WORLD RECORD FOR LONGEST UNINTERRUPTED VENTURE TREK

12 February 1993, Ross Ice Shelf, Antarctica

In November 1992, serial British adventurer Ranulph Fiennes and nutrition specialist Mike Stroud set off from Chile in an attempt to complete an unassisted journey across Antarctica. With each man pulling a 485lb (208kg) sled containing all the supplies the pair would need for the 1,500-mile (2,144km) journey, they reached the South Pole by mid-January – by which time the pair had each lost roughly 25 per cent of their body weight. With Stroud now suffering from hypothermia, and with both men afflicted by frostbite, wind- and sunburn, the pair battled on. On the 95th day, 12 February 1993, stranded on the Ross Ice Shelf and unable to reach the shoreline, they finally called for a plane: they may not have completed their task, but they had travelled a world record uninterrupted distance of 1,350 miles (2,173km).

➲ Stroud took regular blood and urine samples throughout the trek and established that the pair were each burning in excess of 10,000 calories a day, more than the human body is capable of ingesting.

BRAVE GIRARDELLI DEFIES INJURY TO TAKE RECORD FIFTH WORLD CUP

MARC GIRARDELLI BECOMES FIRST SKIER IN HISTORY TO WIN OVERALL WORLD CUP FIVE TIMES

28 March 1993, Are, Sweden

Born in Austria, but electing to ski for Luxembourg, Marc Girardelli first appeared in the World Cup as a 17-year-old in 1980 (competing in slalom and giant slalom – the downhill came later in his career) and recorded his first race win in 1983: shortly afterwards he tore all the ligaments in his left knee. He bounced back in 1985, recording 11 race wins and winning the overall World Cup title for the first time. He repeated the success in 1986 and again in 1989 before suffering another major accident in 1990. He bounced back once again to take a fourth title in 1991 before notching up a record fifth in 1993, despite racing with a ruptured cruciate ligament for the final eight races of the season.

➲ Girardelli finally retired in 1997 when corrective surgery failed to mend his battered knee. His career record reads as one the greatest of all time: 46 race wins (in all five categories) and 13 medals in Olympic and world championship competition.

Marc Girardelli continually bounced back from career-threatening injuries to become the first skier in history to win the overall World Cup competition five times.

PENGUINS GO ON RECORD-BREAKING STREAK

PITTSBURGH PENGUINS BREAK NHL RECORD FOR THE MOST CONSECUTIVE WINS

14 April 1993, Prudential Center, Newark, New Jersey, USA

The Pittsburgh Penguins may have entered the 1992–93 NHL season off the back of two consecutive Stanley Cup wins – the first in the franchise's history – but off the ice they were a team in turmoil. In the space of a few months they had lost their coach Bob Johnson to cancer and their star player Mario Lemieux, temporarily, to Hodgkin's disease. But when Lemieux bounced back fitter than ever, his Penguin team-mates were more than happy to dance to his beat. They ended the season with a 52-21-7 record and broke the NHL record for most consecutive wins (17), which came to an end when they tied with the New Jersey Devils in the final game of the regular season.

➲ However, any dreams of completing a hat-trick of Stanley Cup wins were dashed in the second round of the playoffs when the Penguins crashed in overtime in game seven to the New York Islanders.

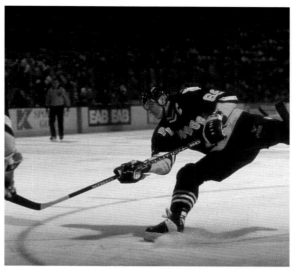

Defending Stanley Cup champions the Pittsburgh Penguins hit a purple patch towards the end of the 1992–93 regular season – winning an NHL-record 17 consecutive matches – before crashing out in the second round of the playoffs.

Ayrton Senna's high-risk driving style, that saw him push his car to the ragged edge and beyond, paid particular dividends at the prestigious Monaco Grand Prix: the Brazilian notched up a record six wins over the street circuit between 1987 and 1993.

AYRTON SENNA: THE MASTER OF MONACO

AYRTON SENNA NOTCHES UP RECORD SIXTH WIN AT MONACO GRAND PRIX

23 May 1993, Monte Carlo, Monaco

Sao Paulo-born Ayrton Senna would feature high up on anyone's list of all-time great Formula One drivers. Worshipped by his home nation, he combined a fearless driving style with a detached introspection, making him one of the sport's most compelling figures. A three-time world champion, he enjoyed particular success over the tight, twisty 2.08-mile (3.34km) Monaco GP circuit, one of the toughest challenges on the F1 calendar. His first win in the Principality came in 1987. He spun out of the lead with ten laps remaining in 1988, but that would be the last taste of Monaco disappointment in his career: he took the race five times in a row between 1989 and 1993 and his total of six wins in the race has never been beaten.

➲ Two other drivers have recorded five wins in Monaco: Graham Hill (1963–65 and 1968–69) and Michael Schumacher (1994–95, 1997, 1999 and 2001). Senna's 1993 win was his last appearance at the race: he was tragically killed in an accident in the 1994 San Marino Grand Prix.

KRONE CONQUERS A MAN'S WORLD

JULIE KRONE BECOMES FIRST WOMAN JOCKEY TO WIN A TRIPLE CROWN RACE

6 June 1993, Belmont Park, Elmont, New York, USA

Julie Krone was a talented rider who was forced to plough a lonely furrow in a sport where the top trainers displayed an alarming reluctance to hand top rides to "jockettes". But Krone fought hard to gain the respect of everyone in the sport and went on to put together an 18-year career of firsts: the first woman to win a race at a major track (1987); the first woman to ride in the Kentucky Derby (1992 – a year in which she became one of only a handful of American jockeys to win six races in a single day); and in 1993 she rode 13/1 long-shot Colonial Affair to victory in the Belmont Stakes to become the only woman in history to win a Triple Crown race.

➲ Two months later she suffered a horrific fall at Saratoga Raceway that left her with a shattered ankle. She returned nine months later, but in August 1996 suffered another heavy fall that left her with two broken hands. She was never the same rider again and retired from the sport in 1999.

At just 4ft 10in and 100lb, Julie Krone showed the racing world that size was not everything and enjoyed a successful 18-year racing career, the highlight of which came when she won the 1993 Belmont Stakes to become the only female Triple Crown winner in history.

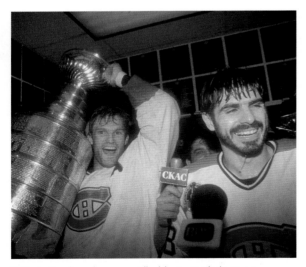

While the Canadiens players were still celebrating inside the Forum, thousands of fans were going wild in the streets, smashing windows, overturning cars and looting shops. The riot lasted several hours and resulted in millions of dollars in damage.

THE CUP COMES HOME – AGAIN

MONTREAL CANADIENS WIN THEIR 24TH STANLEY CUP

9 June 1993, Montreal, Canada

Montreal's win over the Los Angeles Kings in Game 5 of the 1993 series brought Montreal its 24th Stanley Cup, firmly entrenching the team as the franchise with the most Stanley Cup wins in NHL history. After losing the opening game of the finals to Wayne Gretzky and the LA Kings, 4–1, the Habs rallied to win all of the next three games in sudden-death overtime, then reverse the score for a 4–1 victory in Game 5. The series was special in that it was the Cup's 100th anniversary year and the last Cup series to be played in the Montreal Forum before is was decommissioned. It was also Wayne Grezky's last series, though it was the first time the LA Kings had reached the finals..

➲ Though the Habs have won the Cup 24 times, Montreal has been home to the Stanley Cup 37 times, including precursor teams the Wanderers, Maroons, Shamrocks and AAA club. The player with his name on the Cup the most times (11) is the Habs' centre Henri Richard, younger brother of Maurice "The Rocket" Richard.

Renowned for his rigorous training schedule, Kenya's Yobes Ondieki responded to the disappointment of a fifth-place finish in the 1992 Olympic Games 5,000m final by moving up a distance to the 10,000m and breaking the world record within a year.

CHANGE OF PLAN PAYS DIVIDENDS FOR ONDIEKI

YOBES ONDIEKI BECOMES FIRST RUNNER IN HISTORY TO RUN 10,000M IN UNDER 27 MINUTES

10 June 1993, Oslo, Norway

Kenya's Yobes Ondieki travelled to the 1992 Olympic Games in Barcelona as the reigning 5,000m world champion and fully expecting to add an Olympic gold medal to his haul of international titles. But his hopes fell away in the final, when his opponents exposed his lack of "kick" and he finished in a disappointing fifth place. It led to a change of plan: he decided he would move up to 10,000m. After three months' training at high altitude, he travelled to the 1993 Bislett Games in Oslo to compete in the 10,000m with lofty ambitions and did not disappoint, breaking fellow countryman Richard Chelimo's world record – set just five days earlier – by an astonishing nine-and-a-half seconds with a time of 26m58.38s.

➲ Ondieki's mark would stand as a record for over a year until fellow countryman William Sigei clocked a time of 26m52.23s in Oslo on 22 July 1994.

STORMIN' NORMAN ROMPS TO OPEN GLORY

GREG NORMAN RECORDS LOWEST FOUR-ROUND TOTAL IN OPEN CHAMPIONSHIP HISTORY

19 July 1993, Royal St George's Golf Club, Sandwich, Kent, England

Queensland-born Greg Norman began playing golf at the age of 16 after caddying for his mother and was playing off scratch within two years. He won his first professional tournament in 1976 and by 1982 topped the European Order of Merit. He collected his first major in 1986, winning the Open Championship, and although wins continued to flow, the man dubbed the "Great White Shark" seemed to lose his bite when it really mattered in major tournaments. But despite finishing runner-up eight times in majors – he is one of only two men in golf history (Craig Wood being the other) to appear in playoffs in all four major championships and lose – Norman added to his major tally, and in some style, at the 1993 Open Championship at Royal St George's, shooting 66-68-69-64 for a four-round total of 267, the lowest in the tournament's history.

Greg Norman's legend may well be as a major tournament "choker", but when he got it right there was no finer player: one such example came during his second and final major tournament win at the 1993 Open Championship when he tore up the Royal St George's course for a four-round record total of 267 – the lowest in the tournament's storied history.

➲ But Norman will always be remembered for his major tournament final-round meltdowns. In 1986, he led all four majors after three rounds but won only the Open Championship. Ten years later, he famously blew a six-stroke final-round lead in the 1996 Masters.

JUMPING JACKSON FLASHES TO WORLD CHAMPIONSHIP GOLD

COLIN JACKSON SETS 110M HURDLES WORLD RECORD MARK THAT WILL STAND FOR 13 YEARS

20 August 1993, Stuttgart, Germany

Colin Jackson was a talented all-round sportsman with a preference for athletics and in particular the 110m hurdles. After a brilliant junior career, he won his first major international medal (silver) at the 1986 Commonwealth Games and would go on to finish on the podium at every major athletics championships for the next 17 years. However, Jackson's career was not always lined with glory. Considered favourite for the title at the 1992 Olympic Games in Barcelona – he was the reigning European and Commonwealth champion – he finished in a disappointing seventh place. He bounced back in style at the World Championships in Stuttgart the following year, however, taking gold and breaking Roger Kingdom's world-record time of 12.93s by two one-hundredths of a second.

➲ China's Liu Xiang equalled Colin Jackson's record time (12.91s) at the 2004 Olympic Games in Athens before going on to break it on 11 July 2006 with a time of 12.88s in Lausanne, Switzerland.

An electric starter and the master of the closing "dip", Colin Jackson took every honour available to him in the 110m hurdles, bar Olympic gold, but his crowning moment came at the 1993 World Championships in Stuttgart when he set a world-record time that would last for 13 years.

In a performance that triggered huge controversy – with many claiming rigorous training alone could not produce such sensational results – Wang Junxia became the first woman in history to run the 10,000m in under 30 minutes at the 1993 China National Games in Beijing.

WANG JUNXIA CRUSHES 10,000M WORLD RECORD

WANG JUNXIA BREAKS 10,000M WORLD RECORD BY A STAGGERING 42 SECONDS

8 September 1993, Stuttgart, Germany

Wang Junxia's reign at the top of the women's 10,000m event was as glorious as it was brief. Renowned for her demanding training schedule – she would run some 25 miles per day, every day – she first came to prominence when she took the 10,000m junior world championship crown in 1992 at the age of 19. A year later she was the best distance runner on the planet: in April she broke the Asian marathon record (running the fastest time of the year); in May she broke the Asian 3,000m record; and in September, at China's National Games, held just a month after she had become 10,000m world champion, she shattered Ingrid Kristiansen's "impregnable" 10,000m world record (30m13.74s) by a staggering 42 seconds.

➲ Wang's time of 29m31.78s stands as a world record to this day. She retired from competition in 1996 after taking 5,000m gold (and silver in the 10,000m) at the Olympic Games in Atlanta.

THE RYAN EXPRESS FINALLY RUNS OUT OF STEAM

NOLAN RYAN RETIRES FROM BASEBALL WITH RECORD HAUL OF 5,714 STRIKEOUTS

22 September 1993, Kingdome, Seattle, Washington, USA

After winning a World Series with the New York Mets in 1969, Fall Classic success eluded Nolan Ryan for the rest of his 27-year career, but he bowed out of baseball in September 1993 with numerous all-time records to his name.

Nolan Ryan spent his early career with the New York Mets transforming himself from an inconsistent flamethrower into a formidable all-round pitcher. He moved to the California Angels in 1972 and started to set the baseball world alight. In 1973 he broke Sandy Koufax's single-season strikeout record with 383 and during his eight-year stay with the Angels, led the American League in strikeouts seven times. In 1980 he moved to Houston and became baseball's first $1-million-a-year player: the strikeouts, if not World Series glory, continued to come his way. He played out the last five years of his 27-year career with the Texas Rangers, before his arm finally gave out two games before his planned retirement. Ryan left the game with 5,714 strikeouts to his name, a figure many believe will never be beaten.

➲ Nolan Ryan is the only pitcher in history to have recorded in excess of 5,000 strikeouts. He also holds the all-time record for no-hitters (he has seven; no other pitcher has more than four) and bases on balls.

VINTAGE FLOYD PLAYS LEADING ROLE IN US RYDER CUP SUCCESS

RAY FLOYD BECOMES OLDEST COMPETITOR IN RYDER CUP HISTORY

24 September 1993, The Belfry, Warwickshire, England

A surprise captain's selection for the 1993 Ryder Cup, Ray Floyd became the oldest competitor in the event's history and played a leading role in the United States' first win on European soil for 12 years, collecting three points out of a possible four.

He may have been a veteran of seven Ryder Cups, but when captain Tom Watson selected Ray Floyd as one of his two wildcard picks for the 1993 event, several eyebrows were raised. Floyd, a seven-time major winner, had won only once on the PGA Tour in six years and was by then plying his trade on the Senior Tour. He became the oldest competitor in Ryder Cup history (aged 51 years, 20 days) when he partnered Fred Couples during a 4&3 defeat to Nick Faldo and Colin Montgomerie, but then found his form, collecting three points (two in partnership with Payne Stewart and a singles win, by two holes, over Jose-Maria Olazabal) to help the United States to a 15–13 victory.

➲ Floyd went on to enjoy considerable success on the Senior Tour, collecting four major championships: The Tradition in 1994, the PGA Senior Championship in 1995 and the Senior Players' Championship in 1996 and 2000.

Never a world champion, but ever-present on the Formula One grid for over one-and-a-half decades, Riccardo Patrese finally bowed out of F1 having competed in a record 256 grands prix.

PATRESE COMES TO THE END OF THE FORMULA ONE ROAD

RICCARDO PATRESE RACES IN THE LAST OF HIS RECORD 256 GRANDS PRIX

7 November 1993, Adelaide, South Australia, Australia

Riccardo Patrese first appeared in the Formula One ranks at the 1977 Monaco Grand Prix and finished ninth. It was the start of an incredible 17-year, six-team journey in the sport that saw the Italian become the best "team man" Formula One has ever seen. Often quick – fast enough to claim six grand prix wins throughout his career – he twice finished third in the drivers' championship (in 1989 and 1991) and played a crucial role in developing the Williams car that took Nigel Mansell to the 1992 world championship. He moved to Benetton in 1993, but failed to live with the pace of new boy Michael Schumacher and was dropped at the end of the season. After competing in a record 256 grands prix, he announced his retirement shortly afterwards.

➲ Patrese's record of 256 grands prix has stood for 14 years, but seems destined to be broken in 2008 by Brazilian driver Rubens Barrichello.

KANKKUNEN COASTS TO FOURTH WORLD TITLE

JUHA KANKKUNEN BECOMES FIRST FOUR-TIME WORLD RALLY CHAMPION

24 November 1993, Birmingham, England

Juha Kankkunen's stunning performance at the 1985 Safari Rally to secure his maiden rally win played a large part in him securing a move to the all-powerful Peugeot team for 1986. It was a marriage made in heaven: Kankkunen took three race wins and marched to his first world championship. A move to Lancia in 1987 failed to knock him out of his stride and he defended his title, before a fall-out over team orders saw him switch to Toyota for 1988. The move was not a happy one and Kankkunen sought to resolve his differences with the Lancia team to resurrect his title hopes. It worked. In 1991, back with Lancia, the Finn won on five occasions to become the first man in history to win the world championship three times; three years later, now back with Toyota, he added title No. 4.

➲ Tommi Makkinen has since equalled Kankkunen's record haul of titles, winning four consecutive championships between 1996 and 1999.

Competitive and always fast, Finland's Juha Kankkunen was rally's first four-time world champion.

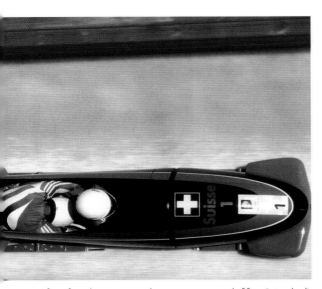

SWEET COMEBACK AT LILLEHAMMER

CANADIAN MOGULS WHIZ JEAN-LUC BRASSARD BECOMES FIRST NORTH AMERICAN TO SCORE OLYMPIC FREESTYLE GOLD

12 – 27 February 1992, Lillehammer, Norway

What a difference two years makes. After finishing a distant six spots behind French skier and hometown favourite Edgar Grospiron in the first official men's moguls event at Albertville in 1992, 21-year-old Canadian freestyle skier Jean-Luc Brassard came roaring back at Lillehammer to become the first North American Olympic freestyle champion. By earning a spot on the top step of the podium, the skier from Grosse-Ile, Quebec, also became the first male Canadian skier ever to take home Olympic gold. The charismatic and boyish Brassard attributed some of his luck that day to three special people cheering him on from the stands. Both of his parents, as well as his girlfriend at the time, Olympic figure skater Isabelle Brasseur, witnessed him race past silver- and bronze-medallists, Sergey Shupletsov of Russia, and Brassard's old rival Grospiron. In 1998, Brassard was chosen to be Canada's flag-bearer at his third and final Olympic Games, at Nagano, Japan.

Brassard, who at age 18 became the youngest skier to win the World Cup, was brought up in an athletic family. His older sister, Anne-Marie Brassard, is a former aerialist for the Canadian team.

➲ Brassard, who retired from competitive skiing in 2002, remains active as a sports broadcaster. He is also associated with a number of charities, including Operation Enfants du Soleil, which raises money to help sick children throughout the province of Quebec.

WEDER AND ACKLIN COMPLETE TWO-MAN BOB DOUBLE

GUSTAV WEDER AND DONAT ACKLIN BECOME FIRST IN HISTORY TO DEFEND OLYMPIC TWO-MAN BOBSLEIGH TITLE

12–27 February 1994, Lillehammer, Norway

In 1986, the International Olympic Committee decided to change the Olympic schedule so that the summer and winter games would be held alternately every two years. The result of this was that two years after the Olympic flame was extinguished in Albertville it was reignited in Lillehammer, Norway; it also meant that, with only two years between events, Switzerland's Gustav Weder and Donat Acklin, having pipped Austria's Rudi Lochner and Markus Zimmermann to the two-man bobsleigh title in 1992, had a genuine shot at becoming the first pair in history to defend it. They did not disappoint, edging compatriots Reto Götschi and Guido Acklin by five one-hundredths of a second to defend their title.

Benefiting from the two-year gap between events instead of four, Switzerland's Gustav Weder and Donat Acklin became the first two-man bobsleigh pair in history to make a successful defence of their Olympic title.

➲ Weder and Acklin's win in Albertville in 1992 was the first Swiss victory in the event for 12 years and only the country's third in two-man bobsleigh history.

LIFE IN THE RECORD BOOKS BEGINS AT 41 FOR COUGHLAN

EAMONN COUGHLAN BECOMES FIRST OVER-40 ATHLETE TO RUN A SUB-FOUR-MINUTE MILE

26 February 1994, Harvard University, Cambridge, Massachusetts, USA

After winning the Irish 1,500m and 5,000m titles in 1971, Eamonn Coughlan won a sports scholarship to Villanova University in Philadelphia and went on to win four NCAA Championships in the 1,500m and mile. In 1975 he recorded his first sub-four-minute mile, and a year later suffered the acute disappointment of a fourth-place finish in the Olympic 1,500m final. He suffered the same fate in Moscow in 1980, this time in the 5,000m final, but made amends in the inaugural World Championships in Helsinki in 1983 when he took the 5,000m gold medal. A better performer indoors than out – he was a six-time winner of the Wanamaker Mile held each year in Madison Square Garden – it was over the boards of Harvard in 1994 that he forged a place for himself in the history books: on 26 February, aged 41, he became the first over-40 athlete in history to clock a sub-four-minute mile (3m58.15s).

Known as the "Chairman of the Boards" throughout his career because of his consistent success in indoor tracks, four-time Olympian Eamonn Coughlan became the first over-40-year-old in history to clock a sub-four-minute mile, at Harvard in February 1994.

➲ Coughlan's time was still some 15 seconds shy of Hicham El Guerrouj's current mile world-record time of 3m43.13s set in Rome on 7 July 1999.

NIEMINEN BECOMES FIRST MEMBER OF THE 200 CLUB

TONI NIEMINEN BECOMES FIRST SKI-JUMPER IN HISTORY TO JUMP BEYOND 200M

17 March 1994, Planica, Slovenia

Toni Nieminen caused a sensation in 1992 when he led Finland to victory in the team K120 ski-jumping event in Albertville to become, aged 16 years, 259 days, the youngest Winter Olympian in history to win gold. Two days later he recorded the two highest scores in the individual K120 and became the youngest winner of an individual Winter Olympic event. A star before the age of 17, he had not since lived up to his early promise, but on 17 March 1994 in Planica, Slovenia – and just moments after Austria's Andreas Goldberger had crash-landed following a leap of 202m – Nieminen produced a legal leap of 203m to become the first ski-jumper in history to pass the magical 200m mark.

➲ Nieminen's world-record mark did not last long. Later the same year, at the same venue, Norway's Espen Bredesen leapt to 209m.

After a sensational start to his ski-jumping career that saw him become the youngest Winter Olympic champion in history, in Albertville in 1992, Finland's Toni Nieminen added another page in the history books when he became the first ski-jumper to leap beyond 200m.

THE GREAT ONE BECOMES THE GREATEST

WAYNE GRETZKY BREAKS GORDIE HOWE'S ALL-TIME NHL RECORD FOR MOST GOALS
23 March 1994, The Forum, Los Angeles, California, USA

Ever since his debut in the NHL with the Edmonton Oilers in 1979, Wayne Gretzky had made a habit of pulling rabbits out of a hat on the ice and had spread the game's popularity beyond more boundaries than anyone had thought possible. The Great One had developed an appetite for breaking records and had shown a flair for the dramatic that would shame even the greatest of Hollywood scriptwriters. Having led the Los Angeles Kings to a first Stanley Cup finals appearance in the franchise's history the previous season, Gretzky entered the 1993–94 NHL season within sight of one final milestone: hockey's unbreakable record – Gordie Howe's career total of 801 goals that had stood as an NHL all-time best for over 30 years. Gretzky tied his childhood hero's mark on 21 March 1994. Three days later, a packed Forum cheered their hero onto the ice as the Los Angeles Kings prepared to face off against the Vancouver Canucks. After 14m47s of the second period, the Great One flicked a shot from the edge of the left face-off circle and past Canucks goaltender Kirk McLean. Hockey's ultimate record was his.

➲ It took Gretzky 1,117 games to achieve the mark, some 650 games fewer than it had taken fellow Canadian Gordie Howe: Gretzky's scoring rate during that time was an average of 55 goals a season over a period of 15 years.

Breaking records seemed an everyday occurrence for Wayne Gretzky, but none was sweeter than those he stole from his childhood hero Gordie Howe and one record in particular caused him tremendous satisfaction: on 24 March 1994 he surpassed the sport's unbreakable mark of 801 career goals.

RECORD-BREAKING BORDER CALLS TIME ON CAREER

ALLAN BORDER PLAYS WORLD-RECORD 93RD AND FINAL TEST AS AUSTRALIA'S CAPTAIN

25–29 March 1994, Kingsmead, Durban, South Africa

After making his Test debut in the 1978–79 Ashes series against England, Allan Border established a reputation as a somewhat limited batsman, but whatever he may have lacked in his attacking armoury he more than made up for with an abundance of steely determination: few wickets in world cricket were prized so dearly. Not a natural leader, he reluctantly took over the captaincy in 1984–85, but he brought a sense of pride and determination into Australian cricket and played a huge role in transforming his nation's cricketing fortunes: under his charge they won the World Cup for the first time in 1987; regained the Ashes in 1989; and by the time he retired in 1993–94 (having captained his country a record 93 times), Australia were challenging the mighty West Indies to the right to be called the greatest team in world cricket.

➲ Border played in 156 Test matches for Australia (a record since broken by Steve Waugh) and scored 11,174 runs (since surpassed by Brian Lara) at an average of 50.26.

One of the true greats of world cricket, Allan Border had a simple, reserved and passionate approach to the game that is one of the main reasons Australia are the dominant force in world cricket today. He captained Australia a record 93 times and brought the good times back to cricket Down Under.

RECORD FOURTH TITLE FOR FJELLERUP

EVA FJELLERUP BECOMES FIRST FOUR-TIME MODERN PENTATHLON WORLD CHAMPION

April 1994, Sheffield, Yorkshire, England

Invented by Baron Pierre de Coubertin to mirror the ancient pentathlon (five events that were supposed to test the military skills of the competitor), the modern pentathlon was based on skills employed by a nineteenth-century cavalryman trapped behind enemy lines. Featuring fencing, pistol shooting, swimming, show jumping and a cross-country run, it first appeared on the Olympic timetable in 1912. However, almost 70 years would pass before women had a chance to compete in a modern pentathlon world championship and a further decade would pass before one woman, Denmark's Eva Fjellerup, took a hold on the event. Between 1990 and 1994 she won a record four world championships.

➲ The modern pentathlon appeared on the women's Olympic program for the first time at Sydney in 2000, by which time Fjellerup had long since retired.

Wheelchair racing handed Jean Driscoll a zest for life she never thought possible and she used her newfound energy to great effect to become the only athlete in history to win the Boston marathon on eight occasions.

DRISCOLL SHATTERS HER OWN WORLD MARATHON BEST

JEAN DRISCOLL BREAKS HER OWN WHEELCHAIR MARATHON WORLD RECORD EN ROUTE TO FIFTH BOSTON TITLE

17 April 1994, Boston, Massachusetts, USA

Born with spina bifida, Jean Driscoll did not start to use a wheelchair until her sophomore year in high school and prepared herself for a life of torment and frustration. That all changed when a friend introduced her to wheelchair soccer and a whole new world of possibilities opened up before her. She started training for wheelchair racing while a student at the University of Illinois and competed in her first marathon in Chicago in 1989: she finished second and her performance earned her a place in the following year's Boston marathon. After six months of gruelling training she won and broke the world record by seven minutes with a time of 1h43m17s. She lowered her world-record mark in each of her next four marathons, culminating in a time of 1h34m22s that still stands to this day.

➲ Driscoll would go on to become the only athlete in any division to win the Boston marathon on eight occasions.

BRILLIANT LARA SETS NEW TEST-BEST MARK

BRIAN LARA BREAKS GARFIELD SOBERS'S RECORD FOR THE HIGHEST TEST SCORE

18 April 1994, St John's, Antigua

Brian Lara went into the fifth Test against England in April 1994 with a single-minded determination to do something he had never done before: to score two Test centuries in a series (he had scored 167 in the second Test). He came to the crease like a man on a mission and ended the day on 167 not out. The crowds grew on day two as Lara passed 200, then 300, and ended the day just 46 runs short of Garfield Sobers's all-time Test high of 365 not out. The third day dawned. Sobers stood among the vast crowd. Lara equalled his mark with a blistering cover drive. The tension was unbearable, before the left-hander unleashed a savage hook to the boundary. Brian Charles Lara had broken Test cricket's greatest record.

➲ Lara's total of 375 not out stood as a Test best until 9 October 2003 when Australia's Matthew Hayden scored 380 against Zimbabwe in Perth.

Brian Lara confirmed his reputation as one of the most exciting batsmen in world cricket when he plundered a world-record 375 not out (off 538 balls) against a beleaguered England attack in St John's, Antigua, in April 1994.

DEVASTATING LARA HITS FIRST-CLASS CRICKET'S HIGHEST SCORE

BRIAN LARA BREAKS WORLD RECORD FOR HIGHEST FIRST-CLASS SCORE

2–6 June 1994, Edgbaston, Birmingham, England

A few weeks after breaking Garfield Sobers's world record for the highest score in Test cricket, Brian Lara arrived in England to great fanfare to take up his position as Warwickshire's overseas professional in the County Championship and got off to a blistering start, registering scores of 147, 106, 120 not out, 136, 26 and 140 in his first six innings. The best was still to come. In his seventh innings, Lara came to the crease with Warwickshire on 8 for 1, chasing Durham's first-innings total of 556, and ended the day (the second of four) unbeaten on 111. The third day was lost to rain, but on the fourth, Lara smashed a sensational 390 runs to take his score to 501 not out and break the record for the highest first-class score (held by Hanif Mohammad with 499 for Karachi against Bahawalpur in 1958–59).

Less than two months after breaking the world record for the highest Test score, Brian Lara etched his name further into the annals of cricket legend when he scored a record-breaking 501 not out for Warwickshire against Durham in the County Championship.

➲ Lara faced 427 balls for his 501 not out which included 62 fours and ten sixes. Dating back to his record-breaking knock of 375 not out against England, it meant Lara had completed another record: he became the first batsman in history to score seven centuries in eight first-class innings.

THE GREATEST ALL-ROUND FEMALE ATHLETE OF ALL TIME

PAULA NEWBY-FRASER BREAKS THE WOMEN'S IRONMAN WORLD RECORD

June 1994, Roth, Germany

Born in Rhodesia (now Zimbabwe) in 1962, but raised in Durban, South Africa, Paula Newby-Fraser was a nationally ranked swimmer in her childhood before dropping out of sports completely during her college years. In 1985 she bought herself a bicycle and, three weeks later, entered her first triathlon and demolished the field: she had found her true calling. Later that year she entered the Ironman World Championships in Kona, Hawaii, and finished third. Before long she was the dominant figure in the sport, winning in Hawaii a record eight times and going on to set numerous world records, the culmination of which came in June 1994 when she set the women's Ironman world record in Roth, Germany, completing the 2.4-mile swim, 112-mile bike ride and marathon run in 8h50m24s.

Considered by many the greatest all-round female athlete of all time, Paula Newby-Fraser dominated the women's Ironman competition, winning the infamous Hawaii event a record eight times and setting a world-record time in 1994 that stands to this day.

➲ Newby-Fraser's record of eight world championship wins is twice the number won by the next-greatest Ironman champions, Mark Allen, Erin Baker and Dave Scott.

GEBRSELASSIE SHOWS SIGNS OF GREATNESS

HAILE GEBRSELASSIE BREAKS SAID AOUITA'S SEVEN-YEAR 5,000M WORLD RECORD
4 June 1994, Hengolo, the Netherlands

Born in Asella in the Arsi Province on the central plateau of Ethiopia in 1973, Haile Gebrselassie had to run 20km a day as a child simply to get to school and back. He entered the Addis Adaba marathon at the age of 16 and, without any training or coaching, clocked a time of 2h42m. He first came to international prominence in 1992 when he took gold in both the 5,000m and 10,000m at the World Junior Championships. The following year he became 10,000m world champion at Stuttgart (as well as picking up a silver in the 5,000m) and in 1994 he confirmed his enormous potential by breaking Said Aouita's seven-year-old 5,000m world record (12m58.39s set in Rome 1987) by over one-and-a-half seconds with a time of 12m56.96s.

➲ Gebrselassie's mark would stand as a record for a little over a year until Kenya's Moses Kiptanui clocked 12m55.30s in Rome on 6 June 1995.

A two-time Olympic and four-time world 10,000m champion, Haile Gebrselassie set the first of his 25 world-record times in the 5,000m in June 1994 in the Netherlands.

Once described by French coach Jacques Fouroux as "having the strength of a bull and the touch of a piano player", Philippe Sella became the first rugby player in history to win 100 international caps.

SELLA FIRST IN RUGBY HISTORY TO REACH 100-CAP MILESTONE

PHILIPPE SELLA BECOMES FIRST RUGBY PLAYER IN HISTORY TO WIN 100 INTERNATIONAL CAPS
26 June 1994, Lancaster Park, Christchurch, New Zealand

Philippe Sella made his debut for France against Romania in 1982, and although he won his first few caps on the wing, his supreme athleticism, sharp running angles and watertight defence soon precipitated a move to centre and it was in that position that he became a fixture in the French line-up for the next 13 years. In 1986 he became one of only five players to score a try in every game of the Five Nations; the following year he played a huge part in France's journey to the World Cup final; in 1994, 12 years after his debut, he became the first player in history to win 100 international caps: his teammates helped him celebrate the milestone in style, running out 22–8 winners over New Zealand in Christchurch.

➲ Sella retired from international rugby following the 1995 World Cup in South Africa with 111 international caps to his name. The mark stood as a record until October 2003 when England's Jason Leonard won his 112th cap.

MILLA BOWS OUT OF WORLD CUP DUTY WITH A FLOURISH

ROGER MILLA BECOMES THE OLDEST PLAYER TO SCORE IN THE WORLD CUP FINALS

28 June 1994, Stanford Stadium, Palo Alto, California, USA

Roger Milla played for Cameroon in his country's first-ever appearance in the World Cup finals in 1982 as a 30-year-old, but when Cameroon failed to qualify for Mexico '86, Milla retired from soccer, moved to Reunion Island in the Indian Ocean and settled down for a quiet life. However, when Cameroon made it to the 1990 World Cup finals, Milla was lured out of retirement: he played a starring role, scoring four times as Cameroon became the first African side in history to make it through to the quarter-finals. He appeared for the Lions in USA '94, aged 42, and although he scored against Russia to become the oldest goalscorer in World Cup history, the tournament was a disappointing one for both Cameroon and Milla: they finished bottom of their group.

➲ In 2004, Pele named Roger Milla among his greatest 125 living soccer players (one of only five African players on the list) and in 2006 he was voted the greatest African player of the last 50 years.

Roger Milla added a sense of style to both the 1990 and 1994 World Cups and his goal-scoring exploits made him the first superstar of African soccer.

Russia may have been playing for little more than pride, but their striker Oleg Salenko was at his sharp-shooting best in his country's final group match of the 1994 World Cup, netting an all-time tournament single-game record five goals in his country's 6–1 demolition of Cameroon.

FIVE-STAR SALENKO SINKS CAMEROON

OLEG SALENKO BECOMES ONLY PLAYER IN HISTORY TO SCORE FIVE GOALS IN A WORLD CUP FINALS MATCH

28 June 1994, Stanford Stadium, Palo Alto, California, USA

After two games the 1994 World Cup was still very much alive for Cameroon: a win against Russia (coupled with a victory for Brazil over Sweden) could see them progress beyond the group stages for a second successive tournament. But Russia – and their striker Oleg Salenko in particular – killed the dream: playing solely for pride, they led 3–0 by half-time with Salenko completing his hat-trick. Roger Milla pulled one back for Cameroon, but the Russian juggernaut rumbled relentlessly on. Salenko added goals four and five in the 72nd and 75th minutes, before Dmitri Radchenko completed the 6–1 rout nine minutes before time. The plaudits, though, lay with five-goal Salenko: no player has scored more goals in a World Cup finals match.

➲ Remarkably, even though Russia were eliminated from the tournament following the group stages, Oleg Salenko (with six goals; he also scored against Sweden) shared the Golden Boot award – awarded to the tournament's leading scorer – with Bulgaria's Hristo Stoichkov.

After 120 minutes of mostly forgettable soccer, the 1994 World Cup final burst into life with the first-ever final shootout in the event's history. It was a nervy affair before Italy's tournament hero Roberto Baggio blasted the ball over the bar to hand Brazil a fourth World Cup win in the most torturous of ways.

BRAZIL SURVIVE SHOOTOUT LOTTERY TO WIN FOURTH WORLD CUP

BRAZIL BECOME THE FIRST TEAM TO WIN THE WORLD CUP ON PENALTIES

17 July 1994, Rosebowl, Pasadena, California, USA

On paper, at least, the 1994 World Cup final was a clash of the giants: three-time winners Brazil against three-time winners Italy. But the two teams' routes to the final could not have been more different: Brazil, without a World Cup win since 1970, powered through their group, dismissed the Netherlands 3–2 in the quarter-finals and edged past Sweden in the semi-finals. Italy, on the other hand, had staggered through the group phases – they qualified as the last of the four third-place finishers – before Roberto Baggio picked them up by the scruff of the neck and hauled them through to the final. The match, played in 40°C heat, was no classic and a stalemate after 120 minutes led to a World Cup first: a penalty shootout. Brazil won the shootout lottery 3–2 to become the tournament's first four-time winners.

➲ Italy gained some measure of consolation when they went on to beat France 5–3 in the second-ever World Cup final penalty shootout in Germany 2006.

DEADLY DJERNIS DELIVERS RECORD THIRD WORLD TITLE

HENRIK DJERNIS BECOMES FIRST THREE-TIME MOUNTAIN-BIKE WORLD CHAMPION IN HISTORY

18 September 1984, Vail, Arizona, USA

Born on the Danish island of Zealand in 1966, Henrik Djernis started road racing at the age of 12 and turned his attention to cyclo-cross racing only after one of his friends paid him a visit bearing a huge trophy he had just won in a local cyclo-cross tournament. Djernis won the first of his ten consecutive Danish national cyclo-cross championships in 1989 and enjoyed his first taste of international success when he won the third-ever mountain-bike world championships held in Bromont, Quebec, Canada in 1992. He retained the title the following year in Métabief, France, and again in 1994, in Vail, Arizona, to become the first three-time mountain-bike world champion in history.

➲ Djernis's feat was surpassed in 2007 when France's Julien Absalon won his fourth consecutive mountain-bike world title in Fort William, Scotland.

A supreme athlete with unmatched bike-handling prowess, Denmark's Henrik Djernis won in many forms of cycle racing, but truly made his name when he collected three consecutive mountain-bike world championships between 1992 and 1994.

STOCKTON NOTCHES UP RECORD 9,922ND CAREER ASSIST

JOHN STOCKTON BREAKS MAGIC JOHNSON'S NBA CAREER RECORD FOR MOST ASSISTS

1 February 1995, Delta Center, Salt Lake City, Utah, USA

John Stockton was selected by the Utah Jazz in the 16th round of the 1984 NBA Draft and for the first two seasons of his career found himself playing second fiddle to Jazz's incumbent point guard Rickey Green. Green's departure from the club prior to the 1987–88 season was the turning-point in Stockton's career: that year he broke the single-season record for assists (1,128) and forged a partnership with Karl Malone that would form part of NBA legend. Fast, gritty and above all durable, Stockton would enjoy 1,000-plus assist seasons for the next four years, breaking his own single-season record in 1989–90 with 1,134. In 1993 he became only the third man in history – along with Magic Johnson and Oscar Robertson – to pass the 9,000 career-assist milestone and it was only a matter of time before he broke Johnson's all-time NBA record of 9,921 assists. The moment finally came on 1 February 1995, when Stockton registered his 9,922nd career assist in a regular-season clash against the Denver Nuggets.

➲ Stockton retired from basketball with 15,806 career assists to his name, over 5,000 more than the next player on the all-time list. He is also the career leader in steals, with 3,265.

The greatest point guard to have played the game, John Stockton used his eye for the killer pass to great effect during his 19-year career with Utah Jazz, registering an all-time-record 15,806 career assists.

ALL BLACKS CRUSH HAPLESS CHERRY BLOSSOMS

NEW ZEALAND BREAK RECORD FOR MOST POINTS IN A RUGBY WORLD CUP MATCH

4 June 1995, Free State Stadium, Bloemfontein, South Africa

Having already qualified for the quarter-finals of the 1995 Rugby World Cup in South Africa, by virtue of their two opening Pool C victories over Ireland (43–19) and Wales (34–9), New Zealand saw their final pool match against Japan as an ideal opportunity to rest their big guns before the business end of the tournament began: Japan had, after all, conceded 107 points in their first two matches. A virtual All Black Second XV it may have been, but the match turned out to be a no-contest. New Zealand ran in tries from all quarters, 21 of them, with Marc Ellis (6), Eric Rush (3), Jeff Wilson (3), Robin Brooke (2), Glen Osborne (2), Richard Loe, Simon Culhane, Paul Henderson, Craig Dowd and Alama Ieremia all crossing the tryline. Culhane kicked 20 of 21 conversions to leave Japan reeling. The final score: New Zealand 145, Japan 17.

➲ Simon Culhane's haul of 45 points in the match and Marc Ellis's six tries are both individual Rugby World Cup records. However, the All Blacks' 145–17 win is not the biggest winning margin in the tournament's history: the record for that belongs to Australia, who beat Namibia 143–0 on 24 October 1993.

New Zealand sent Japan spinning out of the 1995 Rugby World Cup when they crushed the Cherry Blossoms 145–17 in their final pool match. The All Blacks' points haul is a tournament record and one of only five instances of a team scoring in excess of 100 points in RWC history.

Lammtarra and Walter Swinburn defied the bookmakers' 14/1 odds to chase down Frankie Dettori and Tamure in the final furlong to win the 1995 Epsom Derby in a record-breaking time, some 1.5s faster than the previous record.

LAMMTARRA SHATTERS DERBY COURSE RECORD

WALTER SWINBURN AND LAMMTARRA WIN EPSOM DERBY IN RECORD-BREAKING TIME

10 June 1995, Epsom Downs, Surrey, England

Foaled in 1992 by former Derby winner Nijinsky, Lammtarra was two years old when he lined up for his first race, with Walter Swinburn in the saddle, at Newbury and won. His trainer Saeed Bin Suroor had one race in mind for him: the 1995 Epsom Derby. Lammtarra came very close to not making it: a combination of injury and illness meant that when he lined up at Epsom on 10 June 1995, it was his first race for 302 days and only the second of his career. With two furlongs to go, Lammtarra lay six lengths behind Tamure, but then Swinburn guided him into clear air and he tore into the gap, chasing down Tamure with every step before overtaking him in the final furlong to win by a length. The winning time of 2m32.21s was a race record.

➲ Lammtarra went on to win the King George VI and Queen Elizabeth Diamond Stakes at Ascot and the Prix de l'Arc de Triomphe later in the year before retiring to stud.

Sean Fitzpatrick's (centre, black shirt, facing camera) record-breaking 19th and final appearance in the Rugby World Cup ended in disappointment when the All Blacks fell 15–12 to an inspired South Africa in Johannesburg.

SOUTH AFRICA RUIN FITZPATRICK'S RECORD-BREAKING DAY

SEAN FITZPATRICK MAKES RECORD 19TH APPEARANCE IN A RUGBY WORLD CUP MATCH

24 June 1995, Ellis Park, Johannesburg, South Africa

New Zealand had been playing the most destructive rugby of the tournament and had unleashed Jonah Lomu, the most devastating player the game had ever seen, onto the world. So it came as little surprise when the general consensus was that All Black captain Sean Fitzpatrick would celebrate his record-breaking 19th appearance in a Rugby World Cup match by lifting the William Webb Ellis Trophy. But the 1995 World Cup final for South Africa was far more than just a rugby match – it was about the re-birth of a nation and, inspired by a 65,000-strong crowd, the Boks held New Zealand's much-vaunted attack at bay and kicked their way to a surprise 15–12 victory. Fitzpatrick's record-breaking day had turned into a nightmare.

➲ Fitzpatrick's record was destined to be eclipsed: England's Jason Leonard holds the current record for the most appearances in the Rugby World Cup finals with 22, between 1991 and 2003.

Tim Henman shook the world of barley water and strawberries and cream to its very core in June 1995 when he became the first player in history to be defaulted from the Wimbledon Championships.

HENMAN SUFFERS WIMBLEDON DEFAULT WOE

TIM HENMAN BECOMES FIRST PLAYER IN WIMBLEDON HISTORY TO BE DEFAULTED FROM THE TOURNAMENT

June 1995, Wimbledon, London, England

It was hardly the first major career headline Tim Henman would have wanted, but the man who would go on to carry a nation's hopes for two weeks of every summer for the best part of a decade – and who would even have part of the All-England Club unofficially named after him – hit both the back pages and the front during what turned out to be a miserable tournament at Wimbledon in 1995. Having been knocked out of the singles tournament by eventual champion Pete Sampras in straight sets (6–2, 6–3, 7–6), Henman turned his attentions to the doubles tournament. His involvement was short-lived: in a fit of anger he smashed a ball, which crashed into a ball girl's head. Henman was defaulted from the match: it was the first instance of such a case in the tournament's history.

➲ Henman, of course, would go on to enjoy considerable success at the Wimbledon Championships, reaching the semi-finals of the tournament on four occasions.

FIVE IN A ROW FOR INDURAIN

MIGUEL INDURAIN BECOMES FIRST RIDER IN HISTORY TO WIN TOUR DE FRANCE FIVE YEARS IN A ROW

23 July 1995, Paris, France

Capable of gulping eight litres of air into his lungs and with a resting heartbeat of just 29 beats per minute, Miguel Indurain was born to race and made history between 1991 and 1995 when he became the first rider in history to win the Tour on five consecutive occasions.

Miguel Indurain's early outings in the Tour de France gave little indication of what was to come: he failed to finish in his first two attempts (1985 and 1986) and then suffered 97th-, 47th- and 17th-place finishes. In 1990 he rode in support of team captain Pedro Delgado and his tenth-place finish convinced many observers, including his team bosses, that he was now strong enough to win the race himself. In 1991, now Banesto team leader, he took the title and established a formula he would stick to for the rest of his career: blitz the time-trial stages and hold on to the lead in the mountains. Defensive it may have been, but the Spaniard defended his title four times to become the first man in history to win the Tour in five consecutive years.

⮑ Miguel Indurain joined Jacques Anquetil, Eddy Merckx and Bernard Hinault as the only riders to have won the Tour de France five times. Lance Armstrong obliterated their record when he won the race seven consecutive times between 1999 and 2005.

EDWARDS TAKES GOLD WITH TWO RECORD-BREAKING LEAPS

JONATHAN EDWARDS BECOMES FIRST TRIPLE-JUMPER TO LEAP BEYOND 18M BARRIER

7 August 1995, Gothenburg, Sweden

Without any doubt the greatest triple-jumper of all time, Jonathan Edwards broke the world record twice in the space of a few minutes at the 1995 World Championships in Gothenburg.

Jonathan Edwards first came to international prominence when he picked up the triple-jump bronze medal at the 1993 World Championships, but his real breakthrough year came in 1995. Early in the season he produced a staggering wind-assisted leap of 18.43m: the wind speed may have disqualified it from the record books, but it was a sign of things to come. On 18 July he broke Willie Banks's world record (17.97m) with a leap of 17.98m in Salamanca, Spain. Three weeks later, at the World Championships in Gothenburg, he produced the most staggering performance in the event's history. He broke his own world record in the first round with a leap of 18.16m and nailed his second jump as well, raising his arms in celebration as he landed – 18.29m. Edwards had broken the world record twice in the space of a few minutes.

⮑ Edwards went on to produce five of the longest six jumps in triple-jump history (his two jumps in Gothenburg remain the best two jumps of all time). He became Olympic champion in 2000 and regained the World Championship title he had lost in 1997 and 1999 with victory in Edmonton, Canada, in 2001.

CAL RIPKEN JR: "THE STREAK"

CAL RIPKEN JR BREAKS LOU GEHRIG'S ALL-TIME CONSECUTIVE-GAME RECORD
6 September 1995, Oriole Park, Baltimore, Maryland, USA

Cal Ripken Jr made a career out of an extraordinary work ethic and a simple rule: to be ready to play every day. He made his debut for the Baltimore Orioles in 1982, hit a home run in his first at-bat, ended the season as the American League's Rookie of the Year and, on 30 May, started what became known as "The Streak". The following year he earned the first of 19 All-Star selections, was voted the AL's MVP and picked up his first World Series ring. The years rolled by: his father came and went as the Orioles' coach, but Cal Jr stayed right where he was. The Orioles moved from Memorial Park to Camden Yards in 1991: Ripken packed his bags and went with them. By the start of 1995, he was fast closing in on Lou Gehrig's 56-year record of 2,130 consecutive games played and viewing figures hit an all-time high on 6 September when Ripken took to the field for the 2,131st time: he hit a home run in the fourth inning – called over the radiowaves by President Clinton – and when the game became official after the Angels' half of the fifth inning, the 50,000-strong crowd erupted. Cal Ripken Jr had broken baseball's unbreakable record.

⮑ On 14 June 1996, Cal Ripken Jr went on to break Japanese player Sachio Kinugasa's world record for consecutive games (2,216). On 20 September 1998, Ripken Jr brought "The Streak" to an end at 2,632.

Cal Ripken Jr had to shake off minor injuries and occasional illness over 17 years of 162-game-per-season schedules to break Lou Gehrig's consecutive-game record. It could well end up being baseball's longest-standing record.

Jim Kelly was one of the NFL's great quarterbacks: he passed for more than 3,000 yards on eight occasions – only three players in history have reached the 30,000-yard career passing mark faster – and made history in 1995 when he broke the record for most yards gained per completion in a single game with 44.

KELLY SETS NEW NFL SINGLE-GAME MARK

JIM KELLY SETS NFL SINGLE-GAME RECORD FOR MOST YARDS GAINED PER COMPLETION

10 September 1995, Orchard Park, Buffalo, New York, USA

After a stellar college career with the University of Miami and two successful seasons in the short-lived United States Football League, Jim Kelly signed for the Buffalo Bills shortly before the start of the 1986 season and was an instant hit in the NFL. His fast-paced, no-huddle offence terrorized opposing defences and helped transform the Bills into one of the most powerful attacking units the game has ever seen. With Kelly pulling the strings, the Bills made the playoffs in eight of 11 seasons, including four consecutive (losing) Super Bowl appearances between 1991 and 1994. On 10 September 1995 – in the Bills' second match of the season, against the Carolina Panthers – Kelly finally made his way into the record books, setting an all-time NFL high for most yards gained per completion in a single game with 44.

➲ However, the Bills' earch for an elusive Super Bowl win ended in the divisional playoffs when they lost 40–21 to Pittsburgh.

GRAF COMPLETES QUADRUPLE CAREER GRAND SLAM

STEFFI GRAF BECOMES ONLY TENNIS PLAYER IN HISTORY TO WIN ALL FOUR GRAND SLAM TOURNAMENTS FOUR TIMES

10 September 1995, Flushing Meadows, New York, USA

If winning a grand slam tournament on all four surfaces – carpet, clay, grass and hard courts – is the true measure of tennis greatness (only 14 players have achieved the feat) then, by numbers alone, Steffi Graf put together the greatest career of all time. By the start of the 1995 season she was just two wins away (the French Open and US Open) from becoming the first person in history to win all four grand slam tournaments four times. After missing the 1995 Australian Open through injury, Graf outlasted Spaniard Arantxa Sanchez-Vicario in the final of the French Open final. She beat the same opponent in the Wimbledon final less than a month later and travelled to New York in September with history beckoning. She did not disappoint, beating Monica Seles 7–6, 0–6, 6–3 to take her unique place in the record books.

Steffi Graf put the icing on the cake of her extraordinary career in 1995 when she won both the French and US Opens to become the only tennis player in history to have won all four grand slam tournaments on at least four occasions.

➲ Graf's winning ways did not end there. She continued her dominance in 1996 by defending her French Open, Wimbledon and US Open crowns (having missed the Australian Open once again through injury) and collected the last of her 22 grand slam singles titles in 1999 when she beat Martina Hingis in the French Open final.

IT'S A RECORD – AGAIN

DONOVAN BAILEY BREAKS TWO RECORDS IN ONE YEAR

9 February 1996, Reno, USA and 27 July 1996, Atlanta, USA

Donovan Bailey was magic on the track. 1996 saw him break back-to-back records, first at a 50m sprint at an indoor event in Reno, Nevada (where he clocked 5.56 seconds), then by clocking a 9.84 second 100m at that summer's Olympics in Atlanta. He would also bring home gold in the Olympic 4x100m relay. Bailey's Atlanta time would stand as a record until 1999, when his arch-rival, America's Maurice Greene, would break it with a time of 9.79 seconds. The next year, Bailey defended his title as the world's fastest man against the US's Michael Johnson in a 150m event at SkyDome in Toronto. Johnson pulled out at the 100m mark with to a pulled quadriceps muscle, though Bailey was already ahead of him at that point. Bailey was the second runner to hold the titles of World Champion, Olympic Champion and world record-holder at the same time.

Bailey displays his signature intensity on his way to setting his world record in the men's 100m at the Atlanta Olympic Games of 1996, in which he won gold with a time of 9.84 seconds.

➲ A ruptured Achilles tendon and pneumonia ended Bailey's career after the 1997 season, and he finally retired from running in 2001. He now runs a successful sports services company in Toronto, offering a personal fitness programme book, an apparel line and several charitable initiatives.

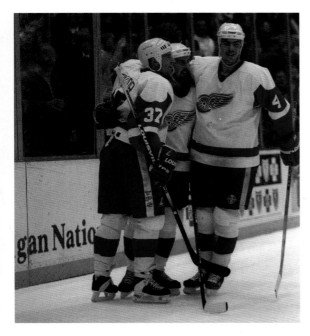

Coached by the legendary Scotty Bowman, the Detroit Red Wings recorded an all-time NHL record 62 wins during the course of the 1995–96 season, but still failed in their quest for a long-overdue Stanley Cup win: a blemish they would rectify the following year.

RED WINGS FIND THEIR WINNING WAYS

DETROIT RED WINGS REGISTER AN NHL ALL-TIME RECORD 62 REGULAR SEASON WINS

14 April 1996, American Airlines Center, Dallas, Texas, USA

Detroit Red Wings coach Scotty Bowman's response to his side's 4–0 1994–95 Stanley Cup massacre at the hands of the New Jersey Devils (in what had been the Red Wings' first Stanley Cup appearance in 29 years) was simply to add more reinforcements to his team's armoury. He added Slava Feistov, Igor Larinov and Mike Vernon to an already impressive cast list and unleashed a revitalized Detroit side onto the Western Conferences Central Division. They marched through the regular season in fearsome style, notching up 131 points to top the table – the second-highest total in NHL history, bettered only by the 132 points scored by the Montreal Canadiens (also coached by Bowman) – and, following a 5–1 victory over the Dallas Stars in the final game of the regular season, registered an all-time record 62 wins en route to the playoffs.

➲ The Red Wings could not carry their momentum through to a first Stanley Cup success in more than 40 years, though. They lost the final series in six games to the Colorado Avalanche.

RECORD-BREAKING BULLS MARCH TO FOURTH TITLE

CHICAGO BULLS RECORD THE BEST REGULAR SEASON IN NBA HISTORY
22 April 1996, United Center, Chicago, Illinois, USA

In 1993, after leading the Chicago Bulls to the NBA's first "three-peat" since the legendary Celtics side of the 1960s, Michael Jordan announced his retirement from the game. And although the Bulls may have gone on to record a 55-win regular season, they were not the same team without their talisman and slumped to defeat in the second round of the playoffs. They did not get off to the best of starts to the 1994–95 season either, but received a major fillip in March 1995 when Jordan announced he would be coming out of retirement. The Bulls suffered another early post-season exit, but by the start of the 1995–96 season Jordan was back to his formidable best and, joined by the likes of Scottie Pippen, Dennis Rodman, Luc Longley and co, the Bulls were unstoppable, posting an all-time record 72 regular season wins en route to claiming a fourth NBA Finals win.

➲The Bulls set many all-time NBA records that year: they produced the best on-the-road performance in history (33 wins and eight losses); the all-time best start to the season by a team (41 wins, three losses); and the longest home-game winning streak in history (44 games, including seven from the previous season).

Michael Jordan may have been the linchpin of the Chicago Bulls' record-setting 72-game winning regular season in the NBA, 1995–96, but he was ably assisted by Scottie Pippen (on floor, front) and the outstanding defensive play of the charismatic Dennis Rodman (91).

LAKERS' PLAYOFF DEFEAT SPELLS END OF LINE FOR RECORD-BREAKING JOHNSON

MAGIC JOHNSON BOWS OUT OF BASKETBALL WITH ALL-TIME NBA RECORD FOR CAREER ASSISTS

2 May 1996, Toyota Center, Houston, Texas, USA

Dubbed "Magic" by the local Michigan press after he had notched up a triple-double for his high-school career as a 15-year-old, Earvin Johnson enjoyed a short but spectacular college career for Michigan State University before joining the LA Lakers in 1979. It was show time: the Lakers marched to the 1980 NBA Championship with Johnson, voted Finals MVP, excelling. It set the tone for his career: by the time he retired for good in 1996 (he had had a brief stint out of the game in 1992 after being diagnosed HIV-positive) following the Lakers' playoff loss to the Houston Rockets, he had collected four more NBA Finals rings (1982, 1985, 1987, 1988), appeared in nine NBA Finals and collected an all-time record 2,346 playoff assists.

➲ At 6ft 9in the largest point guard ever to appear in the NBA, Magic Johnson played a huge part in the United States' renewed interest in basketball in the 1980s.

One of only four players in the history of the game to have won the NCAA Championship and the NBA Finals in consecutive years, Magic Johnson was one of the giants of basketball. An integral part of the LA Lakers' huge success in the 1980s, he retired from the game in 1996 with an all-time record 2,346 playoff assists to his name.

ZELEZNY SHATTERS HIS OWN WORLD BEST MARK

JAN ZELEZNY BREAKS JAVELIN WORLD RECORD WITH A THROW OF 98.48M

25 May 1996, Jena, Germany

Jan Zelezny first came to international prominence when he broke Klaus Tafelmeier's world record (85.74m) for the new-specification javelin (introduced earlier in the year) with a throw of 87.66m. The mark would stand as a record until 1990, but was then broken in quick succession by Patrick Boden, Steve Backley, Zelezny himself and finally by Seppo Raty, whose new mark of 96.96m led to another javelin specification change in November 1991. Britain's Backley set the new mark with a throw of 91.56m in January 1992, but in April the following year Zelezny hit back with a throw of 95.66m. The Czech star had finally made the record his own, increasing the mark to 95.66m in August 1993 and then to a staggering 98.48m in May 1996, a mark no one has come close to matching.

Javelin world record holder Jan Zelezny threw in excess of 90m 34 times during his career, more than the total of any other javelin thrower in history. He is also the holder of the Olympic record (90.17m)

➲ Zelezny ended his career in 2006 aged 40 with three Olympic titles (1992, 1996 and 2000) and three World Championship titles (1993, 1995 and 2001) to his name.

THE LION OF CULIACAN FINALLY LOSES RECORD-BREAKING ROAR

JULIO CESAR CHAVEZ'S RECORD-BREAKING RUN OF 27 CAREER TITLE DEFENCES COMES TO AN END

7 June 1996, Caesar's Palace, Las Vegas, Nevada, USA

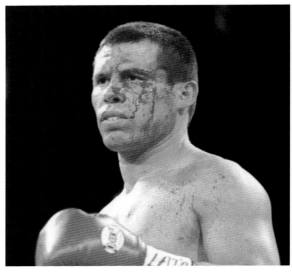

Julio Cesar Chavez, nicknamed the "Lion of Culiacan", drifted between weights but found his inside fighting style was too much for many boxers en route to defending various world titles a record 27 times without defeat. Oscar de la Hoya brought the historic streak to an end in June 1996.

A 44-bout unbeaten streak brought Mexican-born Julio Cesar Chavez a first shot at a title belt in September 1984, and he knocked out Mario Martinez to win the WBC super featherweight title. He went on to defend it ten times before moving up a weight to lightweight and taking the WBA title in 1987 before claiming the WBC belt the following year to unify. The title defences continued to mount up: he took the WBC super lightweight title, then the IBF junior welterweight title, earned a controversial draw against Pernell Whitaker for the WBC welterweight title, before taking his career total of title defences to an all-time record 27. The streak came to an end when he lost by TKO to Oscar de la Hoya in June 1996.

➲ In the early stages of his career, the rugged Chavez put together an 89-bout winning streak: it is the second-best streak in boxing history, behind Sugar Ray Robinson who put together a winning streak of 165 fights, 40 professional and 125 amateur.

Alex Greaves made history when she rode filly Portuguese Lil at the 1996 Epsom Derby, but the race ended in disappointment for the pair when they finished in 20th and last position.

FIRST WOMAN TO RIDE IN THE EPSOM DERBY

ALEX GREAVES BECOMES FIRST FEMALE JOCKEY TO APPEAR IN THE EPSOM DERBY

8 June 1996, Epsom Downs, Surrey, England

Alex Greaves started out as an amateur jockey and rode her first winner in 1989. Her first big success came when she took Amenable to victory in the Lincoln Handicap at Doncaster in 1991 although, despite the fact that she became the leading female rider in Britain, she found top rides hard to come by. But then, in 1996, trainer David Nicholls offered her a ride on Portuguese Lil at the 1996 Epsom Derby. It was a history-making moment: there had never been a female jockey in the 216-year history of the race. The bookmakers did not fancy the pair's chances, offering odds of 500/1, and indeed they lived up to the pre-race billing, finishing the race – won by 12/1-shot Shaamit – 20th out of 20 horses.

➲ The following year Greaves became the first woman in history to ride a group one winner when she dead-heated on Ya Malak at the Nunthorpe Stakes at York.

GERMANY'S GOLDEN GOAL GLORY

GERMANY SCORE THE FIRST GOLDEN GOAL IN INTERNATIONAL SOCCER HISTORY

30 June 1996, Wembley Stadium, London, England

Soccer came home in 1996 when England hosted that year's European Championships, but perhaps not in the way home fans would have wanted. Germany had crushed England's hopes in the semi-final with a dramatic penalty shootout win and took their place in the final against a Czech Republic side they had already beaten 2–0 in the group stages. The match ended in a 1–1 stalemate, bringing extra-time and the chance for someone to score the first Golden Goal in international soccer history – the concept whereby the first team to score in extra-time won the match had been brought in for Euro '96. Germany's Oliver Bierhoff found the back of the net in the 95th minute to hand his team the trophy and himself a slice of soccer history.

➲ Introduced prior to the 1996 European Championships, the Golden Goal was intended to reduce the number of matches decided by a penalty shootout. It was amended to a silver goal (the match continuing to the end of the period of extra-time in which a goal was scored) and was scrapped altogether following the 2003 Women's World Cup.

Germany won the European Championships for the third time in 1996, beating the Czech Republic 2–1 and scoring the first Golden Goal (netted by Oliver Bierhoff) in international soccer history.

NEWCASTLE FINALLY GET THEIR £15 MILLION MAN

ALAN SHEARER BECOMES THE WORLD'S MOST EXPENSIVE SOCCER PLAYER

30 July 1996, St James' Park, Newcastle, England

Rejected by hometown club Newcastle aged 15, Alan Shearer joined Southampton and scored a hat-trick on his full debut against Arsenal in March 1988. Impressive performances for the England Under-21 side followed and Shearer made a scoring international debut against France in February 1992. The following year he moved to Blackburn Rovers and became an England regular. In 1993–94 he scored 34 goals to help Blackburn to the Premiership title but although the goals continued to flow at club level, they dried up at international level. By the time England entered Euro '96, Shearer had not scored in 11 outings for his country. But he regained his goal-scoring touch, netting five times in England's march to the semi-finals. He was the hottest property in soccer: too hot for Newcastle to resist; they paid a world-record £15 million for his services.

➲ The figure stood as a world-record transfer fee until 1997, when Inter Milan paid Barcelona £19.5 million for Brazil striker Ronaldo.

After moving to Newcastle in the summer of 1996 for a world-record fee of £15 million, Alan Shearer stayed at the club for the rest of his career, scoring 148 times in 303 league appearances.

1996

200m KING JOHNSON THE TOAST OF ATLANTA

MICHAEL JOHNSON SHATTERS HIS OWN 200m WORLD RECORD
19 July–9 August 1996, Atlanta, Georgia, USA

Though he'd won 200m gold at the 1991 World Championships, food poisoning prior to the 1992 Olympic Games left Michael Johnson weakened and out of form: he crashed out of the 200m competition in the semi-finals. He found his stride once more to take 400m gold in the 1993 World Championships, defended the title two years later in Stuttgart, and ended a memorable competition by taking 200m gold. By the time he travelled to the 1996 Olympic Games he was in the form of his life and seeking to become the first man in Olympic history to complete a 200m–400m double. Running in a pair of custom-made gold running shoes, he completed the first leg of his quest with a comfortable victory in the 400m. Next came the 200m and the American was in blistering form, tearing through the first 100m in just 10.12s before accelerating to the line in a sensational 19.32s. He had completed a historic double and in magnificent style, shattering his own world record – set a few months earlier at the same Atlanta venue – by a staggering 0.34s, the largest improvement in the event's history.

➲ Michael Johnson's time of 19.32s has stood as the 200m world record ever since. America's Tyson Gay is the only man to have come close to it, clocking 19.62s on 24 June 2007.

A five-time Olympic and nine-time world champion, Michael Johnson reserved his greatest performance for the 1996 Olympic Games in Atlanta, clocking a sensational 19.32s in the 200m to shatter his own world record and set a mark that has never since been touched.

1996

LEWIS LEAPS TO RECORD FOURTH CONSECUTIVE LONG JUMP GOLD

CARL LEWIS BECOMES THE FIRST MAN IN HISTORY TO TAKE LONG JUMP GOLD AT FOUR CONSECUTIVE OLYMPICS

19 July–9 August 1996, Atlanta, Georgia, USA

Carl Lewis was already part of track-and-field legend by the time he scraped through the long jump qualifying tournament for the 1996 Olympic Games and gave himself the chance of becoming the first man in Olympic history to win the long jump at four consecutive Games (following his success in 1984, 1988 and 1992). He may no longer have been at the peak of his powers, but was still considered among the favourites for the title, especially considering that his main rivals, world record holder Mike Powell and Ivan Pedroso, were both struggling to shake off injuries. A jump of 8.50m in the third round was Lewis's best effort: it may have been the shortest effort of his Olympic career, but it was still enough to claim an unprecedented fourth consecutive gold.

⮑ Lewis ended his Olympic career with nine gold medals to his name, a figure equalled by Finnish middle-distance runner Paavo Nurmi but never beaten.

Carl Lewis needed all three jumps to qualify for the long jump final at the 1996 Olympic Games in Atlanta, but once he was there he proved the class of the field to take long jump gold for an unprecedented fourth consecutive time.

OLD MAN OF THE SEA COMPETES IN TENTH OLYMPIC GAMES

HUBERT RAUDASCHL BECOMES THE ONLY MAN IN HISTORY TO COMPETE IN TEN OLYMPIC GAMES

19 July–9 August 1996, Atlanta, Georgia, USA

Hubert Raudaschl was no stranger to Olympic competition: he first appeared in the 1960 Games in Rome as a fresh-faced 18-year-old and it was the start of an extraordinary career. He competed again in 1964, again in 1968 (taking silver in the Finn class at the sailing regatta in Acapulco), again in 1972 and 1976, before taking silver again in Moscow in 1980 (this time in the Star class). The Austrian's competitive edge may have started to dwindle, but the man team-mates nicknamed the "Old Man of the Sea" lost none of his zest for Olympic competition: he appeared in 1984, 1988 and in 1992. When he took to the water at Savannah, Georgia, for the 1996 Olympic sailing regatta, he became the first man in history to compete in ten Olympic Games.

⮑ Raudaschl's 36-year Olympic career yielded two silver medals (in Mexico City in 1972 and Moscow 1980).

Austria's Hubert Raudaschl, a five-time European and two-time world sailing champion, finally bowed out of Olympic competition at the tender age of 53 having competed in an all-time record ten Games.

MASTERKOVA ROUNDS OFF VINTAGE YEAR IN RECORD-BREAKING STYLE

SVETLANA MASTERKOVA BREAKS THE WOMEN'S MILE WORLD RECORD
14 August 1996, Zurich, Switzerland

Svetlana Masterkova's breakthrough year had been in 1991 when she took a surprise 800m victory at the Russian national games. The performance earned her a place at the World Championships a month later, but she could manage only eighth place. And then her career stalled: injuries, coupled with the birth of her daughter, kept her out of action between 1994 and 1995, but when she returned in 1996 she was stronger than ever. She completed the 800m–1,500m double at the Russian national games, but was still considered only an outside chance in both events at the 1996 Olympic Games: she took gold in both and rounded off the year in style by becoming the first woman in history to run the mile in under 4m15s, clocking 4m12.56s in Zurich on 14 August 1996.

➲ Nine days later, on 23 August 1996 in Nice, France, Masterkova broke the 1,000m world record with a time of 2m28.98s. Both this and her mile world record stand to this day.

Chris Boardman arrived at the 1996 World Pursuit Championships with a point to prove – he had elected not to defend his 4,000m individual pursuit crown in Atlanta – and did so in style, trouncing newly crowned Olympic champion Andrea Collinelli and shattering his own world record by two seconds in the process.

BRILLIANT BOARDMAN MAKES HIS POINT

CHRIS BOARDMAN SMASHES CYCLING'S 4,000 INDIVIDUAL PURSUIT WORLD RECORD
29 August 1996, Manchester, England

Chris Boardman cut a distinctive figure at the 1992 Olympic Games when he rode his Lotus-made carbon-fibre-framed bicycle to 4,000m individual time-trial gold and etched his name into cycling lore in 1993 when he broke the world hour record twice. He turned his attentions to road racing, winning a stage of the Tour de France for the first time in 1994, but the longer races did not suit him and he enjoyed little success in cycling's greatest race. He passed on the opportunity to defend his Olympic crown in Atlanta in 1996, electing to compete in the time-trial event (he picked up bronze), but showed his talent in the pursuit at the World Championships held a week after the Games. Having broken the 4,000m pursuit world record in the qualifying stages, he set up a final clash against newly crowned Olympic champion Andrea Collinelli and trounced the Italian, clocking 4m11.11s and cutting two seconds off his world record.

➲ Later in the year, again at the Manchester Velodrome, Boardman would reclaim the hour world record setting a mark of 56.375km (1.084km better than Toni Rominger's record) that still stands as a world best to this day.

VILLENEUVE EASES HIS WAY INTO FORMULA ONE

JACQUES VILLENEUVE WINS ROOKIE RECORD FOUR RACES IN DEBUT FORMULA ONE SEASON

22 September 1996, Estoril, Portugal

Jacques Villeneuve first made a splash on the motor-racing scene when he finished second in his first outing at the Indy 500 in 1994 and confirmed his potential by claiming the CART Championship the following year. He switched to Formula One and the front-running Williams team in 1996 and caused a stir in the season-opening Australian GP when he took pole and led for most of the race before an oil leak saw him surrender the lead to team-mate Damon Hill. But his performance set the tone for the season: he recorded his first race victory at the European GP, three more race wins followed (at the British, Hungarian and Portuguese GPs – a record for a rookie driver) and the Canadian shadowed Hill in the drivers' rankings throughout the season, before a retirement in the final race of the season saw him finish second in the end-of-season standings.

➲ Villeneuve did even better in 1997, notching up seven race wins en route to pipping Michael Schumacher to the world title by the slender margin of three points.

In one of the most remarkable days in racing history, the world got used to Frankie Dettori's trademark victory leap when he ran through the seven-race Ascot card and posted a magnificent seven wins.

FRANKIE DETTORI'S MAGNIFICENT SEVEN

FRANKIE DETTORI BECOMES FIRST JOCKEY IN HISTORY TO WIN ALL SEVEN RACES ON A SEVEN-RACE CARD

28 September 1996, Ascot, Berkshire, England

As day dawned over the Ascot racecourse on 28 September 1996 for the first day of the annual festival of British racing, no sense of the unusual hung in the air and Italian-born jockey Frankie Dettori summarily dismissed his chances with a brief "I could have an each-way chance in the first and I may win the third". But the late-September day developed into one of the most sensational in racing history: Dettori won the first race (on Wall Street), the second (on Diffident), the third (on Mark of Esteem), the fourth (on Decorated Hero) and the fifth (on Fatefully). By the time he rode Lochangel to the winning post in the sixth race, Ascot was a scene of hysteria. Could Dettori achieve the impossible? He could: guiding Fujiyama Crest to the spoils and himself to a place in the record books.

➲ It was a dark day for the bookmakers: Dettori's remarkable feat – which had original accumulator odds of 25,091/1 – left the industry some £40 million out of pocket.

AFRIDI BLASTS ONE-DAY INTERNATIONAL CRICKET'S FASTEST CENTURY

SHAHID AFRIDI HITS THE FASTEST CENTURY IN ONE-DAY INTERNATIONAL CRICKET HISTORY
4 October 1996, Nairobi Gymkhana, Nairobi, Kenya

Shahid Afridi made his one-day international debut for Pakistan as a 16-year-old replacement leg-spinner for the injured Mushtaq Ahmed against Kenya in Nairobi on 2 October 1996. He bowled his ten overs for 32 runs and no wickets and sat in the stands as his team-mates secured a four-wicket victory. Two days later, Pakistan faced off against Sri Lanka, won the toss, elected to bat and pushed Afridi up the batting order to No. 3: it was a masterstroke. Playing in his first international innings, Afridi smashed Sri Lanka to all parts of the ground, hitting six fours and 11 sixes to reach three figures in a world-record 37 balls. Pakistan won the game by 82 runs and Afridi had become a household name.

Talk about announcing yourself to the world: in his maiden innings for Pakistan in a one-day international, 16-year-old Shahid Afridi smashed the fastest century in the game's history – off just 37 balls.

➲ It remains the fastest century in one-day international cricket. The closest anyone has come to breaking it is South Africa's Mark Boucher, who reached three figures off 44 balls against Zimbabwe in Potchefstroom on 20 September 2006.

Martin Brundle enjoyed nine visits to the podium but never once tasted victory in a Formula One race and retired in 1996 holding the record for the most career points scored (98) without a victory.

FORMULA ONE'S LEAST-WANTED RECORD

MARTIN BRUNDLE RETIRES FROM F1 HOLDING RECORD FOR MOST CAREER POINTS WITHOUT A RACE WIN
13 October 1996, Suzuka, Japan

Eight years after his Formula One debut, Martin Brundle finally got the car his talent richly deserved. Famous for having pushed a young Ayrton Senna so close in the 1983 British Formula Three championship, the Norfolk-born driver had been forced to suffer seven years driving for also-rans before Benetton came calling in 1992. Brundle produced the best season of his career, visiting the podium five times en route to a sixth-place finish in the drivers' championship. But it wasn't enough for him to retain his seat for the following season and he never found himself in as strong a car again. He retired at the end of the 1996 season having recorded a career total of 98 championship points – the highest total of any driver in history without securing a race win.

➲ Nick Heidfeld, who drove for BMW Sauber in 2007, has since surpassed Brundle's total.

AKRAM FINDS THE BATTING FORM OF HIS LIFE

WASIM AKRAM BREAKS TEST RECORD FOR MOST SIXES IN AN INNINGS

18–20 October 1996, Sheikhupura, Pakistan

Wasim Akram's 414 career Test wickets attest to the fact that he was a magnificent fast bowler and arguably the greatest left-arm bowler ever to have played the game, but if you were going to criticize the Pakistan legend's career, you would say he was a serial underperformer with the bat – with one glorious exception. During Pakistan's first Test against Zimbabwe at Sheikhupura in October 1996, Akram strode to the crease with his side struggling on 183 for 6 (replying to 375) and proceeded to power his way to 257 not out off 363 balls: the innings contained a Test-record 12 sixes, beating the previous record of ten, set by Walter Hammond in 1932.

⊃ It was Wasim Akram's best moment at the crease during his 104-match Test career: he retired in 2002 with 2,898 runs to his name at an average of 22.64.

With his side in some trouble against Test minnows Zimbabwe, Pakistan captain Wasim Akram produced the innings of a lifetime in Sheikhupura in 1996, hammering 257 not out – the highest score by a player batting at No. 8 in Test history. The innings contained a Test record 12 sixes.

SECREST BREAKS THREE WORLD RECORDS IN 24 HOURS

MICHAEL SECREST BREAKS 12-HOUR AND 24-HOUR UNPACED CYCLING WORLD RECORDS

23–24 October 1996, Olympic Velodrome, California State University, USA

A former marathon runner and triathlete, Michael Secrest finally found his niche in long-distance cycling and during 24 hours on 23–24 October 1996 found himself in the record books not once or twice but three times. Pounding his way around the Olympic Velodrome at California State University, the man known throughout the cycling world as "The Hammer" broke the 24-hour unpaced cycling record in an outdoor arena held by Paul Solon (509.29 miles) by 29 miles; broke the 12-hour unpaced cycling world record (held by Solon with 272.06 miles) by over six miles; and the 24-hour unpaced world record in any arena – 530.41 miles set by Rod Evans indoors in Australia on 22 May 1994 – by over two miles.

⊃ With no updates on his progress while he was riding, consistency was the key to Secrest's record-breaking performance: during one six-hour period, his average pace per hour did not vary by more than half a lap.

SWOOPES SIGNS HER WAY INTO THE HISTORY BOOKS

SHERYL SWOOPES BECOMES FIRST TO BE SIGNED BY WNBA

24 October 1996, Houston, Texas, USA

Born on 25 March 1971, Sheryl Swoopes was playing competitive basketball by the age of seven and by 1988 was a senior on the Texas state championship team. She joined Texas Tech University and won rave reviews for her performances, setting numerous NCAA records – most points in a single season (955), the single-game points record for a championship match (47) and the most points in a championship series (177) – en route to leading the Texas Tech Lady Raiders to the NCAA Championship in 1993. Dubbed the "female Michael Jordan" she led the US women's team to gold at the Atlanta Games in 1996 and, a few months later, became the first woman in history to sign for the newly formed WNBA when she put pen to paper on a deal for the Houston Comets.

A star for the Texas Tech Lady Raiders, Sheryl Swoopes made history on 24 October 1996 when she became the first player in history to sign for a newly formed WNBA outfit.

➲ Swoopes went on to lead the Comets to four straight WNBA Championship successes between 1997 and 2000 and was voted WNBA Most Valuable Player on three occasions (2000, 2002 and 2005).

Jeannie Longo put together the greatest career in female cycling history, winning the sweep of national, world and Olympic titles as well as three female Tour de France victories: the icing on the cake came in 1996 when she broke the world hour record.

38-YEAR-OLD LONGO PRODUCES WORLD HOUR BEST

JEANNIE LONGO BREAKS THE WOMEN'S WORLD HOUR RECORD

26 October 1996, Olympic Velodrome, Mexico City, Mexico

Jeannie Longo started her sporting career as a downhill skier, winning the French junior championships and taking three university championships before turning her attentions to cycling at the age of 21. Within a few months she became the French road race champion and went on to become the greatest, and most unheralded, female cycling champion of all time, collecting 52 national titles, three women's Tour de France titles and 12 world championships. Two months after winning the only Olympic gold medal of her career, at the Atlanta Games in 1996, she added another line to her already impressive CV when she broke the women's world hour record at the age of 38, notching up a distance of 48.159km (29.9 miles) in Mexico City that still stands as a record to this day.

➲ Due to the advance in technologies, the world hour record is split into two categories: the official one where competitors use technology akin to that available when Eddy Merckx set the record in 1972; and a "best performance" record open for other technologies. Longo is the holder of the latter record.

KHAN STORMS TO RECORD EIGHTH WORLD OPEN WIN

JANSHER KHAN WINS THE WORLD OPEN SQUASH CHAMPIONSHIP FOR RECORD EIGHTH TIME

17–22 November 1996, Karachi, Pakistan

Born into a talented family of squash players, Jansher Khan won the world junior squash championship in 1986 and turned professional the same year. He immediately became the heir apparent to Jahangir Khan, with the pair's rivalry lighting up the sport in the late 1980s and early '90s: they met in competition 37 times with Jansher winning 19 and Jahangir 18; one of Jansher's victories came in the semi-finals of the 1987 World Open – he went on to claim the trophy for the first time. When Jahangir bowed out of competition, the stage was left to Jansher … and he was more than happy to take sole command of the spotlight. He went on to win another seven World Open titles, the last of his record eight wins coming when he beat Rodney Eyles in the 1996 final held in his native Pakistan.

His rivalry with fellow countryman Jahangir Khan lit up the squash scene for many years, but following Jahangir's retirement from the sport, Jansher Khan picked up the mantle of being squash's world No. 1 in style, winning an all-time record eight World Open titles, the last five of them in consecutive years.

➲ Jansher Khan also won the British Open – often considered the most prestigious event in the sport – six times, four behind the record number of ten won by his great rival Jahangir.

SNOWBOARDING'S FIRST TRUE ICON

TERJE HAAKONSEN BECOMES SNOWBOARDING'S FIRST THREE-TIME HALF-PIPE WORLD CHAMPION

22–26 January 1997, San Candido, Bolzano, Italy

Born in October 1974, Terje Haakonsen was raised in the Telemark village of Amot in southern Norway and by the age of five was capable of performing a 360° turn on a skateboard. He first tried snowboarding at the age of 13, and although already an accomplished skier, was immediately captivated by the freedom of movement available to him on a snowboard. In a short space of time, Haakonsen became a phenomenon. European half-pipe champion by the age of 17, the following year his pioneering moves elevated him to the status of world champion: it was a crown he defended in both 1995 and 1997 to see him become the sport's first three-time world champion.

➲ What made Haakonsen truly unique was the height he could soar to off the ramps. He had an uncanny understanding of how to move and balance his body while soaring through the air and pioneered a number of new moves, among them the "Haakon Flip" – a move that sees him push a fake ollie so that it eventually becomes a caballerial before evolving into a reverse caballerial.

The best snowboarder in the world by the age of 18, in 1997 Terje Haakonsen, still only 22 years of age, became the first man in history to win the half-pipe world championship on three consecutive occasions.

TENNIS'S LONGEST-SERVING WORLD NO. 1

STEFFI GRAF'S RECORD-BREAKING 377-WEEK CAREER STINT AS WORLD NO. 1 COMES TO AN END

31 March 1997, St Petersburg, Florida, USA

Steffi Graf finally dislodged Martina Navratilova as world No. 1 on 17 August 1987. She held on to the position for 186 weeks until Monica Seles overtook her on 11 March 1991. The position yo-yoed between the two: and then tennis went mad. A Graf "fan" stabbed Seles in the back and kept her out of the game for two years. Graf assumed the No. 1 spot for 87 weeks until 1995, when she was challenged by, lost to and then beat Arantxa Sanchez-Vicario for the right to be named the world's best player ... until 15 August that year, when the WTA announced Seles would share the ranking spot on her return to the sport. It was a position they shared for 64 weeks until Graf found her way to the top in early 1997. Her record-breaking 377-week career stint as world No. 1 was ended 18 weeks later by Martina Hingis.

Graf's career 377-week tenure as the No. 1-ranked player in the world beat the existing record held by Martina Navratilova (333 weeks between July 1978 and August 1987). Graf also holds the record for most consecutive weeks as world No. 1 (186 weeks between August 1987 and March 1991).

➲ Steffi Graf lost the world No. 1 ranking to Martina Hingis in March 1997 but remained competitive until she bowed out of the game in 1999 (still ranked the third-best player in the world).

TIGER SAVAGES FIELD FOR FIRST TASTE OF MASTERS GLORY

TIGER WOODS BECOMES YOUNGEST-EVER WINNER OF US MASTERS

13 April 1997, Augusta National, Augusta, Georgia, USA

The whole world knew Tiger Woods was coming, but still no one could quite believe their eyes when he finally arrived on the international golfing scene. The prodigy turned professional shortly after becoming the first player in history to complete a hat-trick of US Amateur championship wins – persuaded to do so in no small part by endorsement deals with Nike and Titleist amounting to $60 million – and went on to win two tournaments in the latter stages of the 1996 season. But still no one really fancied his chances at the 1997 Masters: it was his first major as a professional; the pressure would be too tough for him to handle, the Augusta course too challenging. Woods responded by blowing the rest of the field apart and winning by 12 strokes to become, at 21 years, 3 months and 14 days, the tournament's youngest-ever champion.

➲ Woods's 18-under par four-round total of 270 is the lowest score ever recorded in the tournament's history and the lowest score in relation to par in any of golf's four major tournaments.

Tiger Woods rocked the golf establishment to its very core when he blew the rest of the field away to win the 1997 Masters tournament, his first major tournament as a professional.

THE ROCKET'S FIVE-MINUTE MAXIMUM

RONNIE O'SULLIVAN COMPILES FASTEST MAXIMUM BREAK IN SNOOKER HISTORY

21 April 1997, Crucible Theatre, Sheffield, England

Perhaps the most naturally talented snooker player ever to pick up a cue, Ronnie O'Sullivan got his professional career off to a blistering start when he won an all-time-record 38 consecutive games. He made history in 1993 when he became the youngest player in the sport's history to win a ranking tournament by beating Stephen Hendry in the final of the UK Championships (aged 17 years, 357 days), and although tournament victories continued to come his way, the one he really wanted – the world snooker championship – continued to elude him. He looked to be in blistering form in 1997 and in the 14th frame of his first-round match against Mick Price, hit the fastest century break in the game's history, taking just 5m20s for his 15 reds, 15 blacks and seven colours.

A magician on the table and the biggest drawcard in the game, "Rocket" Ronnie O'Sullivan compiled snooker's fastest maximum break during the first round of the 1997 world championships: just 5m20s – an average of one shot every nine seconds.

➲ O'Sullivan's quest for a first world snooker championship title came to an end in the second round when he lost 13–12 to Darren Morgan. He finally won the world title his talent so richly deserved in 2001.

ROBERTO DI MATTEO SCORES THE FASTEST GOAL IN FA CUP FINAL HISTORY

ROBERTO DI MATTEO SCORES THE FASTEST GOAL IN FA CUP FINAL HISTORY

17 May 1997, Wembley Stadium, London, England

The two teams due to contest the 1997 FA Cup final had enjoyed mixed fortunes in the lead-up to the match. Under new manager Ruud Gullit, Chelsea had enjoyed their best league finish for a decade. Their opponents Middlesbrough, on the other hand, were appearing in the final for the first time in the club's history after having suffered the horrors of Premiership relegation. The game ran to the formbook and Chelsea took less than a minute to assert their authority in the match when Roberto Di Matteo picked up the ball in his own half, charged forward and unleashed an unstoppable 25-yard thunderbolt that crashed off the underside of the bar and into the back of the net. Chelsea 1 Middlesbrough 0 – and the goal had taken just 42 seconds, the fastest in FA Cup final history.

The 1997 FA Cup final got off to a blistering start when Roberto Di Matteo blasted Chelsea into the lead against Middlesbrough after just 42 seconds: it was the fastest goal in FA Cup final history. The Blues went on to win the game 2–0.

➲ Eddie Newton added a second Chelsea goal in the 83rd minute to hand the Blues a 2–0 victory and their first piece of silverware for 26 years.

BARCELONA TAKE RECORD FOURTH CUP-WINNERS' CUP WIN

BARCELONA WIN EUROPEAN CUP-WINNERS' CUP FOR A RECORD FOURTH TIME

14 May 1997, Feyenoord Stadium, Rotterdam, the Netherlands

First held in the 1961–62 season, the European Cup-Winners' Cup, contested annually by the most recent winners of all domestic cup competitions, was in reality the poor man's version of the European Cup, and even though it was ranked above the UEFA Cup, for many it was considered the easiest of the three European competitions to win. Spanish giants Barcelona certainly found it to their liking: they lifted the trophy for the first time in 1979, after a 4–3 final extra-time win over Fortuna Dusseldorf. A second win came three years later when they beat Standard Liège 2–1 in their home Nou Camp stadium. In 1989 they beat Sampdoria to become the competition's first three-time winners before a 37th-minute penalty from Ronaldo in the 1997 final against Paris St Germain handed them a record fourth win.

Barcelona's first taste of Cup-Winners' Cup success came in 1979: they won it twice more before collecting the trophy for a record fourth – and final – time in 1997 (above). The competition was discontinued after the 1998–99 season.

➲ In contrast, Barcelona have enjoyed mixed fortunes in the European Cup/Champions League: the Catalan giants have won the competition just twice (in 1992 and 2006).

ANWAR PUTS INDIA'S BOWLERS TO THE SWORD

SAEED ANWAR POSTS THE HIGHEST SCORE IN ONE-DAY INTERNATIONAL CRICKET HISTORY

21 May 1997, MA Chidambaram Stadium, Chepauk, Chennai, India

An exquisite timer of the ball, Saeed Anwar caressed opposition bowling attacks to all parts of the ground rather than brutalizing them. Although he went on to enjoy a successful Test career with Pakistan (scoring 4,052 runs in 55 Tests at an average of 45.52), it was in the one-day format that he made an indelible mark on the game. His greatest moment came against great rivals India in a group game for the Independence Cup – a four-team one-day international tournament featuring hosts India, Pakistan, New Zealand and Sri Lanka – when he smashed 194 off 146 balls (with 22 fours and five sixes) to break Viv Richards's record (189 scored against England in 1984) for the highest individual score ever recorded in a one-day international.

A wristy, elegant batsman who worked and cajoled the ball around the park, Saeed Anwar prospered in the shorter form of the game and secured his place in the history books with a world-record knock of 194 against India in Chennai – it was the first time a Pakistan player had scored a century against India on Indian soil in a one-day international.

➲ Pakistan went on to win the game by 35 runs and progressed through to the best-of-three match final against Sri Lanka, which they lost 2–0.

BORDERS BREAKS BASEBALL'S GENDER BARRIER

ILA BORDERS BECOMES FIRST WOMAN PITCHER IN MEN'S PROFESSIONAL BASEBALL

31 May 1997, Midway Stadium, Saint Paul, Minnesota, USA

Born and raised in the La Miranda suburb of Los Angeles, Ila Borders got her first sight of baseball aged ten when she went to watch an LA Dodgers game with her father: she loved the experience so much she declared she was going to be a professional baseball player. She became a star in high school and following her final MVP-winning year at Whittier Christian High in California in 1993 became the first woman to be awarded a baseball scholarship. She pitched for Southern California College for three years before signing with St Paul Saints in the independent Northern League in 1997. She made history on 31 May 1997 when she debuted against the Sioux Falls Canaries, hitting a batsman with her first professional pitch, but recovered to give up three runs and a single out.

Ila Borders fulfilled her childhood dream on 31 May 1997 when she pitched for the St Paul Saints in the Northern League: she had become the first woman in history to pitch in a men's professional baseball match.

➲ Borders was traded to the Duluth-Superior Dukes for the 1998 season and made more history on 24 July 1998 when she became the first woman in history to be named starting pitcher.

Wilson Kipketer was the class act of the 800m field in the mid- to late 1990s, and although Olympic gold medal glory never came his way, he left his mark on the event in 1997 when he broke Sebastian Coe's 16-year world record.

KIPKETER MAKES THE 800M WORLD RECORD HIS OWN

WILSON KIPKETER BREAKS SEBASTIAN COE'S 800M WORLD RECORD

24 July 1997, Cologne, Germany

Wilson Kipketer developed his running skills at St Patrick's School in Iten, Kenya – a Catholic school renowned for developing young running talent. In 1990 he travelled to the University of Copenhagen as a foreign-exchange student and liked his surroundings so much he applied for Danish citizenship. He came to prominence at the 1995 World Championships, taking gold in the 800m, and went on to become the world's leading runner in the discipline (he went through the 1996 season undefeated), but his lack of full Danish citizenship prevented him from competing in the 1996 Olympic Games. By 1997 he was closing in fast on Sebastian Coe's 800m world-record time of 1m41.73s (set in Florence in 1981): he tied the mark on 7 July 1997, before going on to break it 17 days later with a time of 1m41.11s.

➲ Kipketer's record stands to this day. He went on to defend his 800m world title in 1997 and 1999, but Olympic gold medal success always eluded him.

Honda was the dominant bike in the 1997 500cc world championship: at the end of the season eight of their riders were placed in the top ten final standings – but one man's performances towered over the rest of the field: Mick Doohan won 12 of the season's 15 races.

➲ Doohan won eight races the following season to become only the second man in history to win five consecutive 500cc world championship titles (the record is held by Agostini who won seven consecutive titles between 1966 and 1972). The Australian retired in 1999 following another heavy crash.

THE THUNDER FROM DOWN UNDER STORMS TO 12 WINS

MICK DOOHAN SETS ALL-TIME 500CC WORLD RECORD FOR MOST WINS IN A SEASON

15 September 1997, Montmelo, Barcelona, Spain

Mick Doohan made his 500cc world championship debut with Honda in 1989 and ended a promising first season in ninth place. He improved dramatically over the next two years, finishing third and second, and looked set to claim his first championship in 1992, winning five of the first seven races before suffering a massive practice crash at the Dutch TT. He returned before the end of the season but lost out on the title by three points to Wayne Rainey. If 1993 was all about recuperation, it worked: in 1994 he won nine times to claim his first world title. Doohan was now the dominant force in the sport: 15 race wins over the next two seasons saw him complete a hat-trick of titles. And then came 1997: Doohan won an astonishing 12 times (out of 15 races) to break Giacomo Agostini's all-time record of 11 wins set in 1972.

THE RYDER CUP'S RECORD-BREAKER

NICK FALDO BREAKS RECORD FOR MOST APPEARANCES AND MOST POINTS IN RYDER CUP HISTORY

28 September 1997, Valderrama, Spain

Through meticulous preparation and sheer determination, six-time major winner Nick Faldo earned the right to be considered the greatest European golfer in history. He also enjoyed considerable success in the Ryder Cup, making the first of his record-breaking 11 appearances in 1977 aged 20 (the youngest at the time to do so). Over the next 16 years Faldo formed the backbone of the European side and played a full part in historic moments such as Europe's first win for 28 years (1985) and Europe's first win on American soil (1987). By the time he played his last Ryder Cup in 1997 – during Europe's 14½–13½ win over the USA at Valderrama – he held the all-time records for most appearances (11), matches won (23) and points won (25).

➲ Sergio Garcia broke Faldo's record as the youngest player to appear in the Ryder Cup when he played in 1999 aged 19 years, 8 months and 15 days.

No one could question the role Nick Faldo played in Europe's Ryder Cup successes of recent times: between 1977 and 1997 the Englishman played in 11 consecutive cups and set the all-time record for points won, matches won and appearances.

THRUSTSCC GOES SUPERSONIC

ANDY GREEN AND THRUSTSCC BREAK THE LAND SPEED WORLD RECORD

15 October 1997, Black Rock Desert, Nevada, USA

Fourteen years after guiding his Thrust2 car to 633.468mph (1019.47km/h) over the sands of the Black Rock Desert to break Gary Gabelich's land speed world record, Richard Noble returned to the dry lake bed in Nevada in 1997 as project manager for the ThrustSCC team with a car – to be driven by former RAF pilot Andy Green – capable of breaking the sound barrier. Powered by two afterburning Rolls-Royce Spey engines, Green took the car to 714.144mph (1149.30km/h) on 25 September to break the record; they returned 20 days later and completed the mission, passing through the sound barrier before reaching a top speed of 763.035mph (1227.99km/h) or Mach 1.016. ThrustSCC had become the world's first supersonic car.

◐ Andy Green achieved the feat 50 years to the day after US Air Force pilot Chuck Yeager had become the first man in history to pass through the sound barrier in his Bell X-1 plane.

Success may not have been immediate, but it was mission accomplished on 15 October 1997 when Andy Green took the 54ft-long (16.5m) ThrustSCC car through the sound barrier over the sands of Black Rock Desert.

One of the most prolific goal-scorers in the game's history, Ronaldo became the FIFA World Player of the Year award's first back-to-back winner when he collected the trophy in 1996 and 1997.

DOUBLE DELIGHT FOR RONALDO

RONALDO IS FIRST SOCCER PLAYER IN HISTORY TO WIN BACK-TO-BACK WORLD PLAYER OF THE YEAR AWARDS

December 1997, Zurich, Switzerland

Nicknamed "The Phenomenon", Ronaldo played just one season for Cruzeiro in the Brazilian league before moving to PSV Eindhoven in 1994. He electrified the Dutch league, scoring 55 goals in 57 official appearances in his two seasons with the club: it was enough to secure him a move to Barcelona and in December 1996 the striker was voted World Soccer Player of the Year. He continued to excel, scoring 37 goals in 34 games for the Catalan giants (including the winner in their 1–0 European Cup-Winners' Cup final win over Paris St Germain) before moving to Inter Milan in the summer of 1997 for £19 million. The goals continued to flow and, in December, he became the first person in history to be voted the world's best player for the second consecutive year.

◐ Ronaldo remains the only player to have won the award in two consecutive years. He became the award's first three-time winner in 2002 after starring in that year's World Cup, a feat since equalled by Zinedine Zidane who picked up the trophy in 1998, 2000 and 2003.

SURF'S UP FOR FIVE-TIME CHAMPION SLATER

KELLY SLATER WINS RECORD FIFTH WORLD SURFING CHAMPIONSHIP

December 1997, Pipeline Beach, Oahu, Hawaii, USA

Born in Cocoa Beach, Florida, Kelly Slater was a keen student of surfing history who studied the moves of heroes of old, added his own style to the mix, changed the face of modern surfing and led wave riding into the 21st century. In 1991 he surfed the qualifying season for the main tour, qualified, and took the world title in his rookie season. He was the class of the field, with his fast and aggressive style impressing the judges wherever he went. He cast aside the disappointment of a sixth-place finish in 1993 to reel off four straight championships between 1994 and 1997 and become the first man in history to win five surfing world championships.

➲ A sixth championship followed in 1998 before Slater announced his retirement from the sport. It was short-lived: he was back in 2003 and not only did he rattle the cages of surfing's new guard, he stole their thunder, adding titles seven and eight in 2005 and 2006.

The greatest surfer in history, American Kelly Slater overtook Mark Richards's record haul of four world championship wins in 1997 and went on to claim another three titles in 1998, 2005 and 2006.

REBAGLIATI WINS FIRST OLYMPIC GOLD IN MEN'S SNOWBOARDING

ROSS REBAGLIATI AND KARINE RUBY MAKE HISTORY AT THE NAGANO WINTER OLYMPICS

7–22 February 1998, Nagano, Japan

When it was announced that the Nagano Games would be see the introduction of snowboarding as a full medal event, Ross Rebagliati from Vancouver, Canada, was fresh off a first-place finish at the 1997 snowboarding World Cup. Here was an opportunity to add yet another medal to the pile he'd been amassing since 1991, including two other World Cup golds and wins at the European Championships and the US Open. Finishing on the podium was what Rebagliati did, and he looked forward to working his magic in Japan. And he *definitely* worked it, slicing to a Giant Slalom gold-medal finish. His a time of 2:03:96 was just a hair quicker than Italy's Thomas Prugger, who clocked in at 2:03:98. On the women's side, France's Karine Ruby swooped her way to gold with a time of 2:17:34, a comfortable win ahead of Germany's Heidi Renoth, who was second in a time of 2:19:17.

When he was 19 years old, the North Vancouver-born Rebagliati picked up his snowboard and moved to Whistler in order to pursue his dream of becoming a world-class snowboarder.

➲ Controversy Strikes: Rebagliati was briefly stripped of his gold medal for having trace amounts of marijuana in his blood, but his disqualification was later overturned and he was re-instated as the world's first Olympic gold medallist in Grand Slalom snowboarding.

CANADIAN SPEED SKATER NABS ELUSIVE GOLD

AFTER A HUMILIATING FALL IN THE 500M AT THE OLYMPICS IN LILLEHAMMER, PRAIRIE SPEED SKATER CATRIONA LEMAY-DOAN WINS GOLD IN THE SAME EVENT FOUR YEARS LATER

7–22 February 1998, M-Wave, Nagano, Japan

After winning gold for the 500m at successive Winter Olympic games held in Nagano and Salt Lake City, LeMay-Doan became the first Canadian athlete to defend an Olympic gold medal in any sport.

Even when luck has abandoned her, Catriona LeMay-Doan doesn't give up. She gets faster. Early in the 500m race at the Lillehammer Olympics, the 23-year-old Canadian speed skater caught an edge of her skate, hit the ice and crashed into the barrier. Four years later at Nagano, Japan, she bounced back in the same event, winning gold – as well as a bronze in the 1,000m. In 2002 at Salt Lake City, where she served as her country's flag-bearer, LeMay-Doan won gold in the 500m for a second time, making her the first Canadian athlete to defend a gold medal in the same event at back-to-back Olympics. Clearly, the 500m distance is one of her favourites: she has set an astounding eight world records in the event. Sometimes called "the fastest woman on ice," LeMay-Doan has also won the speed skating World Cup six times and the world sprint championship five. .

⮡ After her famous tumble in the 500m event, which was broadcast live to millions of television spectators in 1994, LeMay-Doan stopped skating for several months before making her comeback. After retiring from competitive skating almost a decade later, she embarked on a new career: working for charities, in broadcasting and as a public speaker.

A two-time overall World Cup winner, German sensation Katja Seizinger made history in Nagano in 1998 when she became the first skier of either sex to defend an Olympic downhill title.

SEIZINGER SECURES OLYMPIC DOWNHILL DOUBLE

KATJA SEIZINGER BECOMES FIRST SKIER IN HISTORY TO DEFEND OLYMPIC DOWNHILL TITLE

7–22 February 1998, Nagano, Japan

Raised in Dortmund in the industrial Ruhr region of Germany, Katja Seizinger learned to ski on family holidays and finished fourth in the downhill and third in the Super G at the 1992 Olympics. She travelled to Lillehammer two years later without a race win for a year, crashed out of the giant slalom and Super G, but found her form when it mattered to take a shock downhill gold. In 1997 she won six World Cup speed races in a row – to equal Jean-Claude Killy's 1967 record – and travelled to Nagano in 1998 seeking to become the first in history to defend an Olympic downhill skiing title: she did so in style, cruising to victory 0.29s ahead of second-placed Pernilla Wiberg.

⮡ A day after becoming the first female skier to defend an Olympic title (in any discipline – although her record would last only a few days), Seizinger added to her medal collection by grabbing gold in the combined event.

COMPAGNONI'S UNIQUE GOLDEN TREBLE

DEBORAH COMPAGNONI FIRST SKIER IN HISTORY TO STRIKE GOLD AT THREE SEPARATE WINTER OLYMPICS
7–22 February 1998, Nagano, Japan

Deborah Compagnoni's career was a tale of triumph through adversity. Having recovered from a major accident in her youth, she took the Olympic Super G title in Albertville in 1992 before crashing out of the giant slalom the following day and tearing up her left knee. Unable to practise intensely, from that moment on she focused solely on the technical events and made a habit of reserving her best form for the big occasion. She took giant slalom gold at Lillehammer in 1994, became giant slalom world champion in 1996, was the first skier in history to win the slalom–giant slalom double at a world championships in 1997, and became the only skier in history to win three gold medals at three separate Winter Olympics when she defended her giant slalom title in Nagano in 1998.

Deborah Compagnoni battled the odds to become the only skier in history to win gold medals at three consecutive Winter Olympics.

➲ Compagnoni is also the only woman in history to defend her Olympic giant slalom title. She missed out on adding a fourth gold medal to her collection by six-hundredths of a second in the slalom.

THE WINTER OLYMPICS' YOUNGEST CHAMPION

TARA LIPINSKI BECOMES YOUNGEST WINTER OLYMPIC CHAMPION IN HISTORY
7–22 February 1998, Nagano, Japan

Tara Lipinski secured a narrow victory over her great rival Michelle Kwan at the 1998 Games in Nagano, Japan, to become, at the age of 15, the Winter Olympics' youngest-ever champion.

Already an accomplished roller-skater by the time she took to the ice for the first time at the age of six in 1988, Tara Lipinski first came to prominence when she took the now-defunct US Olympic festival of skating competition in 1994. A disappointing fifth-place finish at the 1996 world junior championships prompted a change of coach and a move up to senior level, and she shocked the skating establishment when she landed a triple loop-triple loop combination to become, aged 14, the youngest-ever US champion. Later that year she became the youngest world champion in history. Michelle Kwan beat her to the US title in 1998, but Lipinski reversed the order when it really mattered to take gold in Nagano: aged 15, she had become the youngest Winter Olympic champion in history.

➲ Later in the year, in April, Lipinski announced her intention to turn professional.

Practice made perfect for German luger Georg Hackl: after suffering the disappointment of a silver medal at the 1988 Winter Olympics he bounced back to take three consecutive gold medals between 1992 and 1998.

THREE-TIME OLYMPIC LUGE GLORY FOR HACKL

GEORG HACKL BECOMES FIRST LUGER IN HISTORY TO DEFEND OLYMPIC TITLE THREE TIMES

7–22 February 1998, Nagano, Japan

Slow starts cost Georg Hackl singles luge gold at the 1988 Winter Olympics (he took silver), so he went away, built a starting gate at his home track, and practised until he could be sure he never made the same mistake again. It paid off: four years later he beat Austria's Marcus Prock to gold by the closest margin in the event's 24-year history. He edged another close call with Prock two years later in Lillehammer to defend his title, but it was altogether more comfortable for Hackl in Nagano in 1998: wearing controversial aerodynamic boots, he recorded the fastest time in all four runs – the first in luge history to do so – to become the first luger to defend his Olympic title twice.

➲ In 2002, Hackl took silver in the singles luge to become the only luger in history to win medals at five consecutive Winter Olympics.

RUSEDSKI'S FASTEST SERVE IN HISTORY

GREG RUSEDSKI HITS FASTEST-EVER SERVE IN TENNIS HISTORY

14 March 1998, Indian Wells, California, USA

A promising junior player in his youth who collected his first Tour title at the age of 20, Greg Rusedski caused outrage in his native Canada when he decided to switch allegiance to Britain in 1995. The British tennis fraternity welcomed him with open arms. Renowned for his powerful serve, Rusedski reached the final of the US Open in 1997 – the first Briton to reach a grand slam final for 61 years – and ended the year at a career-high No. 4 in the world rankings. It was the highlight of his career: a couple of tournament wins apart, he was never capable of taking the next step up, although he did make the headlines in 1999 when, during his run to the Indian Wells final, he recorded the fastest serve in history: a staggering 149mph (239.7km/h).

➲ The record stood until 2004 when America's Andy Roddick delivered a 155mph (249.5km/h) thunderbolt during his Davis Cup singles match against Vladimir Voltchkov of Belarus.

Renowned for his powerful serve, Britain's Greg Rusedski powered his way into the record books in 1998 when he recorded a 149mph (239.7km/h) ace in a tournament at Indian Wells.

AUSTRALIA'S MOST SUCCESSFUL SPORTING EXPERIMENT

JIM STYNES BREAKS AFL RECORD FOR MOST CONSECUTIVE GAMES PLAYED

25 April 1998, Princes Park Stadium, Melbourne, Australia

Jim Stynes was already forging a reputation as a Gaelic football player of some renown – in 1984 he had played a full part in Dublin's win in the All-Ireland Minor Football Championships – when he spotted an advert in the paper from AFL team Melbourne Demons seeking players who possessed Gaelic football skills. Stynes tried out for the Demons, impressed everyone with his skills, went on a crash course of Australian Rules training and made his debut for the Demons' youth team in 1985. Progress was steady but slow: in 1987 he made his senior debut and went on to enjoy a record-breaking 11-year career – between round 17 in 1987 and round 4 in 1998 he played in an AFL-record 244 consecutive games.

➲ Stynes retired following the end of the 1998 season. A medal bearing his name is now awarded annually to the best player in the International Series.

It all started with a newspaper advert in Dublin, but Jim Stynes went on to enjoy a successful Australian Rules career and holds the record for most consecutive games played (244).

Jubilo Iwata's Masashi Nakayama made history during 14 days in 1998 when he became the first, and only, professional soccer player in history to score four hat-tricks in four games.

FOUR HAT-TRICKS IN FOUR CONSECUTIVE GAMES

MASASHI NAKAYAMA BECOMES FIRST PROFESSIONAL SOCCER PLAYER TO SCORE FOUR CONSECUTIVE HAT-TRICKS

29 April 1998, Yamaha Stadium, Iwata, Shizuoka, Japan

He was not particularly quick, did not possess the greatest of first touches and was not the sharpest shooter the game has ever seen, but Masashi Nakayama, nicknamed "Gon" on account of his off-the-field tomfoolery, combined a hard work ethic with an uncanny ability to be in the right place at the right time to become a talismanic figure for both his club, Jubilo Iwata, and country. The only player in J League history to score more than 150 goals, Nakayama also achieved something no player in world professional soccer had achieved before, or since: between 15 and 29 April 1998, he scored four hat-tricks in four consecutive games (amassing a total of 16 goals in the process).

➲ Nakayama also holds the record for the fastest-ever hat-trick in international soccer history, netting three times for Japan in 3m03s against Brunei on 16 February 2000.

GEBRSELASSIE COMPLETES WORLD, OLYMPIC AND WORLD RECORD SET

HAILE GEBRSELASSIE BREAKS THE 10,000M WORLD RECORD

1 June 1998, Hengelo, the Netherlands

In the seven years since Kenya's Yobes Ondieki became the first man in history to run the 10,000m in under 27 minutes, the world record had passed between four different athletes until August 1997, when another Kenyan, Paul Tergat, clocked 26m27.85s in Brussels to make the record his own. But throughout that time there had consistently been one class act in the 10,000m field: Ethiopia's Haile Gebrselassie, the reigning Olympic (Atlanta 1996) and world champion (1993, 1995 and 1997), who had himself held the world record for two short periods of time and who was now missing only the title of current world-record-holder from an already impressive CV. That all changed on 1 June 1998 when he clocked 26m22.75s in Hengelo, the Netherlands.

➲ Gebrselassie's mark would stand as a world record for six years until another Ethiopian, Kenenisa Bekele, clocked 26m20.31s in Ostrava, Czech Republic, on 8 June 2004.

The reigning world and Olympic champion, Haile Gebrselassie added the title of current world-record-holder to an already impressive list of accomplishments when he ran the 10,000m in 26m22.75s in June 1998.

JORDAN THREE-PEATS FOR THE SECOND TIME

MICHAEL JORDAN WINS HIS RECORD SIXTH AND LAST NBA FINALS MVP AWARD
14 June 1998, Delta Center, Salt Lake City, Utah, USA

When Michael Jordan announced his shock retirement from the NBA in 1993 following his heroics of three consecutive NBA Finals MVP awards, he could have been forgiven for sitting back and reminiscing about all the glorious basketball moments to have come his way. But that was not Jordan's style, and by the end of the 1994–95 season he was back. In 1995–96 he inspired the Chicago Bulls to a six-game finals win over the Seattle SuperSonics, with his performances enough to earn an all-time-record fourth MVP award. The fifth came the following year as the Bulls edged Utah Jazz in six games. The same teams squared off in the 1997–98 finals as well and once again Jordan was the difference between the two sides, completing the second finals MVP three-peat of his career.

➲ Jordan retired from the NBA for a second time on 13 January 1999 and claimed he was 99.9 per cent certain this time it would be for good: he was back within a year, this time playing for the Washington Wizards, but his best days were by then behind him.

The bigger the occasion, the better Michael Jordan played: he is the only man to have completed a hat-trick of NBA Finals MVP wins twice (1991–93 and 1996–98).

REBOUND RECORD FOR LESLIE

LISA LESLIE PULLS DOWN A WNBA SINGLE-GAME RECORD 21 REBOUNDS
19 June 1998, Staples Center, Los Angeles, California, USA

A legend in the game while still at high school – she scored a massive 101 points in the first half of a high-school game before the other team forfeited the match at half-time – Lisa Leslie went on to excel during her time at the University of Southern California (she was a four-time All-Pacific Ten Conference first-team selection) and played a full part in the United States' gold medal success at the 1996 Olympic Games. One of the original members of the WNBA, the 6ft 5in player showed her class in the professional season as well: in the league's second season, 1998, she pulled down a single-game record 21 rebounds in the Sparks's match against New York Liberty, a record that still stands to this day.

➲ On 30 July 2002, Leslie etched another line for herself in the history books when she became the first player in WNBA history to perform a slam-dunk.

It came as no surprise when Lisa Leslie became one of the WNBA's first standout performers: on 19 June 1998 she set a league single-game record for most rebounds with 21.

GOLDEN GOAL GLORY FOR FRANCE

LAURENT BLANC SCORES FIRST GOLDEN GOAL IN WORLD CUP FINALS HISTORY

28 June 1998, Stade Félix Bollaert, Lens, France

Hosts France had eased through the group stages of the 1998 World Cup, with a record of played three won three, and were strongly fancied to see off the challenge of surprise package Paraguay – who had qualified for the second round at the expense of Spain – in their march to the quarter-finals. But the French, without their talisman Zinedine Zidane, serving a two-match suspension after being sent off against Saudi Arabia, struggled. The match ended in a stalemate after 90 minutes and as the clock ticked down in the second period of extra-time, the dreaded penalty shootout seemed an inevitability. But up stepped veteran defender Laurent Blanc to crash home the ball in the 113th minute. The match was over: Blanc had netted the first golden goal in World Cup finals history and the French dream lived on.

It needed a 113th-minute golden goal – introduced at the World Cup for the first time in 1998 – from Laurent Blanc to take France past tenacious Paraguay in the second round.

➲ France went on to win the World Cup for the first time in their history, beating Italy on penalties in the quarter-finals and Croatia 2–1 in the semi-finals before their stunning, Zidane-inspired, 3–0 final victory over Brazil.

A veteran of five World Cups and the architect of some of the finest moments in German soccer history, Lothar Matthaeus finally called time on his World Cup journey having played in a record 25 matches in the competition.

MATTHAEUS REACHES THE END OF THE LINE

LOTHAR MATTHAEUS PLAYS IN RECORD 25TH AND LAST WORLD CUP FINALS MATCH

4 July 1998, Stade Gerland, Lyon, France

As the final whistle blew and Croatia's players celebrated their stunning 3–0 second-round victory over Germany in France '98, German captain Lothar Matthaeus sank to the turf: his spectacular World Cup odyssey was finally over. He had appeared in the West German squad in 1982, played a pivotal role in his country's feat of becoming the first team in history to reach three successive World Cup finals in 1982, 1986 and 1990, and in the latter had become only the third German in history to raise the World Cup trophy. But they were the good times: the Germans lost in the quarter-finals to little-fancied Bulgaria in 1994; then came the shock loss to Croatia four years later. After a record 25 World Cup finals matches, their talisman had finally run out of steam.

➲ Lothar Matthaeus may hold the all-time record for most World Cup finals appearances, but the record for most minutes played in the competition rests with Italy's Paolo Maldini (2,220 minutes compared to Mattheus's 2,052).

THE MOROCCAN MIDDLE-DISTANCE RUNNING KING

HICHAM EL GUERROUJ BREAKS 1,500M WORLD RECORD
14 July 1998, Rome, Italy

Hicham El Guerrouj first came to prominence when he finished third in the 5,000m final at the 1992 junior world championships. After missing a year through injury, he formed part of Morocco's 1994 world road relay championship-winning team and by 1995 had become the 1,500m world champion. He was starting to challenge Algerian Noureddine Morceli's stranglehold over the event, but suffered heartbreak at the 1996 Olympic Games when he tripped and fell in the 1,500m final and finished dead last as Morceli struck gold. A month later he became the first person to beat Morceli over 1,500m for four years ... and remained unbeaten in the event for the rest of the year (including a second 1,500m world championship gold). He confirmed his domination the following year when he clocked 3m26.00s in Rome to break Morceli's 1,500m world record (set in 1995) by a staggering 1.37s.

Hicham El Guerrouj ended Noureddine Morceli's stranglehold on the 1,500m: in 1996 he became the first person to beat the Algerian in four years and two years later shattered his world record time (2m27.37s) by a staggering 1.37s.

➲ El Guerrouj went on to defend his 1,500m world championship title in 1999, 2001 and 2003 and in 2004 picked up 1,500m and 5,000m gold at the Olympic Games in Athens. He retired from athletics in 2006 as the holder of both the 1,500m and mile world records.

Not every Brazilian prodigy has turned out to be a success: Real Betis paid a world-record £21.9 million for sensation Denilson, but he never lived up to either the hype or the price tag.

REAL BETIS BREAK THE BANK FOR DENILSON

DENILSON BECOMES THE WORLD'S MOST EXPENSIVE SOCCER PLAYER

July 1998, Manuel Ruiz de Lopera Stadium, Seville, Spain

The king of the "stand-still" step-over, Denilson had starred for Sao Paulo since 1995, had made his debut for the Brazilian national team in November 1996 (aged 19) and shot to international attention following some dazzling performances during the 1997 FIFA Confederations Cup, winning the Golden Ball award for the tournament's best player as Brazil won the competition for the first time. The European soccer scouts were salivating at his potential and the money men started to count their pennies. Shortly before the start of the World Cup, it was announced that Spanish side Real Betis had secured his signature for the following season for a fee of £21.9 million, breaking the world-record transfer fee (£19.5 million paid by Inter Milan to Barcelona in 1999 for the services of Ronaldo) by some £2.4 million.

➲ Denilson failed to live up to the price tag: he stayed with the club until 2005 (including a year out on loan at Flamenco), before he was sold to Bordeaux for an undisclosed fee. His fee stood as a world record until 1999, when Inter Milan paid Lazio £31 million for Christian Vieri.

TIME CATCHES UP WITH RECORD-BREAKING DURAN

ROBERTO DURAN BECOMES OLDEST BOXER IN HISTORY TO FIGHT FOR A WORLD TITLE

28 August 1998, Las Vegas Hilton, Las Vegas, Nevada, USA

Born and raised on the tough streets of Guarare, Panama, Roberto Duran became a professional boxer at the age of 16 and impressed everyone with his raw, explosive talent. When he added ring-craft to the mix, the man nicknamed "Hands of Stone" was virtually unstoppable. He enjoyed a five-decade-long career, was world champion four times – lightweight (1972–79), welterweight (1980), junior middleweight (1983–84) and middleweight (1989) – and was still fighting late into his 40s, with his nous and skills more than making up for the substantial age difference. He made history on 28 August 1998 when, aged 47 years 2 months 12 days, he fought 28-year-old William Joppy for the WBA middleweight crown: he lost in three rounds, but remains the oldest boxer in history to fight for a world championship belt.

➲ Duran's last fight came on 14 July 2001 (he lost by unanimous decision to Hector Camacho) and he finally retired in 2002 after suffering severe rib and lung injuries in a car accident.

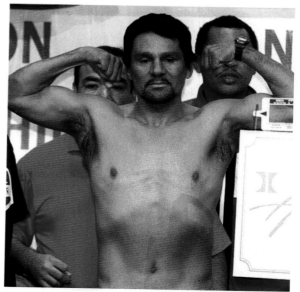

Pound for pound one of the greatest fighters ever to have lived, Roberto Duran made history in 1998 when, aged 47 years, he became the oldest boxer in history to compete in a world championship fight.

THE LITTLE MASTER TOPS THE ODI CENTURY CHARTS

SACHIN TENDULKAR BREAKS RECORD FOR MOST CENTURIES IN ONE-DAY INTERNATIONAL CRICKET

26 September 1998, Queens Sports Club, Bulawayo, Zimbabwe

Only 16 years old when he made his Test debut for India, Sachin Tendulkar was the schoolboy sensation who went on to live up to his billing in the international arena and who continues to enjoy a career of consistent overachievement. Success did not immediately come his way in the one-day international arena: his first hundred came in his 79th match and he followed it up with three successive ducks, but then the three-figure scores started to flow. It was only a matter of time before he would break Desmond Haynes's record for most ODI hundreds (17) and the moment finally came in September 1998, when the "Little Master" recorded his 18th century, against Zimbabwe in Bulawayo.

➲ In September 2006, Tendulkar became the first batsman in history to hit 40 one-day international centuries (with his innings of 141 not out against the West Indies in Kuala Lumpur). A year earlier he also surpassed Sunil Gavaskar's all-time record for most Test centuries (34).

Hailed by Donald Bradman as his modern incarnation, Sachin Tendulkar went on to produce one of the most sensational careers in either form of the game and, in September 1998, he overtook Desmond Haynes's all-time record for most one-day international centuries (17).

THE HIGHEST SPEED ON A SKATEBOARD

GARY HARDWICK RECORDS HIGHEST-EVER SPEED ON A SKATEBOARD

26 September 1998, Fountain Hills, Arizona, USA

There are two competitive types of skateboarding: the technical type seen in specialized parks around the world, and speed skateboarding, a no-thrills alternative requiring little more than the right equipment and the courage to stand upright on a skateboard and watch the speedometer climb higher and higher until you pass through the speed trap. The greatest exponent of the latter was Gary Hardwick and on 26 September 1998 during a race in Fountain Hills, in the McDowell Mountain foothills in Arizona, the Californian, wearing an aerodynamic bodysuit and helmet, clocked a speed of 62.55mph (100.66km/h) to break the world record by some 10mph.

➲ Hardwick's record is for the highest unassisted speed on a skateboard. On 15 May 1998, Billy Copeland had slapped eight jetpacks of fuel onto the back of his skateboard and shot off at a speed of 70mph (112.65km/h).

During a race in Fountain Hills, Arizona, Californian Gary Hardwick clocked the highest speed ever recorded on a skateboard.

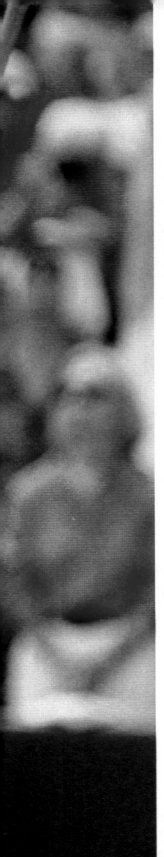

BIG MAC WINS THE GREAT HOME RUN CHASE

MARK McGWIRE BREAKS ROGER MARIS'S SINGLE-SEASON RECORD FOR HOME RUNS

27 September 1998, Busch Stadium II, St Louis, Missouri, USA

As the 1998 MLB season dawned, press speculation reached a fever pitch. This was finally going to be the year when someone finally broke Roger Maris's 1961 single-season home run record (61). The only question was whether Mark McGwire (St Louis Cardinals) or Ken Griffey Jr (Seattle Mariners) would be the man to break it. By the end of May, McGwire led Griffey by 27 home runs to 18 and was on course for an 80-home-run season. Press speculation mounted, and hit fever pitch by the time Sammy Sosa joined the race, to end June tied with Griffey on 33 home runs, four behind McGwire. The three remained competitive entering August, but by the end of the month only two remained in the race: McGwire and Sosa, both of whom were tied on 55. On 8 September, the Cardinals faced off against the Cubs and Sosa was on hand to see McGwire slam his 62nd home run of the season to break Maris's record. The St Louis slugger would end the season with 70; second-placed Sosa had to be content with 66. Griffey finished on 56.

⊃ McGwire's 70 home runs would stand as a single-season record until 2001, when the San Francisco Giants' Barry Bonds hit 73.

In one of the most exciting showdowns in baseball history, St Louis Cardinals slugger Mark McGwire came out on top of the "Great Home Run Race" to break Roger Maris's single-season record for home runs.

RECORD-BREAKING YANKEES SWEEP ALL BEFORE THEM

NEW YORK YANKEES BREAK THE RECORD FOR MOST WINS IN A SEASON
27 September 1998, Yankee Stadium, New York, USA

If 1998 was all about the thrills and spills of the Great Home Run Race between Mark McGwire and Sammy Sosa, the New York Yankees also played their part in what some have described as the greatest season in baseball history and others as the year the sport finally won back the fans after the horrors of the strike-shortened 1994 season. Not for the first time in their history, the Yankees, under the stewardship of Joe Torres, were the class act of the American League, finishing on top of the East Division a massive 22 wins ahead of their great rivals the Boston Red Sox with an all-time-record 114 wins to eclipse the mark set by the Yankees class of 1927.

➲The Yankees continued to sweep all before them in the post-season, beating the Texas Rangers 3–0 in the divisional playoff, overcoming the impressive Cleveland Indians in the championship final 4–2 and then sweeping the San Diego Padres 4–0 in the World Series to collect the franchise's 24th Fall Classic.

The New York Yankees' performances during the 1998 baseball season may have been little more than a sideshow compared to the Mark McGwire–Sammy Sosa home run battle, but they put together the most impressive regular season in baseball history, winning an astonishing 114 games.

450

THE FIRST MAN TO SWIM THE ATLANTIC OCEAN

BENOIT LECOMTE BECOMES THE FIRST PERSON TO SWIM THE ATLANTIC

28 September 1998, Quiberon, Brittany, France

Born in France, Benoit Lecomte emigrated to Austin, Texas, at the age of 23 in 1990. Two years later, after the death of his father from colon cancer, Lecomte decided to do something extraordinary to honour his memory and to raise funds for cancer research: he would become the first man to swim the Atlantic. After two years of hard training, Lecomte, trailed by a support boat, set off from Hyannis, Massachusetts, with eight wetsuits, a snorkel and a pair of flippers. Swimming six-to-eight-hour sessions a day – before resting and sleeping on the boat – he powered his way through rough seas and the threat of sharks and, exhausted, completed his 3,737-mile (5,600km) journey in 73 days.

➲ Lecomte's support boat projected an electromagnetic field with a 25ft radius to ward off the threat of sharks, but the swimmer was tracked for some time by a 10ft shark that hovered some 30ft below where he swam.

To honour his father and in an attempt to raise funds for cancer research, Benoit Lecomte became the first person in history to swim across the Atlantic. He raised $150,000 for his troubles and earned a place for himself in the history books.

Venus Williams underlined her status as the most powerful server women's tennis has ever seen when she unleashed a 127.4mph missile during her quarter-final match against Mary Pierce at the European Indoor Championships in Zurich in October 1998.

WILLIAMS'S SERVE HITS DIZZYING NEW HEIGHTS

VENUS WILLIAMS HITS THE FASTEST SERVE RECORDED IN WOMEN'S TENNIS

16 October 1998, Zurich, Switzerland

Venus Williams turned professional in October 1994 and was playing a full Tour schedule by 1997. The qualities that would see her become one of the standout performers in women's tennis history were soon apparent: quick around the court, a double-handed backhand of tracer-like accuracy and power, a deft touch at the net and a first serve that would put many players on the men's tour to shame. Her breakthrough season came in 1998 when she picked up her first three Tour wins, but it was her performance in the European Indoor Championships in Zurich that set tongues wagging: serving at match point in her quarter-final clash with Mary Pierce, she delivered a 127.4mph (205.02km/h) ace to take the match and a place in the record books: it was the fastest serve in the history of women's tennis.

➲ Venus broke her own record when she blasted a 128mph serve at the 2007 French Open.

Gary Anderson's perfect season also saw him break the NFL record for the most points scored in a season without scoring a touchdown. He ended the regular season with 164 points to his name.

THE NFL'S FIRST PERFECT SEASON

GARY ANDERSON FIRST KICKER IN NFL HISTORY TO POST "PERFECT" REGULAR SEASON

26 December 1998, Vanderbilt Stadium, Nashville, Tennessee, USA

Born and raised in South Africa, Gary Anderson moved to the United States after he had graduated from high school, as a protest against the South African government's Apartheid policy. Although he dreamed of becoming a professional soccer player in Europe, he began practising kicking with an American football and discovered an uncanny talent for kicking goals. He went to Syracuse University and was drafted by the Buffalo Bills in 1982: it was the start of a journeyman career that saw him in and out of clubs – five of them by 1998 when, in what turned out to be his signature year with the Minnesota Vikings, aged 39, Anderson managed to do what no kicker had done before him – he recorded a perfect regular season, kicking 35 of 35 field goals and 59 of 59 extra points.

⊃ Ironically, Anderson's kicking streak came to an end when it mattered most: he missed a crucial last-minute kick for the Vikings in a playoff match against the Atlanta Falcons and saw his team crash 30–27 in overtime. In 2003, the Indianapolis Colts kicker Mike Vanderjagt became the first kicker in history to record both a perfect regular season and post-season.

THE GREAT ONE RETIRES FROM PRO HOCKEY

WAYNE GRETZKY, THE NHL'S MOST HONOURED PLAYER, HANGS UP HIS SKATES AFTER 20 YEARS ON THE ICE

18 April 1999, Madison Square Garden, New York, USA

In a sport long derided for brutish antics, Wayne Gretzky was something special. What he lacked in athletic stature (he was 6 feet tall and weighed 160 lbs in his rookie year), he made up for in style and intuition. And it worked: by the time he retired in 1999, Gretzky was the holder of more records than any other player in NHL history, including most career goals and points and most single-season goals and points. He had also won scads of awards, including the Lady Byng Trophy (for most gentlemanly player) four times and the Hart Trophy (for Most Valuable Player in the League) five times. Gretzky was named an Officer of the Order of Canada in 1984, though it took him four years to get off the ice long enough to attend his own investiture.

Gretzky's climb to glory started early: the 16-year-old was already racking up points galore when he appeared as the youngest player in the World Junior Championships in Montreal in 1978—where he was the top scorer.

⊃ Gretzky's retirement did not end his involvement with hockey. Not only is he coach for the Phoenix Coyotes, but as executive director of Canada's Olympic men's hockey team, he helped bring home gold at the 2002 Winter Olympics in Salt Lake City.

THE QUEEN OF WOMEN'S SOCCER

MIA HAMM BREAKS SOCCER'S ALL-TIME INTERNATIONAL GOAL RECORD
22 May 1999, Orlando, Florida, USA

Capable of keeping up with her older brother and his friends during her childhood, Mia Hamm started to play soccer seriously by the age of 12 and within three years was making her debut for the US national team. She enhanced her reputation at the University of North Carolina, leading the Tar Heelers to four NCAA championships and setting the all-time college record for most goals scored (103), but it was on the international stage that her star shone the brightest. She played in five of six games, scoring twice, as the US won the World Cup for the first time in 1991 (aged 19 at the time, she remains the tournament's youngest winner); won the Player of the Tournament at the 1995 World Cup (the US were eliminated in the semi-finals); and fought off an ankle injury to lead the US to Olympic gold in Atlanta in 1996. By then the most recognized female soccer player on the planet, she went on to break the all-time record, male or female, for most international goals when she netted for the 108th time on 22 May 1999, against Brazil in Orlando, Florida.

⮑ Later in the year Hamm helped the US to the second World Cup win in their history. She retired in 2004 after 275 internationals with a record 158 goals to her name.

More than anyone Mia Hamm propelled women's soccer into the mainstream of American consciousness: in May 1999 she became the most prolific goal-scorer in international soccer when she netted for the 108th time in US colours.

453

LOCKETT ENDS COVENTRY'S REIGN AS ALL-TIME TOP SCORER

TONY LOCKETT BREAKS ALL-TIME AFL/VFL RECORD FOR MOST GOALS

6 June 1999, Sydney Cricket Ground, Sydney, Australia

Tony Lockett first displayed his talents for St Kilda in the opening game of the 1984 season when he scored seven goals against Essendon: in a short time he developed a reputation as one of the AFL's real hard men and as one of the finest full-forwards ever to play the game. He scored 898 goals in 183 games for St Kilda before a shock transfer to Sydney in 1995 and did much to enhance the AFL's profile in the rugby-dominated city. By 1999 he was closing in fast on Gordon Coventry's 62-year-old career scoring record (1,299) and passed the mark to great fanfare on 6 June when he scored his third goal of the match against Essendon – his 1,300th career goal.

➲ Lockett retired midway through the 2002 season with 1,360 goals to his name, a record many consider unlikely to be broken.

Tall and strong, possessing a great leap and one of the most accurate boots in the history of the game, Tony Lockett broke Gordon Coventry's AFL/VFL record for most career goals that had stood since 1937 when he struck his 1,300th career goal in June 1999.

Andre Agassi had the game to trouble opponents on any surface, and in 1999 he became one of only five men in tennis history to complete the career grand slam.

REJUVENATED AGASSI COMPLETES CAREER GRAND SLAM

ANDRE AGASSI BECOMES THE OLDEST PLAYER IN TENNIS HISTORY TO WIN CAREER GRAND SLAM

7 June 1999, Roland Garros, Paris, France

Though he was a three-time grand slam finalist by the age of 21, Andre Agassi's 1992 Wimbledon win from the baseline came as a surprise to many. But Agassi's ability to hit the ball early caused opponents problems on any surface. In 1994 he became the first unseeded player to win the US Open; a year later he entered the Australian Open for the first time and won. In 1997 he slumped to No. 141 in the world rankings. It was a turning-point: he dug deep and trained harder than ever. It paid dividends in 1999 when he came back from two sets to love down to beat Andrei Medvedev in the French Open final to become only the fifth man in history to complete the career grand slam and, at 29 years of age, the oldest.

➲ Agassi went on to add a second US Open title to his grand slam haul later in the year and three more Australian Open titles (in 2000, 2001 and 2003). His total of eight grand slams put him seventh on the all-time list.

MAURICE GREENE BECOMES THE FASTEST MAN ON EARTH

MAURICE GREENE BREAKS THE 100M WORLD RECORD
16 June 1999, Athens, Greece

Maurice Greene's first major international appearance came in the 1995 World Championships: he crashed out of the 100m in the quarter-finals. The following year he failed to qualify for the US team for the 1996 Olympic Games – and sat on the sidelines as Canada's Donovan Bailey clocked a new world-record time of 9.84s. It was time for action: Greene upped sticks and moved to Los Angeles to train with the John Smith camp and in 1997 was transformed, becoming 100m world champion in Athens with a time of 9.86s. Now the dominant force in the 100m, he started to hanker after not only Donovan's record but also the ultimate quest of every 100m runner at the time: Ben Johnson's "illegal" time of 9.79s. He equalled Johnson's time on 16 June 1999 in Athens to break the world record by 0.05s – the largest single improvement in the event since the introduction of electronic timing.

⮊ Later in the year Greene became the first man in history to win the 100m–200m double at the World Championships. His 100m record would stand for almost six years, until Jamaica's Asafa Powell clocked 9.77s in Athens on 14 June 2005.

It had taken 11 years, but on 16 June 1999, America's Maurice Greene matched Ben Johnson's time of 9.79s for the 100m ... and this time it was legal.

Considered the father of skateboarding, Tony Hawk cemented his place in the sport's history in 1999 when he became the first to land the two-and-a-half-rotation "900".

HAWK LANDS SKATEBOARDING'S FIRST 900

TONY HAWK BECOMES FIRST IN SKATEBOARDING HISTORY TO LAND THE "900"

27 June 1999, Pier 30 and 32, San Francisco, California, USA

Tony Hawk's life changed for ever when his older brother handed him a skateboard at the age of nine. A troublesome child, all of a sudden he had found something through which he could channel his considerable energy and search for perfection. He excelled: by 14 years of age he was a professional and by 17 was considered the best in the world. As skateboarding's popularity grew in the 1980s, Hawk was always to the fore and is credited not only as being the father of modern skateboarding but also the creator of over 80 moves. His signature moment came on 27 June 1999 at the X Games in San Francisco when, live on television, he became the first in history to land a "900" – a jump of two-and-a-half rotations (900°).

➲ Hawk entered 103 professional tournaments during his career, won a staggering 73 of them and finished second 19 times. It is the greatest record in skateboarding history.

PALERMO'S PENALTY WOE

MARTIN PALERMO FIRST INTERNATIONAL SOCCER PLAYER TO MISS A HAT-TRICK OF PENALTIES

4 July 1990, Estadio Feliciano Cacares, Luque, Paraguay

The 1999 Copa America had started brightly for Argentina's new scoring sensation Martin Palermo, as the striker hit the back of the net twice during Argentina's 3–1 opening win over Ecuador. But then came Colombia and for Palermo and Argentina it was a day to forget. Argentina were awarded a penalty in the fifth minute: Palermo missed. Colombia took the lead five minutes later, from the penalty spot. Argentina were awarded another penalty in the 47th minute: this time German Burgos missed. Penalty No. 3 came Argentina's way in the 76th minute: Palermo missed. Colombia raced into a 3–0 lead, but the drama was far from over. Argentina were awarded their fourth penalty of the match. Cue Palermo. Cue another miss. He had become the first player in international soccer history to miss a hat-trick of penalties.

➲ The consequence of the defeat was that Argentina failed to win their group and faced a showdown with bitter rivals Brazil in the quarter-finals. They lost 2–1. Palermo was dropped from the side, suffered a serious injury later in the year and never played for the national side again.

In one of the most inglorious moments in international soccer history, Argentina striker Martin Palermo missed a hat-trick of penalties during his country's 1999 Copa America match against Colombia.

EL GUERROUJ CROWNED KING OF MIDDLE-DISTANCE RUNNING

HICHAM EL GUERROUJ BREAKS NOUREDDINE MORCELI'S MILE WORLD RECORD

7 July 1999, Rome, Italy

Hicham El Guerrouj's story is one of banishing the memories of a bitter disappointment through grim determination, sublime talent and a burning desire to end Noureddine Morceli's domination of middle-distance running. The nadir came when El Guerrouj tripped and fell in the Olympic 1,500m final in 1996 and finished last; Morceli took gold. Two months later El Guerrouj ended Morceli's four-year unbeaten streak in the 1,500m; in 1993 he ended the Algerian's reign as world champion; in 1998 he smashed Morceli's 1,500m world record time (which had stood since 1995) by over a second. But the icing on the cake came when he smashed Morceli's mile world-record time (3m44.39s set in Rieti in September 1993) in Rome, clocking the staggering time of 3m43.13s.

➲ El Guerrouj's mile world record still stands to this day and he would go on to dominate the 1,500m event as well: in 2003 he collected a record fourth consecutive World Championship title.

Morocco's Hicham El Guerrouj shrugged off the disappointment of a last-place finish in the 1,500m final at the 1996 Olympic Games by going on to win every honour available to him, including breaking the mile world record in July 1999.

Mario Cipollini (in red, left) showed his mastery of sprint cycling when he emerged from the pack to win the Laval-to-Blois stage of the 1999 Tour de France in the fastest time in the race's long history.

THE LION KING FINALLY FINDS HIS ROAR

MARIO CIPOLLINI RECORDS FASTEST-EVER TIME IN NON-TIME-TRIAL STAGE OF THE TOUR DE FRANCE

7 July 1999, Blois, France

His power and speed had earned him the nickname "The Lion King" and the title of one of the greatest sprint riders ever to have lived, but Italy's Mario Cipollini, a record 42-time stage-winner on the Giro d'Italia, had always enjoyed mixed fortunes in the Tour de France. There had been good times – he wore the yellow jersey for two days in 1997 – and bad – Cipollini withdrew from the race the moment the Tour reached the climbing stages. And the Italian had made a quiet start to the 1999 Tour, finishing the first four stages in 29th, third and tenth places respectively. He roared into life in the 194.5km (121-mile) fourth stage between Laval and the Loire Valley city of Blois, crossing the line in a non-time-trial-record time of 3h51m45s.

➲ Cipollini's average speed during the stage of 50.3km/h (31mph) also exceeded the record of 49.4km/h (30.7mph) set by Belgian Jean Bruynell in the Evreux-to-Amiens stage in 1993.

457

Michael Johnson was the class act of the field in the 400m World Championship final in 1999: he crossed the line some 1.19s ahead of second-placed Sanderlei Clara Parrela in a world-record-breaking time of 43.18s.

JOHNSON POWERS TO 400M WORLD BEST

MICHAEL JOHNSON BREAKS 11-YEAR-OLD WORLD RECORD

30 April 1986, Northlands Coliseum, Edmonton, Alberta, Canada

Michael Johnson set the 1996 Olympic Games in Atlanta alight with his dazzling world-record-breaking performance in the 200m final, taking him to gold and completing a unique 200m–400m double. And his star continued to burn bright, despite a loss to 100m Olympic champion Donovan Bailey in a showdown over 150m for the title "The Fastest Man on Earth", when he pulled up halfway through the race with injury. Johnson recovered in time to defend his 400m title at the 1997 World Championships and travelled to Seville, Spain, for the 1999 championships seeking to become the first man in history to win the event on four consecutive occasions. He did so in style, clocking 43.18s to break Butch Reynolds's world record (43.29s) that had stood since 1988.

➲ Johnson retired from athletics in 2000 having defended his Olympic 400m title in Sydney. His 200m and 400m world-record times still stand to this day.

SOCCER'S £32 MILLION MAN

INTER MILAN PAY LAZIO WORLD-RECORD FEE FOR CHRISTIAN VIERI

August 1999, San Siro Stadium, Milan, Italy

Christian Vieri's climb up soccer's ladder was anything but rapid. The striker's early career path followed a distinct trend: play for one season at a club, show a marked improvement and then get snapped up by another club in soccer's summer sale. But 1997 was the year he finally made his name: aged 23, with seven clubs already behind him, he moved to Atletico Madrid, scored 24 goals in 24 matches and ended the season as La Liga's top scorer. He excelled in the 1998 World Cup, forming an effective frontline partnership with Roberto Baggio. It prompted a move to Lazio: Vieri scored 12 Serie A goals, helped the *biancocelesti* to the European Cup-Winners' Cup and caught the eye of Inter Milan, who, come summer-sale time, promptly paid a world record £32 million for his services.

➲ Vieri remained with Inter Milan until the end of the 2005 season, making 190 league appearances for the *nerazzurri* and scoring 123 goals. His £32 million transfer fee would stand as a world record until the following summer when Lazio paid Parma £36 million for striker Hernan Crespo.

His early career may have resembled that of a journeyman soccer player, but Christian Vieri blossomed into the world's most expensive soccer player when Inter Milan paid Lazio £32 million for his services in the summer of 1999.

THE DOWNHILL MOUNTAIN BIKE KING

NICOLAS VOUILLOZ FIRST FIVE-TIME WINNER OF DOWNHILL MOUNTAIN BIKE WORLD CHAMPIONSHIPS
September 1999, Are, Jamtland, Sweden

Nicolas Vouilloz brought a sense of professionalism and a new dedication to the science of speed to downhill mountain bike racing: he was the first to utilize telemetry and technology in his bike's suspension, for example. It resulted in him becoming not only the standout performer in the sport, but also the dominant force in a sport renowned for its fractions – when jumps and ramps were introduced to the sport in the mid-1990s to satisfy the demands of a growing television audience, Vouilloz coped better than anyone else. A multiple world junior and French national champion, he enjoyed particular success in the downhill mountain bike world championship scene from 1995 to 1999, winning the title a record five consecutive times.

Nicolas Vouilloz confirmed his reputation as the greatest downhill mountain biker in history when he collected five consecutive world championships between 1995 and 1999.

➲ Vouilloz added further titles in 2001 and 2002 before switching his attentions to rally driving. He returned to professional mountain bike racing in 2007.

TEENAGE SENSATION GARCIA MAKES RYDER CUP HISTORY

SERGIO GARCIA BECOMES YOUNGEST PLAYER IN HISTORY TO APPEAR IN RYDER CUP
25 September 1999, The Country Club, Brookline, Massachusetts, USA

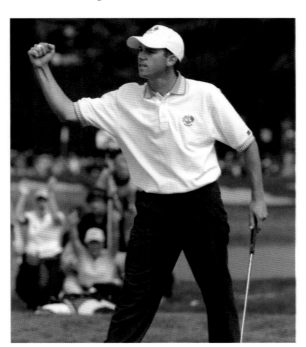

Sergio Garcia burst onto the international golf scene at the 1999 PGA Championships: his second-place finish in the event led to him becoming the youngest Ryder Cup player in history.

Sergio Garcia started playing golf at the age of three and by the age of 12 was his club's champion golfer. Three years later he became the youngest player in history to make the cut at a European Tour event (the Turespana Open) and later in the year became the European amateur championships' youngest-ever winner. He turned professional shortly after finishing as low amateur at the 1999 Masters and shot into the international spotlight at that year's PGA Championships when he pushed Tiger Woods all the way before finishing second. His performance earned him automatic selection for Europe's 1999 Ryder Cup team and he made history on 25 September 1999 when he partnered Jesper Parnevik in the morning fourballs to become, aged 19 years, 8 months and 15 days, the youngest player in Ryder Cup history.

➲ It was a Ryder Cup to remember for the Spaniard. He scored 3½ out of a possible 5 points as Europe lost 13½–14½.

MAKINEN MAKES IT FOUR IN A ROW

TOMMI MAKINEN FIRST TO WIN WORLD RALLY CHAMPIONSHIP ON FOUR CONSECUTIVE OCCASIONS
13 October 1999, San Remo, Italy

A former Finnish ploughing champion (in 1982 and 1985), Tommi Makinen first started rally driving at the age of 21 in 1985 and appeared in the World Rally Championships for the first time two years later. But the Finn's progress through the ranks was far from swift: he recorded his first race win (100 Lakes Rally in his native Finland) in 1994 and didn't get a full-time race seat until the following year. But the moment he was placed behind the wheel of the Ralliart Mitsubishi Lancer Evolution he was unstoppable, holding off the attentions of Colin McRae to claim his first title in 1996 and defending his title over the next three years (1997–99) to become the first driver in history to win the World Rally Championship on four consecutive occasions.

➲ Makinen's career effectively ended following a crash in the 2002 Corsican Rally that left his co-driver Risto Mannisenmaki with a broken back. He stands alongside Juha Kankkunen and Sebastien Loeb as the World Rally Championships' only four-time champions.

Tommi Makinen may have been a relatively slow starter on the World Rally Championship scene, but from the moment he secured a full-time ride with Mitsubishi in 1995 he was virtually unstoppable, collecting four consecutive world championships between 1996 and 1999, a feat since equalled by Frenchman Sebastien Loeb.

The New York Yankees' Fall Classic success in 1999 was their 25th World Series win: it took them past ice-hockey giants Montreal Canadiens' haul of 24 Stanley Cup wins to make them the most successful club in North American sports history.

➲ The Yankees completed a hat-trick of World Series victories in 2000 when they beat the New York Mets 4–1.

NORTH AMERICA'S MOST SUCCESSFUL FRANCHISE

NEW YORK YANKEES BECOME MOST SUCCESSFUL FRANCHISE IN NORTH AMERICAN SPORTS HISTORY
27 October 1999, Yankee Stadium, New York, USA

Think baseball and you think of the blue pin-striped New York Yankees; you think Babe Ruth, Joe DiMaggio, Mickey Mantle et al., but through the 1970s, '80s and early '90s the Bronx Bombers had lost their aim and it wasn't until Joe Torre's arrival in 1995 that a new breed of Yankees finally dared live up to the club's formidable history. They took the title in 1996 to end the 18-year drought and once again two years later – producing the greatest regular season in MLB history (with 114 wins). And although they failed to hit such dizzying heights in 1999, they swept Atlanta in the Fall Classic to claim their 25th World Series. It took them past the Montreal Canadiens' haul of 24 Stanley Cups and confirmed what everybody already knew: the Yankees were the most successful franchise in North American sports history.

THE YOUNGEST SOLO NON-STOP CIRCUMNAVIGATION

JESSE MARTIN BECOMES YOUNGEST PERSON TO COMPLETE NON-STOP SOLO CIRCUMNAVIGATION

31 October 1999, Sandringham Yacht Club, Melbourne, Australia

Born in Germany in 1981 before his family moved to Australia when he was two, Jesse Martin lived a life of adventure from a young age. He sailed for the first time aged 14 and the experience fuelled a passion to sail around the world. Aged just 17, he left Melbourne in a 34ft sloop called *Lionheart-Mistral* on 7 December 1998, sailed south of New Zealand, across the South Pacific, around South America, north through the Atlantic before turning south and passing Africa, via the Indian Ocean and back to Australia. A crowd of 25,000 flocked to celebrate his return on 31 October 1999: aged 18, he had become the youngest person in history to complete a solo circumnavigation.

➲ Martin took 328 days to complete the 27,000-mile journey and documented his progress on both paper (his book *Lionheart: A Journey of the Human Spirit* went on to become a bestseller) and film (a documentary titled *Lionheart: The Jesse Martin Story* was also released).

Claiming "I'm a normal kid fulfilling my dreams", Jesse Martin left Melbourne on 7 December 1998 in an attempt to become the youngest person in history to complete a solo non-stop circumnavigation. He returned 328 days later, aged 18, to the acclaim of the world.

AUSTRALIA CONTINUE NETBALL DOMINANCE

AUSTRALIA FIRST TEAM TO WIN THREE CONSECUTIVE NETBALL WORLD CHAMPIONSHIPS

October 1999, Christchurch, New Zealand

By the time the netball world championships arrived in Sydney, Australia, in 1999, the tournament had been, since its inception in 1963, a primarily antipodean affair, with Australia claiming the title five times and New Zealand three (the 1987 tournament ended in a three-way tie between Australia, New Zealand and hosts Trinidad and Tobago). Playing in front of their home fans, Australia wrested the trophy away from their arch-rivals in 1991, comfortably retained it four years later when the tournament came to England and became the first country in history to complete a back-to-back hat-trick of wins when they fought off a persistent challenge from hosts New Zealand to win the 1999 final by a single point.

➲ New Zealand gained their revenge four years later in Kingston, Jamaica, when they beat Australia 49–47 in the final to win the tournament for the fourth time.

Australia's shock single-point win over strong favourites New Zealand in the 1999 netball world championship final saw them become the first team to win the tournament outright three times in a row.

LOMU BACK TO DEVASTATING BEST

JONAH LOMU SCORES TOURNAMENT-RECORD EIGHT TRIES DURING 1999 RUGBY WORLD CUP
31 October 1999, Twickenham, London, England

Jonah Lomu's power game first came to international attention during the 1994 Hong Kong Sevens tournament and later that year he became the youngest All Black in history, aged 19 years, 45 days, when he made his debut against France. He travelled to South Africa for the 1995 Rugby World Cup with just two caps to his name, but set the tournament alight, scoring seven tries altogether, and although New Zealand lost to South Africa in the final, Lomu's face had become the most recognized in the game. Then disaster struck: in 1996 he was diagnosed with a rare kidney disorder and was out of the game for a year. He was back by 1998, but some way short of his intimidating best. The critics had a field day, but Lomu answered them in style, scoring a tournament-record eight tries in six appearances at the 1999 Rugby World Cup. New Zealand lost in the semi-finals to France, but Lomu emerged from the wreckage of that defeat with his reputation as the world's best player very much intact.

➲ Jonah Lomu's record has since been equalled by South Africa's Bryan Habana, who scored eight tries during South Africa's triumphal march to the 2007 Rugby World Cup.

Having shot onto the international stage in devastating fashion at the 1995 Rugby World Cup, Jonah Lomu was struck down by a serious illness, but he was back to his best in time for the 1999 edition of the tournament, scoring a record eight tries.

THE KING OF EUROPEAN GOLF

COLIN MONTGOMERIE WINS THE EUROPEAN ORDER OF MERIT FOR RECORD SEVENTH TIME

31 October 1999, Montecastillo, Jerez, Spain

Colin Montgomerie put together a promising amateur career (including two appearances in the Walker Cup) before turning professional in 1988. His first Tour win came two years later at the Portuguese Open; he qualified for the European Ryder Cup team in 1991; and in 1993 two victories, coupled with a series of consistent performances, were enough to see him capture his first Order of Merit title. By now the best golfer in Europe, he continually fell short in the major tournaments – he finished runner-up at both the 1994 and 1997 US Opens, the 1995 US PGA Championship and the 1997 US Open – but where he was fallible in America he was invincible in Europe, hanging on to his European Order of Merit title for a record seven straight seasons between 1993 and 1999.

⊃ Montgomerie's reign as Europe's best golfer came to an end in 2000 when England's Lee Westwood captured the Order of Merit title for the first time. Montgomerie reclaimed the title in 2005.

He may have been dubbed the "best player never to win a major", but where Colin Montgomerie failed in America he triumphed in Europe, winning the continent's Order of Merit a record seven years in a row between 1993 and 1999.

Australia benefited from a lacklustre French performance in the 1999 Rugby World Cup final to win 35–12 and become the tournament's first two-time winners.

WALLABIES WALTZ TO SECOND WORLD CUP

AUSTRALIA BECOME THE FIRST TWO-TIME WINNERS OF THE RUGBY WORLD CUP

6 November 1999, Millennium Stadium, Cardiff, Wales

France had little time to celebrate their inspired shock win over New Zealand in the semi-finals of the 1999 Rugby World Cup: their thoughts immediately turned to the final against Australia (world champions in 1991) and thoughts of what had happened to the French team of 1987, who had shocked Australia in the semi-final before feebly falling to New Zealand in the final. But history repeated itself: it was a game too far for Les Bleus and Australia were the beneficiaries, scoring two tries (through Ben Tune and Owen Finnegan) to finish comfortable 35–12 winners and become the first team to lift the William Webb Ellis trophy on two occasions.

⊃ Australia were joined as two-time winners in the tournament by South Africa in 2007 (they also won the trophy in 1995).

THE KING OF THE WAVES

BJORN DUNKERBECK WINS RECORD 12TH WINDSURFING WORLD CHAMPIONSHIP

12 November 1999, Ho'okipa Beach Park, Maui, Hawaii, USA

Born on 16 July 1969 to a Dutch father and a Danish mother, Bjorn Dunkerbeck grew up on the windswept beach of Pozo, Gran Canaria, and first picked up a boom and sail at the age of eight. It was an instant love affair: in 1981, aged 12, he took part in his first windsurfing regatta. Three years later he finished fifth in his first World Cup event; in 1986, still only 17 years old, he was ranked sixth overall in the world; the following year he was second. But by 1988 he was the undisputed king of the waves, winning the overall world title for the first time. And once he got hold of it he refused to let go, dominating the sport for the next 11 years to complete a record haul of 12 titles.

⮑ In addition to his 12 overall world titles, Dunkerbeck has also won 12 world race championships (1988–99), seven wave championships (1990, 1992–95, 1999 and 2001), was the world freestyle champion in 1998 and the world speed champion in 1994.

No one has dominated the sport of windsurfing like Bjorn Dunkerbeck: between 1988 and 1999 he won a staggering 12 consecutive overall world titles.

PINCAY JR PASSES SHOEMAKER'S ALL-TIME JOCKEY MARK

LAFFIT PINCAY JR BREAKS BILL SHOEMAKER'S JOCKEY RECORD FOR MOST WINS

10 December 1999, Hollywood Park Racetrack, California, USA

Laffit Pincay Jr began riding in his native Panama before moving to the United States in 1966 at the age of 19 and winning eight of his first 11 races. It set the pattern for his stellar career, but it was no easy ride: he was plagued by weight problems and had to overcome the tragic loss of his wife in 1985. But the winners kept coming: he rode Swale to victory at the 1984 Kentucky Derby and rode three winners at the Belmont Stakes, though the majority of his wins came on the southern Californian circuit. On 10 December 1999, at the age of 52, he made history when he rode Irish Nip to victory in the sixth race at Hollywood Park Racetrack to break Bill Shoemaker's record for most wins: it was his 8,834th winner.

⮑ Laffit Pincay Jr retired in April 2003 at the age of 56 – after breaking his neck in a fall – with 9,530 winners to his name, a figure surpassed by Russell Baze on 1 December 2006.

It took Laffit Pincay Jr 44,647 rides to record his 8,834 wins; in contrast, Bill Shoemaker had taken just 40,350 races to notch up 8,833 career victories.

Dan Marino finally called time on his legendary career after the 1999 NFL season: he left the game with many records to his name, some of which have since been broken. His passing records of 61,361 yards and 422 touchdowns fell to Brett Favre, who finished the 2007 season with 61,655 yards and 442 TDs.

MARINO CALLS TIME ON RECORD-BREAKING CAREER

DAN MARINO RETIRES FROM NFL WITH ALL-TIME RECORD FOR MOST YARDS PASSED

13 March 2000, Miami, Florida, USA

Dan Marino burst onto the NFL scene in spectacular style: in 1983 he became the first rookie quarterback in history to appear in the Pro Bowl; the following year he broke six NFL single-season records, was voted the NFL's most valuable player and made the one and only Super Bowl appearance of his career (a 38–16 loss against a Joe Montana-inspired San Francisco 49ers). But despite the Miami Dolphins' post-season woes, Marino, with his quick-release arm, remained the NFL's standout quarterback until the latter part of his career, when injuries started to take their toll. He decided to retire, aged 39, before the start of the 2000 season, and although most of his career records have since been broken, his miraculous 1984 campaign and 5,084 passing yards remains.

➲ Marino's single-season record of 5,084 passing yards in 1984 is one of his records to remain unbroken.

BUTTON MAKES FORMULA ONE HISTORY

JENSON BUTTON BECOMES YOUNGEST DRIVER IN FORMULA ONE HISTORY TO SCORE A POINT

26 March 2000, Interlagos, Sao Paulo, Brazil

After a stellar kart career, a switch to cars and Formula Ford in 1998 did little to dampen 18-year-old Jenson Button's progress: he won nine times during the season to win the title. He moved up to Formula Three in 1999, took a poor car to the chequered flag three times and Formula One came calling. He excelled in a test for Prost, outpacing veteran Jean Alesi, and then won a shootout for the vacant Williams seat. He was the youngest driver on the F1 grid at the season-opening 2000 Australian GP but engine failure cut his race short on the 46th lap. He stayed the course at the next race, the Brazilian GP, to finish sixth and become, aged 20 years, 67 days, the youngest driver in F1 history to score a point.

Jenson Button's rapid elevation to Formula One with Williams raised a number of eyebrows, but the Englishman silenced his critics in just his second race when he took his car to sixth place at the 2000 Brazilian GP.

➲ Button's record as F1's youngest point-scorer stood until 17 June 2007, when Germany's Sebastian Vettel, aged 19 years, 349 days, secured a point with an eighth-place finish at the United States GP.

WALSH BECOMES TEST CRICKET'S LEADING WICKET-TAKER

COURTNEY WALSH OVERHAULS KAPIL DEV'S RECORD FOR MOST TEST WICKETS

29 March 2000, Sabina Park, Kingston, Jamaica

One of the most charismatic figures in the game's history, Courtney Walsh was little more than a workhorse when he made his debut for the West Indies in 1984, willingly battling his way up slopes and into the wind to allow the tearaways Malcolm Marshall and Joel Garner the glory of the favourable conditions. But when the two retired, the workhorse morphed into a thoroughbred, forging a deadly partnership with Curtly Ambrose (the pair shared 421 wickets in 49 Tests) and, using his repetitive high action to good use, surged up the all-time leading wicket-takers' list. By 2000 he was closing in fast on Kapil Dev's all-time record of 434 wickets and could have chosen no better venue to break it – his 435th victim (Zimbabwe's Henry Olonga) came before his home fans at Sabina Park, Jamaica.

⮑ On 19 March 2001 at Queen's Park Oval, Trinidad, Walsh dismissed Gary Kirsten to become the first bowler in Test history to take 500 wickets.

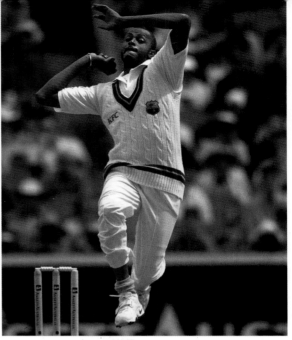

Consistency and an ability to perform through the pain barrier were the hallmarks of Courtney Walsh's 17-year Test career with the West Indies: his reward came when he became the highest wicket-taker in the game's history in March 2000.

When Richard Metcalfe made his Scotland debut in April 2000 against England, the 7ft giant became the tallest player ever to appear in a rugby international.

GIANT METCALFE INSPIRES SCOTLAND TO SHOCK VICTORY

RICHARD METCALFE BECOMES TALLEST RUGBY UNION INTERNATIONAL IN HISTORY

2 April 2000, Murrayfield, Edinburgh, Scotland

Scotland had been in woeful form in the 2000 Five Nations championship, losing their first four games, and few gave them any chance of preventing a rampant England side from claiming their first grand slam since 1995. But wily Scotland coach Ian McGeechan had a few tricks up his sleeve for the crunch match at Murrayfield and one of them would make history. When McGeechan's choice of lock, Richard Metcalfe, took to the field against the Auld Enemy, the 7ft giant became the tallest player ever to appear in international rugby and his debut turned out to be one to remember: Scotland shocked England 19–13 to win the Calcutta Cup for the first time in a decade.

⮑ Metcalfe's did not turn out to be the happiest of careers: he made 11 appearances for Scotland between 2000 and 2002 before a persistent knee injury cut short his career the following year.

Jeff Gordon translated the prodigious talent of his youth onto the Winston Cup stage and developed into one of the greatest drivers in the sport's history. In 2000 he became the youngest NASCAR driver to record 50 race wins.

GORDON CONFIRMS PLACE AMONG NASCAR'S GREATS

JEFF GORDON BECOMES YOUNGEST DRIVER IN NASCAR HISTORY TO WIN 50 RACES

16 April 2000, Talladega Motorspeedway, Alabama, USA

Jeff Gordon's breakthrough year came in the 1992 Busch Series when he secured a record 11 poles. He made his Winston Cup debut the same year and secured a full-time ride in 1993, finishing 14th in his first season. He visited Victory Lane for the first time at the Coca-Cola 600 in 1994 and won the Winston Cup a year later. He won ten times in 1996 but finished second; he won ten times the following year to collect a second title and then came his signature year, 1998, when he equalled Richard Petty's single-season record of 13 wins to defend his title. The championships dried up but, on 16 April 2000, he won the Die Hard 500 to become, aged 28 years, 8 months and 12 days, the youngest driver in NASCAR history to win 50 races.

➲ Six race wins were enough to see Gordon to a fourth title in 2001.

WATER SKIING'S GREATEST LEAP

JARET LLEWELLYN SETS WATER SKI-FLYING WORLD RECORD

13 May 2000, Orlando, Florida, USA

Jaret Llewellyn grew up water skiing on the waters of Lake Sylvan in his native Alberta, Canada, at the age of six and by the age of 17, in 1987, had become junior world champion for the first time. He soon found himself up against the adults and excelled, taking overall and jump gold at the 1990 Pan American Games. In 1992 he broke the world jump record with a leap of 207ft (63.1m); the following year he completed back-to-back victories at water skiing's prestigious US Masters; and by 1997 had become jump world champion for the first time. He won both the tricks and the jump world titles in 1999, but his crowning moment came at the 2000 Big Air Challenge in Orlando, Florida, when he broke the ski-flying world record with a staggering distance of 299ft (91.1m).

➲ Water ski-flying is similar to jumping but the physical jump has a steeper incline to encourage greater distances.

In 2000, Canada's Jaret Llewellyn added the water ski-flying world record to the jump world record he had set eight years earlier.

THE KING OF MOUNT EVEREST

APA SHERPA BECOMES THE FIRST TO SUMMIT MOUNT EVEREST TEN TIMES

24 May 2000, Mount Everest, Nepal/Tibet

Born and raised in the village of Thame in the Everest region, Apa Sherpa carried loads for western expeditions to the world's highest mountain to raise money for his family. After a series of failed attempts, he made the summit for the first time on 10 May 1990, as part of a New Zealand team led by experienced climber Rob Hall. The ascent kick-started his career as a lead sherpa – called sirdar – and he made numerous successful assaults on the mountain, including his first summit from the North Side in 1999. And on 24 May 2000, as part of the Asian-Trekking expedition, he became the first man in history to stand on the summit of the world's highest peak ten times.

Small in stature but a king in the mountains, Apa Sherpa has formed an integral part of many successful assaults on the world's highest peak and in May 2000 became the first in history to reach Everest's summit ten times.

➲ Apa Sherpa continued in his role as sirdar and in 2006 made his 16th successful ascent of Mount Everest.

The 2000 US Open was the moment pundits started to take the idea of Tiger Woods challenging Jack Nicklaus's total of 18 major titles seriously: the young American strolled to the crown by the staggering victory margin of 15 strokes.

TIGER DOMINATES 100TH US OPEN

TIGER WOODS WINS US OPEN BY A RECORD 15-STROKE MARGIN

18 June 2000, Pebble Beach, California, USA

As the new millennium dawned, 24-year-old Tiger Woods had already claimed two majors (1997 Masters and 1999 US PGA), was the No. 1-ranked golfer in the world and was being talked of in the same breath as Jack Nicklaus, but as far as the golfer himself was concerned the best was still to come. Next up on the major tournament roster was the US Open, a tournament that requires ultimate precision and which had already shown Woods's game to be rough around the edges. He had worked on his game – sharpened his driving, perfected distance control with his irons and mastered both putting and chipping – and the results were there for all to see at Pebble Beach: he decimated the field to claim his first US Open by 15 strokes – a record margin of victory in any major tournament.

➲ Woods's four-round total of 12 under was a tournament record (beating the previous record by four shots). He was the only golfer in the field to shoot 72 holes under par.

SAMPRAS BREAKS ALL-TIME GRAND SLAM RECORD

PETE SAMPRAS OVERTAKES ROY EMERSON'S RECORD FOR MOST GRAND SLAM SINGLES TITLES

26 June 2000, Wimbledon, London, England

Rumbles of discontent hung in the air in April 1993 when Pete Sampras made it to No. 1 spot in the world rankings for the first time: consistency rather than big tournament wins had got him there, with his 1990 US Open victory still his only grand slam victory. He silenced his critics with a win at Wimbledon in 1993 and, although success in other grand slams came his way (US Open in 1993, 1995 and 1996 and in Australia in 1994 and 1997), it was on the grass courts of Wimbledon that he showed his class. He defended his All England title in 1994 and 1995, suffered a shock loss to Richard Krajicek, but bounced back in dominant fashion to use the grass courts of Wimbledon as a launch pad for his assault on Roy Emerson's all-time record haul of 12 grand slam titles. He took the title in 1997 and 1998, equalled Emerson's record with a 6–3, 6–4, 7–5 win over Andre Agassi in the 1999 final and saw off the attentions of Pat Rafter in the 2000 final to notch up a record 13th grand slam title win.

Pete Sampras's serve-and-volley game was perfectly suited to the grass courts of Wimbledon and it was appropriate that his seventh win at the All-England club should see him pass Roy Emerson as the most successful male player in grand slam tournament history.

⮑ Sampras picked up the 14th and last grand slam victory of his career when he beat Andre Agassi 6–3, 6–4, 5–7, 6–2 in the final of the 2002 US Open. It turned out to be the last tournament of Sampras's career before he officially announced his retirement in August 2003.

Woods's march to the 2000 Open Championship was flawless: he did not find a single bunker during his four rounds and won by eight strokes to capture the one major tournament trophy missing from his mantelpiece.

OPEN CHAMPIONSHIP WIN COMPLETES THE MAJOR SET FOR WOODS

TIGER WOODS YOUNGEST GOLFER IN HISTORY TO COMPLETE CAREER GRAND SLAM

23 July 2000, St Andrews, Scotland

The press had little time to reflect on Tiger Woods's 2000 US Open win. Next up was the Open Championship, the one major Woods had yet to win, and the general consensus was that the St Andrews course was the perfect match for his game; the pundits were spot-on. It wasn't a one-man field, but it might as well have been. Woods shot 67 in the opening round to trail Ernie Els by one, but subsequent rounds of 66 and 67 took him into a six-shot lead with one round to go. By the time he had finished, the lead was up to eight and Woods, aged just 24, had become the youngest golfer in history to complete the career grand slam.

➲ Woods is one of only five golfers to have completed the career grand slam and at 24 the youngest to do so. In order of youngest to oldest when they completed the slam, the others are: Jack Nicklaus (26), Gary Player (29), Gene Sarazen (33) and Ben Hogan (41).

FIGO SIGNS FOR £37 MILLION

REAL MADRID PAY BARCELONA WORLD-RECORD FEE FOR LUIS FIGO

24 July 2000, Santiago Bernabeu, Madrid, Spain

With his on-the-ball trickery and dribbling skills, Luis Figo was the golden boy of the golden generation of Portuguese players who recorded back-to-back Under-20 World Championship wins in 1989 and 1991. He may have been a standout performer for hometown club Sporting Lisbon, but it was a move to Johan Cruyff's Barcelona in 1995 that kick-started the legend. He helped Barca to two successive La Liga titles, the European Cup-Winners' Cup in 1997, and soon became the first non-Catalan in the club's history to wear the captain's armband: in short he became the club's talisman. And then bitter rivals Real Madrid came calling and their world-record offer of £37 million was enough to turn Figo from the most adored to the most hated Barcelona player in history.

➲ Figo was an instant hit at the Santiago Bernabeu, helping Real Madrid to the La Liga title in his first season. Voted European Soccer Player of the Year in 2000 and FIFA World Player of the Year in 2001, he scored 36 goals in 165 appearances for the Spanish giants.

In one of the most controversial transfers in recent soccer history, Luis Figo left Barcelona for Real Madrid in the summer of 2000 for a world-record fee of £37 million.

123RD TIME LUCKY FOR BARRICHELLO

RUBENS BARRICHELLO BREAKS FORMULA ONE RECORD FOR MOST RACES BEFORE FIRST WIN

30 July 2000, Hockenheim, Germany

Eighteenth place on the grid is not the position from which to launch your first grand prix win, but the 2000 German GP was no ordinary race. Fuelled lighter than his opponents (he was two-stopping to his opponents' one), Ferrari's Rubens Barrichello made the most of his lighter car to be in a points-scoring position by mid-race, though still some way behind leader Mika Hakkinen. Then an intruder got onto the track: the safety car was brought out and the pack closed in behind it. Then Jean Alesi crashed; the safety car was brought out again. Then it rained and everyone flocked to the pits to change tyres. Barrichello stayed out: the rain had affected only one half of the track and the Brazilian held on to win his first grand prix at his 123rd attempt – a Formula One record.

➲ Rubens Barrichello may have been forced to wait seven years before his first race win, but did not have to wait so long to visit the top step of the podium for a second time: his next win came at the 2002 European GP at the Nürburgring.

Rubens Barrichello came out on top of one of the most dramatic races in recent Formula One history, coming through the field from 18th on the grid to take his first race win at his 123rd attempt.

As the spearhead of the most potent team in women's basketball, Cynthia Cooper was the first to pass many scoring milestones in the WNBA.

THE WNBA'S FIRST POINT-SCORING STAR

CYNTHIA COOPER FIRST PLAYER IN WNBA HISTORY TO REACH 2,500 CAREER POINTS

July 2000, Toyota Center, Houston, Texas, USA

Cynthia Cooper started playing basketball at the age of 16 and within two years was her high-school league's most valuable player. She went to the University of Southern California and starred, helping the Trojans to back-to-back NCAA titles in 1982 and 1983. She graduated in 1986 and plied her trade in Europe, first in Spain and then Italy, before signing for the Houston Comets in 1997, the WNBA's first year. And if the Comets were the tournament's first dominant team (winning four successive titles between 1997 and 2000), then Cooper was their spearhead: by the time she retired for the first time at the end of the 2000 season, she had been the first woman in WNBA history to reach 500, 1,000, 2,000 and 2,500 career points.

➲ Cooper went off to become the head coach of Phoenix Mercury, until being lured out of retirement for one final season with the Comets: she ended her WNBA career with 2,610 points to her name.

THE GREATEST SEASON IN AFL HISTORY

ESSENDON BOMBERS BREAK AFL/VFL RECORD FOR MOST WINS IN A SEASON

2 September 2000, Melbourne Cricket Club, Melbourne, Australia

No team has ever recorded a perfect season in the AFL/ VFL since the league's inception in 1897, but the Essendon Bombers went mighty close in 2000. With a dizzying mix of youth and pace, they swept all before them during the regular season (winning their games by an astonishing average of 53 points) and losing only to the Western Bulldogs in the 21st of 22 rounds. But they recovered in the finals series, beating North Melbourne in the elimination finals (198–73) and Carlton Blues in the semi-finals (125–80), before demolishing the Melbourne Demons 135–75 in the Grand Final to complete the most successful season (24 wins) in the 103-year history of the AFL.

The Essendon Bombers class of 2000 have a strong claim to being the greatest team in AFL/VFL history, posting an all-time league-record 24 wins en route to the club's 16th premiership success.

➲ Carlton (1908), South Melbourne (1918) and Essendon (1950) all posted Grand Final wins after suffering a single regular-season loss but, in the days of shorter seasons before the AFL's expansion, none won more than 19 games.

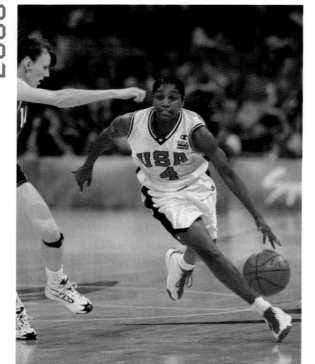

FIVE IN A ROW FOR RECORD-BREAKING EDWARDS

TERESA EDWARDS FIRST FEMALE BASKETBALL PLAYER TO APPEAR IN FIVE CONSECUTIVE OLYMPICS

15 September–1 October 2000, Sydney, Australia

Teresa Edwards first pulled on a US basketball shirt at the age of 17 and enjoyed a standout career at the University of Georgia, but her talents on the hardwood remained largely unnoticed in the United States. A lack of professional game forced to her to ply her trade overseas, but when the Olympic Games came calling, Edwards was a shoo-in for the US team. She made her first Olympic appearance in Los Angeles in 1984 (the US took gold) and played a huge part as the US defended the title four years later. She was part of the bronze-medal team in Barcelona 1992; helped them to gold in Atlanta four years later and made history in 2000 when she became the first female basketball player in history to appear in five consecutive Olympic Games: she celebrated the occasion by collecting her fourth gold medal.

➲ Edwards also holds the distinction of being the youngest (aged 20) and the oldest (aged 36) female basketball player in history to win Olympic basketball gold.

Forced abroad by the lack of a female professional basketball circuit in the United States, Teresa Edwards, the woman known in some quarters as the "Female Michael Jordan", shone in Olympic competition, appearing in a record five consecutive Games and collecting four gold medals.

SOFTBALL'S STRIKEOUT QUEEN

LISA FERNANDEZ RECORDS OLYMPIC SOFTBALL SINGLE-GAME RECORD OF 25 STRIKEOUTS

15 September–1 October 2000, Sydney, Australia

Lisa Fernandez developed a love for baseball as a child and first pitched for her league side at the age of 12, only to be told by her coach that she was too small and should concentrate on batting. She ignored the advice. She attended UCLA, was voted the nation's top female softball player between 1991 and 1993 and led her team to the Women's College World Series Championships in 1994. An automatic selection for the United States team at the 1996 Olympic Games – the first time softball was contested in the Olympics – she starred in the United States' 3–1 final win over China. She was the star four years later in Sydney as well, producing an Olympic-record 25 strikeouts in the United States' semi-final win over Australia before the team defended its gold medal with a win over Japan in the final.

➲ Fernandez formed part of the US team that went on to make it a hat-trick of Olympic gold medals in Athens in 2004 when they beat Australia in the final.

Lisa Fernandez confirmed her reputation as the best pitcher in softball when she produced an Olympic-record 25 strikeouts during the United States' semi-final victory over Australia in Sydney in 2000.

THE IRANIAN HERCULES MAKES LIGHT OF HIS LABOURS

HOSSEIN REZAZADEH BREAKS THREE WORLD RECORDS TO TAKE OLYMPIC WEIGHTLIFTING GOLD

15 September–1 October 2000, Sydney, Australia

The third of seven children born in Ardabil province on the Iranian border with Azerbaijan, Hossein Rezazadeh was encouraged to take up weightlifting by his gym teacher at the age of 15. A devout Muslim, the 345lb (156.5kg) giant, nicknamed "The Iranian Hercules" by weightlifting-mad Iranians, burst onto the international scene at the age of 22 at the 2000 Olympic Games in Sydney: in one of the most dramatic super-heavyweight (105kg and above) weightlifting competitions in recent history, which saw world records tumbling left, right and centre, Rezazadeh lifted a world-record 468 1/4lb (212.5kg) in the snatch and a staggering 573lb (260kg) in the clean and jerk – another world record – and his combined total of 1,040lb (472.5kg) broke the existing world record by 7.5kg. The gold medal was his.

➲ Rezazadeh went on to demolish the rest of the field in Athens four years later, lifting a combined 30lb (13.6kg) more than his closest rival to defend his super-heavyweight title and become the first Iranian double Olympic champion.

Three world records in two lifts (snatch, clean and jerk and combined) were enough to see Iran's Hossein Rezazadeh become the first non-Russian athlete to claim weightlifting gold in non-boycotted Olympic Games since 1960.

RECORD-BREAKING FIVE IN A ROW FOR REDGRAVE

STEVE REDGRAVE FIRST IN OLYMPIC HISTORY TO WIN FIVE CONSECUTIVE ROWING GOLD MEDALS

15 September–1 October 2000, Sydney, Australia

Steve Redgrave narrowly missed out on selection for Britain's rowing team for the 1980 Olympics in Moscow, but made amends four years later when, aged 22, he competed in the British coxed-four team that brought home Britain's first rowing gold medal for 36 years. A switch to coxless pairs in 1988 (with Andy Holmes) did little to slow Redgrave down: the pair took gold. In 1992, this time paired with Matthew Pinsent, he defended the title and again in 1996 (in what would be their 100th race together). Redgrave announced his intentions to try for a fifth gold at the 2000 Olympics, but then suffered a series of setbacks: first he had his appendix removed; then he was diagnosed with diabetes. But he stuck to his training routine and travelled to Sydney as part of a formidable coxless-fours team. The British quartet held off a desperate surge by Italy in the final to win by 0.38s and Redgrave had become the first rower, and the first endurance athlete, to strike gold at five consecutive Olympics.

➲ Redgrave's total of 14 gold medals in Olympic and world championship competition is the largest haul of any rower in history. He was awarded a knighthood for his services to rowing in the 2001 New Year Honours List.

In what has since been voted one of the greatest moments in British sporting history, Britain's coxless four held off a dramatic late surge by Italy to guide Steve Redgrave to a record-breaking fifth consecutive gold medal.

FIRST DESCENT FROM EVEREST ON SKIS

DAVO KARNICAR FIRST TO COMPLETE A SUCCESSFUL DESCENT FROM EVEREST'S SUMMIT ON SKIS

7 October 2000, Mount Everest, Nepal/Tibet

In 1995, after skiing down Mount Annapurna (the world's tenth-highest mountain), Slovenian extreme skier Davo Karnicar decided a descent of Mount Everest was possible. He tried in 1996, but was forced back before reaching the summit. But on 7 October 2000, at 7 a.m., he had made it and, an hour later, started his historic descent. Passing the Hillary step and the south summit – running the considerable risk of avalanches – he made it to Camp IV and attached a camera. He then skied down to Camp III. But the hardest part was still to come, a treacherous route through the notoriously dangerous Icefall. He succeeded and arrived back at base camp at 1 p.m. to joyous scenes. He had become the first man in history to make an uninterrupted descent of Everest on skis.

◗ On 7 December 2006 Karnicar made more history when he became the first person in history to have made a successful descent on skis of all of the Seven Summits (the highest peaks on the seven continents – Aconcagua (South America), Carstensz (Oceania), Denali (North America), Elbrus (Europe), Everest (Asia), Kilimanjaro (Africa) and Vinson (Antarctica).

An experienced skier and climber, Davo Karnicar made history on 7 October 2000 when he became the first person to complete a successful descent from the summit of Mount Everest to base camp on skis. The journey took him five hours.

THE YANKEES' RECORD-BREAKING 14-GAME WORLD SERIES STREAK

NEW YORK YANKEES BREAK RECORD FOR MOST CONSECUTIVE WINS IN WORLD SERIES
22 October 2000, Yankee Stadium, New York, USA

In the 1996 World Series, the New York Yankees had rallied from a 2–0 deficit to win four straight games and stun the Atlanta Braves. Two years later, they swept the San Diego Padres in four games; they handed out similar treatment to the Braves in 1999. It meant they had tied the World Series consecutive win record of 12 set by a previous generation of Yankees between 1927 and 1932. They passed the mark by edging game one 4–3 against the New York Mets in the 2000 Subway Series and extended it with another narrow win (6–5) in game two, before the Mets won game three 4–2 to end the streak at 14.

➲ The Yankees recovered to win games four and five, winning the World Series for the 26th time in the club's history and becoming the first three-peat champions since the Oakland Athletics in 1972–74.

Post-season play seemed to come easier to the Yankees than any other club: between 1996 and 2000 they posted an all-time record 14 consecutive Fall Classic game wins.

Already the holder of the best human effort record, in October 2000 Chris Boardman added the hour record to his collection, breaking Eddy Merckx's mark by a mere 10m.

Ondrej Sosenka notched up 49.70km (30.822 miles) in Moscow. The first recorded world hour record was 26.508km (16.471 miles) set in 1876 by F.L. Dodds on a penny-farthing.

BOARDMAN CLAIMS BOTH VERSIONS OF HOUR RECORD

CHRIS BOARDMAN BREAKS THE "TRADITIONAL" WORLD HOUR RECORD
27 October 2000, Manchester Velodrome, Manchester, England

On 9 September 2000, to cater for the advances in technology, the International Cycling Union (UCI) announced they would be splitting the hour record into two categories: one, called Best Human Effort, to cater for "modern" bikes; and the other, the hour record, to cater for "traditional" ones, the starting point of which would be Eddy Merckx's 1972 record of 49.431km (30.715 miles). The reasons were clear enough: in 1996, Britain's Chris Boardman had travelled 56.375km (35.03 miles) on a bicycle that placed him in a "Superman" position. But the moment the rules were changed, Boardman wanted to have a crack at Merckx's record: on 27 October 2000, riding on a bike similar to the Belgian's, he rode 49.411km (30.516 miles) to break the record by a miserly 10m – an improvement of 0.02 per cent.

➲ Boardman's record stood until 19 July 2005 when Russia's

AUSTRALIA HAMMER WEST INDIES TO BREAK ALL-TIME RECORD

AUSTRALIA BREAK RECORD FOR THE MOST CONSECUTIVE TEST MATCH WINS
1–5 December 2000, WACA, Perth, Australia

Sports operates in cycles: while one suffers another inevitably triumphs. In the mid-1980s, the West Indies were the most feared cricket team on the planet, with their battery of fast bowlers and cavalier batsmen proving too much for the opposition: in 1984 alone they won a record 11 consecutive Test matches. But by 2000 such heady days seemed a distant memory and the West Indies travelled Down Under to face an Australian team on a roll. The Aussies had won ten consecutive matches (including three consecutive series sweeps over Pakistan, India and New Zealand) and were out to break the West Indies' record. The men from the Caribbean put up little resistance, losing the first two Tests by an innings to take Australia's consecutive game streak to 12.

➲Australia went on to win the series 5–0 and continued their winning run in India by winning the first Test, but the record came to an end at 16 matches, when India staged one of the greatest come-from-behind victories in history to win the second Test in Calcutta.

By the turn of the century, the Australian cricket team – with their irresistible blend of stylish batsmen and a bowling attack spearheaded by Glenn McGrath and Shane Warne – were too hot to handle: between October 1999 and February 2001 they won a record 16 consecutive Test matches.

Considered the country's brightest prospect from a young age, Alex Rodriguez inked the most lucrative deal in baseball history when he signed for the Texas Rangers as a free agent in December 2000.

THE RICHEST DEAL IN BASEBALL HISTORY

ALEX RODRIGUEZ SIGNS MOST LUCRATIVE DEAL IN BASEBALL HISTORY

11 December 2000, Rangers Ballpark, Arlington, Texas, USA

A star shortstop in his youth, Alex Rodriguez was drafted first overall by the Seattle Mariners straight from high school in 1993. He made his Major League debut a year later and by 1996 was the Mariners' first-choice shortstop, posting a .358 batting average to become the first shortstop to win the Amercan League's batting title since 1960. He was still only 21 years old. His star continued to shine in Seattle until the end of the 2000 season, when he became a free agent. The race to secure his signature was on and on 11 December 2000 the Texas Rangers announced they were the ones who had won it … at a price. Rodriguez put pen to paper on a deal worth $252 million over ten years: the most lucrative in baseball history.

➲ Rodriguez enjoyed three stellar years with the Rangers – culminating in his winning the American League MVP award in 2003 – before he moved to the New York Yankees on 15 February 2004.

RECORD-BREAKING 151ST CAP FOR HASSAN

HOSSAM HASSAN BREAKS RECORD FOR MOST INTERNATIONAL CAPS

9 January 2001, Cairo, Egypt

Hossam Hassan shared the dreams of any youngster playing soccer on the streets and realized them when, along with his twin brother Ibrahim, he was signed by local club Helwan FC. The striker's first start for Egypt came in 1986 and he went on to represent his country at the 1990 World Cup finals in Italy. But although his talent and appetite for goals were never questioned, his attitude often was, particularly by Egypt's foreign coaches, and Hassan was often omitted from the team. Still the international caps mounted: he was the joint top-scorer at the 1998 African Nations Cup – and was angered when he was overlooked for the African Player of the Year award – but he soldiered on and made history on 9 January 2001 when he played in his 151st international to break Lothar Matthaeus' all-time record of 150 caps.

➲ Hassan retired in 2006 with 170 international caps to his name, a figure since surpassed by Mexico's Claudio Suarez and Saudi Arabia's Mohamed Al-Deayea.

At times Hossam Hassan may well have been the bad boy of Egyptian soccer, but longevity was also a hallmark of the striker's career: in January 2001 he became the most capped player in international soccer history.

JENKINS PASSES 1,000-POINT MILESTONE

NEIL JENKINS BECOMES FIRST PLAYER IN INTERNATIONAL RUGBY HISTORY TO SCORE 1,000 CAREER POINTS

3 February 2001, Millennium Stadium, Cardiff, Wales

Neil Jenkins's inclusion in the Welsh side to face England in 1991 aged 19 caused uproar in the valleys: the Pontypridd fly-half broke the mould of Welsh No. 10s, with his inclusion more about the prowess of his right boot than his dazzling ball-in-hand skills. But through the highs and lows of Welsh rugby fortunes during the 1990s, Jenkins was the one constant, with the points from his boot providing ballast to an otherwise faltering ship. And as his all-round game developed, so the critics were silenced. In 1994 he steered Wales to the Five Nations championship; he starred on the 1997 British Lions tour to South Africa; and in 1999 passed Michael Lynagh's all-time record of 911 points. In 2001, a conversion against England saw him become the first player in rugby history to score more than 1,000 points.

Neil Jenkins spent a career developing his armoury and silencing his doubters, but the effectiveness of his right boot remained constant and ten years after making his debut he became the first player in international rugby history to have scored more than 1,000 points.

⊃ Jenkins finished his international rugby career with 1,069 points to his name. In the 2003–04 season, playing for club side Celtic Warriors, he broke another world record when he slotted home 44 consecutive successful kicks.

FIRST WOMAN TO HIT GOLF'S MAGIC NUMBER

ANNIKA SORENSTAM FIRST WOMAN GOLFER IN LPGA TOUR HISTORY TO SHOOT 59

16 March 2001, Moon Valley Country Club, Phoenix, Arizona, USA

Annika Sorenstam's progress through the professional ranks was as serene as it was spectacular, topping the European Order of Merit in 1995 (in her third year as a pro), winning the Women's US Open in 1996 and becoming the first non-American in history to defend the title the following year. And then the desire seemed to ebb away from her and Australia's Karrie Webb became women's golf top dog. Sorenstam's response was to work harder than ever before, and the results started to show in 2001: during a season in which she became the first woman in LPGA Tour history to earn more than $2 million in single-season earnings, she also became the first woman to shoot 59 – she achieved the feat in the second round of the Standard Register PING tournament in Arizona.

Annika Sorenstam was back to her best in 2001: during the course of her record-breaking season she became the first woman golfer in LPGA Tour history to shoot a round of 59.

➲ Sorenstam's record-breaking round contained 13 birdies – 12 of them coming in the first 13 holes – and no bogeys: her round of 59 beat the previous best score (61 – held by Karrie Webb and Se Ri Pak) by two strokes.

WALSH FAILS TO BOTHER SCORERS FOR RECORD-BREAKING 43RD TIME

COURTNEY WALSH BREAKS RECORD FOR MOST DUCKS IN TEST CRICKET

17–21 March 2001, Queen's Park Oval, Port of Spain, Trinidad

What nature had gifted Courtney Walsh when it came to bowling – his athletic, metronomic action, capable of launching 85mph-plus missiles for 17 years saw him become the world's leading Test match wicket-taker (519 wickets) – it took away when it came to batting. Walsh entertained crowds the world over with his comic incompetence with the bat, scoring a mere 936 runs in his 132 matches and breaking Danny Morrison's unwanted Test-highest haul of 42 ducks. In typical Walsh fashion the record came in a flamboyant manner: ducks Nos. 42 and 43 came when he bagged a pair against South Africa in the second Test against South Africa in March 2001.

He may have been one of the greatest bowlers of all time, but Courtney Walsh also possessed one of the worst batting records in Test history and no one has recorded more ducks.

➲ In the history of Test cricket, only 18 players have completed their careers without a Test duck to their name.

WOODS ACHIEVES THE TIGER SLAM

TIGER WOODS FIRST GOLFER TO WIN FOUR CONSECUTIVE MAJOR TOURNAMENTS

9 April 2001, Augusta National, Augusta, Georgia, USA

A fifth-place finish at the 2000 Masters would give most golfers cause for encouragement, but the world already knew Tiger Woods was no ordinary golfer. He responded by obliterating the field at the 100th US Open to win by a record-breaking 15 shots. He then found the St Andrews course to his liking, winning the Open Championship for the first time and becoming the youngest golfer in history to complete the career grand slam. When he edged Bob May to defend his US PGA title, it left Woods with a shot at history. Could he win the Masters to become the first player in the game's history to hold all four major trophies simultaneously? It seemed the answer would be an emphatic "no" after a first-round 70 left him five strokes behind the leader, but a second-round 66 – replicating the first two rounds of his 1997 tournament success – followed by a third-round 68 handed Woods a one-shot lead with just one round to go. He completed his march into the history books in nerveless style: shooting 68 in the final round to win by two shots.

➲ Not considered a true grand slam because the wins did not occur in the same calendar year, Woods's feat became known as the "Tiger Slam". His next major win came in the 2002 Masters.

Tiger Woods produced arguably the greatest 12 months in golf history between 2000 and 2001, achieving the unique feat of winning four consecutive major tournaments.

Australia eased through the first round of the Oceania 2002 World Cup qualifying process, winning their group with four wins out of four and scoring 68 goals in the process: an international-record 31 of those goals came in their match against American Samoa.

AUSTRALIA 31 AMERICAN SAMOA 0

AUSTRALIA RECORD HIGHEST VICTORY IN INTERNATIONAL SOCCER QUALIFYING HISTORY
11 April 2001, Coffs Harbour, New South Wales, Australia

The Group One qualifying tournament – part of the process to decide which team would represent Oceania in the Intercontinental playoff game for a 2002 World Cup spot – was staged in Coffs Harbour, New South Wales, and there was only ever going to be one winner. Australia had opened the competition with a comprehensive 22–0 win over Tonga. Next up were American Samoa, who had conceded 21 goals in their opening two matches. After nine minutes the match was scoreless. But then the floodgates opened: Australia led 16–0 at half-time, adding another 15 goals in the second half and the winning score, 31–0, was the highest in international soccer history.

➲ Australia's goal-scorers that day were: Con Boutsianis (3), Archie Thompson (13), David Zdrilic (8), Aurelio Vidmar (2), Tony Popovic (2), Simon Colosimo (2) and Fausto De Amicis.

TOGO'S 13-YEAR-OLD STAR

SOULEYMANE MAMAM YOUNGEST PLAYER TO APPEAR IN WORLD CUP QUALIFYING MATCH
6 May 2001, Lomé, Togo

Born on 30 June 1987 in the Togolese capital Lomé, Souleymane Mamam showed an early appetite for the game of soccer, playing for local club sides New Star du Zongo (from the age of 11) and La Modèle do Lomé. But he must still have been somewhat surprised to find himself on the bench for his country's 2002 World Cup qualifying match against Zambia, especially as Togo were still seeking a first victory in group one. But Mamam made history when he was brought onto the field in the second half: at 13 years, 310 days, he had become the youngest player in history to appear in a World Cup qualifying match and to make matters even sweeter, Togo went on to win the match 3–2.

➲ Manchester United signed Mamam in 2003, but problems securing a work permit saw the Togo international loaned out to United's "feeder" club, Royal Antwerp, for whom he signed a permanent deal in 2007.

There may be some discrepancies as to his true date of birth, but according to FIFA at least, Souleymane Mamam became the youngest soccer player in history to appear in a World Cup qualifying match when he took to the field for Togo against Zambia in May 2001 at the tender age of 13.

16-YEAR-OLD CLIMBS THE WORLD'S HIGHEST MOUNTAIN

TEMBA TSHERI THE YOUNGEST PERSON IN HISTORY TO CLIMB MOUNT EVEREST

23 May 2001, Mount Everest, Nepal/Tibet

Temba Tsheri grew up in Tashigaon village in the high Himalayas listening to his father's tales of the fame and fortune achieved by those who had climbed the world's highest mountain and vowed that one day he would be named among the number of successful Everest summiteers. His first attempt in 2000, from the south side, when he was a 15-year-old schoolboy, almost ended in disaster. He was forced to retreat a mere 50m from the summit through bad weather and ended up losing five fingers to frostbite. Undeterred, he returned the following year more focused and determined than ever and on 23 May 2001, approaching the summit from the North Ridge, made the record books by becoming, aged 16 years, 14 days, the youngest person in history to stand on the roof of the world.

➲ Tsheri broke the record of Sambu Tamang who had reached the summit in 1973 at 17 years of age.

A year after battling for his life just 50m short of Mount Everest's summit – the failed attempt cost him five of his fingers – Temba Tsheri returned to the world's highest mountain and became, aged 16, the youngest person in history to conquer it.

AGE NO BARRIER FOR 64-YEAR-OLD BULL

SHERMAN BULL BECOMES OLDEST PERSON TO CLIMB MOUNT EVEREST

25 May 2001, Mount Everest, Nepal/Tibet

Sherman Bull had already stood on Everest's south summit on two occasions (the first time with his son Brad in 1995), but had never completed the final 98m climb to the true summit of the world's highest mountain. But it was the one successful climb missing from his Seven Summit list, and the 64-year-old had a burning desire to complete the challenge. He returned to the Himalayas in 2001 as part of an American team that also included his son and, at 8.15 a.m. on 25 May 2001, became the oldest person in history to summit Mount Everest; an hour and 15 minutes later he was joined on the roof of the world by his son – they remain the only father and son to have summited Everest together as part of the same expedition.

➲ Later that day, Erik Weihenmayer became the first blind person to summit the world's highest mountain. But Sherman Bull's record as Everest's oldest summiteer stood for barely a year: 65-year-old Japanese climber Tomiyasu Ishikawa broke it in 2002.

AUSTRALIA'S WEBB COMPLETES CAREER GRAND SLAM

KARRIE WEBB BECOMES YOUNGEST FEMALE GOLFER TO COMPLETE CAREER GRAND SLAM

25 June 2001, Dupont Country Club, Wilmington, Delaware, USA

Karrie Webb's transition to professional golf was as smooth as her swing: in just her second year she won the Women's British Open title – not then considered a major – and writ her name large when she earned her LPGA Tour card with a second-place finish at qualifying school, despite playing with a broken wrist. She won four times in 1996 to become the first woman to exceed $1 million in single-season earnings and a second British Open title followed in 1997, but she had to wait until 1999 for her first major: the Du Maurier Classic. And then the floodgates opened: in 2000 she won the Kraft Nabisco and US Women's Open titles; in 2001 she defended her US Open title and won the LPGA Championship to become, aged 26, the youngest female in history to complete the career grand slam.

➲ Of the six women to complete a career grand slam (Webb, Pat Bradley, Juli Inkster, Annika Sorenstam, Louise Suggs and Mickey Wright), Webb is not only the youngest to achieve the feat but also holds the record for winning all four tournaments in the shortest space of time: she won her fourth title 1 year, 10 months and 24 days after winning her first.

Karrie Webb's peerless ball-striking ability enabled her to ease into professional golf, and her victory in the 2001 LPGA Championships saw her become the youngest woman in history to complete the career grand slam.

The 1997 British Lions tour to South Africa provided Martin Johnson with his first taste of international captaincy and he made history four years later when he became the first player in history to lead the British Lions on two tours.

CAPTAIN FANTASTIC

MARTIN JOHNSON FIRST PLAYER TO CAPTAIN THE BRITISH LIONS IN TWO TEST SERIES

30 June 2001, The Gabba, Brisbane, Australia

Solihull-born Martin Johnson made a name for himself in New Zealand, where his performances at club level earned his selection for the All Black Under-21 tour to Australia. He returned to England in 1990, made his England debut in 1993 and played two Tests for the British Lions against New Zealand later that summer. By 1994 he was a shoo-in member of England's second row, helping the team to a grand slam in 1995. Two years later, he proved a surprise but inspired choice to lead the British Lions to a 2–1 series win over South Africa, with his no-nonsense leadership providing an example team-mates were only too happy to follow. And he made history in 2001 when he became the first man in history to lead the British Lions for a second tour, this time on their tour to Australia.

⮑ The Lions enjoyed less success in 2001, winning the first Test against Australia before falling in the final two to lose the series 2–1. Johnson would go on to lead England to World Cup success in 2003 before retiring from international rugby after the tournament.

WILDCARD GORAN'S WIMBLEDON FIRST

GORAN IVANISEVIC BECOMES FIRST WILDCARD ENTRY TO WIN WIMBLEDON

9 July 2001, Wimbledon, London, England

The only person who thought Goran Ivanisevic was capable of winning Wimbledon in 2001 was Ivanisevic himself. The big-serving Croat had the pedigree to win the tournament – he was after all a three-time runner-up in the event (1992, 1994 and 1998) and had reached as high as No. 2 in the world rankings – but a combination of injury and poor form had seen his ranking slump to No. 125 and he was only playing at Wimbledon courtesy of a wildcard. No wildcard entry had ever won the title and the Croat's form led no one to think 2001 would be any different. But Ivanisevic delighted in proving everyone wrong: he marched through the early rounds, ended Tim Henman's Wimbledon hopes for another year in the semi-final and edged Pat Rafter 6–3, 3–6, 6–3, 2–6, 9–7 in a three-hour, five-set final thriller to take his place in the history books.

⮑ The 2001 Wimbledon final between Goran Ivanisevic and Pat Rafter lasted 3h01m: the longest final in the tournament's history.

Many thought Goran Ivenisevic's best chances of winning the Wimbledon title he thought his birthright were behind him, but the Croat defied the odds in 2001 and became the first wildcard to win the men's singles title in the tournament's history.

REAL MADRID PAY £45.6 MILLION FOR ZIDANE

ZINEDINE ZIDANE BECOMES WORLD'S MOST EXPENSIVE SOCCER PLAYER
9 July 2001, Santiago Bernabeu, Madrid, Spain

Zinedine Zidane may have shown passion and determination in his early playing days with Cannes and Bordeaux, but it wasn't until a 1996 move to Italian powerhouse Juventus that his career fully blossomed. An artful playmaker, he led Juve to two successive Serie A titles and two successive (losing) Champions League finals in 1997 and 1998, before using the 1998 World Cup in France to stake his claim on being the best player in the world. In a rollercoaster tournament, Zizou went from zero to hero: banned for two matches after seeing red against Saudi Arabia before scoring twice in the 3–0 final win over Brazil that sent France wild. He repeated the dose in the 2000 European Championships, playing a starring role – including scoring a golden goal penalty against Portugal in the semi-final – as France won their second major tournament in a row. The following summer, Real Madrid saw him as a key ingredient of their *galacticos* brand and paid a record £45.6 million for his services: the best player in the world had also become the most expensive soccer player on the planet.

➲ Zidane confirmed his reputation as one of soccer's true greats during his five years with Real Madrid, winning back-to-back Champions League titles in 2001 and 2002 and winning La Liga on two occasions.

2001

Zinedine Zidane became the most expensive player in soccer history in 2001 when he moved from Juventus to Real Madrid for a record-breaking fee of £45.6 million.

£32 MILLION FOR A SAFE PAIR OF HANDS

GIANLUIGI BUFFON BECOMES THE WORLD'S MOST EXPENSIVE GOALKEEPER

July 2001, Stadio delle Alpi, Turin, Italy

Gianluigi Buffon first found himself standing between the posts as a 14-year-old and soon discovered that his sharp reflexes, sound positional sense and ability to command the area made him a natural. He made his Serie A debut for Parma as a 17-year-old in 1995, was part of the Italian Under-21 European Championship-winning squad in 1996 and was soon being compared favourably to Italy's 1982 World Cup-winning goalkeeper Dino Zoff. He made his international debut aged 19 in 1998, was part of the World Cup squad in France (although he did not play a game) and was starting to attract the attention of Europe's biggest clubs. Following some sound performances for Italy during Euro 2000, he moved to Juventus in the summer of 2001 for £32 million: the highest amount paid for a goalkeeper in soccer history.

Flush from the recent £45.6 million sale of Zinedine Zidane to Real Madrid, Juventus paid out £32 million for Parma's goalkeeping star Gianluigi Buffon: the highest amount ever paid for a goalkeeper.

➲ Buffon went on to become a stalwart of both the *Azzurri* and Juventus and played a key role in Italy's 2006 World Cup success.

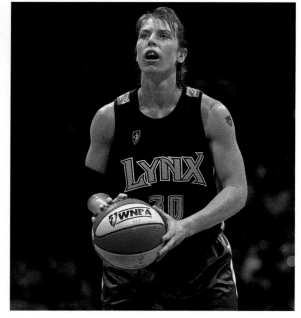

One of the most underrated players in WNBA history, Katie Smith broke the league's single-game scoring record in July 2001 with a 46-point game against Los Angeles.

RECORD-BREAKING 46-POINT GAME FOR SMITH

KATIE SMITH BREAKS WNBA SINGLE-GAME SCORING RECORD

7 July 2001, Target Center, Minneapolis, Minnesota, USA

Katie Smith made a name for herself in her freshman year at the Ohio State University, leading the Buckeyes to the Big Ten and NCAA titles. By the time she graduated in 1996, the sharp-shooting guard had broken the Big Ten Conference all-time point-scoring record. She played for Columbus Quest in the American Basketball League and led her team to two successive titles before joining Minnesota Lynx in 1998 following the ABL's collapse. And although she formed part of the US team's march to gold at the Sydney Olympics in 2000, the greatest moment of her career came in July 2001 when she broke the WNBA's single-game scoring record with 46 points (beating Cynthia Cooper's previous high of 44) in the Lynx's 100–95 overtime loss to Los Angeles.

➲ On 16 August 2007, Smith became the first female basketball player in history to record more than 6,000 career points (counting her performances in both the ABL and the WNBA).

MOST CATCHES IN TEST CRICKET

MARK WAUGH BREAKS RECORD FOR MOST TEST CATCHES BY A NON-WICKETKEEPER

19 July 2001, Lord's, London, England

It was ironic in many ways that Mark Waugh's debut for Australia, in the fourth Test against England in 1990–91, should have come at the expense of his out-of-form older twin brother Steve, the man under whose shadow he would spend most of his career, but the younger Waugh added a touch of polish to an otherwise ruthless Australian team that dominated world cricket from the mid-1990s onwards. An elegant stroke-player and a more than useful bowler, he was also one of the most natural slip fielders ever to play the game. Benefiting from fielding to a bowling attack containing Glenn McGrath and Shane Warne, Waugh snaffled chance after chance and, on 19 July 2001, playing against England at Lord's, he caught Mark Butcher off the bowling of McGrath. It was his 157th catch in Test cricket: a world record.

➲ Mark Waugh ended his Test career in 2002 with 181 catches to his name.

An elegant batsman and an electric fielder, Mark Waugh broke Mark Taylor's world record haul of catches for a non-wicketkeeper with his 157th catch, at Lord's against England in 2001.

The dominant long-distance swimmer of his generation – he remained unbeaten in major finals in the 1,500m freestyle for over a decade – Grant Hackett was at his peak at the 2001 World Championships and broke Kieren Perkins's world record by a staggering seven seconds.

HACKETT SHATTERS 1,500M FREESTYLE WORLD RECORD

GRANT HACKETT BREAKS KIEREN PERKINS'S 1,500M FREESTYLE WORLD RECORD

29 July 2001, Fukuoka, Japan

The imposing 6ft 5in figure of Grant Hackett first cut a dash on the world swimming scene at the 1997 Pan-Pacific Games when he took 1,500m and 400m freestyle gold aged just 17. A year later he was world and Commonwealth 1,500m champion. Although he became the dominant long-distance swimmer of his generation, his first taste of world-record-breaking came in the 200m in 1999. An overwhelming favourite for 1,500m gold in Sydney, he fought off a virus and attacked harder than ever before to hold off the charge of local favourite Kieren Perkins and become Olympic champion. But he was at his peak at the 2001 World Championships in Fukuoka: showing the attacking style he had displayed in Sydney, he shattered Perkins's world record by seven seconds – the new time: 14m34.56s.

➲ In 2005 Hackett took 1,500m freestyle at the world championships for the fourth consecutive time: he is the only swimmer in any event to achieve the feat.

David Toms claimed the 2001 US PGA Championship in record-breaking style in 2001, shooting the lowest four-round total in major championship history (265).

THE LOWEST SCORE IN A MAJOR CHAMPIONSHIP

DAVID TOMS RECORDS LOWEST FOUR-ROUND TOTAL IN MAJOR CHAMPIONSHIP HISTORY

19 August 2001, Atlanta Athletic Club, Georgia, USA

From the moment David Toms won his first PGA Tour event in 1997 – the Quad City Classic – he was being touted as a future major winner. But like so many talented players of his generation, his arrival at the top of golf's pecking order coincided with the whirlwind arrival of Tiger Woods, and major championships were harder than they had ever been to come by. But when Toms finally arrived at the top of a major championship leaderboard, he did so in dramatic style: producing a 243-yard hole-in-one in the third round of the 2001 US PGA Championship. It was a lead he never relinquished: he was a major winner at last and his four-round total of 265 (15 under) was the lowest ever recorded in major championship history.

⟳Although he was a regular in the USA's Ryder Cup and Presidents Cup teams and a consistent performer on the PGA Tour, the 2001 US PGA Championship is the only major tournament to have come Toms's way.

THE MOST SUCCESSFUL FORMULA ONE DRIVER OF ALL TIME

MICHAEL SCHUMACHER BREAKS ALAIN PROST'S ALL-TIME F1 RECORD FOR MOST WINS

2 September 2001, Spa-Francorchamps, Belgium

After becoming the youngest double world champion in Formula One history – a feat since surpassed by Fernando Alonso – with Benetton in 1994 and 1995, Michael Schumacher put his career on the line with a move to the faltering Ferrari team in 1996. And with Schumacher behind the wheel, the Prancing Horse immediately found its zip. The German was competitive from the start, narrowly missing out on the championship in 1997 and 1998, returning from a broken leg to help the Italian team to its first Constructors' Championship for 16 years in 1999 and winning a third Drivers' Championship 2000. During the course of the 2001 season – nine race wins were enough to secure a fourth title – he recorded his 52nd career win (at the Belgian GP) to break Alain Prost's all-time record of 51 victories.

⟳ Now the dominant force on the Formula One grid, Schumacher would go on to defend his title in 2002, 2003 and 2004.

Winning races came naturally to Michael Schumacher, a master driver in all conditions, throughout his career: in 2001 he became the most successful Formula One driver of all time, beating Alain Prost's record of 51 career wins.

THE YOUNGEST PLAYER TO HIT A TEST CENTURY

MOHAMMAD ASHRAFUL BECOMES YOUNGEST CENTURION IN TEST HISTORY

8 September 2001, Sinhalese Sports Club, Colombo, Sri Lanka

News that Bangladesh had been awarded Test status in June 2000 met with a mixed response. For some, Bangladesh's upgrade meant little more than another minnow added to an already over-packed international schedule; for others, here was a rich mine of talent ready to be tapped, and it was only a matter of time before a nation containing 150 million cricket fanatics would be competitive. And in Mohammad Ashraful, the optimists had a shining example. He made his Test debut in the second Test against Sri Lanka in Colombo in September 2001: in the first innings he was dismissed for 26; in the second innings, however, he made history, taking on the Sri Lankan spinners – including the revered Muttiah Muralitharan – to score 114 from 212 balls and become, aged 17 years, 61 days, the youngest player in Test history to score a century.

⮑ Ashraful's heroics in the match did little to save Bangladesh from a heavy defeat: they lost by an innings and 137 runs. They would have to wait until 2005 (and their 35th Test) before tasting victory for the first time (against Zimbabwe at Chittagong).

In his first Test match in Bangladesh colours in September 2001, Mohammad Ashraful broke Mushtaq Mohammad's record as the youngest player in Test history to score a century.

Barry Bonds got better with age: in 2001, aged 37, he broke Mark McGwire's single-season home run record by hitting 73.

⮑ In 2003, Greg Anderson of the Bay Area Laboratory Co-operative (and Bonds's trainer) was indicted for providing athletes with performance-enhancing drugs. As a result, despite never testing positive for a banned substance, a shadow hangs over Bonds to this day.

37-YEAR-OLD BONDS SMASHES HOME RUN RECORD

BARRY BONDS BREAKS MARK McGWIRE'S SINGLE-SEASON HOME RUN RECORD

7 October 2001, Pacific Bell Park, San Francisco, California, USA

By 1999, after 13 years in the Major League, first with the Pittsburgh Pirates (1986–1993) and then with the San Francisco Giants, Barry Bonds had established a reputation as a patient hitter and a great slugger. But although his numbers were consistently impressive – his 30-plus homers per season made him a candidate to break Hank Aaron's all-time home run record (755) – they were never of single-season record-breaking performances ... until the turn of the century. In 2000, aged 36, Bonds posted a career-high 49 home runs. The following year he posted one of the greatest seasons in Major League history: he drew a single-season record 177 walks; had the highest on-base average for over 40 years (.515); and broke Mark McGwire's single-season home run record with a staggering 73.

If by the turn of the century Arnaud Tournant was already considered the best speed cyclist in the business (he had already won every honour available to him), 2001 saw his consecration as the event's king: in October he became the first man in history to clock a sub-60s time in the 1km time trial.

TOURNANT'S CORONATION AS SPEED CYCLING KING

ARNAUD TOURNANT RECORDS WORLD'S FIRST SUB-60-SECOND 1KM TRIAL TIME

10 October 2001, La Paz, Bolivia

Arnaud Tournant's progress through the track cycling ranks was as serene as it was sensational. After finishing second in the sprint competition at the 1996 junior world championships, he played a huge role in France becoming team sprint world champions in 1997 and 1998. In 1999, Tournant became individual sprint world champion for the first time. He defended his title the following year, broke the 1km time trial world record and capped a memorable season by taking sprint gold at the 2000 Olympic Games. Then came 2001: he took three gold medals in the world championships and then travelled to the altitude of La Paz, Bolivia, to try and break his 1km time trial world record: in a lung-bursting effort, he clocked 58.875s, the first sub-one-minute time in history.

➲ Reportedly, shortly after crossing the finishing line, Tournant lost consciousness for 21 minutes before recovering. His record still stands to this day.

YOUNG GUN HEWITT CHARGES TO TOP OF WORLD RANKINGS

LLEYTON HEWITT BECOMES YOUNGEST NO. 1-RANKED PLAYER IN HISTORY

17 October 2001, Sydney, Australia

Lleyton Hewitt shot to international acclaim in 1998, when, as a virtual unknown 17-year-old, he won the Adelaide International title. He turned professional shortly afterwards and his classic counter-punching style, based on supreme athleticism, penetrating groundstrokes and a never-say-die, heart-on-sleeve attitude, proved more than a match for anyone. After impressing in the Davis Cup for Australia in 1999, he claimed his first grand slam singles title the following year, beating Pete Sampras in straight sets in the US Open (7–6, 6–1, 6–1). In 2001, after claiming his sixth title of the year – beating Sebastian Grosjean in the final of the Tennis Masters Cup in Sydney – he became, aged 20 years, 8 months, the youngest player in history to reach the top of the world rankings.

➲ Hewitt remained at No. 1 until 28 April 2003, when Andre Agassi overhauled him. The Australian regained top spot two weeks later for a further month before relinquishing it to Agassi for good a month later. He has never reached as high in the rankings again.

Lleyton Hewitt's pugnacious attitude on the tennis court paid dividends from word go: in October 2001 he became the youngest player in history to be ranked the world's No. 1 player.

GORDON FIRST TO PASS $10 MILLION IN SINGLE SEASON

JEFF GORDON FIRST IN NASCAR HISTORY TO EXCEED $10 MILLION IN SINGLE-SEASON EARNINGS

23 November 2001, New Hampshire International Speedway, New Hampshire, USA

After becoming Winston Cup champion for the third time in 1998 (to add to the championships won in 1995 and 1997), 27-year-old Jeff Gordon had become one of the most feted drivers on the planet and the inescapable face of NASCAR. But then he slumped, finishing sixth in 1999 and a lowly ninth in 2000. And then came 2001: in the year NASCAR mourned the passing of Dale Earnhardt following a crash at the Daytona 500, Gordon eased the pain by returning to form in dramatic style, winning on six occasions – including two back-to-back victories – to ease to a fourth title by 349 points and become the first person in the sport's history to exceed $10 million in single-season earnings.

Thirty years after Richard Petty had become the first NASCAR driver in history to break the $1 million barrier in single-season earnings, Jeff Gordon became the first to pass the $10 million mark.

⮕ Gordon had also been the first to pass the $4 million mark (1995) and the $6 million mark in single-season earnings.

REBORN SORENSTAM BREAKS $2 MILLION BARRIER

ANNIKA SORENSTAM FIRST IN LPGA TOUR HISTORY TO EXCEED $2 MILLION IN SINGLE-SEASON EARNINGS

24 November 2001, West Palm Beach, Florida, USA

Annika Sorenstam's response to losing her iron grip of dominance over women's golf was to go away and work harder than ever before. In came a five-day-a-week program of intense fitness training and, although progress was slow, by 2001 all the hours the Swede had spent pounding the roads and lifting weights started to pay off. Now carrying the ball an extra 20 yards off the tee, she became the first in LPGA Tour history to shoot a 59, set or tied a total of 30 LPGA records, claimed eight tournament victories – including her third major title at the Kraft Nabisco Championship – and ended the season as the first woman in LPGA Tour history to exceed $2 million in single-season earnings ($2,105,868).

Forced to rethink after losing her grip at the top of the women's game at the turn of the century, a reborn Annika Sorenstam bounced back in 2001 to become the first woman in LPGA Tour history to win more than £2 million in prize money in a single season.

⮕ Sorenstam went on to add another six major championships: Kraft Nabisco Championship (2002, 2005), LPGA Championship (2003, 2004), Women's British Open (2003) and the US Women's Open (2006).

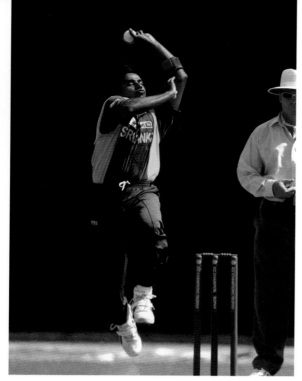

Chaminda Vaas demolished Zimbabwe's batting line-up in Colombo in December 2001, recording the best figures in one-day international cricket history (8 for 19) and becoming the only player in history to take eight wickets in an innings in the shortened format of the game.

VAAS DESTROYS SORRY ZIMBABWE

CHAMINDA VAAS RECORDS BEST BOWLING FIGURES IN ONE-DAY INTERNATIONAL CRICKET HISTORY
8 December 2001, Sinhalese Sports Club, Colombo, Sri Lanka

Zimbabwe warmed up for the LG Albans Triangular Tournament played in Sri Lanka in December 2001 (and also featuring the West Indies) with a four-wicket defeat to Sri Lanka A, and would have entered the tournament's opening game against the Sri Lankan senior side knowing they could do better. But things went wrong for the tourists from the moment their captain Stuart Carlisle lost the toss. Put into bat on a lively pitch, they lost opener Dion Ebrahim lbw to Chaminda Vaas to the first ball of the innings and never recovered. The 27-year-old left-armer tore through the Zimbabwe batting line-up, taking the first eight wickets to fall as Zimbabwe slumped to 38 all out and finishing with 8 for 19, the best figures in one-day international cricket history.

➲ Sri Lanka reached their victory target in just four overs to end the match after just two hours: it remains the shortest one-day international in history.

Salé and Pelletier are a very busy couple: they continue to skate professionally with Stars on Ice and in made-for-TV skating specials — as well as serving as TV skating commentators — toting Jesse along with them wherever they go.

➲ Because Berezhnaya and Sikharulidze were not part of the scandal, they were allowed to keep their gold medals as well, resulting in co-golds being awarded for that year's pairs event. Salé and Pelletier were married on 30 December 2005 and had their first child, Jesse Joe, in September 2007..

OLYMPIC SKATING GOLD GOES TO RUSSIA – AND CANADA?

SALE AND PELLETIER COME THROUGH CONTROVERSY TO BE AWARDED CO-GOLD WITH RUSSIAN RIVALS
8–24 February 2002 Salt Lake Ice Center, Salt Lake City, USA

When Jamie Salé and David Pelletier ended their flawless pairs program at the Olympic Games in Salt Lake City, many thought it was the end of four decades of Soviet domination. The pair left the ice to the sound of a thunderous ovation, which turned to a chorus of boos when the presentation marks were announced. The crowd, the NBC commentators and their CBC counterparts were staggered when the Soviet team of Yelena Berezhnaya and Anton Sikharulidze was announced as the first-place finisher. A storm of controversy immediately erupted, with angry headlines appearing all over the Canadian and US media. The controversy soon engulfed the French judge who, it was discovered, had been pressured by the French skating union's head to vote for the Russians no matter what happened on the ice. The situation was soon rectified with a second medal ceremony in which the Canadian skaters joined their Soviet counterparts as gold medallists.

THE DROUGHT IS OVER

LOONIE BURIED IN THE ICE AT SALT LAKE CITY OLYMPICS HELPS CANADA RISE TO FIRST PLACE A HALF-CENTURY AFTER ITS LAST OLYMPIC GOLD.

8–24 February 2002, Provo, Utah, USA

After 50 years of missing out, Canada's men's hockey squad finally returned to the top of the podium, joining the golden girls to make Canada the first nation to win both ice hockey gold medals at the same Olympics. The men demolished the United States 5–2. The women's team was called for 13 penalties in a hotly-contested gold-medal match, also against the United States, but when the dust settled, Canada had won 3–2. These victories ended a 24-game home-ice unbeaten streak for the US men's Olympic team, which had last been beaten by a visiting team at the 1932 games in Lake Placid, where they lost to – you guessed it – Canada.

➲ It was later revealed that the Canadian icemakers surfacing the rink had placed a lucky loonie under centre ice, ostensibly because the huge logo covering the area was missing the usual circle used for the puck drop. This was the first in a string of lucky loonies that have helped Canada win gold in international hockey or curling events.

The joy of the Canadian men turned out to be fleeting. At Torino four years later, the men's squad finished well off of the podium after back-to-back shutouts by Switzerland and Finland.

Travelling at a staggering 69.6 metres per second, covering 100m in a mere 1.43 seconds, Philippe Goitschel became the first speed skier in history to pass the 250km/h barrier at Les Arcs in 2002.

➲ Goitschel's mark would stand as a record until April 2006, when Italy's Simone Origone clocked an impressive 252.4km/h (156.834mph) over the same Les Arcs course.

GOITSCHEL BREAKS SPEED SKIING WORLD RECORD

PHILIPPE GOITSCHEL BECOMES FIRST SPEED SKIER TO BREAK 250KM/H BARRIER

23 April 2002, Les Arcs, Bourg-Saint-Maurice, France

One of the fastest non-motorized sports on earth – the fastest is speed skydiving, where competitors can reach speeds in excess of 480km/h (298mph) – speed skiing takes place on a specially constructed course 1km in length: competitors use the first 500m to hit their top speed and the second 500m to come to a halt. Wearing nothing more than an aerodynamic helmet and an airtight latex suit, for streamlining, and protected by little more than the mandatory back support, competitors regularly passed the 200km/h barrier – faster than the speed reached by a skydiver in normal freefall (called "terminal velocity") – but it took many years before someone passed through the mythical 250km/h barrier. The man to do so was Philippe Goitschel, a 40-year-old Frenchman, who clocked 250.79km/h (150.53mph) at Les Arcs on 23 April 2002.

Goals from Raul and a scorcher from Zinedine Zidan were enough to secure Real Madrid a tournament-record ninth European Cup/Champions League success in 2002.

REAL MADRID ON EUROPEAN CUP'S CLOUD NINE

REAL MADRID WIN EUROPEAN CUP FOR A RECORD NINTH TIME

15 May 2002, Hampden Park, Glasgow, Scotland

After Florentino Perez was appointed Real Madrid president in July 2000, he used money raised from the club's re-zoned training facilities to fund what would become known as *los galacticos*. In came Luis Figo and Zinedine Zidane to join the likes of Raul and Roberto Carlos. Success was expected. So when Real Madrid lost out to Valencia for league honours in 2002, victory in the Champions League became a basic requirement for Vicente del Bosque's men. They marched through the two group stages to reach the knockout section. They beat old foe Bayern Munich in the quarter-finals (3–2) and arch-rivals Barcelona in the semis (3–1) to face surprise package Bayer Leverkusen in the final: a 2–1 victory – a record ninth in the competition – kept a smile on the president's face.

➲ Despite winning La Liga in 2002–03, Real Madrid's failure to defend their Champions League title – they were knocked out by Juventus in the semi-finals – cost Vicente del Bosque his job.

TIGERS TASTE HEINEKEN CUP GLORY FOR SECOND SUCCESSIVE YEAR

LEICESTER TIGERS BECOME FIRST TEAM TO MAKE SUCCESSFUL DEFENCE OF HEINEKEN CUP

25 May 2002, Millennium Stadium, Cardiff, Wales

Launched in 1995 (although not competed for by English and Scottish clubs until the following year), the Heineken Cup was seen as rugby's answer to soccer's Champions League. Six different clubs had been champions in the first six years, but come the start of the 2001–02 season, Leicester Tigers, who had won the trophy for the first time the previous year, were determined to buck that trend. The Tigers won their group comfortably, but were made to fight all the way to the final – a 29–18 victory over Leinster and a nervous 13–12 victory over Llanelli. And they saw off Celtic opposition in the final as well, grinding out a 15–9 win over Munster to become the tournament's first two-time winners and to date the only side to defend the Heineken Cup.

➲ Leicester Tigers remain the only side to have launched a successful defence of the Heineken Cup, but two other teams have equalled their feat of winning the trophy twice: Toulouse (1996, 2003) and London Wasps (2004, 2007).

Under the phlegmatic leadership of Martin Johnson, Leicester Tigers became the first and to date only team to make a successful defence of the Heineken Cup when they beat Munster 15–9 in the 2002 final in Cardiff.

MILAKOVA BREAKS SKI-FLYING WORLD RECORD TWICE IN TWO DAYS

ELENA MILAKOVA BREAKS WOMEN'S WATERSKIING SKI-FLYING WORLD RECORD

26 May 2002, Pine Mountain, Georgia, USA

Elena Milakova grew up in the Russian town of Rybinsk, near Moscow, and learned to water-ski in a swimming pool at the age of 10. It ignited a dream to become world champion and, 14 years later, she achieved it by winning the 1997 world championships in Colombia, also defending her title four years later in Milan. Sidelined for five months by a serious knee injury in 2000, she was back to her best in 2001, winning the world championships for the third time. On 25 May, at the 2002 US Masters – an invitation-only tournament in which she had enjoyed considerable success – she broke Emma Sheers's water-ski ski-flying world record (66.6m) with a leap of 67.5m. The following day she leapt even further: 69.4m – a record that stands to this day.

➲ At the Malibu Open at Rio Grande, California, July 2002, minutes after seeing Emma Sheers break her jump world record (55.1m set in Lincolnshire in July 2001) with a leap of 55.3m, Milakova produced a jump of 56.6m to reclaim the world record.

THE WORLD CUP'S OLDEST MANAGER

CESARE MALDINI BECOMES OLDEST MANAGER IN WORLD CUP HISTORY

2 June 2002, Asiad Main Stadium, Busan, South Korea

Although good enough as a player to win 14 international caps for Italy, Cesare Maldini made his name as a coach: first as assistant coach to the *Azzurri* (he formed part of the coaching staff when Italy won the World Cup in 1982), then as Italy Under-21 manager and then with the senior national team (leading them to the quarter-finals of the 1998 World Cup). But he was still a controversial choice to take the reins of the Paraguay national side in December 2001: Maldini defied the critics, leading Paraguay to their second successive World Cup finals for the first time in their history. When he led his side out for the opening game against South Africa, he became, aged 70 years, 131 days, the oldest manager in World Cup history.

➲ A win, a draw and a defeat were enough to earn Paraguay a place in the second round, where they lost to Germany (through an 88th-minute goal by Oliver Neuville).

He was a surprise and controversial choice as Paraguay manager in December 2001, but it was mission accomplished for Cesare Maldini when he led Paraguay to the 2002 World Cup finals. It was a history-making moment too: it meant he would become the oldest manager ever to lead a side in the World Cup finals.

FIFTH WORLD CUP AND FIFTH TEAM FOR MILUTINOVIC

BORA MILUTINOVIC FIRST PERSON TO COACH FIVE DIFFERENT SIDES AT WORLD CUP FINALS

4 June 2002, Gwangju World Cup Stadium, Gwangju, South Korea

Serb Bora Milutinovic took the reins of the Mexican national side in 1983 and led them to the quarter-finals of their own World Cup in 1986. But it was as coach of Costa Rica that he earned his reputation, taking charge of the team just five games before the 1990 World Cup: they shocked everyone by reaching the second round. The US Soccer Federation hired the man they called "a miracle worker" to coach the US at the 1994 World Cup: he took them to the second round. He worked his magic with Nigeria four years later as well, taking them to the knockout stages, and when he took China to the World Cup finals for the first time in 2002, he became the first man in history to manage five different teams at the World Cup.

Bora Milutinovic (far right) made history in 2002 when he managed China at the 2002 World Cup finals: he is the only man to lead five different sides in the competition's history.

➲ Having become the first manager in history to lead four different countries to the knockout stages of the World Cup finals in 1998, Milutinovic enjoyed less success with China in 2002: they lost all three of their group games.

Hakan Sukur got Turkey off to a blistering start in the 2002 World Cup third-place playoff, handing them the lead after 11 seconds. It was the fastest goal in the tournament's history, beating Vaclav Masek's record of 15 seconds, set in 1962.

SUKUR GETS TURKEY OFF TO A FLIER

HAKAN SUKUR SCORES THE FASTEST GOAL IN WORLD CUP HISTORY

29 June 2002, Daegu World Cup Stadium, Daegu, South Korea

It was the one World Cup match no one wanted to play in. The 2002 World Cup hopes of South Korea and Turkey may well have been cut short in the semi-finals, but the South Korean fans flocked to the Daegu Stadium in vast numbers to cheer on their side for one last time in the third-place playoff match. The Turkish players took to the field with manager Senol Gunes's words about the importance of silencing the crowd ringing in their ears and got off to a flier: direct from kick-off, Hakan Sukur dispossessed Hong Myung-Bo on the edge of the area and slotted the ball past the keeper to hand the Turks the lead. His goal, in just 11 seconds, is the fastest in World Cup history.

➲ The South Koreans failed to recover from the early setback and bowed out of the tournament with a 3–2 defeat.

BRAZIL FIND FORM FOR RECORD FIFTH WORLD CUP SUCCESS

BRAZIL BECOME FIRST FIVE-TIME WINNERS OF THE WORLD CUP

30 June 2002, International Stadium, Yokohama, Japan

Written off before the tournament started, Brazil found their form when it mattered in Japan and South Korea in 2002 to become the World Cup's first five-time winners.

Having endured a poor qualification campaign that had seen them scrape into the 2002 World Cup, Brazil saw their chances of claiming soccer's greatest prize for a fifth time written off before the tournament started; their edgy opening-game 2–1 victory over Turkey did little to silence the doubters. But then Brazil sprang into life, winning their last two group games 4–0 (against China) and 5–2 (Costa Rica). Belgium and England fell in quick succession in the knockout phases, Turkey were beaten 1–0 in the semifinals and, all of a sudden, the team no one thought stood a chance were in the final. The joy did not end there: two goals from Ronaldo were enough to secure a 2–0 final win over Germany and Brazil had become the World Cup's first five-time winners.

➲ The 2002 World Cup final also marked a record-breaking moment for Brazil's captain Cafu: he became the first man in history to appear in three successive World Cup finals.

At his sixth attempt, Steve Fossett became the first man in history to complete a circumnavigation in a hot air balloon.

AROUND THE WORLD IN 13½ DAYS

STEVE FOSSETT COMPLETES FIRST CIRCUMNAVIGATION IN A HOT AIR BALLOON

4 July 2002, Queensland, Australia

When American adventurer and multi-millionaire Steve Fossett completed the first non-stop crossing of the Pacific Ocean in a hot air balloon in 1998, it became his mission to become the first person in history to guide a hot air balloon around the world. After five failed attempts – one of which saw him dumped into the Coral Sea five miles off the coast of Australia – he hoped it would be sixth time lucky when he launched his ten-storey-high *Spirit of Freedom* balloon in Northam, Western Australia, on 19 June 2002: he completed his 20,482-mile (33,195.10km) journey – reaching 200mph over the Indian Ocean (a record in a balloon) – 13 days, 8 hours, 33 minutes later when he touched down in Queensland.

➲ Steve Fossett disappeared on 3 September 2007 flying his single-engine aircraft over Nevada, although wreckage of the plane has yet to be discovered.

JAPAN 155 CHINESE TAIPEI 3

JAPAN RECORD THE HIGHEST POINTS TOTAL IN INTERNATIONAL RUGBY HISTORY

6 July 2002, National Stadium, Tokyo, Japan

Japan went a long way to restoring their rugby reputation when they demolished Chinese Taipei by a world record score of 155–3 in July 2002.

Although the undisputed kings of south-east Asian rugby (they were the only country from the region to have qualified for the Rugby World Cup), the reputation of Japanese rugby had taken an almighty battering following a 145–17 mauling by a virtually second-string New Zealand outfit at the 1995 World Cup in South Africa. But Japan went a long way to exorcizing the ghosts of Bloemfontein '95 during a qualification match against Chinese Taipei in July 2002. With the match effectively over as a contest after the seventh minute (with Japan already holding a 21–0 lead), the home crowd sat back and watched a try-fest: Japan ran in 23 tries en route to an international rugby world record 155–3 victory.

➲ It may have been the most points scored in an international rugby match, but Japan's 152-point margin of victory only equalled the record set by Argentina a few months earlier when they beat Paraguay 152–0 in Buenos Aires.

SIX IN A ROW FOR THE UNITED STATES

UNITED STATES WIN WORLD LACROSSE CHAMPIONSHIP FOR SIXTH STRAIGHT YEAR

15 July 2002, Perth, Western Australia, Australia

Since the tournament's inception in 1967, the World Lacrosse Championships had provided a platform for the United States to show their dominance in the game. They took the title in the first year, defended it at the next championships seven years later, before tasting defeat for the first time in 1978 when Canada edged them to the title. But from that moment on it had been all America, and they travelled to the 2002 World Championships off the back of five consecutive wins determined to make it six in a row. They did so in style, sweeping through all four of their round-robin games, beating Iroquois Nationals 18–8 in the semi-finals to face off against arch-rivals Canada in the final: the US won 18–15 to win the tournament for an unprecedented sixth consecutive time.

➲ But that was where the run came to an end. In 2006, in London, Ontario, Canada shocked the United States 15–10 in the final to win the tournament for the second time.

THE WORLD'S MOST EXPENSIVE DEFENDER

MANCHESTER UNITED PAY LEEDS UNITED £29.1 MILLION FOR RIO FERDINAND

22 July 2002, Old Trafford, Manchester, England

Rio Ferdinand became the youngest defender in history to play for England when he made his debut for the Three Lions aged 19 in November 1997. His speed, confidence on the ball and ability to read the game impressed everyone and in November 2000 he joined big-spending Leeds United from West Ham for a British transfer-record fee of £18 million (a world-record amount for a defender). It was money well spent: Ferdinand was at the heart of Leeds's march to the Champions League semi-final in 2001 and impressed once more at the 2002 World Cup, but trouble was just around the corner. Leeds was a club in financial straits and, shortly after the World Cup, sold their prime asset to arch-rivals Manchester United for £29.1 million – breaking Ferdinand's own world-record fee for a defender.

⮕ On 15 November 2006, Micah Richards, aged 18 years and 144 days, replaced Ferdinand as the youngest defender to play for England when he made his debut in a friendly international against Holland.

No longer capable of keeping hold of their biggest star, Leeds United could not refuse a £29.1 million offer from Manchester United for Rio Ferdinand in 2002. It meant the Londoner broke the record for being the world's most expensive defender for the second time in two years.

When Matthew Pinsent (right) and James Cracknell were on song in the coxless pairs they were unstoppable: at the 2002 World Rowing Championships, they broke the 2km world record by a staggering four seconds.

PINSENT AND CRACKNELL HIT NEW ROWING HEIGHTS

MATTHEW PINSENT AND JAMES CRACKNELL SHATTER COXLESS PAIRS 2KM WORLD RECORD

21 September 2002, Guadalquivir, Seville, Spain

Matthew Pinsent and James Cracknell had been part of Great Britain's coxless fours team that had carried Steve Redgrave to a fifth consecutive gold medal at the Olympic Games in Sydney in 2000, but when Redgrave retired following the event, Pinsent (now a three-time Olympic champion) and Cracknell decided to switch to the coxless pairs as they set about another four-year build-up to another gold medal quest. On paper, at least, it was a powerhouse pairing: two rowers of awesome ability and strength, both at the peak of their powers, and at the 2002 World Rowing Championships in Seville, the world got a glimpse of just how destructive they could be: the pair clocked 6m14s in the heats to break the old 2km world record by a staggering four seconds.

⮕ However, after a disappointing 2003 season, Pinsent and Cracknell switched back to coxless fours and, partnered by Ed Coode and Steve Williams, went on to collect Olympic gold in Athens in 2004.

THE WORLD'S FASTEST BICYCLE

SAM WHITTINGHAM BREAKS WORLD SPEED RECORD FOR HUMAN-POWERED VEHICLE
5 October 2002, Battle Mountains, Nevada, USA

Canadian cyclist Sam Whittingham's meeting with designer George Georgiev in 1993 changed his life. Georgiev had just designed the world's first two-wheel human-powered vehicle (the others had been tricycles) and Whittingham agreed to become the first to ride the Varna Mephisto in a competition. They won and carried on winning for the best part of a decade. With all the opposition blown away, the only thing remaining for Whittingham and his team was the hunt for records. And how they enjoyed chasing them. At the 2001 World Human-Powered Speed Challenge in Battle Mountains, Nevada, the Canadian clocked a new speed record of 72.75mph (116.50km/h). He returned a year later knowing he could go faster ... and did, clocking 81mph (130.36km/h).

➲ Whittingham is the holder of numerous world records: top speed from 500m flying start (62.34mph/100.32km/h); top speed from 1,000m flying start (79.79mph/128.40km/h); and top speed from 1 mile flying start (78.64mph/126.55km/h). He is also the current holder of the hour record (Best Human Effort category) with 53.917 miles (86.752km).

RECORD-BREAKING 11 WINS SEE SCHUMACHER TO FIFTH TITLE

MICHAEL SCHUMACHER BREAKS FORMULA ONE'S SINGLE-SEASON RECORD FOR MOST WINS
13 October 2002, Suzuka, Japan

The impressive nature of Michael Schumacher's serene rise with Ferrari to the top of the Formula One ladder somehow got lost amid the clamour that such dominance was bad for the sport. After winning his third drivers' championship in 2000 to become the Italian team's first world champion since 1979, no one could stop the German and his Prancing Horse. Nine wins in 2001 – equalling Nigel Mansell's single-season record set in 1992 – were enough to see Schumacher retain his title by a record-breaking 58 points. But that was nothing compared to the 2002 season: the German clinched the title with six races to go (a record); ended the season with a 67-point advantage over second-placed Rubens Barrichello; and won an incredible 11 of the season's 17 races.

➲ Schumacher finished in the top three of each of the season's 17 races, winning 11, finishing runner-up five times and third once.

Michael Schumacher produced the most dominant season in Formula One history in 2002, claiming the title with six races of the season still to run and ending the season with a record 11 race wins to his name.

SMITH EASES PAST NFL'S ALL-TIME RUSHING RECORD

EMMITT SMITH BREAKS WALTER PAYTON'S NFL CAREER RUSHING RECORD

27 October 2002, Texas Stadium, Irving, Texas, USA

Three years of college football was enough to persuade Emmitt Smith that he was ready for the big time and the Dallas Cowboys selected him in the first round of the 1990 NFL Draft. It was a shrewd pick: Smith led them to three Super Bowls in 12 years (1992, 1993, 1995) and broke many records along the way: he started his career with a record-equalling seven straight ten-touchdown seasons; became the only running back to win the Super Bowl, Super Bowl MVP, NFL MVP and NFL rushing crown in the same season (1993); became the first player to post five straight 1,400 rushing yard seasons; and, on 27 October 2002, broke Walter Payton's all-time rushing yard record with the 16,727th of his career.

An uncanny ability to read the game, coupled with a sublime athleticism that helped him to execute his plans, enabled Emmitt Smith to scythe systematically through opponents' defences throughout his 14-year NFL career. In 2002, he broke Walter Payton's all-time rushing record.

➲ Smith retired in 2005 with several all-time records to his name: he leads the NFL charts in most career rushing touchdowns (164) and is the only player in NFL history to post 11 straight 1,000 rushing yard seasons. He ended his career with 18,355 rushing yards.

ROSSI AND HONDA HIT NEW HEIGHTS

VALENTINO ROSSI BREAKS MOTOGP/500CC SINGLE-SEASON RECORD FOR MOST POINTS

3 November 2002, Circuit de Valencia, Valencia, Spain

Valentino Rossi made little impression during his first tryout at the 125cc World Championships in 1996, crashing his Aprilia bike more often than he took it over the finishing line, but he learned his lessons fast and in 1997 won 11 of the season's 15 races. He moved up to the 250cc division in 1998 and struggled, before rebounding with a nine-win season and the title in 1999. His reward was a switch to Honda and 500cc for 2000 and although he finished second in his first season, if the pattern of his early career was to be believed the best was yet to come. In 2001 he stormed to the championship with 11 wins. In 2002 the 500cc championship morphed into MotoGP, but it did little to dampen Rossi's charge: the Italian won 11 times once again and broke Mick Doohan's record points haul (340 in 1997) with a staggering 355 points.

Valentino Rossi and Honda were unstoppable in 2001 and 2002: during the course of two title-winning seasons, the Italian won 22 races and in the latter season broke the single-season record for most points (355).

➲ Rossi retained his title in 2003 and then shocked the MotoGP fraternity by announcing he was leaving the all-powerful Honda team to join the struggling Yamaha outfit. He rose to the challenge, winning the title yet again in 2004 and 2005.

With many fearing his best years were already behind him, Ronaldo ended the 2002 season as the World and European Player of the Year for a record-breaking second time in his career.

RONALDO BACK TO HIS BEST AFTER INJURY NIGHTMARE

RONALDO FIRST TO WIN WORLD AND EUROPEAN PLAYER OF YEAR AWARDS IN SAME YEAR TWICE

December 2002, Santiago Bernabeu, Madrid, Spain

On 21 November 1999, Inter Milan's Ronaldo ruptured the tendon in his right knee and faced a lengthy spell on the sidelines. He made a tentative return on 12 April 2000, but lasted only seven minutes before his knee flared up again. Fifteen months of rehabilitation followed and many feared the Brazilian star would never be the same player again, but he bounced back in style at the 2002 World Cup, scoring eight goals in the tournament – including two in Brazil's 2–0 final win over Germany – and won the Golden Shoe for the first time. Further awards followed later in the year: now playing for Real Madrid, he became the first player win the FIFA World Player and European Player of the Year awards in the same season for the second time.

➲ Ronaldo is one of only two players to win the FIFA World Player of the Year award on three occasions (he also won in 1996 and 1997). The other three-time winner is France's Zinedine Zidane, who collected the trophy in 1998, 2000 and 2003.

BEACHLEY BECOMES SURFING WORLD CHAMPION FOR FIFTH STRAIGHT YEAR

LAYNE BEACHLEY FIRST FEMALE TO WIN FIVE WORLD SURFING CHAMPIONSHIPS

20 December, North Shore, Oahu, Hawaii, USA

With little or no amateur surfing record, Layne Beachley turned professional in 1988 aged 16 and struggled for four years. She finally gained her first Tour victory in 1992 and ended the year ranked sixth in the world. But then two bouts of chronic fatigue (in 1993 and 1996) threatened to end her career. In 1998, she teamed up with Hawaiian big-wave veteran Ken Bradshaw and learned many tricks of the trade from the old master, winning five of the year's 11 events to collect the world championship for the first time. She was now the class of the field: she battled through a knee injury to defend her title in 1999 and carried on winning: further titles in 2000, 2001 and 2002 saw her become the sport's first-ever female five-time world champion.

Having grown up trying to outdo boys on the surf in her native Manley, Layne Beachley translated her competitive spirit into success on the world professional surfing circuit, becoming the first to win five consecutive world championships between 1998 and 2002.

➲ The winning did not end there: she won the world title for the sixth successive year in 2003 and added a record-breaking seventh title to her considerable collection in 2006.

THE RAWALPINDI EXPRESS HITS NEW SPEED RECORD

SHOAIB AKHTAR BECOMES THE FIRST BOWLER TO BREAK THE 100MPH BARRIER

22 February 2003, Newlands, Cape Town, South Africa

Jeff Thompson's legendary delivery clocked at 99.8mph under controlled conditions in 1976 hung heavy in the minds of all fast bowlers, but it wasn't until the introduction of speed guns at grounds that anyone seriously thought of breaking it. And then it became one of cricket's obsessions: who would be the man to record the first 100mph delivery? There were two main candidates: Australia's Brett Lee and Pakistan's Shoaib Akhtar. Lee clocked 98.4mph against South Africa in 2001–02; Akhtar thought he had broken the mark in 2002, only to be told by the ICC that the speed gun used was an unsanctioned model. But the Pakistani tearaway finally achieved the feat at the 2003 World Cup in South Africa, recording a delivery of 100.23mph against England in Cape Town.

➲ Criticized in some quarters for being more interested in breaking the 100mph barrier than in taking wickets for Pakistan, Akhtar has yet to hit the career heights his talent deserves: he is yet to reach the 200-wicket mark in Tests, despite playing in more than 40 matches.

For a short while following the introduction of speed guns at grounds, cricket fans became obsessed with speed and Shoaib Akhtar, known as the "Rawalpindi Express", was more than happy to take centre stage: during the 2003 World Cup in South Africa he became the first bowler in history to deliver the ball at a speed in excess of 100mph.

An inspiration for his country in one-day cricket for 19 years, Wasim Akram became the first bowler in history to take 500 wickets in the short-format game.

WASIM STARTS THE 500-WICKET CLUB

WASIM AKRAM BECOMES FIRST PLAYER TO TAKE 500 ONE-DAY INTERNATIONAL WICKETS

25 February 2003, Paarl, South Africa

Fast-tracked into the Pakistan team in 1984, Wasim Akram proved his worth in just his third one-day international when he took 5 for 21 against Australia at the MCG. He was soon a permanent fixture in the Pakistan team and his haul of wickets rose as sharply as the number of one-day internationals played – including a match-winning three wickets in the 1992 World Cup final. A year later Wasim took his 200th wicket; his 300th came in 1996. Wasim inspired Pakistan to the World Cup final in 1999; they lost, but months later he claimed his 400th wicket. His 500th came during the 2003 World Cup in South Africa against the Netherlands: he became the first player in one-day international history to achieve the feat.

➲ The tournament would turn out to be Wasim's swansong on the international stage. Pakistan failed to progress beyond the group stages and eight players, including Wasim, were dropped from the squad. He announced his retirement shortly afterwards with 502 wickets to his name.

SWITZERLAND: KING OF THE OCEANS

SWITZERLAND BECOMES FIRST LANDLOCKED COUNTRY TO WIN THE AMERICA'S CUP

2 March 2003, Hauraki Gulf, Auckland, New Zealand

On 19 January 2003, Swiss boat *Alinghi* completed a 5–1 victory over the United States' *Oracle* to win the Louis Vuitton Cup and earn the right to challenge defending champions *New Zealand* for the America's Cup. It was a history-making moment. Two Kiwi skippers would be competing against each other for the biggest prize in sailing: Dean Barker for New Zealand and Russell Coutts, who had been a part of the Kiwis' 1995 and 2000 cup-winning teams before, amid great controversy, trading colours to join billionaire Ernesto Betarelli to bring the America's Cup to Switzerland. Coutts had backed the right horse: *Alinghi* trounced *New Zealand* 5–0 and, remarkably, Switzerland had become the first landlocked country in history to get its hands on the America's Cup.

➲ Dating back to 1995, *Alinghi*'s success meant that Coutts had won a record 14 consecutive races in the America's Cup and had become the only person to win as a challenger (twice) and as a defender.

Ernesto Betarelli's millions spawned an unlikely dream in 2003 but, skippered by sailing legend Russell Coutts, Swiss entry *Alinghi* proved unstoppable in the 32nd America's Cup and trounced *New Zealand* to take away sailing's greatest prize.

Michelle Wie burst onto the women's golf scene and in 2003 became the youngest player in history to make the cut at an LPGA Tour event: she ended the tournament tied for ninth place.

➲ Wie's star continued to rise. Backed by massive endorsements from Sony and Nike, she turned professional in 2005 and climbed as high as No. 3 in the world rankings. But in 2006, after a number of ill-advised forays in the men's tour, her form hit a new low. In 2007, she celebrated her 18th birthday with a second-last-placed finish at the Samsung World Championships, 36 strokes behind the leader.

THIRTEEN-YEAR-OLD WIE MAKES LPGA HISTORY

MICHELLE WIE YOUNGEST PLAYER TO MAKE THE CUT AT AN LPGA TOUR EVENT

28 March 2003, Mission Hills Country Club, Rancho Mirage, California, USA

Hawaii-born Michelle Wie first picked up a golf club aged four and knew she had discovered her future trade. In 2000, aged 11, she shot a personal best 64, became the youngest USGA Amateur Championship qualifier in history and then qualified for the Takefuji Classic to become the youngest player in history (since beaten) to qualify for an LPGA event: she missed the cut. In 2002, to great fanfare, she won the Hawaiian State Open women's division by 11 strokes. The following year, by which time the fanfare had become a media circus, she qualified for the Kraft Nabisco Classic (one of the four women's majors), went on to make the cut and became, aged 13 years, 5 months and 17 days, the youngest player in LPGA history to achieve the feat.

WEIR TRIUMPHS AT FABLED MASTERS

CANADIAN LEFTY WINS GOLF'S FIRST MAJOR

13 April 2003, Augusta National Golf Club, Augusta, Georgia, USA

In a nail-biting finish decided on a single extra hole, Mike Weir came back from behind to hold off Len Mattiace and win the prized Masters Tournament in 2003. With his rare playoff victory, the native of Sarnia, Ontario, became the first Canadian to slip on the coveted green blazer at Augusta National. The win transformed Weir into a national hero across Canada, where he was awarded the 2003 Lou Marsh Trophy as the best athlete in the country. The same year also saw him in fifth position on the money list with earnings of $4.8 million. Weir, who won several major tournaments after turning professional in 1992, was also included in the top ten of the Official World Golf Rankings in 2003 and 2004. One of his finest moments came during the 2007 Presidents Cup held in Montreal, when Weir defeated the World No. 1 Tiger Woods in a tense match.

Mike Weir credited his father's calmness on the sidelines for inspiring his Master's victory. "It wasn't until after the (playoff) round that I found out he was probably more nervous than me," he wrote in his public Master's diary.

➲ Weir was also the first left-handed golfer to win the Master's. Although he shoots left, Weir is actually right-handed. When he was 13, he wrote a letter to Jack Nicklaus asking if he should switch to playing right-handed. Nicklaus advised him to keep using his natural swing.

RADCLIFFE ROMPS TO WORLD MARATHON BEST

PAULA RADCLIFFE BREAKS HER OWN MARATHON WORLD RECORD
13 April 2003, London, England

Paula Radcliffe's nodding, plodding but supremely effective style brought her the junior cross-country world championship title in 1992, but it appeared that she might never quite make the transition to winning in the senior ranks. She finished fifth in the 5,000m World Championship final in 1995, achieved the same result in the 1996 Olympics and picked up a silver in the 10,000m at the 1999 World Championships, but when she missed out on the medals altogether at the 2000 Olympics and at the 2001 World Championships it seemed ultimate major championship success was always going to elude her. But a switch to the marathon revitalized her career. In 2002, she won the London marathon by almost three-and-a-half minutes from second-placed Svetlana Zakharova. Later in the year she won the Chicago marathon in 2h17m18s to break the world record by one-and-a-half minutes. Few thought she could improve the mark, but she stunned everyone in the 2003 London marathon, to clock 2h15m25s, destroy the women's elite field and break her own world record by nearly two minutes.

⮑ According to the IAFF, which awards points to each individual performance, Radcliffe's marathon world record is ranked higher than Michael Johnson's 400m record, Martita Koch's 200m world record and Florence Griffith-Joyner's 100m and 200m records. The IAFF rated her performance as the equivalent of a 9.75s 100m run.

A switch to the marathon revitalized Paula Radcliffe's career. It would bring her a world record in 2003 and, in 2005, a first major championship gold medal.

CANADA'S GOLDEN MOMENT

CANADA WINS INAUGURAL LACROSSE INDOOR WORLD CHAMPIONSHIP
24 May 2003, Copps Coliseum, Hamilton, Canada

When Canada met the Iroquois Nationals in the pinnacle game of the first-ever Lacrosse Indoor Worlds, it was with a crash. Canada had previously clocked a convincing 17–9 victory over the USA and the Nats had demolished Scotland 22–8 to move on to the finals. What happened next was nothing short of a complete spanking: The Maple Leafs led 5–0 at the end of the first quarter, then widened their lead to 12–2 by end of the second. In fact, Canada had scored 10 points before the Nats got onto the scoreboard. The second half went no better for the Iroquois team, and Canada ended the series as world champions with a final score of 21–4. Earlier in the day, the US hoisted itself to a 15–9 victory over Scotland to take the bronze.

Team Canada savours its victory. Canada's field lacrosse team has also won two championships: one in 1978 and more recently in 2006 – the only two outdoor championships not won by the USA.

➲ The next Championships, held in 2007, saw Canada fight through a much stiffer Iroquois opposition to again take gold, after both teams had obliterated their respective rivals in the semis. Once again, the US team came away with bronze.

FORMULA ONE'S YOUNGEST RACE WINNER

FERNANDO ALONSO BECOMES YOUNGEST DRIVER IN HISTORY TO WIN A FORMULA ONE RACE
24 August 2003, Hungaroring, Mogyorod, Hungary

Fernando Alonso was forced to wait before Flavio Briatore was prepared to unleash him in one of his Benetton cars. The former junior world kart champion, who had impressed in an underperforming Minardi in 1991 to earn a switch to the Benetton team at the end of the season, had spent a year as test driver, pounding lap after lap, before earning the right to a full-time drive in 2003. Alonso shot out of the blocks: in his second race, at the Malaysian GP, he became the youngest driver in Formula One history to claim pole. Further podiums followed in Brazil (third) and Spain (second), before Alonso struck gold in Hungary: qualifying on pole and leading the race from start to finish he became, aged 22 years, 26 days, the youngest race-winner in Formula One history.

Twenty-two-year-old Fernando Alonso led the Hungarian GP from start to finish in August 2003 to become Formula One's youngest-ever race-winner.

➲ Within two years Alonso had become the youngest world champion in the sport's history and defended the title in 2006.

The undisputed queen of BMX racing, Anne-Caroline Chausson won an unprecedented eight consecutive downhill world championships between 1996 and 2003.

EIGHT IN A ROW FOR RECORD-BREAKING CHAUSSON

ANNE-CAROLINE CHAUSSON WINS EIGHTH CONSECUTIVE MOUNTAIN BIKE DOWNHILL WORLD TITLE

7 September 2003, Lugano, Switzerland

Anne-Caroline Chausson started racing BMXs aged 16, went to the junior world championships in Metabief, France, and won. She defended her title for the next two years and then made a smooth transition into senior racing, finishing second in the World Cup standings (behind American Missy Giove), but winning the downhill world championship. The pattern was repeated in 1997: second in the World Cup (behind Giove) and defending her world downhill title, before she finally captured the double in 1998 and again in 1999 and 2000. From then on she spent less time on the full-time World Cup circuit, concentrating her efforts on defending her world title. She did so in style: in 2003 she collected the title for an unprecedented eighth successive time.

➲ Chausson added a ninth downhill world championship title to her haul in 2005.

Having finished second-best through much of his track career, a switch to the marathon turned Paul Tergat into a big-race winner.

TERGAT EXCELS ON THE ROADS

PAUL TERGAT BREAKS KHALID KHANNOUCHI'S MARATHON WORLD RECORD

28 September 2003, Berlin, Germany

Paul Tergat burst onto the international scene with five successive world cross-country championship wins between 1995 and 1999. But despite the odd moment of glory – such as breaking the 10,000m world record in 1998 – the Kenyan never enjoyed such moments on the track, always destined, it seemed, to miss out on the biggest prizes: he picked up two Olympic and two world championship silver medals – all of them behind Haile Gebrselassie. On the roads, however, it was a different story: he broke the half marathon world record in Milan in 1998; he beat Gebrselassie at the London Marathon in 2002; and, a year later, in Berlin, he broke Khalid Khannouchi's marathon world record (2h05m38s) with a time of 2h04m55s.

➲ Tergat's record stood for over four years until his great friend and rival Haile Gebrselassie clocked 2h04m26s over the same Berlin course on 30 September 2007.

THE GREATEST FORMULA ONE DRIVER OF ALL TIME

MICHAEL SCHUMACHER BECOMES FORMULA ONE'S FIRST SIX-TIME WORLD CHAMPION

12 October 2003, Suzuka, Japan

The characteristics that would mark Michael Schumacher's career were apparent during his early years with Benetton (1991–95): he was quick, fearless and ruthless – a combination that brought him world titles in 1994 and 1995. But then he showed he was a risk-taker, too. In 1996, the German switched to Ferrari – a team that had not produced a world champion since 1979 – and set about waking the sleeping giant. He recorded three race wins in 1996; in 1997 and 1998 he was the championship runner-up. His challenge for the title in 1999 ended with a crash at the British GP, but he returned later in the season to help the team to its first constructors' championship since 1983. By 2000, he was ready to rule the world: Schumacher won nine times to collect a third title; nine wins in 2001 were enough to see him to a fourth title. In 2002 he won a record-breaking 11 times to equal Juan Manuel Fangio's haul of five world titles, and in 2003, notched up six wins to become the first six-time world champion in Formula One history.

By numbers alone, Michael Schumacher is the greatest driver ever to have raced in Formula One: the German holds the all-time record for most race wins (91), most pole positions (68), most fastest laps (76) and most world championship titles (7).

➲ Schumacher extended his record of world championship wins in 2004 when he collected his seventh drivers' title. He retired at the end of the 2006 season.

HAYDEN HAMMERS TEST BEST SCORE

MATTHEW HAYDEN BREAKS BRIAN LARA'S RECORD FOR THE HIGHEST TEST SCORE

9–13 October 2003, WACA, Perth, Australia

Although he'd scored a century in only his third Test match (against the West Indies in January 1997), the form of Australian openers Michael Slater and Mark Taylor suggested Matthew Hayden's international career was over when it had barely begun. But prolific form for Queensland demanded his re-inclusion at the top of the Australian order and by March 2000 he was back in the Australian team. He came of age against India in 2000–01, scoring 549 runs in the series and ending the year with an Australian-record 1,391 runs in the calendar year. Now a standout performer in a dominant Australian team, he produced his finest moment in October 2003 against Zimbabwe in Perth, when he scored 380 runs in the first innings to break Brian Lara's record for the highest Test score.

Matthew Hayden hammered Zimbabwe's bowlers to all corners of the Perth ground in October 2003, smashing a world-record score of 380 off 437 balls.

➲ Hayden's record lasted barely six months before Brian Lara, back to his swashbuckling best, scored 400 against England at St John's, Antigua, in April 2004.

AUSTRALIA 142 NAMIBIA 0

AUSTRALIA RECORD BIGGEST WINNING MARGIN IN INTERNATIONAL RUGBY HISTORY
25 October 2003, Adelaide Oval, Adelaide, Australia

From the moment New Zealand destroyed Japan 145–17 at the 1995 World Cup in South Africa the shadow of how beneficial such massacres were for developing rugby nations loomed large over the game. Fears were raised in 1999 when the tournament was increased from 16 to 20 teams: Italy were the ones to feel the All Black power this time, losing out 101–3. But the difference between rugby's haves and have-nots truly manifested itself for the first time at the 2003 World Cup in Australia. In Pool C, England beat Uruguay 111–13, but that was nothing compared to the thrashing Australia handed out to Namibia in Pool A: the Wallabies scored a tournament-record 22 tries and ran out 142–0 winners – it was the highest margin of victory in international rugby history.

➲ There have been six instances of 100-point totals in Rugby World Cup history: New Zealand 145 Japan 17 (1995); New Zealand 101 Italy 3 (1999); England 101 Tonga 10 (1999); Australia 142 Namibia 0 (2003); England 111 Uruguay 13 (2003); New Zealand 108 Portugal 13 (2007).

Australia scored a World Cup-record 22 tries during their 142–0 win against Namibia in 2003: it is the highest winning margin in international rugby history.

OILERS AND HABS TAKE IT OUTSIDE

EDMONTON AND MONTREAL BEAT ONE ANOTHER IN FIRST NHL REGULAR-SEASON OUTDOOR MATCH

22 November 2003, Commonwealth Stadium, Edmonton, Canada

The Heritage Classic was a special event: an outdoor hockey game played in celebration of the Edmonton Oilers' 25th anniversary as an NHL team. It was, in fact, two games: first was a MegaStars match consisting of two 25-minute halves between squads comprising some of the teams' best alumni, then a regular-season NHL contest. The old-timers game would be remembered not for its so-so scoring or its historical significance, but rather for the fun that the players were obviously having, and the spectacular goaltending on both sides (in the first half alone, Edmonton goalie Grant Fuhr stopped 12 shots on goal, while Montreal's Steve Penney intercepted six of Edmonton's seven tries). At the end of the game, Edmonton was still standing with a score of 2–0 over the old-time Habs, though Montreal's regular team would win the regular-season game later that day 4–3.

The Heritage Classic was played outdoors despite brutally cold temperatures of -29°C (-20°F). Players wore tuques under their helmets and had heaters at their benches. Many of the 60,000 fans who bought tickets left early because of the cold.

➲ This was the first match to be broadcast in the new HDTV television format on the CBC. The broadcast of the Heritage Classic also set a new record of viewers with an audience of 2.75 million across the country. The NHL subsequently held the follow-up Winter Classic on 1 January 2008 between the Pittsburgh Penguins and the Buffalo Sabres with almost 80,000 fans attending the game in Orchard Park, New York.

Karen Stupples may have had to wait five years before collecting her first professional title, but when she finally won she did so in style, shooting an LPGA Tour-record low 72-hole score (258) at the 2004 Welch's/Fry's Championship.

STUPPLES SHOOTS LPGA TOUR FOUR-ROUND TOTAL LOW

KAREN STUPPLES SHOOTS LOWEST FOUR-ROUND TOTAL IN LPGA TOUR HISTORY

15 March 2004, Dell Urich Golf Course, Tucson, Arizona, USA

After an impressive amateur career, England's Karen Stupples turned professional in 1998, but did not have the money to attend qualifying school for the European Tour. Sponsorship duly arrived: Stupples packed her bags, returned to the US (where she had been at college), and gained non-exempt status for the LPGA Tour at the 1998 qualifying tournament. She was back at Q-school after her maiden season, but progressed to earn exempt status for the 2000 season. Progress through to 2003 was slow – seven top-ten finishes in three seasons – before she exploded in 2004, claiming her first Tour title, the Welch's/Fry's Championship, with rounds of 63, 66, 66 and 63: her four-round total of 258 remains the lowest in LPGA Tour history.

➲ Things got even better for Stupples later in the season when she went on to win the Women's British Open at Sunningdale to collect her first major.

LARA REAFFIRMS STATUS AS WORLD'S BEST BATSMAN

BRIAN LARA RECLAIMS RECORD FOR WORLD'S HIGHEST TEST SCORE

13 April 2004, Antigua Recreation Ground, St John's, Antigua

In the mid-1990s, Brian Lara emerged as the most prolific batsman on the world stage. During 1994 he produced two almost-perfect months of cricket, beginning by breaking Garfield Sobers' highest Test score (365) with a flawless knock of 375 against England and ending it by scoring 501 not out for Warwickshire to break the first-class highest record. He was a world star and although the weight of expectation lay heavy on him, and the burden of captaining a West Indies team on a downward spiral sometimes seemed to get the better of him, he proved himself the most proficient run-scorer in Test cricket since Donald Bradman. In 1998–99 he almost single-handedly defied Australia, scoring three centuries in the tied series; in 2001 against Sri Lanka he registered 688 runs (a three-Test series record), 42 percent of his side's runs. In 2003, Matthew Hayden may have broken his Test record (380 against Zimbabwe), but it took a mere six months before Lara's name was back up in lights: he reclaimed his Test record with a peerless 400 not out against England in Antigua.

➲ Lara's accomplishment in Antigua made him only the second player in history to have scored two triple-centuries in Test cricket (the other being Donald Bradman). He also became only the second player in history to have recorded two first-class innings of 400 runs or over (the other being Bill Ponsford).

It took a mere six months for Brian Lara to reclaim the world record he had lost to Matthew Hayden for the highest Test score. In April 2004 he hammered a majestic 400 not out against England in Antigua.

➲ The streak ended at the next race with a fourth-place finish at the Spanish GP, but Rossi would win eight further times that season to win his fourth consecutive world title.

TWENTY-THREE PODIUMS IN A ROW FOR DOMINANT ROSSI

VALENTINO ROSSI BREAKS 500CC/MOTOGP RECORD FOR MOST CONSECUTIVE PODIUM FINISHES

18 April 2004, Phasika Freeway, Free State, South Africa

Valentino Rossi brought his 2001 championship-winning form into 2002, winning eight of the season's first nine races before rear-tyre failure at the Czech Grand Prix brought his momentum to a halt. But Rossi simply shrugged off the disappointment and recorded six successive podium finishes (three wins and three runner-ups) in the last six races to defend the title. He was equally dominant in 2003, finishing on the podium in all 16 races (including nine wins) to stretch his run to 22 consecutive podium finishes – to equal Giacomo Agostini's record that had stood for 34 years. But that's where many people thought Rossi's streak would end: at the end of the year he joined Yamaha. It was a gamble for both team and rider, but they got off to a sensational start at the 2004 season-opening South African GP, as Rossi took the win to extend his streak of consecutive podium finishes to a record-breaking 23.

ZIMBABWE CRICKET HITS RECORD LOW

ZIMBABWE RECLAIM RECORD FOR LOWEST SCORE IN A ONE-DAY INTERNATIONAL

25 April 2004, Harare Sports Club, Harare, Zimbabwe

Zimbabwe's cricketers had tasted ultimate one-day international humiliation before. In 2001 they had crashed to a miserable 38 all out against Sri Lanka in Colombo to collect the record for the worst-ever score. The record may have been broken by Canada (36) at the 2003 World Cup, but the same tournament had seen worrying signs for Zimbabwe cricket. Two of their players (Andy Flower and Henry Olonga) wore black armbands protesting the "death of democracy" in their country and retired after the tournament. Shortly afterwards captain Heath Streak was sacked … and 14 other players followed him. By the time Sri Lanka toured in April 2004, Zimbabwe could muster little more than a fringe XI to take to the field. It showed: in the third one-day international, Zimbabwe slipped to a woeful 35 all out to reclaim the record nobody wanted.

Political problems off the pitch led to major upheaval on it for Zimbabwe cricket in 2004. Fielding little more than a fringe team against Sri Lanka, they slipped to the worst score in one-day international history (35 all out) in Harare.

➲ Zimbabwe's innings lasted a mere 18 overs and none of their batsmen made it into double figures. They lost the one-day series 5–0 and the ensuing Test series 2–0. Later in the year they withdrew temporarily from Test cricket.

MURALITHARAN SPINS HIS WAY INTO RECORD BOOKS

MUTTIAH MURALITHARAN BREAKS COURTNEY WALSH'S RECORD FOR MOST TEST WICKETS

8 May 2004, Harare Sports Club, Harare, Zimbabwe

Muttiah Muralitharan's unusual bowling action, which has caused as much controversy throughout his career as it has gasps of admiration from the crowd for the spin he imparts on the ball, propelled him into the international cricket spotlight. His wickets played a huge part in Sri Lanka's rise up the world rankings, and as he continued to bamboozle batsmen around the world, the records started to fall: he was the fastest to reach the 350-, 400-, 450- and 500-wicket milestones – in 66, 72, 80 and 87 matches respectively – and travelled to Zimbabwe in 2004 fast closing in on Courtney Walsh's record of 519 wickets. He tied Walsh's mark with 6 for 49 in the first innings of the first Test before dismissing Mluleki Nkala in the second to claim the record.

With a viciously turning off-spinner, top-spinner and, later, a mystery "doosra" in his armoury, Muttiah Muralitharan dominated batsmen around the world and, in May 2004, he became the world's leading Test wicket-taker: it was an honour he would enjoy for four months.

➲ Later in the year the Sri Lankan was sidelined for several games through injury and saw Shane Warne break his record. The Australian star finished with 708 Test wickets, a figure Muralitharan passed against England in the first Test at Kandy on 3 December 2007.

In 2003, Pemba Dorji enjoyed the prestige of completing the fastest ascent of Mount Everest in history for just three days. He returned a year later to break the record for a second time: 8h10m from base camp to summit.

FROM BASE CAMP TO SUMMIT IN 8 HOURS 10 MINUTES

PEMBA DORJI SHERPA BREAKS RECORD FOR FASTEST ASCENT OF MOUNT EVEREST

21 May 2004, Mount Everest, Nepal/Tibet

On 22 May 2003, Pemba Dorji broke fellow Sherpa Babu Chiri's "unbreakable" record for the fastest ascent of Mount Everest (16h56m set in 2000) by over four hours, recording a time from base camp to summit of 12h45m. It was hailed as climbing's equivalent of the first sub-four-minute mile, but stood as a record for a grand total of three days, before Khakpa Gelu clocked 10h46m. And then the weather closed in and any thoughts of record-breaking were put on hold for another year. In 2004 Pemba Dorji was back: on 20 May he left base camp at 6 p.m., stopped three times between 8,000m and 8,748m to eat and appease the spirits, and reached the summit at 2.10 a.m: he had completed the climb in 8h10m.

➲ Four days earlier, Appa Sherpa had broken his own world record for the most ascents of Everest when he reached the summit for the 14th time.

WORLD ATHLETICS WELCOMES A NEW STAR

RKENENISA BEKELE SMASHES HAILE GEBRSELASSIE'S 5,000M WORLD RECORD
31 May 2004, Hengelo, the Netherlands

Ethiopia's Kenenisa Bekele burst onto the international scene when he became the first man in history to win both the short race (4km) and long race (10km) at the 2002 World Cross Country Championships in March 2002 in Dublin. He repeated the feat in 2003 and the same year started to show his huge promise on the track, beating his mentor and fellow countryman Haile Gebrselassie into second place in the final of the 10,000m at that year's World Championships in Paris. It was a passing-of-the-torch moment: the following year he broke Gebrselassie's 5,000m world record (12m39.36s that had stood since 1998) by two seconds, clocking 12m37.35s in Hengelo, the Netherlands.

Kenenisa Bekele is the brightest talent to have hit world athletics in recent years. In 2004, aged just 21, he smashed Haile Gebrselassie's 5,000m world record by over two seconds.

➲ Later in the year Bekele broke Gebrselassie's 10,000m world record (26m22.75s set in Hengelo in 1998) by over two seconds, clocking 26m17.53s. He ended the year by winning 5,000m and 10,000m gold at the Olympic Games in Athens.

Drug allegations may never have been too far away from him, but in 2004 French rider Richard Virenque won the polka-dot jersey for a Tour de France record seventh time.

THE KING OF THE MOUNTAINS

RICHARD VIRENQUE WINS POLKA-DOT JERSEY FOR RECORD SEVENTH TIME AT THE TOUR DE FRANCE
25 July 2004, Paris, France

Richard Virenque's four successive polka-dot-jersey-winning performances with the Festina team between 1994 and 1997 (awarded to the King of the Mountains since 1933) marked him out as a potential Tour winner. But then, in 1998, the Italian team was hit by a doping scandal and although Virenque switched teams in 1999 and won a fifth polka-dot jersey, allegations against him would not go away: in March 2000 he was temporarily suspended from the sport. He returned, still under a cloud, only to miss out on the King of the Mountains title in 2001 and 2002, but roared back to win it for the sixth time in 2003 (to equal Federico Bahomontes's and Lucien van Impe's record) and secured a record-breaking seventh King of the Mountain title in 2004.

➲ Virenque announced his retirement from international cycling in September 2004.

A pioneer in vert and mini-ramp skateboarding in his youth, Danny Way brought the concept of mega-ramps to the sport and used them to break multiple distance records, culminating in a leap of 79ft (24.08m) at the 2004 X Games.

THE LARGEST JUMP ON A SKATEBOARD

DANNY WAY BREAKS HIS OWN SKATEBOARD DISTANCE WORLD RECORD

8 August 2004, Staples Center, Los Angeles, California, USA

Born on 15 April 1974, Danny Way started skateboarding at the age of six, entered his first tournament at the age of 12, won it and within two years had turned professional. Described as a daredevil with a showman's spirit, he put his body on the line – he required seven operations in 1997 alone (the same year he became the first skateboarder to drop out of a helicopter onto a ramp) – and pushed his sport to new levels. In 2002 he conceived the idea of mega-ramps and subsequently broke the world distance record with a leap of 65ft (21.03m); he increased the mark to 75ft (22.86m) the following year. In 2004, in the first-ever Big Air Challenge at the X Games, he broke his record again, leaping 79ft (24.08m).

➲ On 9 July 2005, using the Beijing Mega-Ramp, Way became the first skateboarder in history to ollie over the Great Wall of China.

PHELPS STARTS MEDAL QUEST IN RECORD-BREAKING FASHION

MICHAEL PHELPS BREAKS 400M INDIVIDUAL MEDLEY WORLD RECORD

13–29 August 2004, Athens, Greece

In 1996, legendary American swimming coach Bob Bowman spotted 11-year-old Michael Phelps's raw talent and took the youngster under his wing. Four years later, at the 2000 Olympic Games in Sydney, he became, aged 15, America's youngest swimming Olympian since 1934, and finished fifth in the 200m butterfly. A few months later he became the youngest swimmer in history to break a world record (the 200m butterfly, aged 15 years, 9 months); he would break it again in 2001. The records continued to come his way (five of them at the 2003 world championships alone), and expectations were at a fever pitch when he arrived at the 2004 Olympic Games in Athens – with his sponsor Speedo reputedly offering him a $1 million bonus if he equalled Mark Spitz's 1972 feat of winning seven gold medals. He got off to a great start, taking 400m medley gold in a world-record time of 4m08.26s.

Although the ultimate feat of equalling Mark Spitz's haul of seven Olympic gold medals eluded him, Michael Phelps got off to a blistering start in his much-hyped quest at the 2004 Olympic Games by breaking the 400m medley world record in his first event.

➲ The gold trail came to an end a few days later with the US 4x100m freestyle relay team: they finished third behind Australia and South Africa, but Phelps did pick up another five gold medals (100m butterfly, 200m butterfly, 200m medley, 400m medley and 4x100 medley).

QUEEN OF THE CANOE TAKES OLYMPIC GOLD YET AGAIN

BIRGIT FISCHER BECOMES FIRST WOMAN IN HISTORY TO WIN OLYMPIC GOLD MEDALS 24 YEARS APART
13–29 August 2004, Athens, Greece

Birgit Fischer first tasted Olympic success as an 18-year-old in Moscow in 1980, becoming the youngest canoeist in history to take gold when she triumphed in the 500m singles kayak. She was a strong favourite to add to her medal haul in 1984, but the East German team boycotted the Games. She returned in Seoul for a three-medal haul, including gold in the pairs and fours. Representing the unified German team in 1992, she picked up another gold (singles) and silver (fours); she struck gold in Atlanta in 1996 (fours) and picked up gold in both pairs and fours at Sydney in 2000. She was lured back into a boat for the 2004 Olympic Games and, aged 42, led the German four to victory to collect her eighth Olympic gold medal, a record 24 years after she had claimed her first.

➲ Fischer remains the only woman in history to win Olympic gold medals 24 years apart and only Russian gymnast Larisa Latynina (18) has more than her haul of 12 Olympic medals.

MACK BREAKS OLYMPIC RECORD TO CLAIM POLE-VAULT GOLD

TIM MACK BREAKS THE OLYMPIC POLE-VAULT RECORD
13–29 August 2004, Athens, Greece

He may have been a former junior Olympic champion (1991) and NCAA indoor champion, but success on the international stage was limited for pole-vaulter Tim Mack until he recorded a shock win at the 2001 Goodwill Games in Brisbane, Australia. In 2002 he won the world indoor championship and by the end of 2003 was ranked tenth in the world. Then came Athens: with one jump remaining – and with his team-mate Toby Stephenson having already cleared 2.90m – Mack knew he would have to clear Andrei Tivontchik's Olympic-record mark of 2.92m (set in Atlanta in 1996) if he were to claim his sport's ultimate prize. He cleared 2.95m and the gold medal, as well as the Olympic record, was his.

➲ Mack's mark was still some way short of Sergei Bubka's world-record mark of 6.14m set in Sestriere on 31 July 1994.

Tim Mack produced a lifetime best when it really mattered, clearing an Olympic-record 2.95m in his final jump at Athens in 2004 to win pole-vaulting gold.

Yelena Slesarenko's rapid march to the top of the world high-jump ladder was complete when she claimed gold in Athens in Olympic-record-breaking fashion.

SLESARENKO LEAPS TO NEW OLYMPIC HEIGHTS

YELENA SLESARENKO BREAKS OLYMPIC HIGH-JUMP RECORD
13–29 August 2004, Athens, Greece

If a fifth-place finish at the 2002 World Indoor Championships suggested Russian Yelena Slesarenko had a bright future in the high jump then her performances in 2004 proved she was ready to take on, and beat, the world. She started the year by claiming the Indoor World Championship title in Hungary and proved equally impressive outdoors: improving her personal best from 1.97m to 2.04m at the European Cup and then carrying her momentum into the 2004 Olympics. She cleared 2.04m at her first attempt – a height too hot for the rest of her opponents – and with the gold medal already secure, broke Stefka Kostadinova's Olympic record (2.05m set in Atlanta 1996) with an effortless leap of 2.06m.

➲ With the Olympic record and gold medal already secured, Slesarenko made an attempt on Kostadinova's world record mark of 2.09m that had stood since August 1987, but failed in all three attempts.

Roman Sebrle won his first major international decathlon medal in some style at the 2004 Olympic Games, breaking Daley Thompson's Olympic record for the event that had stood since 1984.

SEBRLE FINDS BIG-STAGE FEET TO TAKE DECATHLON GOLD

ROMAN SEBRLE BREAKS OLYMPIC DECATHLON RECORD
13–29 August 2004, Athens, Greece

At the 2000 Olympic Games in Sydney, Czech Roman Sebrle had missed out on decathlon gold by a mere 35 points to Estonia's Erki Nool, but his response to such disappointment was the stuff of champions. The following year he became the first decathlete in history to break the 9,000-point barrier, breaking Tomas Dvorak's world record (8,994 points set in Prague in 1999) with a haul of 9,026 points in Gotzis, Austria. And just when it seemed he was ready to dominate the event, he finished second in the 2003 World Championships. But at the 2004 Olympic Games in Athens he finally found his big-stage feet, recording 8,893 points to win gold and break Daley Thompson's Olympic-record haul of 8,847 points set in 1984.

➲ The 2005 World Championships in Helsinki, Finland, saw a worrying return to the norm for Sebrle: he finished second once again, 211 points behind America's Brian Clay.

Their form elsewhere may have been inconsistent to say the least, but between 1996 and 2004 Denmark's women's handball team put up a determined defence of their Olympic title, becoming the first team in history to win the competition on three consecutive occasions.

DENMARK COMPLETE OLYMPIC HANDBALL HAT-TRICK

DENMARK WIN WOMEN'S HANDBALL GOLD FOR RECORD THIRD SUCCESSIVE OLYMPIC GAMES
13–29 August 2004, Athens, Greece

In 1996 in Atlanta, Denmark – a team with absolutely no Olympic pedigree – shocked South Korea to take handball gold and end the south-east Asians' hopes of collecting a record third consecutive handball gold medal. The Danes confirmed their No. 1 status by winning the World Championships the following year, but after missing out on a medal of any kind at the 1999 World Championships, few gave them a hope of defending their Olympic title. They took gold. They missed out on the medals in both the 2001 and 2003 World Championships and, once again, few gave them a chance of defending their Olympic crown. But it was a tournament they clearly liked: they beat South Korea 38–36 in the final to become the first team in the event's history to win three consecutive gold medals.

➲ True to form, Denmark missed out on a medal of any colour at the 2005 World Championships held in Russia.

MEARES RISES TO OCCASION IN WORLD-RECORD-BREAKING FASHION

ANNA MEARES BREAKS 500M TIME TRIAL WORLD AND OLYMPIC RECORD

13–29 August 2004, Athens, Greece

Australian Anna Meares made tentative progress on the international scene, such as a fourth-place finish in the 500m time trial at the 2002 Commonwealth Games in Manchester, before bursting into the spotlight with a gold-medal-winning performance at the 2004 World Championships in Melbourne: but more challenging times were to come later in the year for the 20-year-old Australian. As she sat preparing herself for the most important run of her career at the Olympic Games in Athens, China's Yonghua Jiang broke the world record with a time of 34.112s. A tough task had just become considerably harder, but Meares's response was sensational: she crossed the finishing line in a staggering 33.952s to break both the Olympic and world record and claim her sport's ultimate prize.

⊃ Meares continued to dominate the women's 500m time trial scene and went on to break her own world record twice: first in Sydney in November 2006 (33.944s) and again in Mallorca in March 2007 (33.588s).

ULMER SHATTERS WORLD RECORD TO TAKE PURSUIT GOLD

SARAH ULMER BREAKS HER OWN 3,000M INDIVIDUAL PURSUIT WORLD RECORD

13–29 August 2004, Athens, Greece

New Zealand's Sarah Ulmer confirmed her status as one of the brightest prospects in world cycling when she took a silver medal in the 3,000m individual pursuit at the 1994 Commonwealth Games at the age of 16. But her arrival into the elite of women's cycling was a long time coming: she placed seventh in the 1996 Olympic Games and fourth in 2000. Her breakthrough year on the international stage came in 2004. In March she broke the world record at the World Track Championships in Melbourne (3m30.604s); she broke it five months later during the qualifying stages at the Athens Olympics (3m26.4s); and again in the final, producing a display of awesome power and speed to clock a time of 3m24.537s.

⊃ Word later emerged that Ulmer had broken her own record a number of times in practice during the build-up to the Olympic Games: such news was, of course, kept from both the public and her opponents.

THE KING OF PRECISION

RALF SCHUMANN BECOMES FIRST THREE-TIME 25M RAPID-FIRE PISTOL OLYMPIC CHAMPION
13–29 August 2004, Athens, Greece

East Germany's Ralf Schumann first picked up a pistol at the age of 15 in 1977 and within no time had become a master of 25m rapid-fire pistol shooting. He travelled to the 1988 Seoul Olympics as strong favourite for gold, but collected silver. Shortly afterwards the targets were changed and, although scores dropped in general, Schumann, the king of precision, prospered. He became world champion in 1990, took Olympic gold in 1992 and, in 1995, broke the world record with 597 points (57 bullseyes out of 60 shots). He defended his Olympic title in 1996 (breaking the Olympic record), but nerves got the better of him in Sydney in 2000, and he finished fifth. He roared back to form in Athens four years later, taking gold to become the sport's first three-time Olympic champion.

⮫ After a major rule change in 2005, Schumann lost his status as world-record-holder to Russia's Sergei Alifirenko, who registered a new "revised" world record of 589 points in August 2005; Schumann equalled the mark in May 2006.

SHARP-SHOOTING PARK SUNG HYUN ON SONG IN ATHENS

PARK SUNG HYUN BREAKS THE 72-ARROW WORLD AND OLYMPIC RECORDS

13–29 August 2004, Athens, Greece

Korea's team of three archers (Park Sung Hyun, Yun Mi Jun and Lee Sun Jin) were expected to dominate the women's archery competition at the 2004 Olympic Games in Athens in exactly the same manner as their fellow countrymen had dominated at the previous four Olympic Games (where they had completed the sweep of individual and team gold medals). And the trio certainly lived up to their billing, occupying the first three positions in the 72-arrow ranking round – used to determine who would play whom in the knockout stage of the tournament – with Yun Mi Jun in third (with 673 points), Lee Sun Jin in second (with 675 points) and Park Sung Hyun at No. 1, having broken the world and Olympic 72-arrow record with a staggering 682 points.

Korean dominance continued in the Olympic archery competition in Athens in 2004, with Park Sung Hyun breaking the 72-arrow world and Olympic records in the qualifying stages of the tournament before going on to claim gold.

➲ The knockout stages of the competition ran true to form with both Park Sung Hyun and Lee Sun Jin making it through to the gold-medal shootout: Park Sung Hyun won the 18-arrow final 110–108 to round off a memorable competition.

KURZER ON TARGET IN WORLD-RECORD-BREAKING STYLE

MANFRED KURZER BREAKS 10M RUNNING TARGET WORLD AND OLYMPIC RECORDS

13–19 August 2004, Athens, Greece

Germany's Manfred Kurzer had finished sixth in the 10m running target competition at the 2000 Olympic Games in Sydney – an event that sees competitors shooting at a sideways-moving target (travelling at various speeds) with air rifles at a distance of 10m. But the man who had dedicated his life to shooting was determined and convinced that he could do better: and proved it in some style during the 10m running target qualifying rounds at the 2004 Olympic Games in Athens, registering a score of 590 points (out of a possible 600) to break Igor Kolesov's world record of 588 points set in 2002.

➲ Sadly Kurzer would not have the opportunity to defend his title. The Olympic Committee announced that the 10m running event would be removed from further Olympic schedules as part of an overall attempt to reduce the number of events contested at the summer games.

A world-record-breaking performance in the qualifying stage of the 2004 10m running target Olympic competition handed Germany's Manfred Kurzer such a commanding lead that even a major slip-up in the final round did not prevent him from winning gold.

FIVE IN A ROW FOR SCHUMACHER

MICHAEL SCHUMACHER WINS RECORD FIFTH CONSECUTIVE F1 DRIVERS' CHAMPIONSHIP

29 August 2004, Spa-Francorchamps, Belgium

After claiming his sixth world drivers' title in 2003 to become the most successful Formula One driver of all time – surpassing Juan Manuel Fangio's mark of five titles – Michael Schumacher would have been forgiven for hanging up his driving gloves and seeking some more leisurely pursuit. But racing was in Schumacher's make-up and as long as he felt he had a competitive car underneath him, he vowed to carry on. His opponents must have wished he hadn't: Schumacher opened the 2004 campaign by winning 11 of the season's first 12 races – he did not finish in Monaco – and went on to claim his seventh world championship with a second-place finish at the Belgian GP: he had become the first driver in Formula One history to win five consecutive world titles.

Michael Schumacher was in typically dominant form in 2004, securing the drivers' title after the 14th race (of 18) of the season to become the first driver in history to win five successive world championships.

⮑ Then Schumacher's fortunes took a downward turn: in 2005 he won just once (at the controversial United States GP). He finished second in the drivers' championship in 2006 (with seven race wins) before retiring from the sport.

A big serve and a devastating forehand have taken America's Andy Roddick into the elite of world tennis: he holds the record for the world's fastest serve with a 155mph (249.4km/h) effort in September 2004.

A-ROD DELIVERS 155MPH BULLET

ANDY RODDICK BREAKS HIS OWN RECORD FOR TENNIS'S FASTEST SERVE

24 September 2004, Family Circle Tennis Center, Charleston, South Carolina, USA

Blessed with an explosive serve and a ferocious forehand, Andy Roddick burst onto the international tennis scene in 2001, reaching the quarter-finals of the US Open and ending the year, aged 19, as the youngest top-20 ranked player in history. In 2003 he equalled Greg Rusedski's record for the world's fastest serve with a 149mph (239.8km/h) bomb at London's Queen's Club and ended the year as US Open champion. Further grand slam success may have eluded him, but his big-serving antics continued: in February 2004 he made the fastest serve record his own with a 150mph (241.4km/h) effort; the following year, during his Davis Cup World Group semi-final singles match against Belarus's Vladimir Voltchkov, he beat it again, improving the mark to 155mph (249.4km/h).

⮑ When Roddick ended 2003 as the world's No. 1-ranked player, he became, aged 21, the second-youngest player since the start of the ranking system in 1973 to achieve the feat, behind Lleyton Hewitt (who was 20 years, 8 months).

SUZUKI SMASHES SISLER'S SINGLE-SEASON RECORD

ICHIRO SUZUKI BREAKS GEORGE SISLER'S SINGLE-SEASON RECORD FOR MOST HITS

1 October 2004, Safeco Field, Seattle, Washington, USA

Ichiro Suzuki's tremendous hitting and fielding abilities, rigorously honed since the age of seven, made him an instant star in the MLB, and a record-breaking one, too: in 2004 he broke George Sisler's 84-year-old single-season record for most hits.

When Ichiro Suzuki signed for the Seattle Mariners on 9 November 2000 after eight stellar seasons with Orix Blue Wave in Japan's Pacific League to become the first Japanese position player to sign for an MLB team, the critics had a field day, suggesting that, at a diminutive 5ft 9in, he was too frail to last in baseball's big time. But the man dubbed "The Human Batting Machine" by the Japanese press thrived, recording a league-high 242 hits (the highest single-season total since 1930) and winning American League MVP and Rookie of the Season honours. The hits continued in record-breaking proportions: 208 in 2002, 212 in 2003 and a staggering 262 in 2004, to break George Sisler's MLB record that had stood since 1920.

➲ Suzuki broke several records that season: on 26 August he became the first person in Major League history to post 200 hits in his first four seasons; on 21 September, he recorded his 207th single of the season to break the single-season record that had stood since 1898.

SEVENTH HEAVEN FOR 42-YEAR-OLD CLEMENS

ROGER CLEMENS WINS RECORD SEVENTH CY YOUNG AWARD

10 November 2004, Minute Maid Park, Houston, Texas, USA

The year Roger Clemens finally evolved from being a "thrower" into a "pitcher" was 1986: his 24 wins helped Boston Red Sox into the World Series and brought him American League MVP honours and a first AL Cy Young Award – given to the best pitcher in the League. He won it again in 1987 and 1991, but by 1996 seemed a shadow of his former headline-making days. A switch to the Toronto Blue Jays revitalized his career: he took Cy Young honours in 1997 and 1998 before moving to the New York Yankees in 1999. World Series rings came in 1999 and 2000; a 20–3 season in 2001 followed: enough to earn Clemens a sixth Cy Young Award. His seventh – but first in the National League – came in 2004 when, aged 42, he posted an 18–4 season for the Houston Astros.

Considered one of the most pre-eminent pitchers in baseball history, Roger Clemens collected the Cy Young Award a record seven times between 1986 and 2004.

➲ Clemens had originally said he would retire following the 2003 season with the New York Yankees but changed his mind and joined the Houston Astros. He stayed with the Texas outfit until 2006 before re-joining the Yankees for the 2007 season.

PATRIOTS BREAK NFL'S WINNING STREAK RECORD

NEW ENGLAND PATRIOTS BREAK NFL RECORD FOR MOST CONSECUTIVE REGULAR-SEASON WINS

24 October 2004, Gillette Stadium, Foxborough, Massachusetts, USA

The New England Patriots started the 2003 NFL season in topsy-turvy fashion, winning two and losing two of their opening four games. But then they seemed to find their stride, winning their last 12 regular-season games on the bounce and taking their form into the playoffs, beating the Tennessee Titans and Indianapolis Colts before securing a last-gasp 32–29 Super Bowl win against the Carolina Panthers – the franchise's second Super Bowl success in three years. The Pats started the 2004 season in similarly impressive fashion, winning their first six games. It broke an all-time NFL record: dating back to the previous season they had won an all-time-best 18 consecutive regular-season games. The streak came to an end with a 30–24 defeat to the Pittsburgh Steelers on 31 October.

➲ Including their 2003 playoff wins, the Patriots are also credited with holding the record for the most consecutive wins (21).

During the course of their back-to-back Super Bowl wins in 2003 and 2004, the New England Patriots broke the NFL record for most consecutive regular-season wins (18), though it was passed by the same franchise in 2006–07, winning the last three games of 2006 and all 16 in 2007.

Between May 2003 and October 2004, Arsenal put together a record 49 unbeaten-game streak in the Premier League and became the first team for 115 years to go through a league season undefeated.

THE PREMIER LEAGUE'S LONGEST UNBEATEN RUN

ARSENAL'S RECORD-BREAKING 49-GAME UNBEATEN RUN COMES TO A HALT

24 October 2004, Old Trafford, Manchester, England

On 7 May 2003, just a week after losing to Leeds to hand Manchester United the Premier League title, Arsenal bounced back with a 7–1 end-of-season thrashing of Southampton. It was the start of great things to come. They started the 2003–04 season with four straight wins, scraped a 0–0 draw at Old Trafford to keep the unbeaten run going and kept it going until the end of the season – the first team to do so since Preston North End in 1889. The streak continued into the 2004–05 season: a 3–0 win over Blackburn took them past Nottingham Forest's 42-game record that had stood for 26 years, before it finally ended at 49 following a 2–0 defeat to Manchester United at Old Trafford.

➲ Arsenal's form slipped away following the defeat and they ended the season as Premier League runners-up, a massive 12 points behind new champions Chelsea.

THE HARD MAN OF IRON MAN

JACQUES FOX BREAKS RECORD FOR MOST IRON MAN TOURNAMENTS CONTESTED IN ONE YEAR

31 October 2004, Honolulu, Hawaii, USA

Iron Man triathlons were first conceived in Southern California in the early 1970s, as an end-of-summer celebration for athletic clubs, but the world had to wait until 1978 before it saw its first international Iron Man competition. Held in Honolulu, Hawaii, the race consisted of a 2.4-mile (3.86km) ocean swim in Kailua-Kona Bay, followed by a 112-mile (180.2km) bike ride through the Hawaiian lava fields and a run of full marathon length. The competition was an instant hit and gained a reputation as one of the most gruelling endurance events on earth. Within no time other Iron Man competitions had sprung up around the world. The record for the most competitions contested in one year is held by Luxembourg's Jacques Fox, who competed in 14 between February and October 2004.

➲ The sport has spawned some of the most legendary endurance athletes in history, such as Australia's Paula Newby-Fraser and America's Mark Allen.

THE PGA TOUR'S FIRST $10 MILLION SEASON

VIJAY SINGH FIRST IN PGA TOUR HISTORY TO PASS $10 MILLION IN SINGLE-SEASON EARNINGS

7 November 2004, East Lake Golf Club, Atlanta, Georgia, USA

In 1963, Arnold Palmer benefited from the new legion of fans he brought to golf – and the television cameras that came with them – to become the first player in PGA Tour history to win more than $100,000 in single-season earnings. Twenty-five years later Curtis Strange became the first to pass the $1 million mark. A decade later the golf world changed for ever with Tiger Woods's arrival on the scene. Interest in the game grew to unprecedented levels, untold riches flowed into the game and the ones to benefit most were the players. Prize funds soared and, in 2004, Fiji's Vijay Singh, with nine tournament wins to his name, became the first player in the game's history to top $10 million in single-season earnings ($10,905,166).

➲ The PGA Tour's all-time list of money winners is dominated by current players: to date, Tiger Woods has earned in excess of $70 million; in contrast, Jack Nicklaus earned $5.7 million in his career.

Sixteen years after Curtis Strange had become the first golfer in history to pass $1 million in single-season earnings, Vijay Singh became the first to pass the $10 million mark.

Jose Luis Chilavert's march up the pitch to take penalties and free-kicks became a common sight in world soccer: the goalkeeper ended his career with a record 62 goals for club and country.

THE GOALKEEPING GOAL MACHINE

JOSE LUIS CHILAVERT RETIRES HOLDING RECORD FOR MOST GOALS BY A GOALKEEPER

11 November 2004, Estadio Jose Amalfitani, Buenos Aires, Argentina

All goalkeepers are frustrated centre-forwards, runs the joke, and although instances of goalkeepers netting last-gasp goals in the final throes of a match occur, they happen only rarely. But Paraguay's Jose Luis Chilavert was a different breed of goalkeeper: as well as performing his duties between the posts, he doubled as a free-kick and penalty-taking specialist for both club and country throughout his 22-year career. He once scored with a free-kick from inside his own half for his club Velez Sarfield against River Plate; in 1999 he became the first goalkeeper in history to score a hat-trick; and when he retired, in 2004, he had a record 62 goals to his name, 54 of them at club level and eight for Paraguay – including four during the 2002 World Cup qualifying campaign.

➲ Chilavert's record stood until 20 August 2006, when Sao Paulo keeper Rogerio Ceni – another goalkeeping free-kick and penalty specialist – scored the 63rd goal of his career.

International soccer has seen no male striker more prolific than Iran's Ali Daei: the first player in history to score 100 goals for his country, he retired in May 2007 with 109 goals in 148 appearances.

DAEI FIRST TO REACH 100-INTERNATIONAL-GOAL MILESTONE

ALI DAEI FIRST PLAYER IN INTERNATIONAL HISTORY TO SCORE 100 GOALS

17 November 2004, Azadi Stadium, Tehran, Iran

He was a centre-forward gifted enough to warrant a £4 million transfer fee when he joined German giants Bayern Munich from Bundesliga outfit Arminia Bielefeld in 1999 – the highest fee for an Asian player at the time. So perhaps it should have come as little surprise that Iran's Ali Daei should have prospered to such an extent on the international stage. He may have had the good fortune to play the majority of his games against lesser opposition, but still the goals kept hitting the back of the net. After making his international debut in June 1993, he had scored an impressive 38 goals in 52 appearances for his country (including 20 in 1996 alone) by 1998. On 28 November 2003 he scored his 85th international goal to overtake Ferenc Puskas's all-time record and, on 17 November 2004, scored four goals against Laos to become the first male soccer player in history to score 100 international goals.

➲ Daei retired from soccer in May 2007 having scored 109 goals in 148 appearances for Iran. The all-time record for international goals, male or female, is held by Mia Hamm, with 158 goals in 275 international appearances.

MANNING BREAKS MARINO'S 20-YEAR TOUCHDOWN PASS RECORD

PEYTON MANNING BREAKS NFL'S SINGLE-SEASON RECORD FOR TOUCHDOWN PASSES

26 December 2004, RCA Dome, Indianapolis, Indiana, USA

After a stellar college career at the University of Tennessee, Peyton Manning was selected first overall in the 1998 Draft by the Indianapolis Colts and stepped straight into the starting line-up, breaking five rookie records in his first season. He became the new quarterback icon, commanding the field and producing excellent if not prolific numbers: four straight 4,000-plus-yard seasons between 1999 and 2003. But the numbers and the performances were enough to make the Colts dig deep into their pockets: in the spring of 2004, Manning put pen to paper on the NFL's most expensive deal. It must have inspired him: he went on to throw 49 touchdown passes that season to beat Dan Marino's single-season record of 48 set in 1984.

➲ Just when it looked as though Manning might share Marino's fate of never having won a Super Bowl, the Colts quarterback led his team to American football's ultimate prize in 2007 with a 29–17 victory over the Chicago Bears. And his touchdown record also fell, to Tom Brady of New England, who threw 50 touchdown passes in 2007.

A quarterback icon in the same mould as John Elway or Joe Montana, Peyton Manning made his mark on the game in 2004 when he broke Dan Marino's single-season record for the most touchdown passes – the record is the NFL's equivalent to baseball's home run record.

THE QUEEN OF THE OCEANS

ELLEN MacARTHUR BREAKS RECORD FOR FASTEST SOLO ROUND-THE-WORLD VOYAGE
7 February 2005, Ushant, France

Frustrated by a lack of sponsorship, Ellen MacArthur travelled to France aged 19, bought a boat, re-fitted it and impressed everyone with her performance in the 1998 junior transatlantic race, including the Kingfisher group, who backed her to the tune of £2 million: the funds kick-started her career. In 2000 she broke the record for the fastest single-handed east-to-west transatlantic crossing in a mono-hull by a woman; in 2001, she finished second in the gruelling Vendée Globe race, breaking the record for a single-handed non-stop circumnavigation by a woman. In 2003, she skippered a crew attempting to beat the round-the-world record, but the quest came to an end when the boat's mast snapped in rough seas. In January 2004, she unveiled a new 75ft trimaran *B&Q*: she tested it by breaking the women's west-to-east transatlantic record, before embarking on her biggest test to date, a shot at the single-handed round-the-world record: this time she shattered it, returning in 71 days, 18 minutes, 33 seconds to beat Francis Joyon's record by 1 day, 8 hours, 35 minutes, 49 seconds.

➲ MacArthur's average speed over the 27,354-nautical-mile (50,660km) journey was 15.9 knots.

Sailing in a boat specifically designed to accommodate her diminutive frame – she stands just 5ft 2in (1.57m) – Ellen MacArthur smashed the single-handed circumnavigation record by over a day in 2005.

AROUND THE WORLD IN 50 DAYS

BRUNO PEYRON SKIPPERS *ORANGE II* TO NEW ROUND-THE-WORLD BEST TIME

16 March 2005, Ushant, France

Ellen MacArthur was not the only one chasing records on the high seas in 2004–05. French master yachtsman Bruno Peyron was determined to regain the Jules Verne Trophy (awarded for the fastest round-the-world time) that America's Steve Fossett had claimed the year before (crossing the finishing line in 58 days, 9 hours, 32 minutes, some six days ahead of Peyron's 2002 record mark of 64 days) and he knew he had the armoury to do it: a state-of-the-art 125ft (38m) catamaran called *Orange II.* Peyron and his 13-man crew obliterated the record, crossing the finishing line off the west coast of France in 50 days 16 hours 20 minutes, to shave more than a week off Fossett's record.

➲ In 1993, skippering *Commodore Explorer* in the inaugural Jules Verne around-the-world race, Peyron had led the first crew to a sub-80-day circumnavigation (they completed the course in 79 days).

In 2005, Bruno Peyron and his crew took *Orange II* – a 125ft catamaran – around the world's oceans in a record-breaking 50 days.

ROMOREN SOARS TO SKI-JUMPING BEST

BJORN EINAR ROMOREN BREAKS SKI-JUMPING WORLD RECORD

20 March 2005, Planica, Slovenia

Bjorn Einar Romoren began ski-jumping at the age of three and although other sports came and went, ski-jumping remained. At the age of 12, at the K120 hill in Lillehammer, he cleared 100m for the first time; eight years later, aged 20, he made his World Cup debut. His first victory came in January 2003 at the Four Hills Tournament in Bischofshogen, Germany; the same year he was part of the Norwegian team to collect bronze at the world championships and ended the season ranked No. 14 in the world. But 2005 was the year the Norwegian with the punk-rocker looks burst into the spotlight: in a season that saw the five longest jumps of all time (all at Planica, Slovenia), Romoren jumped the furthest of all – a staggering 239m.

➲ Known in ski-jumping circles as "the mother of all hills", Planica is the biggest ski-jumping hill in the world. The K185 hill has been the site of every ski-jumping world record since 1986.

Bjorn Einar Romoren's world-record leap of 239m in March 2005 shocked the ski-jumping world: it shattered Matti Hautamaki's previous best by over 3.5 metres.

MAYNARD SHATTERS HIS OWN SPEEDSAILING RECORD

FINIAN MAYNARD BREAKS THE SPEEDSAILING WORLD RECORD
10 April 2005, Le Canal, Saintes Maries de la Mer, France

If you were to build a prototype for the perfect windsurfer it would not look dissimilar to Irish-born but British Virgin Isles-raised Finian Maynard. At 6ft 3in (1.90m) and 258lb (117kg), he was built for speed. On 13 November 2004, already a four-time speed windsurfing world champion (1998–2001) he established a new speed record for sailing vessels (the average speed over 500m), clocking 46.82 knots in the waters of Le Canal, a specially constructed speed canal off the coast of Saintes Maries de la Mer, France. It was the first time a vessel other than a sailing boat had held the record for 11 years. At the same venue six months later, Maynard went even faster, averaging 48.7 knots (56.04mph/90.19km/h).

➲ The women's speedsailing world record also fell that day when windsurfer Karin Jagge averaged 41.25 knots (47.47mph/76.395km/h) over the same Le Canal waters.

Windsurfer Finian Maynard found the conditions to his liking at Le Canal on 10 April 2005, averaging a speed of 48.7 knots over a 500m course to break his own speedsailing world record.

CONSISTENCY THE KEY TO WOODS'S SUCCESS

TIGER WOODS BREAKS PGA TOUR RECORD FOR MOST CONSECUTIVE CUTS MADE
13 May 2005, Las Colinas, Irving, Texas, USA

It all started at the Pebble Beach National Pro-Am Championship in 1998, when Tiger Woods pulled out of the tournament after two rounds – so as not to commit to returning the following year to play the final 54 holes – and was deemed to have missed the cut. Over the next seven years he was a model of consistency, making cut after cut in the good times (including nine major championships) and the bad (he slipped off the top of the world rankings during a swing re-building phase). At the 2003 Tour Championship, Woods made his 114th consecutive cut to break Byron Nelson's all-time record of 113. The streak came to an end at 142 when Woods shot opening rounds of 69 and 72 at the Byron Nelson Classic.

➲ The closest any contemporary golfer has come to matching Woods's total of 142 consecutive cuts is Vijay Singh with 53 between 1995 and 1998.

It says a lot for Tiger Woods's competitive spirit that, over the course of seven years and 142 tournaments, whatever the state of his swing, he continually made the cut.

TOULOUSE CELEBRATE RECORD THIRD HEINEKEN CUP WIN

TOULOUSE BECOME THE FIRST THREE-TIME WINNERS OF THE HEINEKEN CUP

22 May 2005, Murrayfield, Edinburgh, Scotland

Toulouse came out on top of the inaugural Heineken Cup final in 1996, beating Cardiff 21–18 in an extra-time classic at Cardiff Arms Park, but seven long years passed before the French heavyweights graced European club rugby's biggest game for a second time. They beat Perpignan 22–17 at Lansdowne Road, Dublin. They returned the following year, only to taste defeat for the first time with a 27–20 reverse to London Wasps, but they bounced back in style in 2005, marching through the competition and beating Stade Français 18–12 in the final at Murrayfield, Edinburgh, to become the Heineken Cup's first three-time winners.

➲ Leicester Tigers remain the only team to have made a successful defence of the Heineken Cup: they beat Stade Français 24–30 in the 2001 final and Munster 15–9 in 2002.

Toulouse bounced back from Heineken Cup final defeat in 2004 by winning the tournament for a record third time in 2005.

The need to make the books balance struck Rangers FC after their Treble-winning season of 2002–03. The squad was broken up; little money was given to manager Alex McLeish to rebuild and it showed on the pitch. After a bright start to the 2003–04 season, Rangers' form fell away badly and they missed out the title by a country mile. Things looked better the following year, with Rangers staying in contention with Celtic right through the season, but with one match to go, the wise money was on Celtic: they led their cross-town rivals by two points; a win would be enough for the championship; a draw might have been enough. They lost 2–1 to Motherwell. Rangers beat Hibernian 1–0 and secured their 51st title – a record for any league in the world.

➲ Rangers with 51 league championship wins and Celtic with 41 have dominated the 111 seasons of Scottish League soccer: between them, the Glasgow giants have won 82.8 per cent of the championships contested.

A goal by Nacho Novo was enough to hand Rangers a 1–0 victory over Hibernian on the last day of the 2004–05 season. It secured a record 51st championship title for the Glasgow club.

PATRICK DAZZLES INDY 500 WITH FOURTH-PLACE FINISH

DANICA PATRICK RECORDS HIGHEST-EVER PLACING BY A WOMAN IN INDY 500 HISTORY

29 May 2005, Indianapolis Motorspeedway, Indiana, USA

Danica Patrick made history when she guided her Rahal Letterman car to fourth place in the 2005 Indianapolis 500: no woman has finished higher.

After securing Danica Patrick's services on a multi-year deal in 2002, Bobby Rahal made his new addition work for her chance at the big time. In 2003, she competed in the Toyota Atlantic Championship with moderate success; the following year she finished third in the championship, without winning a race. But in 2005, the Rahal team named Patrick as their driver for the Indy Car Series and she chose the biggest stage of all to make an impact. She posted the fastest practice speed in the month leading up to the race; qualified in fourth; led 19 laps of the race; and was still in the lead with eight laps to go before slipping back to fourth place – it was the best result by a female driver in Indy 500 history.

➲ Dan Wheldon's victory in the race saw him become the first British Indy 500 winner since Graham Hill in 1966.

Fu Haifeng marked himself out as a badminton player of both considerable potential and power. In 2005 he hit the fastest smash ever recorded in the game: at an astonishing 206mph (322km/h).

FU HAIFENG SMASHES SHUTTLECOCK AT 206MPH

FU HAIFENG HITS THE FASTEST SMASH EVER RECORDED IN BADMINTON HISTORY

3 June 2005, Beijing, China

Born on 2 January 1984 in Jieyang in the Chinese province of Guangdong, Fu Haifeng first stood out as a badminton player of great promise when he partnered Cai Yun in the 2004 Olympic Games in Athens: the pair reached the quarter-final. But the 21-year-old Chinese star came to the attention of the wider public in the strangest of ways the following year: at the 2005 Sudirman Cup, held in Beijing, badminton officials decided to experiment with measuring devices to ascertain the speed of the shuttlecock during play: Fu Haifeng came out on top of the rankings with a smash recorded at 206mph (332km/h).

➲ Fu Haifeng's record mark gives credence to the argument that badminton is one of the fastest racquet games on the planet: the fastest serve in the history of men's tennis, set by Andy Roddick in 2005, stands at a "mere" 155mph (249.44km/h).

RECORD-BREAKING JOURNEY FOR ENVIRONMENTAL AWARENESS

FLAVIO JARDIM AND DIOGO GUERREIRO COMPLETE THE WORLD'S LONGEST WINDSURFING JOURNEY
18 June 2005, Oiapoque, Brazil

Flavio Jardim and Diogo Guerreiro, both 23 years old, friends, windsurfing champions and icons of the Blue Destination Adventure Education project that highlights environmental awareness, set off on their windsurfers from Chui, the southernmost point of Brazil on the border with Uruguay, with the intention of sailing Brazil's entire coastline, stopping off on the way for rest, food and to give talks in schools about their adventure. Fourteen months later, having windsurfed for up to nine hours a day and having endured two assaults on the land – one of them at knifepoint – and some savage storms, they arrived in Oiapoque on the Brazilian border with French Guyana. Their 4,577-mile (7,367km) journey – the longest in windsurfing history – was complete.

➲ The pair broke the previous record held by America's Steve Fisher who, in 1997, had crossed the Pacific Ocean from California to Hawaii on a highly modified windsurfer: the 2,612-mile (4,203.6km) journey took him 47 days.

SEVENTH LE MANS SUCCESS FOR KRISTENSEN

TOM KRISTENSEN BREAKS RECORD FOR MOST WINS AT 24 HOURS OF LE MANS
18–19 June 2005, Le Mans, Sarthe, France

A junior karting champion and a test driver with the Tyrrell Formula One team in 1998, Denmark's Tom Kristensen never made it in F1's big time, but F1's loss was Le Mans's gain. He won for the first time in 1997; partnered Frank Biela and Emanuele Pirro to a hat-trick of wins in the all-powerful Audi R8 between 2000 and 2002 – the first three drivers to achieve the feat since Jacky Ickx in 1977 – and won the race with Bentley in 2003. A switch back to an Audi R8 with Team Goh helped him to a fifth straight victory in 2004 – his sixth Le Mans success, equalling Jacky Ickx's all-time record of wins. Partnering JJ Lehto and Marco Werner in the ADT Championship Racing Audi R8 in 2005, he made the record his own, notching up his seventh Le Mans victory.

➲ Kristensen remains the only driver in 24 Hours of Le Mans history to have won the race on six consecutive occasions (2000–05).

Formula One may have bypassed him, but Denmark's Tom Kristensen has been a star in the legendary 24 Hours of Le Mans race, winning a record seven times.

A virtual unknown in the world of cycling when he launched an attempt on Chris Boardman's world hour record in July 2005, everyone knew Ondrej Sosenka's name when he shattered the Englishman's mark by 259m.

SOSENKA SMASHES WORLD HOUR RECORD

ONDREJ SOSENKA BREAKS THE WORLD HOUR RECORD
19 July 2005, Krylatskoye, Moscow, Russia

Czech professional cyclist Ondrej Sosenka's first international win of note came with the Polish Intel-Action team at the Peace Race – known as the "Tour de France of the East" during the Cold War – in 2002, but he shot to international acclaim three years later when he took on Chris Boardman's world hour record (49.441km set in Manchester in 2000) on the Krylatskoye cycling track in Moscow. And, riding a carbon-fibre-framed custom-made bicycle (to qualify for the record it had to conform to the characteristics of the bicycle ridden by Eddy Merckx in 1973), he shattered it, leading the Englishman's record-breaking pace at every stage of the attempt and improving the mark by 259m. The new record: 49.700km (30.72 miles).

⮞ The record was not without controversy: Sosenka had used a 3.5kg rear wheel – the theory being that, although it may have been harder to get going, it would maintain speed more easily – whereas Merckx had tried to make his bike as light as possible for his 1973 attempt.

It was perhaps the moment women's pole-vaulting came of age: with the competition already in the bag at Crystal Palace, London, in July 2005 – she had cleared 4.96m to set a new world record – Yelena Isinbayeva raised the bar to 5m and cleared it at her first attempt.

ISINBAYEVA CRUISES PAST FIVE-METRE MILESTONE

YELENA ISINBAYEVA BECOMES FIRST FEMALE POLE-VAULTER TO CLEAR 5M
22 July 2005, Crystal Palace, London, England

After a growth spurt brought a sudden halt to Yelena Isinbayeva's burgeoning gymnastics career in 1997, she took up pole vault and by 1999 she was the World Youth Games champion. But her rise to the top of her sport was far from seamless: championship medals and world records came her way, but there were moments when her lack of technique was exposed, such as her bronze-medal-winning performance at the 2003 World Championships. By 2004, though, the flaws had been ironed out and she broke world records wherever she went – including at the 2004 Olympic Games – but her crowning moment came at an international meet at Crystal Palace, London, in 2005, when she became the first woman in history to clear the 5m mark.

⮞ Twenty-one days later, on 12 August in Helsinki, Finland, Isinbayeva broke the record again, clearing 5.01m.

ARMSTRONG IN SEVENTH HEAVEN

LANCE ARMSTRONG WINS THE TOUR DE FRANCE FOR THE SEVENTH STRAIGHT YEAR
24 July 2005, Paris, France

Lance Armstrong entered his final Tour de France with nothing left to prove: except to himself. And from the moment he finished second in the opening-stage time trial – the fastest in the 92-year history of the event – he had already thrown down the gauntlet to his rivals. Nobody dared pick it up. By the end of the tenth stage, the Texan was back in his familiar yellow jersey and never looked like relinquishing it. The rest of the Tour was as much a celebration of the American's staggering career as it was a race. The final day was unashamedly "Lance Armstrong Day" and, although pouring rain drenched the riders as they rode onto the Champs Elysées towards the finale, it did nothing to dampen the overriding sense of celebration as Armstrong cruised to victory 4m40s ahead of his closest rival and bowed out of the Tour as the greatest cyclist ever.

➲ Four other riders have won the Tour on five occasions: Jacques Anquetil (France, 1957, 1961, 1962, 1963 and 1964); Eddy Merckx (Belgium, 1969, 1970, 1971, 1972 and 1974); Bernard Hinault (France, 1978, 1979, 1981, 1982 and 1985); and Miguel Indurain (Spain, 1991–95 – the first to do so in five consecutive years).

Dubbed by some as the greatest comeback artist in the history of sports, Lance Armstrong beat cancer and returned to win a record seven consecutive Tour de France wins between 1999 and 2005.

545

Despatie was just five years old when his parents noticed his knack for diving in his family's backyard pool. In 1990, he joined the diving team of the Club Aquatique Montréal Olympique (CAMO).

➲ Like race-car driver Jacques Villeneuve, Despatie's "other" competitive sport is downhill skiing. He is also interested in acting and played a role in the 2007 French-language film, *A vos marques! Party!* (Take the Plunge!).

DIVER SEIZES TWIN TITLES

DESPATIE REBOUNDS AFTER OLYMPIC SILVER TO GO FOR GOLD AT THE WORLDS

16–31 July 2005, Complexe Aquatique de l'Ile Sainte-Helene, Montreal, Canada

One year after returning from the Athens Olympics with a disappointing silver medal in the 3m event, two-time diving world champion Alexandre Despatie served notice that he was back by winning not one, but *two* gold medals at the World Aquatic Championships. Diving before friends, family and a hometown crowd, the 20-year-old resident of suburban Laval-sur-le-lac endured sizzling temperatures and occasional drizzle to dominate the 3m springboard event with a world-record score of 813.60 points. Two days later, the athlete known to his fans as "Alexandre the Great" added a second gold, this time in the 1m event. Despatie, winner of more than 30 national and world titles, first made headlines at age 13 when he became the youngest-ever Commonwealth Games champion in the 10m event. When he was just 15, he finished fourth in the 10m at the 2000 Sydney Olympics. He is the only diver to have won world championships in each of the 1m, 3m and 10m categories.

Young gun Kyle Busch started to blaze a trail in NASCAR's top series in his first full season with Hendrick Motorsports in 2005, winning at the California Speedway to become the youngest race winner in the sport's history.

BUSCH MAKES HIS MARK ON NASCAR'S ELITE

KYLE BUSCH BECOMES YOUNGEST RACE-WINNER OF NASCAR'S TOP SERIES

5 September 2005, California Speedway, Fontana, California, USA

A winning reputation in junior racing formulae was enough to earn Kyle Busch his first ride in NASCAR's Craftsman Truck series in 2001: aged 16, he qualified in 23rd and finished ninth. But shortly afterwards NASCAR increased the minimum age of drivers to 18: Busch continued racing in the American Speed Association series. He signed for Hendrick Motorsports shortly before his 18th birthday, impressed in the Busch series in 2003, won his first race in 2004 and was given a full-time ride in NASCAR's big time in 2005. He won pole in his eighth start, at California Speedway, to become, aged 19, the youngest pole-winner in NASCAR history and, later in the year, won his first race – aged 20 years, 125 days – to become the sport's youngest-ever race-winner.

➲ Busch had broken the previous record, held by Donald Thomas, by just four days and went on to finish the season as the Rookie of the Year.

THIRTIETH TITLE FOR RECORD-BREAKING CORK

CORK WIN A RECORD 30TH ALL-IRELAND HURLING CHAMPIONSHIP

11 September 2005, Croke Park, Dublin, Ireland

Against all predictions, the 2005 All-Ireland Hurling Championship – the first to be staged at the newly-refurbished Croke Park – was to be played between defending champions Cork (29-time winners of the competition) and Galway, who had shocked Kilkenny (many pundits' favourites for the title) in the semi-final. And the Connacht men put up a mighty fight, playing their full part in what turned out to be a highly entertaining final, before falling 1–21 to 1–16 to a Ben O'Connor-inspired Cork. It was a record-breaking moment for the Leesiders: they had become the first team in All-Ireland history to lift the Liam McCarthy Cup on 30 occasions.

➲ Kilkenny equalled Cork's feat of 30 wins when they beat Limerick 2–19 to 1–15 in the 2007 All-Ireland final.

Cork's All-Ireland final success over a youthful Galway side in 2005 was a milestone moment: Cork had become the first county in history to become 30-time Liam McCarthy trophy-winners.

PIETERSEN'S RECORD-BREAKING HEROICS SECURE ASHES FOR ENGLAND

KEVIN PIETERSEN BREAKS RECORD FOR MOST SIXES IN AN ASHES INNINGS

12 September 2005, The Oval, London, England

Pietersen eventually fell for 158, by which time England had saved the match and won the Ashes for the first time in 18 years.

Support for the English cricket team had not reached such frenzied levels since Ian Botham's 1981 Ashes heroics. England headed into the final day of the 2005 Ashes series 2–1 ahead and sitting on 35 for 1. If England's batsmen could see out the day, the Ashes would be theirs for the first time since 1986–87 and a country could party. But by lunch, the balance had shifted firmly Australia's way: England sat on a perilous 127 for 5 (a mere 133 runs ahead). Kevin Pietersen returned from the lunch interval like a man possessed, treating the revered Australian bowling attack with disdain: he reached 50 off 70 balls, 100 off 121 balls and 150 off 176 balls, peppering the now-partying crowd with an Ashes single-innings-record seven sixes.

➲ It was one of the most frenzied innings in cricket history: nervous before the lunch interval, but irresistible after it, Kevin Pietersen hammered 158 (including an Ashes-record seven sixes) in the fifth Test against Australia at The Oval to save the match and win the Ashes for England.

RECORD-BREAKING RICE CALLS TIME ON CAREER

JERRY RICE RETIRES FROM NFL WITH NUMEROUS ALL-TIME RECORDS TO HIS NAME

14 September 2005, Monster Park, San Francisco, California

Jerry Rice made an effortless transition from college standout to a San Francisco 49ers star, winning divisional Offensive Rookie of the Year honours in 1985. Over the next decade he led the league in receiving and touchdown receptions, picked up Super Bowl rings in 1988, 1989 and 1994, broke the record for career touchdowns and established a reputation for a strong work ethic on and off the field. He came back from serious injury in 1997; moved to the Oakland Raiders in 2001 and led them to the Super Bowl in 2002; helped Seattle to the Division Championship in 2004; and then called it a day. When he retired in 2005 he was the NFL all-time leader in receiving yards (22,895), touchdown receptions (198), all-purpose yards (23,540) and numerous other categories.

➲ When Jerry Rice caught a touchdown pass in Oakland's losing Super Bowl XXXVII bid in January 2003, he became the first player in history with touchdown receptions in four separate Super Bowls.

Nicknamed "World" during his college days, because there was nothing in the world he could not catch, Jerry Rice enjoyed a stellar 19-year NFL career and broke numerous all-time records along the way.

Three consecutive National League West Division titles between 1991 and 1993, followed by eleven straight NL East Division titles between 1995 and 2005 – no honours were awarded during the strike-shortened 1994 season – made it a record-breaking 14 division seasons in a row for the Atlanta Braves.

14 IN A ROW FOR THE BRAVES

ATLANTA BRAVES WIN MLB-RECORD 14TH CONSECUTIVE DIVISION TITLE

28 September 2005, Turner Field, Atlanta, Georgia, USA

In 1991, the Atlanta Braves and Minnesota Twins became the first teams in MLB history to reach the World Series a year after finishing bottom of their division. The Braves lost, but it signalled the start of great things to come as they became baseball's standout team, winning the division championship in 1992 and 1993 and bouncing back from the strike-shortened 1994 season to win a first World Series in 35 years in 1995. Fall Classic success may have eluded them since, but the Braves remained ever-present in the playoffs (including losing World Series appearances in 1996 and 1999), and although the New York Yankees usurped their place in the spotlight by the turn of the century, division championships continued to come their way: they completed a record 14th straight win in 2005.

➲ The streak came to an end in 2006 when they finished third in the National League East Division behind the New York Mets and the Philadelphia Phillies after posting a 79–83 record.

In September 2005, Real Madrid striker Raul became the first player in history to score 50 goals in the Champions League, passing Alfredo di Stefano's record (49) for most goals in Europe's premier club competition.

RAUL PASSES 50-GOAL MILESTONE

RAUL FIRST PLAYER IN EUROPEAN CUP/CHAMPIONS LEAGUE HISTORY TO SCORE 50 GOALS

28 September 2005, Santiago Bernabeu, Madrid, Spain

A product of the Atletico Madrid youth program, Real Madrid snapped up Raul the moment their cross-town rivals hit financial trouble and handed the young striker his debut in October 1994: aged 17 years 4 months, he became the youngest player to pull on a Real shirt. He soon became Spain's new scoring sensation, his deadly finishing and eye for goal proving a hit in both La Liga and the Champions League. As Real established themselves as one of the tournament's premier teams – they won the competition in 1998, 2000 and 2002 – Raul's shots at goal kept hitting the back of the net. On 28 September 2005, during Real's Group G clash against Olympiakos, he became the first player in European Cup/Champions League history to reach the 50-goal milestone.

➲ Two players since have equalled the feat: Real Madrid's Ruud van Nistelrooy and Chelsea's Andriy Shevchenko.

EIGHTH WORLD TITLE FOR LASER CLASS KING

ROBERT SCHEIDT WINS RECORD EIGHTH LASER CLASS WORLD CHAMPIONSHIP

September 2005, Fortaleza, Brazil

A star sailor in numerous classes of the sport in his youth, Robert Scheidt confirmed his huge potential when he won his first world championship in 1995. He defended his title the following year in Cape Town and added an Olympic gold medal to his haul in Atlanta; the dominant force in the sport, he completed a hat-trick of titles in 1997. But then Britain's Ben Ainslie entered the scene: the Brazilian lost his world crown between 1998 and 1999, and his Olympic crown to the Briton in 2000, and there is no doubt Ainslie's subsequent move up to Finn Class benefited the Brazilian. Scheidt started winning again: three further world championships came between 2000 and 2002; he regained his Olympic title in 2004 and defended his world title; and won a record eighth world championship title in 2005.

➲ Scheidt switched to Star Class keelboat racing following his seventh Laser Class world championship in 2005 in preparation for the 2008 Olympic Games. With his crew Bruno Prada, he won the pre-Olympic tournament in 2006 and the world championship in 2007.

Two-time Olympic champion Robert Scheidt has been the king of Laser Class sailing, collecting a record eight world championships between 1995 and 2005.

ELEVENTH TITLE OF THE SEASON FOR 19-YEAR-OLD NADAL

RAFAEL NADAL BREAKS ATP RECORD FOR MOST TOURNAMENT WINS IN A SEASON BY A TEENAGER
23 October 2005, Madrid Arena, Madrid, Spain

After spending the majority of the 2004 season on the sidelines through injury, 19-year-old Rafael Nadal was raring to go in 2005. He started the season promisingly with two clay-court tournament wins on the South American circuit. Then came the European clay-court season, and Nadal dominated, winning in Monte Carlo, Rome and Barcelona – breaking Andre Agassi's consecutive match-winning streak for a teenager (23) – before collecting his first grand slam win at the French Open. He struggled on the grass, but returned to form with two more titles on clay and carried the momentum into the North American hard-court season, winning in Montreal. A further title followed in Beijing before he brought the curtain down on a sensational season by winning the Madrid Masters – it was his 11th title of the season, a record for a teenager.

Nineteen-year-old Rafael Nadal exploded onto the international tennis scene in 2005, winning 11 times during the season – a record for a teenager – and ending the year as the second-ranked player in the world.

➲ Nadal's record of 11 tournament wins broke the record set by Mats Wilander, who won nine times as a 19-year-old in 1983.

Shipped back to Australia shortly after her birth after no one bid for her in an auction, Makybe Diva became the first horse in history to win the Melbourne Cup three years in a row when she triumphed in 2005.

THREE IN A ROW FOR MAKYBE DIVA

MAKYBE DIVA FIRST HORSE IN MELBOURNE CUP HISTORY TO RECORD THREE CONSECUTIVE WINS
1 November 2005, Flemington Racecourse, Melbourne, Australia

Conceived in Ireland and born in England, Makybe Diva was put up for auction shortly after her birth and did not receive a single bid. It left her owner, Australian tuna fisherman Tony Santic, with little choice but to dig into his pockets and ship her back to his homeland. It turned out to be worth every penny: in 2003, with Glen Boss in the saddle, she streaked to the winning post ahead of She's Archie to win the Melbourne Cup for the first time; she defended her title the following year, beating Irish horse Vinnie Roe into second place; and took top honours in 2005 as well, to become the first horse in Melbourne Cup history to record three consecutive wins.

➲ Tony Santic handed the responsibility of naming the horse to five of his female employees. They came up with a name including the first two letters of each of their given names: Maureen Dellar, Kylie Bascomb, Belinda Grock, Dianna Tankin and Vanessa Parthenis.

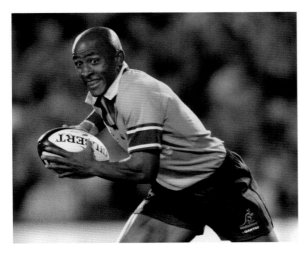

Ever-present in the Australian line-up for over a decade, George Gregan won his 119th cap for Australia in November 2005 to break Jason Leonard's record for the most national caps.

INTERNATIONAL RUGBY'S MOST CAPPED PLAYER

GEORGE GREGAN BREAKS RECORD FOR MOST INTERNATIONAL RUGBY CAPS

5 November 2005, Stade Velodrome, Marseille, France

Born in Lusaka, Zambia, to a Zimbabwean mother and an Australian father, George Gregan grew up in Canberra and excelled in junior levels of rugby, representing both the Australian Under-19 and Under-21 teams. The scrum-half made his senior debut against Italy in 1994 and played a full part in Australia's 1995 World Cup campaign (they lost in the quarter-finals to England). Made the Wallabies' vice-captain in 1997, he enjoyed World Cup success in 1999 before taking over the captaincy in 2001. Still at the top of his game at the 2003 World Cup, he tasted final defeat for the first time, but continued to hold down the Wallabies' No. 9 jersey: on 5 November 2005, he overtook Jason Leonard's haul of international appearances (for a single country) when he won his 119th cap.

➲ Leonard also received five international caps for the British Lions: when Gregan won his 124th cap, against England in Sydney in June 2006, he officially became the most capped player in international rugby history.

THE WORLD'S LEADING TEST RUN-SCORER

BRIAN LARA PASSES ALLAN BORDER'S RECORD FOR THE MOST TEST RUNS

26 November 2005, Adelaide Oval, Adelaide, Australia

On the first day of the third Test between Australia and the West Indies at the Adelaide Oval, Brian Lara had produced a batting master class and hit 202 not out. As he strode to the crease for the start of day two, he received a prolonged ovation from the 20,000-strong crowd who well knew that, at 36 years of age, this would be the last time they would see the leading batsman of his generation – the holder of both the Test and first-class high scores – play on Australian soil. They were mindful of another thing as well: Lara was just 12 runs short of breaking Allan Border's record for most Test runs (11,174). The moment came 22 minutes into the day's play, when Lara paddle-swept Glenn McGrath to fine-leg to complete his 11,175th run.

Already the holder of the highest Test and first-class scores, Brian Lara added another accolade to his considerable collection when he broke Allan Border's record for most Test runs in November 2005.

➲ Lara achieved the feat in 35 fewer Test matches than Border (121 to the Australian's 156) and ended his career after the 2007 World Cup with 11,953 runs to his name at an average of 52.88.

In November 2005, Ruben Wiki, who struck fear into the hearts of opponents for over a decade when he rampaged at them with ball at hand, became the first player in international rugby league history to win 50 caps for his country.

WIKI REACHES 50-CAP MILESTONE

RUBEN WIKI FIRST RUGBY LEAGUE PLAYER TO WIN 50 INTERNATIONAL CAPS

26 November 2005, Elland Road, Leeds, England

Ruben Wiki made the transition from a youngster of huge potential – alongside Tana Umaga (who would go on to captain the All Blacks) he wreaked havoc with the Junior Kiwis – to become one of the most respected and feared opponents in international rugby league for over a decade after his debut in 1994. Putting his longevity down to drinking a bowl of karva – a Pacific Island drink – after every game, he was ever-present for the Kiwis (captaining them on 18 occasions): in October 2005 he won his 47th cap to become the most capped international rugby league player of all time. A month later, during New Zealand's shock Tri Nations final win against Australia, he became the first player in history to reach 50 caps.

➲ Wiki bowed out of international rugby league following New Zealand's 16–12 extra-time golden point defeat to Australia in November 2006 with a record 55 caps to his name.

A ruthless technician and the idol of a nation, no cricketer in history has scored more Test centuries than India's Sachin Tendulkar.

TENDULKAR TOPS GAVASKAR'S RECORD MARK

SACHIN TENDULKAR BREAKS SUNIL GAVASKAR'S RECORD FOR MOST TEST CENTURIES

10 December 2005, Feroz Shah Kotla Stadium, Delhi, India

Brian Lara may have held the ascendancy when it came to building monster innings, but when cricket luminaries such as Donald Bradman and Shane Warne champion Sachin Tendulkar's claims on being the best player of his generation, you sit up and listen. Tendulkar's impeccable technique and full range of shots were on show from the moment he made his Test debut aged 16 and as the runs (and the centuries) accumulated, the Little Master achieved almost god-like status in his country. He achieved in spite of the overwhelming weight of public expectation, continued to thrill a nation and it was only fitting that Tendulkar's faithful should be gathered en masse in Delhi (in the second Test against Sri Lanka) to see him smash 104 (his 35th Test century) to break Sunil Gavaskar's all-time Test record for three-figure scores.

➲ Tendulkar's 35th Test century came in his 125th match for India, the same number Gavaskar had played to score his 34 centuries.

THE BEAST FROM THE EAST WINS WBA HEAVYWEIGHT CHAMPIONSHIP

NIKOLAI VALUEV BECOMES TALLEST AND HEAVIEST BOXING WORLD CHAMPION IN HISTORY

17 December 2005, Max Schmeling Halle, Berlin, Germany

Nikolai Valuev was introduced to boxing aged 20 and it was an instant love affair. What he lacked in ring-craft – his introduction to the sport was late by boxing standards – he made up for with sheer physical bulk: he stood 7ft (2.15m) tall and weighed 325lb (147.5kg) and he turned professional in 1993, after just 14 amateur fights, before spending the best part of a decade honing his trade. His breakthrough came with a nine-round destruction of Paolo Vidoz for the European title in 2004. He started to surge up the world rankings, seeing off opponent after opponent to earn a fight with two-time champion John Ruiz for the WBA Championship belt: the Russian won on points to become the tallest and heaviest boxing world champion in history.

➲ Valuev made three defences of the belt before losing to Uzbekistan's Ruslan Chagaev on a majority decision in Berlin on 14 April 2007.

Not the cutest of boxers ever to take to the ring, but certainly the most formidable, at 7ft tall and weighing 325lb Nikolai Valuev is the tallest and heaviest boxing world champion in history.

WARNE'S WIZARDRY TAKES HIM TO ANOTHER TEST RECORD

SHANE WARNE BREAKS RECORD FOR MOST TEST WICKETS IN A CALENDAR YEAR
26–30 December 2005, Melbourne Cricket Ground, Melbourne, Australia

He may have been in the twilight of his career, but 2005 turned out to be a vintage season for Shane Warne: he took 96 wickets during the course of the season to break the record for the most wickets in a calendar year.

The leading wicket-taker in the history of Test cricket since October 2004, Shane Warne was simply getting better with age. The early zip of the leg-spinner's bowling action may have diminished over the years, but he had added experience to his armoury and that, along with his big-spinning leg-breaks and well-disguised flippers and leg-spinners, was more than enough to bamboozle Test batsmen around the world. During 15 Test matches in 2005, the spin wizard took 96 wickets – including 17 in the three-match series against New Zealand and a sensational 40 in Australia's losing Ashes campaign – to break Dennis Lillee's record 85 wickets (set in 1981) for the most Test wickets in a calendar year.

➲ Only one other player in the history of the game has taken 90 or more Test wickets in a calendar year: Sri Lanka's Muttiah Muralitharan, who took 90 wickets in 11 matches in 2006.

THE IRON WOMAN OF INTERNATIONAL SOCCER

KRISTINE LILLY BECOMES ONLY SOCCER PLAYER IN HISTORY TO WIN 300 INTERNATIONAL CAPS

18 January 2006, Guangdong Olympic Stadium, Guangzhou, China

From the moment Kristine Lilly made her debut for the US soccer team aged 16 in 1987, her career was to become one of milestones. She was part of the United States' Olympic-winning team in 1996; broke Norwegian Heide Shoere's record for international caps in 1998 (151); won the World Cup in 1999, the year in which she won her 165th cap to become the most capped player of either sex in international soccer history. She made her 200th international appearance the following year; became only the fifth player in history to score 100 international goals in 2004; and, on 18 January 2006, during the United States' 3–1 win over Norway in the Four Nations Tournament in China, became the first player in history to reach the 300-cap milestone.

➲ Lilly appeared in her fifth World Cup in 2007 and when she scored against England on 22 September became, aged 36, the oldest goal-scorer in the tournament's history.

Dubbed the "Iron Woman" of US soccer, Kristine Lilly is the only player in international soccer history, of either sex, to have made more than 300 appearances for her country.

GOLD MEDAL NO. 4 FOR RECORD-BREAKING KOSTELIC

JANICA KOSTELIC FIRST FEMALE SKIER IN HISTORY TO WIN FOUR OLYMPIC GOLD MEDALS

10–26 February 2006, Turin, Italy

Janica Kostelic appeared for Croatia in the 1998 Olympics aged just 16 – her best result was eighth in the combined – and went on to win her first World Cup race the following year, but then damaged her knee ligaments. She returned in great style, winning the overall World Cup title for the first time in 2001, and became a national hero at the 2002 Winter Olympics when she won four medals, three of them gold: slalom, giant slalom and combined. A second overall World Cup title arrived in 2003, before injury struck again. She returned to finish second in the World Cup standings in 2005 and in 2006 went on to defend her Olympic combined title – the first woman to do so – to become the first female skier in history to win four Olympic gold medals.

➲ Kostelic ended the 2006 season as overall World Cup champion for the third time in her career before retiring from the sport in 2007.

Considered among the greatest skiers of all time, Janica Kostelic became the first female skier in history to win four Olympic gold medals when she defended her combined title at the 2006 Winter Olympics in Turin.

Philipp Schoch beat off the challenge of his elder brother Simon in the parallel giant slalom final at the 2006 Winter Olympics to become the first snowboarder in history to defend an Olympic title.

PHILIPP SCHOCH BEATS ELDER BROTHER TO MAKE OLYMPIC HISTORY

PHILIPP SCHOCH FIRST SNOWBOARDER IN HISTORY TO DEFEND OLYMPIC TITLE

10–26 February 2006, Turin, Italy

Having taken gold in the parallel giant slalom at the 2002 Winter Olympics, and won the World Cup title in the same event in 2005, Swiss snowboarder Philipp Schoch must have been confident of success in the 2006 Winter Olympics in Turin. He made it through to the final and only one man stood between him and his chance of becoming the first snowboarder in history to defend an Olympic title: his elder brother Simon, who entered the Games as the World Cup leader. Youth won the day: the 0.88s lead Philipp gained from the first run was a margin his elder brother found too immense to overcome, and Olympic snowboarding history had been made.

⮕ The brothers were not the first siblings to win gold and silver medals in the same Olympic event: that honour falls to Christine and Marielle Goitschel of France who took gold and silver in the alpine skiing slalom in Innsbruck in 1964.

Cindy Klassen's decision to switch to speed skating after being overlooked for the 1998 women's ice hockey squad at the Winter Olympics paid dividends eight years later. Her haul of five medals – two bronze, two silver and a gold – is a record for a Canadian at any Olympics.

⮕ Because of her amazing performance, Klassen was dubbed "woman of the Games" by IOC president Jacques Rogge and given the honour of being flag-bearer for the closing ceremony. A day later, Klassen was awarded the most lucrative sponsorship ever for a Canadian athlete when she inked a $1 million deal with a Manitoba telecommunications company.

SHOWING HER MEDALS

KLASSEN BECOMES FIRST CANADIAN TO WIN 5 MEDALS AT THE SAME OLYMPICS

10–26 February 2006, Turin, Italy

Growing up, Cindy Klassen played as many sports as she could fit into a week, but she dreamed of Olympic hockey. She reached the AAAs in boys' hockey before switching to women's at age 16, when she joined Canada's Junior Women's team. When she missed the cut for the 1998 Olympic team, Klassen took up speed skating. As a speed skater, Klassen was a force to be reckoned with: By the time she arrived in Turin, Klassen had racked up three world records and an array of medals on both the national and world stages. In Turin, she shot straight to the head of the pack, winning bronze in the 3,000m and 5,000m events, silver in the 1,000m and team pursuit contests, and glorious gold in the 1,500m. This was a record for medals won at one Olympics by a Canadian, as well as the most medals won by one athlete in 2006.

NICO ROSBERG EMERGES FROM HIS FATHER'S SHADOW

NICO ROSBERG YOUNGEST DRIVER IN FORMULA ONE HISTORY TO SET RACE'S FASTEST LAP

12 March 2006, Bahrain International Circuit, Sakhir, Bahrain

Nico Rosberg enjoyed a stellar junior karting career, won the German Formula BMW title in 2002, spent two productive seasons in Formula Three and won the first-ever GP2 title in 2005 to earn a full-time ride with Formula One outfit Williams in the 2006 season, but he had still not quite emerged from the shadow of his father, 1983 F1 world champion Keke Rosberg. But Nico's first race in F1 did much to change that state of affairs: he finished in the points, in seventh behind team-mate Mark Webber, and recorded the fastest lap of the race – at 20 years, 258 days becoming the youngest driver in Formula One history to do so.

➲ Rosberg ended his first season in 17th place in the drivers' championship; he improved to ninth in 2007.

Nico Rosberg announced his arrival in the Formula One ranks in sensational style: in his first race in the sport's big time – the 2006 Bahrain GP. He became the youngest driver in history to set a race's fastest lap.

THE HIGHEST-SCORING ONE-DAY INTERNATIONAL IN HISTORY

AUSTRALIA AND SOUTH AFRICA BREAK RECORD FOR ONE-DAY INTERNATIONAL CRICKET'S HIGHEST SCORE

12 March 2006, New Wanderers Stadium, Johannesburg, South Africa

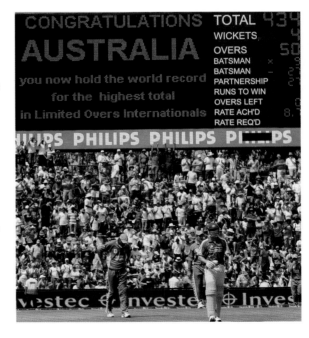

It was one of the most pulsating matches in one-day international cricket history, but at the halfway stage, hosts South Africa were staring down the barrel. Australia, led by captain Ricky Ponting's magnificent 164, had compiled a massive 434 for 4 off their 50 overs – the highest score in ODI history, beating the 398 posted by Sri Lanka against Kenya in 1996. It would take a massive effort by South Africa to get remotely close, but they were up to the task. Buoyed by Graeme Smith's 55-ball 90, Herschelle Gibbs's 175 off 111 balls and the raucous urgings of the home crowd, South Africa reached their unlikely target with one ball to spare. Two world records had been broken in the space of a few extraordinary hours.

➲ South Africa's total of 438 stood as a record for barely four months before Sri Lanka smashed 443 for 9 in their ODI against the Netherlands at Amstelveen in July 2006.

Having just conceded the highest total in one-day international cricket (434), South Africa's cricketers had no time to feel sorry for themselves. Instead they went out and smashed 438 runs to win the match sensationally by one wicket.

THE FLYING TOMATO ROARS DOWN THE SLOPES

SANNA TIDSTRAND BREAKS WOMEN'S SKI SPEED WORLD RECORD

19 April 2006, Les Arcs, Bourg Saint Maurice, France

Just as those attempting an assault on the land speed world record discovered there was no better location on earth than the Bonneville Salt Flats in Utah on which to launch their record-breaking bid, so speed skiers flocked to the slopes of Les Arcs in the French Alps. And conditions for record-breaking were ideal for the Pro Mondial event on 19 April 2006, with 20-year-old Swedish star Sanna Tidstrand, who had broken the junior world record the previous year (with 148.64mph/239.20km/h), chomping at the bit to break Karine Dubouchet's mark of 150.54mph (242.26km/h) that had stood as a record since 2002. The former X Games and Ski X champion flew down the slope and recorded a new world best: her speed – 150.74mph (242.59km/h).

➲ On the same day, on the same slope, Italy's Simone Origone broke the men's speed ski world record with a speed of 156.22mph (251.40km/h).

Dubbed the "Flying Tomato" in the press on account of her bright red racing suit, Sweden's Sanna Tidstrand made the most of ideal conditions at Les Arcs in April 2006 to break the women's speed ski world record.

In the twilight of his sensational Formula One career but still competing at the front of the field, Michael Schumacher recorded the 66th pole position of his career at his final San Marino GP to break Ayrton Senna's all-time record of 65 poles.

SCHUMACHER'S RECORD-BREAKING 66TH POLE POSITION

MICHAEL SCHUMACHER BREAKS AYRTON SENNA'S RECORD FOR MOST POLE POSITIONS

22 April 2006, Autodromo Enzo e Dino Ferrari, Imola, Italy

Any thoughts that 2006 might well be Michael Schumacher's last season in Formula One were pushed to one side when the German clocked 1m22.759s in qualifying for the San Marino GP to edge Britain's Jenson Button into second place and claim the 66th pole position of his storied career. It was a record-breaking moment: Schumacher had finally captured the one Formula One performance record to elude him – he already held the mark for most wins and most championships – breaking Ayrton Senna's all-time mark at the track upon which the Brazilian legend had set the 65th and final pole of his career the day before his untimely death.

➲ Schumacher had taken 235 races to achieve his 66 pole positions; Senna, on the other hand, had taken just 162 races to achieve 65 (an average of 40.1% of his races).

THE WORLD'S MOST CAPPED SOCCER PLAYER

MOHAMED AL-DEAYEA MAKES RECORD 181ST AND FINAL INTERNATIONAL APPEARANCE

11 May 2006, Sittard, the Netherlands

Good enough to have been considered by Manchester United as a possible replacement for Fabien Barthez, Mohamed Al-Deayea first caught the eye as the Saudi Arabian youth squad's goalkeeper on a trip to Scotland in the late 1980s. He made his senior international debut in 1990, came to world prominence with his penalty-saving heroics in 1996 that secured his country a famous Asian Cup victory; and represented his country at three World Cups – in 1994, 1998 and 2002. In December 2004 he passed legendary Mexican defender Claudio Suarez's record haul of 173 international caps, and made his 181st and final appearance for his country in a friendly against Belgium in May 2006.

⮑ Al-Deayea was included in Saudi Arabia's World Cup squad in 2006, but did not play a game. He announced his retirement from international soccer shortly after his country's first-round exit.

Strong, agile and an excellent shot-stopper, Mohamed Al-Deayea made a record 181 international appearances for Saudi Arabia.

MAGIC MANAUDOU BREAKS 18-YEAR-OLD WORLD RECORD

LAURE MANAUDOU BREAKS JANET EVANS'S 18-YEAR 400M FREESTYLE WORLD RECORD

12 May 2006, Tours, France

Swimming sensation Laure Manaudou burst onto the international scene in spectacular style at the 2004 Olympic Games when, aged 18, she won 400m freestyle gold – to become the first French woman in history to win a swimming gold medal – and picked up a silver and bronze medal. Soon pundits were predicting it was only a matter of time before she challenged Janet Evans's 400m freestyle world record (4m03.85s) that had stood since the 1988 Olympic Games. She came close at the 2005 World Championships in Montreal – at the midway point she was inside world-record pace before fading in the closing stages – but the moment finally came at the French national championships held in Tours in May 2006: she clocked an impressive 4m03.03s.

⮑ On 6 August 2006, Manaudou smashed her own world record, clocking 4m02.13s at the European swimming championships held in Budapest.

Olympic, world and European champion in the 400m freestyle, French star Laure Manaudou added the world record to her collection when she beat Janet Evans's 1988 record time in May 2006.

Three tries, including the 65th of his career, for winger Daisuke Ohata in Japan's match against Georgia in May 2006 were enough to see him overhaul David Campese and become the world's leading try-scorer.

Arsenal's hopes of European glory in 2006 were delivered a crushing blow in the 18th minute when their keeper Jens Lehmann became the first player in history to be sent off in a European Cup final.

65TH TRY FOR RECORD-BREAKING OHATA

DAISUKE OHATA BECOMES LEADING TRY-SCORER IN INTERNATIONAL RUGBY HISTORY
14 May 2006, Hanazono Stadium, Osaka, Japan

Daisuke Ohata was first called into Japan's national rugby squad in November 1996 while a 21-year-old third-year student at Kyoto Sangyo University and scored three tries on his debut, against Korea in the Asian Cup. The tries continued to mount and from the moment he broke the Japanese all-time try-scoring record (29 tries) in fewer than 30 Tests, it became a question of when, and not if, he would break David Campese's all-time international record of 64 tries. The moment finally came on 14 May 2006 during Japan's match against Georgia: as the game entered injury time – with the winger already having scored two tries – Ohata burst through a gap in the Georgian defence to score his third try of the game and the 65th of his career.

➲ Controversy was never far from Ohata's assault on Campese's record, with many saying that the inferior level of opposition faced by the Japanese player undervalued Campese's achievements: the critics point out Ohata scored only one-third of his tries against leading rugby nations.

LEHMANN SEES RED ON EUROPE'S BIGGEST STAGE

JENS LEHMANN THE FIRST PLAYER IN HISTORY TO BE SENT OFF IN A EUROPEAN CUP FINAL
17 May 2006, Stade de France, Paris, France

The European Cup had become the Holy Grail for Arsenal manager Arsene Wenger. Years of continued success on the domestic front had translated into no success of any kind on the European stage, but in 2006 it seemed as though the French maestro had finally hit upon the right formula: Arsenal had made it through to the Champions League final for the first time in the club's history and would face off against Catalan giants Barcelona for European club soccer's biggest prize. They got off to a nightmare start: in the 18th minute, goalkeeper Jens Lehmann upended Barca striker Samual Eto'o just outside the penalty area and was shown a straight red card. He had become the first player in history to be sent off in a European Cup final.

➲ Arsenal rallied well from the setback and took the lead through a Sol Campbell header in the 37th minute, but the Gunners' dreams of European glory were dashed when Barcelona scored twice in the second half to win the game 2–1.

THE BASE JUMP FROM THE TOP OF THE WORLD

GLENN SINGLEMAN AND HEATHER SWAN COMPLETE WORLD'S HIGHEST BASE JUMP

23 May 2006, Meru Peak, Uttaranchal, India

Australian doctor Glenn Singleman had made headlines in 1992 when, along with Nic Feteris, he had leapt from the Great Trango Tower in Pakistan to record the highest BASE jump in history – 20,000ft (6,258m). And 12 years later he was in record-breaking mood once again, this time with the intention of leaping from Meru Peak, the world's highest cliff at 21,667ft (6,604m) in northern India, along with his wife Heather Swan. After a 22-day crawl up the near vertical peak – sometimes managing as little as 50m a day on the 80-degree ice slopes – they launched themselves down the near-vertical eastern cliff face wearing wing-suits, hit speeds of up to 200km/h during their descent and were back at base camp just two minutes after jumping: they had recorded the highest BASE jump in history.

➲ The pair were to be joined by cameraman Jimmy Freeman, but he started to suffer from altitude sickness after nine days and returned to base camp, by parachuting down the cliff.

THE KING OF CLAY

RAFAEL NADAL BREAKS GUILLERMO VILLAS'S RECORD FOR MOST CONSECUTIVE WINS ON CLAY

28 May 2006, Roland Garros, Paris, France

If 2005 saw Rafael Nadal make it into tennis's big time, then 2006 was the season he confirmed his potential to become one of the sport's all-time greats. The Spaniard started the year in impressive style, winning 22 of his first 25 matches of the season, including a win over Roger Federer in Dubai. And then came his switch back to clay, the surface upon which he had dominated the previous year – and upon which he had not been beaten since May 2005. Nadal won in Monte Carlo, edged Federer in a five-hour epic in the Italian Open to equal Guillermo Vilas's record for consecutive wins on clay, and made the record his very own following a routine 6–2, 7–5, 6–1 first-round victory over Robin Soderling at the French Open.

➲ Nadal went on to beat Federer 1–6, 6–1, 6–4, 7–6 in the final to defend his French Open crown and his consecutive-win streak on clay stretched to 81 matches – a record on any surface – before Federer beat him in the Hamburg Open final in May 2007.

Unbeaten on clay since May 2005, Rafael Nadal's record-breaking 44th consecutive win on clay came in the first round of the 2006 French Open.

LESLIE PASSES 5,000-POINT MILESTONE

LISA LESLIE BECOMES FIRST PLAYER IN WNBA HISTORY TO SCORE 5,000 CAREER POINTS

23 June 2006, Staples Center, Los Angeles, California, USA

A standout collegiate player and a gold-medal winner at the 1996 Olympic Games, Lisa Leslie was one of the original members of the Los Angeles Sparks team for the inaugural WNBA season in 1997. The 6ft 5in centre was a star from the start, her career littered with achievements: 1,000 career points by her second season; a second Olympic gold in 2000, coupled with a first WNBA title; All-Star Game, WNBA and championship MVP-winning form to lead the Sparks to a second successive title in 2001. In 2002 she registered the first slam dunk in WNBA history; in 2004 she passed the 4,000-career-point milestone; and on 23 June 2006, during a career-high 41-point match against the San Antonio Silver Stars, became the first player in WNBA to pass 5,000 career points.

⮎Leslie also leads the WNBA career marks in rebounds, field goals made and free throws made.

The game seemed to come easily to the Los Angeles Sparks' Lisa Leslie, the most agile centre women's basketball has ever seen: in 2006 she became the first player in WNBA history to score 5,000 career points.

RONALDO NETS RECORD-BREAKING 15TH WORLD CUP GOAL

RONALDO BECOMES THE WORLD CUP'S ALL-TIME LEADING SCORER

27 June 2006, WM Stadion Dortmund, Dortmund, Germany

The World Cup had always been kind to Ronaldo. In 1998, despite Brazil's 3–0 final loss to France, his four goals in the tournament had enhanced his reputation as being the hottest striker on the planet. Four years later, with many writing him off as a spent force following a year out of the game with a serious knee injury, he scored eight goals in the tournament – including two in Brazil's 2–0 final win over Germany – and won the Golden Shoe Award. In 2006, with many questioning his fitness and desire for the game, he scored two goals in Brazil's final group win over Japan to equal Gerd Muller's all-time World Cup record of 14 goals. In Brazil's next match, against Ghana, he scored again to become the leading goal-scorer in World Cup history.

⮑ It would be Ronaldo's final goal of the tournament: Brazil lost 1–0 to France in the quarter-finals.

Ronaldo always seems to have reserved his best form for the World Cup finals and in 2006 netted his 15th goal to become the tournament's all-time leading goal-scorer.

When Adriano slotted home his country's second goal against Ghana on 27 June 2006, it was a moment of history: it was the 200th goal Brazil had scored in the World Cup – a tournament record.

THE WORLD CUP'S GREATEST GOAL-SCORING TEAM

BRAZIL BECOME THE FIRST TEAM TO SCORE 200 WORLD CUP GOALS

27 June 2006, WM Stadion Dortmund, Dortmund, Germany

When you think of the World Cup you almost inevitably think of Brazil; you think of Pele, Garrincha, Zico and Rivelino, Romario and Ronaldo, of samba magic, of fast-flowing, carefree soccer, of carnival-atmosphere stadiums, and of a team that has laid its hands on soccer's greatest prize a record-breaking five times. It seemed entirely appropriate, therefore, that Brazil, a nation whose soccer team had entertained generations of soccer fans, should become the first team in World Cup finals history to score 200 goals: the moment came when Adriano handed Brazil a 2–0 lead in the 45th minute of their second-round match against Ghana at the 2006 World Cup.

⮑ Following the 2006 World Cup, the tournament's all-time leading scorers were as follows: Brazil (201 goals), Germany (190) and Italy (122).

Anchored by innings of 157 from Sanath Jayasuriya (above) and 117 from Tillakaratne Dilshan, Sri Lanka posted a one-day international record total of 443 for 9 against the Netherlands in July 2006.

SRI LANKA POST ONE-DAY INTERNATIONAL CRICKET'S HIGHEST TOTAL

SRI LANKA RECORD HIGHEST ONE-DAY INTERNATIONAL TOTAL IN HISTORY
4 July 2006, VRA Ground, Amstelveen, the Netherlands

Just four months after seeing first Australia and then South Africa pass their one-day international highest innings total (398) in the same match in Johannesburg, Sri Lanka were up to their record-breaking antics once again when they visited the Netherlands in July 2006. After winning the toss, Sri Lanka's batsmen were in buccaneering form: Sanath Jayasuriya, the architect of some of the most devastating innings in ODI history, smashed an imperious 157 off 104 balls; Tillakaratne Dilshan bludgeoned 117 off a mere 78 balls; and by the time their 50 overs were up, Sri Lanka had amassed the mighty total of 443 for 9, to beat South Africa's record by five runs.

➲ In reply, the Netherlands posted a spirited 248 all out, but still ended up losing the match by 195 runs.

Two years after equalling Colin Jackson's 110m hurdles world-record time of 12.91s, China's Xiang Liu made the record his own, clocking a time of 12.88s in Lausanne, Switzerland.

XIANG LIU MAKES 110M HURDLES WORLD RECORD HIS OWN

XIANG LIU BREAKS THE 110M HURDLES WORLD RECORD
11 July 2006, Lausanne, Switzerland

A former national high-school high jump champion before switching his attentions to the 110m hurdles aged 15, Xiang Liu's progress to the top of the event was as smooth as it was spectacular. In 2000, aged 17, he finished fourth in the World Junior Championships. Two years later he broke the world junior and Asian records; in 2003 he won the 60m hurdles world indoor title and picked up a bronze medal at the World Championships. In 2004 he struck gold in Athens, equalling Colin Jackson's world-record time (12.91s set in 1993) in the process. And although he finished second in the 2005 World Championships, he reaffirmed his status as the world's best the following year when he clocked 12.88s in Lausanne, Switzerland, to make the world record his own.

➲ The following year, he added the one title missing from his collection when he became world champion in Osaka, Japan.

TEST BEST PARTNERSHIP OF 624 RUNS

KUMAR SANGAKKARA AND MAHELE JAYAWARDENE RECORD TEST CRICKET'S HIGHEST PARTNERSHIP

27–29 July 2006, Sinhalese Sports Club, Colombo, Sri Lanka

Things were finally looking up for South Africa in the first Test against Sri Lanka in Colombo in 2006. After being dismissed for 169 in their first innings, they had reduced Sri Lanka to 14 for 2 and looked to assert their authority over the game. Kumar Sangakkara and Mahele Jayawardene had other ideas, however, and batted through to the end of the day. They matched each other run for run on the second day too, taking Sri Lanka to 485 for 2, with Sangakkara unbeaten on 271 and Jayawardene on 276. And on they went into day three, passing fellow countrymen Sanath Jayasuriya and Roshan Mahanama's previous world-record partnership of 576 runs (set in 1997) before Sangakkara finally fell for 287 and the partnership ended on 624.

Kumar Sangakkara (left) and Mahele Jayawardene (right) batted for 157 overs to produce the highest partnership in Test cricket history: a mighty 624 runs.

➲ Jayawardene was finally out for 374, at which point Sri Lanka declared their innings on 756 for 5. In reply, South Africa were dismissed for 434 to lose the match by an innings and 153 runs.

FOUR IN A ROW FOR UNSTOPPABLE DAHLE

GUNN-RITA DAHLE FIRST TO WIN FOUR SUCCESSIVE MOUNTAIN BIKE OVERALL WORLD CUPS

24 September 2006, Beijing, China

A trip with her local cycling club in April 1995 ignited 22-year-old Gunn-Rita Dahle's love affair with mountain biking and within five months she had become national champion. But her rise to the top of her sport was far from smooth and it wasn't until she took control of the management of her own affairs in 2002 that her talent started to shine through. That year she won her first world championship title; in 2003 she became overall World Cup winner for the first time; in 2004 she became Olympic champion, and won both the world championship and the overall World Cup. She defended her world titles in 2005 and again in 2006 to become not only the first four-time world champion, but also the first in history to win the overall World Cup on four consecutive occasions.

➲ Gunn-Rita Dahle's run of world championship and overall World Cup wins was brought to an end when she missed a large part of the 2007 season due to a viral infection.

A fourth consecutive overall mountain bike World Cup win in 2006 saw Norway's Gunn-Rita Dahle break Juli Furtado's record of three consecutive titles and assured her legendary status in the sport.

THE WORLD'S TOP-SCORING GOALKEEPER

ROGERIO CENI BREAKS RECORD FOR MOST GOALS SCORED BY A GOALKEEPER

20 August 2006, Morumbi, Sao Paulo, Brazil

Rogerio Ceni was from the same stock as South American goalkeepers such as Jose Luis Chilavert, Rene Higuita and Jorge Campos – goalkeepers who had a little something extra to their games. Ceni's multi-talented abilities came to light when he joined Brazilian league outfit Sao Paulo in 1990: he emerged as a free-kick and penalty specialist and his languid approach to the ball yielded some spectacular results, with the ball flying into the back of the net with delightful frequency. On 20 August 2006, during Sao Paulo's league match against Cruzeiro, he netted a trademark thunderous free-kick – moments after saving a penalty at the other end: it was the 63rd goal of his career, taking him past Chilavert's previous record total of 62.

➲ The crowd did not have to wait long to celebrate Ceni's 64th career goal: he scored from the penalty spot later in the game.

A goalkeeper with a lethal right boot, Sao Paulo's Rogerio Ceni holds the world record for the most goals ever scored by a goalkeeper.

Michael Phelps may have suffered a slump in form following his Olympic heroics in 2004, but two world records inside three days at the 2006 Pan Pacific Championships signalled a magnificent return to form.

PHELPS RETURNS TO FORM WITH TWO WORLD RECORDS

MICHAEL PHELPS BREAKS TWO WORLD RECORDS IN THREE DAYS

17–20 August 2006, Victoria, Canada

In November 2004, just a few months after his Olympic heroics in Athens, Michael Phelps's reputation took a nosedive when he was arrested and charged with driving under the influence of alcohol. The conviction affected him, but if five gold medals at the 2005 World Championships seemed to indicate a return to form, then his performances at the 2006 Pan Pacific Championships reaffirmed his status as the top dog of his sport. He started by registering his first personal best time since 2004 to break his own 200m butterfly world record (1m53.93s set in Barcelona in 2003) – with a time of 1m53.80s – and was up to his record-breaking antics three days later, breaking his own 200m individual medley mark (1m55.94s set in Maryland in 2003) with a time of 1m55.84s.

➲ Phelps's star continued to rise: at the 2007 World Championships in Melbourne he won seven gold medals and broke five world records.

THE HUMAN AQUALUNG

TOM SIETAS BREAKS TWO FREE-DIVING WORLD RECORDS IN TWO DAYS

27–28 August 2006, Tokyo, Japan

Born in Hamburg, Germany, on 12 January 1977, Tom Sietas started free-diving at the age of 23 after taking a course in scuba diving, and his extraordinary ability to hold his breath for immense periods of time – in practice he could remain underwater for up to ten minutes at a time – immediately marked him out as a future star of the sport. He unveiled this huge potential to the world in the space of two days in Tokyo, Japan, in 2006. On 27 August he broke the free-diving depth record without fins, achieving a mark of 183m (600ft); a day later, at the same location, he broke the depth record with fins as well, reaching an incredible 223m (732ft).

➲ Sietas's ability to hold his breath underwater was unveiled on live television on the *Live with Regis and Kelly Show* in the United States on 9 August 2007: he remained underwater for 15m02s.

During the course of two days in August 2006 in Tokyo, Japan, Tom Sietas broke the free-diving dynamic dive world records for both with and without fins.

THE MOST SUCCESSFUL RALLY DRIVER OF ALL TIME

SEBASTIEN LOEB BREAKS WORLD RALLY CHAMPIONSHIP RECORD FOR MOST CAREER WINS

3 September 2006, Obihiro, Hokkaido, Japan

A second-place finish in his first World Rally Championship outing, at the 2001 San Remo Rally, was enough to secure Sebastien Loeb a ride with Citroen for 2002, and although the team ran a limited schedule, he won once. Driving full-time in 2003, Loeb won four times, before dominating the following year: winning six races to become world champion for the first time. The dominance continued into 2005: he won six consecutive races – a WRC record – and ended the season with nine wins and a second world title. There was no let-up in form in 2006: he won five of the season's first seven races, before winning the German Rally to tie Carlos Sainz's all-time record of career wins (26). The record 27th victory of his career came in the following race, the Japanese Rally.

⮕ Loeb won next time out, at the Cyprus Rally, before breaking his arm in a mountain bike accident and missing the final third of the season. No one could catch his points total, however, and he completed a hat-trick of world titles. A fourth world title followed in 2007.

THE FASTEST MOTORCYCLE ON EARTH

CHRIS CARR BREAKS THE MOTORCYCLE LAND SPEED WORLD RECORD

5 September 2006, Bonneville Salt Flats, Utah, USA

On 3 September 2005, at the AMA/FIM International Motorcycle Speed Trials held on the Bonneville Salt Flats in Utah, Rocky Robinson had signalled a new dawn for motorcycle land speed records when he propelled his Mike Akatiff-designed streamliner motorcycle to 342.797mph (551.7km/h) to smash Dave Campos's 1990 record of 322mph (518.2km/h) by some 20mph. His record did not last long. Two days later, on 5 September 2006, seven-time Grand National dirt track champion Chris Carr took his Dennis Manning-designed BUB Enterprises streamliner to an average speed over two runs of 350.8mph (562.6km/h) to earn the title of the fastest man on two wheels.

⮕ The BUB Enterprises streamliner motorcycle was fitted with a V4 engine capable of producing over 420 horsepower.

NAVRATILOVA BOWS OUT IN RECORD-BREAKING STYLE

MARTINA NAVRATILOVA WINS THE LAST OF HER RECORD-BREAKING 177 CAREER TITLES

10 September 2006, Flushing Meadows, New York, USA

In July 2006, after she and her partner Mark Knowles crashed out of Wimbledon's mixed doubles tournament at the third-round stage (losing 7–5, 6–1 to eventual champions Andy Ram and Vera Zvonereva) and then losing with her partner Liezel Huber in the quarter-finals of the women's doubles (to eventual champions Yan Zi and Zheng Jie), it seemed as though time was finally catching up on tennis's very own Peter Pan, Martina Navratilova. But the 49-year-old star, who had collected her first professional title way back in 1974, still had one final trick up her sleeve: later in the year she partnered Bob Bryan to victory in the US Open mixed doubles final – it was the 177th and final title of her glittering career.

➲ Navratilova retired from doubles play at the end of the 2006 season and bowed out of tennis with 18 grand slam singles titles, 31 grand slam women's titles and ten mixed doubles titles to her name.

Just a few weeks short of her 50th birthday, evergreen Martina Navratilova won the US Open mixed doubles title with Bob Bryan to record the 177th title of her career.

FEDERER IN A CLASS OF HIS OWN

SWISS STAR CLAIMS BACK-TO-BACK HAT-TRICK OF WIMBLEDON AND US OPEN TITLES

10 September 2006, Flushing Meadows, New York, USA

At one set all and 0–40 on his own serve things weren't looking so good for the Swiss star. But half an hour later it was all over: Federer crushed an overhead smash into the open court, sank to his knees, lay on his back and stared momentarily into the Manhattan sky, pausing just for a moment to reflect on 30 minutes of almost unrivalled tennis: an incredible array of forehand winners, precise serves and unstoppable returns had seen him become the first player in the history of the open era to win back-to-back Wimbledon and US Open titles three years in a row.

➲ In February 2007, Roger Federer broke Jimmy Connors's 30-year record for the most consecutive weeks as the world's No. 1-ranked player.

A third successive US Open crown in 2006, coupled with a hat-trick of Wimbledon titles, confirmed Roger Federer as not only the finest player of his generation, but possibly of all time.

A stylish, world-class batsman with impeccable technique, Mohammad Yousuf outlined his status as one of the game's best players in 2006 when he scored 1,788 runs to break the record for the most Test runs scored in a calendar year.

MOST TEST RUNS IN A CALENDAR YEAR

MOHAMMAD YOUSUF BREAKS RECORD FOR MOST TEST RUNS IN A CALENDAR YEAR

1 December 2006, National Stadium, Karachi, Pakistan

From the moment he made his Test debut against South Africa in 1998, Mohammad Yousuf's talent was never in doubt, but it took the Pakistan batsman until 2004 to silence those who questioned his temperament to succeed at the highest level. He scored a century against Australia in Melbourne; another century came in the hostile atmosphere of Calcutta; followed by a magnificent double-century against England in Lahore. And then came 2006: he plundered 461 runs in three Tests against India; 631 in the four-match series against England; and then smashed four centuries in three Tests against the West Indies to end the year with 1,788 runs to his credit – breaking Viv Richards's record for runs in a calendar year of 1,710 set in 1976.

➲ Formerly known as Yousuf Youhana before his conversion to Islam in 2005, in his early days Yousuf was one of the few Christians to have played for Pakistan.

Thirty-two years after taking to the saddle for the first time in his career, Russell Baze rode his 9,531st winner to become the world's most successful jockey.

BAZE NOTCHES UP RECORD-BREAKING 9,531ST WINNER

RUSSELL BAZE BECOMES WORLD'S WINNINGEST JOCKEY

1 December 2006, Bay Meadows, San Mateo, California, USA

Russell Baze's first official ride came in 1974 at the age of 16 and he had to wait a mere eight races before recording his first winner. He spent much of his early career plying his trade in Californian racing circles, but came to national prominence in 1995 when he became the first jockey in American racing history to record 400 winners in four straight seasons; between 1992 and 2005 he achieved the 400-mark 11 times – none among his peers could manage more than three. The winners kept coming and on 1 December 2006, at Bay Meadows racetrack in California, he took his fourth mount of the day, Butterfly Belle, to the winning post to record the 9,531st victory of his career, taking him past Laffit Pincay Jr's previous record mark of 9,530.

➲ Brazilian jockey Jorge Ricardo overhauled the mark in February 2007 while Baze was spending a spell on the sidelines through injury.

MAGIC MOMENT FOR MU EN ROUTE TO ASIAN GAMES GOLD

MU SHUANGSHUANG BREAKS WOMEN'S WEIGHTLIFTING'S SNATCH WORLD RECORD
6 December 2006, Al Dana Auditorium, Doha, Qatar

China's women's weightlifting team travelled to the 2006 Asian Games in Doha, Qatar, with a point to prove. Their dominance in the sport, particularly in the super-heavyweight category (75kg-plus), had been usurped by South Korea: China's star Mu Shuangshuang had not beaten the Korean No. 1, Jang Mi-Ran, for over two years. But that was all to change in front of a raucous crowd in the Al Dana Auditorium in Doha: Mu opened up in the snatch section of the competition with a lift of 139kg, breaking the record set by arch-rival Jang the year earlier by 1kg, and hung on in the clean and jerk to claim Asian Games gold.

➲ Mu equalled her world record mark in the snatch at the 2007 World Championships, but could not maintain her advantage in the clean and jerk and lost out on the overall title to Jang. It was the third time in her career she had won a World Championship silver medal.

Mu Shuangshuang opened her super-heavyweight Asian Games campaign with a world-record lift in the snatch and maintained her advantage in the clean and jerk to take her first major championship gold medal.

VALIC BROTHERS SECURE PARAGLIDING WORLD'S BEST

ALJAZ AND URBAN VALIC BREAK PARAGLIDING DISTANCE RECORD TO DECLARED TARGET

7 December 2006, Jamestown, South Africa

As the Bonneville Salt Flats are to those attempting the land speed world record and the slopes of Les Arcs are to speed skiers, De Aar in the northern Cape, South Africa, is the Mecca for paragliders around the world. And in December 2006 conditions were perfect for Slovenian brothers Aljaz (27) and Urban (26) Valic's assault on the declared target world record – 353km (219.34 miles) set in Brazil the previous year. They launched from Vosburg, spent over six-and-a-half hours in the air, battled difficult conditions and reached heights of 5,200m, before landing 200m apart from each other at their declared destination, in Jamestown. They had covered 369.9km (229.85 miles) … and the world record was theirs.

➲ The brothers' journey also broke the world record for the longest tandem flight.

FAVRE OVERTAKES MARINO'S PASS COMPLETION RECORD

BRETT FAVRE BREAKS NFL RECORD FOR MOST CAREER COMPLETIONS

17 December 2006, Lambeau Field, Green Bay, Wisconsin, USA

An injury to Green Bay Packers' starting quarterback Don Majkowski in 1992 opened the door for Brett Favre and once he had gained his place in the starting line-up, the Mississippi-born man refused to give it away. In 1993 the Packers reached the playoffs for the first time in 11 years; in 1995 they reached the NFC Championship; in 1996 and 1997 they reached the Super Bowl (winning one and losing the other). Further Super Bowl success may have eluded him, but Favre continued to post winning seasons, despite a series of personal setbacks: in 2003 his father died suddenly; the following year his wife was diagnosed with breast cancer; but Favre's career rumbled on. On 17 December 2006 he threw the 4,968th completed pass of his career, breaking Dan Marino's previous record.

➲ Just before the start of the football season in his senior college year, Favre was involved in a near-fatal car accident that led to 30in of his small intestine being removed. Legend has it he was back playing within six weeks.

Ever-present for the Green Bay Packers since 1992, Brett Favre was closing in fast on numerous quarterback records by the mid-2000s, and on 17 December 2006 he overtook Dan Marino's mark for most career completions.

At the end of the day's play, Warne told the assembled press he could not have planned his record-breaking moment better if he'd tried: "To do it here in Melbourne ... I don't know who is writing my scripts but they're pretty good."

⮞ Warne's 700th Test wicket was also his 187th against England and came 13 years after his infamous "Ball of the Century" in which he dismissed Mike Gatting with his first ball in Ashes cricket.

MELBOURNE CHEERS ITS FAVOURITE SON

SHANE WARNE BECOMES THE FIRST BOWLER TO TAKE 700 TEST WICKETS

26 December 2006, Melbourne Cricket Ground, Melbourne, Australia

Even the greatest of Hollywood screenwriters would fail to come up with a more powerful denouement to what had been a rollercoaster of a career. With the Ashes already in the bag – Australia had won the first three Tests against a hapless England with ease – and having announced his intention to retire from international cricket at the end of the series, Shane Warne, cricket's enfant terrible, playing in his penultimate Test, and his last in front of his home crowd in Melbourne, stood poised on 699 Test wickets, ball in hand, with England's Andrew Strauss at the crease. Moments later, following one of his trademark big-spinning leg-breaks, the ball squeezed between bat and pad and crashed into the stumps. Warne wheeled away to his left, index finger pointing in the air, his legend as cricket's greatest-ever bowler secure. He had, after all, become the first bowler in the history of the game to take 700 Test wickets.

THE GOLDEN GIRL OF DARTS

TRINA GULLIVER WINS SEVENTH SUCCESSIVE WOMEN'S WORLD DARTS CHAMPIONSHIPS

12 January 2007, Lakeside Country Club, Frimley Green, Surrey, England

Born and brought up in Warwickshire, England, Trina Gulliver first picked up a dart in her parents' pub at the age of two. By age 14 she was playing for her county youth team and soon progressed through the ranks. Despite qualifying as a carpenter and joiner, Gulliver longed to pursue a career in darts and decided to turn professional. Times were tough: women's darts received little exposure and prize funds were small. What's more, she had to wait until 2001, and the inaugural women's World Championship, before she could display her talents to a wider audience. She beat Mandy Solomons 2–1 in the final and went on to remain undefeated in the championship over the next six years, beating the Netherlands' Francis Hoenselaar in five finals and Scotland's Anne Kirk in the other.

The winner of the inaugural women's World Dart Championship title in 2001, Trina Gulliver remained unbeaten in the competition over the next six years to claim seven successive titles.

⮞ Prize money in the women's game falls far behind that of the men's: at the 2006 World Championship, Gulliver picked up a winner's cheque for £6,000; the men's winner that year, Jelle Klaasen, picked up £60,000.

RICARDO BREAKS BAZE'S RECORD FOR MOST JOCKEY WINS

JORGE RICARDO BREAKS WORLD RECORD FOR MOST WINS BY A JOCKEY

5 February 2007, Hipodromo Argentina, Palermo, Buenos Aires, Argentina

Born into a horse-racing family – his father and two uncles were all jockeys – Jorge Ricardo took out his jockey's apprenticeship at the age of 15 in 1976 and earned his journeyman stripes within a year. Based for most of his career in his native Brazil – he moved to Argentina later in his career – he was his country's leading jockey for 25 consecutive years (1982–2006), with his best season coming in 1992–93, when he visited the winner's circle on 477 occasions. On 5 February 2007, in front of a sparse crowd in Palermo, a town to the north of Buenos Aires, he recorded the 9,591st winner of his career to surpass the record total held by still-active American jockey Russell Baze, who at the time was sidelined by injury.

➲ With more rides at his disposal throughout the year in the Argentine racing calendar, the general consensus is that Ricardo, who is three years younger than Baze, will ultimately end up with more career winners than the American.

Thirty years as a professional jockey saw Brazil's Jorge Ricardo become the leading jockey of all time in 2007 when he recorded the 9,591st victory of his career.

THE FASTEST ASCENT OF THE NORTH FACE OF THE EIGER

UELI STECK BREAKS THE RECORD FOR THE FASTEST ASCENT OF THE EIGER'S NORTH FACE

21 February 2007, Eiger, Bernese Alps, Switzerland

The infamous North Face of the Eiger still presented the toughest mountaineering challenge in Europe, but, on 21 February 2007, after waiting two years to witness such a day, Swiss climber Ueli Steck found the normally treacherous rock-face in pristine condition. The time to fulfil a dream had arrived. He set off up the (1,880m) sheer face with the intention of following the legendary Heckmair route – the path taken by the North Face's first four summiteers, Anderl Heckmair, Ludwig Vorg, Fritz Kasparek and Heinrich Harrer, in 1938 – and made it to the summit in 3h54m. It was the fastest ascent of the North Face in history, breaking the record set by Italian mountain guide Christoph Heinz of 4h30m set in 2003.

➲ The placid conditions were not the only reason Steck mastered the Eiger's North Face in record time: he also implemented an innovative technique called "dry tooling".

For one day only in February 2007 the infamous North Face of the Eiger allowed itself to be mastered, and Swiss climber Ueli Steck took advantage of the placid conditions, recording the fastest ascent of the face in history.

GIBBS SMASHES A ONE-DAY INTERNATIONAL FIRST

HERSCHELLE GIBBS FIRST TO HIT SIX SIXES IN AN OVER IN A ONE-DAY INTERNATIONAL

16 March 2007, Warner Park, Basseterre, St Kitts

There had only been two instances of the feat in first-class cricket history: Garfield Sobers (1968) and Ravi Shastri (1985) were the only two players in the history of the game to have hit six sixes in an over. But it had never occurred in international cricket: until South Africa's opening group game against the Netherlands in the 2007 Cricket World Cup when, at the start of the 30th over, Herschelle Gibbs decided the time was right to open his shoulders … and Dutch spinner Daan van Bunge found the South African hitman at his murderous best. Making the most of the smaller, straight boundaries, he smashed every ball of the over for six. It was a first in international cricket and earned $1 million for charity.

Herschelle Gibbs recorded a one-day international first in South Africa's opening 2007 Cricket World Cup game against the Netherlands: in the 30th over he became the first player in international cricket history to hit six sixes in an over.

➲ The previous record for the most runs in an over in one-day international cricket was 30, achieved by Sri Lanka's Sanath Jayasuriya, who achieved the feat twice: against Pakistan in 1995–96 and against New Zealand in 2000–01.

One of the greatest sports stadiums in the world, the new Wembley Stadium is also the most expensive: six years of construction and several delays saw building costs spiral to a massive £778 million.

THE NEW WEMBLEY STADIUM OPENS FOR BUSINESS

WORLD'S MOST EXPENSIVE STADIUM FINALLY OPENS ITS DOORS

24 March 2007, Wembley Stadium, London, England

It took over six years to complete, was the subject of public derision following delay after delay, and became a matter of huge concern as costs spiralled seemingly out of control. But when the Foster and Partners- and HOK Sport-designed "new" Wembley Stadium finally opened for business on 24 March 2007 it made an entire nation proud. Dominated by an arch towering 133m above pitch level, containing 212,000 tonnes of concrete, 23,000 tonnes of structural steel, 80km of speaker cables and 380 floodlights, it also happened to be the most expensive stadium ever built, with the final cost totalling a staggering £778 million: the whole of England hopes it will turn out to be worth every penny.

➲ With a capacity of 90,000, Wembley Stadium is the second-largest soccer stadium in Europe behind Barcelona's Nou Camp, which has a capacity of 98,772.

PRODIGIOUS PRESSEL MAKES GOLF HISTORY

MORGAN PRESSEL BECOMES THE YOUNGEST FEMALE WINNER OF A MAJOR TOURNAMENT

1 April 2007, Mission Hills Country Club, Rancho Mirage, California, USA

Florida-born Morgan Pressel is another prodigy to make waves on the golf world. In 2001, aged 12, she became the youngest player in history – a record surpassed by Alexis Thompson in 2007 – to qualify for the US Women's Open; in 2005, aged 17, she finished second; and later in the year, after seeking assurances from the LPGA that she would receive an age exemption (the LPGA ran a strictly over-18 policy), she turned professional and finished tied for sixth to earn exemption for the 2006 season. But she came of age in 2007, with her first tournament win coming after a final-round 69 brought her the prestigious Kraft Nabisco Championship: she had become, aged 18 years, 313 days, the youngest woman in history to win a major.

➲ Further tournament victories may have eluded her in 2007, but Morgan Pressel ended the season inside the top ten of the money list for the first time.

Final-round nerves may have seen Morgan Pressel lose out on the 2005 US Women's Open (when she was just 17 years old), but the Florida native made no mistake in the 2007 Kraft Nabisco Championship, shooting a final-round 69 to win by one stroke and become the youngest major winner in women's golf history.

THE ULTIMATE IN PEDAL POWER

SAM WHITTINGHAM BREAKS THE BEST HUMAN EFFORT WORLD HOUR RECORD

8 April 2007, Casa Grande, Arizona, USA

American extreme cyclist Sam Whittingham, who since October 2002 could lay a rightful claim on being the fastest man on earth – he set the human-powered speed world record at 81mph (130.35km/h) in his Varna Diablo bicycle – travelled to the 5.6-mile test oval in Casa Grande, Arizona, in April 2007 with the stated aim of reclaiming the Best Human Effort World Hour record – for modified bicycles (the World Hour record for traditional bikes is considered a different record) – he had lost to Fred Markham's 85.991km the year before. And he did just that, powering his five-gear, aerodynamically refined bicycle Varna Diablo III through 86.77km in the space of just 60 minutes.

➲ The conventional World Hour record, held by Czech cyclist Ondrek Sosenka, stands at 49.700km.

If ranking points alone are a measure of a player's dominance, then Roger Federer has been the most secure world No. 1 in modern tennis history: he holds the record for most consecutive weeks as the world's No. 1-ranked player.

FEDERER REVELS IN ROLE AS WORLD NO. 1

ROGER FEDERER BREAKS RECORD FOR THE MOST CONSECUTIVE WEEKS AS WORLD NO. 1

11 April 2007, Ponte Vedra Beach, Florida, USA

On 2 February 2004, Swiss sensation Roger Federer finally rose to the top of the world rankings and, far from being overwhelmed by such a lofty status, relished the role as though it was his birthright, winning three of that year's grand slam titles and adding two more to his growing collection in 2005. He was equally dominant in 2006, reaching all four grand slam finals – winning three of them – and ending the year as comfortable world No. 1, 2,000-plus points ahead of his nearest rival. The steamroller continued into 2007, with Federer defending his Australian Open title, and by April he had overtaken Jimmy Connors's record (160) for the most consecutive weeks as the world's No. 1-ranked tennis player.

➲ Federer went on to collect a fifth Wimbledon and a fourth US Open title in 2007.

ROOKIE HAMILTON AN INSTANT HIT IN FORMULA ONE

LEWIS HAMILTON FIRST ROOKIE IN F1 HISTORY TO OPEN CAREER WITH THREE SUCCESSIVE PODIUMS

15 April 2007, Bahrain International Circuit, Sakhir, Bahrain

History was made in 1998 when McLaren signed 13-year-old karting prodigy Lewis Hamilton to their books: the Hertfordshire star had become the first teenager in history to sign for a Formula One outfit. And with McLaren's financial and technical support, Hamilton rose serenely through the ranks: world karting champion in 2000; Formula Renault champion in 2003; Formula Three Euroseries champion in 2005; and GP2 champion in 2006. By 2007 he was ready for the big time and got his McLaren FI career off to a sensational start: finishing third in the season-opening Australian GP, second in the Malaysian GP and second again in the Bahrain GP to become the first rookie in F1 history to record three podium finishes in his first three races.

➲ Hamilton challenged for the title throughout the season, winning four races and entering the final race of the season leading the drivers' championship before finally finishing second.

Lewis Hamilton's arrival in Formula One generated more excitement than the sport had seen in years and he opened his debut campaign in blistering style, recording a rookie-record three successive podium finishes.

HAAKONSEN THRILLS CROWDS WITH RECORD-BREAKING LEAP

TERJE HAAKONSEN BREAKS SNOWBOARDING WORLD RECORD FOR THE HIGHEST "AIR"

22 April 2007, Oslo, Norway

Terje Haakonsen is the Michael Jordan of the snowboarding world, a man so good they named a move after him (the "Haakon Flip"), and as you trace through the history of snowboarding, the footprints of one of the most iconic and influential figures in the sport's history loom large. A five-time European half-pipe champion, a three-time US Open champion and a six-time winner of the Mount Baker Banked Slalom championship, the Norwegian added another string to his already impressive bow at the 2007 Arctic Challenge, an event he organized back in 1999. Competing against the best snowboarders in the business, he pulled off a 9.8m "air" jump to claim another ground-breaking world record.

⮑ Haakonsen's "air" jump beat the previous record of 9.3m, set by Heikki Sorsa at the 2001 Arctic Challenge.

Terje Haakonsen pulled off a backside 360 9.8m jump from a quarterpipe at the 2007 Arctic Challenge to break the "air" height world record.

AUSTRALIA CLINCH CRICKET WORLD CUP HAT-TRICK

AUSTRALIA BECOME THE FIRST TEAM TO WIN THREE SUCCESSIVE CRICKET WORLD CUPS

29 April 2007, Kensington Oval, Bridgetown, Barbados

The dominant team in world cricket in the Test arena, Australia were able to transfer their class onto the one-day international stage. Winners of the tournament for the first time in 1987, they took the World Cup for a second time in 1999, defended the trophy with some ease in South Africa four years later, and headed to the Caribbean in 2007 determined to achieve what no team had achieved before them: to win the greatest prize in one-day cricket for the third consecutive time. They won it at a canter, marching through the group and Super Eight stages, dismissing South Africa's challenge in the semi-finals and beating Sri Lanka by 55 runs in the final to make history.

➲ The star of the show in the final was Australia's wicketkeeper Adam Gilchrist, who smashed 149 off a mere 104 balls and reached his century off just 77 balls.

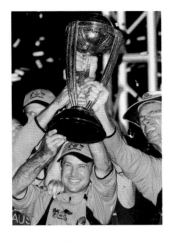

Australia's comfortable 55-run victory over Sri Lanka in the 2007 Cricket World Cup produced a moment of history: it was the first time a team had collected the trophy on three successive occasions.

THE KING OF CLAY EXTENDS HIS REIGN

RAFAEL NADAL BREAKS RECORD FOR MOST CONSECUTIVE WINS ON A SINGLE SURFACE

12 May 2007, Foro Italico, Rome, Italy

Rafael Nadal's start to the 2007 season had yielded a quarter-final exit in the Australian Open and a solitary title before the start of the clay court season handed him the opportunity of extending a single-surface consecutive-game winning streak that stretched back to May 2005, encompassing back-to-back French Open titles, and which had precipitated his majestic rise to No. 2 in the world rankings. He won his third consecutive title at Monte Carlo (the first player to achieve the feat since Ilie Nastase in 1971–73); completed a hat-trick of wins at Barcelona; and, during his march to the Italian Open title, passed John McEnroe's all-time record (set on an indoor carpet) of 75 consecutive wins on a single surface.

➲ A week later the streak came to an end at 81 when Roger Federer beat the Spaniard in the final of the Hamburg Open.

Rafael Nadal's irresistible form on clay continued into the 2007 season: by May, in a streak that stretched back two years, he broke the record for the most consecutive wins on a single surface.

CANADA GETS ITS KICKS

CANADA HOSTS FIFA U20 WORLD CUP FOR THE FIRST TIME

30 June– 22 July 2007, Canada

Argentina's 2–1 victory over the Czech Republic came after Mauro Zarate scored a tie-breaking goal in the 86th minute.

2007 saw two firsts for soccer's highest youth trophy: It was the first youth championship series to be called the "FIFA U20 World Cup" rather than the old title of "FIFA World Youth Championship," and it was the event's first appearance on Canadian soil. And though Canada's players were ousted even before the Group of 16 stage, it didn't stop footie-hungry fans from turning out in droves to watch and cheer on their favourite teams. Games were contested across the country, from Montreal to Victoria and back again, before culminating in a bloody and hard-fought Argentinean victory over the Czech Republic. The 52-match, six-arena tournament is touted as being the biggest single-sport event in Canadian history.

➲ It wasn't all good sportsmanship, though: Controversy erupted after a heated semi-final, when the losing Chilean team was involved in a melee with police officers and destroyed their rented tour bus. Chile went on to beat Austria in the third-place playoff.

In July 2007, Natalia Molchanova cemented her reputation as the greatest female free-diver of her generation by breaking three world records in the space of three days.

MOLCHANOVA REACHES NEW DEPTHS

NATALIA MOLCHANOVA BREAKS THREE FREE-DIVING WORLD RECORDS IN THREE DAYS

5–7 July 2007, Maribor, Slovenia

Already considered the best female free-diver in the world, Russia's Natalia Molchanova, a 45-year-old, seven-time world champion, travelled to Moribor, Slovenia, in July 2007 and produced one of the most sensational weeks in the history of her sport. On 5 July she broke the record for the longest dynamic apnea dive with fins, reaching a distance of 205m (673ft). The following day she broke the record for static immersion (i.e. the time spent underwater without drawing breath) with a world's-best eight minutes. And she had not finished there: a day later she broke the record for the longest dynamic apnea dive without fins, reaching 149m.

➲ Molchanova is also the record-holder for constant weight without fins (any weights the diver used during the descent must be brought back up to the surface) with a mark of 55m set on 7 November 2005 in Dahab, Egypt.

WOODS REVELS IN WORLD GOLF CHAMPIONSHIP EVENTS

TIGER WOODS FIRST TO WIN THREE CONSECUTIVE VICTORIES IN THE SAME TOURNAMENT – TWICE

5 August 2007, Firestone Country Club, Akron, Ohio, USA

Tiger Woods may be in the process of recording the most storied career in golf history, but he has enjoyed particular success at World Golf Championship events – invite-only tournaments for the world's elite golfers – and in particular at the WGC-Bridgestone event played over the Firestone Country Club course in Ohio. Woods took the first three tournaments in 1999, 2000 and 2001, missed out between 2002 and 2004, regained the title in 2005 and 2006 and arrived at the 2007 event looking to make history: no player in PGA Tour history has won the same tournament three times in a row twice. He shot a 72-hole total of eight under par – the only player in the tournament to break par – to create another slice of golf history.

➲ It was Woods's 14th World Golf Championship victory in his 14th start: his WGC-Bridgestone victory in 2007 meant he had claimed $18.5 million in prize money from WGC events alone.

Tiger Woods wrote another entry into the history books with his victory at the WGC-Bridgestone Invitational in 2007: it was the second time he had recorded three consecutive victories in the tournament.

THE MOST PROLIFIC HOME RUN HITTER OF ALL TIME

BARRY BONDS BREAKS HANK AARON'S CAREER HOME RUN RECORD

7 August 2007, AT&T Park, San Francisco, California, USA

As the years passed and as the ravages of time slowly started to catch up with him, Barry Bonds started to edge past the career home run marks of some of baseball's most legendary names. On 20 May 2006 he swatted the 714th home run of his career to pass Babe Ruth's total of 713 and only one person stood between him and the title of baseball's most prolific power hitter of all time: Hank Aaron with 755 (733 in the National League and 20 in the American League). The record finally came at 8.15 p.m. on 7 August 2007 at AT&T Park in San Francisco when he smashed a 435ft home run off Washington Nationals pitcher Mike Bacsik. It was the 756th home run of his career: no player in baseball history has registered more.

➲ The argument still rages as to who is the most destructive power hitter in the game's history. Ruth achieved his 713 career home runs in 8,398 at-bats. It took Bonds 9,246 at-bats to reach the mark; it took Aaron 11,288.

It had been the talk of baseball for some time, but on 7 August 2007, Barry Bonds slammed the 756th home run of his career to become baseball's all-time leading slugger.

SLADE STORMS INTO FASTNET RECORD BOOKS

MIKE SLADE'S *ICAP LEONARD* BREAKS MONOHULL BOAT RECORD IN FASTNET RACE

16 August 2007, Plymouth, England

First contested in 1925 over a 615-mile course starting from the Isle of Wight, racing out to the Fastnet rock off the south-west coast of Ireland and then finishing at the breakwater at Plymouth, the Fastnet Challenge Cup's prestige increased with the spiralling popularity of ocean racing. But it took 92 years before a monohull boat completed the course in less than two days. In 2007, *ICAP Leonard*, a 100ft super maxi sailing in its first offshore race, skippered by Mike Slade, crossed the finishing line in Plymouth in 1 day, 20 hours, 18 minutes, breaking Ross Field's 1999 record by almost nine hours.

➲ The record-breaking journey was not without incident. Midway to the rock, the boat hit a shark which then attached itself to the rudder before a crew-member climbed down and released it.

Mike Slade and *ICAP Leonard* survived gale-force winds and mountainous seasons in the 2007 Fastnet race to set the fastest time by a monohull boat in the race's history.

Between June and August 2007, two wing commanders in the Indian Air Force, Rahul Monga (right) and Anil Kumar (left), piloted a single-engine microlite around the world in 79 days, beating the previous world record by 20 days.

INDIAN AIR FORCE ROUND-THE-WORLD BID ENDS IN RECORD

THE FASTEST CIRCUMNAVIGATION IN A SINGLE-ENGINE MICROLITE

19 August 2007, Hindan Airbase, near Delhi, India

As part of an Indian Air Force round-the-world expedition, wing commanders Rahul Monga and Anil Kumar took off in their microlite from the Hindan Airbase near Delhi on 1 June 2007 with the intention of flying around the world in 64 days. Flying up to ten hours a day, they flew over 19 countries, crossing from Russia to America via the Bering Straits, and then flying across the continent of North America. To save weight, Monga flew single-handed across the Atlantic to the UK via Greenland and Iceland; the reunited pair then flew across Europe, Turkey, Iran and Pakistan before returning home on 19 August. It may have taken them longer than 64 days, but their time of 79 days was still 20 days faster than Briton Colin Bodil's previous record set in 2001.

➲ The microlite's average speed during the 25,164-mile (40,497km) journey was 13.1mph (21.092km/h).

THE CLOSEST RALLY FINISH IN HISTORY

MARCUS GRONHOLM WINS NEW ZEALAND RALLY BY SMALLEST MARGIN IN WRC HISTORY
2 October 2007, Hamilton, New Zealand

The New Zealand Rally, based in the Waikato region, is one of the highlights of the World Rally Championship calendar: the fans love it, the drivers love it and it is often the stage for some spectacular driving. The 2007 rally was no exception, with the fast-flowing gravel roads providing a titanic struggle between Finland's Marcus Gronholm (a two-time world champion) and France's Sebastien Loeb (a three-time and defending world champion). As the pair entered the final stage, Gronholm led Loeb by 1.5s. The Frenchman drove his car to the absolute limit in the final stage, but fell short by three-tenths of a second – the closest margin of victory in WRC history. Gronholm had won the 350km race by less than two car lengths.

➲ Loeb had the last laugh come the end of the season, though, pipping Gronholm to the title by four points (116 to 112).

A titanic battle at the 2007 New Zealand Rally resulted in Marcus Gronholm beating Sebastien Loeb by three-tenths of a second: it was the tightest finish in World Rally Championship history.

POWELL CLAIMS TITLE OF THE FASTEST MAN ON EARTH

ASAFA POWELL BREAKS THE 100M WORLD RECORD
9 September 2007, Rieti, Italy

Asafa Powell first came to the public's attention at the 2003 World Championships when he was one of two athletes to be disqualified for a false start in the contentious 100m final. He clocked nine sub-10s 100m races the following year, but suffered major competition disappointment with a fifth-place finish at the Olympic Games. In 2005 he broke Tim Montgomery's world record (9.78s) with a 9.77s run in Athens; in 2006 he won Commonwealth gold and equalled his world record time twice (as did America's Justin Gatlin). But he would experience major championship disappointment once again in 2007: after picking up bronze in the World Championships, he vowed to eradicate the extreme disappointment by breaking the world record. The Jamaican was true to his word, running 9.74s during an international meet in Rieti, Italy.

➲ Only America's Maurice Greene has registered more sub-10s runs than Asafa Powell. By the end of the 2007 season Greene had recorded 52 to the Jamaican's 33.

The Jamaican seems to freeze on the biggest stages of all, but when it comes to running fast week in week out no man is quicker than Asafa Powell: he is the holder of three of the four fastest 100m times ever, including his world record time of 9.74s set in September 2007.

LUNG-BURSTING EFFORT PRODUCES WORLD RECORD

DAVE MULLINS BREAKS WORLD RECORD FOR MOST DISTANCE SWUM UNDERWATER IN A SINGLE BREATH

23 September 2007, Wellington, New Zealand

In 2004, New Zealander Dave Mullins had made waves in the spearfishing world when, after a two-hour battle, he bagged a 156.6kg striped marlin: the heaviest specimen of the fish ever caught by a spear. Three years later, Mullins's ability to hold his breath for superhuman periods of time manifested in another world record: on 21 September 2007 he broke Stig Severinsen's record (225m) for the longest distance swum with a monofin in a swimming pool in a single breath (swimming 226m). Two days later he was up to his record-breaking antics once again: remaining underwater for 4m02s, completing nearly five lengths of the 50m pool and smashing his own world record by 18m. The new mark: 244m.

➲ The record for the greatest distance swum in a single breath without the use of fins is 186m, set by Stig Severinsen in July 2007.

INDIA BECOME WORLD TWENTY20 CHAMPIONS

INDIA ARE THE FIRST WINNERS OF THE TWENTY20 WORLD CUP

24 September 2007, Wanderers Stadium, Johannesburg, South Africa

An instant hit with cricket fans since it was first played in English county cricket in 2003, it was only a matter of time before Twenty20 proved equally popular on the international stage, and within four years the first Twenty20 World Cup was contested in South Africa. The crash-bang-wallop, 20-over-a-side cricket spectacular was an enormous success: massive hits, drama-filled games and a final worthy of any major sporting tournament. After 13 days of intense competition, India faced off against arch-rivals Pakistan in the final and edged a thriller by five runs in front a packed Wanderers Stadium in Johannesburg to become the first-ever Twenty20 world champions.

➲ In the 27 matches of the 2007 Twenty20 World Cup, an astonishing total of 265 sixes were hit and only 15 maiden overs were bowled.

India emerged on top of the pile after 13 days of razzmatazz cricket to become the first-ever winners of the Twenty20 World Cup.

FAVRE CONTINUES MARCH INTO NFL'S HISTORY BOOKS

BRETT FAVRE BREAKS DAN MARINO'S ALL-TIME RECORD FOR MOST TOUCHDOWN PASSES

30 September 2007, Hubert H. Humphrey Metrodome, Minneapolis, Minnesota, USA

Green Bay Packers quarterback Brett Favre's march towards owning almost every throwing record in NFL history and securing legendary status for himself in the annals of the game continued unabated in 2007. Having broken Dan Marino's all-time mark for most completed yards the previous season, he opened 2007 by posting the 149th win of his career to break John Elway's record mark. Two weeks later, during the Packers' fourth game of the season, against the Minnesota Vikings, he threw an 18-yard touchdown to Greg Jennings in the first quarter. It was the 421st touchdown pass of his career, taking him past another one of Marino's legendary records.

➲ On 4 November 2007, Favre became only the fourth quarterback in NFL history to post a win against the 31 teams in the league. Then, on 16 December, against the St Louis Rams at the Edward Jones Dome, Favre passed Marino for total passing yardage. He completed the 2007 season with 61,655 yards.

Another record bites the dust: Brett Favre completed the 421st touchdown pass of his career on 30 September 2007 to overtake another of Dan Marino's all-time record marks.

GEBRSELASSIE TAKES RECORD-BREAKING WAYS ONTO THE ROADS

HAILE GEBRSELASSIE BREAKS THE MARATHON WORLD RECORD

29 September 2007, Berlin, Germany

By 2004, Haile Gebrselassie's domination over 10,000m on the track was finally being threatened so, after defending his Olympic title in Athens, the Ethiopian four-time world champion decided to leave the track behind and concentrate on road-running: and to some effect. He went through the 2005 season unbeaten on the roads; in 2006 he broke the half-marathon world record (with a time of 58m55s) and set the fastest marathon time of the year in Berlin (2h05m56s); in 2007, he pulled out of the much-hyped London Marathon at the halfway stage, but bounced back in style, breaking Arturo Barrios's world hour record (21,101m) that had stood since 1991, and ending the season with a world record-breaking win in the Berlin Marathon, clocking 2h04m26s to break Paul Tergat's world record by 29 seconds.

➲ Gebrselassie's run in Berlin was the 25th record-breaking performance of his career in distances ranging from 2,000m to full marathon.

A legend on the track (two Olympic gold medals and four World Championship titles), Haile Gebrselassie's switch to road racing following the defence of his Olympic 10,000m title in 2004 did little to stop the accolades coming his way: in September 2007 he produced the fastest marathon run in history.

A handy gloveman and a determined and hard-hitting batsman, Mark Boucher was a vital cog of the South African Test side for over a decade and in October 2007 became the most successful wicketkeeper in the history of Test cricket.

TEST CRICKET'S MOST SUCCESSFUL WICKETKEEPER

MARK BOUCHER BREAKS IAN HEALY'S RECORD FOR MOST TEST DISMISSALS

3 October 2007, National Stadium, Karachi, Pakistan

Mark Boucher made his Test debut as a stand-in wicketkeeper in 1997–98 and took over the reins permanently following Richardson's retirement later that year. He was not everyone's choice for the role, but grabbed the opportunity with both hands: hitting three centuries in his first 25 matches; reaching the 100-dismissal milestone faster than any other wicketkeeper in history; and setting the record for most consecutive innings without conceding a bye. It looked as though his international career might be over in 2004 when he was dropped after a period of poor form, but he fought hard to regain his place and, through the grim determination that has been a hallmark of his career, did so. The reward came in October 2007, when he overtook Ian Healy's all-time record for most dismissals by a wicketkeeper (395).

➲ Boucher is one of three wicketkeepers in the top 20 all-time dismissals list to average more than two victims per innings: the others are Australia's Adam Gilchrist and England's Geraint Jones.

Thirteen years after his departure, Jason Lewis returned to Greenwich having completed the world's first human-powered circumnavigation.

AROUND THE WORLD IN 13 YEARS

JASON LEWIS COMPLETES THE WORLD'S FIRST HUMAN-POWERED CIRCUMNAVIGATION

6 October 2007, Greenwich, London, England

Britain's Jason Lewis departed Greenwich, London, on 12 July 1994 with the stated intention of completing the world's first human-powered circumnavigation: bicycles, in-line skates, swimming, kayaks and a specially designed pedal boat were allowed; motors and sails were not. He crossed the Atlantic in his boat; rollerbladed across North America; crossed the Pacific Ocean in his boat; then crossed Australia; kayaked from Australia to Singapore; cycled to the Himalayas, trekked through them; crossed the Indian Ocean in his boat, cycled through Africa and Europe, crossed the English Channel and returned to Greenwich on 6 October 2007. His record-breaking 46,505-mile journey had taken the resilient Englishman 13 years.

➲ Lewis's epic journey did not pass without incident. He was hit by a car while rollerblading across North America, broke both of his legs and spent nine months recuperating. He also encountered problems with crocodiles, visas, spying allegations and severe bouts of depression.

WILKINSON BACK TO BREAK WORLD CUP POINTS RECORD

JONNY WILKINSON BREAKS GAVIN HASTINGS'S RECORD FOR MOST CAREER WORLD CUP POINTS
6 October 2007, Stade Velodrome, Marseille, France

Jonny Wilkinson made his World Cup debut in 1999, aged 19, and many cite his non-selection against South Africa as the reason for England's quarter-final defeat. But all was forgotten four years later: Wilkinson's sweetly struck drop-goal handed his team World Cup final victory over Australia. But then injuries struck; England's rugby stock fell; and it was 1,169 days before Wilkinson pulled on the white jersey again. Injury almost robbed him of the 2007 World Cup, but after missing England's two opening games, he returned to lead them through the group stages. Next up: a quarter-final clash against Australia. Wilkinson slotted home four penalties in a narrow 12–10 win. It took him past Gavin Hastings's World Cup points record (227), but more importantly for England, the Sweet Chariot rumbled on, and their mercurial fly-half was at the helm.

Jonny Wilkinson has made a career out of producing big performances on the biggest rugby stages and during the course of England's 2007 World Cup quarter-final victory against Australia became the tournament's all-time leading points-scorer.

➲ England continued their march towards an unlikely World Cup defence to the final, before losing 15–6 to South Africa.

COMEBACK KID SETS WORLD SPEED MARK

IN HIS FIRST COMPETITION IN MORE THAN A YEAR, CANADIAN SPEED SKATER JEREMY WOTHERSPOON SETS A NEW WORLD SPEED SKATING RECORD IN THE 500M
9 November 2007, Olympic Oval, Kearns, Utah, USA

Fresh from a season-long break, speed skater Jeremy Wotherspoon marked his spectacular return to the ice with a new world record in the 500m. The 31-year-old Canadian long-track racer, who was born in Humboldt, Saskatchewan, and grew up in Red Deer, Alberta, managed a time of 34.03 seconds at a World Cup event, shattering the previous record of 34.25s. Wotherspoon's feat came during his first race back on the World Cup circuit after sitting out a full season to recover his competitive spirit. With scores of victories, Wotherspoon is the most decorated male speed skater in World Cup history, but his Olympic record is less impressive. After winning a silver medal at the 1998 Winter Olympics, he was favoured to win the same event at Salt Lake City in 2002 but fell during qualifying. He was shut out of the medals at Torino in 2006.

Wotherspoon at Torino in 2006. Disappointed with his own Olympic performance, he has made changes to his training regimen and has high hopes for home-ice gold in 2010.

➲ Wotherspoon first started training in speed skating as a way to improve his hockey skills. A devoted fisherman and outdoorsman, Wotherspoon spent much of his sabbatical from the skating oval fishing in Norway.

INDEX